PE...

THE C...

Peter Clarke is Professor of Modern British History and Master of Trinity Hall, Cambridge. He is the author of a number of important books on British history and politics in the twentieth century, including *Hope and Glory: Britain 1900–1990* (1996) and *A Question of Leadership: Gladstone to Blair* (1999), both available in Penguin paperback. He is a Fellow of the British Academy and reviews books regularly for *The Times Literary Supplement*, the *London Review of Books* and the *Sunday Times*.

PETER CLARKE

The Cripps Version

THE LIFE OF SIR STAFFORD CRIPPS

1889–1952

PENGUIN BOOKS

PENGUIN BOOKS

Published by the Penguin Group
Penguin Books Ltd, 80 Strand, London WC2R ORL, England
Penguin Putnam Inc., 375 Hudson Street, New York, New York 10014, USA
Penguin Books Australia Ltd, 250 Camberwell Road, Camberwell, Victoria 3124, Australia
Penguin Books Canada Ltd, 10 Alcorn Avenue, Toronto, Ontario, Canada M4V 3B2
Penguin Books India (P) Ltd, 11, Community Centre, Panchsheel Park, New Delhi – 110 017, India
Penguin Books (NZ) Ltd, Cnr Rosedale and Airborne Roads, Albany, Auckland, New Zealand
Penguin Books (South Africa) (Pty) Ltd, 24 Sturdee Avenue, Rosebank 2196, South Africa

Penguin Books Ltd, Registered Offices: 80 Strand, London WC2R ORL, England

www.penguin.com

First published in Allen Lane The Penguin Press 2002
Published in Penguin Books 2003
1

In memory of
Winifred Clarke
1917–2000

Contents

List of Illustrations

Every effort has been made to contact all copyright holders. The publishers shall be happy to make good in future editions any errors or omissions brought to their attention.

Cartoons

p. 1 Cartoon by Arthur Wynell Lloyd for *Punch*, 5 August 1931 (© Punch Limited)

p. 95 Cartoon by David Low for the *Evening Standard*, 26 March 1937 (© Atlantic Syndication. Photo: Centre for the Study of Cartoons and Caricature, University of Kent, Canterbury)

p. 181 Cartoon by David Low for the *Evening Standard*, 2 May 1940 (© Atlantic Syndication. Photo: Centre for the Study of Cartoons and Caricature, University of Kent, Canterbury)

p. 255 Cartoon by Shankar for the *Hindustan Times*, 8 April 1942

p. 391 Cartoon by Giles for the *Daily Express*, 21 February 1946 (© Express Newspapers)

p. 477 Cartoon by David Low for the *Evening Standard*, 12 March 1948 (© Atlantic Syndication. Photo: Centre for the Study of Cartoons and Caricature, University of Kent, Canterbury)

Inset Illustrations

(Photographic acknowledgements in parentheses. Unless otherwise indicated photographs are reproduced with permission from the Cripps family archive.)

1. Parmoor
2. Alfred and Theresa Cripps with their children

Preface

The Cripps Version is the first biography of Sir Stafford Cripps to enjoy unrestricted access to his own papers. Why is this so? Why does it matter? And why does Cripps himself still matter?

His death on 21 April 1952 was headline news around the world. For example, all the main papers in Paris broke the news across two or three columns. 'Cripps est mort' was the simple salute in the bold black type of *Le Franc-Tireur*, a paper that had its origins in the left wing of the Resistance. On the right, *L'Aurore*, with its sober republican tradition, splashed a lot of ink on the message: 'En Stafford Cripps l'Angleterre a perdu un de ses grands hommes politiques'. The tabloid evening paper, *Paris Presse*, opted for human interest in its subheading: 'le "chancelier de fer" lutta deux ans avant de succomber à la maladie'. *Le Monde*, as much the organ of the intellectual centre-left as the *Guardian* might be in England, chose a more nuanced headline for its feature: 'Sir Stafford Cripps: un mystique de la démocratie'.[1]

Cripps, who had only recently stepped down through ill-health as Chancellor of the Exchequer, had been featured on the cover of practically every major North American news magazine – *Time* (10 November 1947), *Newsweek* (16 February 1948), *Saturday Night* (Toronto, 7 August 1948), *Business Week* (9 October 1948), *Pathfinder* (21 September 1949), *US News and World Report* (16 December 1949) – as well as headlined and caricatured daily in the British press. Along with Clement Attlee, Ernest Bevin and Herbert Morrison, he had been one of the cornerstones of the post-war Labour Government from 1945 to 1951. Indeed from 1947 he emerged not only as the executive force directing its strategy for economic recovery but also as the public face of 'austerity' – an image that came to characterize a decade. Cripps was remembered too for the extraordinary wartime interlude in his career when, posted to Moscow as a sympathetic

1. All 23 April 1952.

British ambassador while still remaining an MP, he was felicitously associated with Russia's entry into the Second World War in 1941. Linked in the public mind with the resistance of the Red Army, at a time when there were few British victories to record, he was admitted to the War Cabinet on his return to Britain in 1942 and was seen for a while as the only plausible challenger to the wartime leadership of Winston Churchill.

It was an extraordinary reputation; and posthumously Churchill did nothing to diminish it. 'Stafford Cripps was a man of force and fire,' he said in his tribute in the House of Commons, voicing a general perception in adding: 'He strode through life with a remarkable indifference to material satisfactions or worldly advantages.' Even on an occasion when a Prime Minister is hardly on oath to be wholly candid, propriety did not demand that Churchill go to the lengths he did about a determined political opponent:

I suppose there are few hon. Members in any part of the House who have not differed violently from him at this time or that, and yet there is none who did not regard him with respect and with admiration, not only for his abilities, but for his character.

His friends – and they were many – among whom I am proud to take my place, were conscious, in addition to his public gifts, of the charm of his personality and of the wit and gaiety with which he enlivened not only the mellow hours but also the hard discharge of laborious business in anxious or perilous times. In all his complicated political career he was the soul of honour, and his courage was proof against every test which the terrible years through which we have passed could bring.[2]

Yet the reputation did not last well. Partly, no doubt, this was due to the fortuitous impact of relative longevity – relatively short in Cripps's case. This has a direct, if largely unacknowledged, importance in politics in securing the last word for those who succeed in literally burying their rivals. There is also an indirect or secondary effect, in determining who becomes the keeper of the flame and how that flame is kept.

Stafford Cripps had a notably happy family life, owing his wife a domestic debt that underwrote his own notably successful, notably dedicated, notably strenuous public career. It is significant that Isobel Cripps outlived her husband through nearly three decades, during which she kept a tight hold on his private papers. The official biography that she commissioned from the Bursar of an Oxford college – which must have sounded safe – only succeeded in making Cripps dull. A subsequent commission was dogged by

2. 5 HC Debs., vol. 499, col. 219 (22 April 1952).

further adventitious causes of delay. Two recent biographers have pressed on regardless, with an understandable sense of frustration, with commendable enterprise, and with much to show for it – but without the Cripps papers.[3]

The restriction of archival access, as can be seen, has not proved helpful here. In general, it has blighted rather than fostered scholarship. In particular, Dame Isobel's well-meaning efforts to keep alive her husband's flame has had the perverse effect of threatening to extinguish it. As the 1940s passed into history, and new perspectives were established, Cripps has been eclipsed rather than debunked, as other able and authoritative biographers have staked rival claims for their subjects, who are now better documented and better remembered. Thus one remarkable phenomenon has been the continuing rise in Attlee's ratings as Prime Minister, while Morrison has received a full and sympathetic scholarly appraisal, and Alan Bullock's magisterial life of Bevin runs to three volumes. Dalton, abruptly replaced by Cripps at the Treasury in 1947, has been strikingly restored to historical attention, notably through Ben Pimlott's commanding biography.[4]

There may also be other reasons why Cripps's stature has become relatively diminished in comparison with his colleagues in the Labour Government. Their names – and those of Bevan and Gaitskell in the next generation – remain linked with living issues and ideological traditions in a way that his does not. For example, extravagant claims about Attlee's role in the transfer of power in India continue to be made, whereas Cripps's far greater contribution is neglected. Above all, Attlee presided over the creation of the welfare state: first as legislation, then as myth. Fifty years on, Bevan's name remains rightly linked with Labour's dedication to the National Health Service. Crippsian austerity, by contrast, bequeathed no such benign electoral legacy; and those Gaitskellites who were the intellectual heirs of Keynesian policies, as implemented by Cripps, often hankered after a gaiety in politics that his name did not readily evoke. Bevin is saluted as an architect of the North Atlantic alliance, which arguably preserved Western Europe from the Soviet threat. Cripps, however, is charged with having been, for many years, a gullible fellow-traveller of Stalinist Russia. In the internal politics of the Labour Party, both Morrison and Dalton can be identified with consistent strategies that subsequent advocates of moderation and

3. See Cooke, *Cripps* (1957), which is a deeply inhibited work, surely not only because of Isobel Cripps's brooding presence; Bryant, *Cripps* (1997), which is notable in giving insights into Cripps's religious commitments; Burgess, *Cripps* (1999), which provides a full, detailed and well-supported account of Cripps's public life.
4. Harris, *Attlee*; Burridge, *Attlee*; Donoughue and Jones, *Morrison*; Bullock, *Bevin*, i, ii and iii; Pimlott, *Dalton*.

modernization find sensible – rather than silly, like Cripps's well-publicized posturings in the 1930s. Conversely, socialists sympathetic to the pre-war Cripps, the founder of *Tribune*, have tended to deplore his later apostasy. The *Tribune* group were to be identified as Bevanites, but there were no Crippsites in the post-war Labour Party.

Moreover, Cripps's reputation suffered, in death as in life, an even more invidious comparison with that of his great rival on the other side of the House of Commons. Churchill and Cripps provide a nicely stylized study in contrasts. On the right, the leader of the Conservative Party, with strong nationalist and imperialist instincts: a fat man who notoriously enjoyed his cigars, his champagne (other people's too) and his brandy; and who made it a central aim of his post-war policy to give the British people more red meat. On the left, a socialist prig, with a pre-war record as a fellow-traveller of Communism and an increasingly overt Christian commitment: a lean, ascetic man who made a point of abstaining from alcohol, who became a vegetarian, and who ultimately gave up his only conventional 'vice', smoking, on doctor's orders. Churchill's crony, Lord Beaverbrook, distilled this antipathy with a newspaperman's flair for pejorative stereotyping when he told a well-placed American observer that he was ill at ease with socialist teetotallers who were candidates for sainthood.[5]

While Cripps died young, at only sixty-two, Churchill steamed on to the age of ninety, celebrated as the greatest living Englishman, and winning the Nobel Prize for Literature (no less) for his vastly influential history, *The Second World War*. Given the circumstances of its composition, it was hardly likely to be a work that served the reputation of Sir Stafford Cripps flatteringly, or even faithfully. Not that it is ungenerous to him by the standards established in Conservative polemics of the late 1940s, from which one could easily cull dozens of invidious comments on Cripps. 'He has put the cold hand of death on everything he has attempted to reform,' was the verdict of one widely-read publicist. 'Wherever Sir Stafford has tried to increase wealth and happiness, grass never grows again.'[6] Nothing so gross sullies the pages of *The Second World War*; but oral tradition preserved a number of barbs. The most memorable comment on Cripps is still that attributed to Churchill: 'There, but for the grace of God, goes God.'[7]

5. Harriman and Abel, *Special Envoy*, p. 85.
6. Brogan, *New Masters*, p. 159.
7. An early record of this frequently recycled remark is in Hugh Dalton's diary, 24 May 1943: 'Who told me that, when in the presence of the P.M., Cripps asked to be excused to answer the telephone, the P.M. said, when he was gone, "There, but for the grace of God, goes God himself!"?', in Pimlott (ed.), *Dalton: War Diary*, p. 595.

Yet the same man can be described in terms that, by shifting the angle of vision a few degrees, give quite another perspective. 'He was the nearest to a Saint I have ever met,' wrote a junior colleague; 'he was a man of complete selflessness and devotion to humanity. I hope and believe that I am a better man for having known him.'[8] This can be complemented by a perceptive comment from the diary of Lionel Elvin, a pre-war political sympathizer on the left of the Labour Party. Meeting Cripps again on his return from Russia in 1942, Elvin noted that 'the modesty and simplicity of the man charmed me, as they always used to. Yet he is at the same time curiously self-centred. The blend of egoism and the unegotistic is fascinating in most men and especially so in him.'[9]

That Cripps had a strong personality, and was determined to get his own way, is clear. That he was often self-righteous, and sometimes self-deceiving, is difficult to deny. That there was a tension between his background of established wealth and his espousal of Marxist views in the 1930s lends an inescapable piquancy to his ideological formation. That he fitted uneasily into the Labour Party – neither left nor right, neither intellectual nor party loyalist – makes the trajectory of his political career remarkable: lightning promotion to the front bench by 1931, pre-war expulsion, non-membership throughout the Second World War, rehabilitation into the top echelon of government. His ultimate role as Chancellor saw him explicitly adopting a fiscal strategy for the macro-economic management of the economy, which can be termed 'actually existing Keynesianism'. For Cripps, this implied repudiation of his Marxist past; for Britain it marked the inception of a 'post-war consensus' that lasted until Margaret Thatcher.

There are many vicissitudes and surprises, many inconsistencies or at least paradoxes. Previous biographies have wrestled with these in different ways, in a fashioning of Cripps's image that began in his own lifetime – indeed, under his own control. Twice in his political career, in 1942 and 1947–8, he was the beneficiary of a flood-tide that buoyed up his reputation, with talk of him as the next Prime Minister; on each occasion he gave his cooperation to a loyal but doomed work of hagiography, which on each occasion just missed the tide. Though Patricia Strauss bent every effort to rush into print in New York in 1942, her *Cripps* was still not published until after his demotion from the War Cabinet; and Eric Estorick's attempt

8. W. H. Gallienne to IC, 23 April 1952. Gallienne, writing as British Minister in Guatemala, had worked under Cripps at the Moscow embassy in the summer of 1940 before the arrival of his family: 'We had all our meals together and he talked much to me.'
9. Elvin diary, 4 September 1942.

– actually his second attempt – to produce a biography in 1949 was published weeks after the devaluation of sterling, which tarnished Cripps's record at the Treasury. Both were constrained by their partisan status in making use of their selective access to private papers. Both remain interesting documents, not least as evidence of the propagation of the Cripps legend.[10]

The Cripps Version is a different kind of book, speaking to a different generation, asking different questions, using different sources – and using them in different ways.

The events of the public career are now well enough known, yet Cripps remains a two-dimensional, cut-out stereotype who needs to be rescued both from his admirers and his detractors. Previous biographers, to be sure, have made loyal efforts to challenge the legend of 'Austerity Cripps', with his killjoy spirit and his hairshirt policies. In particular, the Labour MP (and later Thatcherite peer) Woodrow Wyatt was an improbable partisan of Cripps, first working for him during the Indian negotiations of 1946 and later writing the biography of Cripps in the *Dictionary of National Biography*. 'The public picture of a Robespierre was belied by the private charm and kindliness,' Wyatt stated, arguing that Cripps 'never believed in austerity for austerity's sake'.[11] Now Wyatt himself can justly be called ebullient, opinionated, vain, snobbish and, above all, counter-suggestible; and he enjoyed improving a story if it would sharpen a paradox. If he latterly relished opportunities for reminiscing about Cripps and 'refuting the legend that he was an austere ascetic', perhaps this does not inspire automatic credence.[12]

Any sympathetic biographer of Cripps is open to the suspicion of protesting too much. As with any successful caricature, there is enough truth in 'Austerity Cripps' to evoke recognition. What is needed is not refutation, which would be unconvincing, but contextualization. The construction of such a potent public image itself requires explanation in its own context,

10. Strauss, *Cripps* (New York, 1942; 1943) – the text of the American and British editions is identical though the format very different. Estorick, *Cripps* (1949), is not to be confused with the same author's earlier book, *Stafford Cripps: prophetic rebel* (New York, 1941), of which only about a dozen pages survived in the second version. All references in my text simply to 'Estorick' are to his widely circulated 1949 volume; otherwise the (highly inaccessible) 1941 edition is specified. There was also another early biography – Tyler, *Cripps* (1942) – which, as one reviewer tellingly demonstrated at the time, 'appears to have been written in a very short time in the library of a Fleet Street newspaper' (Dennis Gordon, *Tribune*, 12 March 1943). Lacking either private information or public impact, it does not rank with Estorick or Strauss.
11. *DNB* 1951–60, pp. 270–74, at pp. 272, 274.
12. Wyatt journal, 5 November 1986, in Curtis (ed.), *Wyatt: Journals*, i, p. 221; see also Wyatt, *Confessions*, p. 140

which this book will attempt, especially through scrutiny of the newspaper press, which was dominant in the opinion-forming media of this era. Discovering the source of common perceptions about Cripps prompts questions about historical sources in general – pausing to ask how we can know what we think we know, or why we privilege one source above another.

In the process, this book shifts the centre of gravity away from the political infighting of the 1930s and the economic policy-making of the 1940s. These were the phases in his career that successively generated the most unflattering stereotypes: first of hare-brained Cripps, then of hairshirt Cripps. Both episodes have already been the subject of much sound historical research, which it would be otiose to replicate and needless to refute. Instead I give close attention to Cripps's involvement with Russia and – still the most neglected aspect of his career – with India. In the process, I explore the personal dynamics of his relationship with Churchill, with Nehru, and with Gandhi.

Biography has always been an elastic form, not least English biography with its A to Z of distinguished practitioners. In the centuries between, say, John Aubrey and Philip Ziegler, the genre has been stretched, not only in the length of treatment but in the range of inquiry and the depth of research. If biographers have learnt from novelists, as many good writers of history surely have, this can be seen in the adoption of different strategies of exposition in telling different kinds of story. Historians rightly honour the discipline imposed by chronology but that does not entail fidelity to a purely chronological scheme of narrative. Readers of this book should not expect to find each year of its subject's life given equal attention, still less equal space. If *The Cripps Version* uses the biographical genre in some unconventional ways, it is with the aim of enriching our understanding of puzzling, neglected or fugitive aspects of one man's life in history.

In particular, it rests to a large extent on diaries. These capture Cripps's personality with a verisimilitude that eludes most other sources, whether speeches, books, articles or correspondence. Views of Cripps, often prejudicial, can be found in the diaries of such prominent contemporaries as Leo Amery, John Colville, Hugh Dalton, Harold Nicolson and Lord Wavell. All these have been published with notable success and have helped to form our judgements on this era. There is also a cluster of diaries by younger men, who worked with Cripps in government during the post-war years: Hugh Gaitskell, James Meade, Robert Hall and Raymond Streat in particular. It is a boon for the biographer that all of their diaries are accessible in good scholarly editions.

It is now possible to provide a fully three-dimensional image through access to a richer range of archival sources than any previous author has been able to draw upon. It is certainly worth consulting some unpublished, and hence less celebrated, diaries by people who had contact with Cripps at various times: the editor of *The Times*, Robin Barrington-Ward; the historian Reginald Coupland, who was part of the Cripps Mission in 1942; the civil servant Frank Turnbull, who went to India with the Cabinet Delegation in 1946, and Cripps's colleague on it, A. V. Alexander; above all, perhaps, the fragmentary but revealing diary kept by Cripps's Canadian personal assistant during the Second World War, Graham Spry.

Moreover, the survival of Cripps's own diaries for pivotal periods of his life allows the reconstruction of his own perspective. There are, too, insights in the diaries kept in Moscow by both his wife, Isobel, and his daughter, Theresa Cripps. Parts of these diaries, covering Cripps's visit to India in 1939 and his time as ambassador to Russia, have already been used in authoritative specialist studies by R. J. Moore and Gabriel Gorodetsky, which draw upon this evidence to elucidate aspects of Indian politics and Anglo-Russian diplomacy.[13] A biographer will naturally interrogate these sources in a somewhat different way, using them to reveal more about Cripps himself.

There are other sections of Cripps's own diaries – notably the important Indian diary of 1946 – that have never previously been available for citation. Furthermore, his early diaries, though fragmentary, throw shafts of light, illuminating his formative years in new ways (especially when read in conjunction with his father's unpublished diary). What Stafford Cripps wrote himself has no peculiar claims to objectivity; it cannot be regarded as simply superior to other accounts – except in one crucial respect, in supplying his own account. Given the way in which the historiography has been constructed, skewed by the necessarily self-interested testimony of others, it is hardly surprising that it is the Cripps version that has hitherto gone by default.

13. Moore, *Churchill, Cripps and India*; Gorodetsky, *Mission to Moscow*.

PART ONE

HIS APPRENTICESHIP
1889–1939

Lord Parmoor to Sir Stafford Cripps. "Glad to see
you've done such a good term's work, my boy, in
your father's old house."

'A normal man'

'I like you and next time I am lonely I shall know I have a dear old friend waiting to hear all my troubles,' wrote Stafford Cripps. It was a comment both in and to the diary that he kept on a visit to Hamburg, undertaken to learn German in July 1910. This is the earliest of his diaries to survive and, though the sentiment may seem somewhat forced, Cripps was accurate enough in foreseeing that he would return to this medium of expression. The Hamburg diary, running to 156 pages, is prefaced with a note: 'Having no one to gossip to, I had to gossip to myself, and so amused myself by writing it all down – or some of it.' The 'strictly private' contents show Cripps warming to the routine of daily entries, which expand from short factual descriptions of his journeys to reflective disquisitions of up to fourteen pages at a time on his views on life. He wrote it quite explicitly because he was alone and thus stopped when a friend came to visit, telling the diary: 'you have been a good friend to me, and listened to everything I have had to say, through thick and thin'.[1]

Though the young man talked of 'all my troubles', his circumstances would have struck most people as enviable. Aged twenty-one in 1910, he was the youngest of five children. His father, Charles Alfred Cripps, son of a well-established ecclesiastical lawyer (*Cripps on Church and Clergy*), himself enjoyed an even more successful legal career. 'I have liked it and prospered by it for 30 years,' he noted on his retirement from the bar, 'making an average income of £10,444.' To put this in perspective, the recently introduced super-tax, with a threshold of £5,000 a year, caught only 11,000 taxpayers, or the top 0.05 per cent of all taxable incomes.[2]

1. Richard Stafford Cripps (hereafter RSC) diary, 31 July 1910.
2. Parmoor diary, 10 January 1914; cf. 4 June, 4 October 1890. Estimates on top incomes courtesy of Professor Sir Tony Atkinson.

Like his own father, Alfred Cripps was the standard authority in his field: in his case through *Cripps on Compensation*, showing the golden touch of specializing in railways. Here was the common interest that had brought him into contact with the entrepreneur Richard Potter, with his nine striking daughters. One of them (Beatrice) subsequently became famous not only for a lifelong partnership with her husband Sidney Webb in propagating Fabian socialism but also for an autobiography of unusual insight, *My Apprenticeship*, based on her diaries. When old man Potter called Alfred Cripps, with his brimming confidence and jutting jaw, 'the little jewel of an advocate', it was Beatrice who embalmed the phrase for posterity (and tactfully suppressed his earlier nickname of 'Chin Chin').[3]

Richard Potter's daughters, as one of them put it, married 'just the sort father likes us to marry, and one likes one's sisters to marry'.[4] Another used to say in old age, 'we gels all married very well'.[5] Beatrice's sisters successively made what contemporaries considered better matches than her own, if seldom happier ones. 'Lallie' had married into the Holts, whose shipping and cotton interests placed them at the peak of Liverpool society; Mary had married Arthur Playne, with his ample estate at Longfords, near Minchinhampton in Gloucestershire; 'Georgie' had married Daniel Meinertzhagen, a merchant banker. So in 1877 it initially (if rather misguidedly) struck the Potters as a come-down when Blanche married Alfred Cripps's elder brother William, who later became senior surgeon at St Bartholomew's Hospital. Margaret was soon to marry Henry Hobhouse, landowner, MP, and Ecclesiastical Commissioner; and later Kate was to marry another MP, Leonard Courtney (eventually Lord Courtney of Penwith), prominent in his day as a highly principled Liberal.

It was the strong-minded Kate who had taken her younger sister Theresa for some months of social work in the East End of London. As a first step, this may seem much like what Beatrice was to do later, leading to her unorthodox marriage to her parvenu socialist husband; but, despite Theresa's stirrings of social conscience and fantasies of establishing a celibate

3. Webb, *My Apprenticeship*. This was first published in 1926, but I have used the republished 1979 edition. This phrase actually appears in the sequel, *Our Partnership*, 29 December, 1894, p. 119, which was edited by her niece, Stafford's cousin, Barbara Drake with Margaret Cole (1948; the reprinted 1978 edition used here). In an earlier entry, originally unpublished, she explained: 'His first nickname in our family was "Chin Chin", afterwards increased in dignity and length to Carlyle's epithet for Jeffrey, "The Little Jewel of an Advocate" ': 22 September 1882, in MacKenzie and MacKenzie (eds.), *Webb: Diary*, i, pp. 59–60.
4. Webb, *My Apprenticeship*, p. 144, quoting her sister Margaret (Hobhouse).
5. Kate Courtney quoted in Caine, *Destined to be Wives*, p. 66.

nursing sisterhood, she stopped well short of rejecting her own class. When she married Alfred Cripps in 1881 she provided her sisters with another suitable brother-in-law: an eligible, highminded, public-spirited man of good family, at the outset of a promising career. This time, moreover, the Potters were gracious enough to acknowledge the Cripps family as their equals. Mary Playne commented: 'We want an Attorney General or even a Lord Chancellor in the family and Theresa won't make a bad Law Peeress.'[6]

From 1884 Alfred and Theresa Cripps took over from grandfather Cripps the country house that he had acquired, with its four hundred acres, at Parmoor in the Chilterns. It was, however, at their London house in Elm Park Gardens that their youngest child, Richard Stafford Cripps, was born on 24 April 1889. He had three brothers, Seddon, Frederick and Leonard, and a sister, Ruth. Only in later years did Beatrice Webb's diary single out her youngest Cripps nephew for attention. As a child, his 'Aunt Bo' struck Stafford as 'rather a terrifying person', altogether different from his aunt Mary, busy with her garden parties and fine lawns at Longfords.[7] One complaint of his elder brother Seddon Cripps about Cooke's biography of Stafford, rather significantly, concerned its 'undue emphasis on the intellectual side of life at Parmoor in the old days. It was not so: in fact, it was rather lacking except for occasional visits of the Webbs, Courtneys, etc.'[8] Still, there was a clannish spirit, well caught in later memories of a family party at the Webbs, when 'Aunt Bo, looking very dashing, mounted on a stone balustrade and addressed us all: "Well, you are a good-looking lot!" she said.'[9]

Parmoor was home. This was where young Stafford was able to exercise his ingenuity in damming streams and to satiate his passion for riding by rounding up as many as thirty horses and ponies on one occasion. He was able to develop his mechanical ingenuity (at twelve) by acquiring a motor-cycle licence and (at fourteen) a motor-car licence which allowed him to accompany the family chauffeur – a family photograph shows him at work underneath the car. When (at twenty) he decided to build a full-scale glider, he commandeered a shed at the foot of the steepest hill on the estate for its construction; it was dragged to the top by an old carriage horse and triumphantly flew on its first flight, only to crash upon landing. 'It was broken to a certain extent on the first trial,' as his father tactfully recorded,

6. ibid., pp. 66–77, at p. 66; cf. Parmoor, *Retrospect*, pp. 35–7.   7. Estorick, p. 31.
8. Seddon Cripps to John Cripps, New Year's Day 1956, copy.
9. Antonia Macnaghten to Isobel Cripps, 25 June 1949, written after the Crippses had likewise held a large family reunion at 11 Downing Street.

'and he is now mending it.'[10] The Parmoor estate's resources amply accommodated these instructive but expensive hobbies. When Alfred Cripps entered the House of Lords in 1914 he took the title Lord Parmoor.

Stafford thus came from a privileged background, as he acknowledged in his diary. He did not take this for granted, and debated with himself over the moral dilemmas that it posed. Yet to what extent he was conscious of the quite exceptional financial circumstances of his family is not altogether clear:

Now I have more money than many people who must be as worthy or more worthy than myself. I have luxuries for instance. I am provided with money to take this tour, that is a luxury. I often travel in motors or 1st class, all those things are luxuries. Now surely I ought to give up these luxuries and give the money away. Yet I am in the middle class of wealth, there are many richer and many poorer. That is to say if the money of those richer than myself were given to those poorer, I should be a normal man.[11]

The notion that the Crippses were merely 'in the middle class of wealth' was, of course, totally misconceived. Did Stafford really think that he was just in the top five out of ten incomes – when in fact he was in the top five out of ten thousand? Even if we make more sophisticated distinctions than he evidently did about the distribution of wealth, or about the difference between a mean and a median, his concept of 'a normal man' is clearly beyond rescue – indeed it is beyond ridicule. Yet it went along with Stafford's facile impression that the fruits of worldly success were simply there for the picking. The experience of his own family showed him as much, especially the example of both his father and grandfather in using their educational advantages to turn academic prowess to pecuniary advantage.

I frankly admit that I am ambitious to make money. I want to have a country home, a dear wife and some children. Further I want to keep my wife with comfort and luxuries and to educate my children in the best possible way. Still further I want to be able to save enough to make our old age happy and if need be provide for my children. Now this is a desire for money and as such it is wrong, *but* surely you would not call a man a good just man if he did not want any of these things.[12]

The earnest, moralizing note was as much a product of the Cripps–Potter family influence as was the assumption of material affluence; and it was

10. Parmoor diary, 20 October 1909; cf. Strauss, pp. 24–7.   11. RSC diary, 25 July 1910.
12. ibid.

reinforced by the trauma of Theresa Cripps's sudden death when Stafford was only four. She had doted on the baby; as Alfred noted in his diary, when Stafford was only fifteen months old, 'his Mother thinks he has too great a brain development, and looks to him as the rising genius among her boys'.[13] Theresa's death marmorealized the family legend of her prescience. This is, of course, a familiar motif in the biographies of famous men, and Cripps himself seems to have encouraged it in later life, judging from the prominence of his early years in the book produced under his aegis by Estorick. Indeed in the magazine serialization in 1949 ('The Chancellor was a Baby') this episode becomes central.[14]

Theresa Cripps was a pious Christian; her relationship with Alfred was manifestly close; and he had a strong belief in the doctrine of personal immortality. Moreover, Theresa left an explicit testament, envisaging if not foreseeing her own death, which her distraught widowed husband enshrined in a slim but impressive memorial volume, copies of which circulated in the family. The combined effect ensured that Theresa's wishes for her children did not die with her. 'I should like them trained to be undogmatic and unsectarian Christians,' she wrote, 'charitable to all churches and sects, studying the precepts and actions of Christ as their example, taking their religious inspiration directly from the spirit of the New Testament.' Her final injunction to them was 'to choose Christ as their sole Hero and Master'.[15]

In Stafford's case (though less conspicuously in the case of all his brothers), this training evoked the desired response. His diary shows no sign that he had ever entertained serious religious doubts: 'I can't conceive what Atheists, Agnostics, and other Dontcares have in the place of this feeling of absolute security, which is given by the knowledge of his care.'[16] He thus regarded God as a friend, so that 'however wretched one may be one can always talk to him and no one in the world can deprive one of his friendship'.[17] This was an intensely personal vision. Moreover, the Christ whom Stafford chose was an *exemplary* hero, calling him not to contemplation but to action, making his life a trial of good conduct in the fulfilment of commitments that were simultaneously challenging yet mundane, demanding yet practicable.

13. Parmoor diary, 4 June 1890.
14. *Leader Magazine*, 17 September 1949; also 24 September, 1 October 1949.
15. Alfred Cripps had the 93-page volume privately printed by the *South Bucks Standard* in 1893, with the title page: 'This memoir of Mother is written for, and dedicated to, her children by Father'. This passage, from a paper left for her children, is taken from pp. 88–9.
16. RSC diary, 26 July 1910.   17. ibid.

What greater proof of God's power can be sought than this. That the love of God felt and known – though he is invisible – has inspired ordinary human beings – with human feelings – to become the greatest and best of men. This is indeed wonderful and ought to teach each one of us that through the knowledge and love of God *alone* can we become worthy to be called to his kingdom. Yet knowing this I wilfully and purposely go and do and say things which can only have the effect of blinding me and sending me further from God . . . Once sin and sin becomes easy. Once conquer sin and the conquest of sin becomes easy. There are always many more opportunites in life of doing good than of sinning. Every moment of every day opportunities for being kind and charitable present themselves, and it is only occasionally that temptations come to one.[18]

The basis of Cripps's Christianity was always social and activist, not contemplative or quietist. All those who knew him well in his later political career saw that this was so. 'He held that there should be no divorce between religion and secular work, but that all our doings should be inspired by the same spirit,' said Attlee. 'His Christianity was essentially practical.'[19] An address that Cripps gave in 1948 simply reaffirmed lifelong beliefs about Christ's ministry. 'Nothing is clearer in the records that have come down to us of that teaching,' he said, 'than that it was aimed at providing us with a way of life on earth which would regulate our relationships with our fellow human beings so that we might play our part in bringing about the Kingdom of God on earth.'[20]

The fact that his outlook here was consistent throughout his mature life needs stressing. His political commitments were to range the ideological spectrum; in his early twenties, partisan Conservatism; in his early forties, dogmatic Marxism; in his early sixties, social democratic reformism. The message was to be the same in public or in private, even in the 1930s.

'Christ's teaching is a tale of life,' was his avuncular advice. 'He taught that we must regulate all our human relationships by love and selflessness. He was not primarily concerned with direct personal salvation.' Cripps could readily argue that 'it is our share in the corporate life and happiness of the world that is of prime importance' and scorned the notion 'that Christ would have approved any religion which stressed the personal and selfish view of salvation'. Hence there was 'no more faithful carrying out of Christ's

18. ibid., 8 August 1910.
19. Lord Attlee, Sir Stafford Cripps Memorial Lecture, given 4 March 1957, p. 5.
20. Address by RSC, Westminster Chapel, 5 January 1948, in *Evangelical Christendom*, January–March 1948, pp. 9–13, at p. 11.

teaching than striving to remedy inequalities in the world' and it followed, for his own part, 'that is why I do what I do in politics'.[21] Here was a commitment licensed – though clearly not required – by the understanding of religion derived from his mother's words and her posthumous idealization.

The concreteness and literalness of this theodicy can hardly be exaggerated. When Stafford, faced with his recurrent digestive trouble in 1910, found that his German hostess had specially ordered veal, and had made rice pudding for him, he was duly appreciative: 'They are so kind and nice here, and it was very nice of God to bring me here.'[22] His sense of the working of a divine plan seems to have encompassed everything from the dinner menu to issues of life and death. In his diary he recollected having a presentiment of evil on a visit that he had made to Portugal: 'I had an unmistakable feeling that I should be drowned in the bay of Biscay, and to this day I believe that providence or God in some way saved me from something by sending me back across land.'[23] Whether providence had likewise saved him *for* something is the unspoken question prompted by such passages. Later in life he privately affirmed: 'We have access through prayer and thought to the divine advice of God and to the inspiration of Christ.'[24] Likewise in a public address: 'We should – if we hold the Christian faith – take advantage of the omni-presence of God to consult with him as to how we should act.'[25]

Early bereavement had several effects upon Stafford. His mother's memory became an ever-burning beacon, kept alive by her sisters as much as her widowed husband. Stafford later acknowledged a great debt to his aunt Mary Playne, whom he liked to visit for holidays at Longfords: 'She more or less adopted me directly my mother died.'[26] She was fun. He admired the energy which she threw into her good works. Reproaching himself for feeling depressed, he remarked in his diary 'what an immensely large and generous mind people like Aunt Mary must have, to be always bright and cheerful.'[27]

Alfred Cripps, however, did not allow the aunts to cramp the freedom of his children at Parmoor. Beatrice Webb noted on a Christmas visit that 'the children revel in high spirits and health', showing great affection for their father, 'the children obeying him implicitly with no consciousness of being ruled or regulated'.[28] Mary Marshall had been appointed as governess

21. RSC to Toby Weaver, 24 December 1932.   22. RSC diary, 26 July 1910.
23. ibid., 27 July 1910.   24. RSC to Toby Weaver, 24 December 1932.
25. 'God is my co-pilot', address to Bomber Command, 8 December 1944, p. 25.
26. Estorick, p. 31.   27. RSC diary, 23 July 1910.
28. Webb diary, 29 December 1894, in MacKenzie and MacKenzie (eds.), *Webb: Diary*, ii, p. 62; also Webb, *Our Partnership*, pp. 118–19.

to Ruth Cripps when baby brother Stafford arrived and, known as 'Mazelle', she became a source of continuity and companionship, aiding and abetting Stafford's daredevil adventures. His father and elder brothers obviously indulged the boy, relishing rather than resenting his precociously solemn wisdom. He was called 'Dad' or 'Daddy', a family nickname that stuck. As his sister Ruth recalled: 'Stafford in those days was very independent and sure of himself.'[29] He grew used to getting his own way through charm, quickness, persistence and a sheer cleverness that impressed everyone.

This showed itself early. He was moved from his first prep school at Reigate in Surrey to spare embarrassment to his elder brother, Len, whom he threatened to overtake.[30] Stafford was sent instead as a boarder to another school in Rottingdean, on the Sussex coast near Brighton, before – like his father and grandfather before him – entering Winchester College. It was an ancient (and expensive) boarding school with a distinctive pedagogic tradition, prizing intellectual achievement rather than sporting prowess, and sometimes thought dry, rigorous and narrow. Stafford was happy there; he remained loyal enough to the old school to send his son there (and to advance a loan to the professional racquets coach, who set up as a sports outfitter). Cripps evinced a low-key acknowledgement of some common bond between himself and such diverse Wykehamists as he came across in later life – for example, Reginald Coupland, D. N. Pritt, Archibald Wavell, Hugh Gaitskell and Douglas Jay.[31]

When Cripps wrote in his diary, 'I wish I had a brain for detail', it was surely a perfectionist comment.[32] His intellectual prowess was the one thing that political opponents never disparaged, whatever they thought of his judgement. His actions, said Churchill, were 'governed by the workings of a powerful, lucid intelligence'.[33] This sort of mental ability, clearly resting on innate endowment, was the subject alike of early appreciation and of purposeful schooling.

Matched against gifted peers at Winchester, Cripps continued to excel. But he showed more than a formidable ability to pass examinations. He played games: both soccer and rugby, but preferred racquets to cricket and,

---

29. Estorick, p. 33; cf. Webb, *Our Partnership*, p. 139.

30. F. H. Cripps, *Life's a Gamble*, p. 29.

31. Jay tells of accompanying Cripps to the opening of the 1945 parliament: 'It was still raining very hard; and A. P. Herbert, whom we passed at the gate of New Palace Yard, remarked to Cripps (they were contemporaries at Winchester): "Our wettest hour, I suppose." ' Jay, *Change and Fortune*, p. 125.

32. RSC diary, 17 July 1910.   33. Tribute, 5 HC Debs., vol. 499, col. 219 (22 April 1952).

denied the opportunity of playing lawn tennis at school, broke the rules by cycling fifteen miles to join a tennis club. It was a sign of the pleasure he always took in coolly defying the conventions and getting away with it. It was striking, however, that he neither took part in the debating society nor evinced any interest in politics.[34] At school, as at home, he remained the golden boy. The headmaster, Dr H. M. Burge, told Alfred Cripps that his son was 'a capital fellow', of first-rate ability in every way: 'He ought to do very well indeed next term: and I hope much will be elected by New College.'[35]

New College, Oxford, loomed as Cripps's natural destination. Sharing the same founder as Winchester, it accepted many Wykehamists, who often hobnobbed with each other as undergraduates. It is hardly surprising that Cripps took the entrance scholarship examinations there in 1907, nor that he was successful. The next step was the unusual one. This was the first scholarship awarded by New College in chemistry, and, rather than take it up, Cripps was persuaded by Professor Sir William Ramsay, Professor of Chemistry at University College, London, to go there instead. In Cripps's generation, even more than later, the natural preparation for a political career in England was an arts degree from Oxford or Cambridge, often considered incidental to the social contacts formed in close-knit residential colleges. Cripps's priorities were otherwise. He had specialized in science at school; in 1907 he crisply chose a university where the laboratory facilities were superior to those in Oxford and went on, in 1910, to take the M.Sc. degree offered at London.

'What a wonderful thing the periodic law is,' Cripps wrote in his diary. 'Cannot think why all the elements were made to fit into a table like that.'[36] The characteristically naive expression may belie, but should not belittle, the intellectual excitement that he found in studying chemistry with Ramsay, who had won a Nobel Prize for his work on the inert gases only a few years previously. When Cripps visited Hamburg in 1910, his future career was on the cusp. His language lessons had a clear scientific utility in an era when British chemistry had much to learn from the German example. Indeed, he had toyed with the idea of going to a German university as an undergraduate; Ramsay had studied in Tübingen and listed his recreations as languages and travelling.

Cripps's achievements as a budding scientist, specializing in the densities of gases, should not be overlooked. A uniquely deep and long-lasting

34. Dr R. Custance (college archivist) to Maurice Shock, 28 January 1991.
35. Burge to C. A. Cripps, 30 July (1907).   36. RSC diary, 15 July 1910.

friendship was forged at University College London with a fellow student, 'Jack' Egerton, who married Ruth Cripps in 1912. 'I was devoted to Stafford,' he wrote forty years later, adding: 'He shaped my life – as he shaped many things – without him I should not have had the glorious companionship of Ruthie throughout my life.'[37] It was their common scientific interests that had drawn the two students together; and if Sir Alfred Egerton (as he became) was to follow a distinguished career as a Professor of Chemistry in London, the potential for Stafford to do the same was clearly there. He was to co-author a research paper, published under the auspices of the Royal Society.[38] It is said that he was the youngest person ever to have a paper accepted and it is undoubtedly remarkable that he was only twenty-two. He was to tell Egerton that he considered his election as a Fellow of the Royal Society in 1948 as the greatest compliment ever paid to him.[39] No other top-ranking British politician has had scientific credentials to match these; and the only graduate in chemistry to exceed Cripps's prominence in twentieth-century British politics has been Margaret Thatcher. Altogether, in 1910 it seemed more likely that Cripps would fashion his career as a scientist – whether academically or commercially – than as a professional politician.

In an era when the notion of a governing class was still potent, it was natural that Stafford's family should be drawn into some kind of political activity: the more so since both Crippses and Potters had sat in Parliament since the early nineteenth century. Moreover, law and politics consorted closely, not least because an able man like Alfred Cripps might hope for preferment as a law officer in the Government. He had first entered Parliament in 1895, as MP for Stroud in Gloucestershire, where the help of Arthur and Mary Playne had proved useful.

Alfred Cripps was a staunch Conservative. This needs to be remembered in view of the fact that he was to end his career as a Labour cabinet minister, and was to leave memoirs that are influenced by that perspective. Thus he later wrote of his early Liberal inclinations becoming overborne by the salience of Irish Home Rule. This may be true so far as it goes; but, as he acknowledged himself, most Liberal Unionists in effect became members of the Conservative Party, unlike his admired brother-in-law, Leonard Courtney, who became a Liberal Unionist in the literal and strict sense, by

37. Egerton to Isobel Cripps (hereafter IC), 24 May 1952.
38. Hubert Sutton Patterson, Richard Stafford Cripps and Robert Whytlaw-Gray, 'The critical constants and orthobaric densities of xenon', *Proceedings of the Royal Society*, A, vol. 86 (1912), pp. 579–90.
39. Egerton diary, 25 April 1948, quoted in Burgess, *Cripps*, p. 9.

remaining 'on most points a Radical'.[40] That would not have been said of
Alfred Cripps. In 1895 Beatrice Webb ruthlessly summarized Cripps's opinion of Courtney as 'an upright but wrong-headed man', whereas 'Leonard
looks on Alfred as a somewhat selfish, thoughtless and superficial conservative' – a view that she shared in the light of Cripps's pragmatic
defence of vested interests.[41] Among these, the Established Church should
be numbered; and in an era when the old cliché still had force – that it
was the Conservative Party at prayer – this bonded Alfred Cripps's Tory
allegiance. Only later did this cement become less strong, as he became more
ecumenical while politics became more secular. Moreover, he had favoured
protection long before Joseph Chamberlain's Tariff Reform campaign was
launched in 1903, and, despite clear evidence that this proved an electoral
handicap, continued to describe himself in private as 'a strong Tariff
Reformer on the grounds of Economic principle'.[42] He was thus a highly
partisan opponent of every Liberal policy: Free Trade and the People's
Budget as much as Welsh Disestablishment and Irish Home Rule.

Until the First World War, then, the Cripps family was unambiguously
Tory. Alfred's political ambitions were strong enough to induce him to
re-enter the House for a Manchester suburban seat after losing Stroud, only
to lose that too in the Liberal landslide of 1906. Hence his availability to
stand for the local vacancy in the Buckinghamshire division of Wycombe in
the General Election of January 1910. The whole family turned out to help,
including Stafford, who (remarkably enough) since the age of sixteen had
been responsible for the business side of his father's paper, the *South Bucks
Standard*, popularly known as the 'Cripps Chronicle'.

It is hardly surprising that Stafford's diary shows him tinctured with
the conventional Conservative catch-phrases of the period. The Liberal
campaign for Free Trade had provided graphic detail of how much lower
food prices were in Britain than in protectionist Germany and had played
on a xenophobic aversion to the sort of rye-bread common there. 'Can't
imagine horror of Liberals if they were here,' Stafford wrote on arrival in
Hamburg: 'black bread and nothing but every day, awfully good too.'[43]
This was an outburst of second-hand slogan-swapping, lacking first-hand
understanding of the realities of the cost of living, as Stafford candidly
acknowledged: 'I tried to gather from the shops comparative prices but I do

40. Parmoor diary, 22 May 1918; cf. Parmoor, *Retrospect*, pp. 49, 51.
41. Webb diary, 28 December 1894, in MacKenzie and MacKenzie (eds.), *Webb: Diary*, ii,
p. 63; also in Webb, *Our Partnership*, p. 121 (but as 29 December); cf. pp. 139–41.
42. Parmoor diary, 17 December 1913.   43. RSC diary, 12 July 1910.

not know the cost of things in England so I could not tell.'[44] He duly railed against having to read 'that lamentable rag the *Daily News*', with its strong support for Asquith and Lloyd George.[45] Yet he had reservations about the popular Tory press, with its scaremongering about the German naval threat – the more so after an agreeable game of bridge with a German naval officer who had befriended a Royal Naval commander while in China. 'I do wish the nations would pal up like this,' Stafford responded, 'it's silly rot the way they go on competing and competing and I am getting more and more angry with the *Daily Mail*.'[46]

These ingenuous and superficial utterances read more like those of a boy than a man of voting age. When he finally got hold of *The Times*, he felt at home. 'What a good paper it is. So thoroughly respectable and English.'[47] There is no stronger term of approbation than 'English'. He was struck with the contrast between the German police and 'that finest force in the world the Metropolitan Police, God bless and preserve them and their traditions!'.[48] He immediately knew whose side he was on when he was confronted with cinema pictures of suffragettes: 'These infernal sexless beasts make England a laughing stock and the whole lot ought to be shot. It was jolly seeing the "Bobbies" marching along solid as rocks.'[49] At twenty-one, Stafford Cripps was very much the callow Englishman abroad, confiding to his diary the unconsidered prejudices of the class into which he had had the good fortune to be born.

Stafford and Isobel: their partnership

It is no more surprising that Stafford happily mobilized the 'Cripps Chronicle' behind his father's election campaign in 1910 than that he should have noticed with approval the presence in the committee rooms of a tall fair-haired girl a couple of years younger than himself. Isobel Swithinbank came from a neighbouring family and had always lived in the country. Prospective heiress to a substantial fortune, she was the unsophisticated product of an upbringing which left her as bereft of academic attainments as of domestic skills. Stafford enlisted the aid of Ruth Cripps in getting to know her. A trip to the Henley regatta broke the ice; there was evidently an understanding that Isobel might write to Stafford during his forthcoming visit to Germany.

His Hamburg diary thus catches him at a moment of tension that had

44. ibid., 22 July 1910. 45. ibid., 20 July 1910. 46. ibid., 31 July 1910.
47. ibid., 21 July 1910. 48. ibid., 29 July 1910. 49. ibid., 13 July 1910.

both a sexual undertow and implications for his future career. He was a young man adrift in a foreign city, lonely, and on tenterhooks about a possible relationship with a girl across the sea. The fellow-students in his language class, especially a couple of Americans, were the only companions of his own age. After evenings spent drinking with them – 'Rather a poor night after a quart of Heller'[50] – Stafford sometimes felt rueful about the company he was keeping. 'They make me quite tired with their rotten talk of women, women, women,' he noted, pausing to add: 'Though women spoken of in a proper way are a very pleasant subject for conversation.'[51] A visit to the cafés of 'the Montmartre of Hamburg' was dismisssed with arm's-length disdain: 'Thank goodness we haven't got such a place in London.'[52] Yet, while himself in London, he had obviously experienced rather more than the salutary exercise of roller-skating at Olympia, which early biographers record. 'I don't mean that I don't laugh at vulgar things & enjoy them but all the time I simply hate myself for it,' he wrote after seeing a German musical comedy which elicited a favourable – and necessarily well-informed – comparison with the atmosphere of the leading London music-halls, 'say Daly's or the Gaiety'.[53]

The timbre of Stafford's emotional responses needs to be judged in context – no easy matter. He had been the spoiled youngest child in a close-knit family, united in compensating for the premature loss of Theresa Cripps as wife and mother. His feelings spontaneously ran to uninhibited expression, within contemporary conventions that are not always easy to decode. For example, he had as a schoolboy formed an evidently close relationship with the father of one of his contemporaries, Stanton Coit. Well-known as a lecturer in the ethical societies of London, Coit was a cosmopolitan aesthete who saw it as his mission to introduce young Stafford to the delights of Florence on the visit they took together in 1906. Coit's subsequent attempts to nourish his friendship with 'dearest Dad' through invitations to the theatre in London may read oddly today. 'Why not come for lunch so that we could have the afternoon together as well,' he importuned. 'It will take us quite half a day to become fully Greek in spirit, Athenian in wit and Attic in idiom again.'[54] If there was a homoerotic charge here, it is likely to have been as fundamentally innocent as Stafford's exposure to the risqué world of the music-hall or his early, fleeting attachments to girls of his own class.

Only after his encounter with Isobel did Stafford's feelings find a focus

50. ibid., 15 July 1910.   51. ibid., 17 July 1910.   52. ibid., 19 July 1910.
53. ibid., 21 July 1910.   54. Coit to RSC, 20 January 1908.

and become serious. Here is the secret ingredient that explains the rather feverish tone of some entries in Stafford's diary, exploring dilemmas that now had an achingly personal inner meaning. Isobel's name is never mentioned but her presence haunts the pages. On Wednesday: 'Still I am just waiting for that one letter to come.' On Thursday: 'I am still expecting that letter but it doesn't seem to come.' It turns out that, in comparison with German girls and American girls, 'the English are the happy mean, they can sit still but they are full of life and they look it'. There are otherwise inexplicable mood swings. 'Ripping family, topping friends, and every chance in life,' Stafford decides on Wednesday. 'I am one of the favoured few!!!' But on Thursday – 'I think it's waiting for that letter that is getting on my nerves' – he is cast down.

If someone came and told me that I was going to stay here 10 years and not see a soul I knew, I should probably remark Oh and commit suicide quite decently. But they won't so why bother. Come now my friend, you will weary Stafford with your chatter. Cheer up and Pretend the sun is shining – light the gas if you like, put on a straw hat and pretend you are in the sunshine. Verruckt alles Verruckt.[55]

On Friday the sun comes out. 'Patience is well rewarded. I got that letter and a topping letter it was, too toppinger than even I hoped.'[56]

Only a week later, Stafford's thoughts were prompted by news from home. Stanton Coit's son, Dicky, announced his engagement to a mutual friend, Violet Slocock – 'two of the most priceless people this world has ever produced' – and threw Stafford into a heady fit of exuberance: 'How ripping it is to know that two really topping people are going to be happy together. I laughed with pure joy for fully half an hour.' That he was undisguisably projecting his own intense feelings is apparent from his reflections over the page. 'I wonder when I shall get engaged and to whom? I only hope God may make me worthy some day to ask some dear soul to share my life with me.'[57] Resolute in not naming names in his diary, where the secrecy of his inner thoughts from his family was now much on his mind, Stafford kept up his fiction of discussing marriage merely hypothetically. 'I really feel as if I ought to fall a victim to some goddess soon,' he wrote. 'It makes me healthier, happier, harder-working and altogether a better man.' He came near to admitting his personal interest in adding: 'Well men may be fools when they are in love, then all I can say is may I be a fool pretty soon.'[58]

55. RSC diary, 20, 21 July 1910.   56. ibid., 22 July 1910.   57. ibid., 30 July 1910.
58. ibid., 31 July 1910.

Stafford asked Isobel Swithinbank to marry him some five months later, in the Alps. Their correspondence had developed wonderfully after its anxious start. 'I do rather object to being called Stafford,' one letter from Hamburg disclosed, 'I simply hate the name, and I am just succeeding in breaking all my friends to the use of Dad, it's shorter and I prefer it – but of course if you insist I can't prevent it!'[59] Ruth Cripps was instrumental in organizing a suitably chaperoned ski party, of which other members were her future husband (Jack Egerton) and her brother Leonard (who had first forwarded 'that letter' to Hamburg), as well as Stafford and Isobel. They all set off for Klosters. Stafford and Isobel came back after only a few days, with the chaperone, of course, and with the sudden news of their plans, which, given that Stafford was twenty-one and Isobel just short of twenty, took both their families aback.

Had they been able to read Stafford's Hamburg diary, they would have had more time to prepare themselves, not just for the match itself but for the urgency of his timetable. He stated baldly: 'I cannot possibly be engaged for 2 or 3 years, how long that sounds, it sounds like centuries.' He was already rehearsing the merits of long as against short engagements, and deciding that true love made the latter desirable, on emotional if not financial grounds. 'I sometimes feel that I shall never be able to afford to marry,' he concluded, but, if faced with the prospect of waiting as long as five years, 'I should simply have to commit suicide.'[60] He had clearly made up his own mind and, as usual, felt fortified that he had been guided to do the right thing. 'How awfully lucky I have been out here,' he wrote, 'oh God is very kind to me, and I feel I never have and never can deserve it but try!'[61]

In this frame of mind, Stafford Cripps was an irresistible force. What ensured that he did not meet an immovable objection – only one that needed focused advocacy and his inflexible will to overcome – was the undeniable fact that both families possessed ample resources. The trump card was his switch from a future career in science to one in law. He later told Estorick that this was just what he had always intended – a kind of claim that Cripps made rather more often than can actually be verified.[62] That he had already begun to read for the bar in 1910, alongside his scientific studies, simply shows that, after meeting Isobel, he kept his options open. What the law offered was not an immediate income: it was the prospect of a secure professional career, following in his father's footsteps, with the same sort

59. RSC to IC (July/August 1910).   60. RSC diary, 8 August 1910.
61. ibid., 30 July 1910.   62. Estorick, p. 32.

of possibility that it might lead Stafford too into politics. This was the scenario that persuaded Alfred Cripps to underwrite Stafford's ambition to qualify as a barrister and thus allow him to marry Isobel in July 1911 without becoming totally dependent on her inheritance.

From the time of their engagement in January 1911, Stafford poured out his heart to Isobel. This early correspondence is what one might expect: copious and cloying – at least when read in the cold light of posterity. But the fact that the letters were written, and kept, tells its own story of young lovers, tense with fraught passions, absorbed in each other, and investing their hopes in an idealized future relationship. Stafford was more than ready to bid farewell to his bachelor freedom. 'After dinner we went to an ordinary pub called Bennetts,' he recounts to Isobel, 'and drank Rhum Punch, which bored me rather as the conversation got very vulgar and when one has a glimpse of Heaven one cannot put up with absolute vulgarity as one used to do. That Darling is one of the ways you have helped Dad to become a little better . . .'.[63]

What cultural interests they shared remains elusive. Isobel had little intellectual discipline; her daughter later commented, while the family was marooned in the Moscow embassy, that 'not being used to learning she can't take up Russian, for example, because a little would tire her out completely'.[64] During their engagement, Stafford told Isobel, 'I love reading with you,' and enthused that 'when we are together we can start reading books on every kind of interesting subject.'[65] There is little sign that this practice was maintained in later years.

Stafford wrote poetry, in an emotionally charged but unmemorable sub-Georgian style, at odd moments throughout his life. The literary influences that shaped him as a young man are not hard to find.

I think really if I were only allowed two books they would be the Bible and Browning. Browning is so full of life. He's like a great city, you can find what suits your mood, grave or gay, sad or happy, serious or frivolous . . . I feel for some inscrutable reason as if I were a second fat monk sitting by a fire with my glass of wine and laughing over some story. Dear Browning, what a good companion.[66]

Yet he wrote later that 'my brain is quite incapable of remembering accurately any phrases and in spite of all the poetry I have read, and some

63. RSC to IC, 25 March 1911.
64. Theresa Cripps diary, 29 November 1940 (passage in secret ink).
65. RSC to IC, 25 January 1911.   66. RSC diary, 27 July 1910.

pieces many times over, there is no single poem that I could repeat by heart'.[67]

Kipling's short story 'The Brushwood Boy' provided the newly engaged couple with an apposite fantasy to live out. In the story, the boy grows up literally dreaming of the girl he will marry: his Annieanlouise, whom he would find waiting for him by the brushwood pile. Back in England, after making his way as a soldier in India, he finds that his brushwood girl has been living all along in his parents' neighbourhood. 'She's one of the Hertfordshire Lacys,' explains his uncomprehending father. 'When her aunt dies –' but at this point the wise mother decides, with a dig of the elbow, to cut short indelicate discussion of the heiress's prospects. Inevitably, and quickly, the young couple discover each other, they make plans ('What's the shortest limit for people to get engaged?') and they fulfil their destiny.[68] 'I wish my Annieanlouise was here to keep me in order,' so Isobel hears 'from the Brushwood Boy' in March 1911.[69] A couple of months later, Stafford tells her that 'I quite agree with your Father, who thinks probably that Pa should give me as much as you get.'[70]

Isobel's family could afford to be generous. Her mother, Amy, was one of two daughters of the businessman and philanthropist J. C. Eno, whose fortune from Eno's Fruit Salts amounted to one and a half million pounds at his death in 1915 (roughly fifty million in today's money). On his daughter's marriage to Commander H. W. Swithinbank in 1883, Eno had made a settlement that offered a direct model for that from which Isobel benefited on her marriage to Stafford Cripps. Family trust funds provided for her (as for her sister and brother) in a complex series of interlocking arrangements that make it difficult to put a figure on the total extent to which Isobel herself benefited from the Eno inheritance. Her father's death at sea in 1928 was to bring about a major transfer (he left nearly £150,000) and Amy Swithinbank's death in 1942 released the rest, over £200,000, some of it direct to her grandchildren. Tax returns put Isobel Cripps's gross income just before the Second World War at just under £6,000 (not far short of £200,000 today). Initially, on her marriage in 1911, she got £500 per annum, which matched what Stafford could expect from his own father, though Isobel's allowance was soon to be increased by £1,000 a year on her grandfather's death.[71]

67. ibid., 28 December 1919.   68. Kipling, 'The Brushwood Boy', at pp. 392, 405.
69. RSC to IC, 21 March 1911.   70. ibid., 4 May 1911.
71. Swithinbank marriage settlement, statement and account, 2 July 1943; Amy Swithinbank's estate, statement and account, 14 February 1950; Bernard Drake to Diana Cripps, 1 May 1941, for IC's income; Swithinbank to RSC, 10 June 1922; RSC to IC, 3, 4 May 1911. His trustees

During their married life Stafford and Isobel Cripps were usually together and their domestic closeness was often remarked upon. Lord Parmoor's diary notes of an early holiday with them: 'Isobel and Staff. very happy together and it was a treat to have them with me.'[72]

Yet it is also clear that Isobel had a hard time, especially when her children were young in the 1920s. They remembered being left to be looked after by the nanny while their mother travelled with their father to London; but she remembered being left alone in the country a good deal while Stafford built up his career. She confessed later that she 'was at times pretty ill, and broke down, though never went deeply over the "border line".'[73] It was not until the mid-1930s that she turned the corner; and not until the Second World War, with her children now grown up, that Isobel emerged also as a political wife with an unusual prominence in her husband's career. For example, the taxing programme of visits that he undertook to wartime factories as Minister of Aircraft Production from 1942 to 1945 saw Isobel almost always at Stafford's side.

Since he had kept his first diary to stave off loneliness, it is not surprising that the habit lapsed thereafter and, once Stafford and Isobel were living together, talking naturally superseded writing to each other. Whenever they were subsequently parted, however, Stafford reverted to his practice of virtually daily letters. Here is the origin of the three big diaries of his mature years, covering his round-the-world journey of 1939–40, his exile in Russia of 1940–42, and his visit to India of 1946. All of these diaries have a complementary and overlapping relationship with his letters to Isobel.

This is not true, however, of the leather-bound quarto diary in which Stafford began writing in October 1917 and into which entries were spasmodically made until they petered out in 1923. 'I should find it much easier to keep a daily journal, than to try to write précis of the happenings of every few months,' he admitted at one point, indicating one reason why he ultimately abandoned his literary experiment.[74] Barely more than a fragment, at forty-seven pages, this diary served as 'a record of my personal doings', often somewhat retrospective; it was for the benefit of the Cripps

---

in this settlement were Leonard Cripps and the solicitor Bernard Drake, whose wife Barbara was their cousin on the Potter side. See also Bernard Harris, 'Cripps: his wealth and his taxes', *Sunday Express*, May 1949.

72. Parmoor diary, 25 September 1912.

73. IC, 'A note on the experience of F. M. Alexander technique', 22 July 1943; cf. Appiah, *Attic*, p. 55.

74. RSC diary, 28 December 1919.

family 'and is not meant to interest anyone else.'[75] It would be as wrong to pretend that this is an undiscovered seam of pure gold as to deny that previous biographies have suffered from not using it. Together with his letters to Isobel, here is our best source for Stafford's own feelings about the phase of his life before he became a full-time politician. It was dominated by four major concerns: the impact of the First World War and his own delicate health; his growing family and their life at their country home (Goodfellows); his career as a barrister; and his quest for fulfilment in public life. These are important themes, each worthy of exploration.

War invalid

That the First World War seriously undermined Cripps's health is beyond doubt. Through Estorick, this story was given currency in bold (but slightly puzzling) terms, asserting that the illness which Cripps suffered in 1916 was wholly unanticipated. 'Up to this time he had been a splendidly healthy person, physically fit, enjoying life to the utmost,' readers were told in 1949. 'He had had no need to think about his diet. He had eaten the food he liked.'[76] This was, perhaps, what it was prudent to tell an electorate of thwarted carnivores, suspicious of the Chancellor's fads; but Cripps's diaries show that it is not the whole truth. 'No lunch today or dinner I think!' he writes after one pre-war stomach upset. 'Better without!'[77] This is exactly the same tone – in Hamburg in 1910 as in Delhi in 1946 – that Stafford consistently struck in dealing with his lifelong digestive problems. He was already telling Isobel in 1911 of his self-invented simple cure: 'eating a decent and not excessive amount and doing a great deal of walking'.[78]

When Estorick came to deal with the outbreak of the First World War, he wrote: 'Without a moment's hesitation Stafford and his brothers volunteered for service in the armed forces.'[79] True, Seddon, the eldest and also a lawyer, became an officer in the Lincolnshire Yeomanry, charged

75. ibid., prefatory note, 1917.
76. *Leader Magazine*, 1 October 1949. This passage is not in the biography.
77. RSC diary, 25 July 1910. 'After eating only one small rusk yesterday and going to bed early I feel much better this morning, though not quite well yet,' he added the next day; and even four days later: 'Not feeling too fit': RSC diary, 26, 29 July 1910.
78. RSC to IC, 28 March 1911.
79. Estorick, p. 45; cf. *Leader Magazine*, 24 September 1949: 'The four Cripps boys sprang to attention, and joined the millions answering their country's call.' Estorick (1941), p. 21, had been even more emphatic – 'all the Cripps sons joined the army' – implying that Stafford was driving ambulances as a soldier.

with court martial duties – desertion was a major problem – throughout the period of hostilities; the dashing Freddie redeemed his playboy reputation by making good as a genuinely heroic soldier in the Royal Buckinghamshire Hussars Yeomanry; and Len, to whom Stafford was closest, resumed a military career begun in the Fourth Hussars. Estorick does not explain why their 'splendidly healthy' fourth brother should not have done likewise.

The fact is that his health was already giving cause for concern. 'Stafford by no means well,' his father noted in March 1914, 'but I hope he may improve quickly if we have good weather.'[80] This hope proved vain, as Stafford's diary shows. 'In June I had a breakdown and was obliged to lie up for a month,' he explained, adding that, when war came in August, 'I was at the time under medical treatment and being married did not think of trying for the army as at that time married men were not wanted.'[81] It is true that the current expectation was that single men would volunteer before married men. It is interesting that Stafford presents this, alongside his already uncertain health, as his reason for not attempting to enlist; and this contradicts the notion, possibly family legend but first published in Cooke's biography, that Stafford was rejected as unfit by the army doctors.[82] He was not held back by doubts about the justifiability of war, such as the freshly ennobled Lord Parmoor increasingly harboured. Instead Stafford threw himself into recruiting activities, showing a readiness to accept sacrifices – 'At this time Allen my chauffeur joined the army' – that was vicarious through no lack of belligerent zeal.[83]

Cripps, true to form, came up with an initiative of his own. Together with Egerton, he crossed to France in October 1914 on a freelance mission to deliver winter comforts to the troops. It was just after the British army had suffered the German onslaught in the battle of the Marne. 'This was the first impression we had of real war and even this seemed in some ways more like manoeuvres,' Cripps wrote, 'though the Hospital trains consisting in most instances of cattle trucks only were very impressive and terribly real.'[84] Once in France, he determined on joining the British Red Cross Society (BRCS) and, kitted out in its khaki uniform, soon became driver of a specially built two-ton lorry which Isobel persuaded her grandfather Eno to donate. For Stafford, it was again time to get out and get under; he

80. Parmoor diary, 29 March 1914.
81. RSC diary, 14 October 1917, retrospective entry.
82. Cooke, *Cripps*, p. 67; cf. Bryant, *Cripps*, p. 53, Burgess, *Cripps*, p.18.
83. RSC diary, 14 October 1917. Estorick (1941), p. 21, gives quite the contrary impression.
84. RSC diary, 14 October 1917.

assured Isobel after six months that 'old Eno is running beautifully – just like new'. He put in almost a year of ambulance service, evacuating wounded men through Boulogne. 'No one who was not there can conceive how dependent the Army were on the BRCS in those early days,' he claimed, recalling that they 'carried nearly every conceivable Hospital requisite, garment and game including also coal, milk, coffins and stretchers with drunken soldiers!'.[85] He told Isobel of shifting six tons of mineral water off the quay in one day; subsequently of having a sore back. It was arduous and unremitting work: 'Our most disagreeable job was coal-carting which took place two or three times a week; on the hot July days tipping sacks of dusty coal in a small cellar was no joke!'[86]

Throughout the summer of 1915, then, Cripps was still in Boulogne, shovelling coal. The received version (originating in Strauss's biography and faithfully repeated since) is that, faced with the use of gas by the Germans at Ypres in April 1915, 'someone in the Government remembered he was a scientist', and that Cripps was accordingly summoned home by telegram, to begin work at once in a munitions factory.[87] Cripps's own wartime record suggests that this account is, at best, a conflation. At the end of May 1915 he made a note of receiving an order: 'Hold yourself in readiness to proceed to St Omer at any time as a chemist in connection with these poisonous gases.' Cripps confessed himself 'flabbergasted' because of the implication that he would thereby be deprived of his first chance in six months' service to get home and moved quickly to secure a week's leave first.[88] Predictably, his week's leave proved 'heavenly'; after which Cripps 'then returned to Boulogne but never heard any more of the chemical job'.[89] In September, however, on leave again in England, he heard from Egerton, now employed in the new Ministry of Munitions, that chemists were indeed needed and Cripps took the initiative in offering his own services. This time he was taken on and sent to the royal gunpowder factory at Waltham Abbey, to train in the manufacture of gun cotton, and later tetryl, necessary in detonating TNT.

Cripps was to spend the next two years working for the Ministry of Munitions, under conditions satisfactory neither to his finances (which

85. RSC to IC, 11 May 1915.
86. RSC diary, 14 October 1917; RSC to IC, April 1915 (probably 1 April) and 19 April 1915.
87. Strauss, p. 30; cf. Estorick, pp. 45–6, Cooke, *Cripps*, pp. 67–8, Bryant, *Cripps*, p. 53, and Burgess, *Cripps*, p. 18.
88. RSC diary, 30 May 1915, misleadingly annotated by Isobel: 'From RSC in France: Letter of recall.'
89. RSC diary, 14 October 1917.

could well bear the temporary strain) nor his health (which could not). He had started off with a few simple axioms. 'I am sure if all the workers in the munition factories were put under military law and discipline it would be an excellent thing and would show a greatly improved output – but I suppose that means national service – and why not?' he wrote, supplying Isobel with the answer: 'Because we've got a sort of Party government still.'[90] This gibe against the Asquith Government shows him more of a hard-line militarist Tory than a champion of Labour, which maintained a strong aversion to industrial conscription; though the good labour relations under Cripps's subsequent management suggest that in practice his methods were tempered by experience.

What gave Cripps his chance was a familiar mixture of his useful family connections, his unusual professional qualifications, plus his own determination. He wheeled out impressive referees to impress the Ministry: not only Sir William Ramsay but Jack Egerton (now his brother-in-law) and Lord Parmoor himself. It was Egerton who secured Cripps's move, after two months' training, to a factory at Queensferry, near Chester on the Dee estuary, ostensibly concerned with installing a tetryl plant. His real task was to help Colonel Waring, the Superintendent, who was single-handed, and Cripps records that he 'put in 12–14 hours work every day – including Sunday – helping Col. Waring generally', since little needed doing on the tetryl plant. 'All Christmas week I worked a night shift managing the gun cotton plant which had just reached the production stage and I had the satisfaction of supervising the packing of the first gun cotton pressed,' he noted. 'I also did my own work in the day time reaching a climax on Christmas Day when I did 20 hours work.'[91]

Conditions at Queensferry, continually under pressure to expand output, were grim enough to tax anyone's health. Colonel Waring took ten weeks' sick leave at the end of January 1916. Shortly beforehand, in Cripps's version, 'I was appointed assistant superintendent and promised a rise in salary from the £125 p.a. I was getting.'[92] In Waring's absence, Cripps moved into his house and took full charge of the factory for six weeks. This arrangement proved unexpectedly beneficial – for production, at least. On his twenty-seventh birthday, and apparently on little over two pounds a week, Cripps found himself running a vital war plant on 140 acres, responsible for 6,000 workers. 'At the end of the six weeks, I had a very bad breakdown which took me four months to recover from,' Cripps reported in his diary. 'When I returned in July I found that the Treasury had repudi-

90. RSC to IC, 29 May 1915.   91. RSC diary, 14 October 1917.   92. ibid.

ated my appointment as assistant superintendent and refused to give me any increase in salary.'[93]

Stafford's condition was naturally a source of anxiety to his family. 'He seems to get on slowly,' his father noted, 'and I hardly know what is really the matter with him.'[94] He was surely correct to say that his son had 'broken down from overwork'[95] and it is easy to see why. Queensferry became one of the three largest munitions factories in the country and, according to the Ministry of Munitions, the most efficient. Cripps remained rightly proud of his record there and did not lack well-placed witnesses to corroborate his claims. 'His breakdown was the direct consequence, as I have always felt, of his zeal,' Waring wrote to the Ministry, with indignation but without effect.[96]

Cripps went back in a subordinate position, his salary still only £700 per annum. Underpaid, overworked, he found that he 'got seedy again' and in January 1917 his condition was diagnosed as colitis, an imperfectly understood affliction of the bowel with symptoms of diarrhoea that resemble dysentery. Characteristically, he did not give up work at once but carried on until June, when he again entered a nursing home and convalesced for three months, with frustratingly little to do. 'On Sept. 1st,' he noted stoically, 'I saw my two doctors and they told me that it was useless my trying to work again at Queens Ferry for at least a year as I could only do light work.'[97] He resigned at once.

This was effectively the end of Stafford's war. 'My health is still bad and there is no immediate prospect of my return to work,' Cripps wrote in October 1918. 'The last eight months I have lived an invalid's life and been able to do nothing to help my Country.' He confessed his worry at remaining in this state 'for the rest of my life'.[98] Even his father, who had repeatedly discerned false dawns over the past months, noted that 'he makes some progress but it is very slow'.[99] Perhaps some sense of anxiety, however misplaced, that he was dodging the column stalled Stafford's recovery; for the remarkable thing, given the seriousness of the prognosis in October 1918, is how quickly he bounced back with the return of peace in the next month. 'Personally I have advanced greatly', he wrote early in 1919, having been given permission to return to work in January by his doctors.[100] Once able to work at all, he worked without stint. According to Strauss's

93. ibid.   94. Parmoor diary, 1 May 1916.   95. ibid., 16 April 1916.
96. Waring quoted in Burgess, *Cripps*, p. 20, which contains an excellent account of this episode, drawing on the Ministry of Munitions archives.
97. RSC diary, 14 October 1917.   98. ibid., 5 October 1918.
99. Parmoor diary, 31 October 1918.   100. RSC diary, 2 March 1919.

authorized version, Cripps 'solved the problem by a daily routine to which he adhered closely for years; rise early, work in Court until about 4 p.m., work in Chambers until about 9 p.m., home, straight to bed, study in bed until 2 a.m.'[101]

Over a period of two or three years, Cripps clawed back lost ground, reserving and rationing all his strength for his legal practice, regardless of other temptations or claims upon his time. 'I have concentrated all my powers on my work up till the present time as I am not really strong enough to undertake anything else,' he explained.[102] This highly disciplined strategy, once adopted, became a way of life. 'We have been out very little as with my work I am not strong enough to go out in the evenings as well,' he reported in 1921. 'I have been however much better and with the exception of my throat which is still very troublesome at times, am nearly my normal self again.'[103]

For Cripps, the First World War was the beginning of a valetudinarian regime that proved lifelong. He had, as one sympathizer told Isobel, 'done his duty equally as if he had become invalided at the front'.[104] His colitis dogged him for the next thirty-five years, sometimes with a dramatic collapse at a moment of stress, more often as a chronic constraint which he battled with resilience, courage and blind obstinacy. The pattern of compulsive overworking, whenever he was fit enough to do so, time and again brought its nemesis in recurrent breakdowns. To say that his susceptibility to illness had a psychosomatic element does not, of course, imply that the physical symptoms were not real; but they came and went, in ways that were surely not just fortuitous coincidence, at significant moments of stress in Cripps's career. As regards his own health, he overtaxed limited resources more blatantly than he ever did as Chancellor of the Exchequer.

Character and circumstance

'For leadership in the labour movement Stafford had a most unfit upbringing,' Beatrice Webb once observed, with her customary crispness. With every advantage in life – 'born and bred in a luxurious Tory household' – he then 'married, at little over twenty years old, a wealthy girl with a millionaire mother. Hence he was able to settle in a charming country home

101. Strauss, p. 33.   102. RSC diary, 26 November 1920.
103. ibid., 31 December 1921.
104. Quoted by Estorick, *Leader Magazine*, 1 October, 1949.

of his own as well-to-do squire.'[105] This was indeed one image that Cripps acquired in the inter-war years – deservedly in some respects and misleadingly in others. His home life discloses distinctive personal attitudes with a public resonance that has often been misperceived.

It is true, as we know from his diary, that he had long thought it a natural ambition to possess a country house; and that, as soon as he could, he took steps to realize it. The fact that Isobel knew no other life made it all the more necessary to provide the sort of support system to which she was habituated by temperament and training (or lack of it). The tribulations of the war years had exposed her domestic deficiencies, notably at the commencement of Stafford's munitions work at Waltham Abbey. Strauss provides one account.

It was a hard period for them both. Isobel Cripps, still in her early twenties, had been brought up in a wealthy home surroundeed by luxury, and had not been taught to cook, wash up, or scrub floors. Now she found herself getting up at five o'clock every morning, wrapping cold sausages in a red handkerchief for her husband's lunch, doing her own housework, and caring for the children without even the aid of gas or electricity.[106]

Whether this is more heart-rending or disingenuous is a nice point. For during this particular period, which actually lasted for only two weeks, Isobel was not left with these chores since Stafford had secretly arranged for her childhood nanny to join them; and, as his diary further makes clear, their two infant children were meanwhile left with relatives in Dorchester.[107]

The fact that Stafford and Isobel had married young did not induce them to defer starting a family. John was born ten months after the marriage, in May 1912, and Diana in September 1913. They were all living at Fernacres Cottage, Fulmer, Buckinghamshire, near the commuter station of Gerrards Cross. Not quite so modest as it may sound, the property had nine bedrooms and was set in three and a half acres of grounds. This was to be let during the war, while Isobel and the children spent much time either with her

105. Webb diary, 9 July 1939, in MacKenzie and MacKenzie (eds.), *Webb: Diary*, iv, p. 436.
106. Strauss, pp. 30–31. With her husband George, she was herself a house-guest at Goodfellows in the 1930s, and thus surely able to observe her hostess's limitations. Theresa Ricketts confirmed during her interview that her mother was incapable of keeping house and that her daughters had to deputize for her.
107. RSC diary, 14 October 1917; cf. Estorick, p. 46, on Stafford arranging for 'Nana' to come and help. Burgess, *Cripps*, p. 19, wrongly suggests it was Mazelle, who arrived later.

parents in Buckinghamshire or at the Playnes' Gloucestershire house, Long-fords. When Stafford began work at Queensferry he was able to reunite his family, if only for a couple of months, at the Grosvenor Hotel in Chester. A furnished house was taken early in 1916, shortly before Stafford's collapse and his first spell in a nursing home nearby.

In July 1916, following his return to work, Stafford moved his family into a new house built for them on factory property at Queensferry. It was, so Lord Parmoor thought when he stayed there, 'quite a comfortable home near the works'.[108] In this convenient, if unwholesome and hazardous, location the family settled down for nearly twelve months, during which Isobel had a mis-carriage. But Stafford's deteriorating health then entailed further moves for the Cripps family. Initially they took a house at Gerrards Cross, combined with a small service flat in Half Moon Street, in the vain hope that Stafford could begin regular work in London. For most of 1918, however, it was an invalid life in Gloucestershire, at the dower house belonging to Longfords called The Chestnuts. Called out of retirement, Mazelle was with the family throughout, still much needed.

Despite worries over his health, Stafford found his months at The Chest-nuts a happy time, watching his own children warm to country pursuits, as he had himself at Parmoor. 'We have lived out of doors as much as possible and have spent nearly the whole of our time in the garden or the field,' Stafford wrote. 'We have started farming in a small way with chickens, pigs, rabbits, cows and bees and hope that the experience will prove of value later on.'[109] It comes as no surprise, then, to find that Stafford and Isobel began looking for a country property of their own, with land that could be farmed. Their quest proved successful early in 1919, with occupation set for September. 'The name is Goodfellows, Lechlade, Glos.; and the village is Filkins in Oxfordshire,' he wrote in his diary. 'The farm is 141 acres and the house a nice old Tudor farm house, small but cosy.'[110] No doubt it seemed small compared with Parmoor or Longfords; but by the time a new wing had been added, faithfully working in Cotswold stone, and with woodwork that satisfied Stafford's standards as an amateur carpenter, Goodfellows was undeniably a substantial property.

As the well-appointed country home of the successful lawyer he duly became, it would have been unremarkable; as the landed estate of a promi-nent champion of the proletariat, Goodfellows was to find itself featured in a number of illustrated magazine or newspaper articles over the years,

108. Parmoor diary, 16 September 1916.   109. RSC diary, 5 October 1918.
110. ibid., 2 March 1919.

though following a major fire after the Second World War little remains today to evoke the legend of the 'Red Squire'.

How did Cripps find the resources to purchase, improve and maintain Goodfellows, at a point when his legal earnings were still scanty and Isobel had yet to come into her inheritance? 'We thought a lot over the plans,' he noted, 'and eventually decided to go in for the most extensive alterations in spite of their expense; as we did not want to have to start altering again, and we preferred to have a really nice home even though we are uncertain as to whether we can really afford it!'[111] All calculations about the scale of expenditure here have to take account of the fact that 1919–20 saw acute price instability, with a brief post-war inflationary boom that particularly affected building costs – as Cripps discovered. The purchase price was £4,500; stocking the farm required a further £2,000; and building costs were originally estimated at £2,500. Cripps records selling all his war loan at £3,800 and borrowing £5,000 from the bank. His mother-in-law paid for the electrical work, at £600 (a gesture that she could well afford, having inherited half of the Eno fortune in 1915). Even so, Stafford needed further loans both from his father and from Isobel's.

Since the renovation work eventually cost £5,000, double the estimate, 'and has quite crippled us financially',[112] Cripps was putting his finances under as much pressure as his health in taking on a commitment that was both heavy and open-ended, albeit potentially worthwhile. 'The work has been well done, however,' he concluded, 'and if we can survive the next few years (financially) all will be well – if not we must sell.'[113] The total outlay was £11,500. Its modern equivalent, at perhaps thirty times as much, may seem a fairly modest price for high-class property. At the time it undoubtedly looked a formidable sum, matched against experience of pre-war prices, and represented a bold decision by Cripps. It would not have been reasonable to foresee that, within a decade, his annual income was to exceed his initial capital investment in Goodfellows.

There is no doubt that family money made Stafford more confident, and credit-worthy, in taking on Goodfellows; but he did not simply regard it as his due. 'I sort of resent the dishonesty of living on money not earned – it isn't dishonest I know but a strong healthy man ought to earn the money for his family to live on and not have it given to him,' he had told Isobel early in the war. 'I know we have had it all given so far but then I am just reaching the earning stage and I want to have something to make an effort for.' He spoke not only of liking his work but of needing an objective to earn money, as the

111. ibid., 28 December 1919.   112. ibid., 26 November 1920.   113. ibid.

provider for his family. 'It'll make me make a huge and mighty struggle when this ghastly affair is over,' he promised, 'to make you happier and to be able to provide you and the children with all the thousands of little luxuries and comforts you deserve.'[114] It hardly seems fanciful to see his acquisition of Goodfellows as the fulfilment of this longstanding goal, as soon as his health had made it feasible to harness his own efforts to this end. He took the decision both anticipating and requiring a highly remunerative career.

The focus of Stafford's hopes and energies was thus his new home and his growing family. Another daughter, Theresa, had been born at The Chestnuts in April 1919 – 'This is the great event of the last four months'[115] – but in the next year the family was finally able to move into Goodfellows. It was there that the birth of the youngest child, Peggy, took place in May 1921 and Stafford proudly recorded that all the villagers came to the christening in Filkins parish church. Satisfied that 'all like it immensely',[116] he was pleased at how quickly they settled down; and the Cripps family were to remain at Goodfellows for twenty years.

For all that, they were in Filkins rather than of Filkins. If John ('Bun') and Diana ('Dinan') first went to school in Filkins, taught by the wife of the village schoolmaster, they did not attend the school itself; and John was soon off to board at Winchester. Theresa ('Tese') and Peggy also went to private schools.[117] Stafford and Isobel might claim an acquaintance with virtually everyone in the village, but their friendships were with people from their own class, who came to Goodfellows as house guests.

Among their relatively small circle of friends, the Weavers were the closest. Lawrence Weaver had had a diverse career as architect, journalist and administrator; it was while he was Controller of Food Supplies that he had met Cripps in 1917. Twelve years his senior, Weaver made efforts to find the convalescent scientist a suitable post in his department, asking him to take over the 'Wart Disease of Potatoes' section.[118] With these inauspicious roots, a warm relationship flourished. Shared hobbies in carpentry and bookbinding saw them together at the workbench in the evenings, and they were later to set up a craft workshop for disabled ex-servicemen, the Ashtead Pottery. After an early visit to Goodfellows by Lawrence and Kathleen Weaver, Stafford recorded that 'one felt at once that they were real friends';[119] and in the following year that 'no one could wish for two better friends'.[120] It was at Good-

114. RSC to IC, 18 May 1915. 115. RSC diary, 7 June 1919.
116. ibid., 26 November 1920. 117. Appiah, *Attic*, p. 57.
118. RSC diary, 1 February 1918. 119. ibid., 26 November 1920.
120. ibid., 31 December 1921.

fellows that the two families spent Christmas together in 1926; there that Kathleen Weaver died after developing pneumonia. The result was that her two adolescent sons, Purcell and Toby, stayed on at Goodfellows and, especially after Lawrence Weaver's death only three years later, were virtually adopted by the Crippses, who paid for their education to be completed.

Stafford was clearly gratified that, after a careful start, the Crippses got to know nearly all the villagers; that Isobel took a great share in the Women's Institute; and that he himself had soon started a village club. Later he was to subsidize the cost difference of building four council houses in Cotswold stone rather than in brick; and in 1935, again at his own expense, he added another stone building, the village centre, to provide a doctor's surgery and athletic facilities.

Noblesse oblige? To a degree. Cripps was now a substantial landowner. He had added substantially to the Goodfellows estate, farming up to 500 acres with the aid of his bailiff or manager, and was accepted by local farmers as a spokesman on current agricultural difficulties. But he did not walk in to Filkins as squire, if only because that role was already pre-empted. 'The neighbourhood is quiet and nice,' he had written on arrival, 'and except for friction existing between the Squire (Goodenough) and the parson (Austen) life seems happy.'[121] It was a classic village feud, which Cripps sought to heal – without, however, playing the squire himself, deferring to Sir William Goodenough on village matters. The fact is that Cripps was wary of distributing largesse, for reasons that reflected deeply held values.

It is worth dwelling on this point. Cripps was not simply a rentier and not simply a paternalist. He might have been easier to understand had he been identified, as many upper-class recruits to Labour were, with a Nonconformist Liberal background in trade, rather than with landed, Anglican Toryism. Stafford's family, Cripps as much as Potter, had been steeped in an ethic that prized hard work – especially by the working class, as Beatrice Webb cuttingly observed. 'The belief – it may almost be called an obsession – that the mass-misery of great cities arose mainly, if not entirely, from spasmodic, indiscriminate and unconditional doles' was a frame of mind that she thought characteristic of 'the Haves' in Victorian England.[122]

She was unafraid to bring such observations very close to home. There are some pertinent remarks in her pre-war diary about Stafford, who (like his brother Seddon) struck her as 'pasty and slack, overfed and under-exercised in body and mind'. This is startlingly unlike the Cripps of the austerity caricature, of course, and perhaps not a wholly fair picture of a

121. ibid., 26 November 1920.   122. Webb, *My Apprenticeship*, pp. 200–201.

young nephew whom she did not yet know at all well; but her strictures made the point that the personal was political.

Stafford has distinct talent, if not a touch of genius, and would naturally be strenuously ambitious. But the indefinite ease of the life, and the very slight demands made on him, are loosening his moral and intellectual fibre. It is odd that exactly the 'school' that thinks the most terrible struggle against fearful odds is good for the poor, take steps to prevent young persons of their own class from having some kind of struggle – even for the pleasures of life! It is strange that these excellent persons should not see that their self-contradictory philosophy of life strikes the ordinary Labour man as hypocritical.[123]

This is a telling point; but more needs to be added before it can fairly be applied to the mature Stafford Cripps. For one thing, it was an anomaly of which he too became increasingly conscious, and not only in his thought but his behaviour. For another, it needs to be remembered that these were not just pious bourgeois platitudes. Part of the nineteenth-century Liberal ethic – the part on which Gladstone founded his politics of moral populism – inculcated pride in working-class independence, including independence of handouts from above. There was a real issue of respect and self-respect here, to which Stafford showed himself attuned in his own peculiar way.

If he accepted the link between effort and reward as a crucial tenet, it was one that imposed exacting demands both on himself and on others. In the pre-war period, he had added a dash of Edwardian anxiety about 'efficiency' that gave a tough-minded edge to his rather callow reflections. Thus 'one of the drawbacks of socialism', he assured Isobel in 1911, lay in the fact that 'if you make things too easy, if you smooth down all the roughness and unpleasantness of life you are so liable to produce a feeble and weak willed race'. True, he did not later choose to talk in this way; but neither did he entirely repent of the view that 'if you do everything for a person and fight all their battles – educate, dress, feed their children, overpay and underwork them you are liable to make them lose the power of doing anything for themselves.'[124]

Surprisingly little of this proved inconsistent with his developing sympathy towards the Labour Party, as reconstituted at the end of the First World War. He still bridled at 'a system of State Philanthropy taking up the

123. Webb diary, 1 December 1909, in MacKenzie and MacKenzie (eds.), Webb: Diary, iii, p. 131.
124. RSC to IC, 31 January 1911.

attitude of "Poor fellow you are very ignorant and boorish but we will do what we can to help you and then you must give us your vote"'.[125] The despicable idea that the working class could be bought off so easily appalled Cripps – the more so, the more he identified their cause as his own.

The point is symbolized in one quintessential part of the Cripps myth. His well-known adoption of teetotalism should surely be seen in this context. This was a step that he was to take when he first joined the Parliamentary Labour Party, on election to the House of Commons in 1930; and he did so, as Beatrice Webb well understood, 'as a protest against the alcoholism of the PLP'.[126] As Cripps privately explained later, he was particularly upset by the 'most demoralizing' spectacle of rich Conservative MPs plying their working-class colleagues with alcohol.[127] This was entirely consistent with his declared policy in Filkins: 'it is our aim to make the villagers pay for their own club and not be dependent on Charity'.[128]

Cripps's mind-set was thus less that of an indulgent rentier than that of a highly motivated entrepreneur – one whose own entrepreneurial nose had led him into the most lucrative branch of the legal profession. Just as Goodfellows was to be relinquished once his legal earnings ceased, so its acquisition had been linked to his own ability to generate the income that provided for its amenities. 'It is great fun and certainly having a "place" of one's own adds a zest to life, though the financial "stringency" which it has entailed is a little trying,' he wrote. 'One thing however is certain and that is that there is no other thing so powerful, as an incentive to work, as a feeling that money *must* be earned.'[129] Cripps resolved what others saw as a troublesome paradox through his ethic of strenuous expectations, which ran as a consistent thread through both his private and his public life.

The choice of a craft

The name of Stafford Cripps would have a cachet as that of a notable twentieth-century lawyer had he never gone near politics. Law was the family business, of course; but in the end Stafford's fame was to exceed that of either his father or his grandfather. Lord Parmoor had retired from the bar on joining the Judicial Committe of the Privy Council in 1914, and Stafford had taken over his chambers; he and his father's old colleague

125. RSC diary, 5 October 1918.   126. Webb diary, 2 September 1934. Cf. Strauss, p. 102.
127. Harriman and Abel, *Special Envoy*, p. 95.   128. RSC diary, 31 December 1921.
129. ibid., 28 December 1919.

Aubrey (Ray) Lawrence also took over the revision of the family law books, *Cripps on Church and Clergy* and *Cripps on Compensation*.

Stafford's diary shows that the early years were not smooth. At the outbreak of the First World War, he wrote, he had 'just begun to see some prospect of getting some work at the bar'.[130] But briefs were hard come by; few came initially in the field of patent law, in which Cripps specialized as a pupil of Arthur Colefax, obviously hoping to capitalize on his own scientific expertise. It was frustrating that offers of two briefs from the Great Western Railway, for whom Cripps had done his first case before the war, did not reach him until after he had gone to serve in France. Only from 1919, therefore, did he get his chance, and even then under unpromising conditions. 'There is very little work to be done at the bar and everyone is slack, so that those who are returning after a long absence find little or nothing to do,' he wrote after three months.[131] Another three months and no improvement: 'Work at the Bar is very slack, slacker than anyone can ever remember.'[132] It is a mistake to think that Cripps's unusual qualifications, or his connection with Colefax, meant that he was able to make his mark at once. 'I have not yet succeeded in obtaining any patent or scientific work,' he noted more than twelve months after returning to his chambers full-time.[133]

How, then, did Stafford survive professionally? His useful family connections again helped out; though it should be said that they were not sufficient to save the legal career of his brother Seddon, who had to become an Oxford don instead. Parmoor had been the great railway lawyer of his day; and, during the bleak year of 1919, the Great Western Railway remembered young Stafford and became his major client. Indeed, apart from this and 'a little work for Eno's', there were only 'odds and ends'.[134] Under the circumstances, it was fortunate that he had a milch cow: indeed two of them.

Cripps records working hard with Ray Lawrence for two years on a new edition of *Cripps on Church and Clergy*. 'It is a great labour, but extremely good practice, it teaches one to read cases and to extract the really valuable portions of the judgments,' Cripps commented.[135] Since this was well received in 1921, it encouraged Cripps and Lawrence to publish a new edition of *Cripps on Compensation* in the following year, again to a good reception. The fact that Lawrence was ready to indulge his young colleague's penchant for practical jokes – he once set fire to the copy of *The Times* that Lawrence was reading – speaks well of their easy relationship.

130. ibid., 14 October 1917.   131. ibid., 2 March 1919.   132. ibid., 7 June 1919.
133. ibid., 9 March 1920.   134. ibid., 28 December 1919.   135. ibid.

Cripps had sufficient faith in his star to turn down a well-remunerated offer to go to India at the beginning of 1920. 'I have now just reached the stage when, if I am ever going to do any good, I might at any moment start getting substantially more work,' he wrote, with a well-founded sense that the tide was about to turn.[136] Slowly at first, it did so, and by the end of 1921 was in flood: 'Work at the Bar has progressed by leaps and bounds, and last term was by far the busiest I have ever had – on several occasions I had to get people to "devil" for me and once or twice I had to return briefs as I was too busy.'[137] As Stafford acknowledged, much of this work came through the firm of solicitors headed by Bernard Drake, his trustee and family connection. At last there was a major scientific brief (concerning Norwegian carbide production) for which Stafford enlisted his brother-in-law Jack Egerton as expert witness. What really made Cripps's name was a long-running case involving the government of the Malayan state of Kelantan, which helped swell his earnings for the tax year 1921–2 to nearly £3,000, enabling family debts on Goodfellows to be repaid.

'Ray Lawrence with his usual kindness has always helped me with my work,' Cripps wrote at the end of 1921, 'and has now with even greater kindness given up his larger room and taken my smaller one as from the beginning of the year.'[138] Lawrence was fourteen years his senior, but it was already apparent that Cripps was leapfrogging into the front rank of barristers; and within six years he became the youngest King's Counsel in the country. It was a step that his father had encouraged; like Goodfellows, it was a bold investment for the future at some risk to immediate income, and again it paid off. By 1930 Cripps's professional earnings topped £20,000, which would be roughly a hundred times as much as a skilled manual worker, and well over half a million pounds in today's money. He cut back somewhat on entering politics, but his earnings were still at least £15,000 a year in the mid-1930s.

Cripps might speak with some contempt of the 'fabulous and fantastic sums' that he was paid by the capitalists whom he represented.[139] Obviously, one reason for his ability to command such high fees was that he was fighting cases where millions of pounds were at stake. But why should Cripps have been singled out and sought out? If he had ever been asked, his uncle Sidney Webb could have explained to Stafford that his was a 'rent of ability', accruing on the basis of an innate or acquired faculty, valuable because it was in short supply rather than rewarded for effort. But Stafford added

136. ibid., 9 March 1920.   137. ibid., 31 December 1921.   138. ibid.
139. *The Times*, *Daily Herald*, 23 September 1935; cf. Strauss, p. 103.

hard work too: fifteen-hour days as a matter of course, meticulously preparing each brief so that every document could be made to count.

'A Rolls-Royce mind, you knew as soon as you met him', was how Cripps struck the young Michael Foot in the 1930s.[140] As a lawyer Cripps became famous for his grasp of evidence. He later said himself that he could re-fight any case of the previous twenty years after an hour with the papers – only to add: 'No, I would not need the papers.'[141] The uncanny accuracy with which he could recollect and pinpoint relevant documents became the stuff of anecdotes, like that which has Cripps telling a nonplussed court: 'If my friend will allow me, I think your Lordship will find that in Bundle 8 of the Correspondence on page 28.'[142] But we have more than admiring, retrospective folklore in testimony. For example, when the historian Reginald Coupland first observed Cripps at work in India in 1942, he recorded on the spot: 'At 7.30 C. dictated his record of the whole day's talks from 10 onwards – without hesitation. A remarkable feat of memory.'[143]

What distinguished Cripps was the way that logic harnessed memory, rather than the way that intuition might inspire more elusive insights. 'There seemed no problem, no issue which he could not strip down to its essentials,' wrote his wartime aide, Graham Spry; 'his power of penetrating to the guts of a problem or a policy, a case at law or a principle in applied science was, perhaps, unmatched among the political leaders and administrators of his time.' Yet Spry prized Cripps's 'powers of analysis and exposition' more highly than his 'powers of creative originality or imagination'.[144] Cripps saw the answer to a problem, even a highly complex problem, with amazing speed – so long as there was an answer. Closed problems, implying specific and determinate solutions, yielded to his methods more readily than open problems, evoking uncertainty and approximation for their resolution.

Geoffrey Wilson, who started work in Cripps's chambers and came to know him well, as will be seen, thought that 'his experience as a lawyer led him to believe that, when he had won an argument, he had also convinced his questioner'.[145] It has rightly been remarked that this was not necessarily a good training for politics. The kind of pleading in which Cripps specialized was not characterized by histrionics, did not involve intuitive judgements on character or motive, and did not depend on persuading a jury of laymen. His was a practical intelligence, highly geared and sharply focused on clearly specified issues.

140. Foot, interview.   141. Plowden, *Industrialist in the Treasury*, p. 20.
142. 'It was usually so,' comments Strauss, p. 37.   143. Coupland diary, 28 March 1942.
144. Spry, obituary for Cripps, Spry papers, 46/10.   145. Wilson, 'My Working Life', p. 16.

Once established as a patent lawyer, what put Cripps's services at a premium was his equal command of scientific and forensic skills. He made a classic contribution to patent law in developing a means of evaluating the 'inventive step', the obviousness of which had to be demonstrated as a requirement for the validity of a patent. Cripps suggested posing the question, whether it was obvious to any skilled chemist in the existing state of knowledge at the date of the patent that he *could* manufacture the relevant product. This approach, subsequently known as 'the Cripps test', is still taught as such to students and practitioners in the field and, further developed in the late twentieth century, enjoyed a renaissance in European patent law.[146] This is surely a remarkable achievement, showing an ability to grasp fundamental issues both of legal procedure and scientific method and to formulate them with precision.

Cripps was known for his patience in expounding a lucidly organized case, sometimes over several days, and occasionally with the result that the other side promptly caved in. He was also held in awe for his hard-fought cross-examination of expert witnesses, when he was never at a loss for the appropriate riposte. What transformed his public image was his appearance in the Gresford public inquiry, a controversial mining disaster with direct political overtones. Yet even here, in his most famous performance as a counsel, his triumph was achieved by enlisting his peculiar aptitude for mastery of a complex technical brief, combined with inexorable cross-examination, so that, even when playing to the gallery, it was on his own terms.

It was the Gresford inquiry that allowed Cripps to parlay his legal achievements into political capital. The death of 266 miners in an explosion in September 1934 at the Gresford colliery, near Wrexham in North Wales, naturally called for a court of inquiry, which met for thirty-eight sessions in all. By prior arrangement, Cripps had already agreed to speak at a Labour meeting in Wrexham; the request of the North Wales Miners' Association to be represented by him at the inquiry duly followed. He agreed to this but refused to take a fee. Part of the myth of Gresford is that a mine manager was imprisoned as a result of Cripps's deadly exposure of wrongdoing in the industry; the fact is that convictions were secured on only eight out of forty-two summonses, with fines of no more than £140.[147]

Cripps's triumph, however, was real enough. What prepared the ground

146. I am indebted on this point to Dr Fritz Dolder, whose forthcoming book on European patent law will elucidate the issue.
147. Williamson, *Gresford*, pp. 202–3, corrects Strauss, p. 80, and Estorick, p. 135.

for it was, as usual, his meticulous technical preparation. Since this largely concerned patterns of air flow and the accumulation of gases in the mine, it directly drew upon Cripps's chemical expertise; and he made Wilson, who was one of his juniors, reduce the mass of statistics to a series of graphs and charts.[148] Armed with sufficient evidence to support his contention that safety had been sacrificed in the pursuit of profit, and licensed by his own rectitude, Cripps went on the offensive from the first. He exploited fifteen years' experience at the bar to force his logic upon shocked and baffled men, especially Bonsall, the manager, whose crime was insufficient attention to a rule-book of which Cripps showed himself the master.

BONSALL: That was an omission on my part.

CRIPPS: And you realize that's a breach of the Act?

BONSALL: I realize that that was an omission on my part.

CRIPPS: And do you realize whether that omission was a breach of the Act?

BONSALL: I can't go any further than that.

CRIPPS: Mr Bonsall, do you know what your duties are as a mine manager?

BONSALL: I do.

CRIPPS: Was it one of your duties to see that this book was filled up after a reading once a month?

BONSALL: It was my duty to countersign –

CRIPPS: I didn't ask you that. I said was it your duty to see this book was filled up once every month after the readings had been taken?

BONSALL: It was my duty to sign the register.

CRIPPS: Are you incapable of answering the question I put to you?[149]

There were, of course, valid points to be made, which Cripps's methods trenchantly elucidated. Thus the contention that the temperature at the bottom of the mine seemed, at 70°F, like that of a cool summer day was exposed to the ineluctable calculation that, since it increased by one degree for every sixty feet, then given a surface temperature of 60°F and a depth of 2,400 feet, the correct answer was 100°F.[150] QED! Cripps's exhibition of intellectual superiority sometimes came uneasily near to an assertion of social superiority. 'I suggest to you,' he told a junior mines inspector, 'that so far as

148. Wilson, 'My Working Life', p. 20; and see Wilson's account, evidently from 1940, in Estorick (1941), pp. 39–41, reproduced in Estorick, pp.134–5.
149. Williamson, *Gresford*, pp. 106–7; these proceedings are taken from the thirty-eight unpublished volumes of evidence held by the North Wales area of the NUM and I rely here on Williamson's careful research in disinterring them.
150. ibid., pp. 105–6.

your supervision of this pit was concerned while you were there it was a farce.' The inspector replied: 'That is wrong, sir.'[151] It is refreshing to find that Cripps occasionally found his overbearing manner resisted. 'I don't know what the term "charter master" means,' he claimed to one miner. 'I'm very ignorant in these things.' 'I know you are,' said the miner. 'I've heard you.'[152]

Gresford saw Cripps at his best and at his worst. In court he was normally subject to more restraint from eminent judges than the lay Commissioner thought fit to impose during the Gresford hearings, which to that extent are not representative of Cripps's ordinary practice. Yet the fact that he had risen to the top in a highly competitive and formally adversarial field carried its own implications. He showed a will to win that was part of his effectiveness as an advocate. His methods won him respect; at Gresford they won him the gratitude of the miners' unions; but they did not win everyone's heart.

In search of a creed

The post of Solicitor-General in a British Government is a hybrid. It is a political appointment to a ministerial office yet legal qualifications are also required. Alfred Cripps nurtured regrets at being passed over as a law officer. The Conservative benches in his day had been replete with ambitious lawyers, confronting the party managers with the problem of awkward choices between numerous eligible claimants. This was a problem escaped by the two post-war minority Labour Governments, recruited from a parliamentary party still containing few university graduates; with a mere four barristers, and only one KC, on the Labour benches in the 1929 parliament, the problem was to find plausibly qualified law officers, however recent their attachment to the party.

In October 1930 Stafford Cripps became Solicitor-General and received the customary knighthood. Legally, he was superbly qualified for the office. Politically, it was another matter. Cripps had not yet entered Parliament; indeed, when that parliament was elected, he had not even been a member of the Labour Party; but following the 1931 General Election, he was regarded as a possible leader of a party that he had joined less than eighteen months previously. How had this come about?

Stafford's diary shows that, while the idea of joining the Labour Party occurred to him at the end of the First World War, it was not mere

151. ibid., p. 149.   152. ibid., p. 104.

negligence that kept him from taking this step for another decade. True, a retrospectively tidied-up account of his tryst with socialism could be formed from fragments like the following letter to Isobel in 1911:

Coming home this evening I saw two poor shivering people – a man & his wife, I think – hobbling along the pavement in the most meagre clothes – cut through by the icy chill of the wind – and looking too wretched and downhearted for words. That's the sort of thing that makes one feel a socialist! I feel somehow they have deserved no worse than I have – probably they have done much better in their fight for life than I should have in their position – yet there they are and here am I. What does it all mean dearest? It is the great puzzle of life and I long to know why God has given us good homes, plenty of money – enough even for luxuries – and those people have nothing.[153]

Yet, cheek by jowl, the overt partisan references speak loyal Toryism. 'Austen Chamberlain made a very good speech this evening on the Canadian question,' Stafford tells Isobel, 'it is so nice to feel that there are *some* patriots left in England.'[154] Again, he reassures her: 'Even if the Liberals do want to kill the Empire and reduce us to little Englandism we will do our very best to thwart them and disappoint them.'[155]

A passage in Stafford's Hamburg diary from the previous summer helps illustrate the tensions in his thinking, especially in his conception of 'social-ism' as an application of the Christian ethic rather than as a political strategy or movement. That evening Stafford had watched the sun setting:

Imagine the joy of the poor slum-beings if only they could see these sort of views. One does not necessarily think that they could appreciate them at once, but it is a regenesis of the divine spirit which is needed and not a genesis. Every child is born with the same amount of divine spirit, that spirit may be crushed or it may be encouraged, or it may succeed or fail in spite of everything – but it cannot die . . . The lowest must possess it and, although it is so weak and paralysed from chronic disease, yet it can & should be made strong & healthy by good and clean surround-ings. This is of course the basis of socialism, and so far every Christian must be a socialist. The means by which this can be done are the stumbling block.[156]

If Stafford was not seriously pushed to the left by the social question before the First World War, nor was he by the immediate issues that the

153. RSC to IC, 2 February 1911.   154. ibid., 8 February 1911.
155. ibid., 28 March 1911.   156. RSC diary, 25 July 1910.

war itself raised, which brought Labour a number of recruits from the upper and middle classes. Lord Parmoor, who was to become one of them, had more qualms about the justice and necessity of the war effort than his youngest son manifested. Stafford's diary contains an account, written in 1917, describing his investigation of some alleged German atrocities during his early days in France. The real cause turned out to be a bursting shell. 'This quite genuine and well intentioned exaggeration,' he noted, 'always recurred to my mind afterwards when I was being told of fresh "horrors".'[157] Yet his own contemporary letters to Isobel hardly show him sceptical of nationalistic fervour. 'Yes, it was awful about the *Lusitania*,' he wrote, referring to the liner's sinking by a U-boat. 'But one can't expect anything else from the Boches . . .'[158] Again: 'The story about the poor Germans is very pathetic but really they don't deserve much pity do they!'[159]

Stafford's interest in politics seems to have quickened in the last year of the war. It did so, however, not so much because he developed new convictions as because he had to consider the practical possibility of how to 'fit myself for a political career if my health were not good enough to return to the Bar'.[160] Hence the significance of his convalescence throughout 1918, in giving him more time to think and read about politics, and in marking a rupture with his previous conventional Conservative allegiance. He wrote in his diary: 'All my bias at the present moment is towards the policy of the Labour Party.'[161] His father's view was similar, applauding Labour for 'putting forward in the main a sensible programme'.[162]

It was at this juncture that his aunt Beatrice and his uncle Sidney belatedly acquired due importance in Stafford's life. Beatrice Webb later wrote that, before joining the Labour Government in 1930, Stafford 'knew nothing whatsoever about the internal life of the labour movement and though our nephew, so far as I can remember, he had never been in our house'.[163] However, Stafford's diary shows that he had had at least a couple of dinners with the Webbs in 1917–18. Through them he met Arthur Henderson, now effectively the leader of the Labour Party and the architect, with Sidney Webb, of its new constitution. What struck Cripps was not its proclaimed commitment to public ownership but the organizational changes, extending direct membership to individuals as well as to trade unions. The key phrase was 'producers by hand and by brain' – a distillation of the Fabian view

157. ibid., 14 October 1917.   158. RSC to IC, 10 May 1915.   159. ibid., 1 May 1915.
160. RSC diary, 1 February 1918.   161. ibid., October 1918.
162. Parmoor diary, 10 December 1918.
163. Webb diary, 9 July 1939, in MacKenzie and MacKenzie (eds.), *Webb: Diary*, iv, p. 436.

that the constituency for socialism was not 'the working class' but anyone who worked. 'As to the reorganization of the Labour Party, the chief point of importance seemed to be the inclusion of the brain-worker,' Cripps commented. 'I think that this will inevitably lead to a split in the party, as the Manual Labourer will feel that he is being imposed upon by his chiefs.'[164]

Here was the making of Cripps's dilemma. 'Trades Unionism is not in reality or should not be a political movement,' he argued. 'The Labour Party since they have decided to admit "Brain-workers" have become the representatives of all those who work for their living and in this respect I feel drawn towards them.'[165] Cripps's suspicion of trade-union domination of the Labour Party was to be lasting. Yet his own work ethic, his constant stress on the need for effort, his reiterated reluctance to rely upon inherited wealth – all pointed to the possibility that 'Labour' might function as both a guiding principle and a party label, even for such a well-born and (prospectively) well-paid recruit as Cripps. In 1918, however, the difficulty that he dwelt upon stemmed from the fact that he was still medically unfit to work himself.

How can I reconcile this with a policy that no one has a right to an income unless he earns it? The only alternative is to give up all my money (and Isobel's) but this is not practicable as I could not do so against my wife's wishes and I would not do so as it would not be of any great benefit to anyone. And yet I could never go into Political life as a representative of Labour, being myself one who 'toils not neither does he spin'.[166]

If what he wrote can be taken at face value, Cripps could not represent Labour unless he were himself fit to labour; but since he regarded Parliament as a second-best career for an unfit lawyer, if he regained his fitness he would practise at the bar rather than go into politics. This does not argue a strong commitment to a political career in 1918. It might, however, explain his concentration of effort upon his legal work, given that he could not do both, in the 1920s; and his attempt to combine a virtually full-time political career with a virtually full-time legal practice in the 1930s. In the end, he did all of this, and had Goodfellows too, and paid for it all out of earned income.

It should also be noted that, for all Cripps's professed sympathy for Labour, his political outlook was still far from radical. The industrial unrest of 1920, with its Bolshevik overtones, led him to write in his diary that 'one

164. RSC diary, 1 February 1918. 165. ibid., 5 October 1918. 166. Ibid.

feels as if one were on the edge of a volcano – at any moment we may come to a crisis leading to revolution'.[167] That this was a rebarbative prospect can be seen by reference to an entry from the previous year. 'Europe has become a chaos of revolution and the outlook is full of anxiety,' he wrote, 'though at present good sense seems to be prevailing in England.'[168] Indeed, Cripps's political perspective seems rather conventional, commending the effort 'to save money in Government departments' when the Lloyd George Coalition signalled its readiness to make heavy cuts in social spending (the policy implemented as 'the Geddes axe').[169]

Unlike the revolutionary utterances that Cripps was to voice in the early 1930s, these were surely the responses of a man who did not look to politics to resolve the world's ills. He wrote in his diary in 1923: 'More and more one sees that the only basis for International Relations is the teaching of Christ and more and more one feels that it is the one thing worth working for.'[170]

In all of this Stafford was at one with his father, with whom he retained a notably close relationship. They corresponded frequently on both private and public matters, and met as often as two crowded diaries permitted. Lord Parmoor had come to the view 'that the [Labour] Party are right in their International outlook, of supreme importance at the present moment'.[171] After the fall of the Lloyd George Coalition, he rejoiced at Labour's political advance. 'For the first time since the war there is a real party of peace in the House of Commons,' he wrote.[172] It was an attitude that led Parmoor, step by step, into the first Labour cabinet in 1924. As Lord President of the Council, he became the British representative on the Council of the League of Nations in Geneva, where he spent much of his ten months in office. But whereas his father was very much the churchman in public life in the 1920s, Stafford was less closely identified with the Church of England as an institution.

Much in the spirit of his mother's testament, Stafford's lifelong Christian commitment had little sectarian flavour. 'It isn't necessary to have elaborate theories or movements,' he affirmed, 'it is the simplicity of Christ's teaching which is its marvel and which so conclusively proves its rightness.' The trouble was that the world had 'long ago left that simplicity – overlayed it with dogma and ritual and theory of every kind'.[173] His own attitude was shown in the conciliatory role he adopted in Filkins. 'I read the lesson in

167. ibid., 9 March 1920.   168. ibid., 2 March 1919.   169. ibid., 31 December 1921.
170. ibid., 6 January 1923.   171. Parmoor diary, 3 November 1920.
172. ibid., 27 December 1922.   173. RSC to Toby Weaver, 24 December 1932.

Church,' he explained, '(1) because I like doing so and (2) because of the friction between the parson and some of the "gentry" and I like to show that though I disapprove of the parson's Anglo-Catholic ritual and ornaments, yet while he is there I like to support him.'[174] This tolerant support was not mutual, since the vicar later took the view that Cripps's political views rendered him unsuitable to read the lesson; so the family started worshipping at a nearby village church instead. There was a pragmatic air to such arrangements, as later illustrated in Moscow, at Christmas 1940, when a plan to go to midnight mass at the Roman Catholic church was put off at the last moment in case it was misconstrued – 'its not being our own church and our not usually going,' Isobel Cripps explained.[175]

Stafford was certainly not Romish in his religious sympathies. On his 1939 holiday, when his party was refused admission to Pisa cathedral because the men's holiday shirts were not 'elaborate or unhealthy enough for the authorities', and Isobel's arms not fully covered, Stafford's sympathy with 'the so-called followers of the simple carpenter of Nazareth' was sorely taxed; as a carpenter himself, he was well placed to suggest that 'the sooner they give up religion and take to something else the better'.[176]

Before the First World War, Stafford's diary shows that churchgoing was not an activity he naturally enjoyed.

I know perfectly myself that the more I cultivate religion, the more I try to do what is right, the happier I am and shall be, and yet when I am at home – or anywhere for that matter – I seem to have distinct disinclination for church. This is wrong and yet even though I go to church I feel then as if I had done someone a favour . . . One may say one gives pause and thanks in private, perhaps so, but the whole spirit of Christianity involves that fellowship which worshipping with others of every class entails . . . Now it is time I pulled myself together and started going to Church regularly.[177]

That his underlying aversion survived his good resolutions to attend is shown by later experience. Peggy's recollection that her family attended the village church every week may be accurate, but it was plainly a habit easily sloughed when they were abroad. On the long voyage to the West Indies in 1938, the family deliberately absented themselves from the Sunday services. Cripps's Christianity was plainly not eucharistic; even the conventional Anglican commitment to taking the sacrament three times a year, above all

174. RSC diary, 26 November 1920.   175. IC to Diana Cripps, Christmas Day 1940.
176. RSC diary, 5 August 1939.   177. ibid., 26 July 1910.

at Easter, seems to have gone by default. In Hong Kong on Easter Sunday 1940, Cripps did not accompany his host, the Governor of Hong Kong, to church but instead began indexing his diary. On Christmas Day it had been much the same – late rising, packing, his usual round of interviews, but no mention of churchgoing. At the Moscow embassy, there is silent testimony in the diaries of Stafford, Isobel and Theresa to the Cripps family's lack of religious observance – they seemed to forget Good Friday altogether in 1941.

Since Cripps's faith seems to have licensed a rather remarkable looseness towards institutional Christianity, it might seem difficult to explain his commitment to the World Alliance for Promoting International Friendship through the Churches. In the history of the twentieth century this is hardly a movement that bulks large. Its importance in Cripps's life, however, should not be underestimated since it was to occupy a large part of whatever spare time he had during the early 1920s. The explanation for his involvement is surely quasi-political – plus the familiar dash of family connection.

In 1919 Lord Parmoor had remarried, much to the pleasure of his family; and his new wife, Marian Ellis, came from an active Quaker and Liberal background that encouraged participation by the happy couple in a network of ecumenical organizations seeking international conciliation. Of these the World Alliance was the most significant; or so Stafford believed in agreeing to become treasurer of its British council. In his diary in 1921 he wrote that he was 'struck by the vast potentialities of the movement', and in 1922, after attending an uplifting conference in Copenhagen with Isobel, repeated that they all 'returned convinced of the vast potentialities of the movement'.[178] Stafford had persuaded Dr Burge, his old headmaster at Winchester and now Bishop of Oxford, to become involved; Burge had officiated at the Parmoors' marriage; they were all drawn together, inspired by personal affection as much as public spirit or religious zeal. For Stafford it was an early experience of how the stage army of the good could persuade themselves of the imminent triumph of righteousness: a fitting prelude to his political campaigns of the 1930s. But Parmoor went off into the Labour Government; Burge died suddenly; the treasurer found it difficult to raise funds; and the potentialities of the movement began to look not quite so vast, after all.

It was, of course, unusual for someone from a family like Stafford's to join the Labour Party. His particular family, however, supplied two Cabinet ministers for the first Labour Government, formed under Ramsay MacDonald in 1924: not only Stafford's father, Lord Parmoor, but his

---

178. ibid., 23 September 1921, 31 December 1922. Cf. Parmoor, *Retrospect*, pp. 130–33, 143, 153–4; Bryant, *Cripps*, pp. 71–7.

uncle Sidney, now Lord Passfield. Five years later, with a General Election in the offing, Herbert Morrison, the alert and pragmatic Labour leader in London, sought Parmoor's support in making a further suggestion. 'It is one of my ambitions to see Stafford Cripps in the Labour Party,' he told him; 'I did sound him on the subject some while ago but he was not clear and I am wondering if it might be useful for me to have another talk with him.'[179] Within weeks Cripps had been signed up. He and Morrison had developed considerable mutual admiration during the hearings of the Railway Rates Tribunal from May 1924 to December 1926, in which Cripps successfully represented the London County Council's view that there was room for reductions in workmen's fares.[180] Not for the last time, Cripps's highly technical pleading, relying on strong inferences from the analysis of complex statistical data, served a cause that carried a clear ideological charge, pitting the pursuit of private profit against the public good. With Morrison's influential support, the new recruit was quickly adopted as prospective Labour candidate for the south-east London constituency of West Woolwich.

Cripps's early biographers make a great deal of his dilemma in deciding whether to join the party. 'He was already overworking,' says Strauss. Estorick adds: 'There were only twenty-four hours in a day and if he decided in the affirmative something would have to go.'[181] Some of this, of course, is undeniable; but it is notable that the option of drastically reducing his legal work is not mentioned; and the acuteness of the dilemma is exaggerated by hindsight. For the only decision that Cripps took in 1929 was to make himself available as a prospective parliamentary candidate; all he could reasonably expect in 1930 was to nurse West Woolwich, which Labour had failed to win in 1929, until such time as its support increased further. 'My own feeling is that with reasonable luck West Woolwich is going to be won for Labour next time,' wrote Morrison, with unconvincing professional optimism.[182] In fact the constituency was not to go Labour until 1945.

It was only the resignation, through ill-health, of MacDonald's Solicitor-General in October 1930 that catapulted Cripps into office so soon; and it was the consequential need to find him a seat in the House of Commons that snatched him from unwinnable West Woolwich and parachuted him into Bristol East, which he won in a by-election in January 1931 and was to hold for twenty years. What got lost in the process were the years of

179. Morrison to Parmoor, 12 April 1929.
180. Burgess, *Cripps*, pp. 30–33; Donoughue and Jones, *Morrison*, p. 123.
181. Strauss, p. 39; Estorick, p. 78.   182. Morrison to RSC, 16 July 1930.

apprenticeship in Labour politics that might have given a forty-year-old lawyer, however brilliant in his own field, the time and experience necessary in mastering his new trade.

Not that Cripps failed to live up to what was expected of him as Solicitor-General. On taking office he was treated in the press as an unknown quantity; most comment centred on the fact that it was the first time since the Chamberlains (Joseph and Austen in 1903) that a father and son had been in the Government together. Cripps immediately attracted curiosity when he was flung into the public inquiry into the R101 airship disaster. Sketch-writers attending the inquiry started looking him over: 'The boyish Solicitor-General, who might be mistaken for a junior, shoots a keen glance towards the dais from his chaos of papers.'[183] His maiden speech in the Commons, on a strictly legal issue with little political charge, was considered 'in its way admirable, clear, concise, perfectly arranged, and delivered in that quiet, unaffected way which always secures a sympathetic hearing from a new member'.[184] It showed that Cripps 'appears to have learned from his father, Lord Parmoor, what the House likes in a novice for he was not merely modest but humble'.[185] One of those deliberately old-fashioned *Punch* cartoons, proudly reproduced in Lord Parmoor's memoirs, shows himself reading young Stafford's glowing school report: 'Glad to see you've done such a good term's work, my boy, in your father's old House.'[186]

The family business was thus in good hands. Yet the acumen that Cripps showed in Parliament quickly established his legal credentials rather than his political credibility. Put in charge of the Government's contentious Trade Disputes Bill, he had to face Winston Churchill across the dispatch box at the end of January 1931. It was the first time, but by no means the last, that observers relished a study in contrasts. To Tory partisans, Cripps's 'downright speech and plain oratorical manner contrasted badly with the dramatic gesture, the fine polished phrase, and the joyous gaiety of Mr Churchill'.[187] To the Labour movement's own *Daily Herald*, however, Churchill's 'wild tirade against the Bill' found an immediate answer in Cripps's 'masterly speech'.[188]

What the loyal *Herald* glossed over, but what virtually every other paper seized upon, was what happened in the course of the Solicitor-General's speech. The Conservatives were predictably pressing him as to

183. Con O'Leary, *Empire News*, 2 November 1930.
184. *Daily Mirror*, 24 January 1931.   185. Eastern Daily Press, 24 January 1931.
186. *Punch*, 5 August 1931, in Parmoor, *Retrospect*, facing p. 304.
187. *Western Daily Press*, 29 January 1931.   188. *Daily Herald*, 29 January 1931.

whether the General Strike of 1926 would have been legal under the Labour Government's new Bill. Since the whole point of introducing it was to legitimate the trade unions' position, an affirmative answer was implicit but there was obviously no profit for the Government in making this explicit. 'Members could hardly believe their ears,' remarked *The Times*, when Cripps not only offered an answer but a negative answer. He plainly stated that, under the Bill, the Trades Union Congress's action in 1926 would have been illegal. 'This opinion by one of their own legal advisers visibly disheartened the Socialists,' the *Daily Sketch* gleefully reported. 'They received it in the silence of blank amazement.'[189] Editorial comment rubbed salt in the Government's self-inflicted wound. 'Sir Stafford Cripps is young in years and still younger in office,' intoned the *Scotsman*. 'The habit of truth-telling has not yet worn off him, and it may be hoped that it never will.'[190]

What Cripps had done was characteristic. He had scorned political prudence in exhibiting his intellectual mastery of the small print and had needlessly engaged with a hypothetical question obviously prone to cause divisions in Labour's ranks. It took MacDonald's well-honed skills in having it both ways to mollify the Trades Union Congress while not openly repudiating his young colleague.

Cripps fared better in his handling of the Government's land tax proposals in the summer of 1931. As was pointed out in the press, his legal experience was directly relevant: 'This training and the fact that he sat patiently through the dreary debate for two days, noting every criticism and objection, accounted for the confident style of his clear-voiced speech, and the rejoinders which he has made to the critics of the proposals.'[191] Again it was his pre-existing lawyerly expertise that served him well. 'Sir Stafford was in his sweetly reasonable mood, anxious to see the point of criticism and meet it,' ran one admiring account in a Conservative newspaper, adding: 'The discussion was detailed and technical almost to unreportability.'[192] But Cripps showed polemical gifts too, with a wide range of newspapers proclaiming that 'the debates revealed a new debating force' or disclosed 'a valuable asset to the Government'; the message was that Cripps had 'made a great reputation in the short period that he has been a member' and that he promised 'to be one of the leading lights of his party'.[193] A fellow

189. *The Times, Daily Sketch*, 29 January 1931.   190. *Scotsman*, 29 January 1931.
191. *Star*, 13 May 1931.   192. *Daily Telegraph*, 12 June 1931.
193. *Christian World*, 14 May 1931; *Bournemouth Echo*, 21 May 1931; *Paisley Daily Express*, 22 May 1931; *Scotsman*, 20 May 1931; cf. *Yorkshire Post*, 27 July 1931.

Labour MP, commenting on 'a series of quite brilliant speeches', summed up Cripps's first six months in Parliament: 'His is the biggest new reputation of to-day.'[194]

Just as the events of the summer of 1931 precipitated an economic and financial crisis for which the Labour Government was lamentably ill-prepared, so they faced Cripps himself with a situation that exposed his lack of political ballast. He was not, like his father and his uncle, a member of the Cabinet and so did not have to wrestle with the problem of how to reconcile social spending on unemployment with a balanced budget and a defence of the parity of sterling. It was the Cabinet's failure to agree on a policy – any policy – that left MacDonald with little alternative but to tender the Government's resignation in August 1931. What was surprising was that he was persuaded to remain in office as Prime Minister of a 'National' Government, with Conservative and Liberal support.

Cripps was abroad. The strain of his first parliamentary session had taken its toll and he had gone to recover in a clinic in Baden-Baden (where he was joined by his similarly invalid father). It was there that Cripps received a terse but significant telegram:

HOPE YOU ARE PROGRESSING STOP WOULD YOU LIKE TO GO ON – RAMSAY MACDONALD.[195]

On returning to London Cripps responded courteously, going so far as to assure MacDonald 'that I admire immensely the courage and conviction which have led you and the other Labour Ministers associated with you to take the action which you have taken'.[196] But Cripps made it clear that he would stick with the majority of the Labour Party, led by Arthur Henderson, and not join the National Government. MacDonald soon came to think this response characteristic of the 'graceless' conduct of such former colleagues as chose to go into opposition – 'those who expected and asked for most now being the meanest, like Sir Stafford Cripps'.[197]

That Cripps stuck with his party rather than with MacDonald is not really surprising. After all, he was at one with both Lord Parmoor and Lord Passfield, who had written to his brother-in-law in Baden-Baden to bring

194. Mary Agnes Hamilton, *The Clarion* (cutting, summer 1931).
195. MacDonald to RSC, telegram, 10.10 a.m., 26 August 1931.
196. RSC to MacDonald, 28 August 1931, copy.
197. MacDonald diary, 12 November 1931, quoted in Burgess *Cripps*, p. 74; but Burgess surely errs in supposing that this constitutes even 'tenuous proof' (p. 49) that Cripps had asked MacDonald to appoint him Solicitor-General in the first place.

him abreast of the Cabinet meetings that he had missed and to declare that 'I have rallied to Henderson and the Party without hesitation.'[198] Though the letter was clearly intended for Stafford too, he was in fact back in London before it arrived; but family solidarity counted for something in his decision. The choice he made, with its far-reaching ideological implications, has often been represented as immediately self-evident. In dealing with the events of late August and early September 1931, Estorick cites 'a letter to a friend' as the source for Cripps's statement: 'The moment had arrived when reformism had to be abandoned.' These were indeed Cripps's own words, but the passage from which they are taken was in an article that he published three years later.[199]

There was no single Damascene moment when all became clear; such a version of events would be both tidied up and speeded up. In a letter of 30 August to his father, still in Baden-Baden, Cripps explained his response at length. They had evidently parted on the assumption that Cripps would decline office and his interviews with Henderson and Morrison served to confirm this resolution. But Cripps gained a strong impression that the ex-ministers were now dissimulating their complicity in MacDonald's policies, with the result that they were 'all to some extent tarred with the brush of acquiescence'. Cripps saw this as one danger now facing the Labour Party. Another was the resort to 'easy meaningless slogans, "a Bankers' ramp" etc.', rather than to 'hard facts'. Admittedly, he suggested that this would make it difficult for a Labour Government to deal with a financial crisis 'most drastically along socialist lines'; but it is wrong to suppose that Cripps was precipitated into an extreme position. The idea of 'continuing in the Labour Party and attempting to rationalize and moderate their programme' was one that he reported sympathetically. 'A third danger,' he told Parmoor, 'is of course TUC domination and I am at the moment very much afraid of this.' His own priority, then, was not solidarity in the class war: it was to prevent Labour from committing itself to 'a lot of sentimental nonsense'.[200]

Cripps's action in refusing office in the National Government counted for more than his own ambiguous words in explaining why he took this decision. It was hardly shameless careerism on Cripps's part, yet the train

198. Passfield to Parmoor, 27 August 1931.
199. RSC, 'Alternatives before British Labour', p. 123, which prints verbatim the whole passage quoted by Estorick, p. 91; no such letter of 1931 has been found in the Cripps archive; and in Estorick (1941), p. 52, the same passage had been correctly identified as what Cripps 'later wrote'.
200. RSC to Parmoor, 30 August 1931.

of events undoubtedly gave a further boost to his political career. Passfield reported to Parmoor from the Labour Party conference in Scarborough in early October that, although the delegates expected to lose the forthcoming General Election, 'Stafford has become their darling idol, and many people speak of him as the future leader.'[201]

Not only had MacDonald's followers quit the party to stay in government: the General Election of October 1931 saw the decimation of the remaining Opposition leadership. More experienced politicians of Cripps's generation, notably Herbert Morrison and Hugh Dalton, lost their seats, as did senior ex-ministers like Frederick Pethick-Lawrence and Albert Alexander (with both of whom Cripps was to go to India in 1946). The net result was that, within weeks, his only remaining colleagues on Labour's front bench were the veteran socialist, George Lansbury, much loved in the party, and the relatively unknown Clement Attlee. Only seven years older than Cripps, Attlee might have been regarded as a dispensable incumbent, to be superseded quickly by a more brilliant and charismatic rival. In fact Attlee and Cripps, though never intimates, developed a mutual respect that sustained political cooperation, off and on, for twenty years.

In 1931 Cripps brushed aside suggestions that he should press his own claims to the leadership. It would indeed have been a wholly precipitate step for a callow recruit. He readily agreed that Lansbury should be elected leader and Attlee deputy leader in the new parliament; and he extended the hospitality of Goodfellows to both of them, in keeping with the good personal relations in this triumvirate. Maybe Beatrice Webb (encouraged by an excluded Morrison) was right to suspect that Cripps preferred Lansbury, not just as a Christian and pacifist whom he respected, but because he was 'intellectually woolly and uncritical and does not curb or check Stafford's advocacy of this or that new project picked up casually from someone'. Her own assessment of her nephew was ambivalent. She acknowledged his leadership qualities – easy sociability, strong personality, 'tall, good-looking, and with a good voice and pleasant gestures'. But she found him 'oddly immature in intellect and unbalanced in judgment'.[202] It was hard to escape a sense that Cripps had been thrust into such prominence *faute de mieux*. Some might say that he was now given his head; others that he was given enough rope to hang himself – and that by 1939 he had almost succeeded in doing so.

201. Passfield to Parmoor, 6 October 1931.
202. Webb diary, 7 March 1932, Passfield papers; partly quoted in MacKenzie and MacKenzie (eds.), *Webb: Diary*, iv, pp. 282–3. Cf. Harris, *Attlee*, pp. 102–4.

The field of controversy

The course of Cripps's career in the 1930s was nothing if not politically controversial. Yet it is not as historiographically controversial as other episodes – his ambassadorship to Russia, his relationship with Churchill, and, above all, his activities in India – which have provoked historians into unresolved arguments, which will be examined at greater length in later parts of this book. The fact is that an extensive scholarly literature has yielded a high degree of consensus about Cripps's erratic and unsuccessful efforts to animate the British Left after 1931: about the failure of the Socialist League under his chairmanship to find a convincing role in the Labour Party; about the misguided moves that Cripps inspired for a united front with the Communists in 1936–7; about his maladroit tactics in advocating a popular front of all non-Conservative parties in 1938–9; and about an incorrigible obtuseness to the effect of his utterances – what Ben Pimlott has called 'the curious combination in Cripps of dialectical brilliance and political innocence'.[203]

It is not the duty of a biographer of Cripps to make a partisan defence of his actions, simply for the sake of it. Still, in seeking to present the Cripps version, it is obviously a pity that no diaries survive – and almost certainly none were written by him – between those of 1923 and 1938: the more so since the most illuminating diary on Labour politics in this period is hostile to Cripps. Hugh Dalton, its author, was another upper-class renegade who had thrown in his lot with the people's party; but his resolute reformism, reinforced by the camaraderie of the committee work in which he revelled, stoked up an acute exasperation – 'This man is really becoming a dangerous political lunatic' – that was only partly political.[204] He exhibited a growing personal antipathy – which his published diary has trumpeted – towards the party's brilliant, wayward, opinionated and arrogant recruit. 'I can't come back this afternoon,' he records Cripps as saying after one adjourned meeting. 'It's cost me £120 to be here this morning and I might just as well have sent my typist.'[205]

We can never know what sense Cripps made of his own actions at this time in the way that we can from his later Russian or Indian diaries. Some idea of his outlook can, however, be formed from his own published writings, which have received relatively little attention.

203. Pimlott, *Labour and the Left*, p. 35.
204. Dalton diary, 4 May 1933, quoted in Dalton, *Fateful Years*, p. 42.
205. Dalton diary, 23 January 1935, in Pimlott (ed.), *Dalton: Political Diary*, p. 185.

Cripps was not a bookish man. This is not contested even in Patricia Strauss's biography, which is particularly useful for the 1930s since, with her husband, George Strauss MP, she was personally involved in all Cripps's campaigns. She states that, by this time, Cripps's political activism had crowded out virtually all his previous recreations (except carpentry).[206] Geoffrey Wilson, who had unparalleled access to Cripps, is more forthright: 'I never saw him read a book or a magazine or an article.'[207] To be sure, when Cripps was travelling he duly packed books in his luggage. At the outset of a rare long holiday to Jamaica, he began the voyage with the intention of reading Virginia Woolf's *The Years*, in addition to the latest novel by the American writer, Waldo Frank, sent to him in proof by its marxisant author. (It does not give an unfair impression of the didactic aim of his work to note that, at a climactic moment, one of his characters affirms: 'I embrace your class.') Cripps thought that 'the two books in a sense are trying to do the same sort of job and Waldo does it very much better'.[208] Discouraged, Cripps did not persist either with Woolf or further ambitious reading.

The habit had atrophied. While Cripps had been convalescent in 1918, he had seriously applied himself to political and historical reading. Indeed he later made the claim: 'At this point my political consciousness was born.'[209] All of this seems to be retrospectively exaggerated. His diary not only shows that, when work was slack at the bar in the following year, he tried 'browsing where the herbiage seems sweetest': it also makes brutally clear his low estimate of the value of this practice.

The result is that I derive very little benefit from anything I read. To a certain extent it tends to broaden one's outlook, and a few of the more important facts may stick in one's brain, but on the whole one derives very little benefit ... Yet I can easily and quickly pick out from a complicated set of papers the essence of their importance, and retain a very accurate idea of their contents, accurate that is in substance and not in words.[210]

As he well recognized, Cripps was highly literate in a technical and utilitarian way: able to absorb masses of information on paper and to

206. Strauss, p. 55.
207. Wilson, 'My Working Life', p. 16. Cf. Jones, *Foot*, p. 29.
208. RSC diary, 30 July 1939. Waldo Frank, *The Bridegroom Cometh* (1938), was the sequel to *The Death and Birth of David Markand* (1934), in which the quoted statement occurs.
209. Estorick, p. 64; this was a statement first printed in Estorick (1941), p. 23, suggesting that it was provided for Estorick in New York in 1940.
210. RSC diary, 28 December 1918.

draft his own memoranda, statements and speeches with great fluency and cogency. But, as a politician, he had long since given up reading for aesthetic satisfaction or intellectual profit. He displayed in his own writings none of the pleasure in words, cadences or phrases that distinguished Churchill: none of his fondness for quotation, resonance, irony, magniloquence – or calculated bathos. Cripps's range of reference was generally restricted to scriptural allusions and the literature of his youth ('the Bible and Browning').

Hence the plausibility of a claim recorded by more than one confidant: that he had never read any of the works of Marx. 'I doubt if, before 1931, he had seriously encountered Marxian ideas,' wrote Dalton. 'But now he knew all the answers.'[211] This might be discounted as unfriendly testimony. But it remains difficult to better the comment offered by Michael Foot, who knew Cripps well and was sympathetic to his outlook: 'His Marxist slogans were undigested; he declared the class war without ever having studied the contours of the battlefield.'[212]

One result is the rather naive quality of Cripps's first book, *Why This Socialism?* (1934). There are no references in it either to works by economists or to the literature of socialism. It is, Cripps explains, 'a short and untechnical description of the economic theory which, as I see it, lies at the root of Socialism.'[213] Having quickly mastered his new brief, albeit in skeleton form, Cripps simply gave it the benefit of his own lucid exposition. Where, then, had he picked up these ideas?

In answering this, it is difficult to ignore the Socialist League. It was a body that had its origin in two distinct impulses. One was a wish to bring research to bear upon policy-making, very much in the former Fabian tradition, which was essentially the project of the Oxford don G. D. H. Cole, patron of the 'loyal grousers' in the Labour Party. The other impulse was more frankly populist and propagandist – a response to the crisis besetting the Independent Labour Party (ILP).

The ILP had, along with the Fabian Society, provided the socialist component of the Labour Representation Committee (soon to become the Labour Party) as founded in 1900, with its preponderent trade-union base. Cripps, of course, had been attracted by the Labour Party's new constitution of 1918 precisely because it reached out beyond trade unionism. This made individual membership of the party possible, whereas previously socialists had had to join as members of affiliated organizations, of which the ILP

211. Dalton, *Fateful Years*, p. 148. Cf. Pritt, *From Right to Left*, p. 98; Woodrow Wyatt, letter to *The Times*, 27 March 1969.
212. Foot, *Bevan*, i, p. 156.   213. RSC, *Why This Socialism?*, p. 7.

was the most important. What role was left, then, for the ILP? Its subsequent wrangles over whether to remain affiliated to the Labour Party, or to strike out as a truly independent socialist alternative, came to a head after the Labour Government's 'great betrayal' in 1931. In the following year the militant majority voted for disaffiliation, leaving a significant minority determined to stay within the Labour Party, with all its many reformist faults.

The 'affiliationists' provided most of the recruits for the newly-formed Socialist League. Cripps, however, had no previous record of militancy and had never been a member of the ILP. He was recruited through an approach from Cole, who had founded a pressure group within the party, the Society for Socialist Inquiry and Propaganda (SSIP). Cole's coup was to persuade Ernest Bevin, the leader of the Transport and General Workers' Union (TGWU), to become chairman of SSIP. The snag was that the ex-ILP affiliationists, with a few thousand supporters, would not simply join SSIP, with its few hundred; so negotiations took place in September 1932 for a merger into what soon became the Socialist League. At this stage it was Cole who persuaded an initially diffident Cripps that the League, unlike the old ILP, would prove loyal to the Labour Party. But Bevin's grievance at being rejected as chairman of the merged body simply reinforced his conviction that the League would 'always have a bias against Trade Unionists'.[214] The fact that, within a year, Cripps had himself become chairman of the Socialist League did not augur well for his relationship with the most massively influential figure in the wider Labour movement.

The Socialist League took shape as a pressure group of intellectuals working within the Labour Party but determined to swing it to a broadly Marxist line. William Mellor and H. N. Brailsford were, together with Harold Laski of the London School of Economics, probably the strongest influences through which a distinctive analysis of the relationship between democracy, capitalism, imperialism and fascism was propagated, though Cripps may also have picked up ideas from more obscure figures, like the ex-Communist J. T. Murphy and the provincial ILP leader, Fred Henderson.[215] Laski offered Cripps the advice, 'as friend to friend', that he should think of himself 'as almost certainly destined in the next years for the leadership of the party' – an expression of esteem reciprocated by the fact

214. See Pimlott, *Labour and the Left*, pp. 42ff., quotation at p. 46.
215. Henderson was based in Norwich; relevant evidence in his papers has been indicated to me by Professor Duncan Tanner.

that Laski is one of the few contemporary authors whom we know Cripps to have read.[216]

Cripps was now receptive to what Marxism had to teach him. He plainly had no answers of his own to the crisis that had paralysed the economic system and the Labour Party alike; he was thus susceptible to the confident appeal of those whose dogma promised salvation – complementing rather than challenging his Christian faith in redemption. His favourite hymn, 'To be a pilgrim', enjoined a robust response to disaster and a peremptory dismissal of dismal stories.

There was no friction between Cripps's religious beliefs and the Marxist analysis that he now embraced: quite the reverse. He continued to declare openly of the New Testament gospel: 'I believe – am convinced – it is the rule of life.'[217] The new twist was, as he explained to his (disconcerted) local vicar, that he saw his religion as 'a great active force for revolutionary change, leading people through political means to an active realization of the principles of Christianity in our everyday life rather than a force enjoining submission to the existing state of affairs'.[218] Indeed he went on to claim that the problem for the Church lay in its 'attempt to harmonize what should be a dynamic and revolutionary religion with a static and reactionary society'.[219]

From September 1931 he moved with characteristic speed and confidence in asserting his new political identity and was soon hailed as the champion of the Left. 'Dear Sir and Comrade', one correspondent addressed him, deference vying with militance.[220] For many intellectuals, especially those younger than himself, the 1931 crisis served to polarize and clarify the choices. It did so for Cripps – at least on second thoughts, since we know that his initial uncertainty was overborne within a matter of weeks by new-found socialist convictions. 'There has been a strong swing to the Left in the Party,' he now told his father, 'and a general feeling of relief that we have shed a number of members who were on the extreme Right.' He was already envisaging 'a direct fight between Socialism and Capitalism' as the means of mobilizing the Labour vote.[221]

'The inevitability of gradualness' had been the Webbs' slogan; but in

---

216. Laski to RSC, 30 June 1932; RSC to Parmoor, 15 April 1935, reveals that, *en route* to Canada, Cripps had read Laski's new book, *The State in Theory and Practice* (1935).
217. Notes for Central Hall address, 13 January 1935.
218. Cripps to Arthur [Austen], vicar of Filkins, 13 February 1935, copy.
219. Cripps, 'The political reactions of rearmament', Fabian Lectures for 1937, *Dare We Look Ahead?*, p. 104.
220. A. Robinson to RSC, 13 June 1932.   221. RSC to Parmoor, 12 September 1931.

October Cripps was assuring the Labour Party Conference that 'the one thing that is not inevitable now is gradualness'.[222] His aunt Beatrice happily concurred in this shift of view, since the Webbs themselves were soon to become apologists for Soviet Communism. 'Sidney and I were so glad at Stafford's attitude towards things,' she told Parmoor, 'and to see the ease with which he gets on with the other leaders and with the rank and file of the Labour Party.'[223] Cripps was soon setting out his position starkly: 'You cannot build a Socialist state within a Capitalist regime, and therefore to help to forward Gradualism is mis-conceived, especially in times of industrial trouble.'[224]

Planning was the new concept (or new rhetoric, at least) that ran as a unifying theme through Labour's economic thinking after 1931.[225] For those on the left, planning was not seen as a remedy for the capitalist system but as an alternative to it. In particular, it was the rationale for Cripps's advocacy of the nationalization of the joint stock banks. In a private letter to a banker friend, Cripps pointed to a fundamental incompatibility between 'the management of "money" and "credit" in the interests of a class (and I use the term advisedly) and of private interests, and its management for the general benefit of a planned and organized state'. Politically, the point was that the state, through the House of Commons, was democratic, meaning that the people could get rid of it as they could not get rid of the bankers; so this was Cripps's preferred democratic socialist alternative to the regime of a Mussolini or a Stalin. Economically, the reality was that a rentier class, living in idleness, consumed two-fifths of the national income, making it impossible to achieve greater equity except at their expense. 'History shows it can't be done,' Cripps claimed, 'at least we see no way of doing it – it is for the Capitalists to show how that can be done.' Moreover, they were ill-advised to suggest that the money would not be forthcoming, which was little more than a declaration of the class war from above. 'It is just this sort of attitude that is playing straight into the hands of communists and revolutionaries,' Cripps admonished. 'Put up what arguments you like but don't threaten class action and class war.'[226]

'Class' underpins Cripps's thinking throughout the 1930s. But not, as is commonly implied, simply as an injunction for the workers to take the offensive: much more as an explanation of why they found themselves on

222. *LPACR*, 1931, p. 205.　　223. B. Webb to Parmoor, 20 October 1931.
224. Answers by RSC to G. D. H. Cole's questions at Easton Lodge, 16–17 April 1932.
225. The indispensable authority here is now Toye, *Labour Party and the Planned Economy*, ch. 2; and see the valuable study by Ritschel, *Politics of Planning*, esp. ch. 3.
226. RSC to Stephen Burge (son of H. M. Burge and a director of Barings), 1932.

the defensive. In that perspective, Cripps's own class position constitutes less of a paradox than has often been claimed; or at least it was one that he was able to rationalize. After all, though the taunts of hypocrisy against wealthy socialists usually come from the political right, it would actually require a belief in hard-line material determinism to claim that Cripps's politics *ought* to have been 'read off' from his own bank account.

Old-fashioned Marxist analysis has often sought to explain the adoption of conservative ideologies by the economically exploited as examples of 'false consciousness'. Perhaps the concept needs to be stretched and adapted – even inverted – if a supposed discrepancy between anybody's economic interest and their 'correct' political outlook is seen as a problem. It is surely obvious that Cripps did not have the option of conducting his life in the egalitarian socialist future of which he dreamt; he had to make his own terms with the (comfortable) circumstances in which he found himself, whatever his opinion of their ultimate moral or economic justification.

As a hard-working if highly-paid professional man, Cripps claimed some degree of exemption from his own strictures on the rentier class. His high income, too, financed extensive philanthropy as well as personal consumption. He also clearly felt himself in a position to stand above the battle: not so much supporting the 'wrong' side in the class war as seeking its just resolution by rallying to the side of an underdog facing class aggression and class oppression. As an admiring American journalist put it, 'he fights entrenched privilege from the inside'.[227] Even so, the owner of Goodfellows was surely subject, in some degree, to 'radical bourgeois false consciousness' in opting for a critique of capitalism so fundamental that its realization was a rather hypothetical issue, while continuing to enjoy the material comforts of the prevailing system. It could thus be said that Cripps was having the best of both worlds, as a member of a privileged class who also relished the psychic satisfaction of repudiating his own class interest.

Cripps took pride in facing up to the consequences of his newly-acquired insight about the potency of class. In the struggle for power, as he saw it, justice would be obstructed by the class that necessarily benefited from the perpetuation of injustice:

To change the existing capitalist system to one in which private property and the private ownership of the wealth-producing resources of the country have no place is a great undertaking. The reins of power must be taken from the hands of those who now own or control practically the whole national wealth. To do this without

227. Gunther, *Inside Europe*, p. 278.

violence the Labour Party must defeat at the polls a coalition of parties each of which can obtain almost unlimited financial support so long as it is pledged to protect the private ownership of property.[228]

The stakes had thus been raised beyond mere reformist tinkering, to which the conventions of British parliamentary government had hitherto been geared. True, Cripps continued to maintain that 'the first and most fundamental' condition for a change of system was 'that a majority of the electorate should desire and vote for change'.[229] Other statements, however, envisaging the lengths to which the struggle might have to be carried, fed a burgeoning reputation for extremism. He suggested that a future socialist government would be unlikely 'to maintain its position of control without adopting some exceptional means such as the prolongation of the life of Parliament for a further term without an election'.[230]

Cripps's outbursts soon became notorious, inevitably stretching the patience of initially well-disposed colleagues. Morrison remained personally cordial; he had been Stafford's patron in the Labour Party; his delicate wife warmed to Isobel's friendship. When Morrison wrote to Cripps, it was with a gentle admonition about 'some of your own speeches, which I hope you will forgive me for regarding as more calculated to help the enemy than the Party (I am sure you never intended it so) . . .'[231] Dalton, less indulgent and more forthright, took the same view. 'It is the *numbers* of these gaffes which is so appalling,' he complained, driven increasingly to despair at the 'stream of oratorical ineptitudes' for which Cripps was responsible, and well aware of the common opinion that 'Tory H. Q. regard him as their greatest electoral asset'.[232]

Cripps had provocatively assured a conference of Labour students: 'There is no doubt that we shall have to overcome opposition from Buckingham Palace and other places as well.'[233] It did not help that Cripps subsequently offered the legalistic disclaimer, that 'I cannot understand why anybody should have thought that I was referring to the Crown.'[234] Naturally the Conservative press pounced – one epithet for Cripps was 'the Middle Temple

228. RSC, 'The Future of the Labour Party', *New Statesman and Nation*, 3 September 1932, pp. 255–6.
229. RSC, *Why This Socialism?*, p. 9.
230. RSC, 'Can Socialism Come by Constitutional Methods?'.
231. Morrison to RSC, 15 June 1937. See Donoughue and Jones, *Morrison*, pp. 173, 231–2.
232. Dalton diary, 19 January 1934, in Pimlott (ed.), *Dalton: Political Diary*, p. 181. See Dalton, *Fateful Years*, pp. 149–51, for a list of a dozen 'choice blooms', with sources.
233. *Morning Post*, 8 January 1934.   234. *The Times*, 8 January 1934.

Trotsky'[235] – but even the left-Liberal *Manchester Guardian* commented that 'Sir Stafford Cripps is rapidly becoming the Labour Party's most dangerous liability.'[236] The repudiation of the speech by Labour's National Executive Committee (NEC) duly followed. Such incidents may have been inflated by the press but they were not simply invented by opponents.

Cripps plainly shrugged them off as tactical skirmishes in a battle to redraw the lines of strategic confrontation. For him, the class struggle now became fundamental, as *Why This Socialism?* makes explicit. 'The existence of class antagonism,' he maintains, 'is a fact which arises out of the social and economic structure of the capitalist system.'[237] It is a result of the maintenance of privilege, which will naturally be defended by the privileged. Some necessary reforms, like Roosevelt's New Deal in the USA, may be tolerated by the possessing class as a means of keeping capitalism going; but if this goes too far capitalism will turn to the use of force. 'When this happens, we refer to it to-day as Fascism or Nazism.'[238] The process could be seen at its most sinister in Hitler's seizure of power in Germany: 'There was no remedy that could save capitalism that could be applied with democratic consent, so democracy was swept aside and its place taken by a dictatorship financed and supported by big business.'[239]

Cripps often seems to be dismissing reformist political strategies with an almost Leninist contempt. 'Reformism Makes More Difficulties' is one subhead in *Why This Socialism?* – a proposition from which he was not weaned by an hour's meeting with President Roosevelt, over lunch in the White House in 1935. 'My whole impression,' Cripps noted, 'was of an honest anxious man faced by an impossible task – humanising capitalism and making it work.'[240] There is a view, propagated by Cooke's biography, that his brief exposure to the New Deal paved the way for Cripps's later conversion to Keynesian strategies; but though he made useful contacts on that visit with sympathetic left-wing New Dealers like Harry Hopkins and Rexford Tugwell, he duly found 'both very pessimistic about the ultimate future', and he seized on the comment from an American economic expert that 'capitalism was unwilling and unable to save itself and that the time had come to change to socialism!'.[241]

---

235. *Evening Standard*, 8 January 1934. 236. *Manchester Guardian*, 8 January 1934.
237. RSC, *Why This Socialism?*, p. 44.
238. ibid., p. 13; reiterated in RSC, 'The political reactions of rearmament', p. 118.
239. RSC, 'Alternatives before British Labour', p. 126.
240. Note, 17 April 1935; this is printed verbatim in Estorick, pp. 136–8.
241. This was Dr Sprague, former adviser to the Bank of England: RSC to Parmoor, 3 May 1935. See Eatwell, 'Labour Party and the Popular Front', pp. 407ff., for Cripps being seriously

Cripps did not want the New Deal to fail; he simply already knew that it must. His conviction on this point was 'reinforced by the conversations which I had when in the United States'.[242] He already knew that attempts to redistribute purchasing power might work in a socialist state, 'but within capitalism they are not possible'.[243] He already knew that this was because they would not go far enough to be efficacious, 'so long as the money power is supreme in the economic and political field, as it is to-day'.[244] Hence *Why This Socialism?* asserts the necessity of a comprehensive transfer of ownership out of private hands. 'Hitherto,' it adds, 'such a change of ownership, and of the economic power that accompanies ownership, has always been attempted by violence.' Inevitably so, then? Cripps takes this corner with some speed and insouciance. If violence is to be avoided, he argues, 'then it is fair and necessary that the owners of the units of production and of the finance power should be compensated for their loss'.[245] His conclusion can be called either bland or menacing: 'The political difficulty of bringing about this change will be measured by the resistance which is offered to this course.'[246]

What was distinctive about the Socialist League's thinking was the integral link it discerned between domestic and international problems. Cripps accepted this. 'The great forces that are inherent in the capitalist system are behind Fascism and war, and British capitalism has much to answer for,' he said, in words often quoted against him. 'You have only got to look at the pages of British Imperial history to hide your head in shame that you are British.'[247] The problem was structural, not the result of individual faults or national failings. Moreover, unlike the analysis of imperialism by J. A. Hobson, a major influence within the ILP, there was no option for capitalist democracy to choose the alternative road of social reform. As Cripps saw it: 'Capitalism inevitably drifts towards war: economic nationalism is the precursor of economic rivalries which are the root cause of war.'[248] His adoption of a Leninist argument that imperialism was the highest stage of capitalism can be seen in his identification of 'the very root causes of

---

impressed by Keynesianism and the New Deal; but the citation of Cooke, Cripps, pp. 166, 178–9, seems to provide little basis for this view.

242. RSC, 'Alternatives before British Labour', p. 127.

243. RSC, *Why This Socialism?*, p. 93.   244. ibid., p. 98.   245. ibid., p. 137.

246. ibid., p. 139.

247. RSC to the Bristol Socialist League, reported in *Bristol Evening World*, 21 October 1935. This speech was used by opponents in the 1935 General Election.

248. RSC, 'Alternatives before British Labour', p. 131.

war' in the imperialist search for monopoly sources of raw materials and markets.[249]

In interlocking ways, war was the product of capitalism, via imperialism, in the international sphere, just as fascism was the product of capitalism at home. Cripps argued, moreover, that 'fascism not only could be started but had been started in England' – a phenomenon that he called 'a country-gentleman form of Fascism'.[250] Fighting fascism was fundamental; but it could not be effectively contested unless imperialism was rooted out (notably in India) and unless bourgeois-capitalist parties were denied power (notably in Britain). It followed that a bourgeois politician like Winston Churchill, who defended the British Raj yet purported to oppose Nazi Germany, was the last person Cripps could imagine working with. His own strategy, implying no remedy short of revolution, staked everything on working-class solidarity and the benign influence of the world's only non-capitalist power, the Soviet Union.

Holding such views – or, at any rate, maintaining them in such a provocative way – Cripps was ill-fitted for office in the basically reformist Labour Party. He seems to have recognized this, notably in refusing to take advantage of Lansbury's invalid status at the end of 1933 to encourage support for himself as an alternative. Attlee told Cripps: 'Personally I think that you are the man who ought to be leading the Party in G. L.'s absence and should he not return you would be his natural successor.'[251] Cripps, however, with his unexpectedly high opinion of Attlee – 'such a first class brain' – thought otherwise.[252] Attlee's own problem in deputizing as leader was financial, as Cripps already realized. It was a problem that he had tried to resolve by indirect means a couple of months previously and one that he now removed by his own direct intervention. He quietly paid £500 into party funds to make it possible for the hard-up Attlee to fill the breach as acting leader. Assuring Cripps that 'any time you wish it I should always be ready to retire in your favour', Attlee thus carried on for the time being.[253]

There were, moreover, important implications for the future. It was as his deputy, when Lansbury resigned in 1935, that Attlee succeeded him as a stopgap leader for the tail-end of the parliament; and it was as the incumbent, following the next General Election, that Attlee was able to

249. RSC, *Why This Socialism?*, p. 148.
250. RSC, 'Alternatives before British Labour', p. 128. Cf. Strauss, p. 69.
251. Attlee to RSC, 30 December 1933.
252. RSC to Bevin, 24 September 1933, Bevin papers, Churchill College, BEVN, II, 9/1/7, which also recounts an earlier attempt to secure a journalistic income for Attlee.
253. Attlee to RSC, 1 January 1934 (misdated 1933).

survive a challenge to his position from Morrison. Acting as Morrison's manager, Dalton was later surprised to hear that his man had had Cripps's silent and unsolicited political support; but Attlee remained indebted to Cripps for his frankly more valuable financial support.[254] As Attlee's biographer acknowledges, 'without this timely help it is unlikely that he would ever have become prime minister'.[255] The arrangement was never publicized; Estorick in 1949 discreetly referred to an unexplained reason for Attlee to have considered stepping down and wrote simply that 'it was Sir Stafford who organized the solution'.[256] None of this looks like naked political ambition on Cripps's part: more like country-gentleman socialism.

Cripps's own priority was his freedom to advocate his left-wing views, which Beatrice Webb now described as 'unhesitatingly revolutionary'.[257] Here too he paid in hard cash, as the major source of funds for the Socialist League. Cripps had a brief spell on the NEC, the party's central committee. He was elected in 1934, despite the lack of support for Socialist League policies in the Party Conference votes. Who had captured whom was a moot point.

That Cripps refused to be stifled through responsibility became clear the next year. The NEC was committed to support the League of Nations, and hence committed to support sanctions against Italy if, as looked increasingly likely, Mussolini launched an invasion of Abyssinia. Public opinion, notably in the so-called Peace Ballot, showed unexpectedly strong support for the League. The vacillations of the National Government, to Bevin's robust mind, were neither here nor there. 'We did not write this document for the National Government,' he told his union conference; 'we wrote it for the Labour Movement.'[258] The issue was thus whether sanctions were in themselves the right policy. To Cripps, by contrast, the existence of a capitalist government was always the real issue, so the logic of his position was to ignore the substantive issue of sanctions. Instead he focused only on *who* would deploy sanctions – to which the triumphant, self-evident answer was: the capitalists! He resigned from the NEC on the eve of the Labour Party Conference at Brighton, rather than support sanctions. This was a

---

254. At the time of Munich, Cripps's view that Morrison should replace Attlee prompted Dalton to remind him that he himself had run Morrison for the leadership – only to receive the reply: 'Yes, and I voted for him': Dalton diary, 6 October 1938, quoted in Dalton, *Fateful Years*, p. 201. There is a conspicuous lack of mention of any attempt to canvass Cripps in 1935; see Dalton diary, 19–24 November 1935, in Pimlott (ed.), *Dalton: Political Diary*, pp. 194–5, and Donoughue and Jones, *Morrison*, pp. 237–8.

255. Harris, *Attlee*, p. 110.   256. Estorick, p. 107.

257. Webb diary, 2 September 1934, Passfield papers.   258. Bullock, *Bevin*, i, pp. 558–9.

policy that Lansbury, too, could not accept; but whereas his objection was pacifist, Cripps's was that the League was acting as the tool of imperialist powers – an 'International Burglars Union' was the taunt he used in the bitter Conference debate.[259] It should be remembered that this was said at a moment when the Italian invasion was obviously imminent, thus undercutting any attempt to deter aggression. It was in this debate that Bevin memorably vented his scorn for Lansbury's position, and contempt for Cripps's.

Far from resiling, Cripps went further the next year. In a speech at Stockport he maintained that the Labour conference's recent acquiescence in rearmament 'showed that the delegates did not realize that the basic cleavage in this country, in the political field, is a class struggle'. The point was that socialists should not put armaments in the hands of a Government that represented the class enemy. 'I would not trust it with a single man in any conceivable circumstances,' said Cripps, 'even if it told me it wanted him to fight Hitler, because I have been told that sort of thing before.' This was the nub of his case, as reported verbatim and subsequently unchallenged. Whether Cripps went on to say, in so many words, that 'he did not believe it would be a bad thing for the British working class if Germany defeated us', is less certain.[260]

These were the words that caught attention and which were to be endlessly recycled thereafter. Either way, literally correct or not, they hardly distort the essential meaning; and again it was a field day for the press. 'Sir Stafford Cripps makes it almost unnecessary to point out Socialist inconsistencies, all but impossible to caricature Socialist policies', was the up-market Tory response, echoed by the down-market taunt: 'Among Socialist MPs "Cripps!" is replacing "Cripes!" as an expletive indicating astonishment.'[261] Labour loyalists blenched: 'Heaven help the Labour Party if this sort of thing continues to be said from a Labour platform.'[262] Unabashed, Cripps continued to denounce rearmament in the Commons on the same reasoning, arguing that the issue was not arms so much as

259. *LPACR*, 1935, p. 158; and see Bullock, *Bevin*, i, pp. 565–71.
260. This is how the *Manchester Guardian*, 16 November 1936, paraphrased his answer to a question from the floor. In a letter to the *Manchester Guardian* on 19 November 1936 Cripps claimed simply to have shown that 'the British working class would not necessarily suffer through the defeat of British imperialism' – and that this was quite a different thing. See also *Manchester Guardian*, 20 November 1936, for the shorthand report of the Stockport correspondent.
261. *Morning Post, Daily Express*, 17 November 1936.
262. *Daily Herald*, 21 November 1936.

power, and judging the National Government 'far more likely to be the allies of Fascism than the allies of Russia or any working-class country'.[263] Throughout 1937 Cripps maintained that 'the only true basis for any coalition of forces is the class basis'.[264]

It was the same resolute class analysis, applied the world over, that underpinned the campaign for a United Front of all working-class parties. Yet this commitment was largely theoretical for Cripps. To some extent it rested on the fact that he had long seen socialism as a project, not for the conventionally defined working *class*, but for a *working* class. 'The general manager of a railway,' he maintained, 'is just as much in the class of salary and wage earners as is the telegraphist or porter, though the present exaggerated differences in reward mask this similarity.'[265] To this extent, Cripps's rhetoric of class meant both more and less than it seemed at first glance.

It remains true that though Cripps talked a good deal about the working class, there was little mutual affinity between himself and authentically working-class leaders, notably Bevin, whose power in the movement was backed by the block vote of the TGWU. It is interesting that the account of Labour's factional politics that appears in the first edition of Estorick's biography, from the perspective of 1940–41, depicts the Unity campaign as essentially 'an attempt to wrest control of the movement from the block vote', on the ground that this had enabled leaders like Bevin and Sir Walter Citrine, Secretary of the Trades Union Congress, to stall a more decisively socialist policy. Thus it was held against the trade unions that 'the party became a purely "class" or "sectional" party, instead of a "national" party appealing both to "investors" and "managers" as well as mere "horny-handed sons of toil"'.[266] That such arguments might justify, by extension, ever more inclusive coalition-building, and all in the name of democracy, was left implicit.

The United Front, publicly launched in January 1937, was a tactic advocated by the Socialist League within the Labour Party. 'Unity of all sections of the working-class movement' was its declared objective and this meant alliance with the (disaffiliated) ILP and the Communists.[267] Harry Pollitt, Secretary of the Communist Party of Great Britain (CPGB), had

263. 5 HC Debs., vol. 320, cols. 1456–63 (18 February 1937). On these arguments, cf. Foot, *Bevan*, i, esp. pp. 266–7.
264. RSC, 'The political reactions of rearmament', p. 120.
265. RSC, 'A word to the middle class, ii', *New Clarion*, 28 October 1933, p. 338.
266. Estorick (1941), pp. 122, 124, 126; cf. pp. 149, 215.
267. Unity Campaign Manifesto, 18 January 1937.

long been pressing for such a move; many saw his influence behind Cripps's conversion, following the 1935 General Election. The ILP preached an independent strain of Marxism that often put it at odds with the Stalinist CPGB. First the Spanish civil war (where the partisans of both factions were actually fighting each other as much as their nominal enemy, Franco), and then the Moscow show trials, set the ILP and the CPGB at each other's throats. Such unpromising demonstrations of working-class fraternity (or its absence) doomed the Unity campaign in 1937.

The impact on Cripps's career was mixed. It was the Unity Campaign that finally shattered the Socialist League, which, now directly pitted against official Labour Party policy, was disaffiliated by the NEC. Moreover, with its flouting of party loyalty the campaign imperilled Cripps's personal support from Attlee, Labour's leader since 1935. 'You talk about driving Cripps out,' Bevin admonished G. D. H. Cole, 'Cripps is driving himself out.'[268] What saved Cripps from disciplinary action in February 1937 was the happy coincidence that, on the day before the NEC met to consider his case, there was a debate in the House of Commons on the report of the Gresford disaster inquiry. Here Cripps was indisputably and indispensably cast in a starring role.

Cripps escaped expulsion at a price. First he wound up the Socialist League; then he abandoned the Unity Campaign. His pure-minded supporters were taken aback by these abrupt decisions, more obviously high-handed than high-minded. By October 1937, Cripps appeared to be back in the Labour Party's fold – indeed, his re-election to the NEC after a two-year gap suggested that he was now a shepherd himself. Reforms of the party constitution, enjoying the double-edged distinction of Cripps's support, had created a new section, elected solely by the grassroots members rather than the unions' block votes. Cripps was joined, among the seven constituency party representatives, by D. N. Pritt and Harold Laski, and, together with Ellen Wilkinson of the women's section, they functioned as a left-wing nucleus on the NEC.

The Socialist League had finally been reduced to what its arch-opponent Dalton called it: 'a rich man's toy'.[269] It is true that Cripps and George Strauss ended up paying most of the bills, as they did for the pro-Unity newspaper they started in January 1937, *Tribune* (or *The Tribune*, as it was known in early days). They found most of the £20,000 start-up capital between them; and this proved to be only the beginning of their liabilities.

268. Bevin to Cole, 25 January 1937, quoted in Bullock, *Bevin*, i, p. 596.
269. Pimlott, *Dalton*, p. 241.

Cripps was covenanting £5,000 a year in donations at this time, as a tax-efficient way of supporting his good causes. Most of his money initially went to three political organizations: to the Socialist League, which received nearly £1,200 from him in its final year; to his constituency party in Bristol East, which got around £300 a year; and, in steadily increasing subventions, to *Tribune* – £683 in 1936–7, £1,250 the next year, and £2,000 in the nine months ending January 1939.[270] Politics was proving an expensive hobby even for a man as rich as Stafford Cripps.

Cripps before 'austerity'

Though Cripps seldom ducked out of professional engagements, he often had to labour against discomfort and pain. His persistent poor health in the 1930s undoubtedly made him receptive to alternative remedies since orthodox medicine seemed unable to help. Advice was proffered from near and far. Purcell Weaver, the more exotic of the brothers taken into the Cripps family, suffered an emotional breakdown in 1934, and took himself, like a latter-day Stevenson or Gauguin, to Tahiti. There he came under the influence of Edmond Szekély, prophet of an 'oranges-only' diet, whose ideas young Purcell henceforth began to proselytize. On returning to England, he naturally first beat a path to the door of Goodfellows with his new recipe for a healthy life: raw fruit and vegetables, combined with cold baths and abstention from tobacco and alcohol. 'Cripps said rather wearily that he had tried everything and found no relief, so he might as well try this too,' Strauss reports. 'He had little faith in "nature cures", but he agreed to give the suggestion a fair trial.'[271]

Cripps persisted with congruent remedies. He established a connection, literally ended only by his death, with the clinic founded in Zurich forty years previously by Dr Max Bircher-Benner, whose theory was that many illnesses, including colitis, could be cured by a strict raw-food diet. Through Isobel Stafford was introduced to the Australian, F. Mathias Alexander, whose eponymous 'technique' they subsequently championed. This was nothing if not a holistic approach. 'Alexander has found the lost chord,' wrote one enthusiast. 'He has found the key to the secret of integrated

270. Deed of covenant, 8 May 1936, drawn up by Bernard Drake; *Tribune* accounts for first three years, up to 24 January 1939. Cf. Foot, *Bevan*, i, p. 245; Pimlott, *Labour and the Left*, pp. 104–5, 107–8.
271. Strauss, p. 102.

behaviour which brings the idea of psycho-physical unity out of the fogs of theory into the light of demonstrable fact.'[272] A three-week course was enough to convert Isobel, who at last found relief from her long-lasting malaise; as she said later, she 'then got Stafford to go and *cannot* be grateful enough for what it has done for us both, though his wrong "use" was not so bad as mine'.[273]

The Alexander technique concentrated on relaxation of the spine and neck so as to produce correct posture. Stafford not only exhibited its benefits in his own notably erect bearing but also lent his name to its propagation. It did 'an immense amount of good in reducing my fatigue and improving my health,' he testified: it was 'the difference between chaos and order and so between illness and good health'.[274] The names of Alexander and Cripps were thus closely linked in public perceptions. 'As a pupil, Sir Stafford is quite a credit,' ran one later newspaper story. 'He gets up at 4 a.m., often works eighteen hours on end, and generally manages to cram two men's work into one man's day.'[275]

Apart from carrying on smoking, Stafford settled into the new health regime and Isobel joined him in becoming vegetarian, initially out of solidarity. Diana became the most fervent convert, later publishing a recipe book on salads for Purcell Weaver's Bureau of Cosmotherapy. There was much family discussion about best practice. 'I entirely agree with the necessity for the bran,' wrote Stafford while on an ocean crossing, 'but unfortunately so far as I am concerned it doesn't function at sea so that I am thrown back on the dear old wash out.'[276] It would, however, be wrong to suppose that Goodfellows was reconstituted as a vegetarian camp or health spa after 1935. Theresa Cripps, though receptive to the Alexander technique, was subsequently to revert to meat-eating, and her brother John's succession of hungry student friends were not required to change their habits.

John Cripps was an undergraduate at Oxford in the early 1930s. Among his contemporaries was Michael Foot, son of the Liberal MP Isaac Foot and himself active in the Liberal Club, of which he became chairman. Though

272. March, *New Way of Life*, p. 4. Bryant, *Cripps*, pp. 271–3, is useful here.
273. IC, 'A note on the experience of F. M. Alexander technique', 22 July 1943. Her introduction seems to have been through the American author Waldo Frank, and his wife Alma Frank.
274. Affidavit in support of Alexander, PRO, CAB 127/118; Cripps quoted in March, *New Way of Life*, p. 13.
275. *Daily Mirror*, 15 April 1948. His attendance at Alexander's eightieth birthday party in 1949 was widely reported.
276. RSC diary, 31 July 1938. Cf. the remarks in his diary on 28 August 1938 about cooked food being bad.

in different colleges, they shared lodgings. Through the Labour Club, John met Geoffrey Wilson, a member of a Quaker family long known to Marian Parmoor. Through John, Geoffrey met Michael; and they became a 'trio' of close friends, broadly united in their radical political views (though Michael did not actually become a member of the party he was to lead fifty years later until after leaving Oxford). John took both of them home to Good-fellows, and they were to be often asked back.

In the 1930s, house parties at Goodfellows were memorable, especially for young guests who had the thrill of mixing on easy terms with well-known political figures. The names of George Lansbury, Herbert Morrison and Clement Attlee are often mentioned; the idea that they might bump into Jawaharlal Nehru, who paid a visit with his daughter Indira in 1938, enhanced the mystique. Memories of Goodfellows were to linger as a warm, active and hospitable family home, where the Crippses lived in great style but without ostentation – 'a place where jaded souls can find peace in beautiful and simple surroundings'.[277]

The household revolved around Stafford, whether at work or play. Once his heavy commitments in law had been augmented by those of an MP in 1930, he took on a full-time secretary, Gwendoline Hill, who received free board and lodging and was thus always on hand when needed by Stafford: a role which may have been resented by Isobel Cripps. Stafford would snatch a weekend at Goodfellows whenever he could, though he often spent much of it toiling away in his study. He extended a convivial welcome to the young people whom he found at Goodfellows and, on departure on a Monday morning, would accompany them as far as the platform for the London train, whereupon he would disappear into his reserved first-class compartment to resume work on his papers.

However busy he was, he would join the family for meals – and immediately take charge. If Stafford suggested tennis, it was tennis; if dancing after dinner – 'and they did a lot of dancing' – then dancing it was.[278] Bedtime was ten o'clock, like it or not. There was a regular pre-breakfast walk with three dogs and a goat; and there were picnics, where Theresa and Peggy exhibited their knowledge of wild flowers.

Geoffrey Wilson fitted in very nicely at Goodfellows, so much so that, in the later 1930s, he felt some guilt at spending more time there than with his

277. Wilson to IC, 21 September 1933.
278. Michael Foot interview; personal information from Margaret Meade and Alice Sutton; also from Geoffrey Wilson, whose unpublished memoirs, 'My Working Life', provide the best written testimony. See Castle, *Fighting All the Way*, p. 80, for a more hostile account.

own parents. Thus began his long and loyal personal and political attachment to Cripps, whom he posthumously celebrated as 'the gay, passionate
Christian crusader who gave me a home more real than my own; who taught
me what forgiveness can mean; who struck fire from all with whom he came
in contact; who set a standard of courage and sincerity which will inspire
tens of thousands of people who never even saw him'.[279]

Brought up in a strict, high-minded, teetotal Quaker family, Wilson
found that the Crippses had much the same values as his parents, 'but softer
and less dogmatic'.[280] Visitors agree that there were always alcoholic drinks
available for guests; some speak of a sideboard with bottles of spirits; others
of beer and cider at the table over delicious and hilarious meals. Stafford
only became censorious about excessively 'well-oiled' imbibers who were
'not in a fit state to dance with sober people after dinner'.[281] House-guests
were conscripted into a variety of games, both indoor and outdoor, and
found Stafford a keen participant. 'Tese and I both lost our competition
shuffle board games,' he noted on an ocean voyage. 'I played a lot of rather
good games of quoits, which I enjoyed.'[282]

Wilson even adopted the family pastime of knitting. When he and Cripps
later went together to China and Russia, they were able to kit themselves
out with hand-knitted ear-muffs (only to find them inadequate against the
Russian winter). Wilson happily joined the Cripps family on their summer
holidays in both 1936 and 1937; and in 1939 the ultimate treat was to
accompany Stafford and Isobel (along with Toby Weaver) on the first leg of
a luxurious Mediterranean cruise – 'I had to pinch myself to make sure that
it was all real.'[283]

This cruise saw the Cripps family at play, for once rather self-consciously
living up to their high income. Cripps had chartered a luxurious motor yacht
of sixty-three tons, the *White Sapphire*, with a skipper and crew of three.
Photographs show 'the Red Admiral' and his wife, 'Madame Butterfly', ready
enough to sample the joys of the Mediterranean in a leisurely and relaxed
style. Stafford relished the ample supplies of fresh fruit on which he and Isobel
dined. They sometimes sought out good restaurants but found that, 'out of
season', some were closed in August – one reminder that pre-war Mediterranean tourist culture did not revolve around the sun. Stafford enjoyed not
only sea-bathing but sun-bathing, preferably in the nude; and one or two
snapshots of Isobel show her rather sparsely clad above the waist. It was a

279. Wilson to IC, 23 April 1952.   280. Wilson, 'My Working Life', p. 14.
281. RSC diary, 4 August 1938.   282. ibid., 25 September 1938.
283. Wilson, 'My Working Life', p. 16.

uniquely happy time – soon only a sunlit memory. St Tropez may, to a modern eye, look distinctly deserted in the photographs he took, but Stafford's judgement in 1939 was that it had 'a nice character of its own which even hoards [sic] of Tourists hadn't been able to spoil'.[284]

Stafford gave up smoking, as usual when he was on holiday, and missed it at first while sitting out in the summer evenings, usually at cafés in the small ports where they put in, immersed in gossip while they watched the world go by. At Viareggio, observing the 'thoroughly happy and care-free' demeanour of the people, he commented wistfully: 'They don't take their leisure and enjoyment so sadly as the English do.'[285] Stafford had no objection to gambling as such: 'Like most things I believe it is a mistake to take up the view that it is forbidden, far better to try and inculcate a spirit of control and restraint.'[286] It is not surprising, therefore, to find that his latent sybaritic tendencies again surfaced after a flutter at the casino at St Juan les Pins, and he thought it 'great fun too seeing the English shocking themselves and feeling obviously frightfully continental and dare devil'.[287] After a while, quantities of the local wines were shipped aboard and, while Stafford did not indulge, he encouraged the rest of his party to do so.

Simply to call Stafford a puritan misses the mark. He was publicly outspoken against sexual prudery: 'We have been half ashamed of our divinely-created animal instincts, and some have tried to hide them or slur over them.'[288] In private, Woodrow Wyatt recalled, he would 'remark how strange it was of God (in whom he unhesitatingly believed) to put the place of supreme emotional and physical satisfaction next to the organs of excretion'.[289] There are sexual allusions in his diaries which suggest that, in an era when middle-class English inhibitions were notorious, the Cripps family enjoyed more frankness and openness than might be expected. Thus in Italy his holiday diary contains a playful entry: 'Mummie keeps saying how nice all the men look and the two boys keep spotting all the winners amongst the girls.' The frustrations of young Geoffrey and young Toby in trying to spot more winners in Monte Carlo elicited Stafford's sympathy, as 'an uglier lot I have seldom seen'.[290]

Treated almost like a son, it would not have been wholly surprising had Geoffrey Wilson become a son-in-law. He was surely eligible, and two years older than John Cripps, whose marriage to Ursula Davy had taken place in

284. RSC diary, 22 August 1939.   285. ibid., 5 August 1939.
286. ibid., 28 September 1938 (on the Jamaican voyage).   287. ibid., 19 August 1939.
288. RSC to the Marriage Guidance Council, reported in *News Chronicle*, 6 February 1946.
289. Wyatt, *Confessions*, pp. 141–2.
290. RSC diary, 5 August, 1 August 1939 (dated 2 August).

1936. Wilson admittedly found Diana Cripps attractive and talks of being 'mildly in love' with her.[291] In the event, in 1938 she was to make a match even closer to home, at least in one sense – a marriage to Purcell Weaver that was sprung upon Stafford and Isobel on their arrival on holiday in Jamaica, where the betrothed couple had been living for several months with their guru, Szekély. Though initially welcomed by her family, Diana's marriage was soon to be annulled because it was never consummated and it seems to have precipitated her increasing mental fragility in subsequent years.

It is likely that Geoffrey Wilson's affections had already shifted to Diana's younger sister Theresa, whose secret diary subsequently alluded to his 'very sweet and self-sacrificing' attitude in not forcing the issue before she completed her degree at Oxford.[292] Here is some of the inwardness to Wilson's comment that Goodfellows 'became my second home and I was more or less adopted as a member of the family'.[293] The diary of the world tour that he was to make with Cripps in the early months of the Second World War stands as evidence of their closeness, as will be seen.

By 1939 Cripps was a well-known public figure. What was printed about his private life centred on Goodfellows, justifiably enough, but was inevitably given news value by dissonant implications about social hierarchy. That he should have become a left-wing socialist was a paradox. That he should have become a teetotaller (for reasons not generally known) likewise jarred with convention. That he should have adopted a vegetarian diet was more unusual in the 1930s than it would have been half a century later, although it could be explained by reference to his known medical condition. That he had taken up the Alexander technique, accounting for his distinctive posture, was not publicized until later. That he wore flat shoes, with no heels, might have been noticed by a quizzical eye. That he was a devotee of knitting was not a foible widely reported at the time.

That Cripps did any one of these things might have passed as an agreeable eccentricity; that he did all of them in succession stored up hazards for the future in forming and projecting his public identity. He was already more liable to be perceived as quirky or priggish than as engaging or congenial. Although Beatrice Webb had privately commented that her nephew 'grows more intense and ascetic every day', Cripps was not generally identified with asceticism until later.[294] It was a rather boyish Cripps, a rather cherubic

291. Wilson, 'My Working Life', pp. 14–15.
292. Theresa Cripps diary, 11 February 1941; passage written in secret ink.
293. Wilson, 'My Working Life', p. 14.
294. Webb diary, 2 September 1934, Passfield papers.

Cripps, with round horn-rimmed spectacles, whom the cartoonists first noticed. The fact that he was becoming thinner in the face was already noticeable in the late 1930s and his increasing severity of countenance was accentuated by his adoption of rimless spectacles. As with his habits, so with his physical appearance: a conjunction of characteristics awaited a unifying theme to fashion them into a distinctive and indelible image.

At sea

In 1939, suddenly but quietly, Cripps took steps to wind down all his commitments, financial and political alike. It soon became apparent that he had reached a crisis in his career; but the nature of that crisis was appreciated by few at the time. To understand it, the events of the previous year need rather closer scrutiny; and luckily this is possible because Cripps again started keeping a diary.

Cripps's health was one problem, and the reason why he had booked a holiday cruise to Jamaica for two months in the summer of 1938. A more pressing problem, however, involved a change of political strategy. Much turned on his decision in the spring of 1938 to support the call for a Popular Front. The cry had become familiar through the example of France, where Blum had achieved a famous electoral victory in 1936, and, above all, through the impact of Spain, where the republic was nominally defended across a spectrum from liberal constitutionalists to Communists. Hitler's annexation of Austria in March 1938 showed how easily fascism could triumph. The dilemma for the left was put to Cripps privately by Kingsley Martin, editor of the *New Statesman*, now uneasily aware that to make 'a class analysis of the situation and leave it at that' seemed cowardly if there were 'half a chance of preventing war by the Winston sort of policy'. Making the distinction 'between a war we ought to risk which would genuinely be in the interests of socialism in Spain, and a war for the British Empire' might have served the left well enough previously. 'It is now, I am afraid, obvious that they would be the same thing,' Martin told Cripps.[295]

Cripps showed a new responsiveness to such arguments. Within days he publicly claimed that the National Government's policy of building up Hitler as a bulwark against Bolshevism had backfired by endangering British imperialism around the world and thereby provoking a significant split. 'Churchill was a Liberal Imperialist,' Cripps explained. 'He would do

295. Martin to RSC, 18 March 1938.

anything to protect the British Empire, and would have no qualms against working with Russia if it would achieve this.' Cripps thus acknowledged that Churchill's sincere commitment to imperial defence might eclipse simple class interest: 'Churchill had been less concerned with the danger of working class power than the safety of the British Empire. That was the fundamental difference between Chamberlain and Churchill.'[296] Moreover, while Cripps had argued strongly against collaboration with a homogeneous capitalist class, once such fissures within it were perceived, it made sense to exploit them.

Events thus called for the consideration of new tactics and the contemplation of new alliances. In May 1938 Cripps was joined by his three comrades on the NEC in declaring that, 'in face of European perils', it was necessary to rally all opponents of the National Government in order to replace it. 'It is better to join forces with anti-Socialist democrats than to see both Socialism and Democracy perish,' they now argued.[297] A Popular Front would, like the United Front, involve cooperation with the CPGB, which supported the proposal (with obvious Soviet inspiration and with Pollitt active as usual). Indeed these points were not lost upon Cripps's critics, who regarded this latest bright idea as tainted by his past record, vitiated by his past tactics, and discredited by his past associates.

In the Commons, Cripps had two loyal supporters through thick and thin: George Strauss and Aneurin Bevan. They sat together on the editorial board of *Tribune* which survived its parent, the Socialist League, as an organ of the Labour Left. Strauss was a wealthy man who could afford to differ from the party line. He would not have been a major figure in his own right; nor would his wife, Patricia, who was to stand for the NEC in 1939 despite being, in Dalton's view, 'completely unknown outside Crippsite and Tribune circles'.[298] With Nye Bevan, of course, it was another matter. The charismatic hero of the Welsh miners from whom he sprang, Bevan was always his own man; and what is remarkable is that in his entire career (as his most objective biographer puts it) Cripps was 'the one senior figure in the Labour Party to whose judgement he was consistently willing to defer'.[299]

296. RSC at Carlisle, *Cumberland Evening News*, 21 March 1938. See also Estorick (1941), pp. 150–61, for a congruent explication of Cripps's thinking, no doubt from the horse's mouth; this is evidently how Cripps explained himself at the time of his journey home through the USA in April 1940.
297. 'The International Situation', submitted to the NEC on 5 May 1938; the other signatories were Laski, Pritt and Wilkinson.
298. Dalton diary, 26 May 1939, in Pimlott (ed.), *Dalton: Political Diary*, p. 266.
299. Campbell, *Bevan*, p. 72.

He did so in 1938-9: Bevan supported Cripps over the Popular Front. But William Mellor, installed as *Tribune*'s first editor, and never an emollient figure, made clear his dissent.

Cripps's next move smacked more of capitalist ruthlessness than socialist forbearance. He had negotiated an agreement with the publisher Victor Gollancz, who, with Harold Laski and John Strachey, selected publications for the Left Book Club, with its pro-Communist line. The deal was founded on a promise and a premise. It promised Cripps some financial relief and *Tribune* the prospect of a larger circulation; it was premised on support for the Popular Front. Anxious to board his cruise ship, Cripps acted quickly to dismiss Mellor and to offer the editorship to his own protégé, Michael Foot – with all of two-and-a-half-years' experience of journalism behind him. Foot, however, in sympathy with the way Mellor had been treated, sent Cripps a principled refusal, thus provoking an affectionate, candid but firmly proprietorial reply:

I think you may give me credit for the fact that I don't propose to pay many thousands a year to run a paper which is not in harmony – broadly – with my views . . . You may be quite assured that I shall not continue putting my money and energies into running a paper for a policy I don't believe in . . . I only elaborate these points, Mike dear, to try and show you that I am not such a completely negligible political factor in the Tribune as you would seem from your letter to think.[300]

It should be added that Foot retained a respect for Cripps, albeit more guarded than before this demonstration that, if the Socialist League had been a rich man's toy, *Tribune* was henceforth to become a rich man's trumpet.

On 25 July 1938, having posted his letter to Foot, Cripps left with his family for Jamaica. It was fifteen years since he had set pen to paper in his last diary; now he resumed – or, rather, he began a new practice. He acquired a typewriter and quickly found it as useful a tool as anything on the carpenter's bench: 'In an aeroplane, in a car, in a train, anywhere, he is always working: either reading, or typing on his portable machine.'[301] In this respect, the four volumes chronicling the Jamaican holiday provide the model for subsequent diaries, notably those running from June 1939 and devoted primarily to political concerns.

The Jamaica diary, by contrast, is the fruit of relaxation. It tells of how a private visit by Stafford, Isobel, Theresa and Peggy, travelling incognito as the Brown family, became a focus of intermittent media attention. That this was not entirely unwitting is shown by Stafford's readiness to speak at a public meeting with Norman Manley, KC, helping to inaugurate the People's National Party. The main object of the trip for Stafford, however, remained a restful family holiday: one in which his daughter Diana and Purcell Weaver would be visited (and during which their surprise wedding took place).

It was only on shipboard, returning home at the end of September, that Cripps got abreast of the international news. As the Sudetenland crisis came to a head, he literally could not help hearing the broadcast of one of Hitler's threatening speeches against Czechoslovakia. Cripps noted that it 'sounded as we walked around the deck not listening like a wild beast show, it was really most unpleasant'.[302] Isolated, out of touch with European news, fed only by rumours from other passengers' portable radios, Cripps was struggling to make sense of the situation as it suddenly thrust itself upon him. On 28 September, uniquely, he wrote at length about politics in his holiday diary, noting that 'it certainly looks to us with the scant knowledge that we have as if there is bound to be war by tomorrow and I suppose that the submarines will get on the job right away'.[303]

Cripps was truly at sea. This is apparent from his contemporary diary, even though he later rationalized his uncharted driftings. In the authorized biography that Estorick was to produce in 1949 under Isobel Cripps's watchful eye, a sharp turn of course is discerned. 'After the signing of the Munich Pact he proceeded to abandon class struggle principles in favour of the national principles of the Labour Party,' wrote Estorick, with the reiterated claim: 'It was "Munich" that changed everything for him.'[304] It took time, however, for this new compass-reading to become established. Cripps's diary shows him at a loss over his response to the crisis and there is an incoherence in his musings that belies his knowing hints that he had foreseen the whole thing. If this was indeed the 'war which we have been pointing out as the inevitable end of the policy of the British Government', one might expect him to have anticipated his own strategy instead of covering several pages of his diary with vacillations.

The position of the Labour Party will I presume be comparatively simple as they will support the government in the policy of protecting Czechoskovakia. The position of

302. RSC diary, 27 September 1938.
303. ibid., 28 September 1938; much of this is quoted in Cooke, *Cripps*, pp. 225–7, which also prints other extracts from the Jamaican diary.
304. Estorick, pp. 169, 361; cf. p. 162. These pivotal passages were carefully scrutinized in the correspondence between RSC, Clem Leslie and IC in early July 1949.

those like myself who have uniformly adopted the attitude that the present Government cannot be trusted to wage a war, because fundamentally they are out after the wrong things, is much more difficult.

I agree that sooner or later it was necesssary to stop the fascist powers. It is a tragedy that the stopping was not done more safely and earlier, but that now is past history and cannot be remedied.

It is difficult to see what might have stopped the fascist powers earlier except the sanctions and armaments that Cripps had resolutely opposed. He now professed himself undecided as to 'whether it is necessary to continue to point out to the workers the acute danger and indeed the uselessness of allowing such a Government as the present to wage any war'. The only redeeming outcome would be the creation of a revolutionary situation, thus enabling a complete change in the economic system; yet victory would make this less likely. Here Cripps's mind went back to the conflicts within the United Front, with the Communists already indicating that they would support a war government. 'The ILP were equally clear that it was wrong to offer support to the Government,' he recollected, 'and we were inclined to the same view though not with the same rigidity as we were not quite so hidebound by theory as they were.'

This line of analysis pointed towards revolutionary defeatism as the correct policy. Reading on, however, it seems no longer axiomatic that this would indeed be Cripps's own view – otherwise he would hardly have explored at such length the hypothesis of supporting a war.

... there is the difficulty as to the attitude that one ought to take up to joining a government either oneself, if asked, or the party. There is always the dangerous but sometimes true argument that if you are going to support it is better to get the advantage of the influence that you may be able to exert from within a Government for the benefit of the workers in a war situation, but then there is also the fact that you must inevitably identify yourself with policies that you disapprove and with the class that you are fighting politically. Although the temptation to join in is very great indeed as one is always inclined to believe that one could do some good yet it is true that there must be a leadership left outside which can watch constantly for the right moment for the workers to exert their power when the war is on the decline.

Here was both an agenda and a dilemma that were to dominate Cripps's career over the next four years. It is not just hindsight to observe this: it would surely have been apparent to any of his political associates, had they read his diary, that his attitude was uncertain. True, he still regarded 'the best solution of the problem for the workers' as the essential criterion, on the ground that 'it is only their interests that really matter in the long run'. Moreover, what camouflaged any change in his outlook was the fact that his position became closer to that of the Communists. It was their support for a Popular Front that coloured the reaction of many other people to the proposal, and thus fostered the image of Cripps as a dupe or fellow-traveller of Communism. Simply supporting moves for a broad-based anti-fascist government, then, did not necessarily mean any lapse from a Marxist analysis, but only a shift in the currently appropriate political tactics.

What Cripps did on his return to London revealed his inner uncertainty. 'He would put Socialism aside for the present,' was how Dalton expressed it at the beginning of October. It was striking enough that the two of them should meet at all on civil terms, still less concert joint political action. But Cripps now proposed that, along with Attlee and Morrison, they should put out feelers to the dissident Conservatives – certainly to Churchill, probably to Leo Amery, another imperialist anti-appeaser, and to Anthony Eden, whose resignation as Foreign Secretary earlier in the year identified him as an opponent of Chamberlain. Cripps also expressed a wish to replace Attlee with Morrison.[305] His main purpose, however, was clearly to get rid of Chamberlain, not Attlee. Though relieved that the Prime Minister's concessions to Hitler at Munich had seen war averted, Cripps intensified his hostility to Chamberlain himself, for the moment envisaging cooperation with Churchill in a ploy to bring down the Government at all costs. For this step, however, the Tory dissidents were not yet ready, fearful of political annihilation if they showed their hand.

The situation was complicated by two tests of public opinion. In October 1938 a by-election at Oxford found the local Labour Party ready to with-draw its own nominee (Patrick Gordon Walker) in order to run an independent anti-Munich candidate, A. D. Lindsay, the Master of Balliol, who was supported also by Liberals and dissident Conservatives, notably Harold Macmillan. The NEC reluctantly acquiesced; but the seat was still held by the Chamberlainite Conservative, Quintin Hogg. A far better result, from Cripps's point of view, was achieved the next month at Bridgwater, Somerset. Here the journalist Vernon Bartlett overturned a Tory majority, enjoying support from local Liberals and Labour as well as from a well-publicized

---

305. Though suggesting a dim view of Attlee's performance, this hardly amounts to 'an attempt by Cripps to remove him from the leadership', as claimed in Harris, *Attlee*, p. 156. See Dalton diary, 6 October 1938, quoted in Dalton, *Fateful Years*, pp. 200–201; cf. Pimlott, *Labour and the Left*, p. 165.

intervention by the Left Book Club. Cripps himself was too busy in London to travel to Bridgwater but sent Bartlett a message. Whereas at Oxford the fall in the Conservative vote since 1935 was 6.7 per cent, at Bridgwater it was a full 10 per cent, compared with an average fall of 5 per cent in all by-elections during 1938.[306] In its best result, then, the Popular Front strategy could be said not only to have healed a split in the anti-Chamberlain vote but to have hit Conservative support twice as heavily as normal.

After Bridgwater, Cripps appears to have decided that the success of his Popular Front did not depend on Conservative support, nor even that of the NEC. Whereas he had appeared willing to work with and through the Labour leadership in his abortive cross-party initiative in October 1938, he soon reverted to his familiar role as gadfly. His renewed advocacy of a Popular Front in a memorandum to the NEC in January 1939 flew in the face of official Labour Party policy, and sought to mobilize grassroots agitation against the leadership in a familiar pattern, with particular emphasis on the activities of youth movements, whether affiliated to the Labour, Liberal or Communist Parties.

Cripps's electoral argument is interesting both for what it did say and what it did not. Instead of a heady invocation of class as the guarantor of ultimate victory, Cripps switched to sober, empirical arguments for doubting Labour's immediate ability to displace the National Government. He pointed to the need to augment Labour's 8 million supporters of 1935 with 'at least another 4–5 million voters who have either not voted before or who have given their votes to other parties, the majority of whom, like many of the Labour Party supporters, are not politically instructed'. He argued that 'we are all apt to over-estimate the degree of political consciousness and intelligence in the electorate and to under-estimate the value of such simple conceptions or slogans as "National", "non-Party" etc., especially in critical times'.[307] His plan, then, depended partly on electoral arithmetic, showing how tactical splits in the Opposition vote might be eliminated, and partly on achieving greater credibility and popularity. Bridgwater provided a model: a constituency where Liberals and Labour had each polled around 20 per cent in 1935, but where Bartlett's campaign as Independent Progressive had put another 10 per cent on top of that, thus overthrowing a previously solid Conservative plurality. For all the noise that was made about the Communists' participation in a Popular Front,

306. Craig (ed.), *British Parliamentary Results*, p. 454; cf. Butler, *Electoral System*, table 32, p. 184.
307. Cripps memorandum, submitted 9 January 1939.

their electoral strength was minuscule. The silent majority were Liberals and 'don't knows', as Cripps implicitly acknowledged. Yet it did not follow – or did not yet follow – that he had abandoned the principled simplicities of Marxism for the pragmatic compromises of bourgeois democracy.

Broad as his anti-Chamberlain coalition purported to be, Cripps envisaged no place in it for the Prime Minister's most trenchant critic. He now wrote disparagingly of Churchill, asserting that his attempt 'to capture the Youth for reactionary imperialism' had to be thwarted.[308] Puzzled as to whether a capitalist could be considered a serious anti-fascist, still less whether an imperialist could, Cripps still found it 'inconceivable that one could approve the policy of any capitalist government toward India'.[309] He was torn between recognizing Churchill's good faith as the foremost opponent of Hitler and denying that political will could override economic determinism. Cripps sought to resolve the dilemma in a long article ('What's Mr Churchill After?') to which a naturally obliging editor devoted the whole of *Tribune*'s front page. 'Fascism arises out of the economic circumstances of capitalism and is not the result of some evil wish of politicians,' Cripps wrote. 'The best intentioned Tory Democrats will be driven into fascism when the economic circumstances call for that type of repression.'[310]

The Popular Front, then, was to be anti-Chamberlain but also anti-Churchill. Cripps presented his memorandum to the NEC in his worst self-righteous, take-it-or-leave-it style. He sat through the meeting, doodling on the back of his agenda papers and making pencilled notes of the comments. Their tone as much as their substance indicates his failure to enlist significant support. Attlee made the standard plea against electoral cooperation by claiming that people were 'more likely to be attracted by a clear-cut programme of socialism'. Morrison, always the party manager, drew on his fund of electoral experience to find reasons why the proposed combination would not work: 'Can't see it is practicable so reject it.' Dalton was likewise sceptical: 'You would get C.P. in but that would lose you support.' There was further disparaging talk about the 'purely anti-official' motivation of Cripps's supporters. Jimmy Walker of the iron and steel workers gave a blunt trade-union view: 'Nothing in document new or original, badly constructed – S.C. still in political childhood.'[311]

308. RSC to Middleton, 9 January 1939, copy.   309. RSC diary, 28 September 1938.
310. RSC, 'What's Mr Churchill After?', *Tribune*, 6 January 1939.
311. RSC, manuscript notes, meeting of 13 January 1939. Pritt, *From Right to Left*, pp. 102–4, has a vivid but not particularly accurate account of the confrontation.

Cripps had provocatively reserved his freedom of action. If defeated, he said, he would circulate his memorandum. He duly was, by 17 votes to 3, and duly did so. Indeed, before the meeting began, he had prepared a mass mailing of his memorandum to Labour MPs and party organizations (without even telling his two supporters, Pritt and Wilkinson) and this was put in the post the same evening. Since the NEC immediately issued a press briefing, both sides sought publicity for their propaganda, while each blaming the other for doing so. The issue at stake was now broadened: on the one side, to the propriety of Cripps's methods, and on the other, to the right to free speech.

The fact is that Cripps's strategic shift can be understood in a much longer historical perspective. The notion of an alliance between the different parties that had inherited a 'progressive' identity had a long pedigree in British politics, one which clearly predated the influence of the CPGB and was more in tune with traditional Liberal values. As the historian of this tradition has put it: 'The Popular Front campaign differed from the United Front campaign in tone, content and context.'[312] Now believing that the fascist threat in Europe was paramount, now believing that the Chamberlain Government would not resist it, now believing that the Labour Party was incapable of forming an alternative Government by itself, Cripps argued for cooperation with the non-socialist left. It is not surprising, therefore, that he now became, at a bound, the champion of this disinherited progressive tradition; and the fact that he soon found himself expelled from the Labour Party simply reinforced his imputed liberal credentials.

The National Petition Campaign, launched at the end of January 1939, was thus deeply ambiguous. In one perspective it was an augmented version of the Unity Campaign, in line with current Communist tactics, and thus excited all the familiar opposition. 'You mustn't start a class war in this country at the present time,' Attlee repeated, exactly as though he were still countering the rhetoric of the United Front.[313] Yet in another perspective, the campaign represented the repudiation of Cripps's class-war stance in face of the pressing external danger of fascism. 'It was only yesterday that Stafford was insisting on uniting in the Socialist League the extreme left – CP, ILP – with the Labour Party against the other two parties, in favour of thoroughgoing socialism with no compromise,' Beatrice Webb noted.

312. Blaazer, *Popular Front*, p. 173. This interpretation is cogently argued in the Introduction and in ch. 7 of this stimulating book.
313. RSC, manuscript notes, meeting of 13 January 1939. Attlee used the opposite (and more apposite) argument the next month in criticizing Cripps for changing his mind; see Harris, *Attlee*, p. 159.

'Today he argues for joining hands with the Liberals and dissentient Conservatives with a moderate programme in another sort of National government, dominated by the Labour Party.'[314]

It is hardly surprising, then, that Cripps both lost and gained allies. Some of his left-wing supporters, like Pritt and Wilkinson on the NEC, remained loyal to official Labour Party policy. Laski, who disapproved of Cripps's new strategy, and had been absent in the USA during the early part of 1939, subsequently sought to play a mediating role within the party to heal the rift. Of his former colleagues, Bevan and Strauss remained notably faithful to Cripps throughout. His new support was exemplified in the person of Lady Violet Bonham Carter, daughter of Asquith and the keeper of his flame. She now joined Cripps in support of a Popular Front, affirming after their first meeting: 'It is so long now since I have met a "great" man – but I know I have seen one to-night.'[315] Cripps likewise now received endorsement from J. M. Keynes, whose economic thinking was nothing if not 'progressive' and whose argument was that the Labour leadership should realize that they were not 'sectaries of an outworn creed mumbling moss-grown demi-semi-Fabian Marxism, but the heirs of eternal liberalism' – a heritage into which Cripps was welcomed like a prodigal son.[316] 'I am in full sympathy with what you are doing,' Keynes told Cripps. 'It seems to me very important not to split existing parties, but to capture them.'[317] The effect of Cripps's activities, however, was almost the reverse.

The Petition Campaign in fact produced the biggest split in the Labour Party since 1931 without coming near to capturing it. Cripps had alienated the leadership while failing to project his strategy successfully to the rank and file. To some the campaign was tainted by its Communist connections, to others by its Liberal associations, and to more by the spectacle of a well-heeled class warrior spurning the ethic of solidarity on which the Labour Movement had been founded. The Party Conference at Southport in May 1939 agreed to hear Cripps in his own defence. It was an opportunity of which he took little advantage, putting points about his own case in a dry and legalistic manner rather than broadening the argument or enthusing his supporters. Conference endorsed the decision to expel Cripps by

314. Webb diary, 21 January 1939, apparently reporting R. H. Tawney's view, in MacKenzie and MacKenzie (eds.), *Webb*; *Diary*, iv, p. 427.
315. This was after Cripps 'determined to put first things first': V. Bonham Carter to IC, 22 February 1942, recalling a meeting at Gollancz's house.
316. Moggridge (ed.) *Collected Writings of Keynes*, xxi, p. 496.
317. Keynes to RSC, 9 February 1939; also printed in Moggridge, op. cit., xxi, p. 502.

2,100,000 votes to 402,000. He was not to be readmitted until the closing stages of the Second World War.

Beatrice Webb concluded *My Apprenticeship* with a statement of 'the successive steps in my progress towards Socialism'.[318] Her enlightenment followed from hard work and hard thinking, as successive chapter headings indicate, whether in grappling with 'character and circumstance', or 'in search of a creed', in her 'choice of a craft' or in her attempts to master 'the field of controversy'. She had surely earned the right to judge the apprenticeship of her nephew in politics; and one considered comment that she made on him is lacking neither in charity, knowledge nor insight.

About Stafford – I think he is an enigma. He is a great lawyer and a good man. But he is ignorant about political social and economic institutions. *And he does not know he is ignorant.* That is his great defect.[319]

As he turned fifty, in April 1939, Stafford Cripps was, in many ways, still an apprentice in politics: but one whose distinctive attributes excited an unusual combination of respect and bafflement. His prodigious endowment of intellectual gifts set him apart, while his obvious personal ambition showed a remarkable carelessness of careerist calculation. Above all, his ideological bearings were a source of confusion – to himself as much as to others.

318. Webb, *My Apprenticeship*, p. 391.
319. B. Webb to Laski, 13 July 1942, in MacKenzie (ed.), *Webb: Letters*, iii, p. 460.

ENTR'ACTE
1939

On the eve of the Second World War, Cripps was as unclear about his own destiny as he was unsure about the course of international developments – much more so than he later cared to admit. Within months he was publicly claiming that 'when I left England at the end of July for a holiday I announced my return for the beginning of September as being the time when war would break out'.[1] No such announcement can be traced. Cripps was speaking with such confidence in that refuge from rapid rebuttal, war-torn China. He had gone there following extensive travels in India, and was to undertake a hazardous visit to Moscow before returning via the USA. The fact that he returned a significantly changed man was masked by his absence, and belied by some of his own public utterances, but acknowledged privately.

Cripps went around the world as a fellow-traveller – of Geoffrey Wilson, whom he took with him as his secretary. Wilson evidently enjoyed both his work and the increasingly close association which it brought. In their diary of the journey, the calculation was that they covered 45,000 miles in all, by land, sea and air. This diary was a more professional successor to Cripps's chronicles of holidays in Jamaica and the Mediterranean, and an immediate continuation of the political record that he had, somewhat patchily, begun to keep from June 1939. The Cripps–Wilson diary was faithfully kept from start to finish, with any break in its sequence the subject of explanation and apology, for example when both were ill (or when the diary itself was temporarily confiscated by the Sinkiang customs officials). It was typed up daily, sometimes on the long flights and the even longer train journeys which they took, or, failing such opportunities, last thing at night. Sometimes Cripps would be up past midnight, tapping out up to half-a-dozen pages. Running to 275 single-spaced pages in all, or 180,000 words, the diary is

1. Kunming speech, 12 January 1940, Cripps papers. All Chinese names as used at the time.

almost as long as this book – long enough to reveal more than was perhaps fully intended.[2]

The two men – one an eminent public figure of fifty, the other not yet thirty – travelled on easy terms of equality with each other, albeit as fellow-Europeans in status-conscious societies. They naturally developed a greater intimacy as they lived alongside each other, often confined to their own company, and sometimes in cramped and primitive conditions. The diary not only supplies interstitial evidence of this: its composition also served as one medium for fostering an already close relationship. Within the convention of a factual report on their doings, they often used the diary for ironical digs at each other. It supplied a frame of reference that allowed for occasional flights of whimsy, for in-jokes, and for allusions that hint at what must have passed between them during long days together, crowded and uncrowded alike. The diary had to serve as a formal record, replete with fact-gathering surveys that mimic a guide-book compiled for and by a committee; and copies of it were intended for private circulation. But it also offers insights about Cripps himself – not only expounding his thinking at this juncture but disclosing his preconceptions, documenting his habits, and showing his temperament.

There was much to attract Cripps in the countries that he visited. In retrospect, the most significant part of his journey was to India, which henceforth had a persistent resonance in his own career. Initially, China was equally salient; indeed it was the diplomatic difficulty of visiting both China and Russia that determined the logistics of his journey. Regardless of the priority between them, China, India and Russia were for Cripps the 'three countries I regard as the most important for the the future'.[3] For all that, a five-month wartime journey would not have been undertaken unless there had been correspondingly little to keep him at home.

There was no opening for Cripps in British politics. So long as peace had lasted, Chamberlain's policy of appeasement seemed like an electoral trump card in his hand. In reading the situation in this way, of course, Cripps was

2. The task was shared and the literary model was initially that of third-person authorship. But it is fairly easy to identify who typed what, if only from the fact that Wilson's typing skills were superior. Clearly some of the diary was typed by Wilson from notes or dictation by Cripps, especially on the latter's discussions with political figures; though Wilson himself was often present at these, taking a record during interviews. While some inextricably joint composition survives, therefore, especially in the early sections, authorship lapsed into a more subjective form, with spontaneous use of the first person; and the transition between Wilson and Cripps is usually discernible even when not explicitly signalled.

3. RSC diary, 23 October 1939.

simply consistent with the analysis which had led him to stake his career on the need for some kind of popular front. It was the inability of the Labour party to offer a credible alternative to the Chamberlain regime that had pushed Cripps in this direction in the first place, first looking to unity on the left, then seeking to consolidate liberal support too, and, by the summer of 1939, envisaging a still broader coalition – what he now called an 'all-in' Government. Though his rhetoric still smacked of the left, his strategy pointed increasingly to the centre.

Cripps's politics had turned on the axiomatic hostility of the Nazi and Soviet regimes. Little wonder that he seemed disorientated by the Hitler–Stalin pact, sprung on the world in August 1939. What should we make of his subsequent hard-nosed extenuation of Russia? Was this simply a hard-line pro-Soviet stance? His public comments certainly left an abiding impression that he was driven by ideology rather than realism. Yet his contacts with the Government suggest otherwise. The air of ambiguity here was sustained by Cripps's prolonged and somewhat mysterious journey, during which the British public heard little of him, apart from headline news of a dramatic visit to the Kremlin. What did Cripps really think? What did he say and write himself?

After the Nazi–Soviet pact, openings for Cripps to influence Anglo-Russian relations were first diminished and then destroyed, at least temporarily. He was to find his new window in India, to which, in the course of the next seven years, he made three visits. The first time his journey was improvised and unofficial. The second time – the Cripps Mission of 1942 – he was to be the emissary of the War Cabinet, to which he was responsible, and by which he was crucially constrained in his effort to negotiate a full settlement. The last time, in 1946, he returned as the key member of a Cabinet delegation sent by the Labour Government to find a path to independence. Cripps thus found himself caught up and progressively enmeshed in the whole complex problem of winding up the British Raj. But not by accident: it all began in 1939 as his own idea.

Cripps's three encounters with India represent three phases of the most important political friendship of his life. Jawaharlal Nehru was a man of the same age as himself, with a provokingly similar background to Cripps's own: from a prosperous, well-established family, educated at an English public school (Harrow), then at Trinity College, Cambridge, and with a career as a barrister that became subsumed in political commitments of an increasingly left-wing nature. Motilal Nehru, like Lord Parmoor, had become more radical in his political allegiance in later life, reinforcing strong bonds between father and son. In the mid-1930s Jawaharlal Nehru, now president of the Indian National Congress, professed a fundamentally Marxist analysis of politics, seeing a decayed capitalism in thrall to imperialism and fascism; he therefore regarded the Soviet Union as a progressive force in the world and favoured a popular front with the Communists. No less than Cripps, Nehru might be considered an example of 'radical bourgeois false consciousness' – as his biographer puts it, 'combining the comforts of a privileged class with the intellectual pleasure of rejecting it'.[4]

Little wonder that Nehru and Cripps found they had much in common. Equally, just as Cripps's sober post-war image came to eclipse his previous record as a maverick, so Nehru's reputation survives in the West chiefly as the elder statesman of independent India, gracefully accommodating to the British when power was finally transferred. Yet this role only looks predestined in hindsight. It needs to be remembered not only how radical and controversial the young Nehru seemed at the time, nor how awkwardly he chafed against the perceived social conservatism of his mentor Gandhi, but also how persistently hostile he remained to the British and their Raj – who, after all, did not finally release him from their prisons until the middle of 1945.

The correspondence between Cripps and Nehru is, under the circumstances, not only extraordinarily full but extraordinarily full of interest. This is not so much the case in the later years, when both men were busy ministers, dictating and signing the official communications that passed between them (some of them dressed up in the form of personal missives). By then, moreover, their friendship had been clouded by confrontation. It is the intermittent correspondence of the early period that speaks to the quality of their relationship at its zenith. Some of Nehru's letters, of up to a dozen pages of his neat, well-formed handwriting, exist in no other copy. This suggests the confidence that he reposed in their recipient not to misuse them – not a trivial consideration given the obvious possibility that Nehru might at some point find himself under arrest.

When Cripps made his first visit to India, he was hailed by one group of well-wishers as 'the Nehru of England'.[5] It was not an innocent compliment; it hints at the extent to which Cripps was co-opted as a partisan of the Hindu-dominated Congress – already a delicate and later an explosive issue. Admittedly, Cripps did his best not only to cover India but to cover the

---

4. Gopal, *Nehru*, iii, p. 285; cf. ibid., i, pp. 203–7. I am naturally flattered that Gopal's masterly analysis has adapted this concept from my own earlier work; cf. *Liberals and Social Democrats*, p. 4.
5. RSC diary, 14 December 1939.

many and various shades of Indian opinion, both official and nationalist. Though he went with preconceptions, these did not remain unchallenged or unchanged by what he observed. We are fortunate, then, that such a faithful record survives of what Cripps made of India in 1939. This had more than an immediate significance – in two dimensions, time and place.

It is commonplace to observe that the impressions that Cripps formed on this first, private, exploratory visit must have influenced him when he returned on official missions, in 1942 and 1946. What seems to have escaped interrogation, however, is the impact of India upon Cripps's perceptions of Western society and its politics. 'An adolescent Marxian miasma!' was how Dalton had dismissed his ideas. 'He seems to be unaware of nationalist passions as a factor in politics.'[6] If Cripps seemed unaware, it was through choice. He himself had identified the 'ultimate question' throughout the world as whether to choose 'a national front, based upon the idea that all classes in the nation must unite against the common racial enemy' or 'a class front based upon the conviction that all the workers must unite irrespective of national boundaries'.[7] Reinforced by Nehru's tutelage, Cripps may have arrived in India confident of his prefabricated, one-size-fits-all, class interpretation of politics. But what when he left?

Here is a topic that is much more important than it may appear at first sight, and one that therefore raises highly charged issues. It would surely be a curious form of 'orientalism' to suppose that Cripps's only alternative to a class analysis was to stereotype the indigenous society as 'other' or alien; or to suppose that recognition of the authenticity of communal allegiances implied complicity in a condescending British propensity to 'divide and rule'.[8] Yet this is how any deviation by Cripps from the bien-pensant preconceptions of his Congress friends has usually been interpreted.

There is, in fact, impressive evidence of Cripps's personal freedom from racial prejudice. This can be found not only in his public declarations or in private incidents like his well-meaning attempts to break down 'the slight colour bar' that he found on his ship home from Jamaica in 1938.[9] More striking testimony comes from the lived experience of his own family, revealing values that were more than lip-service to non-discrimination –

6. Dalton diary, 4 May 1933, quoted in Dalton, *Fateful Years*, p. 41.
7. Cripps, 'The political reactions of rearmament' (1937), p. 116.
8. I refer, of course, to the seminal work of Said, *Orientalism* – or rather to the way that his insights have been debased and generalized as the guiding assumptions of a school of Indian historiography.
9. RSC diary, 25 September 1938; and see his comments on class and colour, and on scapegoating of Jews, ibid., 24 August 1938.

notably the interracial marriage of his daughter Peggy, which was to create a flurry in the British press shortly after Stafford's death. Peggy's decision to marry Joe Appiah and to make her life in Ghana, which admittedly came at the very end of Stafford's life, arose through her prior involvement in a campaigning organization called 'Racial Unity', reflecting an upbringing that had liberated her from many conventional taboos of her generation.

Would Stafford have approved? The couple had only come together at the beginning of 1952, when his fatal illness had just taken him to Switzerland on a stretcher for painful treatment – sufficient reason, surely, for them to keep their recently formed and controversial intention secret. But though it may not have been formally disclosed to the dying man, others in the family believed that 'he knew perfectly well' about the relationship.[10] Moreover, it is certainly the case that the engagement and subsequent marriage were, from the first, sustained by support from the immediate family, led by Isobel with encouragement from Theresa and John, whatever the reservations of a couple of Stafford's more conventional brothers.[11] It is worth recalling the terms in which a visit home (to show Isobel her two grandchildren) was still being reported in the 1950s: 'The two best-connected piccaninnies ever to hit an English village will be getting big hugs and kisses from Lady Cripps, widow of the Iron Chancellor.'[12] If this was the tone in an ostensibly friendly tabloid newspaper, the point hardly needs labouring that Stafford's youngest daughter must have been imbued and fortified with strongly different assumptions about race and ethnicity.

Stafford's religion gave him all the guidance he needed here. In the words of one statement to which he lent support: 'Christian doctrine is quite clear on the subject: All men, being children of God, are brothers one of another.'[13] This can, of course be called a conventional Sunday sentiment. What was unusual was that, here as in other applications of Christian teaching,

10. Information from Lady Ricketts (Theresa Cripps), supported by family testimony. Bryant, *Cripps*, p. 469, seems mistaken in stating that the reason Stafford was not told was that 'they feared that he would not approve of a "mixed marriage"' – apparently citing Peggy Appiah; but she only says: 'Joe and I kept things secret because of my father': Appiah, *Attic*, p. 79. Joe Appiah's claim that 'I entertained no doubts whatsoever about her family raising any objections to our marriage on the grounds of colour' is also corroborative. See J. Appiah, *Autobiography*, pp. 191–6, at p. 195.

11. Peggy Appiah says that Seddon and Leonard Cripps disapproved of the marriage but that Isobel 'gave me her maximum support and love', reinforced by her spiritualist conviction that Stafford 'was doing all he could to help from the other side': Appiah, *Attic*, pp. 56, 77.

12. *Daily Sketch*, 6 April 1957.

13. *In This Faith We Live*, statement by the Parliamentary Socialist Christian Group, foreword by RSC, April 1948, p. 9.

Cripps's literal mind accordingly worked on this hypothesis; his stubborn temperament locked it into place; and his indifference to the tyranny of conventional English upper-class norms insulated him here, as in his other perceived eccentricities. Refusing, then, to embrace the stereotype of Indians as 'other', he was open to the inference that the frailties of Marxist analysis in India had implications nearer home. Was this the hidden factor that precipitated revision of the fundamental postulates that he had accepted since 1931? For if Marx could not adequately explain India, what status had the universal claims and categories of Marxist analysis? Did they any longer serve Cripps as working axioms, even though – vestigially – they were mouthed by him as formulaic professions?

This period saw a major transition in Cripps's career which needs to be explained; and, with the materials now available, his outlook and his thinking can be reconstructed with a new verisimilitude. He walked away from the Labour Party and the factional squabbles that had consumed his attention for years and instead went around the world. He took up a controversial position on wartime relations with the Soviet Union. He consolidated links with India that were to draw him back persistently into the endgame of empire. He made false starts, notably in China, that led nowhere. In the process, he was prompted to adopt a political analysis that allowed more room for realism and relativism. In May 1940, it might seem that he had thrown up his legal practice, relinquished his vast income, and offered his services to the Government – all to no avail. Yet the makings of Cripps as a man of power and responsibility are to be found here.

PART TWO

DISORIENTATION
1939–40

JONAH AND THE WHALE.

I

Cripps's Drift to War

In the summer of 1939 Cripps's life was dominated by the possibility of war. But he considered this an eventuality, not an inevitability; and, even if war should come, it portended a crisis in which he was deeply divided about his own prospective role.

He was no longer a member of the Labour Party. The public position taken up by himself and his fellow-rebels was explained in a widely quoted article in *Tribune*, in which Cripps asked his supporters to 'face the facts. We were badly beaten at Southport.' The lesson was that it was useless to continue in opposition to a party which was the indispensable core to any popular front. Since they had not left of their own volition, it followed that 'all the reasons which would have caused us to remain in the party are also reasons why we should apply to re-enter'.[1]

Press reports interpreted this as capitulation and suggested, often with feline malice, that reconciliation with his old party would quickly follow. 'Sir Stafford Makes Submission' was the headline of one newspaper diary column in early June, claiming that, since he apparently wished to return to the fold, his chances now looked 'rosy'.[2] Harold Laski, preserving his credentials as mediator by publicly keeping his distance from Cripps, assured him privately: 'I care more about you and the things you stand for in the party than any single person in it.'[3] But Laski's formula for reconciliation failed when the NEC met on 28 June and instead set up a sub-committee to consider the applications for readmission from Cripps, Bevan and Strauss. Cripps was told that it would report back at the the National Executive's next meeting, which was not due until the Trades Union Congress in September.[4]

---

1. 'Why we want to get back', *Tribune*, 9 June 1939, reprinted e.g. *Manchester Guardian*, 10 June 1939.
2. *Sphere*, 10 June 1939.   3. Laski to RSC, 27 June 1939.
4. Middleton to RSC, 29 June 1939.

In the meantime, this left the impression that Cripps, having repented sufficiently, was ready to embrace his old comrades and was only excluded because of their determination to keep him out. Cripps made many of the right noises to foster such an impression. For example, he took the whole front page of *Tribune* for a rather vacuous and repetitive string of invocations about current politics, in which he prudently muted his scepticism about Labour strategy. 'To all my friends in the Labour movement I would say: do not take precipitate action because of your disappointment with the progress of the Labour Party.'[5] What his diary reveals is that Cripps had little intention of rejoining himself, even if the opportunity arose. Unlike Aneurin Bevan, with a political career built essentially upon the miners' unions, Cripps was content to keep clear of a party whose prospects he saw as 'poor in the extreme', with the possibility of 'an electoral debacle if there is not a war before the year is out'.[6]

His hopes were no longer pinned on the Labour Party, nor even on a popular front – except as a means to the creation of 'a Government of National Concentration' or an 'all-in' Government. The rationale for such a government was not to wage war but to avert it; it was 'to warn our enemies and encourage our friends, particularly Russia'.[7] Cripps set great store by the methods that had hitherto given him such a high profile: advocacy and propaganda, mobilizing opinion through the sort of dramatic initiative beyond the imagination of the ordinary party wheelhorse.

Cripps believed that ordinary Germans could be disabused of their support for the Nazi regime. He was encouraged in this view not only by his general political outlook but by his specific links, under Christian auspices, with dissident Germans. Of these, the most prominent was Adam von Trott, a contemporary at Balliol of John Cripps and of David Astor, whose family's stake in *The Times* and the *Observer* gave him obvious influence. Geoffrey Wilson, another friend of von Trott, had recently made contact with his circle in Germany.[8] When von Trott visited England in the summer of 1939 he met Cripps, who recorded: 'After long talks during the weekend with A. from Germany I drew up a memorandum upon the question of broadcasting to Germany with a view to divorcing German public opinion from the Government on the war and "encirclement" issue.'[9] These moves were associated with the discreet visit to London of Lieutenant-Colonel Count

5. *Tribune*, 21 July 1939.   6. RSC diary, 27 July 1939.
7. ibid., dated as 8 June 1939, but more likely to be a consolidated entry written on 28 June.
8. MacDonogh, *Good German*, pp. 45, 78, 89, 126, 129–30, 139–40; Wilson, 'My Working Life', pp. 22–3.
9. RSC diary, dated as 8 June 1939.

Gerhard von Schwerin of the German General Staff, who was seeking evidence of British resolution and unity as a means of deterring Hitler, and accordingly was put in touch with anti-appeasers, mainly disaffected Conservatives. Cripps ensured that some Labour MPs were also wheeled out 'to impress on the German Colonel that the British working-class was really serious in its attitude'.[10]

What would have impressed the dissident Germans most would have been a reconstruction of the Government so as to include the pre-eminent anti-appeaser, Winston Churchill. This was what Cripps now advocated (again). Here was the opening to a rapprochement between the two men: one identified with the diehard imperialist right, the other with the fellow-travelling socialist left. Pitted against each other for most of the 1930s, they were to discover common ground over the next six years in giving top priority to stopping Hitler. In *The Gathering Storm*, the first volume of his war memoirs, Churchill acknowledged as much. 'Sir Stafford Cripps, in his Independent position, became deeply distressed about the national danger,' he wrote. 'He visited me and various Ministers to urge the formation of what he called an "All-in Government".'[11] This friendly reference was based on extracts supplied by Cripps from his diary, which records that, in the course of an hour's discussion between the two on 22 June, Churchill claimed that 'but for Chamberlain's switch on Foreign policy after Prague's occupation the Popular front movement would have swept the country and I gathered he would have supported it!'[12] Though there was clearly a good deal of implicit mutual flattery between these two outcast party rebels, and unresolved tensions, the fact that such discussions could take place at all was a piquant development, showing a new responsiveness within the spectrum of opposition to Chamberlain. Cripps used *Tribune* to amplify the message.

Cripps also envisaged using broadcasting to appeal, over Hitler's head, to German public opinion. He made efforts to bring the idea of appealing to 'good Germans' to the attention of the Cabinet through a friendly link with Kingsley Wood at the Air Ministry. Indeed a 22-page draft for such a broadcast by Cripps, in his own hand, gives a revealing guide to his thinking. His theme was the urgency of avoiding 'a mad adventure of mutual annihilation', brought about 'by misunderstandings and distrusts that have grown

---

10. ibid., 29 June 1939. For Schwerin's visit, see Parker, *Churchill and Appeasement*, pp. 230–33.
11. Churchill, *Second World War*, i, p. 279; diary extracts, Churchill papers, CHUR 4/19.
12. RSC diary, 22 June 1939.

up and that have been fostered in some quarters'. Cripps proposed to offer his own contribution towards better understanding and pleaded in characteristic style – 'I could quote to you from many speeches and writings of mine over the last 9 years' – for the authenticity of his peace-loving credentials. Claiming that he, 'like a great mass of my fellow-workers in Great Britain', had deplored the vindictive provisions of the Versailles Treaty, Cripps sought to assuage fears of encirclement while explaining British apprehensions about German expansionism. He proposed instead a joint constructive effort to replace imperialism with an international development strategy.[13]

This approach, which was certainly moralistic though not explicitly Christian, evidently interested the High Churchman Lord Halifax, the Foreign Secretary, enough for him to arrange a meeting with Cripps to discuss it. Cripps privately took credit for influencing Halifax, whose speech to the Royal Institute of International Affairs on 29 June, signalling British firmness against aggression, while holding open possibilities of 'a new world order' by consent, was hailed by liberal opinion as a wholesome new tone from the Chamberlain Government, and was broadcast in German as well as English.[14] Cripps himself took up many of the same themes in a speech at the Forest of Dean Miners' Gala. 'I repeat now what I have said and written a hundred times in the past 8 years,' he claimed, 'that I believe no country is entitled to monopolies of raw materials or market to the cost of others.' Hence the chance for cooperation with Germany in a post-imperial world.[15] Cripps was glad to find the speech well reported, and an extract from the text that he sent to the BBC was used on its European news bulletins.

Cripps always found it easier to state political objectives than to work with the imperfect means available for achieving them. 'The difficulty is to replace the P.M. to make it all possible,' he noted, rather naively. 'This can only now be done by intrigue from within the Cabinet itself.'[16] Halifax understandably refused to become drawn into such seditious talk, instead suggesting that Cripps go to see Chamberlain himself – hardly a practicable proposition.[17] Moreover, the fact that pressure for the admission of Eden and Churchill to the Government was by this time mounting in the press did not gratify Cripps, unwilling to accept that a Churchill Government

13. Draft of suggested broadcast to the German people, RSC diary, sub. 23 June 1939.
14. Chatham House, 9th annual dinner, *Proceedings*, 29 June 1939; leader, *Manchester Guardian*, 30 June 1939; but see Parker, *Churchill and Appeasement*, pp. 229–30.
15. Text, 1 July 1939, Cripps papers.   16. RSC diary, 29 June 1939.
17. Halifax to RSC, 3 July 1939.

was the potential alternative to a Chamberlain Government. 'The present tendency,' he noted in July, 'is to disregard completely all opposition elements and to turn Churchill into the country's saviour – which will be fatal for the opposition parties and the country, in my view. Undiluted Churchill I regard as highly dangerous!!'[18]

Cripps's grand design for political realignment remained a grand illusion, or at best a distant mirage. His thoughts turned to more immediate prospects. Negotiations between Britain and France, on the one side, and the Soviet Union, on the other, had eventually started in Moscow, but were proceeding at a discouragingly low level and at a correspondingly frustrating pace. Cripps's diary for 30 June records his response. 'This morning I rang up K.W. [Kingsley Wood] and offered my services to go at once to Moscow to get the Russian agreement concluded as I feel that I could do this if I were given the authority.' Three days later a message came back from Lord Halifax at the Foreign Office, declining this offer. It was hardly likely that a Conservative Government would seriously have considered sending an erratic left-wing lawyer, without diplomatic experience or party affiliation, on such a delicate errand. Though the position of the Soviet Union was a crucial factor in the defence strategy of the Western powers – and vice versa, of course – neither side trusted the other, and negotiations continued with wariness and suspicion. No doubt this is why the impatient Cripps made his improbable offer to go to Moscow; and its predictable rejection was simply another in a long line of rebuffs to the bright ideas he was constantly dreaming up.

While the fragile peace was maintained through the summer of 1939, Cripps's temperamental inability to sit still drove him to seek a fulfilling role. He even turned to authorship again, with an 'enlarged pamphlet' published at the end of 1939 as *Democracy Up-to-Date*. In size and tone it may seem similar to *Why This Socialism?*. There is the same lack of reference to other authors, the same ambition to provide plain-speaking solutions to problems that had baffled the experts. But whereas Cripps's first book had expounded the case for the necessary failure of reformist strategies within capitalist society, his second book was a practical guide on seeking greater efficiency through incremental improvements of the parliamentary system. 'Civilisation is faced to-day,' he concluded, 'with the necessity of devising forms of government which will weld into one composite whole, the efficiency of totalitarian control and planning in the economic field with the cultural and and political freedom that democracy alone can

18. RSC diary, 3 July 1939.

provide.'[19] This was no utopian hope, incapable of realization without revolution, but an immediate practical possibility. 'I believe,' he now wrote, 'that there is in Great Britain to-day a great fund of genuine desire to maintain and to increase the measure of democratic freedom which the common people enjoy.'[20]

Abjuring sectarian politics, Cripps kept up his contacts with friendly Conservatives in the Government, like Kingsley Wood and Oliver Stanley, the President of the Board of Trade. Above all, he turned frequently to Walter Monckton, an old legal friend and now a political confidant. Monckton's silky handling of the abdication of King Edward VIII was testimony of the trust that the establishment reposed in him, and his influential connections – notably with Halifax – proved useful to Cripps. The more he worked with Monckton, the better Cripps thought of him – 'Most refreshing! He is the real stuff of which rulers should be made!'[21] – a fulsome tribute, privately recorded, and wildly at odds with Cripps's left-wing public image.

An impression of 'the hopeless bankruptcy of ideas and of initiative in the highest quarters' remained with Cripps throughout his discussions. 'It makes me want to yell and shriek to try and wake this country up before disaster overwhelms it,' he wrote at the end of June.[22] Moreover, the lack of a credible opposition sealed his despondency: 'I fear a long period of futility for Labour even if it survives as an effective political party. With its present leadership and direction I cannot see it doing anything effective.'[23] Certainly he wanted no part of it. The brilliant career of Sir Stafford Cripps, MP, KC, was in the doldrums.

Frustrated and under-employed, unheeded and unneeded, Cripps took a step that supplies the strongest evidence that time lay heavy on his hands. It was at the end of July 1939 that he chartered the *White Sapphire* to take his family on holiday for a month. 'I leave for the South of France convinced that at the moment I can do nothing more to push on along the line I have been trying to work on,' he wrote. Despite his subsequent claims, what he wrote privately in his diary suggests that he saw it as more likely that Chamberlain would be able to go to the country that autumn, 'as the saviour of Peace by getting the Russian pact and doing an appeasement with Germany'. The alternative possibility – 'If, unfortunately, war should come

---

19. RSC, *Democracy Up-to-Date*, p. 108. Cripps called it an 'enlarged pamphlet' in his typescript draft of the foreword.
20. ibid., p. 105.　　21. RSC diary, 18 October 1939.　　22. ibid., 29 June 1939.
23. ibid., 27 July 1939.

along,' was how he put it – was admittedly the only way that his project for a Government of National Concentration might, after all, come about. Rather than foreseeing either the Nazi–Soviet pact or a war over Poland, Cripps seems to have been in two minds – like many lesser mortals.

Somewhat ponderously, he weighed up the implications for himself, should war come and thereby change the government:

The problem of my attitude to such a Government I have not yet solved. Shall I be of more use by staying outside or by going in behind it to help in any way that I can?

My primary concern is the British (and secondarily all other) workers, they must after the war find leadership somewhere. Where is [it] to be? Not I believe with the Communist Party, though many left wing Socialists are now going over to that party, and more still will follow especially if Labour does badly at an election. Can I be of any use if I stand aside in a war in helping to create that leadership when the necessity arises? Or would it be better to add any such strength and gifts as I possess to the drive to avoid the most disastrous defeat of this country by Hitler, and if possible, in any way, to influence the terms of peace if I should happen to survive so long?[24]

How far such reflections were a self-consciously theoretical specification of a range of options, and how far a real tool of practical decision-making, is not clear. Since he had so prominently devoted himself to the displacement of Chamberlain by a broadly-based government that would more effectively resist the dictators, it is difficult to see how Cripps could have justified his own refusal to support such a government. To some extent, he seems to have been uncertain over 'what the reaction of the workers will be, whether they will be genuinely captured by the anti-fascist nature of the war or whether they will be suspicious and become disillusioned'. But his dispassionate posture – keeping any formal decision at arm's length – was in fact undercut by his own self-knowledge. 'My urge to join in action,' he admitted, 'will I am certain tend to make me wish to take some active part in the prosecution of the war, and I shall find it difficult to stand out and simply wait.'[25]

From such speculative musings he readily tore himself for the next month. Joined for the first fortnight on the *White Sapphire* by Geoffrey Wilson and Toby Weaver and for the remainder of the holiday by John and Ursula Cripps, Stafford and Isobel devoted themselves to a cruise from Cannes, first down the Italian coast and back to Cannes via Corsica, and then along the French Riviera. 'During the day we seem to have been busy doing

24. ibid., 27 July 1939.   25. ibid.

nothing with great artistry,' Stafford wrote, 'which shews that we are benefitting greatly by the holiday.'[26] The plan was to set politics and international crisis aside for four weeks – and it succeeded for three.

Having completed the first circuit back to Cannes, where John and Ursula Cripps joined the boat on 16 August, the Crippses' plan was for a further fortnight's cruise. After a week, however, *en route* from St Tropez to Porquerolles, progress was barred by mine-laying outside the French naval base of Toulon. The significance of this took time to dawn on him – Cripps was out of touch with the news – until he 'heard the rumours about the new German move towards the Germano-Soviet pact'.[27] The pact that Cripps had expected the Russians to conclude, however belatedly, with the Western powers was now sealed instead with Germany. To the world's astonishment, and to the consternation of the European left, the German Foreign Minister, Ribbentrop, now shook hands in Moscow with his Soviet opposite number, Molotov, on 23 August.

Cripps made no immediate response. He got further news at second hand from other English visitors. There is no record that he telephoned home. Admittedly, a rather laconic comment that 'we gathered that things were a bit tense and that Parliament was being summoned' appears in his diary, well down the page from a vivid account of the mistral that was now blowing up. But even when Cripps had obtained newspaper confirmation of Parliament's recall, he noted that 'it was no good my trying to get back in time and even if I had wanted to I couldn't have managed it, but I didn't want to as it could do no good as I couldn't possibly affect anything now. I made my effort before I left London.'[28]

Naturally Cripps was disappointed that his well-earned holiday might be spoiled. It must have been galling to think of curtailing his expensive cruise before he had got his money's worth. Nor was the mistral a hazard that he could ignore; the search for a safe mooring was made more tiresome by the mine-laying; and it was a bore that the launch now developed engine trouble. All this his diary tells us. It also mentions that the news from London 'was not at all reassuring and made Ursula feel that she ought to get home as soon as she could'. Accordingly, she and John Cripps were dropped off on the mainland, so that they could catch the train home. 'It was very sad to lose them,' wrote Stafford, 'but it was better for them to go rather than worry about the condition of affairs at home.'[29]

These are surely odd reactions. It might have been expected that, instead

26. ibid., 12 August 1939.   27. ibid., 23 August 1939.   28. ibid., 24 August 1939.
29. ibid., 25 August 1939.

of seeing off his apprehensive daughter-in-law on the Toulon train, the MP for Bristol East would himself have returned. It is hard to escape the sense that Cripps was simply irritated by a crisis that caught him off-balance. 'My own reaction is that I wish I could go off with my family to some part of the world where there is some degree of constructive common sense if such a place exists,' he expostulated in his diary. 'I don't feel that I can do any good by going back to England at this moment and I am therefore going to stay until my time is up or else something decisive has happened.'[30] If he had returned, of course, he would naturally have been pressed to give his reaction to the Nazi–Soviet pact – a development which he later affected to regard as predictable, but one which there is no contemporary evidence of his having predicted himself.

Cripps thus decided to sit out the crisis, on a boat caught between a mistral and a minefield. This left him somewhat unsettled, but at any rate totally inaccessible to newspaper reporters, while he pondered his next move. After a couple of days, despite a turn for the better in the weather, allowing a final session of sunbathing, he and Isobel became increasingly restless and returned to Cannes. They arrived home as Germany's mobilization on its eastern border signalled the approach of war.

In September 1939 Cripps was faced with an unanticipated situation. The democratic Western powers had been steeled, however reluctantly, for a war against Nazism – but, now that it was imminent, the Soviet Union appeared to be on the wrong side. Cripps's line, as he belatedly disclosed it, was to credit the Russians with realism in containing a rapidly deteriorating situation where it was clear that Hitler was likely to move east, and likely to do so soon. The German invasion of Poland at the beginning of September duly triggered a declaration of war against Germany by Britain and France. Cripps took the front page of *Tribune* for his own declaration of war, in a joint statement with Bevan. 'Every prophecy that has been made in the *Tribune* over the last years has, unfortunately, come true,' it brazenly claimed. 'The warnings that we have repeated week after week to the people have been disregarded, and now the tragic sequel is upon us.'[31]

Cripps was animated by a new sense of urgency. He cleared the decks (or at least the desk) for action. He retired from his practice at the bar. He returned his outstanding briefs. Though his name remained on the doors of his chambers, at least for the duration of the war, his retirement was to be final. Cripps evidently told his family that he had decided to take an

30. ibid.   31. 'Our duty', *Tribune*, 8 September 1939.

administrative or technical post, building on his record in the First World War. He was reported in the press to have put his services at the disposal of the Government. His offer, however, was not snapped up. A fortnight after making his big gesture, Cripps found that he had given up a substantial income – £25,000 a year was the figure that the press seized upon – and liberated a commensurate tract of his own time, without much to fill the gap. Admittedly, he gave some professional assistance in the drafting of the Board of Trade's anti-profiteering Bill at the end of September, but nothing further came of this by way of permanent employment.

This was Cripps's own 'phoney war'. For the first time in years, he had time on his hands, not least to fill the pages of *Tribune* with his latest thoughts. 'Our enemy is Hitler and the Nazi regime, and not the German people,' he declared in a front-page article. By this he clearly meant that some possibility of negotiation should be kept open – not with the Nazis, to be sure, but by somehow appealing to German public opinion, as he had urged in the summer. He chose to frame this stipulation in a familiar Marxist language, whether through habit or tactics, saying that it was 'not dictation as to their form of government, but merely an insistence upon the necessary steps for safeguarding the freedom of the working class of the world'. The key issue was *who* would make the peace at the end of the war – a peace that needed to be based on economic reconstruction and the end of imperialism. 'The only class that can be trusted to make the peace in this country, as in Germany,' Cripps argued, 'is the working class who will have no vested interests except in peace and in co-operation with their fellows in other countries.'[32]

In private, however, Cripps adopted a different tone in reopening his line to Lord Halifax. Again, he may have tailored his words according to whom he was addressing. Cripps's point was that Soviet policy was 'quite understandable from the point of view of the real-politik that Russia has been pursuing ever since the dismissal of Litvinoff', referring to Litvinov's replacement as Foreign Minister by Molotov four months previously. It was therefore necessary to show that there was some Russian advantage in making terms with Britain and France on the basis of a non-aggression pact, so as to forestall a possible alliance, not only between Germany and Russia but China too.[33]

The Soviet Union's own transgression of Poland's borders, which followed almost immediately, left Cripps unabashed. 'Why Blame Russia?' was the headline over his next front-page article in *Tribune*. Since the

32. *Tribune*, 15 September 1939.   33. RSC to Halifax, 16 September 1939, copy.

Labour Party had at once condemned the Russian invasion, this served to reinforce Cripps's isolation. 'Large numbers of Socialists,' he admitted, 'reacted to the news in a mood composed of bewilderment, dismay and bitter anger at what they could not help regarding as conduct exactly similar to what we have been led to expect from Germany.' Cripps's object was to show the difference. He did so mainly by pointing to the counsels of realism behind the Russians' canny refusal (as Stalin had famously put it) to 'pick the chestnuts out of the fire for the imperialist Powers'. But he reinforced pragmatism with ideology. Cripps suggested that the Red Army would stay put not only for its own protection but also as the agent of a necessary class struggle within Poland. 'The principle for which we Socialists believe it is worth fighting is working-class freedom,' Cripps affirmed, 'and no one will convince me that I can forward that aim by fighting against the Soviet Union.'[34] It is hardly surprising that Cripps's words reinforced his image as a crypto-Communist.

This was, as yet, mainly a war of words for Britain. Cripps turned his attention to three projects – 'all with the same ultimate aim of getting some real advantage for the workers out of the present chaos'. Whatever the rhetoric of ultimate ends, the immediate means were hardly those of the class struggle. First he began exploratory talks among a small all-party group of half-a-dozen like-minded political figures. Secondly, he took steps to improve relations with Russia, despite the existence of the Nazi–Soviet pact, which was no more than Churchill wanted. Thirdly, as Cripps noted with characteristic aplomb, 'I am attempting to organize some sort of immediate alternative Government to the present Govt. and the chaos of the existing state of affairs.'[35]

At first sight the membership of 'The Group' (as Cripps called it) seems disparate. There were MPs from different political parties: Conservative (Walter Monckton and Harold Macmillan), Liberal National (Sir George Schuster), Liberal (Sir Richard Acland and Wilfrid Roberts), together with family – Isobel Cripps and Stafford's brother-in-law, Jack Egerton, as well as Geoffrey Wilson, who was virtually 'family'. What they had in common, it might unkindly be said, was that they were all high-minded toffs, with connections to the aristocracy, landed gentry or haute bourgeoisie; if not ready to join the Labour Party (which several did later), then already critical of the Chamberlain regime; and most of them practising Christians. Here was an early sign of the way that pre-war support for some kind of popular front was now refocusing on centrist proposals for post-war reconstruction.

34. *Tribune*, 22 September 1939.   35. RSC diary, 26 September 1939.

It was also a sign of the direction, as well as the circles, in which Cripps himself was now moving. Apart from Wilson, no current member of the Labour Party attended.

The tenor of the meetings was one of high principle rather than day-to-day politicking. At its second meeting, Cripps led with a memorandum on private property, debating the case for a rentier class as against the alternative incentives for investment that a planned economy would have to rely upon. It was suggested that, as well as a common motivation for efficiency and an impulse to save for old age, there was also 'the impulse of power, which, to the salaried official was really more important than wealth'. This eminently Fabian postulate would have gratified the Webbs, just as the proposal to restrict public ownership and control to the routine industries, while leaving an experimental field to the entrepreneur, was redolent of Hobsonian New Liberalism.[36] All of this was within the mainstream of progressive thinking in Britain over the previous half-century.

Cripps showed himself no economic determinist. 'History I think proves conclusively that men are stirred to their greatest efforts by the force of ideas rather than by force of economic circumstances,' he averred. In support he cited not only the ideals of the French Revolution but the fact that 'the communist revolution in Russia was primarily inspired by a passion for equality and the abolition of the exploitation of man by man'. Economic factors might provide the means but the most potent appeals were always those made by ideas – ideas, moreover, of a particular kind. 'They are primarily spiritual and religious,' Cripps maintained, contending that socialism in Britain had risen on a tide of quasi-religious fervour, whereas 'the slough in which the Labour Party has been wallowing for the last ten years is due to the disappearance of that spirit among the leadership and the adoption instead of a policy of opportunism, uninspired by any spiritual or religious ideals'.

The satisfaction of such a basic need, whether acknowledged in specifically religious terms or not, Cripps argued, was fundamental. Thus the Group needed to recognize that any scheme it formulated had to answer to it. 'It may be called Christianity, morality, justice, or perhaps "fair play", and it is something so deeply embedded in their very natures that, even when they admit that they know of its existence, men do not talk of it easily.' Cripps made his point with direct reference to the Group – members of an elect who needed to find the path to mass salvation.

36. Minutes of Group meeting No. 2, 5 October 1939; cf. summary of discussion by Acland. Blaazer, *Popular Front*, does not cover the period after the outbreak of the war, but this material

Those who take part in these discussions have nothing to gain personally, and everything to lose, so far as material rewards are concerned, from substituting another form of society for the present one. Why then do they do it? Only because the end they have in view is a religious or spiritual one and not a material one. What is the religion or philosophy or whatever else you may choose to call it which will evoke a similar response from the mass of the people in this country?[37]

The role that Cripps envisaged for his Group was in supplying the inspirational thinking necessary to realize an ambition to remoralize society, hardly less. 'We hope to get down to the Philosophic and moral background without which any effort will be fruitless,' Cripps noted, in anticipation of their third meeting.[38] But the ensuing discussion remained focused on economic organization, albeit at a highly abstract level; and by the end of October Cripps realized that other informal groups, fully as high-minded as his own, were also busy conceiving their own misty plans for 'a new world', reinforcing his feeling that 'some kind of popular front movement will be the only alternative to black reaction after the war'.[39]

The meetings and interviews and associated correspondence which were thus generated, as he well recognized, 'have kept me occupied, but not busy in the way to which I have been accustomed!!'.[40] Still, he judged his unofficial activities not only to be worthwhile in lieu of orthodox political employment, but to be more valuable than membership of the Labour Party – at any rate, on any terms that Cripps would now accept.

'Probable Return to the Labour Party' was a frequent newspaper headline in late September, reflecting a real possibility that the National Executive might be ready to readmit him. In mid-September, Cripps was assuring Laski that 'some arrangement will be feasible' and declaring it 'quite immaterial now as to what the Party ask, as circumstances have completely changed'.[41] Laski continued to plead with him: 'Please, please, brush aside all minor considerations, and simply come back with the others.'[42] Cripps's reply was disingenuous. 'I haven't the slightest desire to avoid going back,'

would certainly support his thesis about the existence of a Progressive Tradition in British politics at this time.

37. RSC memorandum on discussion of 5 October 1939.
38. RSC diary, 10 October 1939.   39. ibid., 31 October 1939.
40. ibid., 26 September 1939.
41. RSC to Laski, 14 September 1939, Laski papers, DLA/15/i. I am grateful to Richard Toye and Duncan Tanner for information from the Laski and E. P. Young papers at the University of Hull.
42. Laski to RSC, 27 September 1939.

he claimed; but in his diary he wrote that 'I shall have to do all I can to avoid such a return as it would completely immobilise me for the sort of work I am doing.'[43] Accordingly, he wrote a stalling letter to the Labour Party, elevating his own stand to one of high principle, while concurring in Bevan's tactic of throwing the responsibility for his own decision onto his union. Thus Bevan was readmitted while Cripps publicly scorned the National Executive's condition (drafted by Laski) that he refrain from taking part in campaigns against party policy, saying that this 'might well have formed the *credo* of some totalitarian party in a dictatorship State'.[44] The *Daily Mail*'s report simplified the issue: 'Sir Stafford Won't Say He's Sorry'.

Cripps wanted a free hand, whether at home or abroad. He continued to visualize himself as a roving ambassador, though one as yet without an ambit within which to rove.

Cripps still hankered after going to Moscow. In June he had offered his services as an emissary; in September he again offered to go, this time in a private capacity, and found Halifax unexpectedly agreeable to the idea. As Chamberlain's Foreign Secretary, Halifax had inevitably been closely identified with appeasement of Germany and hostility towards Russia; but during 1939 he had modified his views and subsequently showed himself ready to explore the logic of an Anglo-Russian understanding, if it were on offer.[45] Moreover, if he found Cripps sympathetic, it was not only as a potentially useful left-winger, spoken for by the ubiquitous Monckton, but also as a fellow-churchman (and one whom Halifax knew to be in contact with von Trott and other German Christians opposed to Hitler). There seems to have been a split within the Foreign Office, at least over the tactics of handling the Soviet Union, between the generally hard-line officials and the Foreign Secretary, who inclined towards the more flexible outlook of his junior minister, Rab Butler. For the moment the question remained academic since the embarrassing fact was that the Soviet Union would not give Cripps a visa.[46] But Butler's door remained open to Cripps; sometimes Halifax's too; and he had access to other members of the Government.

Churchill had been brought into the Government by Chamberlain at the outbreak of war. Early in October, Cripps had an hour with the new First Lord of the Admiralty – 'the future Prime Minister', as Cripps now saw

43. RSC to Laski, 28 September 1939, Laski papers, DLA/15/ii; RSC diary, 3 October 1939.
44. *The Times*, 4 October 1939; and see related correspondence in the E. P. Young papers.
45. Cf. Roberts, *Holy Fox*, pp. 253–4.
46. Halifax to RSC, 22 September 1939; Gorodetsky, *Mission to Moscow*, pp. 8–9.

him.[47] What brought them together was mainly their shared view of the Russian situation, on which he thought Churchill 'very sensible on the whole, but quite blind to the reality of the anti-British imperialism attitude of Russia'. This was the context for a pregnant suggestion from Churchill, who 'thought it would be a good thing if I could go to Russia and eagerly threw out the suggestion I might go as Ambassador – which I did not encourage as it would be, I think, of little help'. Stafford and Isobel Cripps did, however, discuss such a possibility afterwards.

Now as later, Cripps and Churchill could find consensus on immediate war priorities. They were firmly agreed on the need to separate Russia from Germany, if at all possible, and also on the need to crush Nazism – hardly trivial issues, of course. Indeed they were the stuff of wartime politics. What was left over from peacetime politics was a tangle of ideological slogans, with which Cripps now showed some impatience: 'He was chipping me and trying to spar about my views – "middle class theorists" sort of line and "What is imperialism?" and "What is capitalism?" etc. etc. but I told him I was not going to argue these points.' That was left, somewhat ritualistically, for the pages of *Tribune*, and Cripps clearly wished that Churchill too could escape from the prison of past preconceptions. He took away from their meeting a strong impression of Churchill's 'utmost determination to support and maintain the most full-blooded British imperialism'. Cripps concluded: 'The whole filled me with fear and foreboding for the future of the world, since I cannot envisage any way of getting a Government that will take a more enlightened view.'[48]

Cripps continued to press his Moscow initiative. It was subsequently refined, partly as a result of discussion with the Russian ambassador, Maisky, who sought to use trade talks as a means of keeping a line open to the West – a reinsurance policy in case of a breach with Hitler. By the time Cripps saw Halifax again at the Foreign Office on 13 October, the proposal was for a trade delegation, of which Cripps might be a member, under the leadership of a Conservative Cabinet minister, preferably Oliver Stanley – 'and that after that the Ambassador should be changed so that better relations could be established through him'. Whether Cripps was cajoled into thinking that an opening might exist for himself here is not clear; but he was plainly gratified that Halifax 'obviously wanted me to act as a sort of go-between for the present', linking the Foreign Office and the Russians.[49] Indeed Cripps subsequently toyed with the idea of manoeuvring himself

47. Theresa Cripps diary, 1 October 1939.   48. RSC diary, 4 October 1939.
49. ibid., 15 October 1939.

into a post in the legal department of the Board of Trade so that it might seem more natural for him to be included in a trade mission to Russia.[50]

This was not the only matter discussed with Halifax on 13 October. That day's issue of *Tribune*, in responding to Hitler's offer of peace proposals, contained a full and schematic disquisition by Cripps on the shape that peace terms might take, emphasizing that 'the key to the whole situation lies in Russia'. This was a distillation of a long note which Cripps had privately sent to Chamberlain, Halifax and Wood, in which he sketched a counter-proposal for a supranational organization of the economic resources of the world, in place of imperialism and subjugation, as the only rationale for a war that was truly for democracy.[51] Similarly, Cripps had spoken in the House on 12 October, with a plea that 'a perfectly clear declaration of our own war aims' should be put forward as a basis for a conference.[52] The following day, he again found a receptive audience at the Foreign Office when he went on to pursue the question of war aims, since Halifax was once more ready to license Cripps as an intermediary, this time in interesting the Roosevelt administration in working towards a conference, on the premise that Hitler would accept an ethnographic limit to Germany's expansion.[53]

The sense of importance with which Cripps had been endowed, as he left the Foreign Office late that afternoon, impregnates the account he gave a couple of days later in his diary. 'After leaving Halifax I went straight on to Maisky and had a long talk with him,' Cripps recorded; and from the Russian embassy, the go-between – busy at last – groped his way home through the blackout to make his telephone call to Washington, DC. Stalled by the censorship, Cripps found that it was midnight before he could contact the Chief Censor – opportunely, his friend Walter Monckton. Despite Monckton's obliging phone call to the Foreign Office, the answer from the Post Office censor was still that nothing could be done that night. But Cripps persisted – 'I explained that I had discussed the question with Halifax and that he had said I might telephone' – and at 2.15 a.m. he finally reached Felix Frankfurter. 'I hope therefore that by now something may be on foot and that it may possibly have done some good.'[54]

But try as he would, Cripps could not conjure up a substantial initiative, still less one which might afford him the prospect of fulfilling employment.

50. ibid., 18 October 1939.
51. RSC, 'Note on Hitler's offer', RSC diary, sub. 10 October 1939; cf. the acknowledgement in Chamberlain to RSC, 10 October 1939.
52. *The Times*, 13 October 1939.   53. RSC to Halifax, 13 October 1939, copy.
54. RSC diary, 15 October 1939; message, 13 October 1939.

The proposal for a Stanley mission was subject to infuriating delay at Cabinet level, though Halifax eventually got his own way. 'It is incredible how long these matters take to get settled!' Cripps expostulated. 'No wonder people complain of the slowness of democracy.'[55] The fact was, however, that autocracy could prove equally dilatory, and equally stubborn in its prejudices.

As Cripps was later to discover for himself in Moscow, the proposal eventually proved abortive because of a lack of mutual trust. Cripps saw the offer to send a mission as a significant change in the position of the British Government, thus promising a breakthrough; but Maisky's evident goodwill could not compensate for his equally evident lack of authority to negotiate without reference back to Moscow, where Molotov continued to manifest invincible distrust of the British. Not only did Molotov publicly express scorn for the idea that Britain and France were engaged in a war for democracy: his dismissal of the legitimacy of 'ideological' war tallied with Cripps's own interpretation of the 'realist' basis of Russian foreign policy.[56] Above all, the proposal for Anglo-Russian trade talks became enmeshed in the developing crisis over Finland – like Poland a stimulus of widespread British suspicion about the real motives beneath the Soviet Union's ostensible concern to secure its western borders.

Cripps was again ready to extenuate the Soviet position. 'Put Yourself in Russia's Place' was the main headline in *Tribune* on 1 December over an article by Cripps that was to be his last public utterance on the issue for several months. In it Cripps sought to challenge 'self-deception' of two kinds: either an idealization of the Soviet Union which sought 'to justify Russia's actions upon quite the wrong lines' or a lapse into bitter disillusionment. Cripps's point was essentially that Russia should be judged like any other great power acting in its own self-interest – certainly no worse than the rest, and actually better because Soviet self-interest embraced a defence of working-class power, in one country at least. 'In a given historical situation it is not always possible for the foreign policy of Russia to be the best,' Cripps claimed – in effect, a second-best argument on pragmatic rather than ideological lines.

By the time this article appeared, it had been overtaken by events on the ground as the Russian invasion of Finland proceeded. Molotov was later to tell Cripps that Britain's anti-Soviet policy had been at work all along in

55. RSC diary, 21 October 1939.
56. See Molotov speech, 31 October 1939, Anglo-Russian News Bulletin text, RSC diary, sub. 1 November 1939.

stiffening Finnish intransigence in face of Russia's legitimate measures to protect its own security. Cripps could not accept this. He maintained that the Red Army's annexation of Finland – soon accomplished in the Winter War of 1939–40 – itself provided an obstacle to cooperation.[57] Whatever the cause, and whatever the ongoing controversy about it, the consequence was a further worsening of Anglo-Soviet relations.

An apparently promising Russian window of opportunity, seemingly ajar in October, was closed by November, only to frost over in the winter of 1939–40. Unabashed, Cripps sought another opening, not only for his restless energy and his immediate sense of political frustration, but for his growing conviction that the war heralded a new democratic era, about which the British Government was proving culpably obtuse. This was why, in the Commons, Cripps put India firmly into the frame of British war aims: 'The avowed objective of the British Government in declaring war had made the treatment of India a test question in the eyes of the world.'[58]

57. See RSC diary, 16 February 1940.   58. *The Times*, 27 October 1939.

2

Indian Window

In 1939 India was at war because the Viceroy had said so – that was the whole trouble, according to supporters of the Indian National Congress. Admittedly, Congress itself was divided between Gandhi's faithful followers, the 'old guard', who were simply pacifists, and politicians like Nehru and Rajagopalachari who were open to persuasion that this war was a struggle for freedom – so long as the struggle embraced Indian freedom too.

How much freedom did India already have? Under the Government of India Act of 1935, which Churchill had vainly opposed at the time, an ambiguous measure of self-government had been instituted, though only in the provinces of British India. These comprised the territory under direct imperial rule; the position of the princes, with treaties with the British giving them a degree of autonomy, was different within their own states, which made up the rest of the subcontinent. In the provinces, Congress had won control of a number of the new governments, and gained thereby a taste for power. The left wing of Congress, headed by Nehru, had initially opposed the Act, root and branch, as yet another British ploy; but pragmatists like Rajagopalachari, who became chief minister of Madras, saw participation in the political process as a Fabian strategy for gradually legitimizing Congress's own credentials. In the states, to be sure, the princes continued to rule; and, with the Act's incoherent scheme for an inclusive Indian federation thwarted by an unresolved clash between their autocratic instincts and Congress's democratic claims, the Viceroy continued to sit in Delhi, responsible for the whole Raj.

Cripps was one of those who hoped that there might be a bridge to genuine Indian participation in a war government for all India; this is how he read Congress's pressure for clarification of war aims, especially over how democracy applied to India. He approved of Attlee's call for 'a more imaginative insight' in appealing to Indians as equals, and he entertained his own hopes of the eagerly anticipated statement from the Viceroy, Lord

Linlithgow.[1] When, on 17 October 1939, the stolidly unimaginative Linlith-gow went no further than affirming that Dominion status, presumably within the Empire, remained the ultimate objective for India, without any reference to practical interim steps, this was all the more of an anti-climax.

Within days of this statement, as his diary reveals, Cripps was secretly toying with the idea of himself undertaking a journey – not only to Moscow, if that were possible, but on to India, thence to the Chinese Nationalist head-quarters at Chungking, and home via Washington, DC.[2] In the Commons on 26 October Cripps made his 'test question' speech. Britain's commitment to democracy, he maintained, could only be validated by a firm commitment to Indian self-government, to be fully implemented after the war, but with an interim instalment at once. What Linlithgow had candidly told Gandhi, by contrast, was that 'it was not a question of fighting for democracy', to which he did not believe the Government committed 'in the slightest degree'.[3] The challenging phrase, 'test question', was henceforth associated with Cripps's name, not least in India, where the speech was widely reported.

This was not the beginning of Cripps's interest in the fate of the Raj. Marian Parmoor was among the group of Quakers who, inspired by Gandhi, supported the India Conciliation Group, with Agatha Harrison as its secre-tary. She was an active and strong-minded figure, with an almost unique ability to remain respected rather than suspected in both countries through-out the vicissitudes of the next decade. 'Agatha Harrison has been an excellent friend of India,' Nehru wrote after independence, 'and has done very good work for her as well as for the maintenance of good relations between England and India.'[4] Cripps did well to rely upon her counsel as well as cultivating official connections. It was while Rab Butler was serving his pre-war ministerial apprenticeship as Under-Secretary at the India Office that Cripps had first established an easy relationship with him. In 1936, for example, they were corresponding frequently about the case of M. R. Masani, General Secretary of the Congress Socialist Party, which functioned at the time as a left-wing pressure group within Congress. His treatment by the authorities raised obvious issues of civil liberty and a reference to 'our friend M. R. Masani', implicitly acknowledging Cripps's help to a fellow-socialist, punctuates the first surviving letter from Nehru to Cripps ('Dear Sir Stafford') in September 1936.

1. See Moore, *Churchill, Cripps and India*, pp. 7–8.   2. RSC diary, 21 October 1939.
3. Reported in Linlithgow to Zetland, 27 September 1939, quoted in Singh, *Origins of Partition*, p. 48.
4. Nehru to IC, 13 November 1949.

An epistolary friendship blossomed. By February 1937, it was 'my dear Cripps' to whom Nehru sent a full account of the recent elections, in the course of which his initial scepticism had been overborne by popular enthusiasm as he spearheaded the sweeping Congress victories. Nehru played up the parallels with 'the joint front of left-wing elements in Britain that you have succeeded in bringing about'. Not only had the election proved a revelation of the strength of anti-imperialist sentiment: 'It had also made clearer the class cleavages among the people.' The wider the electorate, the better for Congress in its crusade against the vested interests. 'But it is true that the Muslim masses are more apathetic,' Nehru conceded. 'They have been too long doped with communal cries.' He looked on this, however, as the last stand of the old communalism, manipulated by its upper-class leaders with their eyes fixed on jobbery.

The extract from Nehru's letter that Cripps chose for publication in *Tribune* pointed buoyantly to the socialist politics of the future: 'As a whole, India is wideawake and expectant. It talks and thinks in terms of the poverty of the masses and how to relieve it, and inevitably it is being driven to a radical solution of our social problems.'[5] Cripps for his part, when solicited for a message to Congress's socialist supporters, proclaimed that 'the empty philosophy of national independence cannot free the Indian people from their age long servitude unless it is associated with a definite economic policy to give the economic freedom both from British and Indian Capitalist landowners'.[6] This was the marxisant argot in which the two men happily conversed. 'Behind the legal and constitutional arguments there lies the real conflict,' as Nehru knowingly assured Cripps.[7]

As early as 1937 Cripps was publicly calling Nehru's friendship the greatest privilege of his life.[8] The two men were not insensible to the genuine mutual affinity they discovered, and they seem to have developed real warmth when they met, first on Nehru's visit to Europe in 1938, when he and his daughter Indira stayed at Goodfellows one weekend, and again in India the following year. After this, it became 'My dear Stafford' and 'My dear Jawaharlal' – a signifier of an intimacy which was, despite obvious conflicts of loyalty, sustained until the face-to-face negotiations of the Cripps

5. Nehru to RSC, 22 February 1937, PRO, CAB 127/143, with marked passage; also in Gopal (ed.), *Nehru: Selected Works*, ix, pp. 31–4.
6. RSC message to the Gujarat Congress Socialist Party, 18 March 1937, copy, PRO, CAB 127/57.
7. Nehru to RSC, 22 April 1937, PRO, CAB 127/57; also in Gopal (ed.), *Nehru: Selected Works*, xii, p. 90.
8. Press cable, 12 March 1937, PRO, CAB 127/57.

Mission put it under fatal stress. There was, in the end, simply too much at stake for each of these ambitious and strong-willed politicians to allow their relationship to be ruled by sentiment. It was a political friendship: one that spoke feelingly of the constrained possibilities of friendship between their two nations.

When Nehru was a visitor at Goodfellows at the end of June 1938, the house-party was mainly of left-wingers, notably Bevan and Laski. It also included Attlee, though there was no official Labour commitment to the Goodfellows concordat. It was here that the outline of a possible way forward in India took shape, providing for a representative constituent assembly to devise a new constitution, which would be guaranteed by a treaty between India and Great Britain during the transition to full self-government.[9] This kind of trajectory towards independence was henceforth the basis of Cripps's thinking about India. It was premised on the recognition of Congress as representing a united India, on the installation in Britain of a sympathetic government, and presumably on the commitment of the Labour Party to such a deal – conditions not easy to foresee in 1938, or, indeed, to fulfil simultaneously in subsequent years.

Cripps and Nehru did their best to maintain an intermittent correspondence, amid their busy lives. While Nehru sought to educate Cripps about Indian politics, Cripps reported on Labour's policy and, after the outbreak of war, offered advice on Congress's tactics in making its case. After an interview with the Marquess of Zetland, the Secretary of State for India, at the beginning of October 1939, Cripps recorded in his diary, blandly enough, that he was 'glad to hear the Viceroy was seeing Nehru and I hope that something may come of that in the direction of freedom for India'.[10]

It was a pious rather than a practical hope. Cripps saw no prospect of accommodation until or unless the British line changed. He implored Congress to stand firm; and there was certainly nothing in the Viceroy's statement of 17 October to dispel suspicion about British intentions. Disappointed, and denied other constitutional expression, on 22 October Congress recommended withdrawal of all its ministers from the provincial governments. While this step successfully masked its own internal tensions, it also had the damaging consequence of marginalizing Congress during the war, if only because the British no longer had to recognize its representative status at a provincial level.

9. Heads of proposals, 13 July 1938. Report by Nehru, 1 August 1938, in Gopal, *Nehru: Selected Works*, ix, pp. 99–102.
10. RSC diary, 3 October 1939.

Cripps next saw Halifax on 23 October. An ex-Viceroy himself, Halifax defended his successor's statement as 'quite reasonable though he might have put it in different terms'. To Cripps, by contrast, it was clear 'that if we believed in Democracy, Congress did represent the majority of British India according to the election results', and he found it 'a depressing talk because it showed the complete inability of the Cabinet to face up to the wholly new situation that has arisen and the attempt to deal with it by masterly inactivity which will of course be fatal'.[11]

What did Cripps really believe? There is some difficulty in reconciling various of his utterances, at least as to the register adopted. Thus he claimed, in a letter to Nehru, that, despite all the propaganda, this was no war of ideologies: 'Some people still think we are fighting for the ideals of Democracy and freedom, but it has now of course become clear that – as on former occasions – that is but the excuse of imperialism fighting for its life.'[12] Yet Cripps could talk differently of British war aims. 'Democracy and freedom must not be merely slogans with which to win the war,' he told the news magazine *Picture Post*, 'but must be realities that we intend at all costs to realise, first and foremost for our own people in this country and the British Empire.'[13] It could be said that the biting candour of the private letter about current Government policy was descriptive, while the aspirational language of the published interview was normative, pointing to desirable change. But it is not surprising that Cripps generated misunderstandings.

Cripps disclosed his geopolitical musings to his constituents on 5 November. The headlines in the two Bristol evening papers were: 'Asia to be Centre of World Politics' and 'Moving Centre of World Politics to Asiatic Side'.[14] If India was salient here, so was China. At a luncheon to celebrate China's national day a few weeks previously, Cripps had supported the Chinese ambassador in warning against any accommodation with Japanese aggression in the Far East if it pitted Britain against 'the struggling democracy of China'.[15]

The Foreign Office, too, soon discovered what was on Cripps's mind. First he revealed that his wanderlust extended beyond Russia, by proposing also to visit China. Butler warned him about the possible diplomatic interpretation put on a direct journey from Moscow to Chungking by such a prominent, albeit unofficial, figure as Cripps. To meet this objection,

11. ibid., 23 October 1939.
12. RSC to Nehru, 11 October 1939, in Nehru, *Bunch of Old Letters*, p. 396.
13. 'What are our war aims?', *Picture Post*, 28 October 1939.
14. *Bristol Evening World*, *Bristol Evening Post*, 6 November 1939.
15. *News Chronicle*, 11 October 1939.

Cripps immediately produced the alternative plan from up his sleeve – that he should instead travel via India, in effect creating a buffer between Moscow and Chungking. This suited Cripps's purposes well enough; he wanted to keep his line open to the Foreign Office; and India was now a high priority. Moreover, Butler, who called the Viceroy's statement 'the worst state document he had ever seen', conveyed the impression that 'he and many of his younger colleagues were not far from my point of view on this matter' and favoured a 'much more imaginative and far-reaching' approach.[16]

It was on this basis that Cripps finally decided to make a private journey, but with official blessing, to India and China, whether or not Moscow figured in the itinerary. Planning and preparations, especially for India, now helped fill Cripps's empty time. His daughter Theresa thought him 'marvellously well and happy to be doing something really important and constructive'.[17] There were to be further visits to the Foreign Office, where Butler was sympathetic to Cripps's plan of working towards a constituent assembly in India, to be followed by a treaty with Britain.

It was at this juncture that the welcome news of Cripps's proposal to visit India reached Nehru. This time he would play host. Cripps was sufficiently encouraged to tell Nehru of his hope that if Linlithgow would only take up the suggestions now in the air, 'there is just a vague possibility that an arrangement might be come to'.[18] Cripps consulted too with a number of acknowledged experts on Indian policy, notably Sir George Schuster, Lord Hailey and the Labour Party spokesman, Wedgwood Benn. Cripps put to them his own scheme for Indian constitutional advance and was gratified at his success ('though I say it who shouldn't') in winning their approval.[19]

Cripps's plan was enshrined in a document that he was to take with him in the form of a draft statement. It proposed offering India Dominion status – with the right to secede from the Commonwealth if so desired – as testimony to the British Government's aims 'in the present war for freedom and democracy'. Within a year of the termination of hostilities, a Constituent Assembly should be summoned, based on the present provincial electorates if no better system could be agreed. The assembly's decisions would be binding if carried by a three-fifths vote; their implementation over a fixed period of, say, fifteen years would be guaranteed by a treaty with Great

16. RSC diary, 26 October 1939. Far from China being an afterthought, it was Cripps's initial proposal; cf. Wilson, 'My Working Life', p. 24.

17. Theresa Cripps diary, 25 October 1939.

18. RSC to Nehru, 16 November 1939, quoted in Moore, *Churchill, Cripps and India*, p. 8.

19. RSC diary, 21 November 1939.

Britain; and during the transitional period the treaty would also protect minority rights.[20]

Before putting his memorandum into its final form, Cripps had an important interview with Sir Findlater Stewart, the Permanent Secretary at the India Office, who was recognized as the most formidable potential critic – not without reason, as it turned out. But Cripps recorded at the time that Stewart 'could not have been more charming or helpful', that 'without committing himself, he was inclined to favour my proposition', and that he promised his good offices in preparing the ground with the Viceroy and the appropriate governors.[21] Whether Cripps read too much into these civilities, intentionally or unintentionally, or whether Stewart subsequently became cooler, is not easy to determine.

The official line was that Cripps was entirely unofficial. Press reports, like that in *The Times* on 1 December, stressed the independent nature of the visit. He stressed it himself, telling his constituency Labour Party that he had 'decided to go to India entirely on my own, not of course in any sense as an agent or emissary for the Government, in order to get first hand knowledge of the situation and do anything I can to assist in a solution'.[22] Despite this, the belief persisted in Bristol, especially among critics of Cripps's record as a constituency representative, that his subsequent long sojourn abroad was at the behest of the Chamberlain Government, and further denials had to be reiterated by his supporters.[23] However, the fact that this story suited both Cripps and the Government – keeping each other at arm's length – concealed a private complicity between them.

Having expected the India Office to wash its hands of any responsibility for his visit, Cripps had found unexpected encouragement in a further interview in late November with the Secretary of State. Cripps recorded that Zetland 'told me that I should not be misleading Congress if I were to say that the Government were prepared to consider the scheme, without of course in any way suggesting that they were at all committed to it'.[24] This tallies with the fact that Zetland, who had already cabled the Viceroy to advocate exploration of the main points of the Cripps plan, now wrote to the Prime Minister; his message was that, in the war situation, many influences made

<hr />

20. Memorandum, 'taken to India 1939' (final draft, 24 November 1939).
21. RSC diary, 21 November 1939.
22. RSC to the General Council of Bristol East Divisional Labour Party, 29 November 1939, copy.
23. See IC to Lilian Rogers, 19 December 1939, copy, and memorandum from Gwendoline Hill, n.d., and her article, *Bristol Labour Weekly*, 30 March 1940.
24. RSC diary, 28 November 1939.

for 'a leap forward' in India. 'The most recent – which is the immediate cause of this letter – is not at first sight of great significance, yet is one that may prove to be of considerable effect,' he told Chamberlain. 'The instrument is Sir Stafford Cripps.'[25]

Even if Zetland was regarded as less influential, when the chips were down, than either Stewart or the Viceroy, there were clearly some members of the Government who thought that an unofficial initiative might be the way to break the official log-jam. Behind the scenes, then, Cripps enjoyed the help of the Foreign Office, where Butler provided a *laissez-passer*, explicitly mentioning the cognisance of Halifax and Zetland. That this degree of accreditation had been won for a potentially unsettling foray by a well-known left-wing critic of the Government is certainly a measure of the effectiveness of Cripps's adroit diplomacy in Whitehall. Equally unmistakably, it is an indication of the depth of the crisis facing the British Raj.

Geoffrey Wilson was a natural choice to accompany Cripps, who confided to his wife, 'what a joy and happiness it is to have him with me'.[26] Son of a prominent member of the India Conciliation Group, Wilson was ready to help with the research for the journey, notably an intensive study of the results of the provincial elections in 1937, which were painstakingly tabulated on a huge sheet (about one metre square) and later produced, with impressive effect, for briefing in discussions on the ground. Called secretary to Cripps, he was treated throughout more as a companion and colleague. When one Indian prince relegated Wilson to a separate motor-car, the protocol was satirized by an embarrassed Cripps – 'being a person of inferior social standing it was of course impossible that he should travel in the same car as so illustrious a person as myself'.[27]

The two men flew out to India – quite a novelty in 1939. The earliest seats that could be booked for them were on a KLM flight from Naples, departing 5 December. Cripps's high spirits – 'I feel like the first day of the new term at school'[28] – were manifest as they made their way overland in some style through France and Italy. Their aeroplane proved comfortable and, in that prelapsarian era of imperial air travel, used luxury hotels as staging posts *en route*. Then the pace changed.

---

25. Zetland to Chamberlain, 1 December 1939, quoted in Moore, *Churchill, Cripps and India*, p. 24.
26. RSC to IC, 17 December 1939.   27. RSC diary, 18 December 1939.
28. RSC to IC, 1 December 1939.

Cripps was to spend a bare twenty days in India. It was his first visit and he may have underestimated the difficulties of forming a faithful impression of the subcontinent in that time. His diary records what he learnt.

Landing on 7 December in Karachi, in what is now Pakistan, they flew east via Jodhpur to Allahabad in the United Provinces; after three days, it was the train up to New Delhi, the capital of British India, and thence an overnight trip to Lahore in the Punjab in the north-west. Returning through Delhi, there was an 850-mile train journey south, via Baroda to the great western port of Bombay. Three days later, they took the train east into Hyderabad, and then north into the Central Provinces for a two-day visit to Gandhi at Wardha. Cripps and Wilson left Wardha on the night of 20 December, sandwiching a day with the Rajah of Sarangarh into a gruelling journey, partly in his car, north-east up to Calcutta, where they spent Christmas Day, before departing for Burma the next morning.

Cripps insisted on having his own meals prepared from salads, fruit and vegetables whenever possible. He also showed a strong self-preservation instinct in foraging for himself, as Wilson – a less rigorous vegetarian, who had been known to eat ham rolls in Europe and was ready to try the local dishes in Asia – wryly observed on one occasion in Lahore. 'The occasion was somewhat marred for me by the fact that S. had eaten the only two chocolate cakes before I had an opportunity to get going. He later gave the somewhat lame excuse that unless he got what he could while the going was good, he might have to eat some of the Indian food.'[29] In a country where vegetarianism was widely practised, and indigenous food free of meat thus available, Cripps's lack of gastronomic enterprise may have been a joke, but one tinged with fastidious ethnocentricity.

'He has an astonishing capacity for acquiring female travelling companions,' Wilson commented when they had reached Delhi.[30] This became an intriguing sub-text in their joint diary. The game began with the flight out from Naples when Wilson was seated next to a 'young and very pleasant' woman passenger – 'described on a card which we have all been given as Miss McLeod, but she wears a wedding ring'.[31] The plot thickened. 'Miss McLeod is certainly Mrs McLeod and is Indian army,' Wilson discovered, somewhere over the Euphrates. 'I sit between her and Stafford and he is always sending her messages through me, but says that he does not want to change places.'[32] By the time the plane had refuelled at Karachi, and Cripps had received his first garlands of welcome, he was showing photographs of

29. RSC diary, 12 December 1939.   30. ibid., 13 December 1939 (misdated 12 December). 31. ibid., 5 December 1939.   32. ibid., 6 December 1939.

his granddaughter Judith to Mrs McLeod and presenting her with his surplus flowers. 'Perhaps it's just as well we get off tomorrow,' put in the superseded Wilson, 'but she really is a most charming person.' It was not a comment that Cripps let pass, on taking over the diary, stating coyly that, while deep in his own converse with an Indian Congressman, he had put the idea of the bouquet into the mind of his young friend; and, 'after a period of somewhat shy hesitation, he plucked up his courage and made the presentation and settled in the next seat to her and had a soul-pour till we arrived at Jodhpur.'[33] For the two men, overtures to the charming Mrs McLeod plainly served as one means of developing their own relationship.

In India, where they criss-crossed the country by train, Cripps – who normally travelled first class in England – made it a principle to book second-class tickets. In practice he was sometimes accommodated in the first class, either through the informal deference granted to an honoured guest of his influential Congress hosts, or through formal arrangements when he was met by the luxurious private carriage of an Indian prince whom he was visiting. Still, when allowed, he had the psychic satisfaction of making his democratic gesture, noting that at Hyderabad they 'stepped out onto the platform from our second class compartment to see a number of officials including a very smart A.D.C. trying to persuade a good looking solitary Englishman in a first class compartment next door that he was Sir Stafford Cripps'.[34]

Cripps's public image was purposefully projected, not least through his own efforts. In Britain, his secretary, Gwendoline Hill, fed the newspapers with press releases. Snippets about his journey continually appeared, keeping his name before the public; for example, the *Daily Express* of 3 January 1940 carried a photograph of Cripps's meeting with Jinnah under the headline 'Sir Stafford Meets a Moslem Leader'. In India, an intensive programme had been arranged: interviews with British officials, Indian nationalists and princes; public dinners and receptions; press conferences, meetings and speeches, especially to university audiences. Why did he receive this VIP treatment? It was, no doubt, partly a spontaneous reflection of Cripps's pre-existing fame among keen students of British politics. But it was also a product of the assiduity of Indian nationalists in purposefully courting an ally on the British left. It was, too, a result of the seriousness with which the

33. ibid., 7 December 1939.
34. ibid., 18 December 1939. This incident prefigures a post-war anecdote of Cripps as Chancellor of the Exchequer. On a visit to Paris Cripps eluded the efforts of the British diplomat sent to welcome him who looked initially in the First Class and only belatedly in the Second, where the Cripps family were sitting: Montague Browne, *Long Sunset*, p. 101.

British, mobilizing for war, took his visit, at a time when Congress had withdrawn in protest from the recently established provincial governments. 'Everybody is wonderfully friendly,' Wilson told Isobel Cripps, 'but I suspect they think S. is on a Govt mission.'[35]

Ostensibly unofficial, Cripps's journey was nothing if not a public event, with full press coverage in India as well as Britain. The first press conference came as soon as he reached India. 'I had a great reception at Karachi from the Raja and everyone else!' Cripps enthused. 'Ten garlands round my neck, a large bouquet of flowers and talk, talk, talk for an hour.'[36] When he arrived in Allahabad, a picture of him with Nehru appeared under the prominent caption, 'Indian Question a Test Case'.[37] When Cripps reached other Indian cities, it was much the same: talks till midnight, then the press for half-an-hour at Baroda; often crowds to welcome him at the station, even when it was an unannounced stop; a battery of movie cameras in Lahore. 'Sir Stafford Cripps Due in Bombay on Friday – Royal Opera House – Brilliant Speaker', ran the headlines in anticipation, while Wilson noted that 'the amount of film used on S. in Bombay must be pretty terrific' – not to mention the attendance of a cartoonist to draw him.[38] In Calcutta, the day started with a press conference; later came a meeting attended by 2,000 students, with a speech that went down well and was extensively reported.

The high point had been at Allahabad, accompanied by Nehru, who was 'received with the same terrific enthusiasm which he has evoked whenever we have seen him'. They first jointly addressed a meeting of over a thousand students – 'Cripps' Homage to Congress Leadership' was one headline[39] – and later went to a Congress rally of over 5,000, where 'Stafford spoke for a few minutes and had a great ovation'.[40] Little wonder, when he was riding on *khadi* coat-tails as expansive as these. Not only did one sympathetic newspaper subsequently devote its front page to a further speech by Cripps: it did so to the accompaniment of a picture of Cripps and Nehru, with the caption 'Spiritual Cousins'.[41]

These were flattering but double-edged compliments. Nehru was already a friend of Cripps, who was now the guest of the extended Nehru family, first in Allahabad and subsequently in Bombay. Their public appearances together signalled their affinity. Nehru's brother-in-law, Ranjit Pandit, was

35. Wilson to IC, 14 December 1939.   36. RSC to IC, 7 December 1939.
37. *Pioneer*, 12 December 1939, PRO, CAB 127/60.
38. *Evening News of India*; RSC diary, 15 December 1939.
39. *Bombay Chronicle*, 12 December 1939, PRO, CAB 127/60.
40. RSC diary, 10 December 1939.
41. *Free Press Journal*, 16 December 1939, PRO, CAB 127/60.

largely responsible for arranging Cripps's itinerary. Little wonder, then, that his visit was perceived as taking place under the auspices of Congress, with its overwhelming Hindu mass support; or that when he went to see Mohammed Ali Jinnah, the leader of the Muslim League, Cripps was met with the suggestion 'that I was being shepherded round the country by Congress and had already made up my mind'.[42] It is fair to add that, from the first, Nehru had thought it desirable for Cripps to meet not only Gandhi but Jinnah.[43] The fact remains that, since Cripps had assured his first press conference, in the largely Muslim city of Karachi, that he had 'come to learn and not to teach anyone anything,'[44] the extent of his prejudice or partisanship was an important issue.

Cripps undoubtedly started with views that he had accepted rather uncritically from his close contacts with Congress. The twelve-page letter that Nehru sent Cripps in January 1939, with a full analysis of the Indian political situation, is a particularly significant document. It can be read as an indication not only of what was in Nehru's own mind at the time but of ideas that he had put into the receptive and retentive mind of his friend, well before Cripps had even set foot in India. This was not, of course, a matter of indoctrination, still less an indoctrination that rode against Cripps's own inclination. Reciprocity was the essence of his relationship with Nehru, who gamely professed how much he enjoyed reading the five-week-old copies of *Tribune* that erratically evaded the incompetence of the postal service and the officiousness of the censorship. It was a similar outlook on politics – as dominated by class struggle, the world over – that had drawn the two men together in the first place. The Congress case was one that fitted Cripps's prejudices as well as appealing to his sense of justice.

In this scenario, a secular and democratic nationalism was seen as uniting India against the British Raj, which classically resorted to two strategies for maintaining imperial control. One was alliance with the parasitic princes who were left in charge of their states, alongside the provinces of British India. The other strategy was 'divide and rule': the manipulation of essentially factitious communal tensions, notably between the Hindu majority and the Muslims, the most sizeable of the minorities. Concepts derived from Marxism all too easily stereotype and pervade such an interpretation. If the Indian masses appeared to respond to the various stimuli of communal

42. RSC diary, 15 December 1939.
43. Nehru to Menon, 8 November 1939, in Gopal (ed.), *Nehru: Selected Works*, x, pp. 230–31.
44. RSC diary, 7 December 1939.

1. Parmoor, Stafford Cripps's childhood home.

2. Alfred and Theresa Cripps with their five children, 1891.

3. Stafford's home-made glider, 1909.

4. Bride and groom: Isobel and Stafford, 1911.

5. *(Above)* Stafford with his children.

6. *(Left)* Ambulance driver, 1914.

7. *(Above right)* 'The Red Squire': Stafford and Isobel at Goodfellows.

8. *(Right)* Farmer Cripps with a prize ram.

9. The youngest KC (centre).

10. Cripps before 'austerity' (early 1930s).

11. Stafford and Isobel at the 1939 Labour Party conference, Southport.

allegiance, this could be dismissed as a form of 'false consciousness', temporarily sustained and exacerbated through social control from above, in the class interest of feudal or bourgeois elements of Indian society and in the political interest of the British Raj.

The integrity of Congress, by contrast, with its heroic efforts to transcend communalism, could not be doubted without giving offence. Moreover, the noble Gandhian myth of Indian unity could not be questioned without giving rise to the imputation that, innocently or malevolently, the question itself must have come from a dupe or stooge of imperialism. In this picture, above all, there was simply no place for the authenticity of the communal experience or its own peculiar histories: rather an impatience with history for so slowly unmasking the 'real issues', essentially those of class conflict on a world scale. Little wonder that one of Cripps's speeches was reported under the blandly approving headline: 'Communal Trouble Shall Go/ But Class-War May Come In'.[45]

Nehru offered Cripps a gloss on this vulgar sketch that was both candid and sophisticated. 'Conflicts and cleavages are developing in our ranks,' Nehru admitted, thus creating difficulties for his own strategy of uniting the left. 'The Congress as a whole is definitely left politically including the old guard,' Nehru assured Cripps, but it was admittedly a problem that 'the emergence of the social issue' now fed disunity. He acknowledged a second problem in communalism, with the new prominence of the Muslim League. 'It almost seems,' Nehru wrote, 'that Jinnah and the other leaders of the Muslim League object to democracy itself in India for democracy means the dominance of the majority.' A final problem was that of the Indian states, where the masses were now stirring against princely rule, prompted by Congress's successes in the provinces of British India.[46] Despite such difficulties, then, Congress alone stood for a democratic solution, in uniting the forces of the political left against the influence of obstructive but essentially obsolescent social forces.

Such were the ideological spectacles which Cripps and his young companion wore on arrival in Allahabad. On happily meeting a young Muslim who supported Congress and a young Hindu who opposed it, Wilson's reaction was simply: 'So much for communalism!'[47] That the situation was rather more complex than they had first envisaged was a part of the wisdom of India that took time to be appreciated.

Cripps did not relent in his suspicion of the Raj and its motives. He

45. ibid., 23 December 1939; *Bharat Jyoti* (Bombay), 24 December 1939.
46. Nehru to Cripps, 21 January 1939, PRO, CAB 127/57; also in Gopal (ed.), *Nehru: Selected Works*, xiii, pp. 706–11.
47. RSC diary, 10 December 1939.

listened respectfully while the widely revered poet Rabindranath Tagore assured him that the British 'were mainly responsible for the communal difficulties and even now were backing up the Moslems against the Hindus'.[48] This tallied with Cripps's own impressions in Calcutta, that British members of the Indian Civil Service were 'rather reactionary and stupid', and that the British journalists whom he met there, writing for the *Statesman of India*, were 'all running the pro-Moslem policy, chiefly I should think on the ground that it will help them to maintain the British Raj and because they are very anti-Congress'.[49]

On other occasions, however, Cripps found more common ground with his fellow-countrymen, notably in Delhi. *The Times*'s correspondent seemed 'sympathetic and fairly enlightened, and, like everybody else that I have seen, took dominion status for granted within the quite near future at the end of the war'.[50] Cripps considered that the legal adviser to the government, Sir Hawthorne Lewis, 'had a progressive mind and was prepared for change, regarding the C.A. [constituent assembly] as merely a further step in the advance of British policy for India'. The Chief Justice, Sir Maurice Gwyer, also 'took an open-minded view of the situation, which he thought that the Viceroy had handled very badly'.[51] In Bombay, likewise, the Governor 'seemed moderate and sensible-minded' – 'perfectly prepared for the granting of Dominion Status immediately after the war' – and dismissed the Muslim League's current complaints against Congress as unjustified.[52] This was, indeed, a view that Cripps publicly endorsed – 'Muslim Charges Baseless' ran the headline report of his press conference in Bombay.[53]

The alleged 'Muslim atrocities' were not, in fact, to be so easily dismissed. With its ministries in office for two years in eight provinces, Congress found that its role in government simultaneously established its credibility and made it the target for the propaganda of the Muslim League, now intent on building itself up as a rival political organization. Underlying conflicts over control of economic resources and political patronage fed more symbolic issues. Several emotive allegations persistently surfaced. Congress was held responsible for offensive music in the vicinity of mosques – its song *Bande Mataram* had Hindu connotations – in much the same way as Ulster Unionist marches are associated with sectarian provocation. There were also complaints about discriminatory school textbooks in Congress-controlled areas like Bombay.

Such stories were retailed with circumstantial details of which Cripps

48. ibid., 25 December 1939.   49. ibid., 24 December 1939.
50. ibid., 13 December 1939 (misdated 12 December).   51. ibid.
52. ibid., 15 December 1939.   53. *Times of India*, 18 December 1939.

vainly tried to keep track from one interview to the next: listening, sympathizing, scrutinizing, as the occasion demanded. It seems to have dawned on him that they were not in themselves particular justiciable issues, to be resolved by his forensic skills, but protean manifestations of intractable inter-communal friction. Meeting the Muslim chief whip of the governing party in Calcutta, Cripps, after a fortnight of rival atrocity stories, noted wearily: 'So far as the complaints by the Hindu community were concerned he dealt with these in very much the same way as the Congress ministries replied about the alleged ill-treatment of Moslems except that he insisted that there existed deep-seated differences and antagonisms right throughout every village and area in the province.'[54]

Cripps made special efforts to establish contact with trade-union and socialist leaders. This was not unnatural in view of the significance he attached to the role of the labour movement, and there was a direct spill-over from his own experience in the advice he gave. As he told one young socialist, 'in my view they should concentrate on the nationalist issue and maintain a united front until that issue was disposed of. In the meanwhile they could continue with their propaganda on the socialist and class basis with a view to benefiting from that propaganda when the real issues emerged.'[55] He said the same to the sectarian Hindu nationalists (Mahasabha), advising them 'to show as united a front as possible with Congress as otherwise those in G.B. who were concerned to deny freedom to India would point with delight to divisions among the Hindus as well as the communal divisions as an argument against self government for India'.[56]

In all of this, Cripps stayed close to the line taken by Nehru and his Congress allies. Indeed, he was endorsing as much as reporting their view that joint action by the Hindu Mahasabha and the Muslim League was actually 'very good proof of the non-communal character of Congress, since these two extreme communalist organisations are both discontented with and combining against the moderates in the centre'. Cripps added: 'It reminds one of the communist and fascist combination in Germany against the social democrats.'[57] The allusion would not have been lost on Nehru, a keen student of European politics who was sometimes reproached for showing more interest in the Spanish civil war than in spinning his own cotton.

There is no disguising the strongly favourable impact made upon Cripps by his privileged entrée to the Congress elite. Perhaps paradoxically, what charmed him about many of these high-caste, patrician statesmen was their

54. RSC diary, 22 December 1939.   55. ibid., 25 December 1939.
56. ibid., 22 December 1939.   57. ibid., 20 December 1939.

attachment to democracy – and a model of democracy, moreover, with which he was familiar at home. 'They have a complete electoral machinery with registers, registration courts, returning officers, polling booths etc. exactly as in English general elections, and provisions for petitions after elections,' he observed with satisfaction. It all went to show 'that the Congress conducts its work on a truly democratic basis'.[58]

Disposed to see Congress in this light, Cripps was naturally inclined to a critical view of its fast-emerging rival, the Muslim League. He listened to the sceptical, marxisant analysis made by members of the Congress leadership – Dr B.C. Roy, Gandhi's physician, and Abul Kalam Azad, himself a Muslim bearing the magisterial scholarly title Maulana, as well as Nehru – who all 'stressed the fact that the M. L. leadership was class as well as communal and that Jinnah never had been prepared for personal sacrifice in the cause of nationalism, much less those who were now associated with him, who were probably pro-British, many of them'.[59] Cripps was ready to credit the imputation that Jinnah was acting as a stooge of the Raj because this consorted with a class interpretation of politics which Cripps had brought in his KLM baggage and simply unpacked on arriving in India.

This analysis, moreover, was not without verisimilitude. It was corroborated by what Cripps heard from Shiva Rao, the correspondent of the liberal *Manchester Guardian*, that 'the M. L. was in fact a class as well as a communal body in so far as its leadership was concerned'.[60] It tallied too with what he had recently found in the princely state of Hyderabad, where 'the Moslem community as a ruling body is identified with a ruling class of feudal landlords', thus maintaining minority rule which democracy threatened.[61] Above all, Cripps was impressed by the testimony of Muslims. He listened with special attention to two prominent Congress adherents in Bombay. 'In their view,' he noted, 'the Moslem League was entirely an upper class organisation, though they admitted it could mobilise the great majority of Moslem opinion on a communal issue by communal propaganda.'[62] No sooner had he been welcomed by Nehru at Allahabad than Cripps was taken to meet representatives of the Momin Conference, representing Muslims enagaged in the weaving industry. Cripps observed that they supported Congress rather than the Muslim League, 'and regard the M. L. as representing the exploiters of their members'.[63]

*

58. ibid., 9 December 1939.   59. ibid., 20 December 1939.   60. ibid.
61. ibid., 18 December 1939.   62. ibid., 16 December 1939.
63. ibid., 8 December 1939.

It is not as though the scales suddenly fell from Cripps's eyes; but, to his credit, Cripps sought to verify such assertions in the course of his travels and interviews. When he met Liaquat Ali Kahn, the secretary of the Muslim League, a rather modifed picture emerged: 'As far as the Momins were concerned, Congress bought their cloth but lower prices were paid to the Momin weavers in Bihar than to the non-Moslem weavers.'[64] Jinnah said much the same: 'The Momins were negligible, and the man whom I saw at Allahabad had been badly beaten by a M. L. man and nearly lost his deposit.'[65] Whether Cripps realized that this was not far from the Viceroy's dismissive view of the Momins, as 'quite uninfluential'[66] is not clear. The tough-minded Muslim Minister of Labour in Calcutta, H. S. Suhrawardy, parading credentials as a former trade-union leader, was most forthright of all. 'The Momins,' he said, 'had been deliberately created by Congress in order to bring about a split in the Moslems.'[67] Here was a new dimension to the protean conspiracy theory of social manipulation.

By the end of his visit Cripps had gained further insight into the labyrinthine complexity of Indian politics. 'We are gradually forming an impression of the situation – which is very difficult indeed – but not I feel hopeless as yet,' Stafford told Isobel, five hard days after his arrival.[68] As he fully appreciated, his opinion was offered before he had seen either Jinnah or Gandhi. Having become almost punch-drunk from another full week of interviews, Cripps declared: 'At the moment I see no solution until the British Govt fairly & honestly decides it will give India freedom & a constituent assembly. Once that is done there will be the hope of a solution.'[69]

While Cripps's sympathies remained with a nationalist movement led by Congress, he became more ready to heed critics of the Gandhian 'high command' which dominated it. Suhrawardy, despite acquiring a reputation as 'one of the most inefficient, conceited and crooked politicians in India',[70] with a callousness revealed during the Calcutta bloodshed seven years later, struck Cripps as worth listening to in 1939. 'As far as a solution was concerned he thought that the essential thing was the recognition of Jinnah as the representative of the Moslems and the sharing of the high command,' Cripps noted. 'In principle there was nothing between the two groups and there should be no difficulty about the sharing of the high command.'[71] This

64. ibid., 11 December 1939.   65. ibid., 15 December 1939.
66. Linlithgow to Amery, 7 March 1942, quoted in Mansergh, *TOP*, i, p. 362.
67. RSC diary, 23 December 1939.   68. RSC to IC, 13 December 1939.
69. ibid., 21 December 1939.
70. Wavell journal, 8 April 1946, in Moon (ed.), *Wavell: Journal*, p. 239.
71. RSC diary, 23 December 1939.

view may have combined cynicism with optimism. In its realism, at any rate, it was fairly close to what Cripps had heard from Sir Reginald Maxwell, a reputedly diehard member of the Viceroy's council, who 're-emphasised the fact that the Indian looked on politics to a considerable extent as a means of getting political appointments and that therefore the communal difficulty was to a considerable extent a question of the competition for jobs between the communities'.[72]

'Congress was a middle class or aristocratic oligarchy which was trying to make contact with the masses,' Suhrawardy maintained, while acknowledging the 'frankly middle class' composition of the Muslim League too.[73] That Congress was likewise in the hands of a hand-picked elite – 'It was in fact Gandhi and Nehru and no-one else' – was testified by more than one informant whom Cripps respected.[74] Meeting the leader of the Harijan or 'Untouchables', Dr B. R. Ambedkar, his 'intense sincerity' struck Cripps. He recorded the Harijan argument against a joint electorate with the Hindus, that it simply allowed Congress to put in its own nominees for the Untouchable seats – 'as for instance in the case of Nehru's butler'.[75]

In this light, Congress's support for simple democracy looked less altruistic and more self-interested, since it was premised on its own control of the majority vote. Sir Sikander Hyet Khan, the shrewd Muslim Prime Minister of the Punjab, where communal difficulties seemed more tractable, put it to Cripps that 'one of Gandhi's motives in insisting on joint electorates for the depressed classes was to preseve the Hindu communal majority, just as the Congress insistence on a move forward now was due to the apprehension that if they waited the depressed classes might come forward and declare themselves in their own interests'.[76] Likewise the audience with Fazlal Huq, the Muslim Prime Minister of Bengal – 'This was one of the high spots of our interviews and reminded me of nothing more than a visit to the robbers' cave in the Arabian Nights' – was as notable for its political insight as its exotic context. Fazlal Huq patiently explained that in the sort of constituent assembly proposed by Cripps, the Hindus would simply gang up and use joint electorates to secure their domination.[77] Both Fazlal Huq and Khan were tactical allies of Jinnah rather than wholehearted followers; in northern provinces like theirs, Muslim strength insulated them from the insecurities of their co-religionists further south, whose acute

72. ibid., cf. 12 December 1939.   73. ibid., 23 December 1939.
74. ibid., 14 December 1939. (Sir V. T. Krishnamachari).
75. ibid., 15 December 1939.   76. ibid., 12 December 1939.
77. ibid., 25 December 1939.

awareness of their minority status created a constituency for the Muslim League.

The fact is that, given his own preconceptions, Cripps had more to learn from the Muslim League than from Congress, and his interviews with Jinnah or Liaquat Ali Khan were thus fully as important as those with Nehru or Gandhi.

Staying at the spacious Nehru residence at Anand Bhawan on his arrival in India, Cripps naturally launched his political discussions with his friend and host, and equally naturally encountered least difficulty. Their initial exchanges left Cripps thinking that 'from the Congress angle it looks fairly hopeful'.[78] Nehru's private opinion was more reserved, not only finding 'two or three fatal defects' in the plan, but warning Gandhi's secretary that 'while Cripps is thoroughly straight and his abilities unquestioned, his judgement is not always to be relied upon'.[79]

On the afternoon of his departure on 10 December, the two men had a full discussion. Nehru was ready to approve the general lines of Cripps's proposal for a constituent assembly, so long as it were based on adult suffrage. This was not, of course, what Cripps's memorandum stated: it had cannily by-passed the long-disputed issue of whether there should simply be universal suffrage by saying that the assembly should be constituted by the present provincial electorates. Cripps deflected Nehru's criticism by complicitly advising him on negotiating tactics: 'I suggested to him that it might be as well if the offer came in the form in the memorandum and that then Congress were to reply stating their demand for adult suffrage, thus putting on the Muslim League the onus of acceptance or refusal, which would be a strong compelling force on Jinnah to give way.'

Nehru in turn advised Cripps not to use the term 'Dominion status', with its imperial overtones, and made it clear that a fifteen-year period of transition to independence was too long. On the minorities, he showed himself conciliatory, short of conceding them a veto. 'There is no doubt about the fact that Congress are doing all they can to minimize the Communal difficulties,' Cripps concluded, 'and are prepared to give the widest possible protection in the constitution to the minorities.'[80]

The following day, on reaching Delhi, Cripps heard a different story

78. RSC to IC, 8 December 1939.
79. Nehru to Mahadev Desai, 9 December 1939, in Gopal (ed.), *Nehru: Selected Works*, x, p. 390; also in Nehru, *Bunch of Old Letters*, p. 413.
80. RSC diary, 10 December 1939.

from Liaquat Ali Khan. 'Communal divisions would persist even in a free India,' he maintained, 'and to-day the bitterness between Moslems and Hindus was more pronounced than ever.' He acknowledged that the League had only turned itself into a mass movement once the 1937 elections had revealed its weakness, but it now claimed a representative status on behalf of the minorities and would only be satisfied with a federation of states. His crucial contention went to the heart of the problem: 'The present form of democracy on western lines was not suitable for India, where the division was such that a minority was a minority for ever and ever and had no chance of ever becoming the majority.'[81]

Cripps had been invited to meet Jinnah on 15 December at his home in Bombay. If Cripps was to leave India still somewhat sceptical of Jinnah and his pretensions, it should be remembered that he had started out simply scornful. He had some acquaintance with Jinnah as a fellow barrister, whose practice in Lincoln's Inn in the early 1930s had provided ample means to sustain an elegant westernized lifestyle. Tall and lean, at sixty-three he was dapper, assured and masterful. Face to face, at his fine house on Malabar Hill, with views of the ocean, Jinnah could hardly have failed to appear more cogent than the so-called British stooge depicted in Congress demonology. After making routine gibes about Cripps's closeness to Congress, Jinnah affirmed that 'in the elections there was a pure communal division with a permanent majority which made democracy, at any rate in the English sense, an impossibility'. So, while professing himself as good a nationalist as Nehru, he warned that 'a permanent majority was always liable to become puffed up and if that majority was a communal one then God help you'.

For Jinnah, these intractable realities were not to be dissolved by fashionable western slogans about democracy, nor the existence of such conflicts dissimulated by a simple reduction to class issues. Hence the fatuity of a constituent assembly until the British had been kicked out; hence too the Muslims' need for entrenched safeguards against swamping by the permanent majority – nominally Congress, actually Hindu – which they always found set against them. He therefore proposed that, in the provincial legislatures, any bill should be susceptible of being blocked on communal grounds if two-thirds of the Muslim members objected to it. 'In the present position you could only have communal parties and either you must trust a bare majority of Hindus or a two thirds majority of Moslems.' He professed readiness to meet Nehru (though the imminent launch of a new phase in Jinnah's anti-Congress propaganda effectively ruled this out). 'Altogether,'

81. ibid., 11 December 1939.

Cripps concluded, 'he gave me the impression of an intensely lonely man in perpetual conflict with himself and with no one in whom he could confide or who could give him reliable advice, but he put his case with great ability and clarity.'[82] At least for the moment, under the force of Jinnah's powerful advocacy of a well-prepared brief, Cripps found his preconceptions shaken.

It was not until 19 December 1939 that Cripps, escorted by Nehru, met Mohandas Gandhi, the Mahatma or 'great spirit' still acknowledged as the real leader of Congress, though, now seventy, ostentatiously holding no official position within it. The widely reported meeting took place at Gandhi's ashram near Wardha. The tiny mud hut was a study in asceticism – 'a little bamboo furniture about, a few books in a packing case on its side, false teeth in a box, some papers, a bed on the floor on which he was sitting, and several rush mats'. Cripps took off his shoes, unlike most English visitors. Wilson lightened the reverential mood not only by recording in the diary that a small stool was provided for Cripps – 'a concession to English middle age!'[83] – but also reserving for Isobel Cripps the news that Gandhi was known by the sobriquet of Mickey Mouse.[84] He was left with the impresion that Gandhi was drawn to Cripps.[85]

Gandhi later came into Wardha itself for dinner with the twenty members of the Congress Working Committee and – again without shoes, and on the floor this time – Cripps thus had an opportunity to meet other members. Of these, the most notable was Chakravarti Rajagopalachari, ex-Chief Minister of Madras now that Congress had withdrawn from government. He was, along with Vallabhbhai Patel, one of the few men to be treated as an equal by Gandhi. What Cripps had previously heard about 'Rajaji' ('who I presume must be very reactionary judging by the universal acclamation of his attainments by all the more reactionary people I have met') was hardly promising.[86] As with Jinnah, a face-to-face meeting generated more positive impressions. Cripps now judged Rajagopalachari 'a very fine and determined type who fears no sacrifice and is rigid in his determination not to compromise'.[87] Their rapprochement was to be consolidated in 1942.

The next day Cripps again met Gandhi, this time with only his secretary, Mahadev Desai, present. Three-quarters of an hour was sufficient to exhaust Gandhi's criticism of the memorandum, which he professed to find an acceptable basis for negotiation, subject to the expected reservations over 'Dominion status'. Cripps took this as a good sign. Gandhi's main point

82. ibid., 15 December 1939.   83. ibid., 19 December 1939.
84. Wilson to IC, 20 December 1939.   85. Wilson, 'My Working Life', p. 25.
86. RSC diary, 18 December 1939.   87. ibid., 20 December 1939.

was that the British Government, by fostering minorities, was itself making this problem insoluble, whether intentionally or not ('though amongst a number of officials it is I am sure intentional,' Cripps added). So the crucial issue was whether to trust Congress. 'Whatever the composition of its membership, Congress was and must remain essentially non-communal because it believed in equality and non-violence,' Cripps was assured.

There were no surprises about Cripps's own reaction. 'One cannot but be impressed with the vigour with which Gandhi holds to his creed and the calmness with which he is prepared for any sacrifice in order to attain it. His whole way of life with its extreme simplicity and selflessness is part of his creed and demonstrates his sincerity.' Encouraged by the reception of his plan, and undoubtedly benefiting to some extent from Nehru's good offices in securing this, Cripps evidently hoped to enlist Gandhi's influence behind it. 'I feel there is a much better chance of solution of the problem while he is still alive and in control than there will be if and when he goes.'[88]

The pilgrimage to Wardha was a happy interlude between 'the rather exaggerated hospitality of Hyderabad' and similar princely entertainment in Saranghar, which was interesting 'but at the same time rather nauseating'.[89] As Stafford put it to Isobel, 'we travel in style and all amidst the infinite sadness of the grinding poverty of the people'.[90] At Hyderabad, the appearance of 'a slightly grubby looking middle aged gentleman in a rather grubby white coat' threw Cripps's expectations for a moment until he realized that he had been ushered into the presence of His Exalted Highness the Nizam of Hyderabad, whose political acumen proved equally unimpressive – not a happy augury, given that Cripps was conferring with the head of the largest of India's princely states.

The advice Cripps proffered to the Nizam was the same as that reiterated a couple of days later to the Rajahs of Sarangarh, Raigarh, Sakti and Khairagah: that the era of British paramountcy over the states was coming to an end, that the day of democracy was dawning throughout India, and that the princes should concert their strategy to get abreast of these developments. 'All the Maharajahs had the best of intentions,' was how Stafford put it to Isobel, 'but I told them it just couldn't go on & they realise the fact.'[91] The imminence of their demise was symbolically brought home by the 'beat' in the jungle that had been laid on for their honoured guests,

88. ibid.   89. ibid., 19, 21 December 1939.   90. RSC to IC, 21 December 1939.
91. RSC to IC, 21 December 1939.

employing 200 beaters to produce a total bag that amounted to one or two small deer and an antelope.

Cripps pulled together his findings at the end of the line in Calcutta, where, as he told Isobel, 'we have to stay one night with the Viceroy, alas!' Here formality was the order of the day – and of the evening too. Luckily for Cripps, who found it awkward having 'no proper clothes', the Viceroy did not expect his visitor to dine with him after their hour's interview.[92] The stiffness and inhibition of the occasion stood in contrast to the hospitable way in which Cripps had hitherto been received in India, especially when affinity of outlook led Congress supporters to reach out to him as the Nehru of England. Conversely, he had been portrayed with suspicion and hostility in the Anglo-Indian press. The *Statesman* had seized on his pro-Russian utterances with the dismissive headline, 'Goodbye, Mr Cripps'. The idiom mimicked the title of a new film (with Robert Donat's Oscar-winning performance as Mr Chips) and lodged the phrase in the mind of the Viceroy, whose own sentiments it caught nicely.

Imposing in stature, aloof in bearing, Victor Alexander John Hope, second Marquess of Linlithgow, had served as Governor-General and Viceroy since 1936. He was undeniably conscientious, deliberately formal and excruciatingly slow in his dispatch of business. 'Heavy of body and slow of mind, solid as a rock and with almost a rock's lack of awareness', was how he struck Nehru, that influential connoisseur of the British upper classes.[93]

Known to his intimates as 'Hopie', this was the man charged with the implementation of the new Government of India Act. Although he had had some initial success in drawing Congress into cooperation, it was hardly through any exercise in personal diplomacy aimed at winning over crucial support.

The Viceroy evinced a grudging respect for Nehru, but the bulk of the Congress Working Committee, as Linlithgow chose to put it later, 'appears more and more clearly as a collection of declining valetudinarians who have no grip on the country, but who, politically, are purely parasitic on Gandhi the spell-binder'.[94] Whereas Halifax, during his period as Viceroy a decade previously, had courted Gandhi to bring him to the conference table, Linlithgow always kept his distance. His meeting with Nehru just after the outbreak of war was only their second – and was to be their last. When Cripps gathered opinions in 1939, the Viceroy remained a notably inscrutable

92. RSC to IC, 17, 24 December 1939.   93. Nehru, *Discovery of India*, p. 374.
94. Linlithgow to Amery, 23–27 January 1942, quoted in Mansergh, *TOP*, i, p. 60; cf. the marginal comments on pp. 55–6.

figure whose real attitude was a puzzle to many, Indian politicians and British officials alike – a general criticism, so Stafford told Isobel, 'and it naturally means he is a bad negotiator!'[95]

At their meeting on 24 December, as Cripps admitted, 'I did all the talking', rehearsing the gist of his discussions, while the Viceroy sat impassively taking notes. Cripps reported his view that Congress would respond favourably to an immediate pledge to convene a post-war constituent assembly and ('provided it was not made an actual public condition') would resume their role in the provincial governments. But negotiations between Congress and the Muslim League would only be possible if the Viceroy himself intervened.

'I am sure that he has got a genuine and impartial desire to settle the differences on a just basis,' Cripps noted – and he evidently conveyed as much to Linlithgow, who none the less remained impervious to cajolery in not disclosing what was in his own mind.[96] Cripps ventured the comment to Gilbert Laithwaite, the Viceroy's private secretary, that 'most people I had met who had seen him were rather dismayed at his sphinx-like manner of receiving their arguments'.[97] Cripps's own arguments were clearly no exception. Linlithgow's subsequent conduct in fact reflected his private view of Congress as 'entirely ruthless politicians;'[98] and, above all, it manifested his own temperament, moving by inches and only when he was pushed.

Stafford gave his private reckoning to Isobel: 'I don't think, as things look at present, that there is any likelihood of much happening in India for a few weeks. I have the impression that my visit has made all parties think again and that the very wide publicity given to it all over India has to some extent helped towards an atmosphere of solution – anyway I hope so.'[99] He had received a friendly valedictory letter from Nehru, making a tactful reference to 'the complexity of our problems' and concluding with the platitude: 'I do not suppose any major problem in the world today is easy of solution.'[100] This was politeness. What Nehru had sardonically told a colleague was that, while Cripps's visit might have made him better

95. RSC to IC, 24 December 1939.
96. RSC diary, 23 December 1939. See also RSC to Nehru, 24 December 1939, quoted in Moore, *Churchill, Cripps and India*, p. 17.
97. RSC diary, 24 December, 1939.
98. Linlithgow to Amery, 21 January 1942, quoted in Mansergh, *TOP*, i, p. 48.
99. RSC to IC, 27 December 1939.
100. Nehru to Cripps, 25 December 1939, PRO, CAB 127/57; also printed in Gopal (ed.), *Nehru: Selected Works*, x, p. 269.

acquainted with these problems, 'it is quite possible that this further know-ledge might confuse him more'.[101]

He came, he saw, he left – not unhopefully. The next steps, Cripps believed, were for others to take. Had he known of the current transactions within government he might have been less optimistic. Even in inaccessible China, he could not fail to become aware of a steady souring of the atmosphere. 'Drift' was how Nehru described a situation in which Linlithgow's inactivity seemed far from masterly. Nehru's analysis of the situation categorized the shifting allegiances, class by class, with Congress attracting mass support, even among Muslims, while the Hindu feudal class gravitated toward the Mahasabha, and the Muslim League's gains were confined to the lower-middle-class Muslims. 'Essentially the conflict between the Congress and the League is a conflict between the lower middle classes with a large mass following and the Muslim feudal and middle classes,' Nehru claimed. 'Of course the religious element confuses the issue and excitement can be roused up in the name of Allah and Islam.'[102]

It was hardly surprising that Nehru became persuaded by the conduct of the British authorities that their policy was one of full-blooded imperialism, 'any profession to the contrary notwithstanding'.[103] In a rapidly deteriorat-ing situation, he made his points with unwonted forthrightness. 'The pro-posals you made when you were here do not help,' he told Cripps.[104] Congress's position had hardened, not only on the already sensitive issue of Dominion status but on its attitude to the war itself – an imperialist war in which, spurred on by Nehru, Congress now declared that it wanted no part. The response from the Muslim League was the Lahore resolution of March 1940, generally considered the decisive commitment to the goal of 'Pakistan' as the means of protecting Muslim identity. By April Nehru was stating that 'an unbridgeable gulf exists between us and the British Govt' and that Cripps's conciliatory efforts were therefore in vain: 'The kind of scheme you proposed when you were here had grave defects even then; now it is completely unthinkable.'[105] He was to be even more blunt behind Cripps's back: 'I fear Stafford has completely failed to understand the elements of the Indian problem!'[106]

101. Nehru to Menon, 21 December 1939, in Gopal (ed.), *Nehru: Selected Works*, x, p. 412.
102. Nehru to RSC, 17 January 1940.
103. Nehru to Gandhi, 4 February 1940, in Nehru, *Bunch of Old Letters*, p. 428.
104. Nehru to RSC, 27 February 1940, PRO, CAB 127/143.
105. Nehru to RSC, 9 April 1940, PRO, CAB 127/143.
106. Nehru to Menon, 16 May 1940, in Gopal (ed.), *Nehru: Selected Works*, xi, p. 33.

Failure to understand, of course, is a relative concept; it depends on what is taken to be correct; and Nehru was a demanding tutor, irritated by the waywardness of his brilliant pupil. Yet the extent to which Cripps was still prepared to take his lead from Nehru can be seen in the way that he promptly adjusted his own views. Nehru, obviously angry and inevitably partisan, now poured out his dark suspicions of the Muslim League. They were accused of abandoning nationalism, of capitulating to the British Government, of not being serious about their new cry for partition, but instead of using it to shore up vested and feudal interests. 'This development will perhaps show you that you were not quite right in the appraisement of the communal situation,' Nehru rebuked his friend. 'I am glad that the clarification has taken place for now it is absurd to talk about our joining hands with the leaders of the Muslim League.'[107]

Admittedly, Nehru found himself pushing on an open door in seeking to persuade Cripps, whose ideological habits predisposed in the same direction. The media brought news of Nehru's position to Cripps well ahead of his personal letter. Halfway across the world, Cripps was already talking in broadly similar terms to the American press: contending that class interest motivated the Muslim League in their 'fantastic' plan of partition to create Pakistan, which merely served to obstruct a settlement, with Jinnah's ego making him irreconcilable.[108]

It was one thing for Cripps to subscribe, virtually point by point, to Congress's reading of the Pakistan campaign: quite another to publish his highly partisan views in *Tribune* in May 1940, since this had a lasting effect on how he was perceived in India, especially by Muslims. Cripps reminded his readers that 'the religious differences are often stirred up and exaggerated to serve what are really class ends', whereas his own belief was that 'once India is self-governing, the lines of political cleavage will tend to become those of class and not religion'. Factitious difficulties were stirred up by a 'class of well-to-do Moslems' who regarded British rule as a lesser evil than that of a democratic India. This was why 'the reactionary leaders of the Moslem League' had come up with 'an impracticable suggestion for the division of India in order to prevent the Indian peasants and workers from obtaining the control of their own country'.

Cripps thus sought to reduce the complex manifestations of nationalism, imbricated with communal tensions, to the simple maxims of democracy, imperialism and class struggle. He not only abandoned his rather vacuous

107. Nehru to RSC, 9 April 1940, PRO, CAB 127/143.
108. Asia Office press conference, 8 April 1940, notes by Agnes Flexner.

optimism about a possible settlement but suppressed the evidence of his own eyes and ears about the intractability of the communal issue. He was thus led to dismiss Jinnah's case as 'a dog-in-the-manger attitude which does not deserve our support'.[109] Unlike Nehru, Jinnah may not have been a subscriber to *Tribune*, but it is little wonder that this article came to his attention – nor that its slighting remarks about the authenticity of Muslim nationalism were still to be a cause of residual bitterness two years later, at the time of the Cripps Mission.

Not until Cripps's return to London in April 1940 was he able to plumb the official mind on India. Zetland, who had been well disposed to Cripps's visit, seemed unmistakably in eclipse as Secretary of State. Indian policy, Cripps gathered, was 'now being conducted by Linlithgow in accordance with the "man on the spot" theory, and he is taking a violently suppressive attitude'; there was little check from the more liberal members of the Cabinet, 'and as a consequence Winston, who of course supports the Viceroy, gets away with it'.[110] This accurately reflected the fact that Zetland had spent weeks vainly seeking Cabinet backing for moves to force the pace of reform and thus circumvent the communal impasse, with one comment attributed to Churchill in the Cabinet minutes – 'He regarded the Hindu–Moslem feud as the bulwark of British rule in India'[111] – sufficiently indicating the timbre of the discussion.

Whereas Halifax proved to be the most liberal member of the British Cabinet, Zetland, as the responsible minister, encountered resistance to proposals for change, not least from the Viceroy, who characteristically judged any such move unnecessary. 'It is no part of our policy, I take it, to expedite in India constitutional changes for their own sake,' was Linlithgow's line.[112] He was dutifully served by the equally cautious Laithwaite, to whom Sir Findlater Stewart, perhaps as a means of absolving the India Office from any suspicion, confided his own epitaph on Cripps's efforts – 'at best he has been guilty of wishful thinking to the point of crookedness'.[113] Very similar comments, by very similar people, were to be made a couple of years later, after the Cripps Mission.

It is not surprising that a debriefing interview with Findlater Stewart at the India Office left Cripps 'extremely depressed about the whole outlook'.

---

109. 'Finding the real India', *Tribune*, 3 May 1940.   110. RSC diary, 25 April 1940.
111. PRO, CAB, 30 (40) 4, 2 February 1940, quoted in Moore, *Churchill, Cripps and India*, p. 28.
112. Linlithgow to Zetland, 21 December 1939, quoted ibid., pp. 25–6, at p. 26.
113. Stewart to Laithwaite, 13 January 1940, quoted ibid., p. 10, n. 2.

Stewart's message was bleak: 'that though he did not like to use the word, he despaired of any solution and did not think I could do anything to assist'. At best, there was some hope that Gandhi's influence might prevent Congress's non-cooperation campaign from creating 'excessive difficulties'; at worst there was now 'the possibility of G.B. going to war with India in order to force her to remain within the Commonwealth of Nations' – though 'British Empire' is surely what Stewart really meant. 'Altogether he seemed to be subdued and hopeless compared to his state of mind at the interview before I left,' Cripps concluded.[114]

The real clash was between different mind-sets in facing the challenge of the Indian situation. Cripps's whole plan depended on a Viceroy who would try to break the impasse with bold new initiatives. The reality was the inert Linlithgow, resolved to stand firm and take no chances with Britain's imperial interests. Cripps appealed over the heads of the India Office, using an interview with Halifax on 3 May to raise the urgent question of India. At Halifax's suggestion, further interviews were arranged with the Home Secretary, Sir John Anderson, and with the Prime Minister, Neville Chamberlain.

Cripps was the go-between once more. He was simultaneously in touch with Agatha Harrison of the ICG, and through them with Gandhi, the one person whose influence might buy time for conciliation. Cripps felt sufficient confidence, when he saw Anderson on 6 May, to show him the sombre letter which Nehru had written the previous month. Anderson, carrying into politics the administrative ethic of his civil service background, had recently served as Governor of Bengal for five years, and now struck Cripps as 'very anxious and also very receptive'. Not only was his view of Jinnah 'very hostile and very similar in some ways to my own': a more striking similarity showed in Anderson's view of the Viceroy as 'so rigid that however good his intentions he was absolutely incapable of bringing about any settlement'.[115] What Cripps proposed was to supersede Linlithgow by sending out an *ad hoc* delegation of three members with plenipotentiary powers to try and arrive at a negotiated settlement – an idea that foreshadows the Cabinet delegation of 1946.

Cripps did not succeed in seeing Chamberlain before he was replaced as Prime Minister by Churchill. Given that Zetland had been a weak Secretary of State for India, the question was whether his successor in the new Government, the veteran imperialist Leo Amery, would be any improvement? When, in an interview within days of his appointment, he told Cripps

114. RSC diary, 1 May 1940.   115. ibid., 6 May 1940.

that he had an open mind about the situation, Cripps commented that 'it will take him a long time to get a picture of it and when he does, it will of course be the India Office picture, and when in doubt he will have to take the Viceroy's views so that I have not any great hope of his open mind receiving anything except an impression adverse to Congress and their views'. That Cripps judged the situation primarily from this standpoint was made clear by his warning to Amery: 'I also said that I had advised Gandhi and Congress to hold their hand till it could be seen what attitude the new administration took up but that I should be bound to tell them what my considered view was on this very shortly and that I proposed to do so quite objectively as I certainly should not be any party to misleading them for the sake of peace in India.'[116]

Cripps had one commanding theme, often repeated. He had broached it in his interview with Anderson, now Lord President of the Council: 'whether they were going to try and hold India by all methods of suppression or, by granting self government, going to arrive at a favourable treaty which would regulate the future relations of both countries'. Anderson seemed 'quite aware of the repercussions of the first line of policy upon American opinion and also volunteered the fact that it was contrary to our own democratic professions'.[117] Cripps put the nature of the choice in the same way to the ICG: everything turned on 'the Cabinet's decision about whether they were going to try and hold India by force or make a treaty with a free India'.[118] With the change of government, Cripps reiterated to Halifax, still Foreign Secretary, 'the need for the Cabinet to make up their minds as to whether they were going to try and force India to remain a part of the dominions or rely upon a favourable treaty with a free India'.[119]

After a final interview with Amery on 23 May, Cripps played no further part in these discussions. The stark choice with which he had sought to confront the Cabinet was subsequently fudged rather than faced. Though Amery was to press Linlithgow hard on a full commitment to Dominion status, on support for a constituent assembly, and on a treaty of guarantee – all items in Cripps's agenda – the scale of any change in British policy was successively minimized by the hesitant foot-dragging of the Viceroy, combined with the obdurate resistance of the new Prime Minister. Indeed Churchill went so far as to accuse Amery of having misled the Cabinet and forced him to back down.

By the time the Viceroy was ready to promulgate his new offer in August

116. ibid., 17 May 1940.   117. ibid., 6 May 1940.   118. ibid., 9 May 1940.
119. ibid., 16 May 1940.

1940, it went no further than an affirmation that the 'objective' remained that of Dominion status and a conditional approval of a post-war constitution-making process, with no reference to a treaty. Moreover, a qualification that power could not be transferred to 'any system of government whose authority is directly denied by large and powerful elements in India's national life' was taken as a pledge that the minorities would be allowed a veto.[120] Cripps's low expectations – 'I am sure that Linlithgow will again, with the help of Laithwaite, destroy the possibilities of settlement'[121] – were thus borne out by the 'August offer', which Congress quickly rejected. By August, however, Cripps was to be British ambassador in Moscow.

---

120. Mansergh, *TOP*, i, pp. 877–9, at p. 878; Cmd 6219, 8 August, 1940; see also Moore, *Churchill, Cripps and India*, pp. 31–8, and Louis, *In the Name of God, Go!*, pp. 130–35.
121. RSC diary, 23 May 1940.

3

False Starts

On leaving India, Cripps and Wilson had arrrived in Burma on 26 December 1939 and left Mandalay for China on New Year's Day 1940. The objective of the second phase of their journey was to reach Chungking on the Yangtze Kiang, the headquarters of Chiang Kai-shek, the Generalissimo of the Nationalist forces, which were currently in a precarious alliance with the revolutionary Communist armies in resisting Japanese invasion. From Chungking, Cripps had planned to visit the province of Sinkiang Uighur. This lay deep in the interior, and was shrouded in mystery, not least about whether it was still under effective Chinese control. The possibility of using this trip, which would take him near the Soviet border, to make contact with the Russians obviously lay at the back of Cripps's mind from the start; but only when he was in Chungking was a plan to be improvised for him to fly to Moscow for talks. This obviously stretched the whole itinerary – and while it proved difficult enough for Cripps and Wilson to get to Moscow in February, getting back again turned out to be arduous in the extreme. After this, the journey home, via Hong Kong, Japan, Formosa and the USA (though not Canada, as at one time envisaged), was to be relatively straightforward.

Cripps was a good traveller. India had consumed his professional interest but once he left it, with the pressure now off for the moment, he obviously took the view that it was the journey as well as the arrival that mattered. The magnificent wooded landscapes in the hills on the Burma Road into China are vividly described in the diary – by Wilson, but in terms that echo those used in the correspondence that Cripps sought to maintain, however intermittently and precariously, with his wife. 'It is indescribably lovely,' he told her, adding that 'it is all in the diary'.[1] The diary likewise records first-hand impressions of 'the most fantastic country' revealed below on the flight to Sinkiang.[2] It was clearly Cripps who subsequently rhapsodized the

1. RSC to IC, 5 January 1940.
2. RSC diary, 6 February 1940; all Chinese names as in original.

'indescribably beautiful' effects of snow and sun upon 'the best piece of mountain scenery I have ever seen', adding that 'even G. thought that we had seen something worth seeing at last'.[3] Cripps's ability to turn from the concerns of his political mission and relish his immediate experiences is caught in his comment at one point that 'it's difficult to believe that one is travelling such a road for the purpose of getting to a definite place and not merely for sightseeing'.[4] That he was enjoying himself more than he would have done in London is evident.

Cripps was uncensorious about petty vices. It was not until Hong Kong, on the way home, that he 'discovered that G. was a born gambler and took, like myself, considerable pleasure in risking small sums on the races, with the net result that we came away about 40 dollars (Hong Kong) up . . .'[5] This was on Holy Saturday. Cripps followed his normal rule when on holiday and gave up smoking. But whether the rigours of an ice-bound journey across Russia could be described as a holiday is a moot point; and by then Cripps had succumbed to the habit, admitting in Moscow that 'we had forgotten our cigarettes so I cadged two more boxes, or rather I only cadged one and incited G. to cadge the other'.[6] His self-denial may have been undermined by the Generalissimo's hospitality, since the fact that they had 'even been supplied with smokes' had been worth noting on their entry to China.[7]

Cripps was a teetotaller, and only later was Wilson weaned to 'serious alcohol'.[8] Their abstinence had passed without comment in India but in China became contentious. Indeed, on the arduous journey by road into China, Cripps and Wilson were induced by their hosts to drink brandy, ostensibly as a means of disinfecting the water. It took a couple of days for the penny to drop with Cripps: 'I think the brandy disinfection theory is really nothing more than an excuse to try and make us drink quantities of alcohol and is part of the entertainment technique of Mr Yang-Heng.'[9] Cripps abstained from alcohol even at public dinners where social conventions, notably toasts, demanded some response from the honoured guest. At one dinner in Kunming the British Consul-General was deputed to take Cripps's part in a drinking game of which the latter mildly observed: 'It is a game that not unnaturally is liable to end in drunkenness.'[10]

'I am devoutly glad that I am a teetotaller,' Cripps commented in a letter

3. ibid., 8 February 1940.   4. ibid., 4 January 1940 (by Wilson).
5. ibid., 23 March 1940.   6. ibid., 16 February 1940.
7. RSC to IC, 14 January 1940.
8. While serving under Cripps at the Moscow embassy: Wilson, 'My Working Life', p. 34.
9. RSC diary, 5 January 1940.   10. ibid., 12 January 1940.

home.[11] Only when he reached Russia did his abstemious habits create difficulty. As the guests of the Soviet Government at the Hotel National in Tashkent, he and Wilson were plied with champagne, vodka and wine, provoking an impeccably dry comment that 'for two teetotallers to be faced with such entertainment and to be waited on by a charming waiter who considers the height of hospitality to press the guests to drink as much as possible is indeed embarrassing'.[12]

In China Cripps seems to have been more relaxed than in India in his appreciation of the local cuisine, even overcoming his suspicion that some vegetable dishes might have been prepared using animal fats. Chinese hospitality and ingenuity combined to give their guest lavish banquets, in which the outward appearance of chicken, ham, bacon, liver and fish dishes belied their vegetarian substance. While Cripps showed himself duly appreciative, it is evident that his distinctive diet excited considerable interest from his hosts. Whether through politeness or conviction, Madame Chiang Kai-shek pressed him for details – 'as they both thought that I looked so well on it' – and threatened to impose it on the Generalissimo too.[13] Indeed, later in the year, when Cripps was ambassador in Moscow, the two of them were still exchanging advice on diet.

Cripps repeatedly reported on his health to his wife, reiterating that he was 'very fit' and telling her at the end of the first month that he had taken no pills since leaving home.[14] He must indeed have been fit to withstand such intensive travel, over a long period, sometimes across exotic terrain, and in climates that varied from the tropical to the sub-arctic. In India he and Wilson had spent ten out of nineteen nights on trains – 'we talk all day and travel all night', wrote a weary Wilson.[15] The rough mountain roads, which they traversed for a week between Mandalay and Chungking, were fatiguing. Above all, the ill-starred journey from Chungking to Moscow and back meant travelling 10,000 miles, with few creature comforts, especially for a vegetarian. At Urumchi Cripps 'dined off bread, potatoes, yoghourt and a curious compote of dried fruits which they serve like tea in a glass', while at Alma Ata, the vegetarian menu initially on offer was bread and lard, until 'some excellent locally tinned apricots, some very good chocolates and coffee made a very adequate dinner for me . . .'[16]

If the fare was peculiar at best, the travelling arrangements on the return

11. RSC to IC, 14 January 1940.   12. RSC diary, 13 February 1940.
13. ibid., 16 January 1940; cf. 17 January 1940.   14. RSC to IC, 31 December 1940.
15. RSC diary, 12 December 1939.
16. ibid., 8, 12 February 1940. There is an account of the journey by Cripps in an undated text headed 'Sinkiang'.

journey from Moscow became makeshift in the extreme. The first stages were in intermittently unheated aircraft, with outdoor temperatures as low as –30C. Cripps and Wilson were stranded at snowbound airfields, on occasion for days at a time, in rough accommodation, and sometimes with only scraps of food. Then, as the temperature rose, the thaw bogged down their aircraft on the grass runways. Instead they took to a car, covering 400 miles in thirty-seven hours on the rocky track between Ili and Urumchi, sometimes with Cripps taking over as driver, and with the windshield open for visibility, and with ropes lashed round the tyres for traction – only to find that the Urumchi airfield was no better. Another drive of equal length therefore faced them, after a day's rest, during which jointly compiling a full record in the diary had clearly become a self-sustaining, time-consuming, tedium-destroying end in itself.

Wilson's account of one overnight stop at Kuybyshev (Samara), after a day with nothing to eat since an early breakfast, captures the mood as much as the conditions:

Before the food came we made enquiries as to the conveniences available and the custodian demonstrated to us by breaking a match in pieces that the toilet arrangments had come to grief, and he then searched in the English–Russian diction-ary until he found the phrase 'the windows look out on the street' and underlined with a match the words 'on the street', meaning thereby that we could utilise the natural resources of the very cold outer world for our needs which we proceeded to do. This is not quite so pleasant as it sounds with a bitterly cold wind and a temperature many degrees below zero and deep snow everywhere except on the well trodden paths just by the house. The rest can be left to the imagination, except that both of us nearly died laughing during the process.[17]

This is a picture of a surprisingly robust and resilient man. There was naturally the odd day of stomach upsets or diarrhoea, when he might turn in early for the night, but Cripps suffered no more illness on the whole journey than his much younger companion. 'Stafford is still bearing up in the most marvellous way and says that he feels as fit as a fiddle,' Wilson told Isobel from his own sickbed in Chungking – and speaking just too soon.[18] For it was now that Cripps succumbed, albeit for only a matter of days. He was diagnosed as suffering from a severe bilious chill, with a temperature of 103F, and noted grimly that his Chinese guide – 'Poor Mr Hsia was taken ill with the same thing the next day but his temperature

17. ibid, 17 February 1940.   18. Wilson to IC, 17 January 1940.

went to 105' – fared no better.[19] Covertly, perhaps competitively, Cripps resorted to homeopathic remedies to restore him to health. 'That is that and I am glad that the incident is closed,' he wrote briskly on resuming his duties in the diary – hardly an exaggerated response to a nasty bout of illness, albeit the sort of affliction liable to beset any traveller.

Cripps missed exercise when cooped up on trains and liked to walk when he could, especially in Chungking where the alternative was being carried in a chair. 'I can't somehow cotton to the idea of making Human beings beasts of burden to that extent.'[20] On arrival at the airport, built on an island in the Yangtze, he made the exhausting climb of 400 steps up to the city on its rocky bluff rather than take a chair; and the British ambassador, Archibald Clark Kerr, at once put himself in Cripps's good books for taking him out for a long walk – 'we did 1¾ hours quite steady going producing so far as I am concerned a very good skin action as my old man used to say'.[21]

Cripps could relax – but on his own terms, in his own way, and in his own time. He was indeed a keen time-keeper, as his officials in post-war Whitehall were to discover if they blundered into a meeting late. On his world tour, Cripps noticed even a few minutes' delay in the appointed time for meals. Once more he found that his Russian experience tempered him, admitting in Alma Ata that 'as far as I was concerned I should regard all my family as models of punctuality when I returned to England'.[22] Though undisguisably taxing in his expectations, Cripps was also manifestly good company. Admittedly, on one long air journey he plainly had little time for 'the "jolly" man of the party who does his best to keep us all amused'; Wilson's comment was that 'S. and I are rather high-hat about it'.[23]

If necessary, Cripps could become 'magnificently haughty' as part of his tactics to avert yet another intensive search of baggage and scrutiny of documents on re-entering China from Russia.[24] But he was far from pompous. At an otherwise intimate dinner where his Chinese hosts punctiliously observed the full etiquette of prepared orations and elaborate toasts, Cripps recorded that 'G. and I were afraid to look at one another as there was something undefinably comic in the formality of a speech at such a small party'.[25] Not only was Cripps able to relate quickly to the dignitaries whom he visited but he also showed himself ready to strike up cordial relations with all sorts of people – old and young, men and women, but especially the latter in each case.

19. RSC diary, 30 January 1940.   20. ibid., 16 January 1940.   21. ibid.
22. ibid., 13 February 1940.   23. ibid., 28 March 1940.   24. ibid., 1 March 1940.
25. ibid., 26 February 1940.

Wilson observed this particular bias with wry amusement. 'We have both been greatly struck especially by the gracefulness of the women, partly due to their costume the sari,' he had recorded judiciously in Hyderabad.[26] And when, after a wearing overnight journey, they reached the Gupta residence in Calcutta to begin the day's work, he noted: 'S. found it considerably lightened by the discovery that our host's daughter was, as he put it, a peach, which he later explained as referring to her cultural and intellectual abilities.'[27] At his leisure on Christmas Day – 'For once we have had an easy day' – Cripps returned to the diary himself in reflective vein. 'One of my major tasks,' he expatiated, 'has been to try and provide suitable young companionship for Geoff and so far it has been fairly successful. Miss Gupta performed the service in Calcutta, young Mrs Desai in Bombay and before that Mrs Bannerjee.'[28] Tongue in cheek, aimed at his co-author rather than any other reader, Cripps's comments adopted a jesting tone; but it was a running joke that he was happy to share and prolong because he always saw the point of it.

Learning in Delhi that Felicity Gwyer, the niece of the Chief Justice, was bound for Burma, Cripps suggested that she join his party. His feeling that she would be 'a nice young girl friend for Geoff.'[29] was duly borne out – 'Felicity, as she has now become, S. and I rode in one car and the others followed independently', on the journey from Mandalay.[30] Cripps himself found her a travelling companion whom he was sad to lose at Chungking; and on the last night, which the Chinese drinking game made more convivial even for non-players, 'F. was very talkative after dinner as the result of playing the game and told me that she was a socialist but never quite understood what socialism was.'[31] No doubt the defects in her political education were agreeably repaired; and, soon enough, Cripps was to discover a more sophisticated political confidante in Chungking itself – the French fiancée of a resident British businessman, Mlle Cosmé, who disclosed Communist sympathies which Cripps enjoyed debating with her.

That intellectual stimulation was not Cripps's only susceptibility was shown on his long Russian journey, in seeking any diversion rather than further endless games of bezique. In Aktiobinsk, Wilson made pointed reference to 'a charming girl whom S. always calls "my dear" and who wears a red handkerchief round her head and has already changed her dress

26. ibid., 17 December 1939.   27. ibid., 22 December 1939.
28. ibid., 25 December 1939.   29. RSC to IC, 31 December 1939.
30. RSC diary, 1 January 1940; cf. 12 December 1939.   31. ibid., 12 January 1940.

for our benefit'.[32] A couple of days later, there was room in the diary for Cripps to record that Wilson had telephoned 'a very fascinating young woman whom he has discovered in the basement and who looks after our arrangements' – a blatant riposte from his co-author. 'Fortunately she has been able to keep him amused most of the day,' Cripps bantered. 'These little events are his only perquisites as secretary.'[33] Another couple of days and it was Wilson's turn to comment, this time on a supper 'which is being produced by another of S.'s young women to whom he proposes to give one of our very precious chocolates'.[34] Six weeks later, now making the long homeward flight across the USA, Wilson paused to observe that 'S. was greatly struck by the charm of the air-hostesses of whom we had four during the course of the trip'.[35]

That such observations were the product of the longueurs of an often tedious itinerary, rather than of any impropriety on Cripps's part, speaks for itself. This was no secret diary; Cripps knew that it would be read by his wife and daughter Theresa, to whom sections were sent via the diplomatic bag. Any mild sexual innuendo simply echoed comments by Cripps in earlier diaries. Equally transparently, behind his rimless spectacles and his dialectical manner, here was a man more attentive to the sexually charged by-play of his social contacts than his public stereotype might suggest.

While in Burma, *en route* to China, Cripps was treated respectfully by the British authorities, though he declined the use of a staff car in Mandalay as 'rather too much of a good thing'.[36] He had been met in Rangoon by the personal adviser to Generalissimo Chiang Kai-shek, William Donald. A former journalist for American and English papers, he quickly won Cripps's confidence as 'a really delightful & humorous person with a bit of "devil" in him'.[37] Donald became Cripps's primary source of information on Chinese politics, especially in relation to the armed struggle for the control of China that had begun with the Japanese invasion of Manchuria in 1932. Donald's own story, Cripps observed on hearing it, was 'so amazing that it would seem incredible unless one were prepared to believe him, which I am certainly prepared to do, as I feel certain that he is perfectly straight and honest'.[38] It was a judgement that became infused with real personal warmth as they worked together in Chungking, and manifestly coloured Cripps's perceptions of China.

32. ibid., 14 February 1940.   33. ibid., 16 February 1940.   34. ibid., 18 February 1940.
35. ibid., 1, 2 April 1940.   36. ibid., 30 December 1939.
37. RSC to IC, 31 December 1939.   38. RSC diary, 9 January 1940; cf. 16 January 1940.

It was Donald who superintended the journey by road from Mandalay to Kunming, but he himself left the party at Lashio, only rejoining it at Kunming. A cryptic telegram informed Cripps of the change of plan but left him in the dark about Donald's reasons.[39] The story he told on their reunion at once tested Cripps's credence and enhanced Donald's romantic credentials. It seemed that there had been a message for Donald from the Generalissimo; 'he was to return to Kunming at once by air as the Japs had a plot to assassinate him on the road'; pausing only to satisfy himself that the rest would be spared, he had complied.[40] Cripps's programme of relevant fact-gathering had meanwhile proceeded in all innocence, with a pause *en route*, to inspect an aircraft factory that had been moved into the safety of the western hills from its exposed position on the east coast at Hangchow.

Whether the guards of honour marked the importance of Cripps's visit for a regime badly in need of international support (as he first supposed) or represented a precautionary tightening of personal security (as he later came to think), the VIP treatment was again clearly signalled. Customs formalities were waived and the government paid for excess baggage on the air flight from Kunming to Chungking. At factory visits banners were hung out, saying in English, 'Welcome Sir Stafford'. Chinese bands struggled with 'God Save the King'.

Donald had been determined to make a success of the visit. With a flat in the building next to the Chiangs, with whom he took all his meals, Donald was clearly in a position of great influence. It was through 'Don', and in his company, that Cripps met the Generalissimo and Madame Chiang Kai-shek, and this doubtless conduced to the highly favourable impression that they made on Cripps. 'They are both dears and I felt completely at home,' Stafford confided to Isobel.[41] 'I have come to love the Chinese more than ever even with all their faults,' he wrote in the diary, 'but especially the young and clean ones that embody the new China and of whom Madame is the outstanding example. She is extraordinarily intelligent and superbly kind to everyone and full of courage and initiative often in the most difficult circumstances.'[42]

Cripps's response may seem unexpected. After all, 'the G.' was the leader, and his (American-educated) wife notoriously the *eminence grise*, of the Kuomintang regime, which was depicted in Communist propaganda as a reactionary force – and not much of a force at that, in view of the Japanese takeover of much of the eastern seaboard of China. Cripps was later ready

---

39. Telegram, 2 January 1940, PRO, CAB 127/59.   40. RSC diary, 8 January 1940.
41. RSC to IC, 16 January 1940.   42. RSC diary, 16 January 1940.

to acknowledge that the Kuomintang was 'a totalitarian party: that is to say it believes in a one-party system'.[43] Precisely because this was so, as Cripps put it in the report which he later presented to the British Government, it had affinities with the Russian Communists; but in comparison, the Kuomintang's relatively looser discipline meant that 'its relationship to its members is much more like that in the British Labour Party' – perhaps an ambiguous accolade from its famous ex-member.[44] Moreover, he applauded Madame Chiang's New Life Movement as 'in essence a puritanical movement' and reaffirmed his confidence that the Generalissimo had a strategic commitment to reform, albeit tempered by characteristically tortuous tactics.[45]

Some of Cripps's early views of Nationalist China were distinctly rose-tinted. The Chinese won his admiration for 'cheerfully making the best of it' under adverse conditions. 'It is a tragedy as they are such gallant and courageous people and one does so long to help them,' he told Isobel.[46] He was progressively led into a rather indulgent account of some of the industrial conditions he inspected, which might not have survived the scrutiny of his trade-union supporters in Bristol. 'In the match factory we saw some little children of ten working 9 hours a day, but they were not being pushed as they were on piece work and could do as much as they liked or as little.'[47]

To a greater or lesser extent, all Cripps's perceptions were influenced by the fact that China was fighting for its survival against Japanese aggression. This was the context, and sometimes the extenuation, for what he observed on his visits to factories and colleges alike. 'To any one who knows the refinements of modern Chemical technique it is amazing that university standards can be taught as they are being under such circumstances,' he wrote after a visit to an improvised laboratory. 'It is only another example of the cheerful determination that we have experienced anywhere [sc. every-where] to continue the cultural and economic life of the country no matter what the Japs do.'[48]

'Japs' haunt the pages of Cripps's diary. They were a constant threat, but one that could, he hoped, be contained and beaten back. Cripps's hopes helped lend credence to a widespread belief, at least in the circles in which

43. 'The situation in the Far East', address distributed by the National Peace Council, 9 May 1940.
44. RSC, 'Report on the Position in China', par. 39. Cripps's report on China, running to 175 paragraphs, was later printed for official circulation.
45. RSC, 'Report on the Position in China', par. 20; cf. par. 5.
46. RSC to IC, 16 January 1940.   47. RSC diary, 18 January 1940.
48. ibid., 9 January 1940.

he now moved, that the war was actually going better for the Chinese than most British sources claimed. The *Daily Herald* carried one optimistic statement from him under the headline 'Cripps Backs Chinese'.[49] In particular, Cripps was persuaded that the extent of Japanese control of mainland China had been exaggerated, and that five-sixths of the country remained under Chinese control. 'One appreciated from the daily News bulletins which I get from Don every day or twice a day that there is continuous fighting going on all over the place, that the Japs are constantly losing men by the hundred and that all this must be wearing them down gradually.'[50] He was therefore ready to subscribe to the opinion that 'the best help that the Chinese had had was from the Japs because their indescribable bestiality had driven the Chinese to combine and to revolutionise their methods for the one purpose of defeating the Jap.'[51]

The friction between the Government and the Communists was obvious to Cripps, who turned initially to Donald to explain it: 'He is very much opposed to the communists, and says that he thinks they are holding up their armies from doing much as they want to have them for action after the Japanese are defeated so as to conquer the rest of China and get power.'[52] Worrying away at this problem, Cripps had pressed for a fuller account. 'The Communists,' Donald said, 'were in possession of a part of the North west and at the beginning of the war could easily have been wiped out by the Central Govt's troops, but they instead came to an arrangement with them.'[53] Formally, there was a common front, but on the ground there was clearly friction, the sources of which it took time for Cripps to discern.

Cripps heartily approved of the British ambassador, Archibald Clark Kerr, who was 'most advanced in his views & very sympathetic with the Communists'.[54] This did not imply, however, that Cripps endorsed the Communist position, still less doctrinaire Marxism. Chiang Kai-shek, of course, was difficult to read, especially by a left-wing westerner whose good opinion the Generalissimo was assiduously wooing. 'He is obviously of opinion that communism is unsuitable for China at this stage and I agree with him,' Cripps noted, rather ingenuously.[55] It was through the British embassy that Cripps met a group of Chinese Communists in Chungking.

49. *Daily Herald*, 13 March 1940.
50. RSC diary, 16 January 1940; cf. RSC, 'Report on the Position in China', par. 27.
51. RSC diary, 17 January 1940; cf. RSC, 'Report on the Position in China', par. 21.
52. RSC diary, 14 January 1940.   53. ibid., 16 January 1940.
54. RSC to IC, 16 January 1940. Clark Kerr subsequently succeeded Cripps as ambassador to the Soviet Union.
55. RSC diary, 16 January 1940.

'They agreed,' he noted blandly, 'that the industrialisation of China had not gone nearly far enough for a proletarian revolution to succeed.'[56] As reported by Cripps, this view was not radically different from the Generalissimo's opinion (again as reported by Cripps). More to the point, it was not far from his own.

The arm's-length nature of Cripps's attitude to Communism needs to be stressed, the more so in the light of his recent experiences in India, inducing scepticism over the universalism of Marxist analysis. When he came up against party-line Communism – as argued (somewhat playfully) by his confidante Mlle Cosmé – Cripps evidently contested its assumptions, noting that Mlle Cosmé 'was obliged to admit that in practice the theoretical marxist view did not seem to work out in its complete absolutism'.[57] Bringing Communists into a popular front, whether in France, Britain, India or China, was another matter. It is not surprising, therefore, to find Cripps advising a Kuomintang Government minister that 'for the good of the Country and even for the Government itself it would be much better if the Communists were to be given a seat in the Executive Yuan [cabinet]'.[58] Cripps stopped short only of actually terming this a proposal for a Government of National Concentration.

The problem – whether obstacle or enigma – that he was increasingly brought to acknowledge lay in the attitude of the Kuomintang leadership. It was not just that 'the old gang' could not appreciate the need for action and would impede any moves by the Generalissimo: even Madame Chiang Kai-shek's credentials lost some of their pristine allure. Cripps approved of the work of the Chinese Industrial Cooperatives, which he knew was suspect in the USA as a communist front, but was at any rate an organization independent of the Government. After seeing their activities in Szechuan, Cripps tried to interest Madame Chiang in their progress, only to encounter a riposte about 'what excellent work her own co-ops were doing'. For Cripps, this simply went to confirm what Mlle Cosmé had alleged only the previous evening:

the fear of the Kuomintang of the effect of any popularly inspired effort by other than themselves is such that it makes them hostile to the effort and leads them to attempt to set up some rival organisation to cope with the same sort of popular feeling – a disastrous policy, I think, as it antagonises incipient effort which might well be harnessed behind the G. if it were treated sympathetically, and also by dividing the effort diminishes the effect. The insistence upon strict orthodoxy reminded me

56. ibid., 18 January 1940.   57. ibid., 1 February 1940.   58. ibid., 19 January 1940.

of the Labour Party's attitude in G.B. – to descend from the sublime problems of China's future to the – from this distance – ridiculous squabbles of British politicians.[59]

He did not turn against the Chiangs. 'They really are perfect dears, so kind and simple and natural and such really good friends,' as Stafford continued to assure Isobel.[60] But, sadly, he came to recognize that a real popular front against the Japanese was impossible. Not only did he prepare memoranda on transport and supply problems that were politely received by the Generalissimo – 'he had my memo. on gasoline and had passed it forward with instructions for it to be put into operation'[61] – but Cripps was also invited to envisage a more permanent role for himself in Chungking.

The invitation was broached as early as 20 January and was to be repeated at intervals. Though it took Cripps by surprise, it caught him at an opportune moment. 'So small a degree of help here might now make all the difference to the outcome of this war and the whole future of the world – yet nothing is done, it is like flogging a dead horse or a dying one,' Cripps wrote home. 'It all makes me feel very inclined to accept the offer to come out here for a year and do my individual best, especially if I can find a really effective group of people who can work with me from the other end.'[62]

Donald apparently infused a note of caution: 'that it was remarkable that the G. should have asked me on his own as this was most unusual, but warned me against the fate of other advisers who had been broken hearted by their inability to get things done'.[63] Since Cripps was charged with producing another memorandum, this time on the role of foreign advisers, his recommendation that there must be a strong chairman can be seen as a draft of a possible job specification for himself. An open-ended invitation to occupy a decisive position in the government of China obviously appealed to Cripps's *amour propre* at a time when nobody in Britain seemed to want his services. So long as he was in China, he took the proposal seriously – for want of alternatives; only later did he recognize it as another false start.

In Chungking, Cripps had made an early call on the Soviet ambassador, to whom Maisky had given him an introduction. Since Cripps's departure from England, the USSR had invaded Finland in the Winter War, and this act of aggression had generated widespread resentment and hostility in

59. ibid., 1 February 1940.   60. RSC to IC, 4 February 1940.
61. RSC diary, 1 February 1940.   62. RSC to IC, 29 January 1940.
63. RSC diary, 3 February 1940.

Britain, in Labour as much as Conservative quarters. The week after Cripps's departure, *Tribune* had carried a manifesto in the name of the board – comprising Bevan, Strauss and, of course, Cripps himself – which was scornful of official Soviet allegations about Finnish provocation. Its scathing tone – 'Chickens don't hunt wolves' – was attributed by the Communist *Daily Worker* to Bevan's alleged readiness, while seeking readmission to the Labour Party, to align himself with 'Lord Halifax, Mussolini and Transport House'.[64]

There remained, however, an intriguing silence over the position of the peripatetic Cripps. In the *Evening Standard*, Londoner's Diary assumed that Cripps must be a supporter of the Finns – 'His newspaper, the *Tribune*, is publishing violent attacks on the Russians' – and reported that the Communists were accordingly now trying to discredit their old comrade.[65] Yet, in the absence of definite news, a quizzical paragraph in another British paper caught a sharper tone of interrogation: 'It would be interesting to know what the Socialist K.C. thinks about Russia now, and whether his allegiance to the Soviet has stood the test of the Russian invasion.'[66]

In the light of the Finnish confrontation, it is understandable that, at their meeting in Chungking, the Russian ambassador should ask Cripps whether there was any likelihood of Britain and Germany combining against Russia. 'I thought this was a rather odd question,' Cripps noted, though had he been more adequately informed of the deterioration in Anglo-Russian relations, he might not have been quite so surprised. Cripps had his own question on Finland: 'I told him that many friends of Russia thought that she should have waited to get the readjustments that she wanted without copying the Nazi methods of aggression, and that I should like to know what he thought was the answer that should be given to those who accused the Russians of imperialism.' The answer he received was that Russia had been forced to act to protect its own security and had no ambitions to annexe territory, only to protect the people of Finland. Cripps seems to have thought – or at least argued – that a categorical and official declaration on these lines would have helped. 'I told him that the Russians often seemed to overlook the difficulties of their friends in other countries who were of some value to them and that they ought to make such a statement for that purpose.'[67]

This was the statement of a temporarily embarrassed and candid friend

---

64. *Tribune*, 8 December 1939; *Daily Worker*, 13 December 1939.
65. *Evening Standard*, 8 January 1940. Estorick (1941), p. 224, likewise argued that, in the absence of any statement by Cripps expressing disagreement with the *Tribune* board, 'it can be assumed that he accepted at least its main outlines'.
66. *Manchester Evening News*, 6 March 1940.   67. RSC diary, 17 January 1940.

of the Soviet Union rather than its suddenly disillusioned critic. No more than the Nazi–Soviet pact, nor than the Russian invasion of Poland, did the Winter War diminish Cripps's ardour for better Anglo-Russian relations. Indeed, by January 1940 he was ready with a full rationale for his pro-Soviet attitude. His journey had given him the time to engage in a formal reappraisal of the course of international relations; invitations to speak gave him the opportunity to expound it. The speech he gave to 1,200 students at Kunming University on 12 January 1940 – expressly without press reporting – and substantially repeated to an audience of 1,500 at Chungking University on 3 February, was hailed in Estorick's biography as 'the greatest of his career'.[68] It remains a revealing text, both lucid and explicit in its exposition.

As usual, Cripps invoked an interpretation of international conflict as a product of capitalism and imperialism. He took it for granted that 'Great Britain had no special advantages in the competition [for markets] except her imperial connections', but argued that there was now a clash of priorities between Britain's interests (in maintaining the Empire) and the interests of a capitalist class, intent since 1931 on confronting the Soviet Union. Hence the Conservatives' loss of confidence, producing a foreign policy that was 'more and more opportune and always hovering between a desire to destroy or to protect themselves from the Russian Revolution and a desire to maintain the integrity of the British Empire'. The policy of appeasement had been adopted not through love (or even fear) of Hitler, but because the Government misguidedly saw Hitler as a bulwark against Bolshevism. And it was this that generated an important division within the Conservative ranks, with Churchill speaking for those who saw the real threat as 'coming from a very rapidly rearming Germany with the result that they were even prepared to combine with Russia to protect the Empire'. The Churchill paradox – that precisely because he was strongly pro-imperialist he was therefore relatively pro-Soviet – informed many of Cripps's perceptions and significantly influenced his relations with Churchill throughout this period.

Cripps adopted a righteous, even self-righteous, tone in explicating the British Government's error. 'You would find if you were to read the Hansard Report of the proceedings of the House of Commons,' he assured the ranks of Chinese students before him, 'literally hundreds of columns of protest by myself and others in the Opposition accompanied by explicit warnings that the end would be exactly as has now happened in Europe.' Chamberlain's failure to offer Poland proper guarantees (backed by Russia), and his

68. Estorick, p. 242. He prints the Chungking speech *in extenso*, pp. 242–9, but omits the pertinent references to Churchill. My quotations are from the Kunming text.

decision instead, for electioneering reasons, to issue an unrealistic pledge was the sorry outcome. It was in this unsatisfactory context that Soviet actions had to be understood. The fact was that 'the Russian foreign policy had completely changed and had become one of true realpolitik in which the safety and peace of Russia was the over-riding factor'. Weighing up the balance of power and advantage, prudential considerations on every side 'made it inevitable almost that Russia would arrive at an agreement with Germany if that were possible'.

Yet the man who claimed to have foreseen the Nazi–Soviet pact, and to have predicted the invasion of Poland, was not prepared to say that the Winter War was also inevitable. Cripps stated the strategic case for the Russians' protection of their own security and blamed the Finns for refusing a negotiated settlement. But he acknowledged that 'Russia then committed the extreme folly of attacking Finland and pretending that she was doing so at the request of the Finnish people.' This was not a cause for indignation so much as for sorrow. Russia had 'thus sacrificed the good opinion, which despite all her mistakes, she had in the minds of millions of people in the world'. The invasion had thus put the Soviet Government on a moral par with 'all the anti-Red Governments of Europe', who now gave Finland a measure of support that they had withheld from the democratic regimes of 'Austria, Czechoslovakia, Abyssinia, Albania, Spain, or even China, when these countries were attacked by fascist aggression'.

Cripps's own view of 'the curious war that is no war between Germany and the western democracies' reflected the detached moral relativism of his analysis. 'I am certain the people of none of the countries want to fight,' he maintained, 'and they don't know what they are fighting about or what good can possibly come out of it.' Cripps offered two speculations about what might happen next: a prescient suggestion that Germany might try to break the stalemate on the western front in the spring, and the less plausible scenario that Hitler might turn Communist.

The fact that Cripps thus maintained his stance as a friend of the Soviet Union throughout the Winter War and the 'phoney war' further isolated him, in his absence, from the British Labour Party and from British public opinion. What he was saying was very similar to what the British Foreign Office was hearing from the Russians themselves: 'that in the jungle the strangest of animals got together if they felt their joint interests made this advisable'.[69]

*

69. Maisky's conversation with Butler, 30 January 1940, quoted in Woodward, *British Foreign Policy*, i, p. 108.

Cripps naturally exploited his sympathetic stance to enlist the help of the Soviet ambassador in Chungking in facilitating further travel. In view of Sinkiang's delicate status, Cripps needed Russian permission to visit the province. This was, to his surprise, quickly granted. Cripps also took his opportunity to ask, somewhat tentatively, if it might be possible to meet Soviet officials – little knowing how opportune such a suggestion was. For his request came at a time when Soviet diplomacy was seeking some way of thawing out relations with Britain and France, which had frozen rock-solid as a result of the Winter War. On the mistaken supposition that Cripps was officially sanctioned by the British Government, an invitation to the Kremlin itself was unexpectedly forthcoming.[70]

Because of the delay in receiving this positive response, the convalescent Geoffrey Wilson had time to complete his recovery in the Chungking Canadian hospital and was, after all, fit enough to join Cripps on the expedition. A fortnight thus elapsed, with constantly changing plans, and an increasing preoccupation with the acquisition of warm clothes and furs – coats, gloves, ear-flaps, knee-boots – all desirable for Sinkiang and, as it turned out, indispensable for Moscow. Madame Chiang Kai-shek took an interest, having both Cripps and Wilson measured for lined suits by her personal tailor. Thus attired, on 6 February 1940 they set out from Chungking, bound for Sinkiang, *en route* to Moscow. 'S. has gone completely native in the matter of clothing, and was wearing Madam's suit of rompers, his fur lined Chinese dressing gown, felt boots, a fur cap, and Don's scarf and walking-stick,' Wilson recorded.[71]

Sinkiang turned out to be the least eventful part of the trip. The flight plan took them north from Chungking to Chengtu, then high over the Himalayas to Lanchow and on to Urumchi via Hami. But starting off thirty hours late they got no further than Chengtu on the first day, then had to divert to Suzhou (now Jiuquan, near Jiayuguan) for another day, and only reached Urumchi, the capital of Sinkiang, on 8 February: a journey of 2,000 miles that should have been a warning about the remaining 8,000. The fact that, although Russian cultural influence was strong, the province was clearly under Chinese control was quickly made clear to Cripps and Wilson. This may have made reassuring news for their Chinese hosts on their return, but since sovereignty was testified partly by an officiously thorough customs inspection of all their baggage, including the precious diary, it was a mixed blessing for the travellers themselves, who began to get bored. Under virtual house arrest, however courteously it was enforced, Cripps threw himself

70. Gorodetsky, *Mission to Moscow*, pp. 19–20.   71. RSC diary, 6 February 1940.

into the composition of his plan for reconstituting the government of China, while itching to get to Moscow.

In the official report later sent to Lord Halifax, Cripps set down his account of how the invitation for talks in the Kremlin had been engineered through the Russian ambassador in Chungking: 'I consequently felt it my duty to undertake the journey to Moscow though it entailed a 6,000 mile flight over some of the coldest and worst country in the world.'[72] He did not add that, in a moment of hubris, he had told the ambassador 'I could only spare five days at the utmost in going to Russia.'[73] Cripps had initially been told that the plane that would pick him up at Alma Ata would take one and a half days to fly direct to Moscow; after talks, and a similarly expeditious return journey, he would thus be back in Chungking by 23 February, seventeen days after leaving. In fact there were cumulative delays that put back this schedule by ten days. Across the Soviet border, Cripps was given unstinting official hospitality (albeit tempered by the often severe climatic and topographical limitations) which was just as well in view of the fact that he and Wilson seem to have had no local currency from beginning to end.

They finally arrived in Moscow on 15 February. The first that Isobel Cripps knew of the visit was from *The Times* report three weeks later, with Cripps's comment that it was 'of a purely private character'.[74] The British ambassador had been withdrawn at the end of December. At no point did Cripps make contact with the residual staff in the British embassy; this was perhaps just as well, given the Government's view that the trip was untimely.[75] The fact remains that, until Cripps arrived in Moscow, there had been virtually no British contacts with the Soviet Government since the ambassador's withdrawal. On arrival, Cripps had been met by Michael Tichomerov of the Soviet Foreign Office. Clearing the agenda with him, Cripps gained an impression of anxiety for some kind of rapprochement with Great Britain, though he was not in a position to appreciate what the Russian concern really was. 'I told him of the current belief in G.B. that Hitler might turn communist in order to get a military alliance with Russia,' Cripps wrote in the diary; and the dismissive response to this suggestion was consistent with the tenor of the whole conversation in suggesting that 'the German association was only looked upon as a temporary expedient'.

72. Report on meeting with Molotov, copy in RSC diary, written 3 March 1940; also FO 371/24846, 4 March 1940 (N 2779).
73. RSC diary, 1 February 1940.   74. *The Times*, 6 March 1940.
75. Gorodetsky, *Mission to Moscow*, p. 22.

Molotov agreed to see Cripps at 5 p.m. on 16 February in the Foreign Minister's magnificent office in the Kremlin – 'very up to date and most beautifully furnished and decorated, the best government offices I have seen anywhere in the world'.[76] They talked for one and three-quarter hours. The topics they covered were circumscribed by what Cripps had outlined the previous day, and he found Molotov unwilling to be drawn further without the kind of close and cautious preparation for which he was famous. What came across was Molotov's view that, all along, the British Government had been hostile to Russia, and that this was why initiatives for détente, notably the proposed Stanley trade mission, had come to nothing. Finland constituted a problem on both sides: Molotov arguing that there was no plan for sovietization and that Britain had been meddling here in a way inimical to Russian security; Cripps arguing that it was the Finnish war itself that had changed the situation and made a rapprochement more difficult. While Cripps made sure that he represented Molotov's points in his report to Halifax, he also made it clear there – and much more fully in his own diary account – that he disagreed with Molotov on this point and had contested it with him. When Cripps also pressed about fears of Russian designs on either India or China, Molotov dismissed these as equally ridiculous in either case.

'Throughout his conversation,' Cripps's report concluded, 'Molotov seemed to speak quite frankly to me as a friend of the Soviet Union in spite of my criticism of Russia's action in Finland, and I think that what he told me was with a genuine idea of giving me to understand the Russian attitude.'[77] It was two weeks before this report could be typed up on Cripps's return and transmitted from Chungking to London. In the Foreign Office it evoked a sceptical reaction, of which Cripps naturally had no inkling at the time. The official view was that, since immediate Soviet interests were well served by the pact with Hitler, the Russians were, as usual, simply reinsuring themselves through a purported readiness to talk to the Allies – and 'appear to have found a willing tool in Sir Stafford Cripps'.[78]

On the spot, Cripps's own response was optimistic, perhaps determinedly so. 'I feel that the interview was worth while, not only in elucidating the present Russian position vis-à-vis G.B. but also in establishing a relationship between myself and the Russian government which should enable me to

76. RSC diary, 16 February 1940.
77. Report on meeting with Molotov, copy in RSC diary.
78. Fitzroy Maclean, 6 March 1940, FO 371/24846, quoted in Hanak, 'Cripps as British ambassador' (part 1, 1979), p. 55, which provides a useful account.

work more effectively for Russian British friendship.'[79] Having gone to such lengths for the sake of a hundred minutes of conversation, Cripps stuck to this view, despite the escalating difficulties of the journey home.

Departing from Moscow on 17 February, Cripps and Wilson took five days to fly back in short hops to Alma Ata as the weather closed in, only to meet further disappointments as they struggled on to Ili, and then, abandoning the plane, going on by car. 'And so back to Urumchi 13 days after we had left it, when we expected to be back in a week at the very outsider.'[80] Not until reaching the Singkian city of Hami, on the old silk road, did they take to the air again and manage to reach Lanchow on 2 March.

At Lanchow Cripps was received by the Governor, whose good news from the front – 'the Japanese had shot their bolt' – was as cheering as his hospitality. Their stressful journey behind them, it became transmuted, understandably enough, into an epic tale. It may have appeared 'much more romantic to others than it does to us', as Cripps modestly put it.[81] None the less it made a story which he was induced to 'tell on at least a dozen occasions with only minor variations of detail', according to Wilson. ('Sometime I'm thinking of trying to tell it to someone myself,' he added.) 'It all seems so hum-drum to us now that it's difficult to realize that all these people regard it as the most terrific adventure and treat us as though we had just returned from the South Pole or a successful expedition up Mount Everest.'[82]

On his return to Chungking on 3 March, Cripps was distressed to learn that Chinese politics had meanwhile taken a turn for the worse from his point of view. A representative of the Chinese Industrial Cooperatives, Rewi Alley, joined with John Alexander of the British embassy, whom Cripps likewise regarded as a trustworthy source, to tell him of the growing hostility between the Kuomintang and the Communists. Alley's story, that 'the forcible suppression of the Communists is going to be continued, many having already been liquidated by violent means', was apparently confirmed by documents from the Generalissimo's headquarters. 'Both he and Alexander thought that the only person who could do anything was the G. but that he was himself too much imbued with the feudalist ideas to tackle the problem with any thoroughness.' This betokened a wholly different political configuration from that which Cripps had hoped might develop

79. RSC diary, 16 February 1940.   80. ibid., 24-25 February 1940.
81. ibid., 3 March 1940.   82. ibid., 4 March 1940 (dated 3 March).

(possibly under his own benign tutelage). 'Apparently the words "unity front" are now prohibited in the press,' he noted sadly.[83]

In his subsequent formal report on the situation in China, Cripps mentioned this incident, apparently crediting at face value the assurances of Han Lih Wu, one of Chiang's lieutenants, that the offending circular had been issued in contravention of the Generalissimo's own wishes, 'but that somehow or other it had got out'.[84] The contemporary diary gives a different impression of what passed between Cripps and Han, a liberal official of anti-Communist disposition, with Cripps lecturing him 'that it was no good talking of unity and combination unless the KMT were prepared to make some concessions to the demands of the communists, and certainly you could not get unity on the basis of the suppression of the communists'. According to Cripps's diary, Han professed that someone should talk to the Generalissimo about it, 'but in view of my known political sympathies he doubted if I was the right person'.[85]

This was hardly a promising prelude to Cripps's farewell dinner with the Generalissimo on the evening of 4 March. Cripps's views were solicited, as before, and his latest memorandum, that on foreign advisers, duly commended. Indeed there was a reiterated invitation for Cripps to serve as their chairman. But there was, too, a sense of the situation slipping away.

The next morning, before his departure from Chungking, Cripps had a final meeting with Dr Sun Fo, seemingly one of the most attractive members of the Government and – unusually – sympathetic to the Communist leadership. 'The communist programme at the moment,' he maintained, 'is merely for a democratic government carrying on the war against the Japs, the liquidation of feudalism, and getting rid of the old evils of Chinese officialdom.'[86] In claiming this as 'really the succession policy to that of Sun Yat Sen', Sun Fo spoke as his son and as a possible future leader himself. Sun Fo impressed upon Cripps that he should accept the Generalissimo's invitation and that (as Stafford put it to Isobel) 'he thought I was perhaps the only man, if in that position, who could bring about a solution of China's very acute internal political differences (between the Kuomintang & Communists) which are at the moment a very urgent and dangerous threat to Chinese unity!'[87] Moved and flattered by this appeal, and otherwise unemployed, Cripps yet again felt the tug of temptation.

Escaping the political field of force in Chungking, which he found

83. ibid., 3 March 1940.   84. RSC, 'Report on the Position in China', par. 40.
85. RSC diary, 4 March 1940 (dated 3 March).
86. ibid., 5 March 1940 (misdated 7 March)   87. RSC to IC, 5 March 1940.

intriguing in more senses than one, Cripps still toyed with the idea of returning. He took away with him not only a hope that the Kuomintang could be brought to see the necessity of democratic reforms but also a reading of the Communists' outlook that identified them as the obvious partners in a common front against the Japanese. Reaching Hong Kong, at a lunch with Madame Sun Yat Sen, Cripps found that the talk round the table 'confirmed that the objectives of the Chinese communists are not really communist at all but are democracy, the abolition of feudalism, the cleaning up of the administration, as their main plank, and the intensification of the anti-Japanese drive'.[88] And speaking subsequently in Tokyo to the Japanese Foreign Minister, Cripps naturally put the best gloss on the situation, maintaining that no peace could be bought through an anti-Communist pact since 'although Chiang was of course against communism, he had the whole-hearted support of the Chinese communists at the present time, most of whom were not communists at all but at most rather advanced liberals.'[89]

Determined not to give comfort to the Japanese, Cripps adopted this optimistic line. But his final meetings on 6 March with Madame Chiang Kai-shek and William Donald, who had also made the journey to Hong Kong, struck a different note. 'She and Don were very frank about the possibility of sabotage by some of the ministers,' Cripps recorded. 'They described the attempts they had made to clean up the administration in certain quarters and their failure and made it quite clear that Madame's power with the G. was nothing like as much as was generally supposed. She furthermore warned me that the G. had an oriental mind and that it was very difficult for any westerner to appreciate its workings.'[90] If there was a final moment when Cripps's occidental mind dismissed the chimera that he could serve as the saviour of a democratic China, this was probably it. Back in London, on the same day that Cripps finally told the Chinese ambassador that he could not return to Chungking, a telegram from Donald arrived, later followed by an explanatory letter. Not only did Donald now firmly advise against Cripps's return to the Generalissimo's side: he revealed that he himself, under pressure, was bowing out.[91] The Chinese window too was shut.

Cripps had gone around the world in quest of a significant political role and had failed to find it, despite all his efforts. He and Wilson had spent December 1939 travelling to and around India; they had spent January

88. RSC diary, 6 March 1940.   89. ibid., 14 March 1940.   90. ibid., 6 March 1940.
91. ibid., 14 May 1940.

1940 travelling to and around Nationalist China, and most of February travelling to Moscow and back. Now they were heading home, though it was to take them another seven weeks to get there. It was only when Cripps returned to Britain that his luck began to change, and, even then, only after a further chapter of disappointed hopes.

Arriving in Hong Kong on 5 March, Cripps and Wilson stayed with the British Governor, who had to issue an order to the General Officer Commanding and the Admiral before they would meet Cripps. Never was the story of the Russian journey more necessary to break the ice; never was it more potently deployed – 'and at last to my surprise both of them said that if the British Government did not seize the opportunity they would be fools'.[92] Subsequent offers of naval transport attested to the efficacy of Cripps's charm; but of course he had bigger diplomatic triumphs in mind. He had offered to return home at once if the Foreign Office desired; on 12 March he heard that Halifax saw no point in this. Cripps was subsequently to be assured that this was because the Foreign Office thought his presence would be even more valuable in the USA than at home.[93] The fact was that the Foreign Office wanted Cripps anywhere but on their doorstep while the final stages of the Winter War still remained unsettled and controversial (though by the time that Halifax's telegram actually reached Cripps, a Finno-Soviet agreement was virtually concluded).[94]

In Hong Kong Cripps's search began for a homeward means of transport, and one that would square speed with economy. He had financed his own journey. True, he had received much official hospitality along the way; in China he had been a guest of the Government; the journey to Russia had been entirely at state expense; but getting home was his own responsibility. The idea of writing lucrative articles for American publications like *Time/ Life* came to nothing. The *deus ex machina* had the name of Rogers, chairman of the currency stabilization fund in Hong Kong, who came up with an offer to subsidize air tickets for Cripps and Wilson. 'I stated that I should not make any enquiries as to where the money came from as I was certain that it was only being put up because of the international implications and not because of me personally,' Cripps noted.[95] With no apparent qualms – and no summons from London either – Cripps evidently felt himself free to clinch this handsome offer.

Before departing, Cripps pulled in further visits. He and Wilson spent a couple of days at sea, going to Shanghai, where a Japanese military plane

92. ibid., 6 March 1940.   93. ibid., 25 April 1940.
94. Gorodetsky, *Mission to Moscow*, pp. 23–4.   95. RSC diary, 8 March 1940

collected them. After a couple of days of talks with officials in Tokyo, they were flown out of Japan, this time to the island of Formosa, and thence to Canton – 'our fifth entry into China'[96] – and back to Hong Kong on Good Friday, 22 March. The faithful Rogers had meanwhile arranged for tickets with Pan-American Airways, costing 'with the various reductions, 992 dollars each all the way to Lisbon'.[97] This was a substantial sum – say, £6,000 each at today's prices; and it remains unclear exactly what Rogers hoped to get for his money.

On 25 March Cripps and Wilson left Hong Kong, hopping each day across the islands of the Pacific, a distance of 8,700 miles, before arriving six days later in Los Angeles. Cripps spent one night in California. He had arranged to have dinner in Hollywood with Charles Chaplin, who gave him an enthusiastic account of his forthcoming film *The Great Dictator* – 'he said that he thought Hitler would never dare to make a public speech again after the film was shown'. The two men were obviously content to bask in mutual esteem. 'He told me many times that he had always considered me the white hope of western civilisation and expressed his sympathy with the Russian experiment though he is not a communist by any means.'[98]

Cripps's objectives in the USA were publicity and propaganda. As usual, he handled journalists adroitly in talking up his news value and meting out tantalizing morsels. In the British press, he was widely quoted as telling reporters: 'I could say a great deal, but I shan't.'[99] After a two-day flight to Washington, expanded by the three-hour time difference, Cripps was immediately pitched into a round of public engagements. The National Press Club lunch, said to be the largest they had ever had, was attended by over 400 people. Cripps was pleased with his address on China, the more so since the secretary 'went out of his way to point out how much better it was than the one which Eden gave'.[100]

This programme of engagements had been organized by Eric Estorick, a young American admirer, who already had the idea of becoming Cripps's biographer. The form such a work might take was still in the air; one proposal put to a New York publisher was for a three-generation study, not only of Cripps but his aunt Beatrice Webb and his grandfather Richard Potter.[101] A conventional biography was finally agreed, published in the following year – to very little effect – in New York but not in England,

96. ibid., 21 March 1940.

97. ibid., 23 March 1940. Who paid what finally is not clear; and the Atlantic was to be crossed by boat, not air.

98. ibid., 31 March 1940   99. For example, *Evening Standard*, 1 April 1940.

100. RSC diary, 3 April 1940.   101. See PRO, CAB 127/62.

where it was (and is) virtually unobtainable.[102] A curious twist in Estorick's relations with Cripps is the fact that the man who had first introduced them, the author Waldo Frank, had subsequently turned violently against Estorick. Indeed Frank had recently warned Cripps that 'Estorick is an utterly discredited and dangerous individual with but one gift: the vile one of ingratiating himself with generous men and with generous, motherly women, in order to exploit and abuse the good impulses he has awakened.'[103] Cripps none the less deliberately ignored this letter, probably judging that any risk was offset by the value of the publicity generated.

The terms in which Estorick could serve as the great man's publicist are illustrated by a press handout which Cripps preserved in his papers. It repays attention as an early draft of the authorized version of Cripps's career; much of it was reproduced or expanded in the 1941 biography.[104] Headed 'The Cripps "Mission"', it introduced this subsequently irresistible phrase, successively applied to Cripps's posting to Moscow and to both of his official visits to India. 'Unlike Ramsay MacDonald, born of lowly estate, who loved nothing better than to bask in the smile of Duchesses,' Estorick's handout claimed, 'Cripps has reversed the historic order of British working class leaders by coming of distinguished aristocratic stock.' His breach with the Labour Party was dated to his opposition to sanctions over Abyssinia, whereupon he 'resigned from the National Executive of the Party and was majorly vindicated by Prime Minister Baldwin's confession of duplicity the following year'.[105]

Cripps's expulsion from the party in 1939, and his failure to be readmitted, were both attributed by Estorick to the machinations of the National Executive, backed by the block vote of the trade unions. 'Convinced, as a result of first hand information, that Hitler would strike within the next two months,' Cripps had spent the summer of 1939 campaigning for a National Government, though with 'absolutely no idea at all in Sir Stafford's mind that he should personally go into such an enlarged Government'. Estorick claimed to have heard from Cripps in July 1939 of his plan to

102. Estorick (1941). Its significance lay in what Cripps wanted to be purveyed rather than in its popular impact, which was virtually nil.

103. Frank to RSC, 8 September 1939. Whether this animus fed on political disagreement about the war, of which Frank was now a supporter, is unclear.

104. Press handout, 4 pp., under the letterhead of the Chinese Industrial Cooperatives, n.d. but during Cripps's visit to New York.

105. This was Baldwin's 'appalling frankness' in subsequently alluding to the electoral context – 'his famous confession', as Estorick (1941), p. 100, calls it, which was notoriously twisted out of its context by many of Baldwin's critics, including Churchill, *Second World War*, i, pp. 169–70.

travel to China, to see Nehru in India, and to visit Russia – an uncanny anticipation of a journey actually improvised in response to the exigencies of the war crisis.[106]

What Estorick was at pains to confute here was the notion that his hero could have been brought to 'perform in an official capacity a "mission" of colonial appeasement for the Chamberlain Government, as has been suggested'. On the contrary, it was 'the fact that his incorruptibility, his greatness of mind and thought, and his steadfastness in the face of opposition are so strongly respected by the peoples with whom he has come into contact' that gave Cripps his influence.[107] Waldo Frank may have provoked momentary doubts as to whether Estorick was the right man to produce a fitting biography; but of his aptitude for hagiography Cripps could surely have been left in little doubt. Estorick continued to receive encouragement, and his draft manuscript was checked for accuracy by Wilson in New York before being updated for publication the following year.

What struck Cripps most about his ten days on the east coast was the extent of distrust of Britain, or at least of the current British Government. Conversely, the anglophiles whom he encountered were more than once given the dismissive label 'reactionary'. The British ambassador, Lord Lothian, impressed Cripps with his open-mindedness but also with 'a certain quality of fixed woolliness about his ideas which is perhaps typical of his liberalism'. Lothian expressed support for Cripps's Indian plan, 'but he was afraid that Linlithgow was too wooden to deal with the situation'.[108] Neither wool nor wood appealed to Cripps, for whom they symbolized the failures of traditional British diplomacy in a dangerous new world where democracy was on the march. Lothian's antagonism to using publicity to influence American opinion was all of a piece with this, as against Cripps's view that the need was for careful propaganda, 'largely based on stressing the democratic issue'.[109]

Cripps's thoughts on the boat home – he and Wilson eventually took an Italian liner from New York to Naples – reflected not only his own values and predispositions but a keen tactical appreciation of British interests. 'There is a very strong feeling for democracy which the Americans believe they enjoy and far the best line of appeal to them is on a basis of common democratic interests,' he wrote in his diary. These values had a worldwide resonance, and the trick, therefore, was to mobilize them in Britain's favour,

---

106. Estorick (1941), pp. 218–19, and p. 220, repeats both of these implausible claims.
107. Estorick (1941), pp. 228–9, toned down this rhetoric.   108. RSC diary, 6 April 1940.
109. ibid., 10 April 1940.

as he claimed to have done himself, through 'quiet and continual propaganda on the common interests of democracies in a rather general way'.[110]

Cripps embodied these musings in a formal memorandum for the Ministry of Information and the Foreign Office, warning them that the two issues which were liable to have an adverse effect on American perceptions were 'British policy in the Far East, and British policy towards India'. In both cases Britain needed to reconcile its policies with American opinion. Moreover, 'the common task of the two great democracies' needed to be stressed through purposeful but subtle propaganda. 'Americans must come to look upon themselves as partners in this task and they will then when the need arises be easily led into the paths that are necessary for the implementation of the common work.'[111] This was the message that Cripps preached at the end of his expedition to those countries which he had picked out as 'the most important for the future'. It was a message opportunely relevant to the needs of his own country, if it were now truly engaged in a war to uphold democracy.

Back in London, via Paris, on 23 April 1940, Cripps had a lot of catching-up to do. There remained a wide gap in attitude between him and his old party. During his absence, Laski had been impressing on Isobel Cripps the case for Stafford's return to the Labour Party, now that Bevan had been readmitted in December and Strauss in March. Press reports had speculated about reconciliation, but Cripps himself remained unimpressed and unrepentant. When he met again with his colleagues on the board of *Tribune*, he was dismissive of Labour, which could 'concert neither political nor industrial action against the government'. His fellow-rebels (now ex-rebels) could not openly advocate a coalition since Bevan and Strauss had given a pledge not to do so, as the condition of their readmission. 'I told them that the present was the time when it was impossible for socialists to come out with any programme and that the only thing to do was to bide our time until much later on some opportunity might occur,' was all Cripps could advise.[112] This frank opportunism was easier for him to sustain because of his independent status – and, of course, his independent means.

Suddenly, the phoney war was over; Hitler was on the move; the German armies swept through western Europe. Following the conspicuous collapse of the British intervention at Narvik, Chamberlain was faced with a debate on Norway in the House of Commons, to take place on 7 and 8 May.

110. ibid., 19 April 1940.
111. Memorandum, 24 April 1940, sent to Sir John Reith and Lord Halifax, PRO, CAB 127/62.
112. RSC diary, 1 May 1940.

Here was the moment Cripps had long awaited. At the May Day demonstration, organized by the Bristol labour movement, to which Cripps had been invited, he found the atmosphere 'rather hostile and generally confused'[113] but he was allowed to address a large crowd on Durdham Down and used his first public speech since his return to call for the overthrow of the Chamberlain Government. 'The events in Norway were, in my view, inevitable, given the Government that we have got,' he argued – if not inevitably then predictably. A change of government was essential not only to promote efficiency but to turn this from an imperialist war into one for democracy.[114]

Over the previous few days Cripps had made efforts to compile and publicize a list of an alternative Cabinet – floating an idea so as to prompt an overdue deed. Since *The Times* would not oblige, Cripps settled for publication in the *Daily Mail*, which on 6 May printed his suggestions on the front page as a letter from 'a leading member of the House of Commons whose name is known throughout the world but who wishes for the moment to be anonymous'. Not Churchill but Halifax was listed as the alternative Prime Minister, with Churchill, Lloyd George, Morrison and Eden as ministers without portfolio, Attlee as Chancellor, Bevin at the War Office, Anderson at the Home Office, Monckton as Minister of Information.

The *Mail* ran a supportive leading article, claiming that 'the enemy within' did not comprise a fifth column of 'Nazi agents, pacifists and Communists', but took the form of complacency and muddle. This was a significant endorsement from a major Conservative newspaper which might have been expected to round on the fellow-traveller Cripps as insufficiently patriotic. With his practised touch for press management, Cripps had primed other papers; and the liberal *News Chronicle* and its sister paper, the *Star*, both gave prominent editorial support. Cripps was, however, unmasked in a double sense by the Chamberlainite *Daily Telegraph*, which not only revealed him as the author of the list but asserted that there was 'no man in public life with as little title to undertake the role of Cabinet-maker'.[115]

Cripps was now in touch with leading critics of the Government, notably Lloyd George. The first day of the Norway debate, 7 May, left the Government relatively unscathed; but on the second day, the stakes were raised with Labour's decision to make this a vote of no confidence. Now it was 'Ll.G.'s brilliant speech, which was an almost perfect parliamentary performance',

---

113. ibid., 5 May 1940.
114. *Bristol Evening Post*, 6 May 1940; cf. *Western Daily Press*, 6 May 1940.
115. 'London day by day', *Daily Telegraph*, 8 May 1940.

that Cripps considered decisive.[116] After Lloyd George had sat down – to loud Opposition cheers for his final sally, that Chamberlain should 'give an example of sacrifice' by sacrificing the seals of office – there was a short and ineffective reply from a Government supporter. Then Cripps rose.

Cripps's intervention figured among 'the hardest hits' of the debate in press comment, which noted that 'in his precise and damaging way' he mounted a case for greater initiative in the war effort which was taken up in subsequent speeches.[117] Cripps showed himself ready enough to enter into a detailed tactical argument over the mining of the fjords; but the real impact of his speech rested on his concluding suggestion, echoing Lloyd George, that when Chamberlain had used the words 'my friends' in asking for support, he was making an unworthy 'appeal upon personal grounds and personal friendship to the loyalty of the House'.[118] This may have been little more than a lawyer's trick, investing a well-established parliamentary expression, which Chamberlain had been unwise rather than improper to employ, with a sinister connotation.

The rhetoric worked, however, because it pitted self-interest against a wider patriotic duty, consonant with the fact that Cripps now invoked public spirit rather than the logic of the class war. The Government was not defeated in the vital vote at the end of the Norway debate on 8 May but, ostentatiously deserted by over a hundred of his own followers, Chamberlain found that his friends proved too few. A new Prime Minister was needed to make a coalition acceptable.

The outcome did not, however, fulfil Cripps's hopes. Talking again with Lloyd George on the morning after the vote, Cripps 'told him that I had gathered from the Labour people I had talked to that they did not want Halifax and that many of them were frightened of Winston with the result that suggestions were being made that he might take the job on'.[119] Though recalling Lloyd George was hardly a serious possibility, Cripps's qualms about Churchill did not evaporate, even when Churchill quickly succeeded in forming a new Government – but one with the Chamberlainites still inside it. They were 'trying to force the Labour Party into a cabinet which would retain all the reactionary elements,' Cripps wrote. 'This was the end that I had prophesied and foreseen for some years and has since become the accomplished fact, Churchill having chosen the leaders of various power groups in the House as a coalition, irrespective of their qualifications in a war cabinet.'[120]

Cripps revealed, not for the last time, a rather naive sense that wartime

---

116. RSC diary, 8 May 1940.   117. *Star*, 9 May 1940.   118. *The Times*, 9 May 1940.
119. RSC diary, 9 May 1940.   120. ibid., 10 May 1940.

politics could leave out the politics. It was true that the Churchill coalition was founded on a shrewd appreciation of party balance and party interests, with a premium, therefore, on party loyalty. Far from being hailed for his prescience by his old comrades, Cripps found that there was no place for himself in the new Government for the simple reason that the Labour Party had quite enough loyal claimants on the places made available to it. So once Churchill had formed his Government, there was little point in Cripps taking the Labour whip – as a backbencher, he might as well retain his independence of action. He pointedly approached the Speaker of the House of Commons with the question – now that Labour was within the Government – of who could properly constitute His Majesty's Opposition.[121] On meeting the council of his constituency Labour Party in Bristol on 15 May, Cripps noted that he had 'expressed my determination not to go back to the Party' and secured a vote of twenty-four to two in his favour.[122]

Having renounced party in order to campaign for an all-in Government, Cripps found that, once the all-in Government was formed, party remained the passport to power. One of his old political associates, Edgar Young, wrote to him: 'It's funny to think that it's only a year since we were excluded from the Labour Party for daring to propose common action with Liberals, isn't it?' Whether it seemed funny or a bitter paradox was obviously a matter of taste. Had Cripps decided to use his convenient absence from the country as a smoke-screen for repositioning himself within the Labour Party, his obvious front-bench quality could hardly have been ignored in May 1940. As it was, the new Government (so Young put it) were 'adopting towards you an attitude somewhat like that which they seem to have definitely adopted towards the USSR: "if we need your help to win this war, we'd rather lose it without you".'[123] The formation of the Churchill coalition apparently offered Cripps nothing: no job, no movement on India, no rapprochement with Russia. That it was headed by the arch-opponent of the sort of Indian initiative that Cripps saw as desperately urgent soon became clear. So the best he could hope for was that, over Russia, Churchill's realism under the duress of events might prevail over his prejudices. Thus the political crisis initially seemed like another false start to Cripps, whose peregrinations left him a sadder and a wiser man.

121. RSC to Speaker, 14 May 1940, copy.   122. RSC diary, 15 May 1940.
123. E. P. Young to RSC, 16 May 1940, copy in Young papers, DYO 2/25.

ENTR'ACTE
1940

In 1940 Cripps was in England for hardly more than one month, though a decisive one not only in the European war and in British politics but also in his own career. On his return Stafford was reunited with Isobel and Theresa Cripps, who had seen him off nearly five months previously. Within days, a family conference, including also Diana and John, was convened. The statement that Cripps had given up an income of £25,000 was frequently recycled through press cuttings over the years, and the family understood that this was, if anything, an underestimate. The question was, whether to give up Goodfellows. Theresa's diary expressed their feelings.

It isn't possible to realize it yet, or even believe it, but there are various reasons why it isn't quite as bad either as it sounds when put baldly and even more as for many people who have had to leave their homes. Firstly, we have known for a long time that one day it would be beyond our means, and also it would be walking out and not being kicked out in a hurry – at the moment at any rate – because actually as things are at present we could probably afford it, but it would be an awful tie and it would be tragic to see it all 'go back', and even after the war D. won't be earning his £30,000 again – he says he won't earn anything again.

From this point of decision, itself evidently long in the making, developments moved quickly. The initial alternative considered was a new house – 'built at once while one can apparently still get the material if one knows the right people'.[1] Such a pre-emptive claim on fast-disappearing resources, with its black-market connotations, might well have aroused adverse comment. Within a week, however, Stafford and Isobel were looking at an old farmhouse between Cirencester and Stroud, and within a month they had secured it. It turned out to be Stafford's last month of residence at Goodfellows before he was again on his travels, this time at public expense.

1. Theresa Cripps diary, 29 April 1940.

Cripps served as British ambassador in Moscow from June 1940 to January 1942. His appointment at last provided a suitable response to the offer he had made at the outbreak of war, some eight months earlier, to put his services at the disposal of the Government. It was a curious but also a momentous interlude in his career. Exceptionally, he was allowed to remain a Member of Parliament throughout this time – thus permitting his easy re-entry to British politics at a moment of his choosing.

The record of this hybrid politician-ambassador can be studied with two questions in mind. First, what was the impact of Russia on Cripps? How did his experiences affect his political views and the subsequent course of his career? Cripps went to Moscow with the reputation of being an extreme left-winger, an advocate of a popular front with the Communists and an uncritical apologist for the Soviet Union. When he returned, it soon became apparent that this was not so, or no longer so. The inference has often been drawn that he must have suffered an abrupt disillusionment while in Moscow. This ignores, of course, a number of prior signs that his ideological position had already been shifting, as more than one perceptive historian has already observed.[2]

Secondly, what was the impact of Cripps on Russia? His ambassadorship constitutes a significant episode in the diplomatic history of the fraught period from Dunkirk (when Britain apparently faced defeat) to Pearl Harbor (when Churchill scented 'certain victory').[3] During Cripps's first twelve months in the Soviet Union, it often seemed that nothing was happening and that his role was marginal. Then with the German invasion in June 1941, code-named Barbarossa, the Russian front became the crucial theatre of the world war. How far did Cripps foresee this? Was he alive to the warning signs? Did he expedite or impede communication between Churchill and Stalin? In the final six months of Cripps's ambassadorship, Russia became Britain's much-needed ally. How far did he deserve his burgeoning reputation as architect of Anglo-Russian solidarity?

One theme running through the story of Cripps's ambassadorship concerns his wartime relations with Churchill. Here perceptions have been strongly influenced by the account Churchill himself gave when he published the six volumes of *The Second World War* between 1948 and 1954. In particular, volume 3, *The Grand Alliance*, was composed at a time when Cripps was Chancellor of the Exchequer in the Labour Government and

2. Addison, *Road to 1945*, p. 192; Gorodetsky, *Mission to Moscow*, p. 30; Eatwell, 'Labour Party and the Popular Front', pp. 408–10, esp. p. 410, n.2.
3. Gilbert, *Churchill*, vi, p. 1274.

Churchill was his bitter critic as Conservative Leader of the Opposition. The effect of the treatment in that volume is, not unnaturally, to diminish Cripps.

On the publication of *The Grand Alliance* in 1950, one allegation became headline news: Cripps's culpable delay in forwarding a 'cryptic warning' of Barbarossa from Churchill to Stalin. It should be noted that Cripps had agreed to publication of the relevant documents. ('Which was sporting of him,' Churchill was reminded by one of his aides, 'because you might not have told the story without his consent, and you hesitated even when he gave it.') Churchill agreed that 'taken out of their general context, these statements are undesirable', and exerted his veto on prior serialization in the *Daily Telegraph*, seemingly reluctant, as Lord Ismay had put it, 'to make political capital out of those great days when we all worked together'.[4] Publication therefore had to await the appearance of this volume in print but the incident has remained controversial.

Cripps's side of the story is poorly represented in the public archives, and consequently in the official history. The most authoritative monograph on his ambassadorship has noted that his unconventional methods created gaps in the Foreign Office papers 'which can only be bridged by Cripps' meticulously kept daily letter-diary' and that, as Foreign Secretary, Anthony Eden came to rely upon the extracts that Isobel Cripps read to him after her return.[5] Gorodetsky's scrupulous scholarship makes out the case for a more sympathetic reappraisal of Cripps's diplomatic role, but it has not stilled academic criticism. The fact remains that the most vehement charges have continued to be pressed without the benefit of testimony from the Cripps papers.[6] Yet these are surely indispensable to the formation of a balanced judgement here.

Not only does Cripps's own record, covering his entire tour of duty, survive in his papers; during the eight months that he was joined in Moscow by Isobel, Peggy and Theresa, their stay is documented from three subtly different angles. Stafford had been writing almost daily to Isobel since he left home. Once she herself was in transit to Russia, he switched his epistolary attentions from her to his remaining daughter Diana. This self-consciously complementary series of letters, intended for preservation, constitutes Stafford's Moscow diary. But there were now two other diarists in the

---

4. Denis Kelly to Churchill, with Ismay note, 6 January 1950; Churchill to Kelly, 1 March 1950, Churchill papers, CHUR 4/250 C.
5. Gorodetsky, *Mission to Moscow*, pp. xiv, 206, esp. n.143 (on p. 329).
6. This is a major theme of Miner, *Between Churchill and Stalin*, and, in a more moderate vein, Gardner, *Spheres of Influence*, pp. 75–89.

household. Isobel wrote an account that was also sent to Diana, its episodes likewise collected in batches for the diplomatic bag; and there was a tacit division of labour between her domestic chronicle and Stafford's political record. Moreover, Theresa kept her own meticulous daily journal, its secrets guarded by her for the next half-century – not because these were scandalous but because confidentiality permitted candour in the observations of a perceptive young woman of twenty-one.

Diplomatic life in Moscow, as one visitor put it, 'was about as close to prison as anything outside of bars'.[7] These sources offer not only insights into Stafford Cripps's public life but also opportunities to explore the private life he enjoyed with his family under the constraints of their isolated existence: cocooned in a bizarre enclave of anomalous privilege and, to an unusual extent, thrown upon each other's company.

7. Harriman and Abel, *Special Envoy*, p. 95.

PART THREE

RUSSIAN MYTHS

1940–41

ANYBODY HOME?

I

Staring in the Face of the Kremlin

It created quite a sensation, even amid other pressing war news, when Cripps went to Moscow. How this remarkable appointment came about was not straightforward. The fact that his interest in Russia was well known was a mixed recommendation in the Foreign Office; the officials had not been much impressed by his meeting with Molotov in February, though they had to admit that no other Briton had had any direct contact with the Kremlin. Nor had Cripps's lightning visit to Moscow won him many friends in the Labour Party. In his widely read column in the *Daily Mirror*, 'Cassandra' had a paragraph on the theme, 'Come off it, Stafford': 'It's like travelling a thousand miles to reproach a burglar whom you introduced to a party at which he promptly stole the spoons.'[1]

Labour's National Executive, with its full support for the war against Hitler, opposed negotiations with Hitler's unlikely new friend, Stalin. Cripps, conversely, argued for rapprochement. On his return to London, therefore, he kept up cordial relations with Harry Pollitt, whose dissent from his party's official anti-war line had occasioned a break (that was to last until 1941) in his long period of service as General Secretary of the Communist Party. Cripps had also gone to the Soviet ambassador, Maisky, to be brought up to date on 'the Russian business'.

The history of this since I left is that for 3½ months Maisky did not see Halifax at all and there was the most intense anti-Russian feeling in all quarters but he maintained contact with Butler continuously, though Rab was strongly criticised for this, and on the 22 February Maisky got telegraphic instructions from Moscow to approach the British Government with terms for the Finnish settlement. These were rather more favourable to Finland than the ones eventually agreed, but the Cabinet decided they would have nothing to do with them. I think this approach probably followed my explanation to Molotov of the

1. *Daily Mirror*, 8 March, 1940.

impossibility of any sort of agreement with this country till the Finnish affair was out of the way.

This account seems to be substantially accurate on the sequence of diplomatic exchanges; and, finding that moves towards a rapprochement on trade had been sanctioned by the British Cabinet in March, Cripps was also satisfied that 'my telegram started things on the move again'.[2]

Even if there is here some natural tendency towards exaggeration of his own part, it is significant that Cripps believed himself capable of influencing the responses of both the Soviet and British Governments at the highest level. He considered himself uniquely capable of playing such a role because he was simultaneously free of Marxist dogma and of Labour Party attachments. As he saw it, one thing that stood in the way of better Anglo-Russian relations was the doctrinaire approach of the Communist Party of Great Britain. 'Their attempt to interpret events according to a political theory when they are really influenced by power politics has led them into an anti-British and pro-Nazi line of argument which becomes a grave embarrassment to the Russian government,' Cripps wrote in his diary.[3]

It was Cripps's realism, not his ideology, that finally opened the door of the Foreign Office. The warmest supporter of his conciliatory approach was the junior minister, R. A. Butler, with Halifax, as Foreign Secretary in both the old and the new Government, reserving his position. It became increasingly plain that something needed to be done about British relations with Russia, if only because it could exploit its neutrality to import strategic goods while offering (if not always delivering) economic assistance to Germany. Hence the potential importance of an Anglo-Soviet trade agreement. Cripps had impressed upon Halifax 'the urgency of the Russian situation and I hope convinced him' at a frustratingly short formal interview on 3 May, feeling the need for an evening together to win him over.[4]

Cripps was fortunate in having influential friends. It was Walter Monckton, now a political confidant, who apparently persuaded Halifax to invite Cripps to dinner on 16 May. Cripps took his chance with the two issues he thought most important: India, of course, but also Russia. 'As to the last,' Cripps noted, 'I impressed upon him again the need for quick action and offered to go out to Moscow if he thought it would do any good.'[5] It was

2. RSC diary, 25 April 1940. Cf. Gorodetsky, *Mission to Moscow*, pp. 23–4.
3. RSC diary, 25 April 1940.
4. ibid., 3 May 1940. There is disappointingly little about Butler's extensive contacts with Cripps in the authoritative biography by Anthony Howard, *RAB; the life of R. A. Butler*.
5. RSC diary, 16 May 1940; cf. Hyde, *Monckton*, pp. 2–3.

an opportune moment. The previous day Attlee, now a member of the small War Cabinet, had proposed sending 'an important figure in public life' to begin negotiations in Moscow; Halifax now waived any preconditions; and early on the morning of 17 May he sought Butler's reaction to the idea that Cripps might head such a mission. Butler was predictably supportive, and the proposal went forward to the Cabinet.

Churchill later commented in *The Second World War*: 'We did not at that time realise sufficiently that Soviet Communists hate extreme Left Wing politicians even more than they do Tories or Liberals.'[6] The implication was that he himself had made a misjudgement in selecting Cripps. Admittedly, as First Lord of the Admiralty six months previously, he had toyed with the idea of Cripps as ambassador; but, now suddenly Prime Minister, beset and engrossed by the calamity of the German invasion of France, Churchill had played little part in the decision, and ideological considerations less.

The main opposition to Cripps's appointment, especially if it were to entail a wide-ranging brief, came from a familiar quarter. Hugh Dalton had just taken office as Minister of Economic Warfare and he made sure that his new colleagues at the Foreign Office were duly warned about his old comrade in the Labour Party. Telling Halifax that his relations with Cripps were now 'rather sketchy', Dalton assented to the plan only on condition that 'if he goes, he must have a policeman from my Ministry' – a role into which he drafted Munia Postan, whose career as a distinguished economic historian was temporarily punctuated by war service. Thinking he had sufficiently reined in Cripps, Dalton did not make a fight in the Cabinet when the appointment went through, even though more latitude than he would have liked was allowed to the envoy. When Dalton said, 'if it goes wrong, don't blame me', Churchill replied with a grin, 'You're on velvet.'[7]

On 20 May Cripps was summoned to the Foreign Office. A leak from the War Cabinet, through the Labour deputy leader Arthur Greenwood, had already alerted him to what was proposed. Cripps was received by Halifax and Butler, together with Dalton. Cripps readily agreed to go to Moscow as an envoy, with a brief to explore political or trade matters, 'provided I was assured there was a genuine desire to treat Russia as a friendly neutral and not in any way an underlying hostility, as I would not allow myself to be used as a camouflage to attempt to deceive the Russians'. Halifax met this condition and 'stated that I was at liberty to discuss any

6. Churchill, *Second World War*, ii, p.118; Gorodetsky, *Mission to Moscow*, pp. 29, 31–2; Woodward, *British Foreign Policy*, i, pp. 455–60.
7. Dalton diary, 17, 18 May 1940, in Pimlott (ed.), *Dalton: War Diary*, pp. 10, 12.

political or trade matters that I liked but that I must not commit the government to any arrangements without prior consultation with them'.[8]

It was eventually agreed that Cripps's delegation should include not only Postan but also a Foreign Office aide – perhaps just as well, since Postan, with his compromising pre-revolutionary Russian background, was to be refused entry to the Soviet Union. Cripps himself insisted that he be accompanied by Geoffrey Wilson. Since returning from their world tour, Cripps had been making fruitless efforts to secure an official post for Wilson and the Foreign Office's qualms about accepting 'a henchman of Sir S. Cripps' could now be overborne.[9]

When the news of his appointment broke, it was well received. There was a half-page story in Beaverbrook's *Evening Standard*, possibly by Michael Foot, under the headline 'Britain's Man for Moscow', which put a surprisingly favourable gloss on his career: 'He has the self-confidence of a Messiah, the conviction that he is right when all the world appears to pronounce him wrong, amazing energy and powers of concentration to continue working in the face of constant rebuffs, a burning belief in the rectitude of his cause.'[10] More soberly and predictably, the *Manchester Guardian* called it highly satisfactory that Cripps should go to Russia since he was untarred with the imperialist brush.[11]

The Russians adroitly took the opportunity of declaring that they would only treat with someone of ambassadorial rank. They had been pressing for Britain to send an ambassador to Moscow, where Britain had been unrepresented since the end of 1939. The subtlety of their move was that, while formally it meant a promotion within the diplomatic hierarchy for Cripps, it was actually a demotion of the special status of his mission – or could be presented as such to Hitler by the ever-fearful Russians. They calculated that a demand congenial neither to the British Government nor to Cripps himself might now become a *fait accompli*, given that Cripps was already *en route*.[12] He had indeed set out for Poole on 24 May to catch a flying-boat to Athens, and concluded his diary that night, with misplaced confidence, by writing: 'Now we are off.'

In fact Cripps was not 'off'. He was still in England; his aircraft had been delayed in Poole; but the momentum was now self-sustaining. The new Russian condition about his status was speedily met, with Cripps, Halifax

8. RSC diary, 20 May 1940.
9. Note by Howe for Butler, 7 May 1940, Butler papers, RAB E3/3, 138.
10. *Evening Standard*, 29 May 1940.   11. *Manchester Guardian*, 25 May 1940.
12. Gorodetsky, *Mission to Moscow*, p. 34.

and the Cabinet agreeing to it in quick succession. As Gabriel Gorodetsky, the historian of this diplomatic episode, puts it: 'Thus the Russians gained the unprecedented achievement of not only forcing the British to return an ambassador to Moscow but also securing the appointment of their own candidate.'[13]

Cripps had never intended to become an ambassador and assumed the title with reluctance. 'It would be purely ad hoc for the duration of the mission,' Geoffrey Wilson assured Isobel Cripps when the possibility first arose.[14] But, as Stafford himself later told her, while kicking his heels in Athens, waiting for his status to be resolved, things were not so simple.

The Russians have refused to accept an Ambassador 'on special mission'; which means that either someone else must go (with whom I could go as legal adviser) or else if I go I must give up my seat in the House of Commons. I wired Halifax to say I would do either but strongly recommended the first and now am waiting to know what the government's decision is and whatever it is I shall accept it as obviously the national interest is at the moment much more important than my own position, though of course I dont want to give up my seat in the House unless it is necessary, as it will be very difficult if not impossible for me ever to get back in.[15]

The matter-of-fact way in which Cripps revealed his readiness to bring his political career to an end is striking, even in the context of the war crisis. He was not, however, faced with this drastic step. Like Sir Samuel Hoare, who became ambassador to Madrid, Cripps was allowed to retain his parliamentary seat. The arrangement was that, by forgoing the diplomatic salary, Cripps did not acquire an 'office of profit under the Crown' which would have debarred him from sitting in the House.[16] In compensation, as he told his wife, he was offered 'an "allowance" of £6,000 which I consider excessive and I have said I will take the £4,000 which the last man had as an allowance'.[17] Of course, the last ambassador, Sir Wiliam Seeds, had had his salary in addition. Cripps thus needed to be a wealthy man to make possible this whole arrangement, let alone his own self-denying gesture on the scale of his expenses allowance.

Cripps, not for the first time, escaped a dilemma. One might speculate that, had it been foreseen that Cripps would come back in 1942 as Churchill's

13. ibid., p. 36.   14. Wilson to IC, 26 May 1940.   15. RSC diary, 3 June 1940.
16. See Butler to RSC, 18 June 1940, copy, Butler papers, RAB E3/3, 146. Gilbert, *Churchill*, vi, p. 1016, comments on Churchill's speech in February 1941 in defence of the arrangement for Hoare, Cripps and MacDonald.
17. RSC diary, 13 July 1940.

rival, the Government might not have been quite so ready to find this neat solution. But actually both Cripps and Churchill, to their credit, had more urgent problems on their minds at the time. Although the two men did not meet before the ambassador's hasty departure, Churchill sent an appreciative telegram, on which Stafford commented to Isobel: 'Very nice of him to telegraph me when he must be so desperately het up and worried about things.'[18]

On the way to Sofia, Cripps's party suffered two inauspicious blows. Not only was the plane struck by lightning – a serious incident, attracting press coverage – but Postan was told that he must return home. Cripps called this 'awkward but understandable'.[19] It meant that he had lost his official 'policeman'. He told Isobel that 'I feel very odd indeed being given precedence as an Ambassador and called "Excellency" all the time. I dislike it immensely but it can't be helped.'[20] He now realized that being an ambassador meant kitting himself out with full evening dress and that perfecting his French would be essential. He worked on this almost daily as soon as he was settled into the embassy and by the end of August reported that 'I am at last beginning to get a little better knowledge of the language and occasionally get a tense and a person right when I am talking!'[21]

The British embassy in Moscow, formerly a merchant's residence, was a building that set out to impress, if only through its opulence. The decor appalled Stafford: 'terribly over-decorated, gold and flowers and paint and Louis 15 furniture ormolu etc. and all jammed full of stuff'.[22] The best feature was the location, with the principal rooms looking across the narrow Moscow river to the crenellated walls and onion domes of the Kremlin. A good sense of the place was later captured in the photographs taken by Theresa Cripps. She was to consider her own room 'much the nicest, with plain cream walls and only a moderately elaborately moulded ceiling', not to mention 'a bathroom as big as my room at Goodfellows and twice as high'. A fine dining-room ('though of course very ornate'), a formal drawing-room (with 'ghastly painted ceiling'), a cosy family sitting-room, a further sitting-room for her mother, and her father's study ('with striped silk walls which make it look rather shabby') comprised the main features of a house in which Stafford lived for sixteen months, until the evacuation of Moscow, literally staring in the face of the Kremlin.[23]

18. ibid., 23 June 1940.   19. ibid., 6 June 1940.   20. ibid., 7 June 1940.
21. ibid., 20 August 1940.   22. ibid., 13 June 1940.
23. Theresa Cripps diary, 3 October 1941.

Communication with the staff presented him with an initial difficulty since German was the house language. Not until the installation of the Greek butler, Timoleon, in August did things shake down. Cripps's diet was, as always, a concern, especially since fresh vegetables were hard to obtain. But after a few weeks he told Isobel: 'As to myself I am really very fit only in danger of getting too fat as they will insist on feeding me much too well and a raw diet isn't possible though latterly I have been having lots of fruit.'[24] He asked for photographs to be sent, to remind him of home and family. Above all, he settled down to work as soon as he could.

Molotov saw Cripps for an hour on 14 June. With France clearly about to fall and the British forces preparing for evacuation, Cripps took the opportunity to affirm that Britain would fight on regardless. After what seemed a reasonable start, Cripps held himself ready for the further interview he had requested. He waited in the embassy, at first not daring to leave for even an hour in case a sudden summons should arrive. But he waited in vain. Days passed. At first Cripps made light of the difficulties, telling Isobel: 'I am still waiting for my interview with Molotov but I do not think the delay means anything as he is terribly busy over the Baltic and if favourably disposed to us would be afraid to show it openly by seeing me unless it was necessary.'[25] A second request was met with the bland comment that Molotov was very busy. A third request became necessary.

Admittedly, there was protocol to observe, since sending Cripps's credentials from London was not easy and these were not ready for presentation until 28 June. Much has been made of this subsequently, to suggest either that the Foreign Office was actually making difficulties or at any rate that Cripps blamed it for doing so.[26] Although Cripps was naturally anxious to have proper accreditation, his lack of deeper concern about it is shown by the way he put it to Isobel: 'Technically as my letters of credence have not yet come I dont exist but they dont pay great attention to such formalities here, fortunately.'[27] As Cripps well appreciated, the real difficulties were political. With Britain's very survival in doubt, the Russians were using any excuse for keeping their distance.

It is just as well that Cripps did not know that the Foreign Office evinced mixed feelings about their ambassador's plight. Sir Orme Sargent, Deputy Under-Secretary, found time to gloat that Stalin had now 'got Sir S. Cripps

24. RSC diary, 13 July 1940.   25. ibid., 21 June 1940.
26. Miner, *Between Churchill and Stalin*, p. 64, for this view, but see Gorodetsky, *Mission to Moscow*, p. 50.
27. RSC diary, 24 June 1940.

exactly where he wants him, that is to say, as a suppliant on his doormat holding his pathetic little peace offerings of tin in one hand and rubber in the other'. It was left to Butler to enjoin the officials to be 'very careful about comments on such Envoys who with complete disregard for their own private convenience undertake duties such as this which might at times be odious'.[28] The lack of confidence in Cripps on the part of the Foreign Office establishment, and his corresponding impatience with their rigid methods, was a tension implicit in the entire terms of his appointment. It was not lost upon the Russians.

Cripps's isolation – diplomatic, political, personal – could hardly have been more complete. If he had naively imagined that the workers' state was so eager to throw its weight against fascism that his mission would speedily be accomplished in an intense whirlwind of amicable negotiations, he would have been quickly disillusioned. Contemporaries who knew his reputation were inclined to attribute such views to him, on the basis of their own surprise at the tough-minded tenor of some of Cripps's reactions. The American ambassador, Laurence Steinhardt, though never an intimate, became an assiduous Cripps-watcher of this kind. Such recorded impressions, chiming in with those of the Foreign Office, have naturally influenced later historians who have relied upon them.[29]

Yet by the time Cripps arrived in Moscow, his outlook was far from dogmatic. As he told Isobel: 'In the welter of events I have lost all my preconceived notions of what ought to happen.'[30] Naturally his experience in the Soviet Union from 1940 modified Cripps's views; but it was a year previously that the decisive shift had occurred in his understanding of Stalin's foreign policy – abandoning ideology as the key in favour of Realpolitik.

What was certainly brought home to Cripps in Moscow was the intractability of the Russian way of doing business. If, to someone of Cripps's temperament, this was inevitably taxing, it was also, to someone with his lack of governmental experience, starkly instructive. Cripps had an unusual apprenticeship as a minister in that his first real lessons in executive government came not on the nursery slopes of municipal administration or junior ministerial office but by confronting that Everest of bureaucracy, the Kremlin. He quickly learnt that it was going to be difficult to get anything done; even more so to get anything done quickly. It was a lesson that he

28. Quoted in Miner, *Between Churchill and Stalin*, p. 65; cf. Gorodetsky, *Mission to Moscow*, pp. 50–51.
29. See esp. Miner, *op. cit.*, pp. 73, 75, 85, 97, 101, 110–11.
30. RSC diary, 29 June 1940.

accepted, if not happily, then stoically, telling Isobel Cripps after little more than a fortnight in Moscow: 'I am afraid it looks as if I am settled here for a long spell as nothing much can be done at the moment except to work quietly and patiently at better relations from which later on something may eventuate.'[31]

Stafford put his time to the best use he could. With diplomatic activity in Moscow largely suspended, he found that there was initially little for him to report in telegrams, and no point in writing dispatches at a point when routing the diplomatic bag across the war zone had become so precarious. 'I seem to spend most of my time now doing French exercises in translation; as you know I cannot bear idleness and so whenever work stops I just go on with my French!'[32] He made efforts to keep up the staff's morale, generating some feeling that he was attempting to over-organize their spare time. He cast about for suitable games to play after dinner. Bridge? No – 'everyone will always be wanting to play it all day when the weather gets bad!' Shuffle-board, perhaps? Billiards, if possible, 'as it is a healthy amusement'.[33] And all the while, the worrying war news was buzzing in the background, with an invasion of England thought likely at any moment.

Stafford was lonely. He thought it acceptable to have breakfast with Geoffrey Wilson but they both felt that they should keep their distance socially to avoid impressions of favouritism. He clearly missed Isobel a great deal and without her felt insufficiently motivated for outdoor tasks like gardening. 'I don't mind how long and late I work,' Stafford told her, 'what riles me is that I can get so few opportunities to work – and as you know I've been accustomed to pretty high pressure in the past and I find it very difficult not having anything to do and having to invent jobs for myself.'[34] The solution he came up with was to get a dog for companionship. He chose a ten-month Airedale, which featured not only in many family photographs of Cripps in Moscow but also in press coverage – not least because he further chose to call it 'Joe'.

It was a name much on the ambassador's mind. He had finally been granted an interview with Stalin on 1 July in order to present a message from Churchill. Indeed the message had been drafted by the Foreign Office largely in order to secure the interview. This, their first face-to-face meeting, showed Cripps hopeful but frustrated in his attempts to achieve any sort of personal breakthrough. True, the meeting began at 6.30 p.m. and lasted

31. ibid., 30 June 1940.   32. ibid., 24 June 1940.
33. ibid., 1 July 1940; cf. Theresa Cripps diary (from Wilson), 4 October 1940.
34. RSC diary, 2 July 1940.

until 9.15 p.m., allowing for a discursive and often repetitive conversation, which Cripps distilled into half-a-dozen telegrams for the Foreign Office. 'The general tenour of the whole talk was friendly and quite frank,' he assured Halifax, 'and as a result I think that trade negotiations may start shortly.'[35]

The full record, as kept by the embassy staff, suggests that this was an optimistic reading. The key issue here concerned British sanctions on Russian imports of non-ferrous metals. These were liable to find their way via the Soviet Union into the hands of its German partners – as Stalin readily admitted, arguing that raw materials had to be made available if the Germans were to manufacture essential supplies for Russia. Since Stalin also affected to believe that there could be no German domination of Europe without command of the sea, Cripps tried to turn the edge of the argument, saying that this was exactly why the British blockade had to be maintained. But, professing confidence that there was no overriding difficulty here, he undertook to go back for specific instructions from his own Government. Stalin then said: 'I could of course give a promise that not a single pound of metal would go to Germany; but that would be dishonest. A promise is no use which is not fulfilled.' With whatever private feelings, Cripps seized upon this magnificent response to voice the hope that 'this extremely useful discussion' would lead to the long-awaited trade talks. The official record concludes: 'To this M. Stalin merely intimated his assent.'[36] The embassy staff were on this occasion better than the optimistic ambassador in reading the signs and it is difficult to quarrel with their later summary: 'Nothing of importance emerged from this interview.'[37]

The root of the trouble was that Britain had little to offer and that Russia was certainly not going to choose this moment to offend Germany, now at the peak of its power in Europe. Objectively, Cripps saw that the situation was highly unpromising; but subjectively the sense of crisis braced him.

The whole tempo of the political atmosphere is increasing and everyone is expectant and waiting for a new development at any moment. Probably Germany's attack on England will be the sign for the outbreak of hostilities by Japan in the Far East, America will not come in and we shall be left isolated as a result of the insane policies of the last 10 years. All one can do here at the moment is to try and get things better

35. Cripps to Halifax, 1 July 1940, FO 371/29464, ff. 134–5 (copy).
36. Note of interview with Stalin, 1 July 1940 (by Dunlop), enclosed with Cripps to L. Collier, 16 July 1940, FO 371/24845, ff. 9–22; also copied in FO 371/29464.
37. 'Summary of events since the arrival of Sir Stafford Cripps in Moscow', 17 March, 1941, FO 371/29464, f. 128.

in this particular sphere, but it is very late to hope for anything effective unless we can hang on for a long and very terrible and trying time in England. However, though we all realise fully the seriousness of the situation, we also try to keep 'our peckers up' and do not allow our morale to be undermined.[38]

It was a relief, at any rate, to be busy at last: so busy that even Stafford's letters to Isobel were suspended for a couple of days. The volume of cipher work vastly increased, bringing home how understaffed the embassy was, and meaning that most of the diplomats were working seven days a week into the small hours. Cripps complained to the Foreign Office that all but one of his staff had to spend nine-tenths of their time in purely mechanical tasks of ciphering.[39] At one point he did not even have his own secretary and had to write everything by hand. This situation actually suited Cripps far better, at least in the short run. 'Just every now and then I turn around and look at myself and say, "What odd chance has brought you here as an ambassador?" and it all seems so very odd, artificial and out of place altogether.'[40]

In the long run, however, the looming prospect of a prolonged sojourn in Moscow was hardly what he had originally contemplated.

There is a feeling here now – which I have – that we shall not get much further with the Soviet Government until the present phase of the war has crystallised. They are not going to do anything to antagonise Germany in such a way as to make possible a German attack before the Winter and so will do all they can to appear to be on the best terms. This means they will avoid all contacts with us and I doubt very much whether we shall even get so far as any Trade talks. We were too late to do any good in this place and can now only stand by in the hope that in the next phase, when it comes, things may alter, but this, I think, definitely means staying here until next year at any rate. It all rather alters my ideas of my activities and I do very much dislike being away from England now. I wish they had accepted my suggestion to send another person as Ambassador and let me come just as an adviser, free to go back if nothing was happening. However things have turned out differently and it is no good worrying about them.[41]

The diplomatic stalemate, implying a long stay in Moscow, also entailed a welcome reassessment of whether his family should now join him. At the outset it had been agreed, with some reluctance on Isobel's part, some

38. RSC diary, 3 July 1940.   39. Cripps to L. Collier, 16 July 1940, FO 371/24845, f. 9.
40. ibid., 6 July 1940.   41. ibid., 10 July 1940.

breeziness on Stafford's, that she should stay at home with the girls. Although they wrote practically every day, their letters had to await the highly uncertain diplomatic bag, and he received none from her until the middle of July. Meanwhile, Isobel had been relying for news on the Foreign Office, and snippets from Stafford's official telegrams had been passed on to her by R. A. Butler. It was 'Rab' and Walter Monckton, in post at the Ministry of Information, who now facilitated arrangements for not only Isobel but also Peggy and Theresa Cripps to go out to Moscow – news which greatly cheered Stafford and helped persuade him to stay there. Had the Foreign Office calculated how best to keep him at his post, it could have come up with no better suggestion.

'I am quite reconciled to a long stay here,' Cripps now assured Butler. His hardheaded analysis was that 'these people will put up the maximum camouflage of German friendship without in the least believing in it but in the hope that it may save them from any attack before winter'. As one Christian to another, Cripps put it this way: 'I believe they earnestly pray every night (!!) that we may hold our own and weaken Germany but they daren't show a sign of it to anyone.' So the Russians – 'in a blue funk of Germany' – had to dissimulate their position, while the Germans, on their side, were equally mistrustful. 'It is a marriage of convenience,' Cripps concluded, 'in which each spouse is tucking away all the valuables possible against the inevitable moment of divorce!'[42]

This fairly cynical appraisal of the wicked ways of the world was built on the same principles of Realpolitik that Cripps had, ever since the Nazi–Soviet pact, proclaimed as the foundation of Rusian foreign policy. Thus it was not the will-o-the-wisp of Marxist ideology that made Stalin chary of an alliance with imperialist Britain: it was the iron grip of circumstances. When the circumstances changed – when the snows came, or when the British showed themselves able to defy Germany, or when Hitler's hungry eyes turned east – the whole situation might disclose new hopes.

An unusually reflective account of his impressions, which he sent to his daughter Diana after three months in Moscow, is worth quoting at length as first-hand evidence of his current view of Soviet Russia.

There is every reason to criticise a great deal that they do – they do it in 'Asiatic' ways which are not our ways and which are often cruel and undesirable ways. Their methods often differ hardly at all from the Tsarist methods, in fact they are Russian methods! Their lack or organisation, their way of doing or neglecting business is all

42. RSC to Butler, 13 July 1940, Butler papers, RAB E3/3, 156.

of it quite devastating at times, but in spite of all that one can either look upon them as people broadly groping after something which is in the right direction or as wicked and malevolent destroyers of world civilisation.

It should come as no surprise that Cripps opted for the former view and criticised the tendency, common in the British diplomatic corps, to put the worst interpretation on Russian actions. To this extent he might be called naive, but hardly in a way that blinded him to the obvious failings and barbarities of the Soviet system.

This régime certainly suffers from a very great many most grave defects. Partly due to inherent characteristics of the people, partly due to external circumstances and perhaps partly inherent in every form of dictatorship . . .

If to all these difficulties you add the government by secret police and spies which is the only method for a dictatorship then in such a country as this with a people of this kind, apt to intrigue and brought up in 'underground' revolutionary activities, you get perpetual change of personnel and 'liquidation' of many of the more intelligent people, creating new difficulties of organisation.

Was the dictatorship, then, a Stalinist perversion that betrayed the revolution? A later comment by Isobel, clearly influenced by Stafford, speaks of sadness 'that many things had gone awry and those who had followed Lenin had "erred and strayed" a long way from the path he meant them to follow'.[43] But, rather than blaming some corruption of revolutionary ardour, Stafford also manifested an inclination, which his aunt Beatrice would have approved, to identify the flaw in what she had dubbed the 'new civilisation' as its inadequacies in Fabian-style managerialism. 'The thing that seems to be most required is a really efficient staff of organisers and experts who will take steps to prevent wastage,' Stafford assured Diana. Nor was he immune to the Stalinist cult of personality.

Stalin and his fellow workers, but Stalin first and foremost, is making a tremendous effort to stimulate activity. His methods have been very many of them excessively cruel by our standards, others have been attempts to substitute some other form of competition or instigation for the profit motive.

As in China, he thought that 'they must work out their own salvation in their own way'. Also as in China, 'a whole host of things have happened and

43. IC to Diana, 27 November 1940.

will happen that I and most others will regard with horror and intense dislike'. Yet, just as Cripps had faced a dilemma some months previously in deciding whether to become Chiang Kai-shek's adviser, he now posed the question: 'if Stalin were to ask me tomorrow for my advice (which he won't do!!!) what should I say about it?' Claiming to be 'more than ever convinced of the undesirability of dictatorship and totalitarian regimes', Cripps also affirmed that 'some better forms of democracy must be invented if we are to give democracy the right form of government – not for some ruling class – but for the people as a whole'. His conclusion, therefore, was a fairly direct snub to Aunt Bo, or at least to her part in fomenting a Panglossian view of Soviet Communism.

One thing has been proved here – so far – and that is that you cannot leap into Utopia in one bound. It's a long and painful journey whatever route you travel and it is always difficult to tell whether you are on the right road. A great deal of harm has been done to the reputation of this country by its over-enthusiastic supporters who have pictured it as proceeding at full speed along a broad and beautiful highway.

Cripps obviously did not subscribe to a naive Communist vision, that he had seen the future and it worked. He was ready to put his finger on all sorts of ways in which it did not work; he did not envy the lot of the Soviet citizens he saw around him and admitted, 'I dislike the whole atmosphere.'[44] But whether he was any longer a fellow-traveller is less easy to determine. The classic posture of the fellow-traveller was to maintain that the Soviet system was a noble experiment – or at least a necessary one – for a backward country with an autocratic history, and thus an inspiration for the liberal socialism that might yet be realized at home. It was Utopia at arm's length.

What needs to be appreciated is that Cripps could simultaneously write of the Soviet Union as 'the future' while denying any determinist or exemplary imperative for replication, imitation or even emulation. For it was not a benignly beckoning future at all, but a chillingly dystopian future represented not only by Stalin's Russia but by Hitler's Germany. As he intimated to his friend Monckton:

historically they are both an attempt to get away from an effete civilisation which the countries we represent are trying desperately hard to cling to and to revivify. It is indeed a revolutionary war and we are on the side of the past – at the moment.

44. RSC, 8 September 1940, to Diana, which is the source for all otherwise unidentified quotations; much of this letter, though not the paragraph quoted above, is printed in Estorick, pp. 259–62.

Neither a Communist nor even a fellow-traveller, Cripps seems to have been moving, if he had not already moved, to a third possible position. He wanted 'the new world of the post-war period', now in its pre-natal stage, to be born with 'a moral and intellectual attitude which will encourage the right line of development'. If he anticipated a revolutionary situation in post-war Britain, it was hardly a prospect that he now relished – 'I shall probably get back in plenty of time to enter a concentration camp!!'[45]

These were not unspoken assumptions in shaping Cripps's position; but he spoke only to family and friends already disposed to his way of thinking; and his long-familiar public image misled alike former followers (notably on the far left) and current critics (notably in the Foreign Office). Cripps's Russian sojourn provided the occasion, not the cause, for a reformulation of his views, not least about the regime under which he lived. For him, it was precisely the utopianism of the Soviet experiment that flawed it as a response to the Russian predicament – and likewise invalidated it as a model for western democracy. Yet he persisted in finding extenuations for Russia, with a historical relativism that can be regarded as fairly sophisticated, even if his ethnic stereotyping was less so. Psychologically, maybe Cripps identified with Soviet Russia because they both had so many of the same enemies, from capitalists and Conservatives to the Foreign Office and (as he still believed) Hitler. Above all, he believed that strategically Britain could not write off Russia, and that their mutual interest in offering a common front against the Nazis was the crux.

This was Cripps's outlook as he dug in for a vigil suddenly made more bearable by the imminent arrival of his family. His Excellency leapt into action, with a stream of telegrams to Filkins.

PLEASE ARRANGE THROUGH FOREIGN OFFICE SEND AT ONCE BEST ROUTE TRUNK MY WINTER CLOTHES COATLINING ALL TIDY AND TWEED SUITS THICK UNDERCLOTHES AND CELLULAR SOCKS SHIRTS PYJAMAS TWO NEW WOOLLEN SCARVES NEW BLACK SHOES GALOSHES INDOOR SHOES ALSO FROM CHINA TWO SILKSUITS FURCAPS SOCKS TOPBOOTS FELTBOOTS USE WHITE FOX YOURSELF.[46]

It is interesting to see the list of supplies that he considered essential for a winter in Moscow.

---

45. RSC to Monckton, 25 September 1940, copy; part of this letter is cited incorrectly as 25 November 1940 in Burgess, *Cripps*, p. 141.
46. Telegram, 18 July 1940.

CHIEF REQUIREMENTS DRIED FRUITS VEGETABLES GOOD DEAL ENTERTAINING
SMALL SCALE TOBACCO TEN POUNDS THREE NUNS EMPIRE THOUSAND LARGE
MILD CIGARS LEN'S CHOICE THOUSAND MANILLA CHEROOTS TEN THOUSAND
PLAYERS CIGARETTES BEER TOMATO AND FRUIT JUICES LIME JUICE CASE KNIT-
TING WOOL AND MATERIALS YOURSELF POSSIBILITY GOOD SEAMSTRESS HERE
WINE AND SPIRIT ORDER FOLLOWS DIRECT . . .[47]

With ten thousand Players on hand, the ambassador was evidently ready
to smoke out the Russians. The trouble was that they were adept at this sort
of waiting game, where inscrutability was at a premium and paranoia
informed every tactical move. Such halting progress as Cripps supposed
himself to have made was soon cancelled. Unknown to him, the Russians
had passed an account of his interview with Stalin to Berlin; with rumours
leaking into the international press, the Foreign Office sought to pre-empt
their effect by giving the story to the BBC. Since this was the source from
which an unprepared Cripps, tuned in to the overseas service as usual, heard
the news of his secret talks broadcast to the world, he was understandably
upset, wrongly suspecting 'sabotage somewhere' or 'leakage of information
through drink in the Cabinet!!'[48] Despite such setbacks, Cripps tried to
retain his equanimity. 'Sometimes I think I may be of some use here and
sometimes I don't!!' he wrote home. 'I suppose history will decide in the
long run.'[49]

Listening to the BBC news was one of the major rituals of a day otherwise
programmed around Joe the dog, French practice, briskly taken vegetarian
meals, French lessons, telegrams, tennis, more French practice . . . It was an
innocent regime – 'My French mistress is coming to lunch with me
tomorrow' – of which Stafford gave a full account to Isobel.[50] During the
hot weather there were regular trips to the embassy's dacha, an equally
welcome destination for winter sports later as a refreshing break from the
claustrophobia of diplomatic life in Moscow. The continual presence of two
'secret police' added an exotic touch, or perhaps a surreal one when 'the
YMCA boys', as they became known, joined them in picking flowers.[51]
There was a picnic given by the press representatives for the diplomatic
corps – 'of course we didn't "see" the Germans'.[52] Above all, Stafford doted
on Joe, especially once the animal had been house-trained. 'We have great

47. Telegram, 27 July 1940.
48. RSC diary, 19 July 1940; see also Miner, *Between Churchill and Stalin* pp. 75–6.
49. RSC diary, 22 September 1940.   50. ibid., 15 July 1940.
51. ibid., 18 June, 6 July 1940.   52. ibid., 16 July 1940.

games in the garden chasing one another, jumping the tennis net together and rolling him on the ground,' wrote a more relaxed ambassador. 'To such simple pleasures are we – I was going to say reduced – but they are so preferable to others that I think I should say elevated!'[53] This was hardly why Cripps had come to Moscow; but it all helped make life tolerable while he awaited his family.

53. ibid., 20 July 1940.

2

Winter in Moscow

The safest route for Isobel, Peggy and Theresa Cripps to travel to Moscow in 1940 was via Canada. They set off for Montreal in late August on a ship carrying evacuated children – 'the whole boat was like Blackpool, complete with orange peel and chocolate paper', Isobel observed.[1] It was an interesting trip, with the Canadian Pacific Railway taking them to the dramatically sited hotel at Lake Louise in the Rockies before going on to Vancouver, where the press reports – 'Lady Cripps Here, Tells of British Will-to-Win' – were larded with the latest news on Joe ('the dog', as Isobel carefully explained). Then it was another ship to Shanghai and the long journey on the trans-Siberian railway. Stafford, now fully prepared for their arrival, was impatient at every delay. 'Today I've felt rather like an elderly hen wanting to fuss but nothing to fuss about!' he wrote on the eve of their arrival.[2] On 2 October, hours behind schedule, he went down to the station, with Joe in the car, for an affectionate family reunion and late supper at the embassy.

For the Cripps family, the embassy was to be home for the next eight months. Theresa and Peggy had each other to confide in. They agreed that their mother, stepping into the role of His Excellency's hostess, was 'feeling her new position rather', and had become touchy and 'overpowering'.[3] It is not surprising that a family that had spent only one month together during the previous year should have encountered some stress when suddenly thrown together again while adapting to a wholly new way of life under wholly unfamiliar conditions. Isobel told Diana:

The whole situation is unnatural and a nervous strain, from the 'scheming' of our foreign household entourage to the tension of an intensely overworked staff. This I feel has put great strain on D. and I have a good deal to which to get adjusted before

1. IC diary, 22 August 1940.   2. RSC diary, 2 October 1940.
3. Theresa Cripps diary, 4, 5, 30 October 1940.

I can get started at doing what I do hope I can mitigating various difficulties. An Ambassador is in a v. isolated position and I think the effects of these matters on D. will take a little time to work out.[4]

In fact the family quickly shook down to a curious but not uncongenial existence. At home they ate vegetarian meals together but there were also concessions to the conventions of Moscow's diplomatic life, especially as Theresa and Peggy, though resisting being stereotyped as 'the Cripps sisters', were carving out a niche for themselves. Their father later joked that their parties had given him good training for air raids.[5] They initially felt awkward that they did not drink alcohol, given that 'unfortunately all the young people seem to'; but they quickly found that Vuka Gavrilovic, daughter of the Yugoslav ambassador, disapproved too, and she soon became a close friend, especially of Peggy.

Stafford's view, unsurprisingly, was equally disapproving, finding 'too much drinking and drunkenness throughout the diplomatic circle here'. But he was relaxed about the consumption of the ample stocks he had himself laid in, content to note that ' "chez nous" I have never seen anyone the worse for drink yet and I hope I shan't do so!'[6] Whether he knew that his daughters had been initiated into the delights of a midnight swig of neat brandy, straight from the bottle, along with Geoffrey Wilson, may be unlikely. But it must have been obvious that they soon graduated to drinking wine in public, though still finding it a relief at a diplomatic gathering when 'for once people didn't drink too much'.[7] Likewise, Isobel Cripps's modestly calibrated social drinking – 'I must own myself to have had more than I approve of! i.e. 1 cocktail, ½ glass of beer and 2 glasses (small) of red wine' – showed that the ambassador's abstinent habits were not imposed upon the household.[8]

In some ways it was a highly privileged life. On the diplomatic round, an informal dinner could comprise eight courses with champagne.[9] This had never been the Cripps style; in 1940, it was a jarring anomaly. Isobel wrote home:

All this – as you can imagine – talk of food, in times like this, and this kind of life, makes things seem so unreal, and sometimes we feel 'awful' about it. Everyone

4. IC to Diana, 11 October 1940.   5. Appiah, *Attic*, p. 66.
6. RSC diary, 25 December 1940.
7. Theresa Cripps diary, 11 October 1940, 11 February 1941; cf. 21 November 1940, 18 December 1940.
8. IC to Diana, 18 March 1941.   9. RSC diary, 17 October 1940.

201

struggles to keep from putting on weight. We've both gained, but not too badly! and Geoffrey is looking better than I have seen him for a very long time.[10]

Within the embassy, the Crippses, conscious that, 'as Ambassador, Stafford *must* (more or less!) ask the staff to dinner now and again, and they (more or less!) *must* accept', struggled to break down barriers of formality.[11] They seem to have had some success, especially over the Christmas holiday in 1940. Moreover, Cripps displayed his talent for inspiring teamwork around his own leadership. When he stepped down, the career diplomat left in charge of the embassy took the unusual step of officially recording 'the regret that I and others who have served under him feel at the departure of one to whom we are indebted for constant kindness and consideration, as well as the tributes to his qualities which I have received from all quarters in the diplomatic corps'.[12] Such opinions became widespread among Cripps's subordinates. One of them later wrote: 'I got to know him very well, and only those who knew him well could realise, not only his wit and charm, but his kindness and human warmth.[13] He made this impression despite inevitable differences of outlook between himself and career diplomats with a Foreign Office pedigree.

'What a set of museum pieces!' Peggy commented to Theresa after their introduction to the embassy staff.[14] Geoffrey Wilson, with whom Theresa had at one point teetered on the brink of a romantic attachment, was another matter. Picking up an intimacy with him, she quickly gained the benefit of his impressions, few of them very encouraging. In Wilson's opinion, Cripps should now be in England and was wasting his time in Moscow, where a trained diplomat could do the job equally well.[15] Still, she found it 'gratifying to think that any definite step in the right direction on the part of this country will at home be attributed almost entirely to D.!'[16]

Cripps was no ordinary ambassador and he flouted the ordinary rules. In the letters he sent home to Diana, he was astoundingly open. To some extent, he chafed at the restriction of his own letters to political topics, which he then strove to make as interesting as he could; and perhaps spilling the beans to Diana was a means of fostering his intimacy with her across the gulf of distance. Maybe there was a frisson in telling her that an approach to the Russians 'will all have to be absolutely secret and confidential as

10. IC to Diana, 15 February 1941.   11. ibid., 28 November 1940.
12. Lacy Bagallay dispatch, 14 January 1942, FO 371/32941, f. 37.
13. W. H. Gallienne to IC, 23 April 1952.   14. Theresa Cripps diary, 3 October 1940.
15. ibid., 4 October 1940.   16. ibid., 7 October 1940.

otherwise they will run out of it through fear of Germany', or in writing that 'absolute secrecy is essential if we are to accomplish anything in the present state of fear of this country'. He showed himself conscious in another letter 'that a great deal of this is becoming quite secret though by the time you get it will be out of date'. But enjoining her to 'use the greatest discretion' was hardly a sufficient precaution.[17]

Here is a disconcerting puzzle. Did Cripps's sense of the need for secrecy not extend to an awareness that the Germans were intercepting diplomatic messages? We now know, if he did not, that their knowledge of his own moves came partly from reading his confidant Gavrilovic's dispatches to Belgrade.[18] Did Cripps's knowledge of how difficult it was for the diplomatic bag to get through – especially once the 'northern route' through Sweden was closed and the 'southern route' had to skirt hostilities in Greece and the Middle East – not give him pause? The British ambassador might naughtily scribble to his daughter: 'I suppose really it is a crime to write it even to you!'[19] But it could easily have been worse – a blunder which would have put this information at the disposal of German intelligence. The British war effort could no doubt have survived the spilling of the meagre secrets of the Moscow embassy. But could the career of an embarrassed ambassador?

Cripps saw himself as a major political figure with his own mission to accomplish – to ease relations between Britain and Russia pending the eventual 'divorce' between Hitler and Stalin. If the British Government had wanted an obedient messenger boy instead, it should not have chosen Sir Stafford Cripps. He said as much himself on occasion and implied it in all his dealings with London. Cripps's impatience with the Foreign Office was no secret to his family. There were routine references to 'the F.O., who are I think being stupid on this as on other things!'.[20] To Theresa, it was what her father told her 'about the fatuousness of the Foreign Office that really made me wonder what we had been let in for coming out here'.[21] Taking her cue from him, she expostulated that 'the F.O. really are the limit'.[22]

It was hardly surprising that Cripps should take the initiative with proposals to break the log-jam in Anglo-Soviet relations. One immediate issue to settle was the status of the Baltic states (Latvia, Lithuania and Estonia). Their occupation by Russia in June had appeared to Cripps as evidence of Russia's security worries rather than of its own imperialist

17. RSC diary, 17, 19, 23 October 1940.   18. Gorodetsky, *Mission to Moscow*, p. 58.
19. RSC diary, 23 October 1940.   20. ibid., 1 October 1940; cf. 11 October 1940.
21. Theresa Cripps diary, 4 October 1940.   22. ibid., 11 October 1940.

expansion and Churchill had likewise conceded that the annexation was 'dictated by the imminence and magnitude of the German danger'.[23] The issue became highly polarized on ideological lines, however, especially after the states were absorbed into Russia following elections that were staged under Soviet auspices in July. Cripps privately acknowledged his differences with a Foreign Office still under Chamberlainite control. 'There is not the slightest likelihood of this bunch ever wanting me to help in any situation where I could have any influence on policy,' he told Monckton, 'nor could I as they are about 100 per cent against all my political views.'[24]

Some of Cripps's old supporters on the left, professing concern that he was being used as a tool of Halifax's reactionary anti-Soviet policy, were to reproach the British Government for showing 'affection for the Baltic Fascist regimes by refusing to recognise the decision of those States to enter the Soviet Union'.[25] But it was a mistake to suppose that the ambassador privately shared this indulgent view. Instead, he acknowledged that 'everyone looks on it as a tragedy that the Baltic states should be Russianised'; faced with a choice of evils, he wrote that 'for the ordinary people it will be hard and difficult but better than being Nazified which was the only possible alternative for them'.[26]

Given the realities of the situation, then, why should not Britain recognize the Russians' *de facto* sovereignty? This was Cripps's persistent line. He could argue that, since they effectively controlled these states anyway, recognition would change nothing on the ground. As for the disputed assets (bullion, merchant shipping) that were in British hands, Cripps saw these as chips on the board, to be played in a bigger game, calling them 'the insignificant stake of recognising the *de facto* right of the Soviet Government to the Baltic gold and Baltic ships'.[27] The reservations of the Foreign Office, backed up by American concerns, centred on the all too close analogy between the Soviet takeover and the Nazi occupation of Poland – for the sake of which Britain had ostensibly gone to war.

In the middle of October, Cripps won crucial support for a new approach to the Russians. He had sent a long private letter to Halifax, explaining his thinking. The key point was that the Soviet Union had good reason to suppose the British Cabinet fundamentally hostile – as he chose to put it, with 'the attitude of a Nazi to a Jewish shopkeeper', merely exploiting a

23. Churchill to RSC, 22 June 1940, quoted in Gorodetsky, *Grand Delusion*, p. 37.
24. RSC to Monckton, 11 October 1940, copy.
25. D. N. Pritt, 'An open letter to Sir Stafford Cripps', *New Statesman*, 14 September 1940.
26. RSC diary, 17 July 1940.
27. RSC to Butler, 5 October 1940, Butler papers, RAB E3/3, 159.

distasteful arm's-length relationship. Instead, he argued, what the Russians needed, since they desired 'ultimate protection by the success of Great Britain, U.S.A., Turkey and China', was reassurance that 'in so far as they are prepared to "go in" with us and America and the others', they could expect to be treated as partners 'if and when we are victorious'.[28] It is notable that Cripps was not only counting on some degree of American participation but also on the willingness of the world's leading socialist and capitalist powers to work together – a potential grand alliance that in 1940 looked like a grandiose chimera.

Halifax, who had few better cards in his hand, persuaded the War Cabinet to support the proposals that Cripps now put forward: proffering assurances on British friendship for Russia in the uncertain future in return for an attitude of benevolent neutrality in the precarious present. The build-up of pressure in the Balkans and Turkey made this opportune. To clear the way, Cripps was authorized to make concessions on the Baltic issue. This was done in the text of a document finally handed over in Russian translation on 22 October. Cripps had requested an interview with Molotov; instead he was fobbed off with his deputy, Vyshinsky, and Cripps was right to sense pro-German proclivities behind this. But he pressed on regardless, exploiting the latitude he had been given, in an effort to tempt and mollify the Russians. Thus he talked about conceding *de facto* 'sovereignty' rather than 'control'; and, when pulled up by the Foreign Office in London, resorted to the line that the Russian term used in the text could be translated either way.[29] As a negotiator – a role that he later played in India, and in similar style – Cripps was ingenious in stretching to its utmost the brief he had been given, and indefatigable in his pursuit of a settlement. He had a lawyer's confidence that a clever form of words could be found to satisfy all parties.

Would the Russians take the bait? A further meeting with Vyshinsky left Cripps not unhopeful. His buoyant mood can be gauged from an entry in his daughter's diary at the time of the United States presidential election: 'If Roosevelt is returned, D. thinks they will be in the war by the New Year.'[30] This balloon of misplaced optimism was soon deflated with the announcement on 9 November that the elusive Molotov was off to Berlin, for the first top-level talks since the Nazi–Soviet pact had been signed fifteen months

28. RSC to Halifax, 10 October 1940, copy; summary in Woodward, *British Foreign Policy*, i, pp. 498–500.
29. See Woodward, op. cit., pp. 475–96; Miner, *Between Churchill and Stalin*, pp. 88–94; Gorodetsky, *Mission to Moscow*, pp. 76–80.
30. Theresa Cripps diary, 28 October 1940.

previously. The Cripps family were at the US embassy, watching Cary Grant and Katharine Hepburn in *Bringing Up Baby*, when the news came through. Theresa's cool comment, recorded the same night, that 'it is not a good sign for us, and D. fears there may be going to be some "arrangement" about Turkey and the Balkans', hardly suggest that Cripps flew off the handle, as one later American memoir contended.[31]

'We were glad to hear Berlin was bombed whilst Molotov was there and hope he saw something of it,' Isobel Cripps remarked in her diary a couple of days later.[32] She doubtless knew of Stafford's prior suggestion to the War Cabinet that the RAF should make Berlin a special target during the visit. If he had known that Molotov and Ribbentrop had to meet in an air-raid shelter, Cripps would have felt gratified that the British could not altogether be ignored. He had other ways of relieving his feelings of impotence, notably an angry exchange with Vyshinsky. Yet Cripps remained confident in dismissing 'the view that this country will or can ally herself permanently with Germany'.[33] Everything still depended on weakening Germany's hold, albeit in a longer game than he had recently hoped. It was his refusal to admit that his proposals for an Anglo-Russian rapprochement were now dead, his continued hope that they were simply dormant, that explain his reaction to his own Government's next step on 16 November.

'Today is quite the worst I have had since I came here!' Stafford declared.[34] Sensing an opening for a propaganda coup, the Foreign Office had released details in London of the proposals made to Vyshinsky. The effect was to demonstrate that the ungrateful Molotov had not lacked overtures from the British before choosing to go off to Berlin. Once more, however, Cripps had not been informed in advance. Once more, it was the BBC that brought the news to the Moscow embassy. Once more, Cripps exploded with pent-up exasperation, of which he made no secret. The various explanations canvassed within the Cripps family for the Foreign Office's actions – 'prize stupidity', 'lunatic folly', 'sabotage' – were uniformly unflattering. As Isobel's summing-up makes clear, in a sense it was a choice between resignation and resignation:

If Stafford were to resign it would have *such* international repercussions that all know it must not be considered, for the sake of one's country; so now – and nothing

---

31. ibid., 9 November 1940; cf. Gorodetsky, *Mission to Moscow*, p. 82, esp. n. 3 (on p. 312) about the account in Bohlen, *Witness*, p. 103.

32. IC to Diana, 12 November 1940; cf. Gorodetsky, *Mission to Moscow*, p. 82, and Gorodetsky, *Grand Delusion*, p. 75.

33. RSC diary, 13 November 1940.   34. ibid., 16 November 1940.

can undo what's been done – we must resign ourselves and make the best of what can be picked up out of the wreckage.[35]

This thunderstorm served to obscure the whole issue of who was responsible for the failure of Cripps's initiative. It is hard to escape the suspicion that, for a few hours, it allowed him to displace the burden of his immediate feelings of frustration from the Soviet foreign ministry to his own. But the thunderstorm evidently cleared the air, and Cripps's mind too. He did not cease reprimanding the Foreign Office but his real wrath was now directed against the Soviet Government. The significant point is that, within days, he was seeking permission to withdraw the British proposals, so as to show Molotov that he could not expect them to remain on the table whatever his own conduct. It was thus Cripps who now became the hawk and the Foreign Office that switched to a more conciliatory position. There is more than one irony in these shifts of stance. 'It is amusing,' ran one Foreign Office memorandum, 'that after only six months in the Soviet Union the Ambassador should have become so strong an advocate of a firm line with the Russians.'[36]

For once, Cripps literally did not know what to do next. In the prevailing 'atmosphere of fog', he thought it necessary to be 'a mixture of a crystal-gazer and a prophet to do any good at this job!'[37] Seeking to exploit his private line to Butler, Cripps rehearsed his grievances. Lack of proper consultation by the Foreign Office, he wrote huffily, 'makes me look a complete fool – not that I mind that personally a pin! – but I object to the British Ambassador in Moscow being made to look a fool publicly to the whole diplomatic corps'. Unconvincing as his professions of personal unconcern may be, he surely had a point in maintaining that 'it is no good my creating a negative atmosphere here, if a positive one of courting is made in London'.[38]

The candour of these comments was licensed by the private status ascribed to this correspondence. Cripps always put informal contacts at a premium in doing business. In later political crises, he was often to resort to a letter marked 'personal' – Nehru, Gandhi, Churchill, Mountbatten were all privileged recipients at crucial moments – in an effort to cut through an issue of confidence. It may not have been clear even to Cripps himself how far this was a manifestation of his own innocence – or of the lengths

---

35. IC to Diana, 17 November 1940; cf. RSC diary, 16 November 1940; Theresa Cripps diary, 16 November 1940; RSC to Butler, 22 November 1940, Butler papers, RAB E3/3, 165.
36. Fitzroy Maclean, 3 December 1940, quoted in Miner, *Between Churchill and Stalin*, p. 97.
37. RSC diary, 22 November 1940.
38. RSC to Butler, 22 November 1940, Butler papers, RAB E3/3, 165.

to which he would resort in his manipulation of private relations for public ends. At any rate, it did not wash with the Foreign Office. The Permanent Secretary, Sir Alexander Cadogan, who was the draftsman of ostensibly personal replies to Cripps's missives from Halifax and Eden successively, was prudently made aware by Butler of the letters he had received unofficially from the disaffected ambassador. Cadogan simply commented: 'I am sorry for him – reading between the lines one can see his disillusionment, which has made him peevish.'[39]

If Stafford had not been depressed at this juncture, he would have been the only member of the household to escape the pervasive malaise that hung over the British embassy. Theresa and Geoffrey Wilson mooned around, raking over the embers of a love affair that had never quite caught fire. At a loose end, Isobel recurrently took to her bed. 'She misses her political activities which we always said were bad for her,' Theresa commented.[40] The upsetting news came from London that Stafford's chambers had been bombed and all his books destroyed. Nothing seemed to be going right for him. His normal expedient for low spirits was to throw himself into his work; but his work was just the trouble.

Cripps was feeling embattled on at least two fronts: against the gentlemanly Foreign Office and against the streetwise Russians (not to mention Hitler, of course). If he went to the root of the matter in saying that 'the best diplomats are the events, they alone can bring about any decisive change here', he found it temperamentally difficult to live up to this maxim.[41] Cripps may have been right to blame poor communications with London for some of the tactical disagreement, which he thought could have been resolved in minutes by telephone.[42] But there was a disabling clash of styles between the Foreign Office's timeless, impervious detachment and his own urgent itch to do something.

This was a token of Cripps's lack of aptitude for a regular diplomatic post that he had never sought in the first place. He was neither happy to represent his own government's views nor able to change them. Having spent four months persuading the Foreign Office to offer concessions over the Baltic states, Cripps found that it could not abruptly be unpersuaded, even though by December his own line had changed. That his line was liable to change, all too disconcertingly, now became part of the received wisdom

39. Cadogan note, 21 January 1941, Butler papers, RAB E3/3, 164; cf. Woodward, *British Foreign Policy*, i, p. 500; Gorodetsky, *Mission to Moscow*, pp. 95–6.
40. Theresa Cripps diary, 29 November 1940 (passage in secret ink).
41. RSC to Butler, 22 November 1940, Butler papers, RAB E3/3, 165.
42. RSC diary, 20 December 1940.

about this wayward ambassador. His telegrams to a bemused Foreign Office lectured it on how 'un-sentimental, realist and nationalist' the Soviet Government was, and how it was inclined to 'attribute "gentlemanly" diplomatic methods to weakness'.[43]

Cripps privately justified stern measures, which he now urged, by appealing to the half-Asiatic propensity of the Russians to admire a strong and cruel ruling hand.

It is no good being too kind and nice, they merely look upon it as feebleness, one must be firm and forcible at times and then they sit up and take notice of you and probably secretly rather admire it, though openly they will pretend to be very cross and hurt! One has to remember too that like most Asiatics they are great bargainers and love a bargain and bargaining for its own sake, apart from what they get out of it.[44]

Realism tempered with impatience, or optimism tempered with petulance, seem better ways of describing Cripps's outlook than putting down everything to 'disillusionment'. None the less, his attitude to Russia – or how to deal with Russia – had indeed altered. Whereas he had been accustomed since 1939 to invoke realism in order to evoke sympathy for the Soviet Union, by the end of 1940 he was invoking it to enjoin a degree of cynicism. Correspondingly, his conviction that his own Government was doing the right thing – if often in the wrong way – had been strengthened. His ambivalence about Churchill was still there; absent from England during the summer, Cripps was slow to appreciate the new Prime Minister's hold on the public. But their common commitment to the war acted as a solvent of other disagreements. Speaking on the BBC on 11 September, Churchill spoke of fighting on 'until the last vestiges of Nazi tyranny have been *burnt* out of Europe, and until the Old World – and the New – can join hands to rebuild the temples of man's freedom and man's honour, upon foundations which will not soon be overthrown'.[45] These words reached – and touched – the British ambassador in Moscow.

I've just listened to Winston's broadcast – I think it was an absolute masterpiece in every way, he really comes out as a great man on these occasions. If only he were not so reactionary! he would be a great leader. I fear very much his influence in the post war period if we succeed. But that is a long way off.[46]

43. RSC to FO, 23 December 1940, quoted in Miner, *Between Churchill and Stalin*, p. 106.
44. RSC diary, 3 December 1940.   45. Gilbert, *Churchill*, vi, p. 779.
46. RSC diary, 12 September 1940.

As Cripps put it to Monckton, since the real political difficulties were postponed, it was 'perfectly plain sailing for the moment – to win the war and subordinate all effort to that accomplishment'.[47] Likewise, Theresa Cripps, always finely tuned to her father's mood, wrote of a subsequent broadcast speech by Churchill as 'so different from all the propaganda from the other side and making our cause and the struggle sound really worth while'.[48]

In a statement on war aims that Cripps sent to Halifax (and Monckton) in December 1940, he likewise depicted the war as a struggle for a better world, led by his own country, and appealing to 'the community of sentiment of the ordinary people of all countries'. This was, of course, a good propaganda line – and later used as such by Halifax in the USA – with Cripps in his best aspirational, exhortatory mode. But it is significant that there was no reference to the Soviet Union. 'Come what may, Great Britain and her allies will fight on in their crusade to free the world,' Cripps wrote, 'not seeking to preserve unchanged the past, but determined to save the world from the savage inhumanity which now threatens it so urgently, and then to join with the free and freed peoples of all nations to build up a better, saner and safer international and national order.'[49]

Winter in Moscow saw Anglo-Russian relations frozen into immobility once more. When the British ambassador to the USA, Lord Lothian, suddenly died, there was some talk in London of transferring Cripps instead. Churchill, genially and post-prandially, responded that 'he was a lunatic in a country of lunatics and it would be a pity to move him.'[50] He took this opportunity to demote Halifax to the Washington embassy while putting Anthony Eden into the Foreign Office. It was a switch that Cripps had contemplated as possible for some months, remarking that 'though I think a change would be good, not that one I hope'.[51] Accordingly, he was unenthusiastic when the change actually came, if only because he feared losing an 'indirect channel of approach' in view of his lack of previous personal contact with Eden.[52] 'We had "other hopes" for home,' was Isobel Cripps's gnomic comment, 'but can but hope for the best and the first telegrams to Daddie show some hope anyway and that's all one can say. Daddie is playing a waiting game now.'[53]

47. RSC to Monckton, 25 September 1940, copy.
48. Theresa Cripps diary, 27 April 1941.
49. Draft statement on war aims, 7pp., 3 December 1940; cf. RSC diary, 9 December 1940.
50. Colville diary, 12 December 1940, in Colville, *Fringes of Power*, i, pp. 367–8.
51. RSC to Monckton, 31 August 1940, copy.   52. ibid., 5 February 1941, copy.
53. IC to Diana, 18 December 1940.

At Christmas there was a determined effort to lift everyone's spirits, with thirty-six of the staff and their families invited to dinner. The Cripps family hobby of knitting occupied many hours indoors, while skating offered outdoor amusement once their kit had arrived from London. Skiing was a tempting idea – but how to get hold of skis? Here the enterprising Greek butler came into his own, mysteriously but triumphantly bringing home a pair of foreign skis, to his master's mock dismay: 'I told Timoleon he mustn't do that sort of thing and anyway he mustn't tell me of it if he did!!'[54] Stafford took to skiing at the dacha with a vigour that cheered Isobel – 'he really is splendidly hardy in this way at present with his early morning outing with Joe followed by – *still* – a cold bath!'[55]

There was a clear need to keep occupied, to keep cheerful – and to keep better informed. 'It's very trying sitting here waiting for things to happen!' he told Monckton.[56] One minister who talked with Cripps on his visit to London a few months later formed the impression that he literally did not know any Russians:

he was not allowed to meet or talk to Russians. He had had one meeting with Stalin, two with Molotov and perhaps half a dozen with Vishinsky and one or two other people. He had Russian guards always, but they were not allowed to have any talk with him or the embassy staff. The result was inevitably that he simply could not have any first-hand knowledge of things in Russia.[57]

Even if not literally true, this was worrying. Cripps admitted to Eden: 'There is an almost complete lack of contact and therefore the views I express are perforce gathered by piecing together opinions, rumours and facts gathered from various sources.'[58]

Cripps took what steps he could to counter diplomatic isolation. He brought together the ambassadors from the three countries that were now the cockpit of the polarizing conflict in south-east Europe: Christophe Diamantopolous of Greece, Haidar Aktay of Turkey, and – already a close friend of the Cripps family – Milovan Gavrilovic of Yugoslavia. Sometimes the Iranian ambassador joined them. All of them were pro-Allied, often more so than their governments; and since Molotov would only see the Axis ambassadors, Cripps ensured that he and his 'cronies' at least saw each

---

54. RSC diary, 30 December 1940.   55. IC to Diana, 17 January 1941.
56. RSC to Monckton, 5 February 1941.
57. Sir Archibald Sinclair recorded in Crozier diary, 18 July 1941, in Taylor (ed.), *Off the Record*, p. 231; cf. p. 232.
58. Cripps to Eden, 26 January 1941, FO 371/29464, f. 151.

other. This was 'the club' that met almost daily in Cripps's room: comparing notes, talking politics, assessing the latest intelligence.

It is now known that, from the beginning of 1941, the Russians were receiving intelligence reports pointing to a German attack upon them. Hitler had switched from the view that he first needed to defeat Britain and had decided that war against Russia would be 'like child's play in a sand box'. Consequent preparations for 'Barbarossa', as the operation was code-named, could not wholly be masked from the Russian intelligence network.[59] For the moment, Cripps remained in the dark about all this, enjoying hardly more contact with the Russians than with the Germans themselves. He was granted an interview with Molotov on 1 February, but only because Eden insisted upon it as a matter of protocol; they had nothing to say to each other. Cripps expected the Germans to move into the Balkans; he could not read Russian intentions beyond suspecting that they were keeping these to themselves. 'At the moment these people seem more sphinx-like than ever and I doubt if even the Germans know what they are thinking!' he wrote, little knowing what an understatement this now was.[60]

At the end of February came an interlude which, though it amounted to little in itself, restored Cripps's sense of purpose. He set off to meet Eden in Turkey, flown out by the Russians on a pioneer flight to Istanbul, and then rushing to catch the train to Ankara. Cripps 'spent the usual comfortable but rather sleepless night that I get on trains', arriving for a late breakfast at the British embassy, only to find that Eden was still asleep ('after being at a Cabaret till 5 a.m.'). Their encounter did not begin well; Eden was late that morning and still tired later in the day; and he seemed unfamiliar with the letter Cripps had sent him in January. But Cripps's decision to join Eden on the first leg of his onward journey to Athens provided the opportunity for relaxed talks the following day on 'a most luxurious train well stocked with food, drinks and smokes'.[61]

This, the first tête-à-tête between Cripps and the new Foreign Secretary, was an opportunity to establish a degree of personal rapport. Monckton had encouraged Cripps in thinking that he would find Eden congenial, and so it turned out. More than twenty years younger than the Prime Minister, Eden was the rather self-conscious representative of youth, of progressive Conservatism, of a more constructive view of post-war politics than Churchill embodied, and of more sympathy for Russia than Halifax had manifested. Cripps found that he could do business with this man and their

59. See Gorodetsky, *Grand Delusion*, pp. 85–6, 130ff.   60. RSC diary, 13 February 1941.
61. ibid., trip to Istanbul and Ankara.

developing relationship, forged in Ankara, was to be important in the politics of the next eighteen months. For Cripps, this was worth the long return journey, for all its broken nights in transit. It left him cheered 'that we are back in an atmosphere of possibility and not of impossibility so that now there is at any moment the *chance* of something turning up which makes life much more interesting and less depressing!'[62]

It was during March 1941 that Cripps became convinced that a German attack on Russia could be expected within the next few months. His hardest, most specific source was probably the Swedish ambassador. Cripps first alerted the Foreign Office on 24 March, though without persuading the Joint Intelligence Committee that this was anything more than a war of nerves.[63] The information was not what the Foreign Office wanted to hear; their line was that the Nazi–Soviet pact would hold firm. Conversely, Cripps's forecast was just the sort of thing they expected to hear from him since he had maintained all along that there was no love lost between the Germans and the Russians. For the moment, Cripps does not seem to have pursued the point; he was used to being ignored in London; and in any case he had a more urgent crisis on his doorstep.

Pressure on Yugoslavia had induced the regent, Prince Paul, to accede to a pact with Germany. When the news reached Moscow on 22 March, while Cripps at once began plotting busily with Gavrilovic to enlist Russian influence, their families sought to console each other. 'It's my first experience,' wrote Isobel, 'of being close to people with breaking hearts because they feel their country has been betrayed and taken a step leading to ignominy, especially when it is a stab in the back to valiant Greece.'[64] Within days, the news changed again; a coup in Belgrade brought hope of resistance to Hitler and incidentally restored Gavrilovic to favour. Though he was formally successful in signing a pact with the Soviet Union, this proved of little effect in preventing a German invasion on 6 April. Gavrilovic's efforts were again abetted by Cripps, with an inevitable backwash of suspicion, in Russian eyes, that this was because of an obvious British interest in fomenting discord between Germany and the Soviet Union.[65] Personal (and political) sympathy with the Gavrilovic family could not obscure the diplomatic reality that any moves by Cripps were bound to be read in this light by the Russians, as he was not allowed to forget.

*

62. ibid., 8 March 1941.
63. Gorodetsky, *Grand Delusion*, pp. 157–8; cf. Gorodetsky, *Mission to Moscow*, pp. 114–15.
64. IC to Diana, 27 March 1941.   65. Gorodetsky, *Grand Delusion*, pp. 141, 147–50.

Here was the context for an incident that has bulked disproportionately large in subsequent accounts of Cripps's stewardship during the
build-up to 'Barbarossa'. In *The Second World War*, Churchill wrote of
receiving, at the end of March, an intelligence report which 'illuminated the
whole Eastern scene like a lightning-flash'. It revealed that, when
the Germans supposed that Prince Paul had delivered Yugoslavia to
them without a fight, they began moving three Panzer divisions to Poland,
only to countermand the movement following the Belgrade coup.
Churchill's inference, 'that this could only mean Hitler's intention to invade
Russia in May', may have seemed remarkably prescient when it was first
published in 1950.[66] At this time, the fact that the British had broken the
German Enigma codes, and that the Prime Minister had access to the
decrypts, remained a closely guarded secret. Once the story of Enigma and
Ultra intelligence from Bletchley Park had been told, Churchill's powers
of intuition might seem less impressive; but his reasons for passing on
information from a unique source might appear correspondingly more
imperative.

Churchill decided to send a personal message to Stalin. Transmitted on
3 April, it was 'short and cryptic', by intention. It simply reported the troop
movements, adding: 'Your Excellency will readily appreciate the significance
of these facts.'[67] It is, however, by no means obvious what that significance
was. Churchill's initial conclusion was that it could 'only mean in my
opinion the intention to attack Yugo at earliest or alternatively act against
the Turk'. Deputizing at the Foreign Office for Eden, who was abroad,
Churchill was given further briefings, including the telegram conveying
Cripps's previous warning. Only then did the Prime Minister settle on the
interpretation that, despite what the Foreign Office kept telling him, it
actually meant an attack on Russia.[68] But how was Stalin supposed to divine
that? Only in hindsight did these points seem obvious.

When Cripps received the cryptic message, with instructions to deliver it
personally, he was unimpressed. He was purposely denied any knowledge
of Enigma; still more, of course, were the Russians; so the force of the
warning was liable to be lost on those who literally did not have a decrypt.
Instead, as Cripps well realized, its authority was likely to be impugned by
its British source. It is understandable that such considerations weighed

66. Churchill, *Second World War*, iii, p. 319.
67. ibid., p. 320; Woodward, *British Foreign Policy*, i, pp. 604ff.
68. RSC to Eden, 30 March 1941, quoted in Gorodetsky, *Grand Delusion*, pp. 160–61; cf.
Gorodetsky, *Mission to Moscow*, p. 117.

heavier in Moscow than in London. An obedient diplomat would none the less have tried to deliver the message at once.

Not Cripps. On 5 April – the same day that his friend Gavrilovic was engaged in frenetic activity to enlist Soviet support against the imminent German invasion of his country – Cripps told Churchill that these were not circumstances in which it was possible for him to deliver any message personally. But Cripps made sure that Gavrilovic used his access to Stalin to pass on a report that Hitler had told Prince Paul of his plan to attack Russia on 30 June.[69] This was a sharper version of what Churchill was now telling Cripps he wanted the Russians to realize: 'that Hitler intends to attack them sooner or later, if he can . . .'[70] A couple of days later, following Stalin's signature of the pact with Yugoslavia, it seemed to Cripps that things were going well, since the Russians had at last shown some sign of resistance to German designs. Told now that it would suffice to deliver the message to Molotov, Cripps still demurred, arguing that further interference by Britain at this juncture would be unwise. It was a view that the sceptical Foreign Office readily accepted. Eden supported Cripps, whose own efforts were now directed to making a reality of the Soviet commitment in the Balkans. Denied even a proper interview with Vyshinsky, a frustrated Cripps wrote him a long personal letter instead. In it he argued that the Russians should act themselves rather than wait for Hitler to attack them.[71] Cripps was thus taking a lot upon himself: playing it by ear with the Russians, sensitive to the need to strike the right note, and confident that he could do so himself.

The Prime Minister, however, still wanted his own message to be delivered. Eden's bland suggestion that it would now be better to await a response from Vyshinsky was brushed aside by Churchill. Cripps was therefore instructed to deliver the cryptic warning on 18 April and did so the following day. There is no evidence that it made any particular impression upon Stalin.

What Churchill later alleged was that, had there been no delay in delivering it, it might have done so: 'If I had had any direct contact with Stalin I might perhaps have prevented him from having so much of his Air Force destroyed on the ground.'[72] What we now know is that Stalin had a range of much more circumstantial intelligence reports available, and from

69. Woodward, *British Foreign Policy*, i, pp. 604–5.

70. Churchill to RSC, 5 April 1941, Churchill papers, CHAR 20/37, f. 34.

71. Gorodetsky, *Grand Delusion*, pp. 164–7.

72. Churchill, *Second World War*, iii, p. 323; his account prints the later telegrams but is, of course, wrong to state that Cripps made no reply until 12 April.

sources that were not compromised, as any anti-German communication from the British was bound to be. We also know that, for his own reasons, he chose to ignore them all.[73] It is true that Churchill's early appreciation of the likelihood of a German attack showed unusual acumen – unusual, that is, in London. In Moscow, however, his was one of many similar messages to reach Stalin.

Churchill's warning exposed not only a minor difference on tactics between the Prime Minister and his ambassador but also a major divergence between Churchill's strategic view of German intentions and that of the Foreign Office. That he later chose to accentuate the former (and minimize the latter) by a noisy chastisement of the disobedient Cripps was a function of their subsequent rivalry. As early as November 1941, Churchill had become worried that Cripps was 'preparing his case against us'; it was then that he prepared his own riposte, which became the draft of the war memoirs.[74] Conversely, the proposed newspaper serialization in 1950 would have excised altogether the references to dissent from Eden, currently heir apparent to the Conservative leadership, showing that it was the partisan impact of this tale that was subsequently judged explosive. By contrast, the diplomatic impact of the incident in 1941 was negligible.

On the British side, the substantive difference of opinion had been between the Foreign Office, backed by military intelligence appraisals, tending to dismiss an imminent German attack as a phantom;[75] and, on the other side, Churchill and Cripps, who both now thought this likely – but who took different views of how to get through to the Russians. In every sense, it was frustrating that London and Moscow were so far apart. When Isobel Cripps reported at this juncture that 'Daddie is longing and "aching" for closer contact with those at Home in authority', she was, as usual, faithfully reflecting Stafford's mood. Had he evinced hostility to Churchill, she would hardly have written: 'I wish D. could have an hour or two's talk with the P.M.'[76] Correspondingly, when Churchill was writing to his ambassador on another matter later in the year, he blandly assured him: 'It

73. Gorodetsky, *Grand Delusion*, p. 133. A point which, rather inconsistently, Churchill recognized in writing: 'Nothing that any of us could do pierced the purblind prejudice and fixed ideas which Stalin had raised between himself and the terrible truth.' Churchill, *Second World War*, iii, p. 328. Likewise Churchill records Stalin as saying later, when challenged about the warning: 'I remember it. I did not need warnings': ibid., iv, p. 443.

74. The fullest treatment of this issue is in Gorodetsky, *Mission to Moscow*, pp. 116–25. Cf. Gorodetsky, *Grand Delusion*, pp. 177–8.

75. Hinsley, *British Intelligence*, i. pp. 453–9.   76. IC to Diana, 17 April, 1941.

is never necessary for you to deliver my telegrams to Stalin personally unless you wish to do so.'[77]

Cripps's own view of an unfolding situation is fully conveyed in his letters to his daughter. On 12 April he anticipated the possibility of an evacuation of Moscow within a couple of months, despite the Russians' wish to avoid war, because 'if the Germans attack as is now anticipated by many people then they will fight'.[78] A few days afterwards, he reported Moscow 'full of rumours of German attacks'.[79] Later in the month, having been sent by the Foreign Office a summary of the relevant evidence, Cripps spoke of 'waiting to see what demands Germany is going to make here and whether she is going to attack this country'.[80] The point on which he remained unclear was not whether the Germans were ready to go to war but whether the Russians were ready to give in. 'I still think there won't be any war now but there is no doubt a danger of it and every one is talking about it not only amongst diplomats but amongst the Russians as well,' he wrote on 30 April. 'I expect these people will be able to do enough appeasing to avoid it – if Hitler lets them.'[81]

If intelligence on German war preparations was becoming more compelling, readings of Russian intentions remained as ambiguous as ever. Only with the opening of the Soviet archives has it become evident that Stalin himself had little idea what to do next, beyond hoping against hope that his concern to avoid provocation of the German military would succeed in averting catastrophe. When there were talks between the two sides in May, Cripps wrote: 'I have the feeling that somehow or another the Russians will avoid a war!!'[82] At 'the club', he argued for this view, albeit with 'little enough grounds of any solid kind', as Theresa Cripps noted – 'though it may be perfectly correct, I certainly don't regard Daddie's judgment as infallible'.[83]

The Cripps family seems to have sensed that, with the onset of spring, one chapter was coming to an end. Isobel wrote:

We walked thro' the Kremlin gardens & right round home by the other Bridge. As I crossed it and saw all the light reflected in the river, and the always beautiful vista

77. Churchill to RSC, 4 September 1941, Churchill papers, CHAR 20/24, ff. 120–22.
78. RSC diary, 12 April 1941.   79. ibid., 15 April 1941.
80. ibid., 24 April 1941; cf. Woodward, *British Foreign Policy*, i, pp. 612–13.
81. RSC diary, 30 April 1941.
82. ibid., 2 May 1941; he told Monckton much the same: RSC to Monckton, 3 May 1941, copy.
83. Theresa Cripps diary, 10 May 1941.

of the Kremlin, I realized how the charm of it had grown with me and what a comfort it had been all those months to live opposite to it, instead of in some of the other Embassies or Legations right in the town. For the rest of my life I shall feel a harmony with Moscow.[84]

This was, alas, the fatal hour for 'the club', since the Russians withdrew accreditation from the Yugoslavs, along with the Belgians and Norwegians (and soon the Greeks too). The Gavrilovic family sadly prepared to pack their bags: Milovan glum at the prospect of joining the exiled government in Jerusalem, Vuka disconsolate at the thought of losing her friends, especially Peggy. Attending what Theresa called 'the maddest party I've ever been at', held in the Yugoslav embassy, she found that 'three glasses of wine in ten minutes or so' set the tone for a night that ended 'making whoopee in the garden' at 4 a.m.[85] It was a last fling.

The signs were confusing but bleak. The closing of the missions and Stalin's formal assumption of the premiership seemed to Cripps to point towards appeasement of Germany. When the news reached Moscow that Rudolf Hess, Hitler's deputy, had flown to Scotland, it created a stir: not only in the British embassy, where Isobel Cripps excitedly recalled having met Hess in 1935, but also in the Kremlin, where a less innocent story appeared plausible. Did Hess bear peace terms for Britain? Was the British War Cabinet split over whether to accept them? Would the British save themselves – at Russia's peril? It is true that Cripps himself had, in April, already given the Russians an admonition lest protracted war should tempt 'certain circles in Great Britain' to seek a separate peace; and it has been argued that this ploy proved counter-productive in exciting the Russians to jump to just such a conclusion – the more so after Hess's flight.[86] The Foreign Office regarded this as a 'very dangerous and wholly unauthorized threat', but whether the Russians needed Cripps to nourish their already fertile capacity for suspicion is a moot point.[87] In any case, their continued determination not to allow the wily British to manipulate them into a war against Germany is clear enough.

Plans for evacuation from Moscow had long been spoken of; but, with the exception of Peggy, that is not why the Cripps family left. On 2 June, Theresa, hearing that Geoffrey Wilson was going to Teheran with the

84. IC to Diana, 1 May 1941.   85. Theresa Cripps diary, 28 May 1941.
86. See Gorodetsky, *Grand Delusion*, pp. 174, 265; Gorodetsky, *Mission to Moscow*, pp. 126, 135.
87. Sir Orme Sargent memorandum, 26 April 1941, printed in Ross (ed.), *Foreign Office and the Kremlin*, p. 73.

diplomatic bag, recorded that 'the Great Idea came to me' – she would accompany him for a holiday in Persia. She quickly got her way – 'Daddie agreed readily, his only doubt being whether it was quite proper for me to go with Geoffrey' – and there was no suggestion that, in the ambassador's mind, an imminent invasion was a bigger threat to this proposed jaunt than 'the proprieties'.[88] On the same day, news came through that the ambassador had been recalled for consultation in London. He held a farewell dinner for 'the club'. After a day or two of uncertainty, it was arranged that Isobel should accompany Stafford, with the cover story of a weekend visit to Stockholm. From Sweden they were flown home. 'BRITAIN!' wrote Isobel in the train from Scotland to London. 'We both say we "don't feel anything", it all seems a ridiculous dream, specially for me.'[89] Their time together at the Moscow embassy was over; Stafford's return was to be under altogether different circumstances, personal and political alike.

88. Theresa Cripps diary, 2 June, 1941.   89. IC to Diana, 11 June 1941.

3

Withstanding Barbarossa

Many subsequent legends spoke of Cripps forecasting 'Barbarossa', some-times down to the very day. If he did so, it was in a hit-and-miss way, with no better accuracy the nearer the invasion came. His real claim to vindication came through the consistency with which he had predicted that, despite the Nazi–Soviet pact, Hitler would turn aggressively upon the Soviet Union. Whether that might lead to Russian capitulation, as Cripps feared, or to the making of a grand alliance with Britain and the USA, as he hoped, was a question on which he wobbled this way and that. On 12 June, when the Joint Intelligence Committee finally came round to the view that the evidence pointed to an imminent German invasion, Cripps seems to have swung the opposite way. The next day he was confiding his fears about the Red Army to his aunt Beatrice. When he attended the Cabinet on 16 June, he spoke of the uncertainty of Stalin's intentions, given the likelihood that Russia could not hold out for more than three or four weeks in a war with Germany.[1] This was the conventional military assessment at the time. The phrase that was already in the air – and subsequently attributed to Cripps – was that the Germans would go through the Red Army 'like a knife through butter'.[2]

There was much speculation as to why Cripps was in London. The Russians interpreted his visit, almost through force of habit, as a hostile move; they had been told of Cripps's true destination only on the eve of

---

1. Hinsley, *British Intelligence*, i, pp. 478–82; Webb diary, 14 June 1941, in MacKenzie and MacKenzie (eds.), *Webb: Diary*, iv, p. 470.
2. For example Sir Archibald Sinclair recorded in Crozier diary, 18 July 1941, in Taylor (ed.), *Off the Record*, p. 231. Gorodetsky, *Mission to Moscow*, pp. 170–71, suggests Cavendish-Bentinck, chairman of the JIC, as the source, while Ismay, *Memoirs*, p. 229, suggests Sir John Dill, Chief of the Imperial General Staff (until the end of 1941, when he was succeeded by Sir Alan Brooke). After dining with Dill and Cripps, Brooke noted that the latter 'on the whole did not throw much light on the probability of military resistance on the part of Russia if pressed'. Danchev and Todman (eds.), *Alanbrooke: War Diaries*, p. 165 (17 June 1941).

his departure for Stockholm. The truth was that he had been recalled as a disciplinary step.[3] The Foreign Office had built up a formidable dossier against the behaviour of their eccentric ambassador. The indictment centred on his 'occasional unwillingness to carry out his instructions, combined with his tendency to take independent and unannounced action of his own', which were justifiably identified as sources of confusion in British foreign policy.[4] The Foreign Secretary himself was by no means hostile to Cripps, often adjudicating between his suggested line and that urged within the Office. Likewise the Prime Minister was notable within his own Government for his relatively pragmatic view of the possibility of alliance with Russia, for his early alertness to the likelihood of a German attack, and for his refusal to write off Russia's chances completely if war came.

As events turned out, Churchill and Eden found it easy to close ranks with Cripps. On Sunday, 22 June, the day that 'Barbarossa' was launched, they were both at Chequers for the weekend. They were to be joined during the day not only by Cripps but by Lord Beaverbrook, the flamboyant Canadian newspaper proprietor and old friend of the Prime Minister, who left more than one retrospective account, heavily coloured by his desire to show himself from the outset a better champion of aid for Russia than his obvious rival, the ambassador to Moscow.[5] It seems safer to rely upon what John Colville, the Prime Minister's private secretary, recorded at the time in his diary, an amended version of which was later quoted in Churchill's memoirs. Colville's diary makes it clear that, at dinner on the previous evening, Churchill announced a German invasion of Russia to be certain ('and Russia will assuredly be defeated', he added, in an aside not quoted in *The Second World War*). Still, Churchill declared that Hitler was wrong to count on 'enlisting capitalist and right-wing sympathies in this country and the US' and that he would go 'all out to help Russia'. It was after dinner that Churchill, warming to his theme, said: 'If Hitler invaded Hell he would at least make a favourable reference to the Devil!'[6] Accordingly, when the

3. Gorodetsky, *Mission to Moscow*, pp. 146–9. However, Gorodetsky is wrong to suggest that Cripps's daughters were deliberately evacuated, cf. p. 154.

4. Sir Orme Sargent memorandum, 26 April 1941, printed in Ross (ed.), *Foreign Office and the Kremlin*, pp. 72–4.

5. Beaverbrook recorded in Crozier diary, 19 February 1942, in Taylor (ed.), *Off the Record*, p. 284; this was, of course, at just the moment when Beaverbrook was effectively superseded in the Government by Cripps. See the post-war narrative, 'The Second Front', in Taylor, *Beaverbrook*, pp. 474–5. Cf. Gorodetsky, *Mission to Moscow*, p. 163.

6. Colville diary, 21 June 1941, in Colville, *Fringes of Power*, i, p. 480; Churchill, *Second World War*, iii, p. 331, quoting an account by Colville which is only a paraphrase of his diary.

news of the German attack came through the next morning, Eden was told in his dressing-gown that Russia must be treated as a partner.

Cripps was summoned at once. He and Isobel drove down from London, and it is a mark of how well the day went that they ended up staying not only for lunch but for dinner too. On arrival, Cripps supported Churchill in scorning the notion (put forward by the American ambassador, Winant) that the news might be a 'put up job'. True, at lunch, the Prime Minister duly trailed his coat about Communism. Colville noted: 'Cripps took it all in good part and was amused.' But we also have Colville's contemporary record that, on the serious issue of policy towards Russia, Cripps and Churchill sided together (with no mention of Beaverbrook) in the 'extremely vehement' argument, over dinner that night, with Eden and another Conservative minister, Lord Cranborne, who both wanted to keep their distance from the Soviet regime.[7]

Whatever their differences of emphasis or subsequent recollection, Beaverbrook, Eden and Cripps were probably the three most prominent pro-Russian figures in British politics. These were the men with whom Churchill chose to closet himself, while he spent this crucial day pacing around the house and garden in the midsummer sunshine, preparing the speech that he gave on the BBC that evening. 'I knew that we all felt the same on this issue,' was how Churchill explained not having consulted the War Cabinet; and his own actions made this true.[8]

The Prime Minister's broadcast, by general consent, was a masterpiece. It struck Theresa Cripps, listening to it at the British Consulate in Shiraz, as 'a very clever speech', in squaring twenty-five years of Churchill's anti-Communist sayings (which he declined to unsay) with his immediate commitment to help Russia and the Russian people. 'The Russian danger is therefore our danger,' he concluded.[9] Not only the fervour of this appeal but also its realism tallied, of course, with Cripps's own analysis. As he had told Eden, Stalin was not 'affected by any pro-German or pro-anything feeling except pro-Soviet and pro-Stalin'.[10] After 22 June, enlightened self-

His acknowledgement (to Beaverbrook in 1960) of some discrepancies is noted in Taylor, *Beaverbrook*, n.1, p. 475, and Gorodetsky, *Mission to Moscow*, n.2, p. 163 (on p. 324) – both written several years before Colville's diary was published. None of this makes Beaverbrook more plausible. Gilbert, *Churchill*, vi, pp. 1118–20, is based chiefly, and surely rightly, on the original Colville text.

7. Colville diary, 22 June 1941, in Colville, *Fringes of Power*, i, pp. 481–2.
8. Churchill, *Second World War*, iii, p. 331.
9. Theresa Cripps diary, 22 June 1941; Churchill's speech is printed in Churchill, *Second World War*, iii, pp. 331–3.
10. RSC to Eden, 27 May 1941, quoted in Gorodetsky, *Grand Delusion*, p. 285.

interest drew Stalin and Churchill together in a way that Cripps had prophesied. Like many prophecies, it embodied a good deal of wishful thinking
and its fulfilment proved to be highly imperfect.

If Cripps was not feted, he certainly avoided being carpeted. Nobody
could suppose that this was the week to replace the British ambassador in
Moscow. On Sunday he had been at Chequers. Speaking in the House of
Commons on Tuesday, the Foreign Secretary claimed that 'by his influence,
and by his example, my honourable and learned friend has shown to
the Soviet Union the fundamental desire of His Majesty's Government to
maintain our relations upon a normal footing'.[11] On the same day Cripps
received notice that he was to be sworn in as a Privy Councillor, clearly
marking his front-bench status. By Friday he was back at the embassy in
Moscow, with VIP treatment on his journey from the British and Russians
alike.

Eden had assured the House that Cripps would now 'be able, with his
marked ability, to advise and direct the help which it is the declared intention
of His Majesty's Government to give to the Soviet Union at the present
time'.[12] He was joined by a British military mission, headed by Lieutenant-
General Noel Mason-Macfarlane, later augmented by Rear-Admiral
Geoffrey Miles and Air Vice-Marshal A. C. Collier. These heads of missions
were to accompany Cripps throughout his remaining stay in the Soviet
Union and came to form a close bond with him. This was one sign of the
new agenda for the British ambassador.

Britain and Russia were not allies – yet. Here was the task facing Cripps,
and bracing him for renewed efforts. 'I am very glad I came back,' he wrote,
'as though I may not be able to do a great deal I think I can probably do
more than anyone else could!'[13] The change in atmosphere since spring was
palpable. There were to be no more mysterious hindrances in gaining access
to Molotov, whom Cripps saw almost daily in the first fortnight back, or
even to Stalin, whom Cripps now found 'much more friendly and frank'.[14]
An agreement on mutual assistance was finalized with unwonted speed on
both sides. Cripps wrote on 10 July:

I have just had a 'most immediate' through from Winston that they are prepared to
enter into the agreement that Stalin suggested to me and I am hopeful that it will
have a very great effect upon World opinion when it becomes public. I am now

---

11. Eden in 5 *HC Debs.*, vol. 372, col. 974 (24 June 1941); wrongly attributed to Churchill in
Estorick, p. 271, and Cooke, *Cripps*, p. 271.
12. ibid.   13. RSC diary, 28 June 1941.   14. ibid., 9 July 1941.

waiting to go and see the great man and tell him the good news. Once that it is done I think that all our difficulties should be out of the way.[15]

12 July was a day to remember. Cripps was cheered by a prompt telegram from London – 'This is really good work on the part of the government and I give them full marks for it!' – giving him authority to sign at once. A meeting between him and Stalin settled remaining issues. Then, in the afternoon, Cripps's entourage swept back to the Kremlin in thirteen cars, with the lights switched to yellow at all the road junctions, for the official signing. 'No festivities of any sort at my request,' Cripps had specified; but, what with it being his thirtieth wedding anniversary too, he was apparently induced to take a glass of champagne. 'I feel at last that I have accomplished something worth while,' he recorded.[16] Eden sent his 'warmest personal congratulations on the success of your negotiations over the Alliance, as we now dub it'.[17]

A year after his first arrival in Moscow, Cripps saw a second chance for a mission of high importance but limited duration, in which he would bask in the confidence of the two governments whose amity he had helped seal. This was indeed a honeymoon, and it duly lasted about a month. 'I am trying to curb the P.M.'s desire for sending rather emotional messages,' Cripps noted at the end of July, 'as it is not a good thing to make them too frequent as they tend to lose their effect at this end.'[18] If he was soon becoming wary of the Prime Minister's warm words, it was because he feared they were a substitute for action in support of the Russian war effort. Whatever Eden had told the House about Cripps's ability to 'advise and direct' the course of British assistance, it was made obvious that the real decisions would be taken by the man with the big cigar in London, not by the man on the spot in Moscow.

On 30 July there was a flurry among the diplomats when Harry Hopkins arrived in Moscow on a brief visit. His importance lay in the fact that he was at this time Roosevelt's special envoy, allowed a good deal of initiative in the moves he made. He had been in London for talks on lend–lease supplies for the United Kingdom, which clearly would be affected if it were decided to supply the Soviet Union too. So he decided to visit Stalin in Moscow in preparation for his master's forthcoming summit meeting in

15. ibid., 10 July 1941.
16. ibid., 12 July; cf. RSC to Peggy, 13 July 1941; Cassidy, *Moscow Dateline*, p. 52.
17. Eden to RSC, 15 July 1941, PRO, CAB 127/64.   18. RSC diary, 29 July 1941.

Placentia Bay with Churchill (whom Hopkins would accompany on the sea voyage to Newfoundland). Cripps knew Hopkins as a left-wing New Dealer in Washington; he liked him and saw eye to eye with him politically, unlike Steinhardt, the US ambassador. Cripps pounced on Hopkins for private briefings – snatching him from under Steinhardt's nose – and made the most of this conduit to Roosevelt. Cripps was encouraged by Hopkins's assurance 'that in his view the Americans would be in the war by the 1st of September'.[19] Perhaps also Cripps sought to emulate Hopkins's glamorously untrammelled role.

For, on the eve of Hopkins's arrival, Cripps sent an important ('personal and private') letter to Eden. Not only did it report on the general problems in liaising with the Russian forces, but it also turned to his own concern 'about the length of my stay here'. The plan that he wanted put to the Prime Minister was that he should quit as ambassador after another month, freeing him to take up an unspecified job in England; but that he should return to Moscow 'as a person specially instructed to discuss with Stalin the post-war problems', with a wide-ranging political brief.

I dont want personally to get stuck here doing nothing all through the winter, as I explained to Winston before I came back and as I think he realised. Nor do I want to consult my own wishes but only what is best for the conduct of the war and of the peace. I feel that I have got a position with Stalin now that would enable me if I were to come back clothed with special authority to make some real progress towards an understanding of our ideas of post-war Europe.[20]

One does not have to accept the Foreign Office's view that Cripps was suffering from delusions of grandeur to think that he was now misjudging his own potential. Lacking an appreciation that such decisions would now be taken by the leaders themselves, lacking the temperament for a subservient role, and, above all, lacking ideological affinity with Churchill, Cripps could never have served as his Hopkins. Eden's reply, when it came some six weeks later, was predictably cool. He appealed to Cripps's sense of duty to stay at his post while Russia's fate hung in the balance. 'At the same time you will not want to come back here and do nothing,' Eden added pointedly. 'There is not, Winston asked me to say to his regret, at the present time any vacancy in the Government nor any immediate prospect of there being one.'[21] Cripps sharply fired back: 'Quite specifically you can tell Winston that I

19. ibid., 30 July 1941; cf. Gorodetsky, *Mission to Moscow*, pp. 198–203.
20. RSC to Eden, 29 July 1941, copy.   21. Eden to RSC, 25 August 1941.

do not expect him to find me any job, that sort of attitude is not my form!'[22]

These exchanges were conducted in slow motion, entailed by Cripps's ploy in styling them personal letters, which meant that they went in the diplomatic bag rather than as official telegrams. It was, as he recognized, an unsatisfactory medium, what with letters crossing and the bag's delays, which spun out the correspondence into the autumn. The upshot was that Eden renewed his appeals, at first personally, and in the name of the Prime Minister, and finally in the name of the Cabinet; and he found events conspiring with him in parrying a further letter from Cripps suggesting that he should return to London for consultation.[23] Invoking the German thrust on Moscow that had meanwhile been mounted, Eden telegraphed in mid-October: 'I feel sure that you will agree that in present circumstances it would be impossible for you to leave the Soviet Government.' To which Cripps answered: 'Of course I agree.'[24]

It was, inexorably, the war that drove all other events and decisions. The German advance, though worrying, was less swift and sure-footed than had been anticipated. This war was not to be over in three to four weeks after all. Cripps's diary contains a repetitive refrain, cumulative in its sense of triumph, as days spread to weeks, and weeks to months. 'Quite frankly I never expected to be still in Moscow undisturbed on the 24th day of the war!' (15 July). '. . . I did not expect still to be unbombed in Moscow after 4 weeks!' (17 July). After a month, there were still neither air raids nor evacuation – 'and I regard that as a distinct victory for the Russians' (20 July). Even after the raids began, enduring a week of nightly bombing spoke of Russian fortitude, enjoying a week with no bombing spoke of German fallibility. 'This is the beginning of the sixth week of the war, and here we still are in Moscow' (27 July). 'Well here we are at the last day of August and still in Moscow' (31 August). 'Here we are at the end of the first three calendar months of the war and still going strong' (20 September).

The real test, Cripps wrote at one point, was 'to remember what one's expectation was when one came back and then measure the gains and losses against that standard'.[25] He was often subsequently mocked for sharing the common view that the Red Army would suffer speedy reverses; but his own conduct on his return to Moscow hardly suggests that he thought that the

---

22. RSC to Eden, 16 September 1941, copy; also RSC to Eden, 10 September 1941, copy, reiterating request to leave.
23. Eden to RSC, 18 September 1941; RSC to Eden, copy, 1 October 1941.
24. Telegram, with reply, 14 October 1941, copy.   25. RSC diary, 9 August 1941.

Russians would quickly be out of the war. 'Never have I doubted their capacity or their determination,' he said later. 'I was always confident that in the long run they would be victorious, at whatever cost, over the aggressive hordes of the Nazis.'[26] This tallies with what he recorded in his diary during 1941. Torn between his fears and his hopes, Cripps hesitantly allowed himself to become more confident, writing at the end of the year: 'I thought that they could not hold the Nazi advance until it got further into Russia but I never wavered for a moment in my view that they would go on fighting and that in the end they would wear down the Germans.'[27]

There is certainly no room for doubt that Cripps felt invigorated in sharing dangers of which his diary makes light. On the first night of bombing, there was a direct hit on the roof of the embassy and 'had it not been for the magnificent work of all the personnel led by the heads of the Military Mission the place would probably have been burnt out'. Cripps was prominent in giving moral support, moving among his staff in the basement: 'They were all splendid and there wasnt a whimper even from a child.'[28] The building inevitably suffered from the vast quantities of water pumped to the roof. Strengthening of the cellars was put in hand, and retreat to them henceforth often broke a night's sleep. 'I should go out to the Datcha,' Cripps admitted, 'were it not for the fact that other people are bound to stay and cannot get away and so I feel that I must not desert them.'[29]

His identification with the sufferings of the Russian people was translated into lessons for grand strategy. Stalin had first asked for a second front to be opened in the west, then for British troops to be sent to Russia itself. 'One doesn't wonder at their feeling of disappointment that we can do nothing to draw off the weight of the German attack when even the difference of a comparatively few divisions might make a critical difference,' Cripps wrote.[30] Even if direct military intervention were impossible, it should surely be feasible to expedite supplies from Britain and the USA, if only because they stood to lose from their own delays: 'Each day we are throwing away the help of thousands of Russian soldiers and a mass of material and equipment.'[31]

Cripps was anxious to show the Russians that the British were giving them both moral and material support. The storm over an ill-judged remark by one Conservative minister – 'There was a time when I hoped that the Germans and Russians would exterminate each other' – showed the

26. Red Army Day speech at Sheffield, 21 February 1943.
27. RSC diary, Christmas Day 1941.   28. ibid., 22 July 1941.   29. ibid., 23 July 1941.
30. ibid., 13 September 1941.   31. ibid., 21 September 1941.

potential for mischief and misunderstanding. Cripps's impulse to send his 'personal word of explanation' to the Soviet Government had to be restrained by Churchill.[32] More constructively, Cripps's pressure to implement plans for military aid through Anglo-American talks with the Russians yielded results when such a conference was finally convened in Moscow. He wrote on 28 September:

Today is the 99th day of the war. And at last the British and American delegations are due to arrive. I wish it had been fifty days ago as it might and should have been.[33]

Cripps had played a significant part in getting this conference off the ground. It had been proposed in one of the two joint statements by Churchill and Roosevelt to come out of their Placentia Bay conference (the other was the Atlantic Charter). When Steinhardt and Cripps had to deliver this message to Stalin in the middle of August, Cripps noted with satisfaction that it was 'based on the draft I gave Harry Hopkins when he was here.'[34] Cripps's own reward, as it turned out, was to be exclusion from the conference itself. Instead, the entire discussion of supplies for Russia was to be kept in the hands of the visiting dignitaries: the British Minister of Supply, Lord Beaverbrook, and the American roving ambassador, Averell Harriman. Yet again, Cripps heard the news first on the BBC. 'It is curious,' he commented, 'but you might think that it was of sufficient interest to send us a telegram about so that we could tell the Russian Government before it was announced on the Radio. But apparently the British Government don't think so and we have no news from them at all.'[35]

Even Cripps's warmest admirers acknowledged his 'insensitivity to the feelings of others'.[36] The corresponding virtue of this defect was that he was almost as oblivious in receiving slights as in giving them. He was thus still capable of affirming: 'I am glad Beaverbrook is coming as he is of sufficient importance and enough of a realist to get on well with the job here.'[37] Cripps appreciated that Beaverbrook was currently the champion of the Soviet Union – his 'tanks-for-Russia' week was a prelude to his Moscow visit – but perhaps did not yet appreciate the extent to which that made the two rivals. The way that Cripps put it was that 'they will have enough

32. Correspondence between Cadogan, Cripps and Churchill over the speech by Moore-Brabazon, 2, 3 September 1941, Churchill papers, CHAR 20/24, ff. 104–22.
33. RSC diary, 28 September 1941.
34. ibid., 15 August 1941; cf. Gorodetsky, *Mission to Moscow*, p. 205.
35. RSC diary, 4 September 1941.   36. Strauss, p. 12.
37. RSC diary, 4 September 1941.

people without me to take part in the conferences'.[38] It was just as well that he accepted this, given Beaverbrook's determination to shut out the ambassador, whom he always claimed the Russians disliked: 'When I went to Moscow it was necessary for me to see Stalin alone – without Cripps – I had to.'[39]

The second honeymoon of Cripps's ambassadorship was well and truly over. If he could just about bear feeling slighted he could not abide feeling redundant. It was conspicuous on all sides that he was not involved in preparations for the forthcoming conference. He noted acidly that his Government might have felt that it could benefit from his advice: 'But the P.M. thought otherwise.'[40] He had been on the point of flying home in early September, taking Mason-Macfarlane with him, to drive home the arguments for urgent assistance to Russia: only to be forbidden to leave his post.

There was undoubtedly some friction between Cripps and his own Government, but it would be a mistake to suppose that he was isolated in his pro-Soviet stance. In fact Eden's position, here as on other issues, was very little different from that of Cripps, both of them scornful of the reactionary Tories and hopeful of getting the Prime Minister to match the bounty of his rhetoric about their Russian ally with practical assistance. Here the signs were mixed: some foot-dragging by Churchill but also enough progress on delivering supplies to make Cripps think that 'Winston ... is really doing very well in the efforts that he is making to make good the losses of material that the Russians have suffered.'[41]

Nor were differences in policy towards Russia ideologically driven in any simple way. Cripps's diary leaves no doubt of his distaste for Beaverbrook's right-wing politics. Yet, paradoxically, it was this millionaire capitalist, this crony of Churchill, who took the uncritical pro-Soviet line, as Cripps wryly appreciated in making an after-dinner story of the spectacle of 'Stalin "selling" Russia to "the Beaver"'.[42] Whereas Beaverbrook was ready to nod along while British Communists bathed in the glow of Soviet resistance, Cripps had taken up a combative stance: 'They certainly must not be allowed to walk away with the credit for it!'[43] All this needs to be

38. ibid., 16 September 1941
39. Beaverbrook recorded in Crozier diary, 19 February 1942, in Taylor (ed.), *Off the Record*, p. 284.
40. RSC diary, 7 September 1941.
41. ibid., 10 September 1941. On the differences between Churchill and Eden see Lawlor, 'Britain's entry into the War', esp. pp. 175-7.
42. Coupland diary, 26 March 1942.   43. RSC to Monckton, 14 July 1941, copy.

remembered in understanding the complex relationship between Cripps, Churchill, Eden and Beaverbrook as it unfolded during the following twelve months.

Though Cripps vigorously represented the demands of the Soviet Government, he was by no means its creature. In the economic negotiations with the tough-minded trade minister Mikoyan in August, Cripps chided the Foreign Office for wanting 'to give in on everything in case it may cause unpleasantness if they dont' and wrote that they were 'still imbued with the appeasement attitude and dont see that people respect you if you stand up to them in a dignified way'.[44] He was glad to score minor victories on these issues – 'I appealed to Stalin and got a decision against Mikoyan on every point' – not only in themselves but to establish a businesslike approach.[45] In his diary he often noted the need for 'a frank talk', preferably with Stalin, to sort out problems.[46]

Cripps thought the Russians were 'a bit childish over their disappointment at our not being able to take any more active steps to draw off the pressure on them'.[47] Above all, he was well aware of the frustrations faced by the British military mission in being denied the relevant information on which to base any assessment of what was needed. 'The most that one can get,' he told the Foreign Office, 'is an occasional piece of gossip through the Russian chauffeurs or *dvorniks*, or possibly through foreign journalists.'[48] Little wonder that he later leapt to the defence of British officers whom he felt unjustly accused of impropriety when they were simply trying to do an impossible job. He again charged that 'the weak-kneed attitude of the F.O.', as he saw it, was 'the worst form of appeasement and most undignified and goes back on all that I have done so far in the matter'.[49]

Cripps's tough tactics in handling the Russians went along with his strategy for forging a robust alliance of equals. Hence the hopes that he invested in the Harriman–Beaverbrook talks. With an appointment to see Stalin a few days before the conference, Cripps worked on the hypothesis 'that they have definitely decided that we are not acting as full allies' and found the meeting 'very satisfactory'. Faced with a 'very frank note' from Cripps, Stalin apparently 'responded equally frankly so that we now know where we are'.[50] Cripps accepted that there was nothing more that he could

---

44. ibid., 11 August 1941.   45. ibid., 26 August 1941.
46. For example ibid., 16 September 1941.   47. ibid., 12 September 1941.
48. Report, 15 September 1941, in Woodward, *British Foreign Policy*, ii, p. 28.
49. RSC diary, 15 October, 4 October 1941.   50. ibid., 19, 20 September 1941.

do. 'I hope that Beaverbrook will be able to clear the matter up,' he wrote, 'as I have not been able to as I havent got the power or authority to make the statements that are necessary to convince them.'[51] As usual, he professed not to care 'two pins' about his own position, so long as the conference was successful.[52]

Beaverbrook's whirlwind visit was conducted with ruthless charm. Cripps was not taken in by his claim that 'he and Anthony were the only two Crippsites in the cabinet!'[53] Behind his back, Beaverbrook disparaged Cripps, not only to Harriman (as a socialist teetotaller) but to Stalin (as a bore).[54] More important, Cripps was denied any proper account of the business conducted in private sessions from which he was purposely excluded. Cripps did not object to Beaverbrook's attempt to strike a deal with Stalin – this was how he had envisaged the conference working – but to the air of illusion that was engendered. 'It was to be a Christmas-tree party,' as Beaverbrook put it or, as Cripps recorded with distaste, 'a sort of Father Christmas party', patronizing the Russians while dazzling the press.[55] Though Cripps conceded that 'the atmosphere was so genuinely friendly' at the lavish farewell banquet, he regarded the final communiqué as 'quite false in saying that we had satisfied the wishes of the Russians'. It was prescience as much as sour grapes that led him to remark: 'I am afraid that after the spectacular success of the conference the time of disappointment will come when the things do not arrive.'[56]

Cripps had successfully been kept in the dark. Given 'little except scraps of information at mealtimes from Beaverbrook', Cripps admitted that 'now I feel right out of the picture' over future dealings with Stalin. He had, however, seen enough of Beaverbrook to form a very clear view of him, especially as the prospective colleague in Government that he now purported to be. 'I more and more doubt whether it is possible for me to work with the present Government in any way,' Cripps concluded, 'especially since my experience here of the Beaver, who is about the most reactionary person possible.'[57] His influence on the Prime Minister was as disturbing as his methods were distasteful. Cripps's judgement was to guide him some four

51. ibid., 24 September 1941.   52. ibid., 27 September 1941.
53. ibid., 29 September 1941.
54. Taylor, *Beaverbrook*, p. 490; Chisholm and Davie, *Beaverbrook*, p. 416; Harriman and Abel, *Special Envoy*, p. 94.
55. Taylor, *Beaverbrook*, p. 487; RSC diary, 29 September 1941.
56. RSC diary, 2 October 1941.
57. ibid., 1 October 1941. This episode is well treated in Hanak, 'Cripps as British ambassador', part 2 (1982), pp. 339–41.

months later: 'The more I see of B. the less possible it seems to me that I should ever be in the same cabinet as he is.'[58]

The Moscow conference was the moment of truth in Cripps's ambassadorship. Following his abrupt departure on 4 October, Beaverbrook apparently sent Cripps a telegram: 'The corner-stone had been laid by you and the bricks were at hand when I reached Moscow.'[59] But the whole conduct of the conference showed that Cripps was not to be entrusted with defining the terms of Anglo-Russian cooperation. His personal treatment by Beaverbrook was hardly the main point, though it left Cripps deplorably and avoidably under-informed about the course of the discussions. What little he learnt came from Harriman. Left to themselves for an hour of after-dinner conversation at a farewell party at the American embassy, the two men overcame the personal friction that had bedevilled the visit and found much common ground. They agreed, in particular, that it would be easier to satisfy Russia's territorial demands at this moment of crisis than in the event of a victory later contrived by Russian efforts.[60] Irrespective of whether this seems wise in hindsight, it is hardly just a pro-Soviet line.

Within days of the departure of the Harriman–Beaverbrook delegation, the whole war situation deteriorated in ways that further marginalized Cripps. The German advance resumed; at the beginning of October Hitler announced Russia's defeat; the mood in Moscow turned from sombre to panic-striken; plans for evacuation of the Government and the diplomatic corps were laid. 'It is today the 109th day of the war and as yet nothing that could make any difference has been sent or at least has arrived,' wrote Cripps. 'If only we had taken the matter as seriously in the first days of the war as we are doing now it might have made a difference.'[61] The Russians asked for a large British force to be committed; Churchill countered that this was logistically impossible. Instead he switched attention to Iran (which had been in joint Anglo-Russian occupation since August), offering to release the Soviet troops stationed there by undertaking that the British would take over full responsibility. Did they not have a common interest in safeguarding this crucial supply route? Or, as the Russians predictably suspected, were imperialist ambitions behind it? Cripps intervened by introducing the idea that if Churchill could spare troops for Iran, perhaps he could spare them to send a small British force to the Caucasus. This was

58. ibid., 3 October 1941; cf. 29 September, 4 October 1941.
59. Gorodetsky, *Mission to Moscow*, p. 208; original not found.
60. RSC diary, 4 October 1941: Harriman and Abel, *Special Envoy*, p. 95.
61. RSC diary, 8 October 1941; and on this crisis see Overy, *Russia's War*, pp. 94–8.

Cripps the clever lawyer mediating between two obtuse clients. If only Churchill would listen to his official advice on Russian psychology! If only Molotov would accept his unofficial advice on how to respond![62]

It was never likely that Cripps would be allowed to play the role he wished in such negotiations. It became all the more unlikely when he was told, at eight hours' notice, to evacuate the embassy on 15 October. Members of diplomatic staff locked themselves in their rooms, burning official papers.[63] A delegation from the TUC, led by its General Secretary, Walter Citrine, had arrived in Moscow only three days before; Cripps took them under his wing, as the safest way of getting them back home. Accompanied by a hundred British personnel and mountains of luggage – and of course the faithful Joe – Cripps spent the next five days on a slow journey to Kuibyshev, 500 miles to the east on the River Volga. Travelling on the enormous diplomatic train with his friend Gavrilovic, restored since July as Yugoslav ambassador, Cripps regretted that their daughters Peggy and Vuka were not there to cheer them up.[64] The butler, Timoleon, was happily in attendance, producing coffee and food with Figaro-like panache, while his master indomitably brought his diary up to date. He was observed by Citrine, 'sitting in a compartment looking nearly frozen with his coat collar turned up, but clicking away steadily at the keys of a typewriter on his knee'.[65]

Conditions on arrival proved primitive, with dormitory accommodation for displaced diplomats overflowing. Worst of all, though the diplomatic corps was now in Kuibyshev, the Soviet Government was not. Stalin had changed his mind at the last minute and decided, after all, to stay behind to rally resistance. This may have been a heroic decision; but Cripps felt tricked that Stalin and Molotov were still in Moscow, leaving only Vyshinsky for Cripps to remonstrate with in Kuibyshev. The contrast between his position and that of his counterpart, Maisky, Soviet ambassador in London, was brought home sharply. It meant, Cripps concluded after a few days, that 'I am just wasting my time here and that anything I want to say might just as well be said to Maiski in London and telegraphed here as said to Vyshinski and telegraphed by him to Moscow.'[66]

Unable to get back to Moscow, unclear about whether he could leave the country, undecided about whether he should resign, Cripps diverted his

62. RSC diary, 14 October 1941. Cf. Miner, *Between Churchill and Stalin*, pp. 164–7, and Woodward, *British Foreign Policy*, ii, pp. 41–2.

63. Citrine, *In Russia Now*, p. 60.   64. RSC to Peggy, 23 October 1941.

65. Citrine, *In Russia Now*, p. 68.   66. RSC diary, 26 October 1941.

energy into setting up a small house as headquarters for himself and the military mission. He busily laid hands on furnishings, he enlisted the resourceful Timoleon in securing creature comforts, he took Joe for walks, he was even reduced to playing patience – all in his efforts to avert boredom. His diplomatic duties now reduced to a humdrum level, Cripps focused his ideas by starting to write a book (of which nothing apparently survives) for several hours a day.

By the end of October, Cripps's outlook was settled, even if he had not yet also settled upon a feasible plan to achieve his objectives. For the first time since going to Russia, he looked hard at his own political prospects. He recorded the suggestion of Philip Jordan, a sympathetic journalist from the *News Chronicle*, that he might form an alternative government: an early mention of such a heady possibility. But Cripps worked on the assumption that Churchill's support was still rock-solid in the country (if less so in the Commons) and thus thought the problem easier to state than to resolve: 'We must try and get something more progressive than Winston and Beaverbrook to conduct the peace-keeping for us when it comes and that means a change of Govt during the war, which at present looks to be an impossibility.'[67]

Cripps's increasingly sharp clashes with Churchill thus had a political undertone, of which both men were aware. When Cripps reported the impression made by German propaganda, that Britain was prepared 'to fight to the last drop of Russian blood', Churchill was moved to make a full reply. If this reads like a draft of the case he might have made in a parliamentary debate, perhaps it is because he now envisaged the possibility of facing just such a challenge from Cripps. In his missive, the Prime Minister delivered telling reproaches to the Russians for bringing their own fate upon themselves through the Nazi–Soviet pact and, while he professed to give such aid as was practicable now, he asserted that 'it would be silly to send two or three British or British-Indian divisions into the heart of Russia to be surrounded and cut to pieces as a symbolic sacrifice'.[68] Cripps privately called this telegram 'petulant and irrelevant', though conceding that 'he has been and is awfully good on the supply side'.[69]

It is notable that, in mounting his alternative case for intervention, Cripps carried with him all his own colleagues in Kuibyshev, not only

67. ibid., 28 October 1941; cf. 14 August 1941.
68. Woodward, *British Foreign Policy*, ii, pp. 43–5 and n.1, p. 45.
69. RSC diary, 30 October 1941.

Mason-Macfarlane and the military mission but also the Foreign Office regulars. For Cripps, the issue was more than an argument about British military commitment: it was his exclusion from the policy-making process. For what he did not know, because he had not been told, was that some of the same ground had been covered in Beaverbrook's discussions in Moscow. It was not until 1 November that a copy of Harriman's notes was telegraphed by a shamefaced Eden. Cripps exploded. He drafted a telegram ('which if I send it is a flat resignation'), but thought better of it overnight after long discussions with his friend Monckton, who was passing through Kuiby-shev.[70] The redrafted reply was none the less strong. 'I am amazed that these most important conversations should now be reported to me for the first time,' Cripps expostulated. He gave the warning: 'I can see no use in my remaining here to act as an occasional post-box (for messages to Stalin about the formulation of which I am not consulted and which I am not instructed to discuss with him) . . .'[71]

Though addressed to Eden, the real target was Churchill. 'Beaver and Winston are apparently running the policy as regards this country,' Cripps noted in his diary, 'and I gather that the F.O. and Eden are having very little to do with it.' Still, if he were to be allowed to negotiate a treaty of post-war collaboration, Cripps declared himself prepared to soldier on – 'but if not,' he mused, 'then I must either get them to sack me which I should prefer or else I must go home myself. I prefer the former as it would prevent Winston using my resignation against me which of course he will do if I have to resign on a difference with him.'[72] Here was an open acknowledgement that they were now locked in a tactical struggle for position. Stafford took the opportunity to send Isobel, who was busy on his behalf in London, a candid warning: 'I am pretty sure that the major part of Winston's desire for me to remain here arises from the domestic political situation and not from his view as to the needs of the position out here.'[73] What with Halifax's exile to the Washington embassy, not to mention Samuel Hoare's to Spain, posting awkward persons abroad now looked like 'the technique that is becoming so common with Winston'.[74]

Cripps thus saw himself as a political exile. He was stuck in Kuibyshev with only Vyshinsky as his contact with the Soviet Government, and neither of them was informed of the messages now being exchanged directly between

70. ibid., 4,5 November 1941.
71. RSC to Eden, 5 November 1941, quoted in Ross (ed.), *Foreign Office and the Kremlin*, p. 76.
72. RSC diary, 5 November 1941.   73. ibid., 5 November 1941.
74. ibid., 6 December 1941.

Churchill and Stalin.[75] Eden was right to suppose that 'there will surely be more trouble from Cripps, whose one idea is to come home and play a part here'.[76] Monckton's role as an informal go-between was enhanced by his current visit to Kuibyshev. Advised by him, Cripps pondered his position, and on 13 November sent a telegram. It pointed out that he was not a career diplomat; it said that the policy of the Government meant that there was nothing more that he could do; and it was, as Cripps put it privately, 'to all intents and purposes a resignation of this job'.[77]

The battle lines were drawn for the sort of debate that Churchill was already rehearsing in his head – and now on paper too. The minatory and provocative tone of his draft reply, had it been sent, would surely have provoked an open clash. In it Cripps was warned 'that it would be a mistake from your point of view to leave your post and abandon the Russians and the Soviet cause' – evidently how Churchill would have portrayed a resignation. He claimed to act 'not from any fear of political opposition', which he could face without embarrassment, since Cripps could hardly expect the Soviet government to side with him, though he would inevitably be saddled with their misdoings. 'You must not underrate the strength of the case I could deploy in the House of Commons and on the broadcast,' Churchill threatened.[78]

In Kuibyshev the War Cabinet's response was anxiously awaited. Cripps wanted to know what they were going to do about Stalin's demands 'and also incidentally about me'. He correctly expected 'that they will take up the attitude that I must stay here and leave it to me to resign if I want to do so, and then they will raise difficulties about a successor and make me appear the most selfish and inconsiderate person!'[79] This scenario did not allow for the fact that Eden had been busily deploying his consummate emollient skills. The upshot was his offer to travel to Russia himself. Though Eden recorded some growls from Churchill – 'Winston said he would not have me go to Moscow to keep Cripps quiet'[80] – in fact he got his way. The War Cabinet opted for conciliation – of Stalin primarily but concomitantly

75. ibid., 10 November 1941.
76. Eden diary, 11 November 1941, in Eden *Memoirs*, ii, p. 281.
77. RSC diary, 13 November 1941; the telegram is quoted in Gorodetsky, *Mission to Moscow*, p. 270.
78. Churchill draft telegram, 15 November 1941, quoted *in extenso* in Miner, *Between Churchill and Stalin*, p. 179; also partly quoted in Gorodetsky, *Mission to Moscow*, p. 272. Throughout 1941, Churchill's poor strategic record generated an undercurrent of criticism which can readily be invested with conspiratorial overtones, as suggested (rather often) in Day, *Menzies and Churchill at War*.
79. RSC diary, 17 November 1941.
80. Eden diary, 14 November 1941, in Eden, *Memoirs*, ii, p. 282.

of Cripps too. Meanwhile Eden had played down the significance of Beaver-brook's indiscretions and he calmed down the excitable Prime Minister too. It was judged better to keep Cripps, for the moment, on the other side of the Volga Hills than to face him on the other side of the House.

The turn in policy was enough to satisfy Cripps – or to trap him, at any rate. With Eden now about to visit Moscow, Cripps was browbeaten, yet again, into staying at his post; he would not, after all, be back with his family for Christmas. He thus had mixed feelings about the forthcoming conference: 'This is the step I suggested too so that it would hardly be possible for me to go off just when they are doing what I have suggested in this matter.'[81] Eden had put himself out to charm Isobel Cripps in London, though Stafford ruefully told her: 'I am afraid that he cannot have supported my demands to return very strongly or else Winston was more insistent on keeping me out here than I thought!'[82] Now Eden exerted his charm on Stafford, who, though aware of it, none the less to some extent succumbed.

Eden's visit to Moscow in December 1941 was a notable event, if only because the meeting took place at all and did so within forty miles of the front. Cripps set out gladly enough from Kuibyshev to meet the Foreign Secretary and found Moscow surprisingly undamaged. The British embassy was uninhabitable because of looting and Cripps was put up in a luxurious hotel suite. Arriving a few days early, he was able to join Eden on the last lap of his own rail journey from Murmansk in the north, for a few hours of discussion before confronting the Russians. Cripps thought that there should have been more preparations for the conference and that he should have been entrusted with them. None of this dulled the mood of elation in which he recorded the positive atmosphere at the opening session: 'Yesterday was a most important day in the history of the world!'[83]

Cripps suddenly sensed an alleviation of his anxieties, not only about the future of the world but about his own. His dilemma had seemed acute. 'My own view is that when I insist on coming back either Winston will feel obliged to try and get me into the Cabinet or else he will attack me for deserting my job so as to do all he can to destroy any influence I might have,' Stafford had confided to Isobel. 'I dont know which he will do; it will depend on the exact circumstances at the time and how strong and much threatened he feels his position.'[84] This disenchanted view can be compared with the anodyne account in Churchill's memoirs, which had the great man reflecting

81. RSC diary, 23 November 1941.   82. ibid., 3 December 1941.
83. ibid., 17 December 1941.   84. ibid., 3 December 1941.

on poor Cripps's plight (especially after his move to Kuibyshev 'in the crisis of December') and reflecting that 'there was nothing inappropriate in a political personage of his quality seeking to return to the House of Commons' – hence the Prime Minister's agreement ('early in January') to Cripps's plea.[85] Both dates are incorrectly given, though convenient in conveying a blandly disingenuous impression of what happened.

It is arguable whether Churchill came to think Cripps a bigger menace in Russia than at home. What seems to have been decisive is that the context changed, with startling abruptness. While the Foreign Secretary was setting out for Moscow, the Prime Minister had impulsively decided to visit Washington, following the dramatic entry into the war of the USA. This news had made surprisingly little direct impact upon Cripps – in sharp contrast to Churchill, who telegraphed to Eden on 12 December that it 'will give certain victory'.[86] The indirect impact upon Cripps, it seems, was to allow him, within days, an honourable discharge by a Prime Minister who no longer felt so beleaguered. So on joining the Foreign Secretary's train from Murmansk, as Cripps recorded with satisfaction, 'Anthony told me that they now agreed to my return which was great news as I had decided to tell him that I was going anyway.'[87] The path was thus clear for Cripps's re-entry to British politics.

The Moscow talks, starting on 16 December, constituted the finale to Cripps's diplomatic career. Eden had been faced with Stalin's suggestion of their beginning with a tête-à-tête (without Cripps) but persuaded him otherwise.[88] In contrast to the Beaverbrook–Harriman negotiations, therefore, Cripps was a participant throughout, flanking Eden alongside Cadogan of the Foreign Office, and facing Stalin and Molotov on the Russian side, with Maisky as interpreter. At a personal level the meetings began in an atmosphere of cordiality, even gaiety, sitting late into the night over champagne and caviar with Stalin.

We got quite hilarious at the end and I asked him to give a judgment on a very difficult and vexed question for me which was whether caviar was fish or eggs. This

---

85. Churchill, *Second World War*, iv, pp. 55–6; cf. iii, p. 470, which has Cripps in Kuibyshev in November in a highly selective reprinting of telegrams.
86. Gilbert, *Churchill*, vi, p.1274; cf. the curious reference in RSC diary, 8 December 1941: 'Just heard of Japan's war with U.S.A.'
87. RSC diary, 16 December 1941. Cf. Gorodetsky, *Mission to Moscow*, p. 280, which notes that Churchill and Eden recognized the 'potential danger of having a politician in Moscow'.
88. Cadogan diary, 16 December 1941, in Dilks (ed.), *Cadogan: Diaries*, p. 421; Oliver Harvey diary, 14 December 1941, in Harvey, *War Diaries*, p. 73.

amused him greatly and he decided it was eggs. They tried to make me drink the numerous healths that they drank and eventually I promised that I would if they signed two agreements but only after the signatures and not before.[89]

Britain and the Soviet Union were seeking to negotiate an alliance. Eden came with instructions to build on the Anglo-Russian agreement that Cripps had signed in July through a joint declaration associating Russia with the principles of the Atlantic Charter. Stalin dismissed a mere declaration as 'algebra', whereas he wanted the 'arithmetic' of a formal agreement recognizing the Soviet Union's 1941 frontiers. On this there was no prospect of immediate agreement, however much Cripps may have desired it. Yet it is hardly too much to describe the Moscow conference as the makings of an Eden–Cripps axis, not only over recognition of Soviet frontiers, but on a broad range of political issues during the coming months.

Working together, Cripps found his respect for Eden's diplomatic skills reciprocated by a respect for his own arguments, which avowedly influenced the Foreign Secretary's thinking. In particular, it was in the aftermath of the conference that Eden came round to the view that it would be more advantageous to settle Russia's territorial demands sooner rather than later – a shift of position that he has been criticized for retrospectively extenuating on the ground that it might have acted as a restraint upon Soviet expansion.[90] Whether or not it would have done so, this was not simply a retrospective view, generated by the Cold War, but a fear expressed at the time. Cripps was increasingly conscious that the Russians' success in seeing out the war for the winter had made it more difficult to reach agreement except on their terms. 'What disturbs me most is that they have obviously got their tails up now,' he noted, and took refuge in the thought that 'I am sure however that I can do more at home now than I can here on this matter.'[91]

For the moment the official line prevailed and the British ambassador punctiliously supported it. While Eden went on a visit to the front, Cripps was allowed to try his luck with Molotov. The official record kept by the Russians shows that Cripps loyally contested their insistence that frontiers should be determined in these negotiations, and claimed that, had he known that to be their position, he would have tried to prevent Eden's visit.[92] Though Cripps's forthcoming return to Britain was quite unrelated to the

89. RSC diary, 17 December 1941.
90. Cf. Miner, *Between Churchill and Stalin*, pp. 197–9, who calls the Eden–Cripps position a 'deceptively convincing argument'.
91. RSC diary, 18 December, 1941.   92. Rzheshevsky (ed.), *War and Diplomacy*, pp. 46–7.

negotiations, so he now told Molotov, the problems that had now arisen would make it much more difficult for him to work for further improvement in British–Soviet relations. The impasse would simply gladden the hearts of those in Britain who opposed the agreement.[93] If Cripps hoped that such an appeal would thaw out the unsentimental Molotov, he was to be disappointed; he recognized that he had made little impression.[94] Privately, he thought his own Government at fault for its lack of foresight.

This is the first outward result of Winston's folly in refusing to think about the post-war situation. He will have to do it now but in a condition of affairs that will make it impossible to modify the Russians' claims as they might have been modified some time back . . . We shall fight two separate wars and we shall suffer as a result.[95]

The conference did not result in the signature of any agreements so Cripps was spared the duty of drinking champagne. His first reaction was to regard the outcome simply as failure. Possibly his mood was influenced by his health, which suddenly broke down after the final interview with Stalin. It was a recurrence of the sort of fever which had afflicted him in Chungking and it confined him to bed for several days in his hotel room. He was cheered by Eden's assurance, before leaving for home, that he would continue to press in Cabinet for consideration of a post-war settlement. 'I think that in view of all that has happened,' Cripps wrote on his sickbed, 'I took rather too tragic a view of the failure to get an agreement and that perhaps it will not turn out so badly after all.'[96] None the less, when later pressed by the Foreign Office for a final dispatch, he declared that the prospect 'fills me with gloom and apprehension!'.[97] At any rate, the Anglo-Russian treaty that emerged from the continuing negotiations a few months later was no longer Cripps's direct responsibility.

'All the romance of the last six months seems to be distilled into this Xmas Day at Moscow,' wrote Cripps: still convalescent, undeniably weary, somewhat deflated, increasingly lonely, but mainly relieved to be going home soon. He recorded his sense of triumph over all the false prophets who had predicted an easy victory for Hitler – 'and a lurking fear from time to time that after all perhaps they might prove not so wrong.' What he found inspiring was the fortitude with which 'this despised and rejected regime' had withstood the onslaught.

93. ibid., pp. 46, 48.   94. RSC diary, 20 December 1941.   95. ibid., 19 December 1941.
96. ibid., Christmas Eve 1941.
97. Cripps to O. Sargent, 2 February 1942, FO 371/32941, f. 20.

No one can now say that such a regime is rotten or that it has sapped the vitality of the country. No, but for that regime and all that it has done over the last 20 years Hitler would now be the undoubted conqueror of the whole of Europe and our chance of ever being victorious would be precisely nil. That is why I feel this Xmas night a sense not only of intense relief but also of triumph. With all its imperfections and anyone who has lived here knows that they are many this Soviet regime has shown itself the triumphant saviour of all that we profess to uphold in our democracy.[98]

Cripps's warm valedictory feelings were entirely one-sided, evoking not even a formal response from the Soviet regime. He felt put out that, on his departure from Moscow, Stalin should refuse to see him to say goodbye, and wondered whether this was a personal slight or a sign of deteriorating Anglo-Soviet relations.[99] After this, it was simply a question of a brief return visit to Kuibyshev to put his affairs in order and take his leave of his companions in exile. This was the opportunity for Timoleon's last hurrah: the farewell party for the diplomats, with twenty bottles of whisky, 120 of beer and 100 of Nazan – 'everyone said that nothing like it had ever been seen in Kuibyshev'.[100] Joe was eventually to be left behind in Timoleon's care (and died shortly afterwards). At New Year 1942, Cripps had had a telegram from the heads of the military mission, signing themselves 'your three chiefs of staff' – 'because [as he explained in his diary] we have so often had jokes about the need for all of us to go home to take over and they always say that they will serve with me as the chiefs of staff if I want them when I get into the saddle as P.M.!'.[101] As Cripps sailed from Murmansk to Scapa Flow in the middle of January, it remained to be seen how well this joke would travel.

98. RSC diary, Christmas Day 1941.
99. ibid., 30 December 1941; Cripps to O. Sargent, 2 February 1942, FO 371/32941, f. 22.
100. ibid., 6, 7 January 1942.   101. ibid., 2 January 1941.

ENTR'ACTE
1942

Within a month of Cripps's return from Russia in 1942, he had been brought into the War Cabinet as Lord Privy Seal and Leader of the House of Commons. He was to hold ministerial office – with some vicissitudes and with one short break – for the next eight years. No longer the prophet of the left, he was to become the advocate of political consensus; and with the transformation in his public career went a modulation in his private life. In the 1930s his egalitarian professions and his patrician lifestyle had presented a vulnerable paradox. In particular, Goodfellows had functioned as an opulent country house, not only accommodating a large extended family but receiving a regular stream of influential weekend guests (including many whose politics scorned such opulence). The 1940s did not see Goodfellows revisited but Goodfellows repudiated.

That there was a religious dimension to this change is clear, though whether as cause or effect is less so. Cripps turned towards the Church of England, as an institution, with a respect that he had not accorded it since the 1920s. Many of his associates, especially those Conservatives (like Monckton or Butler) whose supposed 'change of heart' so impressed him, were Anglicans.

William Temple is correctly identified as 'the most conspicuous of all churchmen in promoting the vision of a New Jerusalem' – even by those who apply that term pejoratively to a vision of post-war reconstruction.[1] His Penguin Special, *Christianity and the Social Order*, became a bestseller in 1942. Cripps had made contact with him during 1941 while he himself was still ambassador and Temple Archbishop of York. Building on their shared emphasis on 'the need for a spiritual basis for our political changes', Cripps argued that 'the time has now come when a start should be made with the organisation of public opinion along the right lines'. What concerned him

1. Barnett, *Audit of War*, p. 15; and see the perceptive treatment of Temple in Calder, *People's War*, pp. 482–7.

was that, whereas 'many people are ready rather ostentatiously to make theoretical sacrifices so long as they are under the immediate influence of the fear and horror of war and its consequences', the moment needed to be seized to campaign for post-war reforms.[2]

The fact that Churchill thought it fitting – perhaps necessary – to appoint Temple Archbishop of Canterbury in the same month that Cripps was brought into the War Cabinet was a sign of the times. 'Of the Archbishop it is being said that he has put the Church on the map,' stated one newspaper article later in the year. 'And of Sir Stafford Cripps many are saying that he may put it on the march.'[3] In allying himself with Temple, notably in a joint meeting that packed the Albert Hall in London that autumn, Cripps gave a new prominence to his Anglican commitment. Mervyn Stockwood, the left-wing vicar of a large parish in Bristol, told Cripps: 'I believe that the immediate future of the Church in Britain can rest largely in your hands.'[4]

Cripps, however, was less interested in bringing the Church into politics than in bearing witness to the living reality of its teaching. No longer believing that the kingdom of God on earth could be postponed to a utopian future, the personal became political for Cripps in a new sense. Henceforth he made Christ his reformist hero, adopting an exemplary way of life in the imperfect present, with the good book in one hand and a ration book in the other.

Henceforth Stafford and Isobel lived simply, and on their own. Peggy had stayed in Teheran, following the German invasion of Russia, and only got home several months later, joining Stafford en route on his return passage from India in April 1942. Theresa had joined the WRNS and was to be away for the rest of the war, meeting her future husband, the country solicitor Robert Ricketts, on a posting to Gibraltar. In 1940 arrangements for leaving Goodfellows had been made and it was subsequently to serve as a hostel for the Women's Land Army. With her sisters now abroad, Diana was left winding up arrangements for the move, and John, who took over the farm, led an active life throughout the next half-century as a protagonist for rural interests – long after the rest of the Cripps family had left Filkins.

Frith Farm, in the village of Far Oakridge, between Cirencester and Stroud, had undergone a wartime conversion as a comfortable, though more modest, country home. It was in the Anglican church at the nearby village of Sapperton, rather than in the parish church at Oakridge, that the Crippses

2. RSC to Temple, 8 August 1941, copy.
3. Hugh Redwood, 'Britain is waiting for a prophet', *News Chronicle*, 30 July 1942.
4. Stockwood to RSC, 4 August 1942.

subsequently chose to worship; there that they felt most at ease; and there that Stafford was to be buried. He had had no time to visit his new house in June 1941 – his priority had been to pay a last visit to his dying father – and the couple of weeks' holiday Stafford spent in Gloucestershire on his return from Moscow was his first experience of Frith. He had little enough time to enjoy it, given the urgent claims of politics.

It should be remembered that Stafford had spent hardly more than a month in England between November 1939 and January 1942. Isobel had joined him in Moscow, leaving home in August 1940 and returning with him in June 1941. Apart from those ten months, she had had to manage all their affairs in England, including an increasing amount of political business. It was during this time that Isobel derived further benefit from lessons in the Alexander technique, especially after her return from Russia. Though subsequently 'working at a tension and pressure I had never coped with in my life before', she found fulfilment in 'meeting a diversity of personalities, and *trying*! to understand enough in the hope of giving encouragement instead of being a drag'.[5]

The fact is that Isobel flourished during their enforced separation. She became Stafford's eyes and ears, especially during his exile in Kuibyshev: watching over his interests with a keener intuition than his for the political salience of human nature and personal ambition, and with a constant concern to cultivate allies. When she was in London, at a flat chosen for its proximity to Westminster and Whitehall, she made herself available for lunch with a wide range of politicians (even including the egregious Beaverbrook). Together with her wartime work for the China Relief Fund, this gave her a much more active and prominent public role, which she did not subsequently relinquish. Visitors for Stafford in the two-room flat at Whitehall Court found, with mixed feelings, that they had the pleasure of Isobel's company too. Hence Hugh Dalton's jaundiced comment: 'The inevitable Lady Eno sits in.'[6]

Isobel Cripps was thus fully involved in the activities of the coterie of Stafford's intimates which coalesced at the time of his re-entry to British politics. Several names recur in the fragmentary records that survive. That of Geoffrey Wilson was naturally one, at least initially, until he was given (partly through Cripps's patronage) a Foreign Office posting. Another was that of Wilson's friend from Oxford days, David Astor, with his family links

5. IC, 'A note on the experience of F. M. Alexander technique', 22 July 1943. Some of this plainly has special reference to her work with Stafford in visiting aircraft factories.
6. Dalton diary, 19 May 1942, in Pimlott (ed.), *Dalton: War Diary*, p. 439.

to the *Observer* and, above all, *The Times*: a newspaper which, under its new editor, Robin Barrington-Ward, became strongly Crippsite. It was Astor who made the initial link between Isobel Cripps and David Owen. Formerly a labour economist, Owen was to be promptly snatched by the new Lord Privy Seal from his desk as a leader-writer on *The Times*, rather to its editor's dismay, as a personal assistant and publicist; the arrangement was initially that Owen would work part-time for each of them, though Cripps soon pre-empted all Owen's time. He continued throughout 1942 to act as a go-between for his two masters, 'leaking' high-level political gossip to Barrington-Ward (as the latter's diary shows) and ensuring Cripps favourable coverage in *The Times*.[7] Two sympathizers who also recorded meetings with Cripps in their respective diaries were Lionel Elvin, a veteran of the Socialist League, and Patrick Gordon Walker, who had withdrawn as Labour candidate in the Oxford by-election of 1938.

More significant than any of these, however, was Graham Spry. A former Rhodes scholar from Manitoba, Spry had useful political credentials, not only through lobbying, with striking success, for the establishment of the Canadian Broadcasting Corporation but also through his involvement in the formation of a new social democratic party in Canada (the CCF). The two men had met during Cripps's visit to Canada in 1935; his presence, along with that of the American socialist leader Norman Thomas, had 'made our hasty and rather unimportant annual meeting a great occasion, the influence of which constantly fortifies and encourages the movement throughout the provinces,' Spry told his hero.[8] Spry was forty-two in 1942, and was currently employed by Standard Oil of California. He was to work on secondment for Cripps for the rest of the war. His wartime broadcasts from London for the CBC might have roused queries about his political impartiality but nobody questioned his shrewdness in using the media to project the desired message: an aptitude that Cripps well appreciated.

It is Spry's diary that best captures some revealing glimpses of Cripps at work and at play. Both he and Owen were to go as part of the Cripps Mission to Delhi, where their constant attendance upon their master, in a committed and supportive advisory role, generated the nickname 'the Crippery'. It is fortunate, too, that the Crippery's activities in Delhi are chronicled not only in Spry's diary but in that kept by its house historian, Professor Reginald Coupland. Working closely with Cripps, with a low

7. Barrington-Ward diary, 22 February, 28 April, 2 June, 1 October 1942. Spry diary, 20 February 1942, on links.
8. Spry to RSC, 15 May 1935.

degree of formality and a high level of trust, they developed strong mutual loyalties. Convinced of Cripps's qualities – 'incisive intelligence, enormous courage, superlative confidence, energy'[9] – they were not only encouraged to engage in robust argument with him but also licensed to indulge in gentle mockery of his foibles.

The Crippery – to apply the term more loosely to his London-based supporters – thus comprised a cabal of subordinates ten or twenty years younger than himself. Like the famous 'Kindergarten' that the pro-consul Milner assembled in South Africa (including the young Leo Amery), they became a well-identified group of partisans with whom Cripps succeeded in establishing an easy rapport often lacking in his relations with senior colleagues. This tallies with George Orwell's first impressions of a man 'more approachable and easy-going than I had expected', and still, at fifty-three, 'almost boyish' in his demeanour.[10]

If Spry supplied the image of a Messiah for the returning ambassador, he did so with his tongue in his cheek, aware that the messianic bearing observed so often in public consorted with a playful demeanour in private. He records leaving an evening meeting at David Astor's flat:

RS [Cripps] wanted to make D's bed – apple pie or loosen one leg. At the elevator, 'in you get, boys.' He was jovial, confident, and somehow, in other ways, different – more grip, less impatience, less defensiveness, and as always, no egotism, whatsoever.[11]

The question has often been raised: what was Cripps's game in 1942? For example, in Chris Bryant's broadly sympathetic biography there is a chapter called 'Challenging Churchill', organized around the twin themes of 'activity and conspiracy'.[12] Given his high profile, his dramatic rise to power, his known impatience with the British war effort, his record of hostility to the political establishment and his manifest self-belief, it was only natural that politicians and journalists should impute to Cripps the obvious ambition to become Prime Minister himself. It is apparent, too, that there was talk of such a possibility within the Crippery, notably in stray remarks attributed to David Owen and to Isobel Cripps. In particular, historians have often cited the pages of Dalton's diary, highly readable and widely read in a fine published edition. A party warhorse, who craved but

9. Spry diary, 20 February 1942
10. Orwell diary, 15 May 1942, in Davison (ed.), *Orwell: Complete Works*, xiii, p. 322.
11. Spry diary, 27 January 1942.   12. Bryant, *Cripps*, ch. 19, at p. 296.

seldom enjoyed the sort of favour that Churchill was temporarily lavishing upon the undeserving Cripps, Dalton preserved his deeply-felt account for posterity (though hardly on acid-free paper).

Yet if Cripps really wanted to displace Churchill, he went about it in a very odd way. One explanation is incompetence, given Cripps's somewhat naive appreciation of the political process. Another explanation is that Cripps baffled the sophisticated political classes by living up to his own rhetoric about the priority of winning the war, and conceded vital support to Churchill on that basis. The two explanations are not incompatible.

At this juncture, Cripps gloried in being 'a man without a party' – a phrase loyally and uncritically picked up in early hagiographical works by Patricia Strauss and Eric Estorick.[13] Indeed this was self-evidently part of what Dalton called his 'mystique'. But just as Cripps's current popularity inevitably cast him as a rival for Churchill – a point lost on neither of them – so the non-party nature of Cripps's appeal was likewise double-edged. 'Stafford is really at odds with the central forces in party politics,' Spry had noted. 'He has been expelled by the principal movement on the left and he is suspected by the right.'[14] Buoyed up by a wide, if fickle, public following, Cripps was pitted against the institutional loyalties engendered by party – much as Churchill had been at an earlier moment. These points are vital to an understanding of the two crises to which he was central in 1942: that over the conduct of the war and the Cripps Mission to India. Each, separately, has been the subject of numerous accounts; but to understand the Cripps version it is necessary to understand their interwoven nature.

The Cripps Mission attempted to find a single answer to two pressing problems: world war and Indian independence. It is elaborately documented. A whole volume of nearly a thousand pages in the official series, *The Transfer of Power*, edited by Nicholas Mansergh, prints the official documents on the British side. This magnificent edition allows every nuance in the procedural and constitutional wrangles to be examined; and since its publication there has been a succession of scholarly studies of the Cripps Mission which have shown admirable expertise in exploiting this rich source. One problem, indeed, is to tell the wood from the trees; and one danger is to reconstruct the preoccupations of Cripps and Churchill as though everything were in Mansergh. For example, the telegrams between them that have been chosen for publication are quite properly those that cover their discussion of Indian political issues; but Churchill's own papers include an appreciably thicker file of communications with Cripps during March

13. Strauss, p. 170; Estorick, pp. 296–7. 14. Spry diary, 22 October 1941.

and April 1942. These are concerned with a whole range of vital and pressing military and strategic issues, on which Churchill sought Cripps's first-hand impressions and advice – readily given in copious technical detail. Oppressed by the exigencies of war, both of them had more on their minds than pleasing Gandhi or even President Roosevelt.

'The Cripps mission,' its leading historian has concluded, 'was crushed by the monolithic millstones of Churchillian Conservatism and Congress nationalism.'[15] Each undoubtedly exerted a negative influence. But did this preclude a settlement altogether? Was the outcome the result of sabotage in high places – by Churchill, perhaps, or by Gandhi? What was the role of Cripps and his friend Nehru, caught between the millstones? How did the politics of India and Britain impact upon each other – and thereby determine Cripps's fate?

It is often said that Cripps played a double game in Delhi. Even sympathizers readily assume that, straitjacketed by Churchill, he turned a blind eye to his instructions. Allegations and recriminations abound since Cripps was the man in the middle, the target for sniping shots from both sides, in subsequent accounts as much as at the time. The result has been a good deal of innuendo against Cripps and a failure to grasp some of the inevitably subtle distinctions at stake. Much turned on what the Indian politicians had been offered – as members of the Viceroy's Executive Council, they would be treated 'as if' they were a cabinet, or as 'a quasi-cabinet'.

How 'quasi' is a quasi-cabinet? It was an issue much debated subsequently. Furthermore, the aftermath of the Cripps Mission, meshed into the war crisis of 1942, can be regarded as a quasi-war of words, politics, tactical advantage and personal ambition. Quasi-war can be regarded as an inversion of Clausewitz's dictum: as the pursuit of war by other (political) means.

Nehru was not alone in subsequently probing the motivation of the Cripps offer, raising a question that has never gone away: 'had all this been done merely as a propaganda stunt for the people of the USA?'[16] It is undeniable that the Cripps Mission led two lives: one as negotiation and one as propaganda. It will be argued that Cripps tried to make a success of each, the more so since each, in his view, would help to win the war. Propaganda could to some extent be used to improve the chances of a successful negotiation: notably by bringing the pressure of American public opinion to bear on the Indian National Congress and by holding the Churchill Government to its own claims about a war for democracy. All

15. Moore, *Churchill, Cripps and India*, p. 122.   16. Nehru, *Discovery of India*, p. 399.

this Cripps welcomed as giving him greater leverage. But how far was negotiation used to serve the ends of British propaganda? That it did so is unmistakable; that it was intended to do so is also surely plain, if only from Cripps's own activities. That the negotiation was intended to fail in order to achieve a propaganda coup, however, is the really contentious claim.

There are two puzzles here. The first and more significant concerns Cripps's position in the Government, his standing in the country and, above all, his relations with Churchill. We need to understand what was at stake for both men, not only in India but in British politics in 1942. In the inception and execution of the Cripps Mission, their uneasy working relationship and potential rivalry undeniably bulked large. In its aftermath, however, what is striking is their ostensible agreement over its import. Though the Cripps Mission may have entailed a tragedy in Delhi, it came to achieve a triumph in the West, as propaganda. In this Cripps was instrumental: partly protecting his own position, perhaps, but mainly with the effect of shoring up Churchill's. Now this was surely a remarkable and ill-judged exercise of magnanimity on Cripps's part if he secretly felt that the Prime Minister had stabbed him in the back – or indeed if Cripps was secretly scheming to stab Churchill in the back.

The tension between Churchill and Cripps constitutes one tantalizing theme. Over India, as over Russia, they started from very different premises, bringing different ideological preconceptions and prejudices. Over Russia, they had found common ground through grim realism under the pressure of events, and Cripps had respected Churchill for not allowing his utterances about the Bolshevik menace to stand in the way of alliance with the Soviet Union. Over India, likewise, their common commitment to winning the war created a moment of opportunity for seeking a settlement – or so Cripps believed.

The tension between Nehru and Cripps is equally salient. The two men had been on the same wavelength in 1939–40, but found their ability to communicate troubled by a good deal more atmospheric interference by 1942. The inherent delicacy of their relationship in the negotiations needs to be appreciated. Their friendship was well advertised, and generally presumed a bonus, but it also raised expectations that were difficult to meet. Cripps seemed to be at the peak of his power when he faced Nehru in Delhi in April 1942. He appealed for trust and courage, telling his old friend that he himself 'had entered the War Cabinet knowing that he couldn't get *all* he wanted, but seizing the opportunity to get what he could'.[17] This was a

17. Coupland diary, 9 April 1942.

political judgement, offered with confidence and good faith, but vulnerable to the turn of events. By the end of 1942, Churchill was more obviously the beneficial legatee of the turn of events than either Nehru or Cripps.

PART FOUR

CRIPPS VERSUS CHURCHILL
1942

I

Messiah

When Cripps arrived in London on 23 January 1942, he was a prominent public figure without a public role. His political stock was now booming, while Churchill's was sliding. There was no longer any need for Cripps to apologize for his record as a fellow-traveller of the Soviet Union. It was not just Russia's entry into the war that rubbed off favourably on the British man on the spot: much more important was the subsequent dogged resistance of the regime that he had championed. Conversely, the sorry list of British reverses in the field could not but tarnish the reputation of a Prime Minister who had staked everything on victory. In his war memoirs, written eight years later, Churchill still wrote feelingly:

The Leftists and their press in Britain had built up the story that he more than any other living man had been responsible for bringing Russia in to the war on the side of solitary, hard-pressed Britain. There were some on the extreme Left who appeared to regard him as worth running as an alternative Prime Minister, and in these circles it was said that he would lead the new group of critics of the Government, which it was hoped to organize into an effective Parliamentary force.[1]

Churchill's exasperation is understandable, and it colours many of his references to Cripps, despite professions to 'liking him personally'. But it is not the case that Cripps simply represented a political threat from the left. Such a threat would have been easier to contain and to counter than the pervasive disenchantment over the course of the war and the widespread disaffection with party politics that was apparent by 1942. Cripps may have done little to create this political atmosphere but, from the time he stepped off the plane in London, he became its outstanding beneficiary.

Opinion polling was in its infancy and there was a war on to inhibit its

---

1. Churchill, *Second World War*, iv, p. 56. The idea that Cripps simply represented a threat from the left colours the secondary literature, e.g. Gardner, *Spheres of Influence*, pp. 121–2.

use. None the less, enough polls were conducted to give some scientific backing for otherwise impressionistic assertions about public opinion. When the public was asked in November 1941 whom they favoured as Prime Minister if anything should happen to Churchill, 38 per cent had said Eden, only 1 per cent Cripps. When the same question was asked again in April 1942, Eden was still ahead with 37 per cent but Cripps was now second with 34 per cent. In November, it was Beaverbrook who had lain second, with 11 per cent, whereas by April his standing was a mere 2 per cent, showing that his mantle as the champion of Russia had meanwhile been appropriated by Cripps – a point that obviously influenced their personal relations.[2] The fact that Cripps was not a member of the Labour Party was no mere technicality at this juncture; it was integral to his political appeal. While apparently representing a radical, left-wing, Soviet-tinctured challenge to the Churchill Coalition – to its official Labour component as much as to its Conservative core – Cripps also seemed an attractive alternative precisely because he was non-party.

A string of press reports talked up Cripps's prospects. The left-wing *Daily Mirror* splashed Cripps's arrival on its front page. The photographs that were used usually showed him in a Russian fur hat, which sufficiently made the point. For example, the Liberal *News Chronicle*, which Churchill came to regard as 'one of the most critical and hostile newspapers'[3] published a prominent feature article on Cripps under the headline 'Man of the Week'. It was not alone in calling him 'the mystery man of British politics'; but its author, Vernon Bartlett, who had been a supporter since popular-front days and had seen a fair amount of Cripps in Russia while working for the Ministry of Information, was egregious in his adulatory tone. 'Humble people in Moscow adored him and gave me examples of his unobtrusive generosity and thoughtfulness,' Bartlett reported. 'One very important officer said to me almost reverently: "The man's a saint." '[4]

Churchill needed to buttress his position. He had himself only recently returned to London after an arduous month-long journey to Washington, accompanied by Beaverbrook, and felt the need for a vote of confidence in

2. Cantril (ed.), *Public Opinion*, pp. 279–80. This poll was conducted by the British Institute of Public Opinion, which used random sampling, not by Mass-Observation, with its less rigorous methods, as cited by Addison, *Road to 1945*, p. 200; his ch. 7, 'Stafford Cripps's Progress', remains a pathbreaking study, as does the section on 1942, also drawing on Mass-Observation, in Calder, *People's War*, pp. 270–305. Fielding, in 'The Second World War and popular radicalism,' makes excellent use of the original BIPO data archive in stressing the non-party nature of the current disaffection.
3. Churchill, *Second World War*, iv, p. 63.   4. *News Chronicle*, 24 January 1942.

the Government. A motion was tabled in the House of Commons, to be debated on 27–29 January. Churchill acted quickly to make sure that Cripps did not use this to make himself into a real leader of the Opposition. On Sunday, 25 January, Stafford and Isobel Cripps were invited to lunch at Chequers (of which they gave the Crippery a full account the next day). 'Well, Stafford,' the Prime Minister greeted him, 'how have you returned? Friend or foe?' Cripps answered: 'a friendly critic or a critical friend', and told Churchill that he was riding roughshod over both the House of Commons and public opinion. In the course of a long talk after lunch – 'W[inston] had four different wines, and several brandies' – the Prime Minister became romantic and emotional, even weeping at one point. 'I have my niche in history, nothing can displace me,' he assured his guests. 'I am England.' Cripps's response was equally characteristic: 'but winning the war comes first'.[5]

The upshot was that Cripps was offered the Ministry of Supply. He realized that he would not have a seat in the War Cabinet, whereas Beaverbrook would; and that Beaverbrook's appointment as Minister of Production, coordinating supply for all the armed forces, was imminent. From Churchill's point of view, it was the least he could offer Cripps. *The Second World War* presents himself as acting 'wholly on the merits of the case', rather than for political reasons. In one of his drafts he could not resist putting his presumptuous rival in his place by saying that in the First World War 'Cripps had managed a small munitions factory' – a description changed in the published version to 'the largest explosives factory in the British Empire'.[6] The amendment was in the interests of both accuracy and verisimilitude, since Churchill could hardly simultaneously diminish Cripps's reputation for executive efficiency while citing it as the reason for taking him into the Government.

Why, though, should the offer have presented attractions to Cripps? Spry's diary suggests how Churchill set out his stall.

The conversation was very frank and very friendly. W. behaved well. He made it quite clear that he wanted RS [Cripps] and would support him. He also made it clear that he did not like MA's [Beaverbrook's] methods, respect his administrative capacity, or his results, but that he was essential to him – W. – as driver stimulus and friend.

---

5. Spry diary, 27 January 1942, reporting 26 January.
6. Churchill, *Second World War*, iv, pp. 56–7; cf. draft in Churchill papers, CHUR 4/300B.

Moreover, following Beaverbrook's successful visit to Washington, the proposal was that he should return there for up to six months to help coordinate Allied war production, while Cripps would be left free to run the Ministry of Supply along his own preferred lines. Nationalization would not be vetoed if it were for war purposes. The Prime Minister 'more or less indicated that he knew vast changes were coming; that was not his pigeon, younger men would have to be responsible for the post-war situation'. Finally, the whole proposal was attributed to Eden and was supported by two other members of the War Cabinet, Sir John Anderson and Ernest Bevin.[7]

It was the potential of this combination that impressed the Crippery. Eden had apparently told Cripps, 'you and I could swing things after the war'. Both he and Bevin were natural allies in any struggle with Beaverbrook, and the importance of cultivating their support was evident.[8] Cripps agreed to consider the proposal and the fact that an offer had been made was reported in the press. Barrington-Ward, who also talked with Cripps at this point, counselled him that 'he must not expect the P.M. to part forthwith with all his stimulants, his "necessities" – to wit, his Beaverbrooks'.[9] This was the dilemma. Would Cripps have to swallow working with or under Beaverbrook? Or was his position strong enough to face Churchill with choosing between them?

Cripps received conflicting advice. Isobel Cripps was in favour of accepting office. Geoffrey Wilson was against, sensing a trap set by Beaverbrook, with a threat to Cripps's working-class support. Graham Spry argued the other way: that from inside government Cripps would be better able to gain it, hold it and lead it. David Astor was torn between the temptation of power and his own family's hatred of Beaverbrook. What seems to have swayed Stafford against accepting was a breakfast meeting that he and Isobel had with the MPs Nye Bevan and George Strauss on 27 January, the first day of the no-confidence debate. Spry, anxiously recording everyone's views, had sufficient realism to recognize that the bargaining in which Cripps was now engaged was 'dependent on his real strength and W.'s needs – we could not determine that; only S. and in conversation with W.'.[10]

Although Churchill had not yet secured Cripps's services, he had effectively secured his silence in the no-confidence debate. The Government won by the misleadingly wide margin of 464 to one, but it did so only because Churchill adroitly gave ground, asserting his own authority while yielding

7. Spry diary, 27 January 1942.   8. ibid., 27 January 1942.
9. Barrington-Ward diary, 26 January 1942.   10. Spry diary, 27 January 1942.

on substantial criticisms over the Government's direction of the war. Hearing him from the gallery, Barrington-Ward noted: 'The House and the critics have, in essentials, had their way or look like having it.'[11]

It was in this atmosphere, on the last day of the debate, that Cripps replied to the Prime Minister. At Westminster rumours circulated, eagerly propagated and zealously recorded by an envious Dalton, about what had happened. It was alleged that Cripps wrote three successive letters: the first accepting the Ministry of Supply, and the second and third raising tactical difficulties, thus enraging the Prime Minister. In fact there seems to have been a single reply, though it evidently went through several drafts.[12] The point on which Cripps seized was that, under the proposed arrangements, the Minister of Supply would be relegated to a subordinate position, subject to Beaverbrook's control. 'The least that is necessary in order to make it possible to get the increased production looked for,' Cripps argued, 'is that the Minister of Supply should be complete master in his own department, a member of the War Cabinet and responsible for allocations and priorities.'

These were hardly unreasonable conditions. Cripps had come to the conclusion in Moscow that he could not work with Beaverbrook, whose idiosyncratic and erratic behaviour was acknowledged even by Churchill himself. But the tone of Cripps's letter was cooperative. Indeed he held out the hope of remaining 'a frank and I hope helpful critic' and left the Prime Minister with the assurance: 'if there are any special tasks that I can usefully undertake (as for instance with regard to the Indian question) I am of course always at your disposal'.[13] Churchill's reply likewise closed no doors, though he claimed to be unable to unlock the door of the War Cabinet itself, arguing that the admission of Cripps would in turn require a further and disabling increase in its membership, currently nine (including Beaverbrook, of course). 'I shall always be ready to receive your friendly advice,' Churchill concluded, 'though what I had wanted was your active help. Perhaps I may be able to obtain this some day.'[14]

*

11. Barrington-Ward diary, 29 January 1942.
12. See Dalton diary, 4–5 February 1942, in Pimlott (ed.) *Dalton: War Diary*, pp. 360–62. The source was Maurice Webb of the *Daily Herald*, which was hostile to Cripps and had an obvious interest in creating bad blood. The letter of 29 January which survives in the Cripps papers is marked 'copy as sent', implying that there had been earlier drafts. But if Churchill had had an earlier letter he would surely have used it – as he evidently contemplated using the existing exchange – to convict Cripps of tergiversation; yet his *Second World War*, iv, p. 63, only cites the single 'friendly letter declining my proposal'; cf. ibid., p. 69, for the veiled threat to publish 'your letter of January 29 and my reply of the 31st'.
13. RSC to Churchill, 29 January 1942, copy.   14. Churchill to RSC, 31 January 1942.

While these exchanges remained private, press speculation continued that weekend. The mass-circulation *Sunday Pictorial*, sister to the *Daily Mirror* devoted a double-spread article, under the headline 'Cripps Gets His Chance', to 'The Astonishing Story of – The Man Who Came Back!'. It can be seen as a milestone in the making of the Cripps myth. In a biographical piece aimed at a popular readership, Anthony Hern dwelt on the great man's links with Filkins, where 'Stafford and Isobel are – there is no doubt about it – loved by the people'. Their former 'red squire' was now said to have 'taken a small cottage in the locality'.[15] This description, though it would have surprised anyone who had seen the well-appointed farmhouse at Frith, later found its way into an Indian paper under the caption 'Cripps' Cottage Home – as simple in its western way as Gandhi's hut'.[16]

Naturally, Hern's article mentioned Cripps's vegetarianism, which was attributed to illness contracted during his time with the Red Cross. 'He usually has one meal a day, consisting of vegetable, sour milk, wholemeal bread and butter, and an occasional baked potato.' In politics, his commitment and idealism were paralleled by modesty of manner: 'A man of simple tastes, Cripps has no "side".' Though his popular-front supporters might have been disappointed in 1939 by the low key of his representations at the Southport Conference, the reason now given was that 'although a tub-thumping speech would have had more effect on the Conference, Cripps could not go against his nature to win a political victory'.

Cripps's integrity, attested by his renunciation of 'a cool £50,000 a year' at the bar, had found its true métier in Moscow, according to Hern's account, which chiefly relied on evocation rather than evidence.

I can imagine the meetings between Cripps and Stalin. The Russian premier, super-ficially solid, with an alert mind, immense knowledge and lightning grasp of the realities that lie under the surface of things. Opposite him, the British Ambassador, quite different physically, but with something approaching Stalin's own view of affairs.

This, then, was the man who, having helped bring the weight of the Red Army into the struggle against the Nazis, had come home, that job now done. 'His career has been fascinating so far,' Hern concluded. 'HIS FUTURE MAY BE MORE FASCINATING STILL.'[17]

Cripps's admirers, however, were not all on the left. Later that week, the

15. *Sunday Pictorial*, 1 February 1940.   16. *Illustrated Weekly of India*, 6 December 1942.
17. *Sunday Pictorial*, 1 February 1942.

news that he had in fact turned down the Ministry of Supply was broken in a banner headline across the front page of the *Daily Mail*: 'Cripps Returns to Back Benches'. Normally a reliable Conservative paper, the *Mail* too was now in Churchill's bad books for its hostile tone towards his Government. In the course of its exclusive interview with Cripps, his own wartime sacrifices were assessed on a less dramatic scale than in the *Sunday Pictorial* – his former bar earnings were halved to £25,000, and his new home was described as a farmhouse rather than a cottage – but the effect was similarly positive. If much was left implicit in the text, the accompanying picture, again showing Cripps in his Russian fur hat, spoke for itself. 'It was typical of the modesty of Britain's ex-Ambassador,' the journalist noted, 'that not once during the interview lasting more than an hour did he make any reference to his work in Russia.' It would have been otiose to do so. Here was a man whose modest demeanour belied his heroic stature, as he calmly awaited a suitable opportunity to serve his country. Significantly, India was prominently mentioned; Cripps made it clear that, although he had no current intention of making another visit himself, he was ready to go to India if asked to do so. 'When Britain has settled her policy,' Cripps said, 'then I think the Indians can be persuaded to agree.'[18] The fact that it was front-page news that Cripps was not, after all, to join the Government shows how high his profile was.

There were thus high expectations for Cripps's radio broadcast on 8 February, in the 'Postscript' series that J. B. Priestley had made famous as a platform for leftish pro-war views that often annoyed Churchill. Cripps spoke as the returning ambassador, acknowledging the privations that war had brought to his listeners, but intending to make them realize 'the differences between the fortunes of war as you have experienced them and as they have been suffered by millions of our Russian allies'. The Russians' response had been to turn one hundred per cent to war work, and, faced with black marketeers, to abjure 'the tolerance which is shown in this country to these fifth columnists!' Likewise, the moral was that they should not just be helped but emulated. 'It is a total war and demands our total effort,' Cripps asserted, calling for 'unstinted sacrifice', untainted by 'slackness or selfishness', in surviving 'this ghastly war, itself the brutal negation of every teaching of our Christian civilisation'. With its plea pitched at this level of personal ethics, tinged with religious rather than class appeals, the political charge of Cripps's broadcast was implicit but unmistakable. 'I have felt in this country since my return a lack of urgency,' he told listeners; 'I

18. *Daily Mail*, 6 February 1942; cf. Gilbert, *Churchill*, vii, p. 56.

may be wrong but I feel it in the atmosphere in contrast to what I felt in Russia.'[19]

'Postscript' went out in the prime slot after the 9 o'clock news and thus gave Cripps the opportunity to reach millions of listeners. Within days he had received 400 letters, with a common refrain that management of the war effort made it impossible for people to give a hundred per cent effort.[20] The amateur opinion surveyors of Mass-Observation estimated that the talk had been heard by about half the adult population, of whom over 90 per cent approved of it.[21] Cripps seems to have evoked this striking response as much through the manner as the content of his talk. 'He bore himself as though he had a message to deliver,' was how Churchill put it later.[22] Here was a challenge which the hard-pressed Prime Minister found as hard to meet as it was dangerous to ignore. Cripps was riding a wave of disillusion that was all the more politically potent for being non-party. A Gallup Poll a few weeks later showed only 35 per cent saying they were satisfied with the Government's conduct of the war, 50 per cent dissatisfied.[23] Cripps thus seized the moment, created by his Soviet connections, for going as far as wartime decencies allowed in voicing vague and general – but widely resonant – criticisms of the war effort.

There was a lot to criticize. It was undeniable that the USSR was now doing most of the fighting against Germany and that there was no immediate prospect of a second front in western Europe. Britain's military effort seemed to be concentrated in the Middle East and North Africa, and with little to show for it. Moreover, the crucial development was the spread of hostilities to Asia, making this truly a world war. Until 7 December 1941, Pearl Harbor was an exotic mid-Pacific location known to a few privileged European tourists – Cripps had touched down for a press conference, a bath, and a speech in March 1940 – but it had become a household name after the Japanese attack brought the USA into the war. The British Empire now joined its new ally and China in a full-scale war, by land and sea, against further threats of Japanese advance. Once again, Britain was thrown onto the defensive. On 15 February Singapore fell – as decisive a setback in Asia as Dunkirk had been in Europe. Churchill did not make light of these reverses, publicly warning: 'Australia is threatened: India is threatened.'[24]

19. BBC text, 8 February 1942.   20. Theresa Cripps diary, 12 February 1942.
21. Fielding, 'The Second World War and Popular Radicalism', p. 45.
22. Churchill, Second World War, iv. p. 69.
23. 1 April 1942, in Gallup, Gallup Poll, i, p. 328.
24. Speech, 26 March 1942, Gilbert, Churchill, vii, p. 78.

The pressure on Churchill was thus unrelenting, not least to strengthen his Government at this bleak moment. 'The public hopes more and more for new blood,' Spry reported. 'Hence, the swing to Cripps.'[25] It was a sentiment echoed, with both weariness and wariness, in Churchill's war memoirs: 'The most noticeable new blood available was of course Sir Stafford Cripps.'[26] On 11 February Churchill renewed the offer of the Ministry of Supply and Cripps repeated that his condition was membership of the War Cabinet.[27] This was not a refusal but a bid in a haggling process. As Spry put it: 'W. will try to take him into the govt and will on S's terms.'[28]

The underlying difficulty was the temperamental Beaverbrook: purportedly Churchill's liveliest ally, potentially his deadly rival, his hypochondria cloaking an intermittent inclination to lead a challenge to the Government. With Beaverbrook now locked in dispute with Ernest Bevin, Cripps's leverage was increased. 'SC has been constantly with W for the last few days and has kept in close touch with EB,' Spry reported; 'he has in fact seen him five times.'[29] Faced with this formidable pincer movement, Beaverbrook began to talk of resigning from the post to which he had so recently been appointed.

This left Churchill free to execute a bigger reshuffle of his Government. But he was not free to do so just as he pleased. He needed to take account not just of the war emergency but of the domestic political balance on which the coalition rested. Having predicted that His Majesty's ambassador in Moscow would prove 'a damned nuisance' and 'a frightful bore' on his return, Dalton found a ready subject for malicious and inaccurate gossip in the machinations over Cripps's entry to the Government. But he showed a firm grasp on political realities in warning that there would be 'a riot in the Labour Party' if – as one wild rumour had it – both its leader and its deputy leader, Attlee and Greenwood, were to be spurned in favour of one famous, but famously unrepentant, expelled member.[30] Rumours reached the Crippery. 'The major [Attlee] has said that he would resign if Arthur were dropped,' Spry noted. 'And this threat alarmed W.'[31]

Churchill worked out his own answer to the problem. On 19 February he reconstructed the War Cabinet by bringing in Cripps as Lord Privy

---

25. Spry diary, 16 February 1942.   26. Churchill, *Second World War*, iv, p. 65.
27. Gilbert, *Churchill*, vii, p. 55.   28. Spry diary, 16 February 1942.
29. Spry diary, 20 February 1942. There is no mention of this link in the discussion of the crisis in Bullock, *Bevin*, ii, pp. 148–54.
30. Dalton diary, 25 August 1941, 2 January, 9, 11 February 1942, in Pimlott (ed.), *Dalton: War Diary*, pp. 272, 339–40, 364, 369.
31. Spry diary, 17 February 1942.

Seal in succession to Attlee. Cripps also became Leader of the House of Commons, nominally succeeding the Prime Minister, though the duties had in practice been performed by Attlee. To persuade him to give way to Cripps in this double role, it was clearly necessary to offer Attlee more than his new departmental post of Secretary of State for the Dominions. Giving him also the new title of Deputy Prime Minister, however, not only mollified him personally: it sufficiently signalled his importance as leader of the Labour Party to make it safe to sack his deputy, the incompetent Greenwood. This was an ingenious solution which squared the political circle. Attlee's support was thus secured for Cripps's appointment, though Beaverbrook – with some inconsistency and more mischief – sought to maintain otherwise; and the arrangement had Eden's support, once he had suppressed his own fleeting ambition to serve as Leader of the House of Commons.[32] Five previous members of the War Cabinet – Churchill, Attlee, Eden, Bevin and Anderson – were joined in the reconstructed body of seven by the Conservative Oliver Lyttelton and by Cripps.

Cripps was in, Beaverbrook was out – a switch with both a personal and a political dimension. Churchill, who still professed reluctance to lose an old friend, offered Beaverbrook the option of ministerial office outside the War Cabinet, but within a week his resignation (partly in objection to Cripps's appointment) was finally accepted. It meant, as his faithful biographer A. J. P. Taylor put it, that Beaverbrook's 'days of power were over' – or, at least, his days of high office.[33] The reality was that, in or out of office, he remained an intimate of Churchill, as Cripps never had been nor ever would be; and the influence of the *Express* group of newspapers, indulging in a lifelong disparagement of Cripps, represented power of a different kind. Moreover, although both were seen at this point as champions of the Soviet Union, Beaverbrook was right to maintain that 'it isn't an exchange, as between him and me, that the Russians like'.[34] The reason was to become increasingly apparent during 1942: that Cripps showed no inclination to support the opening of a second front in the west, which was Stalin's key demand and the cause that Beaverbrook now took up in his newspapers.

Cripps's promotion thus brought a marked shift in the centre of gravity of the Government. To the Crippery the signal was that 'Winston took SC's advice and the new cabinet is, indeed, a Winston–Stafford affair.'[35]

32. Eden, *Reckoning*, p. 321; cf. Taylor, *Beaverbrook*, pp. 507–8, 513–15.
33. Taylor, *Beaverbrook*, pp. 514–20 at 520, and Gilbert, *Churchill*, vii, pp. 63–4; cf. Chisholm and Davie, *Beaverbrook*, pp. 428–31, for a more balanced perspective.
34. Crozier diary, 19 February 1942, in Taylor (ed.), *Off the Record*, p. 284.
35. Spry diary, 20 February 1942.

Perhaps the Prime Minister's qualms were eased by the advice he received from his wife. Writing once it was clear that Cripps would join the Government, Clementine Churchill demanded, 'why not put all your money on him' – thus excluding altogether her *bête noire*, Beaverbrook. Cripps she described as 'a new personality equal perhaps in power to him & certainly in intellect', who might provide 'a new accession of strength'. Evidently echoing a phrase the Prime Minister had used, she concluded: 'And you don't mind "that you don't mean the same thing." You both *do* in War, & when Peace comes – we can see. But it's a long way off.'[36] It was a theme which her husband soon picked up himself, privately reassuring a Conservative colleague: 'In spite of all the differences in our lines of approach, I have entire confidence in his overriding resolve to beat Hitler and Co. at all costs.'[37]

Cripps's hope was that he would displace Beaverbrook as the confidant and lieutenant of a Prime Minister whose immediate war aims he fully shared. Isobel Cripps was soon ready with the optimistic gloss: 'SC's influence with WC had reduced and was reducing the Beaver's.'[38] A measure of personal cordiality, whether or not totally spontaneous – and nurtured on both sides by their wives – could be observed at the lunch that the Churchills gave for the Crippses at 10 Downing Street on the day the news of the Cabinet reshuffle broke. Churchill's only other guest was the editor of the *Manchester Guardian*, who recorded: 'As we went in for lunch he and Cripps stopped to glance at a morning newspaper and Churchill said, "We'd a pretty good press this morning?" and Cripps agreed with great heartiness.'[39] If the editor of *The Times* thought it 'a large sweep, capable of reinvigorating the conduct of the war and public confidence', the reason was not hard to find: 'Most of what *The Times* has asked for has been conceded.'[40]

At a stroke, Cripps had become one of the most prominent ministers in the Government. It had been a piquant moment when the new Lord Privy Seal and his wife went to lunch with the King and Queen. Churchill asked pointedly afterwards, 'Well, did you make your peace with Buckingham Palace?' to which Stafford responded that it had all been very pleasant and

---

36. C. Churchill to W. Churchill, dated 'Thursday' (12 February suggested, but almost certainly 19 February 1942), in Soames (ed.), *Speaking for Themselves*, pp. 463–4.
37. Churchill to Linlithgow, 10 March 1940, in Mansergh, *TOP*, i, pp. 394–5; and see Rhodes James, *Eden*, p. 263.
38. Gordon Walker diary, 4 March 1942, in Pearce (ed.), *Gordon Walker diaries*, p. 109.
39. Crozier diary, 20 February 1942, in Taylor (ed.), *Off the Record*, p. 293.
40. Barrington-Ward diary, 19 February 1942.

Isobel commented that the Queen had been very charming.[41] These were not quite the terms which Stafford had used in his comment to the Crippery: 'the K. – not bright but progressive, and the Q. – intelligent but reactionary'.[42]

The King evidently fully appreciated the importance of publicly receiving and entertaining his new minister. When his daughters asked him if they had to attend the lunch, he had insisted that they must, even though they had to leave early to accompany Queen Mary the Queen Mother on a visit to the Kayser Bondor stocking factory at Baldock. The present Queen recalls getting up to go at the end of lunch, and Cripps saying: 'Don't forget your clothing coupons!' The impression it made on a girl of sixteen was that he was 'a dry old stick'. If the name of Stafford Cripps became a byword in the royal family, it was more because they were put out that their vegetarian guests consumed the whole week's egg ration than because they feared for the throne.[43]

The position in which Cripps now found himself was curiously ambiguous. 'The fact that such a man, without any party machine backing him, can be put into the Government in direct response to the wishes of the common people,' George Orwell proclaimed, 'is a testimony to the strength of British democracy.'[44] Not everyone saw it in such clear terms. 'All very odd,' Harold Nicolson, now himself an ex-minister, commented. 'The proletariat seem delighted, although it is a snub for the Labour people and the reinstatement of the upper class.'[45] In the end, Cripps had been brought in by an ambivalent Prime Minister, less for any acknowledged executive talent, which might have marked him out for the Ministry of Production, than as a concession to public opinion, stoked by a supportive press. Conservative papers like the *Daily Mail* and *The Times* had been among Cripps's warmest advocates, whereas he and Churchill agreed about the 'rather grudging' tone in the Labour *Daily Herald*.[46] It was a sign that Cripps continued to be viewed with some suspicion in the Labour Party – one reason, indeed, why the Conservative chief whip found him acceptable.[47]

41. Crozier diary, 20 February 1942, in Taylor (ed.), *Off the Record*, p. 293.

42. Spry diary, 20 February 1942

43. Personal information and see Curtis, *Wyatt: Journals*, i, p. 310.

44. Broadcast to India, 21 February 1942, in Davison (ed.), *Orwell: Complete Works*, xii, p. 187.

45. Nicolson diary, 23 February 1942, in Nicolson (ed.), *Harold Nicolson: Diaries and Letters*, ii, p. 213.

46. Crozier diary, 20 February 1942, in Taylor (ed.), *Off the Record*, p. 293.

47. Stuart; see Eden diary, quoted in Eden, *Reckoning*, p. 321.

'The entry of Cripps as L.P.S. is very interesting,' Dalton had to admit. 'If he has grown out of being a bloody fool, he will be first-class, and, in any case, if things go badly for a few months, his stock, now artificially inflated, will fall heavily and he will have to bear a large part of the responsibility.'[48] The fact that Cripps did not owe his position to the Labour Party, and that it owed as little to him, is easily overlooked. He might profess amusement at his own position: 'At last, I have a party that cannot be split and is in total agreement.'[49] But it vitally affected his political leverage over the next few months, as a minister whom grudging or unenthusiastic colleagues regarded as having been imposed upon them by an evanescent wave of ill-informed outside opinion.

The Crippery had reason to rejoice. 'As a little group we can say we established essential contacts, influenced the timing of S's return, reported on opinion and the general situation, and stopped a few possible entries to blind alleys,' Spry noted. He felt that they could take credit for some, though far from all, of the publicity that had strengthened Cripps's position; and he attributed most influence to an almost providential pattern of external events, which 'erected SC into a Messiah, made the PM change his attitude, and the two produced the complete change in the structure of the government'. Much turned not only on Cripps's own qualities but on whether he had indeed established 'an intimate and powerful relationship with Winston'.[50]

'The appointment of Cripps has placed in our hands a propaganda argument that could not possibly be more favourable,' Goebbels wrote in his diary. Regarding Cripps as 'Stalin's emissary in London' and as 'the prototype of the Bolshevik in England', Goebbels immediately reorientated Nazi propaganda so as to make Cripps the prime target.[51] BBC radio monitoring on the days after the Cabinet reshuffle reported that the Germans 'almost forgot Mr Churchill and concentrated on Sir Stafford Cripps and the Bolshevisation of Britain'. German radio in occupied France talked of the basic unity of plutocracy and Communism, with a symbolic incarnation in Cripps. 'Sir Stafford owns one of the finest castles in England,' asserted an article in Le Petit Parisien, evidently unimpressed by Cripps's new penchant for cottage life. 'His hatred of Germany has completely adulterated

48. Dalton diary, 19 February 1942, in Pimlott (ed.), Dalton: War Diary, p. 373.
49. Spry diary, 20 February 1942.   50. ibid.
51. 'Im Falle Cripps haben wir überhaupt ein Propaganda-Argument in die Hand hineingespielt bekommen, wie man es sich günstiger gar nicht denken kann'; 'Cripps ist der Abgesandte Stalins in London'; 'der Prototyp des Bolschevismus in England', Goebbels diary, 21, 20, 22 February 1942, in Fröhlich (ed.), Tagebücher von Goebbels, pp. 350, 347, 355.

his judgement and inspired his blind policy which, under the guise of an alliance between London and Moscow, is throwing open the gates of Britain to Bolshevik propaganda.'[52] Such attention, of course, was a backhanded tribute to the position that Cripps had carved out.

British propaganda, conversely, now got to work on an equally purposeful enhancement of the Lord Privy Seal's reputation. In this process, Cripps was hardly a passive object of press attention but an active collaborator, with his longstanding belief that 'the things we do now, the attitudes we take up, the propaganda we make, the forces we strengthen or weaken will all of them play their part in the formation of the new world'.[53] Convinced that he embodied such aspirations for a better future, Cripps was conscious of the role of publicity in advancing his own case and in fostering his own fortunes.

This process can be observed in an unusually revealing and explicit way in an interview that he gave in June, following the abortive Cripps Mission, to D. V. Tahmankar of the United Press of India. The exclusive terms on which the interview was granted meant that Tahmankar had to clear the text with Cripps before publication. The fact that this became a controversial news story may account for the fact that all the documents were kept in this case; but what they show, albeit in peculiar detail, is the care with which Cripps was accustomed to control presentation of his views in the press.

On this occasion, as often happened, Cripps spoke freely with a journalist whom he evidently trusted, in a complicit bargain whereby remarks that would catch the headlines were traded for a sympathetic presentation.

Outside the flaming June sun swam in a clear blue sky as we talked together freely and frankly for an hour or so in Sir Stafford's room. His room is a small and modestly furnished one. The walls were bare and the writing table had neither books nor files; a couple of telephones but none of which rang during my interview.

With a cordial hand-shake which conveys a sense of sincerity and strength of character, Sir Stafford puts his visitor at ease. There is nothing in his manner or speech which can be described as other than a warm and human understanding. But Sir Stafford's charm is not like an evening dress put on for the occasion, it is natural. As he talks with ease, calm and clearness, one is apt to forget that one is in the presence of an intellectual giant and the near-Prime-Minister of Great Britain![54]

---

52. War Cabinet: report on foreign broadcasts, 21–23 February 1942, Churchill papers, CHAR 20/65 f. 2.
53. RSC to Monckton, 25 September 1940, copy.
54. Tahmankar interview, final version, sent 18 June 1942, PRO, CAB 127/81. Tahmankar later became Vallabhbhai Patel's biographer.

That Tahmankar's scene-setting pleased Cripps is evident, if only because a comparison of the successive drafts of the interview that survive in his papers show no substantive emendations in this passage, whereas the published quotations from Cripps are by no means faithful to the original transcript (into which Tahmankar himself admitted 'I have put into your mouth one or two sentences.').[55] It is not just that the minister had to be protected, against himself or others, by apprehensive officials: most of the extensive emendations are in Cripps's own hand. Some remarks were struck out altogether; names were omitted; new passages of explication were inserted or substituted. Numerous statements were more persuasively presented – or more tactfully rephrased. To call such a process distortion is hardly apt; but to imagine that Cripps actually uttered every word attributed to him in exclusive press interviews is naive.

When Cripps entered the War Cabinet, then, he was fully conscious of the importance of shaping his own public image. 'Cripps – day after day the name hits the headlines in Britain's newspapers,' ran one Ministry of Information handout; 'day after day when men talk about war or politics they talk about Cripps.' The effortless string of successes, which told 'the same story all through the life of this very remarkable man', were invoked to explain how he had 'risen so suddenly to occupy almost the very centre of the British political stage.'[56] As Mass-Observation confirmed, in a series of reports that were sent to Cripps and probably commissioned by him, his initial appeal made much of 'brains'.[57] This might easily be seen as elitist. The crucial twist, however, was to link Cripps's clear thinking with his plain living, at a time when rationing and restriction had become a way of life in Britain and the lifestyle of a privileged elite a vulnerable target for popular resentment.

Early Cripps hagiography was not chary of making this explicit. Patricia Strauss's *Cripps: Advocate and Rebel* was published in New York in 1942, in a handsomely produced fat volume, poised to cash in on Cripps's sudden transatlantic prominence; though its British publication, in the mean war-economy format, was delayed until the next year – a victim of austerity, of course. Written by the wife of George Strauss, MP, Cripps's loyal supporter throughout the last decade and now his Parliamentary Private Secretary, it was conceived in mutual self-interest. As the author told her husband at the

55. Tahmankar to RSC, 5 June 1942, PRO, CAB 127/81.
56. Sidney Horniblow (MoI), copy for files, 9 March 1942, PRO, CAB 127/76.
57. See Tom Harrisson, 'Trusting the brains', for the *New Statesman*, February 1942, Mass-Observation Archive, FR 1118.

outset, 'if you could get anecdotes and stories from Stafford himself, or his family, and friends, it might well become a best seller which would be invaluable to Stafford'. Barely pausing to dismiss Eric Estorick's first attempt at a biography as 'completely ignored, so it doesn't matter very much', Patricia Strauss scribbled away in New York, while in London her husband hosted supportive lunches in the Cripps cause. 'It should at least appear to be an objective account of Stafford's life and attitude,' was how George Strauss put it.[58]

In what would now be called a campaign biography, Patricia Strauss sought to feed the public appetite for information about their famously frugal hero. She wrote of life in 'his two-room apartment' in Whitehall Court: 'He and Lady Cripps prepare their own meals, and together wash up the dishes.' This was not fabricated – visitors who interviewed Stafford in the bedroom might assist in the washing-up in the hand-basin while Isobel packed next door – though Strauss's claim that Cripps 'could not afford' a secretary strains credulity.[59]

What fixed the Cripps image was the use of one subsequently inescapable word. It was a word that, in racking the thesaurus for suitable adjectives, journalists had inevitably applied to him before. On his return from Russia, for example, he had been called by Vernon Bartlett, in an awed compliment, 'one of the most austere men I have ever met'.[60] But the *locus classicus* was Cripps's first Commons performance as Leader of the House, on 25 February 1942. Winding up for the Government – 'drily, meticulously, helpfully, but without inspiration', Nicolson thought – Cripps declared the Government's intention 'to treat this grave situation with all the seriousness and austerity that it undoubtedly demands'.[61]

In yoking the language of austerity with the measures to enforce it Cripps invested himself with a powerful symbolism. He claimed that there was as little place in wartime for 'pleasure as usual' as for 'business as usual' and invoked the sanction of majority opinion to curb abuses by 'small or selfish' groups bent on personal extravagance. In the authorized version, according to Strauss: 'He promised an immediate reform, which was immensely

58. George Strauss to IC, 24 March 1942, quoting two letters from Patricia Strauss. On G. Strauss, Dalton diary, 2 June 1942, in Pimlott (ed.), *Dalton: War Diary*, p. 451.

59. Strauss, p. 169; cf. Barrington-Ward diary, 26 January 1942; Pearce (ed.), *Gordon Walker diaries*, p. 110; Elvin diary note, 4 September 1942.

60. *News Chronicle* 24 January 1942.

61. Strauss, p. 171; Cooke, *Cripps*, p. 281; Burgess, *Cripps*, p. 161; this passage omitted in Estorick, p. 298. Nicolson diary, 25 February 1942, in Nicolson (ed.), *Harold Nicolson: Diaries and Letters*, ii, p. 214.

popular – the curtailment, or if necessary the abolition, of dog-racing, big boxing tournaments, and similar wasteful diversions from the war effort.'[62] Tighter restrictions on private motoring and clothes rationing were part of the package.

The comfortable myth is that the British people put up with wartime privations cheerfully, even when they grumbled. Historians have demonstrated that this is too simple and that different views at different times were taken by different groups in the population. Thus attitudes towards food rationing at this time showed that among the professional and managerial classes there was an approval level of 68 per cent (with only 7 per cent dissatisfied), whereas among workers in heavy industry barely 40 per cent approved – and 30 per cent were dissatisfied, mainly because manual workers felt their diet inadequate. Moreover, what working-class men missed most was meat.[63]

Such findings may indicate some mismatch between Cripps and the constituency for austerity. His appeal was disproportionately to high earners and the professional classes. The Mass-Observation files contain evidence that respondents thought him popular with the workers (though few of the remarks recorded apparently came from workers themselves), on the pattern: 'As a left-winger he should appeal to the factory workers.' Yet it is open to doubt whether an admiring comment, 'fine man, understands the working class', proves that Cripps really did so.[64] It is not wholly surprising that a vegetarian toff preaching austerity should have found a better reception almost anywhere than in the heartland of the Labour movement.

It was the tone as much as the substance of the 'austerity' speech that created an indelible impression.[65] Averell Harriman, currently in London as Roosevelt's envoy, was quizzical rather than hostile in reporting the impact of Cripps at this juncture: 'He is personally austere in his habits and wants the British people to wear the hair shirt for the sake of wearing it.'[66] Once this connection had been made by Cripps himself, the ascetic features of his own lifestyle were inevitably stressed, in implicit contrast to the presumed habits of the dog-racing classes, or indeed the parliamentary classes. Cripps

62. Strauss, p. 172.

63. Zweiniger-Bargielowska, *Austerity in Britain*, pp. 72–80.

64. 'Stafford Cripps', 7 December 1942, Mass-Observation Archive, FR 1524; and see the analysis in Fielding, 'The Second World War and popular radicalism', p. 47.

65. For example Dalton diary, 27 March 1942, in Pimlott (ed.), *Dalton: War Diary*, pp. 404–5.

66. Harriman to Hopkins, 7 March 1942, in Harriman and Abel, *Special Envoy*, p. 128; similar to Harriman to Roosevelt, 6 March, in Harriman and Abel, op. cit., p. 127.

himself escaped the obvious imputations against luxury feeding – off the ration, in smart restaurants – pilloried in one satire:

> Come share at the *Savoy* with me.
> The menu of austerity.[67]

Nobody accused him of hypocrisy. 'He is a man of great personal austerity, a vegetarian, a teetotaller and a devout practising Christian,' Orwell assured Indian radio listeners. 'So simple are his manners that he is to be seen every morning having his breakfast in a cheap London eating house, among working men and office employees.'[68] If Cripps was depicted as heroic by Patricia Strauss, it was to be on his own terms, in repudiation of the conventional criteria: 'There is about him a dignity, an austerity, an almost inhuman rectitude, which contrast starkly with the expansive warmth, the joviality, the histrionic flair, of the legendary popular hero.'[69]

With 'austerity', then, the word was made flesh. There are indications that, within a couple of weeks of the notorious speech, both Stafford and Isobel Cripps were conscious of the dangers of its killjoy overtones. Significantly, in publicity that Cripps's own department commissioned, determined efforts were made to back-pedal.

Don't be misled by his pictures. They make him look austere and aloof. He's nothing of the sort. He's frank and kindly, a very human and humorous person. He's a teetotaller, but he smokes a good deal and he takes a cold bath every morning.[70]

The trouble was that the more that was said, the greater the reinforcement of the flinty stereotype – a caricature maybe, but one by which Cripps was subsequently recognized, and one that did not necessarily exclude feelings of affection and respect. Anecdotes proliferated. Barrington-Ward, as a good journalist, knew how to encapsulate a story in a terse report: 'In the interests of "austerity" (now a boss word) Cripps got the sit down lunch altered to a buffet affair.'[71]

In a desperate situation, Cripps's reputation for remorseless efficiency did him little harm if it was perceived as the steel that reinforced his resolute commitment to the war effort. In the spring of 1942, opinion polls gave him

67. Quotation from Sagittarius in Zweiniger-Bargielowska, *Austerity in Britain*, p. 78.
68. Weekly News Review, 14 March 1942, in Davison, *Orwell: Complete Works*, xiii, p. 225.
69. Strauss, p. 1.
70. Sidney Horniblow (MoI), copy for files, 9 March 1942, PRO, CAB 127/76.
71. Barrington-Ward diary, 8 May 1942.

an approval rating that had leapt from nowhere to around 70 per cent, whereas the Prime Minister's rating had now fallen to around 80 per cent.[72] Such was Cripps's standing at the time of his heroic return from Russia. For the time being, he was taken on trust. As Spry recognized, even in the Crippery's moment of euphoria, the hard days were now to come. 'The Messiah is arrived, and responsibility is his.'[73]

72. Fielding, 'The Second World War and popular radicalism', p. 43.
73. Spry diary, 20 February 1942.

2

Origins of a Mission

Even while still in Moscow, Cripps's name had already been linked with India in the press, with talk of him as a daring and imaginative choice as next Viceroy.[1] His first two months as a minister were absorbed with the affairs of India which became in every sense his first task. If this came about partly through his own choice, it was also partly through the initiatives of others, not only in Britain and India but in China and the USA – and, not least, in Japan.

The idea of sending 'someone' to India, 'charged with a mission to try to bring the political leaders together', was already in the air at the time that Cripps returned from Moscow. This was what Attlee had proposed to Amery, the Secretary of State for India, as a response to the cross-party dissatisfaction with the policy of simply sitting tight on the August offer of 1940, with its conditional, deferred and plainly half-hearted offer of Dominion status.[2] The state of public opinion made an initiative opportune, just as it made Cripps's incorporation into the Government opportune. There is evidence that the India Conciliation Group was attempting to interest Cripps in making another unofficial journey to India; Cripps had himself raised the possibility both in private correspondence with Churchill and in his *Daily Mail* interview; and a Reuters report to that effect elicited the Viceroy's howl that any such visit 'in existing circumstances would be in my view disastrous'.[3]

Lord Linlithgow was still in post, and his influence militated against any change in policy, especially in view of India's new peril. 'I am carrying here, almost single-handed, an immense responsibility,' he reminded Amery the day after Singapore fell, moved by his sense that 'the key to success in this

1. Spectator's Diary, *Spectator*, 25 September 1941.
2. Attlee to Amery, 24 January 1942, in Mansergh, *TOP*, i, p. 75.
3. Linlithgow to Amery, 7 February 1942, in Mansergh, *TOP*, i, p. 127; cf. Moore, *Churchill, Cripps and India*, pp. 54–5.

war is now very largely in my hands'.[4] That this was the context in which all the decisions had to be made, by hard-pressed men who had other legitimate worries than the shape of a post-war Indian constitution, is an important consideration, sometimes too easily overlooked. There was, however, a breach between those who thought that the *status quo* ought to prevail while there was a war on, and those who thought that a war for democracy could best be won by enlisting democratic aspirations on the side of the Allies. Cripps was identified with the latter analysis, Linlithgow with the first, as he made clear: 'India is hopelessly, and I suspect irremediably split by racial and religious divisions which we cannot bridge, and which become more acute as any real transfer of power by us draws nearer.'[5]

Two recent political developments within India, however, required attention. One was the reconvention of the Congress Working Committee, after a virtual abdication of fourteen months during which its functions had been exercised by Gandhi, while its members had spent varying periods in prison. In December 1941 the meeting of the Congress Working Committee at Bardoli took a line that can be called canny or disingenuous. While in form duly deferential to Gandhi and his commitment to non-violence, the Bardoli resolutions expressed support for 'the peoples who are the subject of aggression and are fighting for their freedom', while contending that 'only a free and independent India can be in a position to undertake the defence of the country on a national basis'.[6] Under the influence of Nehru, Rajagopalachari and Azad, all more committed to resisting fascist aggression than to Gandhian non-violence, Congress thus formally professed readiness to support the war, if given the chance. The second initiative came within days from a distinguished group of Indian moderates, headed by Sir T.B. Sapru, in the form of a telegram to Churchill, calling for the Indianization of the Viceroy's Executive Council so as to form an interim national government.

None of this had impressed the Viceroy. Congress was seen as untrustworthy in the task of shoring up the defences of the British Raj. The essential issue, then, was 'whether in such circumstances, whatever the feelings of India, we intend to stay in this country for our own reasons'.[7] Linlithgow had largely got his own way hitherto, little troubled by the presence of Labour ministers in the Coalition, and still made the assumption that his outlook was shared by his political masters in London in writing scornfully

4. Linlithgow to Amery, 16 February 1942, in Mansergh, *TOP*, i, p. 186.
5. Linlithgow to Amery, 21 January 1942, par. 13, in Mansergh, *TOP*, i, p. 48.
6. Bardoli resolutions, 30 December 1941, in Mansergh, *TOP*, i, pp. 881–4, at p. 882.
7. Linlithgow to Amery, 21 January 1942, par. 15, in Mansergh, *TOP*, i, p. 49.

of the need to resist 'Left Wing pressure and pressure from academic theorists or sentimentalists, reflected even in such papers as *The Times*'.[8]

But the ground on which the hard-pressed Hopie stood was slipping from under his feet. It was to slip further. The Viceroy had confidently asserted:

Cabinet will I think agree with me that India and Burma have no natural association with the Empire, from which they are alien by race, history and religion, and for which as such neither of them have any natural affection, and both are in the Empire because they are conquered countries which had been brought in by force, kept there by our controls, and which hitherto it has suited to remain under our protection.'[9]

By the beginning of 1942, public opinion in Britain, let alone the USA, was not receptive to this kind of restatement of the rules of the great game of empire, as the normally circumspect Attlee well appreciated. Belatedly stirred to action, he became unwontedly forthright. He scouted Linlithgow's analysis as 'an astonishing statement to be made by a Viceroy', saying that it sounded 'more like an extract from an anti-imperialist propaganda speech' and, if true, 'would be the greatest possible condemnation of our rule in India'. In a Cabinet paper, Attlee spoke now as the faithful product of a public school (Haileybury) which had specialized in instilling a high-minded code of British imperial service. He argued that it was precisely the 'acceptance by politically conscious Indians of the principles of democracy and liberty which put us in the position of being able to appeal to them to take part with us in the common struggle'.[10]

Rival analyses of the Indian position were thus already before the War Cabinet at the time that Cripps joined it: in Linlithgow's appreciation, broadly endorsed by Amery, and in Attlee's critique. Amery, as Secretary of State, had started by backing up the Viceroy, claiming that the political deadlock in India, though ostensibly concerned with 'the transfer of power from British to Indian hands', was in reality 'mainly concerned with the far more difficult issue of what Indian hands', if anarchy or civil war were to be avoided.[11] This pointed to the difficulties of doing anything at all, and led Amery to conclude that 'we can, I believe, weather the immediate storm which is sweeping down upon India'.[12] Attlee, by contrast, found it 'quite impossible to accept and act on the crude imperialism of the Viceroy, not

---

8. Linlithgow to Amery, 21 January 1942, par. 16, in Mansergh, *TOP*, i, p. 49.
9. Linlithgow to Amery, 21 January 1942, par. 14, in Mansergh, *TOP*, i, p. 49.
10. WP (42) 59, 2 February, 1942, par. 10, in Mansergh, *TOP*, i, p. 111.
11. WP (42) 42, 28 January 1942, in Mansergh, *TOP*, i, p. 81.
12. WP (42) 42, 28 January 1942, in Mansergh, *TOP*, i, p. 90.

only because I think it is wrong, but because I think it is fatally short-sighted and suicidal'.[13] He therefore rejected Amery's 'hand-to-mouth policy' as inadequate in a world where Britain had to look for support from the USSR, from China, and from the USA, all of them sensitive to the claims of the East against the long dominance of the West.[14] A reference to 'the increasingly large contribution in blood and tears and sweat made by Indians' turned Churchill's rhetoric against its begetter; and Attlee formally reiterated his proposal of sending out 'some person of high standing', rather as Lord Durham had been sent to Canada a century before, 'with wide powers to negotiate a settlement in India'.[15]

In retrospect, Amery was to reflect to Linlithgow that when they took the view that nothing was to be done, they had done so on the merits of the situation, 'and also in view of Winston's own vehement attitude'. But, whatever the Prime Minister's prejudices, the fact that, especially since Pearl Harbor, he had to bend his mind to the problem of Anglo-American grand strategy now made a difference, as Amery subsequently recognized: 'the pressure outside, upon Winston from Roosevelt, and upon Attlee & Co. from their own party, *plus* the admission of Cripps to the War Cabinet, suddenly opened the sluice gates, and the thing moved with a rush'.[16] The Government's readiness to respond to pressure was as much a cause as a result of Cripps's appointment, and, ten days before it took place, the official line on India was already shifting.

On 9 February Churchill took the War Cabinet by surprise with his own proposal. Cripps was not surprised. His long lunch at Chequers two weeks previously, so he told Spry, had seen the Prime Minister agreeing with him 'to make a new gesture on India'.[17] In fulfilling this promise, despite not having Cripps aboard yet, he was surely sending a signal. What Churchill proposed was to expand the Viceroy's Defence Council on a representative basis, both as a means of bringing Indian opinion behind the war effort and as a conduit to post-war constitutional change. At short notice, plans were improvised for Churchill to make a broadcast explaining what he had in mind. Naturally, Amery had already heard of this plan, which he was charged with springing upon the Viceroy, whom he expected to 'throw a fit'.[18] Remarkably, Amery's diary records Churchill as convening a meeting

13. WP (42) 59, 2 February, 1942, par. 10, in Mansergh, *TOP*, i, p. 111.

14. WP (42) 59, 2 February, 1942, at par. 8, in Mansergh, *TOP*, i, p. 111.

15. WP (42) 59, 2 February, 1942, pars. 7, 12, in Mansergh, *TOP*, i, p. 111–12.

16. Amery to Linlithgow, 10 March, 1942, in Mansergh, *TOP*, i, pp. 403–4.

17. Spry diary, 27 January 1942.

18. Amery diary, 8 February, 1942, in Barnes and Nicholson (eds.), *Empire at Bay*, p. 770.

to refine these proposals at 10 Downing Street, with Cripps taking a full part alongside Attlee and Anderson, on 11 February.[19] This was the same day that Churchill renewed his efforts to bring Cripps into the Government. 'This Indian problem must be solved,' he had told the Prime Minister.[20] Was Cripps drawn into this discussion simply for expert advice – or to give him a taste of the influence he might hope to deploy as a minister? Cripps's obvious concern with India may well have been used to bait the hook of office.

The Viceroy, who had been left in the dark, trundled into action to head off trouble. He saw it as 'a fatal defect of the Prime Minister's proposal that it precipitates the whole constitutional controversy, which is so largely communal and on a present view irreconcilable, into the conduct of the war'.[21] Linlithgow was already plagued by the difficulty of explaining how the democratic principles asserted in the Atlantic Charter, to which Churchill and his friend Roosevelt had blithely set their names six months previously, applied to the British Raj. Protectively, Linlithgow talked of saving the Prime Minister 'from exposing himself to the criticism that only when the enemy was at the gate and British power to hold India already flagging did he hear her cry for freedom'.[22] This ideological twist to the Indian problem, turning on the Allies' championship of the principle of self-determination, and reinforced by Britain's need to appeal to American democratic sentiment, was neither new nor unanticipated. But by 1942 it became a crucial dimension in the whole story of the Cripps Mission, from beginning to end.

The Viceroy's objections were thus enough to thwart Churchill's half-sheet-of-notepaper scheme but not to halt the growing momentum for reform in India. It made interesting news that Chiang Kai-shek was currently taking two weeks away from Chungking 'to meander through India with Nehru sticking to him like a burr' (as the Governor of the United Provinces put it)[23] in an effort simultaneously to enlist Indian nationalism behind the common cause and to alert Britain to the need for Indian self-government. Chiang cabled to London, advising the Chinese ambassador to convey his concern about the state of morale in India by talking first to Cripps – no longer, as in 1940, the putative right-hand man of the Generalissimo but,

19. Amery diary, 11 February, 1942, in Barnes and Nicholson, op. cit., p. 772.
20. Reported to Hodson on arriving in Delhi, in Hodson, Great Divide, p. 91.
21. Linlithgow to Amery, 13 February 1942, in Mansergh, TOP, i, p. 167.
22. Linlithgow to Amery, 16 February 1942, in Mansergh, TOP, i, p. 181.
23. Sir M. Hallett to Linlithgow, 21 February 1942, in Mansergh, TOP, i, p. 219; cf. ibid., pp. 348–50.

by 1942, the new colleague of Churchill, for whom (along with Roosevelt) the message was intended.[24]

As Minister of Supply, or Minister of Production, Cripps would have had little time to pursue the Indian initiative, even if he had been in the War Cabinet. But as the new Lord Privy Seal, he found the door already ajar, and made it his brief to push it open wider. 'India will be the first big task,' he said on the day he took office.[25] Prompted by events as much as by contacts with the ICG, with which Isobel Cripps had kept in touch, Stafford's mind went back to the plan he had taken with him on his journey to the East two years previously. Its imprint was to be stamped upon the papers that soon flowed from the office of the Lord Privy Seal.

Within a week of his appointment, Cripps became one of the key members, along with Attlee and Amery, the Secretary of State for India, of the newly-established India Committee of the War Cabinet. As Prime Minister, Churchill had the right to attend, rarely exercised. Three other ministers sat on this committee. The Lord Chancellor, Viscount Simon, having begun his glittering career as an Asquithian Liberal, had served fifteen years previously as chairman of a Commission on India that included Attlee; and the recommendations of the Simon Report in 1930 had to some extent inspired the 1935 India Act. The two remaining seats on the India Committee went to Sir John Anderson, Lord President of the Council, and Sir James Grigg, Secretary of State for War – both of them ex-civil servants with administrative experience in India. Cripps had already established a rapport with Anderson over the Indian issue in 1940; and, though Grigg's hard line in defence of the Indian Army made him a tougher nut to crack, he was Cripps's ally against Churchill on other war issues.

This was not a committee on which partisan Conservatives, still less diehards, were at all well represented. In retrospect, Attlee called the committee 'pretty good', and justifiably made a point of embracing Amery within this favourable assessment, whereas he remembered 'a constant struggle between the Committee and Winston' whom he regarded as 'both obstinate and ignorant on the subject'.[26] Looking round the table, Cripps could not have failed to observe the erosion of the blocking power of the political right in the two years since he had unavailingly pressed the Government for a new démarche over India.

The committee was first convened with Churchill in the chair on 26

24. *FRUS*, 1942, i, p. 605 (24 February, 1942).   25. Spry diary, 20 February 1942.
26. 'As It Happened', draft memoirs (1951–4), Churchill Archives, ATLE 1/13, f. 7.

February. Amery was disconcerted by 'Winston's complete inability to grasp even the most elementary points in the discussion' and imagined that an outsider ignorant of his reputation 'would have thought him a rather amusing but quite gaga old gentleman who could not understand what people were talking about' – an impression evidently shared by Cripps, who said that 'he had been nearly as bad at a meeting earlier in the day'.[27] This was a discouraging start, though Cripps and Amery at least forged agreement on giving any dissenting province a right to opt out of any new constitution (but not to prevent the others from going ahead with it).

The committee had seven further meetings in the next eleven days, each time with Attlee in the chair, and accordingly made better progress. The drafts initially before it naturally emanated from the India Office. The plan was at first for a statement that Churchill might broadcast direct to India. This created an air of expectancy which further unsettled the Viceroy and which was fuelled by a statement that Cripps had made, as Leader of the House, in the Commons on 25 February. For the third meeting, on 28 February, Cripps prepared his own alternative draft, evidently with back-room support from Geoffrey Wilson and Agatha Harrison of the ICG.[28] Amery, by now on cordial terms with Cripps, seems not to have resented the fact that this draft henceforth replaced his own as the master text.

It was largely an updated version of the Cripps plan of 1939. It affirmed the Government's decision 'to lay down in precise and clear terms the steps which they propose shall be taken for the earliest possible realisation of self-government in India'. As a Dominion, India would be 'equal in every respect to the United Kingdom and the other Dominions of the Crown, and free to remain in or separate itself from the equal partnership of the British Commonwealth of Nations'.[29] This clearly spelt independence. There would be a post-war constituent assembly, subject only to the right of any province not to accede. This provision in effect entrenched the right of predominantly Muslim provinces not to be coerced into an Indian union, opening the door to some kind of 'Pakistan' option. The position of the princely states was likewise left unresolved: they were to be free to stand out but encouraged to go in. While these were provisions for future constitutional arrangements, the declaration concluded with a short paragraph concerned with immediate wartime defence, reserving this responsibility to

27. Amery diary, 26 February 1942, in Barnes and Nicholson (eds.), *Empire at Bay*, p. 779.
28. Moore, *Churchill, Cripps and India*, pp. 64–5.
29. Draft declaration, 28 February 1942, in Mansergh, *TOP*, i, p. 266.

the British Government, but inviting 'the immediate and effective participation of the leaders of the principal sections of the Indian people in the
counsels of their nation'.[30]

Churchill, when he was shown it, declared himself 'favourably impressed
by the draft'.[31] He had, as Amery put it, 'seen the red light (especially the
American red light) overnight', and was now ready to support many of
the same proposals he had so recently obstructed.[32] Churchill still put all
the traditional difficulties before Roosevelt: in particular he dwelt on the
position of the Muslims, whose contribution as a major section of the
'martial classes' was currently at a premium, given Churchill's unsubstan-
tiated but forceful contention that they comprised 75 per cent of the Indian
troops; and he did not omit the perils of upsetting the Gurkhas, with 'their
somewhat childish mentality'.[33] These atavistic perceptions, however, now
constrained rather than drove the policy of the War Cabinet, which had to
confront the reality of reverses in the field, with Rangoon now abandoned.
'We have resigned ourselves to fighting our utmost to defend India in order,
if successful, to be turned out,' was Churchill's mordant comment to the
Canadian Prime Minister.[34]

Along the way, to be sure, Amery appealed to Churchill for support
'against being rushed by Cripps and Attlee'.[35] There was much feverish
tinkering over secondary issues: some of substance, some of detail, and some
mainly symbolic. The connotations of 'Dominion status' were elaborately
rehearsed, provoking even Linlithgow at one point to cable: 'Having gone
so far why boggle at the word "independence" with all its appeal to India?'[36]
With such diverse support, adroitly managed by Attlee, it was essentially
Cripps's version of the draft Declaration that was adopted by the War
Cabinet.[37]

Amery had suspected from the outset that Cripps and Attlee wanted to
get rid of Linlithgow, and a private chat with Cripps on 28 February had

---

30. Draft declaration, 28 February 1942, in Mansergh, *TOP*, i, p. 267 ('Councils' subsequently
corrected to 'counsels').
31. Prime Minister's minute, 1 March 1942, in Mansergh, *TOP*, i, p. 272.
32. Amery to Linlithgow, 2 March 1942, in Mansergh, *TOP*, i, p. 295.
33. Churchill to Roosevelt, 4 March 1942, in Mansergh, *TOP*, i, pp. 312–13. In fact, on
Linlithgow's own estimates (6 March 1942), there were more Hindus than Muslims in the
Indian Army: 41 per cent to 35 per cent, with 10 per cent Sikhs and 8.5 per cent Gurkhas. See
Rizvi, *Linlithgow and India*, p. 176.
34. Churchill to Mackenzie King, 18 March 1942, in Mansergh, *TOP*, i, p. 440.
35. Amery to Churchill, 2 March 1942, in Mansergh, *TOP*, i, p. 280.
36. Linlithgow to Amery, 2 March 1942, in Mansergh, *TOP*, i, p. 286; cf. ibid., p. 332.
37. Draft declaration text, 7 March 1942, in Mansergh, *TOP*, i, pp. 357–8.

confirmed his suspicions.[38] Cripps envisaged the new policy statement as implying the need for a new Viceroy: one who would be more sympathetic than the old to the aspirations for Indian independence embodied in the bulk of the text; one, moreover, who would be better able to improvise arrangements – specified with deliberate vagueness in the Declaration's final paragraph – for the representation of Indians in 'the counsels of their nation'. But how many of them? And in what capacity?

The War Cabinet had pressed the India Committee as to what this vital paragraph really meant. At the committee's meeting on 3 March, Cripps, as usual, had his own draft ready: this time 'Draft Instructions to the Viceroy', authorizing him to negotiate with 'leaders of the principal sections of Indian opinion' by offering them posts on his Executive Council.[39] Though British members still controlled its key portfolios, notably Defence, there had been an Indian majority on the Council since July 1941; and Linlithgow had not had to resort to his formal power to overrule it. Under the new Instructions, the Viceroy – a creative Viceroy, an imaginative Viceroy, a forward-looking Viceroy – was licensed to turn his Executive Council into something like an Indian Cabinet, with members who represented the political parties replacing its existing hand-picked members.

But though the India Committee accepted Cripps's draft on 3 March, his own implicit assumption that this was intended to facilitate full Indianization of the Council was called by Amery, in his private diary, 'the very thing which the Government have decided not to do'.[40] Whether this was a simple misunderstanding between the two men – Amery was notoriously hard of hearing – or a silent agreement to differ, is not clear. Moreover, it was significant – or became significant – that Churchill was not present at this meeting, and thus subsequently relied on Amery's sense of what had been determined. Furthermore, Linlithgow later claimed never to have been told of instructions which he would self-evidently have been the wrong man to implement.[41] None of this augured well for the consistency with which the policy would be implemented, in a context where any inconsistencies would readily be attributed to dissimulation.

At its last hurdle in London, the draft Declaration ran into serious trouble. Cripps had remained ready with further drafting amendments to get round awkward issues as they arose, for example meeting Linlithgow's

38. Amery diary, 19, 28 February 1942, in Barnes and Nicholson (eds.), *Empire at Bay*, pp. 777, 781.
39. Committee on India, 5th meeting, 3 March 1942, in Mansergh, *TOP*, i, pp. 304–6.
40. Amery diary, 4 March 1942, in Barnes and Nicholson (eds.), *Empire at Bay*, p. 783.
41. See Moore, *Churchill, Cripps and India*, p. 80.

sensitivity about the minorities by explicitly covering their rights under the proposed treaty guarantees.[42] Within the India Committee, he and Attlee could, in Churchill's absence, generally secure Amery's and Anderson's support to carry the plan forward; and within the War Cabinet, Attlee, Cripps and Anderson could expect little dissent from Bevin, Eden or Lyttelton, and only token head-shaking from Churchill. But at a meeting of all Cabinet-rank ministers on 5 March, it was evident that the new policy initiative dismayed many Conservatives, who looked in vain to Churchill for reassurance, and a meeting of all Conservative backbench MPs gave Amery a rough ride, clearly believing that Government policy had been captured by its left-wing members.[43]

Moreover, the Viceroy, slow to move as ever, and having failed to emasculate the drafts, was plainly preparing for the kill, with a pointed reminder to the Cabinet that he was still not in favour of making a Declaration at all.[44] The plan of simply presenting the Declaration to the House of Commons looked increasingly risky. Yet Amery nourished hopes that, if only it could be properly explained, 'the thing can go through and will satisfy Moslems, and just possibly some of Congress, as well as Americans and Left Wing here'.[45] He toyed with the alternative of deferring publication until he had himself gone out to India to prepare the ground. Meanwhile the political strains in the coalition Government, never far below the surface in 1942, were becoming more obvious.

It was Cripps who broke the log-jam. On Saturday, 7 March, Cripps apparently made a remark about possibly going to India himself – 'I think he did, but that I didn't hear this', Amery noted[46] – thus raising the stakes in a way that alarmed the Secretary of State. The following day, the Crippses were again at Chequers and stayed overnight with the Churchills. Cripps affirmed his willingness to go to Delhi as an emissary, with authority to disclose the plan in due course rather than publish it first in London. Amery joined them and found Churchill, who was tired of 'trying to grasp the problem to which he has given so little thought' and pained at 'abandoning his old die hard position', now 'resolved to get clear of it at all costs'. In this mood, 'he wanted Cripps to go out and carry through our plan by negotiation'.[47]

42. cf. Mansergh, *TOP*, i, pp. 329, 352, 358.
43. Cadogan diary, 5 March 1942, in Dilks (ed.), *Cadogan: Diaries*, p. 440; Amery diary, 5 March 1942, in Barnes and Nicholson (eds), *Empire at Bay*, pp. 783–4.
44. Mansergh, *TOP*, i, p. 332.
45. Amery to Churchill, 5 March 1942, in Mansergh, *TOP*, i, p. 324.
46. Amery diary, 7 March 1942, in Barnes and Nicholson, *Empire at Bay*, p. 784n.
47. Amery diary, 8 March 1942, in Barnes and Nicholson, op cit., p. 785.

Negotiation, in order to secure consent, rather than the imposition of a predetermined plan, was implicit in the Cripps Mission. At Chequers that same day, Cripps drafted a Commons statement, announcing that the Government had 'decided to send immediately to India a member of the War Cabinet with full power to discuss with the leaders of Indian opinion the scheme upon which the War Cabinet has agreed'.[48] Amery, who had come to see the tactical advantages in sending Cripps, none the less thought him 'quite capable of deliberately trying to provoke Linlithgow's resignation'.[49] Indeed a cable from Linlithgow, fulfilling his threat to resign as Viceroy, was already on its way to the India Office.

At the War Cabinet meeting on Monday, 9 March, Cripps's offer to go was accepted. As the meeting broke up in 10 Downing Street, Graham Spry, now on the Lord Privy Seal's staff, was waiting in the dining-room of No. 11. He recalled Cripps appearing through the connecting door, playing with the familiar black cat, which he picked up and placed on Spry's shoulders. 'We are going to India', he said. 'I am leaving Wednesday.'[50]

The problem was to define Cripps's brief, so as to give him some chance of success. The War Cabinet minutes stressed that he would be taking with him a specific, agreed scheme: 'Otherwise, it would be said that he was going out to negotiate.'[51] Amery, however, sought to soften this impression in the forthcoming public statement, telling Churchill:

While it is essential that Sir S. Cripps should work to a definite set of instructions, and that there should be no idea that he is going out on a purely roving commission, I think there are serious objections to referring to his instructions as if they were an absolutely cut and dried plan (even though from our point of view they are something fairly near that). To do so seems to me to fetter the Cabinet emissary's discretion too much . . .[52]

In working over Cripps's own draft for the Prime Minister's statement, Amery thus argued for greater licence. Only when Cripps talked of calling into 'immediate consultation all the principal sections of Indian opinion, whether in British India or in the Indian States', did Amery seek to apply the brakes.[53] He insisted that in the States, any consultation should be with

48. Suggested lines of Indian statement, 8 March 1942, in Mansergh, *TOP*, i, p. 377.
49. Amery diary, 8 March 1942, in Barnes and Nicholson, op. cit., p. 786.
50. Spry memoirs, Spry 84/25.
51. WM (42) 31, 9 March 1942, in Mansergh, *TOP*, i, p. 378.
52. Amery to Churchill, 9 March 1942, in Mansergh, *TOP*, i, p. 387.
53. Suggested lines of Indian statement, 8 March 1942, in Mansergh, *TOP*, i, p. 377.

the princes themselves or their ministers, rather than Congress.[54] Such amendments reflected the India Office's solicitude for the position of the princes – and for that of a Viceroy whom they still wished to retain. Amery also held a brief for the Muslims, with their image of Cripps as 'a pure Congress-man, a close friend of Nehru, etc.'.[55] Official circles were well aware of Linlithgow's view of Nehru: 'he has not changed an atom and he is so obsessed by his hatred for us – or what he calls British Imperialism – that he is blind to the harm that he is doing to his own countrymen'.[56] Little wonder that Amery was worried about this potentially explosive mixture.

Churchill took over the drafting of his own statement, delivered to the House of Commons on 11 March. He spoke of an emissary going to India 'to satisfy himself upon the spot by personal consultation that the declaration upon which we are agreed, and which we believe represents a just and final solution, will achieve its purpose'. This struck a nice balance, conveying the 'atmosphere of precision and finality' which the India Committee had agreed was important,[57] while implying some latitude. As to who would be consulted, Churchill abandoned euphemism: the task, his statement said, was 'to procure the necessary measure of assent not only from the Hindu majority but also from those great minorities amongst which the Muslims are the most numerous and on many grounds pre-eminent'.[58] Then Churchill announced to a crowded House of Commons: 'My Right Honourable Friend the Lord Privy Seal has volunteered to undertake this task.' Apparently, there was a moment of anti-climax – eyes habitually turned towards Attlee – but the mood of the House turned to delight as the word went round, 'he means Cripps'.[59] The significance of Cripps's absence – he was already in the air – suddenly dawned. It was at this point that Agatha Harrison, sitting in the gallery, 'realised that the age of miracles has not passed' – or so she reported to Gandhi in a letter assuring him that Cripps was 'the "man of the hour" here; desperately needed and trusted by all alike'.[60]

The choice was undoubtedly popular, warmly welcomed not only on both sides of the House but equally widely in the press. The subtlety of the position was not lost on the politicians with the most immediate stake in

54. Amery to Churchill, 9 March 1942, in Mansergh, *TOP*, i, pp. 387–90.
55. Amery to Churchill, 4 March 1942, in Mansergh, *TOP*, i, p. 316.
56. Linlithgow to Sir M. Hallett, 24 February 1942, in Mansergh, *TOP*, i, p. 236.
57. Minutes, 3 March 1942, in Mansergh, *TOP*, i, p. 305.
58. Churchill statement, in Mansergh, *TOP*, i, pp. 407, 408.
59. Nicolson diary, 11 March 1942, in Nicolson, *Diaries and Letters, 1930–64* (condensed edn.), p. 226.
60. Agatha Harrison to Gandhi, 12 March 1942, copy sent to IC same date.

the fortunes of the Cripps Mission. Churchill cabled to Linlithgow that his resignation 'might be the signal for a general collapse in British Indian resistance with serious rupture of political unity here'. He appealed for the Viceroy's support in the 'thankless and hazardous task' that Cripps had undertaken. 'The announcement of his mission will still febrile agitation and give time for the problem to be calmly solved or alternatively proved for the time being to be insoluble.'[61]

Ironically, the launching of the Cripps Mission helped Churchill to persuade the Viceroy to stay on, whereas Cripps, who would have been only too happy to see the back of Linlithgow, was forced to bide his time. It was Amery who, in no fewer than seven telegrams to the Viceroy during the course of 10 March, put the right-wing case for the Cripps Mission, developing the view that the policy was 'in essence a fairly conservative one, at any rate as compared with what everybody seems to be expecting'.[62] Admittedly, the choice of Cripps might upset the Muslims 'who will think we are selling out to Congress', but on closer inspection it would be discovered 'that the nest contains the Pakistan cuckoos' egg'.[63] He maintained that there was an essential continuity of policy between the present policy and that implied in the August offer of 1940, flattering the Viceroy into complicity with the very different sort of offer now proposed. On the eve of the Commons statement, Amery told Linlithgow of having had a 'long talk with Cripps who I am convinced is determined to be helpful and quite prepared to face unpopularity with the left wingers which may result from identifying himself with a policy falling so far short of their crude ideas'.[64]

It would be naive simply to take such utterances at face value, as unmasking the real purpose of the British Government from its own secret documents.[65] These were reassurances tendered by a shrewd minister, himself more machiavellian than diehard on Indian policy, deploying his own longstanding Tory credentials to assuage the fears of a reactionary Viceroy who was threatening to jump ship at any moment. 'What we have been up against all the time is the hope on the part of Congress that its influence with the members of the Left Wing here and in America would push us into going back on the pledge of 1940,' was how Amery read the position. So

61. Churchill to Linlithgow, 10 March 1942, in Mansergh, *TOP*, i, pp. 394–5.
62. Amery to Linlithgow, 10 March 1942, in Mansergh, *TOP*, i, p. 396.
63. Amery to Linlithgow, 10 March 1942, in Mansergh, *TOP*, i, p. 396.
64. Amery to Linlithgow, 10 March 1942, in Mansergh, *TOP*, i, p. 401; cf. ibid., p. 400.
65. See e.g. Patel, *Cripps Mission: the whole truth*, esp. pp. 19–20 on 'the non-availability of secret British documents' until published by Mansergh, and pp. 47–9 for a literal interpretation of Amery's gloss.

these elements needed to be 'definitely told in so many words, and by someone whom they regard as not unsympathetic, that their game is up and that they must either find ways and means of compromising with the minority elements, or face the disadvantages of a divided India'.[66] In this context, Amery argued, 'there is much to be said for sending out someone who has always been an extreme Left Winger and in close touch with Nehru and the Congress. The immediate effect on your Muslims, as with my Tory friends here, may be alarming, but the result in the end should be both to increase the chances of success, slight as they are, and to mitigate any blame thrown upon the Government as a whole for failure.'[67] Here was one dimension of the Cripps Mission, but hardly the whole truth about it.

Why, then, had Cripps been chosen – and why had he agreed to go? The inescapable fact was that Cripps was now Churchill's most serious rival, indeed the only serious rival to emerge since the crisis of May 1940. Talk of him as the next Prime Minister was common, recorded by parliament-arians like Dalton and Nicolson who remained sympathetic towards Chur-chill and, at best, sceptical towards Cripps.[68] It was the private opinion of David Owen that 'if he brought this Indian settlement off, C. would certainly replace Winston'.[69] Both Cripps and Churchill must themselves have appreciated such a possibility.

'You performed a miracle in Russia', Gandhi told Cripps when they met in Delhi; and asked him 'to perform a miracle here too'.[70] A double miracle-worker would, of course, assume heroic stature, but only by per-forming feats that were commonly considered impossible. The Viceroy, in his initial musings on the Cripps Mission, took it for granted that 'if he wants to be Prime Minister, what sensible politician would take the immediate risks of failure over this just when his stock is very high?' Linlithgow was driven to the conclusion: 'No, I think he realised that India might take things from him which they wouldn't take from anyone else, and he is coming out here in a genuine public-spirited attempt to solve the problem'.[71] Better disposed

66. Amery to Linlithgow, 10 March 1942, in Mansergh, *TOP*, i, pp. 401–2.

67. ibid., p. 402; and see the perceptive comments in Louis, *In the Name of God, Go!*, pp. 129, 154–7.

68. Dalton diary, 5 March 1942, in Pimlott (ed.), *Dalton: War Diary*, pp. 389–90; Nicolson diary, 25 February 1942, in Nicolson (ed.), *Harold Nicolson: Diaries and Letters*, ii, p. 214.

69. David Owen, reported in Coupland diary, 3 April 1942; cf. Coupland, *Cripps Mission*, pp. 23–4.

70. Fischer, *Week with Gandhi*, p. 19.

71. Hodson diary, 14 March 1942, in Hodson, *Great Divide*, p. 95.

towards Cripps, the editor of *The Times* privately took the same view: 'It is an exemplary act of courage and selfless public spirit.'[72]

An interesting exchange of letters, at the time of the Mission's inception, survives in Isobel Cripps's papers. She had written to the Prime Minister before she left Chequers the previous weekend, asking if she might see him from time to time during Stafford's absence. She was at pains to 'emphasize Stafford's, & my own, deep desire to cooperate with you & share in any way possible to lighten the biggest burden one man can have been asked to bear & which you have shouldered all this time'. It seems unlikely that she would have written without Stafford's knowledge, the more so since she made a point of mentioning how closely she and he worked together. 'We do ask you to believe that, with all that is in us, our desire is to help & not hinder.'[73] It may have been over-effusive for Isobel to say this; the point is that she felt it needed saying. The Prime Minister left Clementine Churchill to reply, knowing that their wives reciprocated a warmth that he and Stafford found it difficult to engender face to face. Isobel was invited to spend further weekends at Chequers during the period of the Mission, which she did on at least one occasion.[74]

In domestic politics, Churchill needed all the support he could rally, but particularly from the left, his strongest supporters in 1940–41, but now growing restive. This was the symbolic aspect of Cripps's accession to high office. He had been given an impressive post in the Government, a self-proclaimed friendly critic who now had to shield the Prime Minister from further criticism. 'As Leader of the House SC will have to both defend W to the Commons and interpret the C to W,' Spry recognized. 'It will be no mean task and presents no mean opportunity for a false move.'[75] It was a post, too, essentially empty of executive responsibilities. Harold Laski expressed the ambivalence of many on the left. 'I find everywhere profound interest in Stafford, immense faith in his determination to get something done quickly,' he told Isobel Cripps. 'But I find also wide doubt whether he can get anything done quickly, or whether the system will not break him first.'[76] From Churchill's point of view, though, Cripps was dangerously under-occupied, and threateningly free to carve out his own role. After talking to Churchill on the day the Mission was dreamt up, Amery noted: 'I am by no means sure too that Winston doesn't think it a good thing to

72. Barrington-Ward diary, 11 March 1942.
73. IC to Churchill, 8 March 1942, copy (left for him on 9 March).
74. C. Churchill to IC, 10 March 1942.   75. Spry diary, 20 February 1942
76. Laski to IC, 9 March 1942.

send off this dangerous young rival on the errand of squaring the circle in India.'[77] India served to mop up his attention and – for a month as it turned out – keep him out of the way and out of mischief.

Yet this was no factitious diversion. The centrality of the Indian problem was now recognized on all sides. A military preface to the Cripps Mission was provided by the fall of Rangoon on 8 March and a postscript by the evacuation of Mandalay on 29 April. Chiang Kai-shek's farewell message to India, published on 23 February, not only invoked the Atlantic Charter but specifically called on Britain to hand over real political power as speedily as possible, linking the struggle against aggression with that for India's freedom – Nehru's line, of course.[78] American opinion was a crucial pressure in the same direction. Externally, Churchill needed to satisfy his allies that Britain's real commitment was to democracy and self-determination rather than to imperialism – a task made the harder by his own past record.

Churchill's agonized misgivings over the framing of the draft Declaration showed him torn between his rooted attitudes and his conviction that a major war crisis had to be faced. More was required than a mere propaganda ploy. Only an initiative with a real chance of success, however slight, would serve to improve the war situation, not only on the ground in Asia but in consolidating the grand alliance on which final victory depended. These objectives became more attainable with Cripps as the emissary; but he would not have agreed to act as emissary unless he had himself thought a settlement attainable. Success, as he must have realized, would accrue to him personally as well as help to win the war. If, however, the Cripps Mission were to fail, in what everybody acknowledged as a desperate attempt to 'square the circle', then the position was less easy to foresee. A great deal would depend on how the cause of failure was perceived, not only by the parties to the negotiations but by public opinion at home and overseas.

77. Amery diary, 8 March 1942, in Barnes and Nicholson (eds.), *Empire at Bay*, p. 786.
78. Mansergh, *TOP*, i, pp. 232–3.

3

Tragedy in Delhi

The agenda of the Cripps Mission was ambiguous from the outset. Conservative MPs were apprehensive that it meant a lurch to the left in British policy; and whereas many on the left hoped that this was true, others feared that Cripps had been compromised. Amery rationalized it as an extension of the enlightened Conservative policy that he had vainly been urging on Churchill (and the Viceroy) for nearly two years; and what others called the Cripps offer he plainly regarded as the Amery offer. Now that they had to work together, the carnivorous Amery invited his new colleague to dinner – 'Do you include fish and eggs in your diet (when procurable) or are you a vegetarian of the straiter sect?'[1] – incidentally demonstrating that differences of diet and culture were not a peculiarity of India. Cripps cordially reciprocated Amery's goodwill and a *modus vivendi* was established.

Cripps was not, however, gullibly co-opted into the India Office scheme nor confined to the official channels which it preferred. Having decided not to resign, the Viceroy reconciled himself to receiving Cripps with a good grace. Although many of Linlithgow's detailed suggestions, especially over invitations to make representations to the Mission, were adopted by Cripps, from the start he showed himself determined to maintain an independent presence in Delhi. He plainly took a dim view of the Viceroy's Executive Council as it was currently constituted, and ruffled its feathers by failing to pay it the due deference it expected. His policy of keeping at arm's length from the Raj is attested by Linlithgow's subsequent reproach: 'How could I help when I was consulted by Cripps about nothing?'[2]

The plan for the Cripps Mission was essentially that which he himself settled with Amery on the day after it was announced. Cripps would arrive in India on 22 March. The first couple of days were to be spent on official

1. Amery to RSC, 9 March 1942, in Mansergh, *TOP*, i, p. 390.
2. Annotation by Linlithgow on cable from Amery, 11 April 1942, in Mansergh, *TOP*, i, p. 756.

briefings; then Cripps would move to his own house for the rest of his talks, just as Chiang Kai-shek had done. Cripps's intention was to stay no more than a fortnight 'unless it becomes clear that there is a definite prospect of doing business'.[3] In the event, he was to stay on for a further week – making this visit to India almost exactly the same in length as that of 1939.

This important mission depended, to an extent difficult to imagine today, upon a single missionary. No great diplomatic entourage flew out; just three middle-ranking aides. David Owen and Graham Spry went as personal assistants. Frank Turnbull, a rising civil servant who after twelve years in the India Office was now Amery's principal private secretary, was sent as the official minder. 'We went out to India together as strangers,' Cripps subsequently wrote (to 'my dear Frank'); 'we returned . . . as friends . . .'[4] The strength of their working relationship is testified by the fact that Cripps was to choose Turnbull to accompany him again in India on the Cabinet delegation four years later. Once in Delhi, the Mission was reinforced by Reginald Coupland, Beit Professor of Colonial History at Oxford, who had been in India writing a report on the constitutional problem for Nuffield College, Oxford, and who became their house historian. It was now that they acquired the name, 'the Crippery'.[5]

It took Cripps six days to reach India, flying through Gibraltar, then with a long southern loop across Africa to reach Cairo. He was only in Egypt for a couple of days but he was determined to put them to fullest use. Meeting his old friend Walter Monckton, who was serving as a resident minister in the Middle East, Cripps advised Churchill that Monckton's status should be enhanced by immediately announcing his appointment as Minister of State. After discussions, not only with him but with the commanders of the British forces, Cripps telegraphed an appreciation assuring Churchill, who was understandably impatient for a decisive victory in the desert, that General Sir Claude Auchinleck's caution was well justified. 'Your Cairo telegrams do not convince me,' Churchill replied, brushing aside Cripps's case about the present insufficiency of *matériel*, backed as it was by detailed evidence from his own inspection of tank modifications.[6]

Cripps was to maintain this interest in immediate defence requirements while in India. The take-it-or-leave-it style of the taciturn Commander-in-

3. Amery to Linlithgow, 12 March 1942, in Mansergh, *TOP*, i, pp. 411–12.
4. RSC to Turnbull, 30 June 1942
5. Coupland diary, 4 April 1942. For the Crippery, see above p. 248.
6. Churchill to RSC, 22 March 1942, T. 445/2; cf. RSC to Churchill, 21 March 1942, T. 438/2 and 441/2; Churchill papers, CHAR 20/72, ff. 55–7, 61, 66. cf. Churchill, *Second World War*, iv, pp. 263–4.

Chief in India, General Sir Archibald Wavell, had not ingratiated him with Churchill. Cripps readily added his own advocacy to Wavell's appeals for the diversion of bombers from Europe to the defence of India. Certainly Cripps arrived in India immersed in practical military problems, whether of strategy or supply. It would be a mistake to think that, in his subsequent discussions of the defence issue with the Congress leaders, Cripps was abstracted from those difficulties on the ground with which the Prime Minister, the Viceroy and the Commander-in-Chief were so evidently pre-occupied.

On the eve of his arrival in India, Cripps finally had time to take some Mission work up to bed with him and told his wife from Basrah: 'I am full of excitement at the magnitude of the effort that will be needed & feel keyed up at the prospect of "going over the top" tomorrow.'[7] He touched down in Delhi on 23 March, 'looking very fit', according to the Viceroy, who had insisted that he remain in Karachi the previous night, ostensibly because of quarantine regulations, perhaps to keep him away from the press.[8]

Linlithgow saw the problem, as usual, in terms of applying the brakes. Above all, he sought to pre-empt any move to entice Congress into a settlement with offers of executive posts. His attitude was charged with a defensive caution and an undertow of suspicion lest he was being kept in the dark (which to some extent he was). The 'Draft Instructions to Viceroy', drawn up by Cripps and forming part of his own terms of reference, pointed in just the direction that Linlithgow feared, though it was only cabled out to him some days later.[9] Just as Cripps felt himself licensed to speak of Indianization in general terms, so the Viceroy felt himself justified in drawing the line at promising specific posts. 'That's my business,' he told Cripps, apparently after handing back a document in which Cripps showed a possible allocation of twelve seats on the Council: four to the Congress, three to the Muslim League, with two representatives of the states (one Hindu and one Muslim), one Sikh, one for the Depressed Classes (Ambedkar) and one other (co-opted).[10]

As well as talking to Linlithgow and Wavell, Cripps explained his plan to the Executive Council, but was clearly impatient to get down to what he saw as the real business with those who were vital to its accomplishment. He spoke also to a press conference, said to be the largest ever held in

7. ISC to IC, misdated 22 March, but 21 March 1942.
8. Linlithgow to Amery, 24 March 1942, in Mansergh, *TOP*, i, p. 466.
9. Moore, *Churchill, Cripps and India*, p. 80.
10. Viceroy quoted by Hodson, *Great Divide*, p. 98; drafts, including one in Cripps's handwriting, n.d., but 23 March 1942, PRO, CAB 127/70.

Delhi, the first of seven. The give-and-take between him and the assembled journalists, mainly Indian, was a clear breakthrough in public relations. Spry, who called Cripps 'the newspaper man's dream', noted how his props – the pipe, 'the box of matches tossed' – were deployed to reinforce 'the ready, measured flow of words'.[11] Cripps relied on his practised ability to keep reporters happy even when he had little to divulge.

I suppose that somebody is going to ask whether I had a cheerful talk with Mr Gandhi yesterday. I notice that the Press observes the appearance of the face of each person as he comes out of the house (laughter). I am afraid I have been diddling some of you on that. Just as he is going out each time I tell my visitor that he has got to smile broadly (laughter) ... Perhaps you would ask me what I talked to Mr Gandhi about. We had a talk about the weather, about Wardha, and food, and health and some other matters (renewed laughter).[12]

Cripps established a striking contrast to the aloof Viceregal style. After a couple of days, he moved into 3 Queen Victoria Road, which had been put at the disposal of the Crippery. This was a pleasant house, with gardens that were still in flower, although the erection of tents for extra office space, and the presence of bearers, guards, newspaper reporters and photographers, meant that these seemed thronged with people at all hours. It was here, or at the house of G. B. Birla, the wealthy industrialist and Congress supporter whom Cripps had met in 1939, that he met about forty separate individuals or delegations. 'We have all been very busy but I do not think all of us together have worked so hard as Stafford,' Graham Spry told Isobel Cripps. Reassuring her that 'it is amazing how well and how fresh he has been able to keep', Spry insisted that 'Stafford has always been in top form and has never let up for a minute.'[13]

The list of those whom Cripps wished to see was strongly influenced by his own earlier contacts and experience. Of the four Governors whom he initially specified, three had previously been interviewed by Cripps.[14] Likewise, among the six Congress leaders whom Cripps listed, he already knew Azad, Nehru and Rajagopalachari. And a meeting with Gandhi was desirable, if he would agree to come to Delhi (which he did, thus avoiding

11. Spry diary, 27–28 March 1942.
12. Official press handout, 28 March 1942, PRO, CAB 127/71.
13. Spry to IC, 6 April 1942.
14. Sir Bernard Glancy of the Punjab, Sir John Herbert of Bengal and Sir Roger Lumley of Bombay had been interviewed by Cripps before, while the fourth, Sir Maurice Hallett, had only been in the United Provinces since 1939.

the impression that any kind of pilgrimage to Wardha was demanded – another delicate issue during Chiang Kai-shek's recent visit). Cripps wanted to see Jinnah again, of course, and also the Muslim chief minister of Bengal, Fazlul Huq. Dr B. R. Ambedkar, for the Depressed Classes, and Narayan Joshi, for Labour, were also on Cripps's list, as were the Diwans of Hyderabad and of Baroda, among the representatives of the States. All of these were interviewed during the Cripps Mission, forming a strong core of persons whom Cripps had met before. The various political parties were invited to nominate their own representatives, though Cripps was not thereby precluded from seeing anyone whom he specially wanted.

Memories of his 1939 visit were not always to his advantage. 'He forgot then that the depressed classes existed,' said one of their representatives; 'he saw a few Congressmen and went away.'[15] Either at the Viceroy's prompting, or because he realized the necessity himself, Cripps sought to calm Muslim apprehensions about his record. 'My association in the past has been more close with my friends in the Congress than with the members of other parties or other communities,' he stated in his first press release, 'but I am duly impressed with the need in any scheme for the future of India to meet the deep anxieties which undoubtedly exist among the Muslims and the other communities.'[16] Jinnah's response was conciliatory, saying that although Cripps had been a friend of Congress, he came now as the representative of the British Government.

Cripps conducted the interviews alone. The record of each long day's proceedings was dictated in the evening, a practice that largely followed the routine established with Geoffrey Wilson. Indeed these notes read more like an extension of Cripps's diary than a series of official minutes. In pride of place on 25 March were the authorized representatives of Congress and the Muslim League.

First came Azad, the President of Congress. The fact that he was accompanied by his secretary, Asaf Ali, who acted as interpreter, raises an important question about the adequacy of Azad's English. Jinnah's dismissive assessment – 'he's like my bearer. He can understand a few words of English but he can only answer "Yes" or "No"' – need not be accepted literally since the hostility between these two irreconcilable Muslims stemmed from more than their respective linguistic competence.[17] None the less, everyone

15. Rao Sahib Sivaraj, quoted in Mansergh, TOP, i, p. 419.
16. Press statement, Delhi, 23 March 1942, in Mansergh, TOP, i, p. 463.
17. Jinnah's comment in 1946 is quoted in Wyatt, Confessions, p. 149, and may be taken from his contemporary diary.

agrees that, although Azad could follow English conversation and could scrutinize a written text, he felt inhibited by his grasp of spoken English. So, rather than attempt to speak it himself, he used others, including Nehru, to translate his Urdu.[18] But on 25 March 1942 Nehru was absent.

These were hardly ideal conditions under which to elucidate the carefully formulated proposals in the draft Declaration, still unpublished. When Cripps slowly read it out, Azad let all the projected constitutional arrangements go by until reaching the final paragraph, containing the vaguely specified proposals for interim wartime arrangements. In a letter from Azad to Cripps, written after the breakdown of negotiations, the allegation was made: 'You told me then that there would be a National Government which would function as a Cabinet and that the position of the Viceroy would be analogous to that of The King in England vis-à-vis his Cabinet.'[19]

If Cripps said exactly this, he was stretching his brief, or at least straining the concept of analogy. Azad's memoirs, dictated in Urdu during his last illness, contain an elaboration of this account. It is not surprising that this testimony has been seized upon by those who have accused Cripps of 'not running straight' with Congress, and by extension, of deceiving the Viceroy.[20] In this way, the allegation that Cripps exceeded his mandate was to provide a convenient alibi for the two parties which subsequently repudiated the lines of a proposed settlement that they came to find embarrassing: for the Viceroy and Churchill on the British side as much as for the Congress leadership on the Indian side.

Such charges have become commonplace; even accounts sympathetic to Cripps often accept them.[21] Yet it should be remembered that the crucial

18. Graham Spry, 'A British reply to Louis Fischer', *Nation*, 14 November 1942, p. 501, describes Asaf Ali acting as interpreter; this is one point on which he and Fischer, who met Azad shortly afterwards at Wardha, are not in dispute; see Fischer, *Week with Gandhi*, p. 110. See also Alexander diary, 3 April 1946; RSC diary, 5 May 1946; Molesworth, *Curfew*, p. 220.
19. Azad to RSC, 11 April 1942, in Mansergh, *TOP*, i, pp. 743–5; see Gopal (ed.), *Nehru: Selected Works*, xii, pp. 209–11, for drafting by Nehru.
20. See Glendevon, *Viceroy at Bay*, pp. 237–8; and p. 231 for his reliance on the misdated account of this interview in the 1959 edition of Azad's memoirs, *India Wins Freedom*; see the 1988 revised edition, published as 'the complete version', p. 50. But Azad's memoirs have met telling criticism for their inaccuracies in quite other respects, esp. in Rajmohan Gandhi, *India Wins Errors*; and see French, *Liberty or Death*, p. 107.
21. In particular there are frequent citations of the influential opinion of Stokes, 'Cripps in India', esp. pp. 431–2. But this is actually a cautiously phrased hypothetical question about whether Cripps exceeded his brief; and other scholars with a close command of the relevant documents take the opposite view, notably Moore, *Churchill, Cripps and India*. It is, however, certainly worth pondering Stokes's suggestion (p. 430) that Azad imagined he was being offered (verbally but officially) what Cripps had shown him in writing on his private visit in 1939.

evidence on the supposedly misleading nuances of Cripps's proposal rests on an English translation of the heavily retrospective, self-interested testimony of what a terminally ill Urdu speaker claims to have remembered of verbal exchanges conducted, fifteen years previously, through an interpreter. It is a pity that Nehru, who accompanied Azad in all subsequent meetings with Cripps, and who drafted all the letters sent over Azad's signature, did not arrive in Delhi until 29 March. The marriage of his daughter Indira had detained him in Allahabad (though it is canard that his friend Cripps so forgot his official responsibilities as to attend a Hindu wedding at this juncture).[22]

What is indisputable is that, in his talks with Congress, Cripps held out the prospect of a fully Indianized Executive Council, which was itself not the way that Amery and Churchill had envisaged implementing the draft Declaration, though it was consistent with it. At their first meeting, Cripps thought Azad 'extremely friendly throughout'. Apparently somewhat surprised that the interim arrangements were of most interest to Congress, Cripps noted: 'My general impression was that Congress wanted the appearance and name of an Indian Defence Minister while at the same time realising that he could not take any effective part in ordering the movement of troops or other military arrangements.' The impression Cripps gained here was to govern his strategy over the next weeks, in bending every effort to meet Congress on this point, if this were seen as the main impediment to a settlement. He recorded that he pressed Azad on 'whether he could suggest any other way in which we could have demonstrated more decisively our intention to give India full self-government at the earliest possible moment. He had no further suggestions to make.'[23] Since previous initiatives, notably the August offer, had foundered through vagueness and dissimulation on the British side, and consequential cynicism and lack of confidence on the part of Congress, this seemed a promising beginning.

In his next interview Cripps took the bull by the horns. The previous day's newspapers had carried reports of a speech by Jinnah in which he had brandished a copy of Cripps's strongly anti-League article in *Tribune* of May 1940; one headline read 'Cripps – a Friend of Congress'.[24] True, Jinnah had gone on to advise his supporters not to get 'cold feet'; but plainly some fence-mending was necessary. 'Directly Mr Jinnah arrived,' Cripps noted, 'I broached the question of my past attitude towards the Muslim League

22. Contra French, *Liberty or Death*, p. 144.
23. RSC note, 25 March 1942, in Mansergh, *TOP*, i, p. 479.
24. Unidentified cutting, 24 March 1942.

and told him that the views I took two and a half years ago were sincerely taken and represented my judgement of the situation as it then was and that I had regarded the Pakistan propaganda as pure political pressure.' But now, he claimed, he knew better. What made the difference was 'the change in the communal feeling in India and the growth of the Pakistan movement', Cripps told Jinnah, and noted that the draft Declaration 'rather surprised him in the distance it went to meet the Pakistan case'. It was naturally this part of the scheme that mainly interested Jinnah; he could not see insuperable difficulties in devising ways 'to mobilise the whole of India behind her own defence'. Again Cripps was encouraged. 'On the whole I was hopefully impressed by his general attitude and his lack of pernickety criticism of phrases and words which I had rather expected.'[25]

It was a curious kind of negotiation. The rival Indian leaders were so antagonistic that they never met each other; yet when Cripps did so, the atmosphere was hardly adversarial, perhaps because Cripps's real adversary was the absent Viceroy, with whom daily consultation was expected. The official memorandum of Cripps's report to the Viceroy on his first day of talks conveys the tenor of their exchanges, at once polite and prickly. The question of the future role of the Executive Council continued to trouble Linlithgow, in view of his forthright objections to appointing representative Indian members, as specified in his telegrams home.

His Excellency . . . observed that though he had nothing firm from His Majesty's Government, his own position was clear enough. Sir Stafford Cripps recalled these telegrams, and agreed that his Excellency had made his own position perfectly clear. His Excellency, pursuing the matter, observed that he knew the people concerned better than Sir Stafford Cripps did. He knew how little administrative experience they had, and how prejudiced they were both in their own minds and by statements made so often to their followers.

He left Cripps in little doubt of his attitude: 'His Excellency, as a last word, remarked to Sir Stafford that he would forgive him almost anything except stealing His Excellency's cheese to bait his own trap.'[26]

It was only at this point that it was agreed that the moment had come to publish the draft Declaration. There were two last-minute changes in its text: one to please the Muslim League and one to propitiate Congress. Jinnah's keen legal mind was satisfied by a tightening of the wording on the

25. RSC note, 25 March 1942, in Mansergh, *TOP*, i, pp. 480–81.
26. Memorandum, 25 March 1942, in Mansergh, *TOP*, i, pp. 484–5.

provisions for non-accession. More significant was the revision of the final paragraph on defence.

This change in Cripps's approach arose out of a meeting with Rajagopala-chari. His dissent from Gandhi's anti-war line had already become apparent and he was not an official Congress representative; but Cripps had arranged interviews with all provincial ex-Chief Ministers, mainly as an excuse to meet the ever-helpful Rajaji. He explained to Cripps what Congress needed in order to give 'some clarion call to the Indians which would stimulate them from their present defeatist attitude'.[27] This reinforced other advice from sympathetic Indian contacts, like Shiva Rao, who acted as correspondent for the *Manchester Guardian*, that Congress was less interested in the proposed post-war promises than in immediate changes.[28] Accordingly, new wording was devised over defence, with competitive drafts within the Crippery from Coupland, Turnbull and Owen, and a composite version was itself amended by agreement with the Viceroy and the Commander-in-Chief.[29]

An explicit distinction was introduced into the Declaration. The responsibility for defence, it now explained, was retained by the British Government 'as part of their world war effort', whereas 'the task of organising to the full the military, moral and material resources of India must be the responsibility of the Government of India with the co-operation of the peoples of India'.[30] Linlithgow, Wavell and himself were united, so Cripps put it to Churchill, in doing their utmost 'to deprive Congress of any excuse for refusal under this head'.[31] Armed at last with Churchill's approval of the altered clause, Cripps became more confident. Coupland reported him as saying that 'the proposed settlement is just and final: there is no more that C. would concede, even if he were a wholly free agent'.[32]

There was a general sense of expectancy, driven by a sense of urgency about India's defences. In London, a cartoon in the *Daily Mail*, with the caption 'The tide is rising', showed Cripps urging a hesitant elephant (India) to embark in an ark named 'The Democracies', with the words: 'Come on, make your mind up. I haven't much time to spare – but you have less.'[33] Reports of Japanese advances came in daily, vying with the Cripps Mission for the main headlines. Cripps later claimed that he was 'fully expecting the Japs to make large-scale landings in India' during his stay.[34] The *Hindustan*

27. RSC note, 28 March 1942, in Mansergh, *TOP*, i, p. 512.
28. Rao in Philips and Wainwright (eds.), *Partition of India*, p. 428.
29. Drafts in PRO, CAB 127/70.   30. Text in Mansergh, *TOP*, i, p. 566.
31. RSC to Churchill, 29 March 1942, in Mansergh, *TOP*, i, pp. 525–6.
32. Coupland diary, 28 March 1942.   33. *Daily Mail*, 25 March 1942.
34. Tahmankar interview, United Press of India, 18 June, 1942, PRO CAB 127/81.

Times, which was owned by Birla and edited by Gandhi's youngest son, while voicing worries about a 'scorched earth' policy in the event of a British withdrawal, had been calling for speedy action: 'Everything depends on how quickly Sir Stafford Cripps gets through his task in this country.'[35] The centrality of the defence issue, for Congress as much as for Cripps, was a function of the war situation. 'The supreme issue before this country,' the paper argued in another leader, 'is the Japanese threat, which is today at our doorsteps, and how to meet it.'[36]

Cripps conducted a well-publicized interview with Gandhi, who had reluctantly travelled to Delhi for the occasion. 'Gandhi–Cripps Meeting: Fateful Political Talks' was the front-page banner headline in the *Hindustan Times*. It carried a photograph of a beaming Cripps, attentively escorting his diminutive visitor out of 3 Queen Victoria Road after their meeting, amid the throng of reporters and cameramen who besieged them. Gandhi at first stated, 'I am observing my silence.' But when a journalist responded, 'Oh! is the news so good as that', Cripps intervened with the retort: 'You bad boy.'[37] Much cheerful banter ensued. 'Look at the sharks. I am sure you like them,' said the Mahatma, and Cripps replied: 'You like them more.'[38] Both men were playing to the gallery, concealing for the moment what an awkward couple of hours they had just spent together.

From first to last, the Cripps Mission did not impress Gandhi. His loyal supporter Agatha Harrison had sent her own testimonial with Cripps: 'Our "best Englishman" is now coming – Gandhiji.'[39] If not unread, such appeals were certainly unheeded by the old man. He scouted the draft Declaration as soon as Cripps showed it to him, saying later:

He gave it to me, and after a brief study, I said to him, 'Why did you come if this is what you have to offer? If this is your entire proposal to India, I would advise you to take the next plane home.' Cripps replied, 'I will consider that.'[40]

According to Cripps, when he asked Gandhi, 'as a friend', for his advice, Gandhi said that 'it would have been better if I had not come to India with a cut and dried scheme' – which was certainly at odds with what Gandhi had contended on their previous encounter in 1939, when he had insisted

35. Leader, *Hindustan Times*, 21 March 1942.   36. ibid., 24 March 1942.
37. Spry diary, 27 March 1942   38. *Hindustan Times*, 28 March 1942.
39. A. Harrison to Gandhi, 12 March 1942, copy to IC stating this had been dispatched by hand via Cripps's secretaries. It is not, however, printed in the relevant volume of Gandhi, *Collected Works*.
40. Fischer, *Week with Gandhi*, p. 15.

that it was up to the British Government to take the initiative. Cripps was now met with a hail (or at least a drizzle) of objections from Gandhi, including an objection to publishing the Declaration at all. Faced with this unpromising response, Cripps warned that this was the only scheme on offer, at least until the end of the war, 'and that those people who had taken the Congress point of view in the past, like myself, would not be in a position to exercise further influence in England as regards the solution of the Indian problem, as it would be generally thought that this offer was one which Congress should have accepted'.[41]

Banner headlines across the Indian newspapers anticipated the publication of Cripps's proposals. In giving copies of the Declaration to the politicians whom he had seen, Cripps had made it clear that the wording in each copy was distinctively and identifiably different; and he was pleased that his little ruse had helped to keep the actual contents of the Declaration from the Indian press.[42] One cartoon by the *Hindustan Times*'s talented cartoonist, Shankar, captioned 'The Cat is in the Bag', had shown Cripps with a stick over his shoulder, carrying a mysterious bundle which formed the object of universal curiosity.[43] Cripps took a close interest in the media arrangements. He had, as usual, handled the press attentively, giving a good deal of access, with much informal give and take, even when there was little hard information. Now that it was time to let the cat out of the bag, he sought to ensure that publication of the Declaration be simultaneous in Delhi and London, and that the text appear in the newspapers before it received comment on radio. The 'spin' put upon it was regarded as crucial; this was coordinated through Spry and the Ministry of Information so as to take the lead from Cripps's Delhi press conference. The top priority was for the Indian public to receive the first news from Indian sources; the next priority for the message to reach the USA. Indeed, it seems likely that the Ministry of Information had already primed some American newspapers, since the *New York Times* was commending the Cabinet's proposals five days before they were published.[44]

The Declaration, in its amended form, was finally published on Sunday, 29 March. Cripps held a press conference in which his mastery of the issues

---

41. RSC note, 27 March 1942, in Mansergh, *TOP*, i, p. 500; Gandhi was subsequently induced to acknowledge that he acquiesced in Cripps's 1939 proposals. Coupland diary, 29 March 1942.

42. Report to Cabinet, in Mansergh, *TOP*, ii, p. 321.

43. *Hindustan Times*, 26 March 1942; the phrase had been put in circulation by the Hindu Mahasabha two weeks previously; see Patel, *Cripps Mission*, p. 53.

44. *New York Times*, 24 March 1942, quoted in Mishra, *Cripps Mission*, p. 113

12. Geoffrey Wilson with Cripps at Urumchi, 1940.

13. The Cripps version in the making: at his typewriter.

14. Moscow souvenir, 1941: signed by Beaverbrook, Stalin, Harriman, Voroshilov, Litvinov, Molotov.

15. Days with Joe: outside the Kremlin, 1941.

16. Recalled to London: leaving Downing Street, June 1941.

17. The rivals: Cripps and Churchill, 1942.

18. The Crippery: Stafford Cripps in Delhi with Graham Spry, Reginald Coupland, Frank Turnbull and David Owen

19. *(Above)* Bad news from 'Hopie': with the Marquess of Linlithgow, 1942.

20. *(Right)* Laughing it off: with Gandhi, 1942.

21. *(Above)* Still friends? With Nehru, 1942.

22. *(Above right)* Cripps takes questions, 1942.

23. *(Below right)* Wartime factory visit.

24. *(Above)* Smiles around the table, 1946: (clockwise from left) Pethick-Lawrence, Wavell, Alexander, Jinnah and Cripps.

25. *(Right)* Congress leaders: Patel and Azad, 1946.

26. *(Below)* Cripps and Pethick-Lawrence hog the limelight; Alexander (right) 'the silent man'.

impressed everyone even more than his ability to make the reporters laugh. 'At one point he took off his coat – it was getting hot, he said – and squared up to the questioner,' an admiring Coupland noted. 'An old trick, no doubt, but it elicited friendly laughter.'[45] The tone was firm and constructive, seeking conciliation between parties whose past dealings had been bedevilled by mistrust but whose common interest lay in reaching an interim agreement. The text was exhaustively examined, clause by clause, and sometimes word by word. The post-war proposals for an Indian union with a constituent assembly, and the right of provinces to non-accession, received most attention; then Cripps turned to the interim arrangements, on which there were further questions.

'You cannot change the constitution,' Cripps replied to one reporter. 'All you can do is to change the conventions of the constitution. You can turn the Executive Council into a Cabinet.'[46] These pregnant words were later to receive wide currency and have been quoted in virtually every historical account of the Cripps Mission as the gist of Cripps's message. He certainly meant what he said; it was no more than he had already told Congress in private; and he must have known what he was doing in putting these expansive hints on the record, perhaps to pin down the Viceroy, certainly with Congress in mind. Yet his words elicited no comment from Linlithgow and were not picked up at the time in the press reports. The *Hindustan Times* said only that, while nothing was obligatory on the Viceroy, it would be possible for him to Indianize the Executive Council through changes in its composition.[47] It was left to the *Statesman* to pick up the point a couple of days later, with the parenthetical comment: 'Sir Stafford used the word Cabinet, not "Executive Council".' Here was the established press organ of the British community in India, which had mocked Cripps in 1939, now voicing loud support of his proposals as the only means to wartime unity in India – and whispering, too, its suspicions that 'the diehards' in London were denying him a free hand.[48]

Cripps undoubtedly felt some sense of frustration. 'If I were free, if I were PM,' he told the Crippery, 'I could make a broadcast that would lift the whole of India to its feet.'[49] Still, his radio broadcast, on the day after his press conference, reached a wide audience, overseas as well as within India. The initial reaction of most of the Indian press was favourable, with the

45. Coupland diary, 29 March 1942.
46. Press conference, 29 March 1942, in Mansergh, *TOP*, i, p. 547.
47. *Hindustan Times*, 30 March 1942.   48. Leader, *Statesman*, 1 April 1942.
49. Spry diary, 26 March 1942.

Bombay Chronicle an apparent exception.[50] In London, *The Times* gave a predictable welcome to the plan, and sought to attribute the credit for it jointly to Cripps's 'initiative and determination' and to Churchill's 'insight and imagination' in seizing the moment for change.[51] The Cripps offer was front-page news in the USA, and the tone of the *New York Times*, with its longstanding record of support for Congress, was notably favourable to the proposed arrangements for coping with the immediate problem of defence. American press comment, expressing optimism about a settlement, was widely reported in the Indian press. The fact that the Hindu Mahasabha remained notably wholly negative, dismissing the non-accession provisions as a threat to Indian unity, did not upset Cripps's calculations. He was tipped off that the Muslim League was ready to accept; he knew that the attitude of Congress was the crux; and he expected the rest to fall like dominoes, one way or the other.

The negotiations now hinged on Cripps and Nehru. They at last met on 29 March, when Nehru arrived at the Crippery only minutes after his arrival in Delhi on the overnight train from Allahabad. Coupland, breakfasting on the verandah with Cripps, noted that he 'talked of his coming contact with Nehru as decisive and reminded me that this was the day of National Prayer at home'.[52] Cripps and Nehru talked privately for forty-five minutes before going together to a large gathering of Congress leaders at Birla House. Cripps concluded that 'quite frankly they were trying to face up to the difficulties of combining an actual British control of the Defence forces and a publicly acknowledged position in which an Indian Member [of the Executive Council] could really lead the Indian people to their defence'.[53]

From the moment he arrived in Delhi, Nehru became the cynosure of the negotiations. When he dined at 3 Queen Victoria Road, the Crippery felt the thrill of proximity. According to Spry, 'we juniors withdrew' to the garden and saw, through the open windows, Cripps in serious conversation with Nehru – 'they were old friends and they were talking as old friends'.[54] Yet the known friendship between Cripps and Nehru excited suspicions that were not helpful to a negotiation where neither could appear compromised in the eyes of his own colleagues. Gandhi subsequently professed to find it discouraging 'that the man who was a friend of Jawaharlal's and

50. See Mishra, *Cripps Mission*, p. 79, citing the *Bombay Chronicle* in support of the contention that the Declaration 'was not well received in India'.
51. Leader, *The Times*, 30 March 1942.
52. 'Spry tells me he is a deeply religious man', he added. Coupland diary, 29 March 1942.
53. RSC note, 29 March 1942, in Mansergh, *TOP*, i, p. 529.
54. Spry, CBC broadcast, 26 April 1942, CBC archives.

had been interested in India should have made himself the bearer of this mission'.[55] This was, in its inimitable way, an implied rebuke to Nehru's gullibility, reflecting the fact that the Mission put him as well as Cripps on trial. Certainly it put their friendship to the test, as Nehru ruefully acknowledged afterwards.

Cripps surprised me greatly. I have liked Cripps as a man, though I must confess that I have considered him a somewhat muddleheaded politician. But on this occasion I was surprised at his woodenness and insensitiveness, in spite of his public smile . . . I made it perfectly plain to him that there were limits beyond which I could not carry the Congress and there were limits beyond which the Congress could not carry the people. But he thought that all this was totally beside the point.[56]

To Cripps, conversely, Nehru seemed below par. He had not been well and appeared to be unable or perhaps unwilling to exert his full strength in the Congress Working Committee, which was now reported to be heading towards rejection. Cripps gathered from Nehru ('though he did not say so precisely') that this was due to Gandhi's influence, and to the reluctance of his supporters, with their belief in non-violence, to become enmeshed in the armed defence of India.[57] It was all very civil, almost unnervingly friendly.[58] By this stage, however, Gandhi's aphorism, that the Cripps offer was 'a post-dated cheque' (with the journalistic improvement 'on a failing bank'), was already in circulation; so was his phrase about a 'vivisection of India'.[59] If Nehru's privileged contacts with Cripps were no secret, neither was the political gap between them. A cartoon by Shankar, usually well informed, depicted Nehru dining disdainfully at 3 Queen Victoria Road, with Cripps as a waiter showing him 'Menu (after War)'.[60]

With this sort of evidence now before him, Cripps realized that there was little further hope, as he did not disguise from the quizzical Viceroy on 31 March:

Sir Stafford replied bluntly that he thought Indian leaders had missed an excellent offer . . . He added that Nehru had been fighting hard for the scheme, but that

55. Fischer, *Week with Gandhi*, p. 20.
56. Nehru to Evelyn Wood, 5 June 1942, in Gopal (ed.), *Nehru: Selected Works*, xii, pp. 241–2.
57. RSC note, 30 March 1942, in Mansergh, *TOP*, i, p. 558.
58. See Coupland, *Cripps Mission*, p. 188.
59. Spry diary, 27 March 1942, records both of these phrases; this is earlier than in other sources, e.g. Pinnell note, 30 March 1942, in Mansergh, *TOP*, i, p. 561; Coupland diary, 31 March 1942; reports in New York papers on 30 March, cf. Gopal, *Nehru*, i, p. 279n.
60. *Hindustan Times*, 31 March 1942.

Gandhi had made up his mind to reject the organisation of India for war, and was prepared to use any means to thwart it. The Congress would not split.[61]

Cripp's reading of the Congress position was too simple. He saw Gandhi's hand behind every move to thwart a settlement and speculated that the old man 'may be actually desirous to bring about a state of chaos, while he sits at Wardha eating vegetables'.[62] Conversely, Cripps saw Nehru's influence behind every move to bring Congress behind the war effort. No doubt Cripps observed that when Nehru talked to his countrymen of the need to oppose fascist aggression, he told them of how his heart bled for China, and of what a calamity it would be for the Soviet Union to fall.[63] It was a selective language, with which Cripps was familiar because he had used it himself; and perhaps he accepted it too readily as tactically coded support for Britain's position.

Cripps and Nehru misread each other in 1942. They did so not because they were so distant but because they had been so close, thus leading each of them to suppose that he understood the other more completely than turned out to be the case. Cripps was inclined to forget that Nehru had often been more radical than Gandhi in opposing collaboration with the British Raj, not least over the control of defence, and inclined to overestimate Congress's readiness to assume governmental responsibility, especially at such a dire moment. Nehru, for his part, underestimated how much Cripps had changed, now that he was driven by the imperatives of national unity and world war. Gandhi, meanwhile, having made it sufficiently clear that he favoured rejection of the Cripps offer, privately relied on Nehru to persuade Rajagopalachari – who, with his consistent wish to defer other quarrels in face of the Japanese threat, was actually the leading advocate of acceptance. 'If you are inclined to agree with Rajaji,' Gandhi had conceded to Nehru, 'then the matter deserves further consideration.'[64] As events showed, Nehru remained closer to Gandhi than to Rajagopalachari, and thus closer to the mainstream of opinion in Congress.

While Cripps's prospects of pulling off a settlement suddenly plummeted, his standing correspondingly soared in the eyes of the Viceroy; it was, he told Amery, 'certainly no fault of Cripps', for he has handled a difficult and wearing job with skill, courage and imagination. I have watched his

61. Note by Pinnell, 31 March 1942, in Mansergh, *TOP*, i, p. 572.
62. Coupland diary, 31 March 1942.
63. For example Gopal (ed.), *Nehru: Selected Works*, xii, p. 249.
64. Gandhi to Nehru, after 27 March 1942, in Gandhi, *Collected Works*, lxxv, p. 440.

technique with interest and admiration, and hope I may have learnt a little in the process.'[65] Linlithgow was ready with his own epitaph on the Mission – a catchphrase from 1940, of course – 'Goodbye Mr Cripps.'[66]

If the Viceroy thought that Cripps would give up at this point and quietly go home, however, he was shortly to be disabused. Fed by leaks from Congress, suggesting that Gandhi would not actually block such a settlement, Cripps encouraged Shiva Rao to get together with Rajagopalachari and others to produce some potentially acceptable formula covering India's wartime role. Their draft had three points. One was that India be treated as a free member of the Commonwealth. The second was that the Executive Council would 'function on the principle of joint responsibility in the manner of a Council of Ministers'. Coupland, the constitutional expert, commented for Cripps that, as the maximum practicable concession, 'it should be understood as a matter of convention' that the Viceroy would treat members 'as if they constituted a Cabinet' – or, as Coupland shortly formalized the concept, as 'a quasi-cabinet', such as Rajagopalachari and the other provincial chief ministers had operated from 1937 to 1939.[67] The third point of the Rao formula covered the respective responsibilities of an Indian Defence Member and the British Commander-in-Chief.

Cripps decided on 1 April to prolong his visit. He seized on a long leading article in the *Hindustan Times*, or 'the Hindu Press', as he unwisely termed it in a letter to Azad (thus offending Congress's pride in its non-communal credentials).[68] The article had expressed guarded satisfaction over the post-war arrangements, but had focused concern on the immediate defence situation. 'We are bewildered that one so sensible, so honest, so broad-minded as Sir Stafford,' it said, 'should have lulled himself into the false belief that a scheme based on the complete control of India's defence by the British Government would prove acceptable to Indian opinion.'[69] He set about arranging a meeting between the Commander-in-Chief, General Wavell, and the Congress leaders, in the hope of dispelling unnecessary misconceptions.

Cripps also sought authority from London for talks with Congress to

65. Linlithgow to Amery, 31 March 1942, in Mansergh, *TOP*, i, p. 592.

66. Marginal note on Amery telegram of 3 April 1942, in Mansergh, *TOP*, i, p. 634.

67. Shiva Rao's formula with Coupland's note, n.d. but 1 April 1942, PRO, CAB 127/70; cf. Coupland diary, 6 April 1942, in Coupland, *Cripps Mission*, p. 22, and Rao in Philips and Wainwright (eds.), *Partition of India*, pp. 430–31.

68. RSC to Azad, 1 April 1942, in Mansergh, *TOP*, i, p. 598; in the published text 'the Hindu Press' was changed by Cripps to 'the Press'. Original in PRO, CAB 127/70.

69. *Hindustan Times*, 31 March 1942.

see if an acceptable division of authority could be devised. He painted a melodramatically bleak picture – morale was deplorably low, only Indian leadership could do the job. The War Cabinet minuted that, although 'there could, of course, be no question of our accepting a nominee of Congress' to a defence post, the appointment of 'some suitable Indian, selected by the Viceroy himself' met no objection.[70] Amery saw no difficulty in supporting Cripps's suggestion, which was implicit in the Indianization policy, and he already had some suitable names up his sleeve.

The inherent difficulties of long-distance negotiation now became increasingly apparent, though they have too easily been ignored in accounts of the Cripps Mission which prefer conspiratorial interpretations. The fact that Cripps did not have plenipotentiary powers was brought home by the stipulation that any arrangement remained subject to approval by the War Cabinet. Even given goodwill at each end, this was liable to create difficulties. Some gap in perceptions between London and Delhi was only to be expected, especially as time passed and the negotiating process created its own momentum. When similar problems arose during the visit of the Cabinet Delegation in 1946, these were solved within hours by immediate two-way traffic on the new teleprinter link that had been installed. 'It entirely justified my insistence before we came on having some special machines put in here by which we could communicate secretly and rapidly with the Prime Minister,' Cripps wrote on that occasion. 'Without them we should have been done – in point of time.'[71] He could draw on bitter experience. Delhi was four and a half hours ahead of London time; in 1942 all communications were by telegraph; there was no possibility of talking by telephone; under war conditions, the telegraphic links were circuitous; and every cable had to be coded and decoded, with obvious possibilities of corrupting the text. It was virtually impossible to get an answer out of London the same day; and meanwhile the mood could change in Delhi.

The members of the India Committee in London found themselves increasingly out of touch with the situation as conveyed by the Lord Privy Seal. In turn, the absence of Cripps's moderating influence in London made it more difficult to restrain the Prime Minister's suppressed hostility to negotiating with Congress at all. 'Winston's draft struck us as rather crude and negative,' Amery noted on 2 April, 'especially if all these telegrams come to be published some day.'[72] The cable as it was sent to Cripps read:

70. WM (42) 40, 2 April 1942, in Mansergh, *TOP*, i, p. 612.
71. RSC diary, 15 May 1946; cf. Turnbull diary, 15 May 1946.
72. Amery diary, 2 April 1942, in Barnes and Nicholson (eds.), *Empire at Bay*, p. 789.

'Everyone admires the manner in which you have discharged your difficult mission, and the effect of our proposals has been most beneficial in the United States and in large circles here.'[73] Though the Prime Minister might still appear supportive, the new note was his complacent assumption that the Cripps Mission had already achieved its objective on the propaganda front. It is true that even the *Hindustan Times* reported: 'India's Cold Reception of Cripps Plan – U.S. Circles Surprised – Press Comments – All Aspirations Met'.[74]

The last phase of the Cripps Mission was dominated by arcane issues over the putative status, responsibilities and authority of a Defence Member of an Indianized Executive Council. These were important matters, no doubt, and ones that raised real qualms both on the British side and within the Congress Working Committee. But the bewildering proposals and counter-proposals need to be understood as manoeuvres undertaken in a context where the negotiations were already deadlocked. The British Government had already made its final offer and Congress, as well as the Hindu Maha-sabha, had already decided that it was not good enough within ten days of Cripps's arrival in Delhi. That he now decided to stay for another ten days was a triumph of optimism and – in a benign sense – opportunism.

On 2 April Cripps received the formal Congress response from Nehru and Azad. It was an interim statement, withheld from immediate publication, and covered four areas where there were predictable difficulties. One was over British reluctance simply to use the word 'independence'; Cripps did not judge this vital either way. A second was over the position of the Indian States, where Cripps knew that his hands were bound by British obligations to the Princes. The third was Congress's fear of partition; but the right of provinces to 'non-accession', as stated in the Declaration, was essential to its acceptance by the Muslim League. The final point was, of course, devolution on defence. 'It is only thus that even at this grave eleventh hour it may be possible to galvanise the people of India to rise to the height of the occasion,' declared the Congress Working Committee; and said that 'on this ultimately depends what advice they should give'.[75]

Cripps knew that the other points were either not substantial or not negotiable, whereas here lay a dilemma that, just possibly, might be resolved. Within the Crippery he had talked of a 10 per cent chance of

73. Churchill to RSC, 2 April 1942, in Mansergh, *TOP*, i, p. 607.
74. *Hindustan Times*, 1 April 1942.
75. CWC resolution in RSC to Churchill, 2 April 1942, in Mansergh, *TOP*, i, p. 618.

agreement.[76] Cripps accordingly telegraphed his analysis to Churchill on 4 April. Congress was divided; Gandhi's supporters were hostile but 'definitely a minority'; the rest were all in favour of fighting the Japanese but were in turn divided on whether the Declaration went far enough to make their participation in the war effort effective. The only negotiations that could proceed were therefore on the final paragraph of the Declaration, 'which as you know was purposely left vague apart from the general principle of the retention of defence'.[77]

Now was the moment to clothe this principle in suitable administrative garb. There were two possible ways forward (given that the *status quo* was unacceptable to Congress). Either an Indian could be appointed as Defence Minister, subject to a convention that he would respect the Commander-in-Chief's responsibility to the British War Cabinet on military issues; or a new defence portfolio could be devised, to which the Commander-in-Chief would hand over certain functions. Cripps preferred the former and thought that it would have the best chance of acceptance, but clearly regarded it as a non-starter. In effect, he pressed for authority to work with Linlithgow and Wavell on the latter option, 'on the off chance of acceptance and in any event to show we have done our utmost to reach an accommodation'.[78]

Churchill's immediate response was outwardly cordial. It was Easter Sunday, and Isobel Cripps was at Chequers. Her message – 'All my love and undaunted confidence' – was officially cabled back to Delhi. Churchill promised to put the proposal to the War Cabinet the next day, adding: 'I hope by then we shall have heard from the Viceroy and the Commander-in-Chief.'[79] The right of both of them to submit their own advice, independent of Cripps, had been proposed by Linlithgow three days previously, as Cripps knew; but he did not know that in the meantime Churchill and Amery had also acceded to Linlithgow's request to send telegrams *without showing copies to Cripps*, whose influence with his colleagues at home was inevitably impaired thereby – as, in the course of the following week, was their confidence in his judgement.

The responsibilities of a new defence member of the Executive Council proved less troubling than the conventions under which that body would operate. Cripps's telegram made a reference to 'the new arrangement whereby the Executive Council will approximate to a Cabinet'.[80] This was

76. Coupland diary, 3 April 1942.
77. RSC to Churchill, 4 April 1942, in Mansergh, *TOP*, i, pp. 636–7.
78. ibid., pp. 638–9.
79. Churchill to RSC, 5 April 1942, in Mansergh, *TOP*, i, p.653.
80. RSC to Churchill, 4 April 1942, in Mansergh, *TOP*, i, par. 18, p. 638.

the sort of language – encouraging but guarded – which he had been using to cajole Congress, adumbrating Coupland's more rigorous concept of a 'quasi-cabinet'. One danger in talking in this way was that it encouraged Congress into more ambitious extrapolation, with the *Hindustan Times* now writing of the new Council functioning simply as 'a Cabinet', with 'full and joint responsibility to the Legislature'.[81] Another danger was that it was the sort of talk liable to over-excite a truculent imperialist like Churchill – especially late at night, as Amery discovered when he received a telephone call from Chequers.[82]

The result was that, although the War Cabinet gave its approval to a scheme for dividing defence responsibilities, it did so in a telegram that plainly showed apprehension about the course of the negotiations. Linlithgow, now with his own channel for airing his growing disquiet, had warned that 'the position of the Executive Council should not be glozed over'.[83] It was a mark of Cripps's new insecurity rather than his strength that he should, for the only time, have activated his personal cipher to the Prime Minister. Cripps attempted to provide reassurance that there were no differences between himself and the Viceroy, telling Churchill: 'I know your views on this and you can rely on me.'[84] But what Cripps said was bound to be undercut by the fact, as well as the content, of Linlithgow's rival communications. If at one level the issue was military security and constitutional safeguards, at another it was political trust.

In Delhi, however, the prospect of a settlement began to look brighter, not least because, over the Easter weekend, Cripps found himself able to mobilize a new source of support. Roosevelt's personal representative in India, Colonel Louis Johnson, had arrived in Delhi on Good Friday, 3 April. Launched in Washington at the same moment as the Cripps Mission, the Johnson Mission was plainly intended to cover more than advice on munitions supply, its ostensible cover. In fact, Johnson's career had been made in law and politics, rather like that of Cripps himself. When the two men met on 4 April at the Viceroy's residence, they hit it off. Cripps felt no compunction in disclosing the nature of the authority he was seeking from London over defence. The next morning, the ubiquitous Shiva Rao met Johnson and, learning of the expansive nature of the American commitment

81. Leader, *Hindustan Times*, 3 April 1942.

82. Amery diary, 5 April 1942, in Barnes and Nicholson (eds.), *Empire at Bay*, p. 790, phone call late Sunday night.

83. Linlithgow to Amery and Churchill, 6 April 1942, in Mansergh, *TOP*, i, p. 654.

84. RSC to Churchill, 6 April 1942, most secret – cipher telegram, Churchill papers, CHAR 20/73, f. 64.

– 'we are fighting this war,' he said, 'more than the British' – arranged a clandestine introduction to Nehru.[85]

The American connection soon became overt. There were few secrets in Delhi, and Nehru later noted 'much silent amusement at the underlying friction between the newcomers and the official class'.[86] His own meetings with Johnson were prominently reported in the press, feeding existing suspicions about the use of American muscle. 'Hinduphobia in American Press,' reported the *Hindustan Times*: 'Tirades Against India; Threats and Assurances'. In a leading article, it marvelled at the attention India was belatedly claiming in the world's press but warned that 'threatening is not the very best way of getting things from a people who have been threatened for the last century or so'.[87] The paper reported the long discussions in the Congress Working Committee under the headline: 'War Cabinet's Reply "Not Satisfactory" '. Its leading article, too, showed that the mood within Congress had swung into pessimism: no longer personally complimentary to Cripps but bracketing 'the British Imperialists and their American friends' together.[88]

The fact that, within a couple of days of his arrival, Johnson was at work as an active go-between was thus potentially embarrassing – not only to his own government and the British authorities but also within Congress. In public, Cripps always stood by the story that, at his invitation, Johnson was 'merely acting as a personal friend who happened to come along at an opportune moment when he thought he could help';[89] but Johnson's forte did not lie in delicate personal diplomacy, still less in any expertise about Indian political or constitutional matters. 'The magic name over here is Roosevelt,'[90] he reported to Washington, and, failing the official intervention he pleaded for, he resorted to unofficial arm-twisting, and sometimes word-twisting too.

The result was 'the Johnson formula'. The British proposal on defence was that the Commander-in-Chief would sit on the Executive Council as War Member, while an Indian would take over certain specified defence functions. This was given to Congress (and also the Muslim League) on Tuesday, 7 April. It quickly became apparent that Congress could not honourably accept from the hands of the British a new (inferior, subsidiary)

85. Rao in Philips and Wainwright (eds.), *Partition of India*, pp. 431–2.
86. Nehru, *Discovery of India*, p. 387.
87. *Hindustan Times*, 5 April 1942; Leader, *Hindustan Times*, 6 April 1942.
88. Leader, *Hindustan Times*, 8 April 1942.
89. Press conference, 22 April 1942, Mansergh, *TOP*, i, p. 819.
90. Johnson report, 9 April 1942, *FRUS*, 1942, i, p. 630.

defence post, to which certain powers would be transferred. Johnson had the answer: 'dressing the doll up another way' was how he put it to Cripps.[91] Why not offer an Indian the existing defence post, in all its prestige and dignity – but transfer the war powers to the Commander-in-Chief? Linlithgow and Wavell had already agreed on a division of defence functions; they now accepted the 'Johnson formula' but safeguarded any possible residual powers to the Commander-in-Chief by saying that he would exercise all powers *except* those specified to remain with the new appointee.

Cripps knew that this was the crisis. On Tuesday, 7 April, he made a personal appeal to his friend – 'My Dear Jawaharlal' – saying that leadership could alone accomplish the result: 'It is the moment for the supreme courage of a great leader to face all the risks and difficulties – and I know they are there – to drive through to the desired end.'[92] Cripps was taking risks, pushing Churchill hard; he relied on Nehru doing likewise, in pulling away from Gandhi. Talk of a possible 'fast unto death' spelt out the worst case.[93] Nehru wrote back later the same day, saying that he had not given up hope. 'But I am convinced that it is beyond my power, even if I wished, to get any considerable number of people to agree to the present offer,' he explained. 'That is a tragedy for all of us.'[94] The cartoonist Shankar, who was in Nehru's confidence, picked up this theme in the *Hindustan Times*, over the caption 'Trapeze Tragedy?'. On the high trapeze, Cripps has already launched himself, but his mouth is agape as he looks towards an appalled Nehru on the other trapeze, unable to catch his partner because his own hands are tied, immobilized by a heavy weight which renders him helpless. 'Is the weight Gandhi?' wondered Spry.[95] The cartoon was at once economical, subtle, ambiguous – and prescient.

Cripps's mood was difficult to gauge. He cared deeply about the outcome of the negotiations, of course; but having played his part (and his cards) to the best of his ability, the advocate became detached, even playful, while the jury was out. Sitting after a long lunch, the Crippery enjoyed a debate over whether the Indian pacifists could be equated with Pétainistes, as David Owen maintained. Cripps argued the other way, claiming that he wanted to fight 'because I think that on the whole the civilisation which will emerge from a British victory will be better than the civilisation which will emerge

91. Coupland diary, 7 April 1942.
92. RSC to Nehru, [7] April 1942, Nehru, *Bunch of Old Letters*, p. 478.
93. Coupland, *Cripps Mission*, p. 213.
94. Nehru to RSC, 7 April 1942, PRO, CAB 127/73. Spry's diary, 7 April, reports much the same.
95. Spry diary, 8 April 1942. Cartoon reproduced on p. 255.

from a German one'. But, he put it to them, why should an Indian think that? How could a people be asked to fight for a freedom they had never known? Were not pro-Japanese Indians therefore entitled to their opinions? Why should intelligent Indians not assume all anti-Japanese statements to be propaganda?[96] If Cripps had not forgotten how to argue a brief nor was he beyond sharing the Crippery's amusement at the idea that he too like Gandhi might undertake a 'fast unto death'. 'I'm sure I could out-fast him and bring him to terms,' Cripps said. 'He would call begging me to take a sip of orange juice and be ready to sign the proposals.'[97]

The negotiations make a complex story, but one made familiar through many previous accounts. The plan was for the redrafted Johnson formula, as finally settled late on 7 April, to go back to Johnson, to give to Nehru, to be discussed by Congress, and to come back from the Working Committee as its own counter-proposal, but one presumed to be acceptable to the British Government. A now impatient Spry commented, 'it is all "Face"'.[98]

Wednesday, 8 April saw eighteen hours of agitated progress, inching towards agreement. Other sources show that Johnson gave Nehru the draft at 7.20 a.m; but the next twist relies on Spry's own contemporary record. Twenty minutes later, Shiva Rao turned up at 3 Queen Victoria Road, with a note dictated by Rajagopalachari, whom Cripps knew to have been working for a settlement. This simply suggested turning the definition of functions inside-out, this time by listing those powers to go to the Commander-in-Chief – plainly seeking to escape any invidious implication that an Indian would merely be delegated certain responsibilities. Spry showed the piece of paper to Cripps. 'He said (1) definition was required, and added (2) discussions could not be carried on by "finesses".' If Rajagopalachari, as Spry thought, 'wanted some dope on Cripps's view' before the Congress Working Committee met at 8.15 a.m., he now had it.[99]

There had been talk in the Crippery about 'zero hour'; in fact one zero hour ran on to the next.[100] Cripps had to wait all day, in the mounting heat of the sultry Delhi spring, while the Committee deliberated. In the afternoon, Nehru sent Johnson the latest proposal on defence functions, commenting: 'You will notice that this does not differ materially from your

96. Coupland diary, 7 April 1942.
97. Spry diary, 7 April 1942.
98. ibid. Moore's account in *Churchill, Cripps and India*, pp. 106–13, is exemplary in its clarity.
99. Spry memorandum, 8.05 a.m., 8 April 1942, PRO, CAB 127/70; Spry diary, 8 April.
100. Coupland diary, 7 April: 'It is zero hour.' Spry diary, 8 April: 'This is zero day and zero hour.'

formula.'[101] Cripps finally rang up Johnson, who came round to show him the redrafted proposal. This was essentially an elaboration of the Rajagopalachari finesse – as Cripps could see at once, since he had had the day to think about it. This explains the apparent impulsiveness of his response. It was still a black-and-white definition, but instead of describing white as not-black, it described black as not-white. Thus the substance of the revised formula did not come as news to him – only the exciting suggestion that, armed with it, Nehru and Rajagopalachari could get the committee to clinch on these terms: by 7 to 5 votes at least, perhaps unanimously. When Johnson said that 'Nehru was fighting 100 per cent for settlement', Cripps remarked to Coupland that 'he thought this was due to his personal appeal.'[102]

What became known as the Cripps–Johnson formula was drafted by them in (at most) one hour on Wednesday evening.[103] Like the Johnson formula before it, it was to be unofficially passed to the Congress Working Committee so that it could become their formal (and presumably acceptable) proposal. To Cripps, impressed all along with the importance of appearances, this final revision was a cosmetic touch behind the scenes, to be ratified in due course. H. V. Hodson, then a confidant of the Viceroy as his Reforms Commissioner and later the rather sour historian of these events, was momentarily caught up in the optimism of the moment, marvelling at Cripps's lack of resentment at being upstaged by Johnson.[104] With Hodson at his elbow, Cripps redrafted the list of specified functions, which was not difficult since the Viceroy had himself drawn up such a list already. Indeed, alternative drafts must have been ankle-deep by this stage.

Cripps made light of his next step in his cable to the War Cabinet. He wrote that 'since the annexed list of functions of War Member was identical in terms with that in Viceroy's original draft, I suggested to Congress tentatively that I would consider such a formula if they were prepared to accept it'.[105] What this meant was that, on Wednesday evening, he had let Johnson shuttle a copy back, in Cripps's own handwriting, to be shown to

101. Nehru to Johnson, 8 April 1942, in Gopal (ed.), *Nehru: Selected Works*, xii, p. 198; cf. *FRUS*, 1942, i, p. 630.

102. Coupland diary, 8 April 1942; corroborated by Spry diary.

103. 6–7 p.m., Turnbull note, PRO, CAB 127/73. According to Coupland, it was 5.30 p.m. when Cripps telephoned Johnson, who then came round; and that Cripps also saw Jinnah at 6 p.m. Spry says Johnson arrived at 6 p.m., Jinnah at 7 p.m. Hodson's account, in *Great Divide*, pp. 99–100.

104. Hodson, *Great Divide*, pp. 99–101.

105. RSC to War Cabinet, 10 April 1942, in Mansergh, *TOP*, i, p. 716.

Nehru – before the Viceroy himself had formally approved it. No doubt he was encouraged by Johnson's plea, that 'from a publicity point of view, this formula was just what Nehru needed'.[106] Cripps later explained to the War Cabinet that 'unless action was taken at once it was probable that the Congress would finally reject the proposals'.[107] As he put it to the Viceroy, 'the situation was getting hot and he had to do something'.[108]

The Viceroy's reaction quickly lowered the temperature. At first he said he was too tired to deal with the matter until the following morning. Reluctantly, he saw Cripps at 10 p.m. on Wednesday, 8 April, and kept a full record. He confessed himself 'nervous' about this fresh draft, which he had only just seen.

Sir Stafford then said that he thought Congress would come in on this formula and Johnson had gathered that from them. I asked how Congress had come to know about this formula. Cripps replied that Johnson had shown it to them, but that they had not got it.

Consternation! The Viceroy's complaint was not only that he (and Wavell) had been passed over, and that Congress now knew their position, but that it was Johnson who had been the intermediary. 'If I were now to differ from the draft,' Linlithgow expostulated, 'my position might well be rendered intolerable, as I ran the risk of being held up to the USA as the obstacle to a settlement.'[109]

Cripps's exemplary patience now snapped, if not in the presence of the Marquess of Linlithgow then as soon as he returned to the Crippery. 'M.L. is becoming a bloody nuisance', he told Spry, insisting that the Viceroy had been shown everything courteously. 'I am giving a lead – why the bloody hell should he hold up agreement between HMG and the parties?'[110] The Viceroy's bruised feelings would not have mattered if Cripps had succeeded, and on the night of 8–9 April he felt close to success. At 1 a.m. he sent a telegram saying as much to Churchill; an hour later Linlithgow telegraphed his assent to the new formula; Wavell agreed the next morning.

On Thursday, 9 April, therefore, everything now depended on Congress. The banner headline across that morning's *Hindustan Times* read: 'Congress–Govt Settlement in Sight?'. Not only did it write of 'a dramatic change in the political talks': it revealed a detailed knowledge of the negotiations,

106. Spry diary, 8 April 1942.   107. Report, in Mansergh, *TOP*, ii, p. 328.
108. Linlithgow note, 8 April 1942, in Mansergh, *TOP*, i, p. 695.
109. ibid.   110. Spry diary, 8 April 1942.

including Johnson's role. American influence was benign in sweetening a settlement for the benefit of nationalist opinion. 'If, as is now considered very probable, agreement is reached on the Defence question,' the paper reported, 'there is not likely to be any difficulty in settling other matters so as to ensure that the new Viceroy's Council composed of political representatives functions as a national Government on the same lines as a Dominion Government.'[111] 'C. very cheerful,' Coupland observed.[112] The only cloud in the sky that morning was a tactless speech in Washington by Lord Halifax – 'The silly fool,' said Cripps.[113] Throughout Thursday, reports continued to suggest that Congress would accept. Johnson had received an encouraging letter from Nehru that morning, which he gave to Cripps, telling him that he was 'keeping his fingers crossed all day'.[114] In mid-afternoon Cripps got the news that Rajagopalachari had told the press, off the record, that agreement was now certain. 'We were all too cautious to cheer or rejoice,' Spry noted. 'Is it really true?'[115]

There was a price to be paid for the breach with the Viceroy. At noon he had given Cripps a pointed reminder of the War Cabinet's view (in fact, his own) that 'the constitutional position of the Viceroy's Council cannot be altered' and asked him to make this clear to the Congress leaders when he saw them later that day.[116] When Nehru and Azad arrived at 3 Queen Victoria Road at 5.35 p.m., Cripps met them on the steps. Azad seemed 'sententious as usual' and Nehru 'dignified' when Spry ushered them into Cripps's room.[117] They spent two and a half hours with Cripps, pressing him time and again on how the Viceroy would actually operate the constitution. 'They spoke of differences with the Viceroy and C-in-C,' Spry was told afterwards, and he found them looking 'tired, even gloomy' as they left.[118] Cripps had had to be guarded. He had kept saying that it was for the Viceroy to decide, and that 'the Viceroy would doubtless do all he could by means of appropriate conventions'. Even this seemed a bit much to Linlithgow when Cripps reported back later, and he grumbled that 'he did not want to get into the position afterwards where he would be held up as the bad boy responsible for wrecking at the stage of practice the wonderful settlement arrived at by Sir Stafford Cripps'.[119]

111. *Hindustan Times*, 9 April 1942.   112. Coupland diary, 9 April 1942.
113. Spry diary, 9 April 1942.
114. Nehru to Johnson, 9 April 1942 (1), PRO, CAB 127/73; Johnson in Spry diary, 9 April 1942.
115. Spry diary, 9 April 1942; cf. Cabinet report, in Mansergh, *TOP*, ii, p. 329; Coupland, *Cripps Mission*, p. 223.
116. Linlithgow to Cripps, 9 April 1942, in Mansergh, *TOP*, i, p. 709; orig., PRO, CAB 127/70.
117. Spry diary, 9 April 1942.   118. ibid.
119. Pinnell note, 9 April 1942, in Mansergh, *TOP*, i, p. 711.

So long as the definition of defence responsibilities remained unresolved, it had seemed crucial; with its apparent resolution, the focus disconcertingly switched. Now feeling 'somewhat depressed', Cripps told Coupland that Nehru 'had gone right back on fundamentals', even reviving the claim for immediate independence, as well as asking for a prior definition of the constitutional conventions and making clear his distaste for the Viceroy.[120] Only Johnson still continued to believe that Nehru would settle, scurrying from Birla House back to 3 Queen Victoria Road. According to Spry, 'SC had a chat and later with Nehru and left him more cheerful.'[121] This otherwise unrecorded encounter suggests that their personal relationship had survived their rather frosty formal interview; but Cripps and Nehru were not to meet again until 1946.

The latent issue of distrust had suddenly but decisively tainted the whole negotiating process. For Congress it meant a loss of nerve. 'They have come to the edge of the water, and stripped, but hesitate to make the plunge because the water looks so cold,' Cripps surmised.[122] Nehru always acknowledged how near they had come: 'For the first time I felt, and so did others, that a settlement was probable.'[123] He said that, before the fateful interview, he would have put the chances of agreement at 75 per cent.[124] Cripps claimed that the Congress leaders, having been satisfied by the Cripps–Johnson formula on defence, now seemed determined to break on the wider question of the executive's powers.[125] Again in retrospect, Nehru contended that Cripps was 'not a free agent', and hence changed his tune 'under threats of resignation which Wavell and the Viceroy telegraphed to Churchill'.[126]

Behind Cripps loomed the figure of Linlithgow. If Cripps's answers seemed increasingly evasive to Nehru and Azad, thus bearing out all their worst fears about the British Raj, it was no doubt partly because he felt constrained in what he now said – the more so, the more he was pressed, in a vicious circle of disintegrating mutual confidence. Cripps expostulated, 'he is impossible'.[127] Though he had not secured the Viceroy's replacement in advance, it was no secret – or rather it was a secret – in the Crippery that he planned to do so.[128] Moreover, there is evidence that he had at some stage said as much to Nehru. Cripps later made a comment so pointed that he decided against publishing it while Linlithgow remained in post: 'In order

120. Coupland diary, 9 April 1942.   121. Spry diary, 9 April 1942.
122. Coupland diary, 10 April 1942.   123. Nehru, *Discovery of India*, p. 395.
124. Nehru, press conference, 12 April 1942, in Gopal (ed.), *Nehru: Selected Works*, xii, p. 216.
125. Report, in Mansergh, *TOP*, ii, pp. 329–30.
126. Interview with Fischer, 24 May 1942, in Fischer, *Nation*, p. 620.
127. Spry diary, 9 April 1942.   128. ibid. Coupland diary, 9 April 1942.

to get over suspicion and distrust I went so far as to assure Jawaharlal that I will not allow any British official, however highly placed he might be, to jeopardise a reasonable chance of a settlement.'[129] To complement this, there is a cryptic, private, retrospective note in Nehru's papers: 'If our proposals accepted no chaos – no disruption &c. Cripps – No Viceroy &c!'[130]

For Cripps, the political reality was that Congress would have had far more leverage once inside the Executive Council. He had banked on the view that 'they were realists' and therefore knew how hard it would be for the Viceroy to prevail against a National Government of party leaders.[131] Cripps extrapolated from his own experience in exploiting an opening, as he told Nehru and Azad when they pressed him for formal guarantees. 'They should take the power and make the most of it, aware as they were how difficult it would be for the V. to override them,' Cripps reported to Coupland. It was now that he reinforced the point by an appeal to his own experience in entering the War Cabinet.[132] Though this argument was obviously infused with the optimism of his own recent accession to power, he never repented it.

'The tragedy of it from the Indian standpoint,' he later commented, 'is that had there been an agreement Indians would have had absolute control of the situation.'[133] Had not Linlithgow himself been treating his already largely Indianized executive, albeit comprising his own nominees, as if it were a cabinet?[134] The gist of Cripps's position was later stated by Graham Spry: 'Not in law, not constitutionally, but in practice, that executive council would have been the supreme government of India, and so long as it resisted the pacifist wing of the Congress Party and co-operated duly in waging the war, there would have been no interference.'[135]

A majority of Indian party leaders on the Council would be in an immensely strong position, backed by the ultimate sanction of resignation if the Viceroy proved obstructive in practice – just as Linlithgow feared. As Johnson bluntly put it: 'Since the Congress rejection seemed mainly due to distrust of the V., why not get rid of him and clear the situation

129. Tahmankar interview, original draft, 4 June 1942, PRO, CAB 127/81.
130. Note, 4 August 1942, in Gopal (ed.), *Nehru: Selected Works*, xii, p. 435.
131. Coupland diary, 7 April 1942.   132. ibid., 9 April 1942.
133. RSC interview with Dewett Mackenzie, *Manchester Guardian*, 24 October 1942.
134. cf. Coupland, *Cripps Mission*, p. 55.
135. Spry, first draft of reply to Fischer, October 1942. This document undoubtedly represented Cripps's position; the published version was marginally more prudent in its phrasing; see Spry, *Nation*, p. 504.

up?'[136] Cripps knew that it was not so simple. He could not change the Viceroy in order to clinch the deal, only rely on Congress to clinch the deal first, with a new Viceroy to follow. But in asking Nehru simply to trust him on these matters, Cripps was asking too much. 'Viceroy high principled but wooden – incapable of conference,' was the view in the Crippery, provoking an unflattering comparison with his more adroit predecessor: 'Willingdon would have put the interim plan of government, with its conventions, across.'[137] Had Cripps been able to wheel out a Willingdon, let alone a Mountbatten, to charm the Congress leaders at this point, their distrust might have been allayed; but the actuality was Hopie, who refrained throughout from intervening.

Through lack of mutual confidence, the whole position was now spiralling towards collapse. Late at night on 9 April, a bundle of telegrams arrived from London, impugning Cripps's own credibility. First, Churchill told him shortly that everything must await the War Cabinet's decision, and the independent advice of Linlithgow and Wavell. A second barrel from Churchill – MOST IMMEDIATE. CLEAR THE LINE – said that Colonel Johnson had no authority from Roosevelt – a half-truth, if that.[138] Two cables from the War Cabinet picked up on points raised by Linlithgow and told Cripps: 'It is essential to bring the whole matter back to Cabinet's plan which you went out to urge, with only such amplifications as are agreed to be put forward.'[139]

Now it was Cripps's turn for a display of his well-developed faculty of self-righteousness – well justified on this occasion. Spry observed Cripps's reaction when he realized that the Viceroy had sent cables to London without informing him – 'it means I can no longer trust him'. The two of them sat up till 2 a.m. drafting an immediate and indignant response. 'Halifax speech, fussiness in India Office, and H.E.'s cable without copy to S.C. all suggest "ganging up",' Spry noted.[140] As well as giving Churchill a full statement of the position and asking for the War Cabinet's authorization to proceed, Cripps made clear his resentment against the Viceroy's conduct. The War Cabinet's telegrams, he noted icily, 'apparently refer to some sent from here which I have not seen, and therefore I find difficulty in understanding them'. Linlithgow's complaints about Cripps going behind his back had involved the Viceroy in going behind the back of the Lord

136. Coupland diary, 10 April 1942.
137. David Owen reported in Barrington-Ward diary, 28 April 1942.
138. Churchill to RSC, 9 April 1942, in Mansergh, *TOP*, i, p. 704.
139. War Cabinet to RSC, 9 April 1942, in Mansergh, *TOP*, i, p. 707.
140. Spry diary, 9 April 1942; cf. Coupland, *Cripps Mission*, p. 226.

Privy Seal, who now put his own account before his colleagues, reproaching them for presuming to distrust him and concluding: 'Unless I am trusted I cannot carry on with the task.'[141]

What task was left? Friday, 10 April gave the final answer. The gap between the War Cabinet and Congress was now widening, leaving Cripps stranded. 'He and Nehru could solve it in 5 minutes if Cripps had any freedom or authority,' wrote Johnson.[142] Only the Viceroy could have saved the situation at this point. The *Hindustan Times* was to supply an insight into Congress's thinking, marshalling the evidence from Cripps's own statements to show that a scheme of Indianized cabinet government had indeed been envisaged: one operating for the time being on the basis of conventions which only the Viceroy could make clear. It pointed out a parallel with the India Act of 1935, which similarly reserved overriding authority to the Governors; but here Linlithgow had paved the way for Congress to accept office in the provincial governments by himself making a statement declaring that normally such powers would not be exercised. 'It is now for His Excellency to rise to the height of the occasion,' the leading article concluded, 'and prevent what may well prove a major national disaster to his country as well as ours.'[143]

By the time these words were published, it was too late. Cripps knew from Johnson of Nehru's negative reaction to their interview the previous evening. It was hardly surprising that, during a long meeting on Friday, the balance within the Congress Working Committee shifted against acceptance; nor that there was an inclusive broadening of the reasons for rejection, picking up every objectionable aspect of the Declaration, if only to secure a future bargaining stance. A letter from Azad to Cripps was drafted. Coupland records its delivery.

At last, about 7 p.m., a sealed envelope arrived. Turnbull opened it and handed C. a typescript of 4 or 5 pages. He read it sitting in the corner of the sofa in the hall, the rest of us sitting round in complete silence. As C. read the first page with a serious face and saying nothing, it seemed probable that it was rejection. When, on the second page, he said 'That's quite untrue', it was certain.[144]

---

141. RSC to War Cabinet, 10 April 1942, in Mansergh, *TOP*, i, pp. 715–17.
142. Johnson to Secretary of State, 11 April 1942, in *FRUS*, 1942, i. p. 631.
143. Leader, *Hindustan Times*, 11 April 1942; cf. Coupland's very similar argument: Moore, *Churchill, Cripps and India*, pp. 123–4; also comment by Sir M. Hallett, in Mansergh, *TOP*, i, p. 767.
144. Coupland diary, 10 April 1942.

The same evening Cripps sent a cable to Churchill, telling him that the rejection was on the 'widest grounds', not just defence. 'There is clearly no hope of agreement and I shall start home on Sunday.'[145] This he did. The Cripps Mission had failed.

145. RSC to Churchill, 10 April 1942, in Mansergh, *TOP*, i, pp. 730–31.

4

Picking Up the Pieces

There was an authentic tragedy in Delhi when Cripps came unstuck on the high trapeze; but not everyone took it tragically. For Gandhi, it served to confirm his consistent view that 'Sir Stafford Cripps, having become part of the Imperial machinery, unconsciously partook of its quality.'[1] As he put it to an English friend: 'How nice it would have been if he had not come with that dismal mission.'[2] Likewise, Churchill did not wholly suppress his inner feelings about Cripps's failure when he came to write in his war memoirs: 'I was able to bear this news, which I had thought probable from the beginning, with philosophy.'[3]

Churchill's chapter on the Cripps Mission in Volume IV of *The Second World War* is uncharacteristically circumspect. After ten pages of expatiation on 'the loyalty of the Indian Army to the King-Emperor' and delicate mockery of Roosevelt's idealistic ingenuousness, the account is suddenly truncated on the plea of lack of space, leapfrogging to lengthy quotation of Cripps's account of the breakdown, dated (or misdated, as will be seen) 11 April. In a six-volume work, notorious for its citations from the Chartwell Papers in settling old scores, this is a remarkable display of restraint; and the great man's loyal biographer likewise could spare only a dozen lines, amid the fourteen hundred pages of his own seventh volume, for the Cripps Mission.

It must be remembered that Churchill put together his story in 1949–50. At the time of writing, not only was Gandhi now a martyr in an independent India (of which Nehru was Prime Minister) but also NATO was in the process of creation. Churchill, Leader of the Opposition and still hungry for power, clearly had to reconcile inner tensions between what he wanted to say and what it was politic to say. A tribute to Nehru, for speaking out

---

1. Article for *Harijan*, written 13 April 1942, in Gandhi, *Collected Works*, lxxv, p. 28.
2. Gandhi to Horace Alexander, 22 April 1942, in Gandhi, *Collected Works*, lxxv, p. 60.
3. Churchill, *Second World War*, iv, p. 192.

in favour of resistance to Japan (as Cripps had predicted he would), was drafted for Churchill by his assistant F. W. D. Deakin, in order to focus the chapter on the way that American criticisms were met.[4] The implicit contrast with Gandhi (so Churchill decided in revising the proofs) might be made explicit by adding the comment that Gandhi 'did not reveal what was no doubt the truth, that he himself was willing to give the Japanese free passage across India to join hands with the Germans in return for Japanese military aid to hold down the Muslims and secure the All India Dominion of the Hindu Raj'.[5] Six months after writing this, with a General Election now putting Churchill within grasp of the premiership, he was firmly advised not to 'give offence to millions in India who revere Gandhi's memory', with Lord Ismay, Mountbatten's former chief-of-staff as well as Churchill's, weighing in about Gandhi: 'With all his faults he was NON-COMMUNAL.'[6] Churchill backed down; the comment was omitted.

In dealing with the end of the Cripps Mission – in 1949 as in 1942 – the key point for Churchill was to cement Anglo-American relations. His best alibi, if he were suspected of un-American activities like imperialism, was to maintain his united front with Cripps, whose famous offer had played so well in Washington. As is often the case with alibis, fine matters of chronology bulk disproportionately large in evidence. Cripps's telegram reporting Congress's rejection of the offer on 10 April was sent off the same evening and received in London before midnight local time. Indeed, because of the time difference, allied with Churchill's nocturnal work pattern, the copy of this telegram that he forwarded to Roosevelt actually arrived at 9.28 p.m., Washington time – still on 10 April. It is curious, then, that this telegram should be dated 11 April in *The Second World War*. The innocent explanation is that, after coding, it was dispatched from New Delhi half-an-hour after midnight. Curiouser, this and a subsequent telegram that Cripps actually did send on 11 April are printed together, separated only by the rubric: 'And further on the same day.'[7]

Why dwell on a trivial discrepancy in dating? It is the loose thread one notices on a shoddily made garment: if it is pulled, the stitching begins to

4. Deakin to Churchill, 27 July 1949, Churchill papers, CHUR 4/264.
5. Churchill amendment to proof, 3 August 1950, Churchill papers, CHUR 4/264.
6. Ismay note on proof, 23 February 1950, Norman Brook note, 15 March 1950, Churchill papers, CHUR 4/264.
7. Original telegrams, with times of despatch and receipt, Churchill papers, CHAR 20/73/78 (10 April 1942, in Mansergh,*TOP*, i, pp. 730–31) and 20/73/82 (11 April 1942, in Mansergh, *TOP*, i, 740–41). Churchill to Roosevelt, forwarding Cripps of 10 April 1942, in Kimball (ed.), *Churchill and Roosevelt*, i, p. 444.

fall apart. For the effect is that an unsuspecting reader of Churchill's chapter is thereby seamlessly taken from events in Delhi to their impact in Washington – without noticing that in London a whole day's business had meanwhile been transacted. It is these unreported transactions that jar with Churchill's bland account, notably in giving a less benign impression of the patience, magnanimity or unity of the British Government. The response of Cripps's ministerial colleagues in fact reveals that there was an attempt to thwart his efforts, just as some Americans suspected at the time and some historians have later argued.

Was the Cripps Mission in fact deliberately sabotaged? Herein lies the importance of what actually happened on 10 April 1942. When the consequences of the rupture between Cripps and his colleagues are examined closely, it does not appear that what happened in London at this juncture was decisive. Assertions that a veto from Churchill determined the fate of the Cripps Mission seem to rest on an insecure grasp of relative chronology. It is plain that by 3.30 p.m. London time on 10 April, when the India Committee convened, it was 8 p.m. in Delhi and Cripps had therefore already received Congress's letter of rejection. Moreover, he did not receive the telegrams generated that day in London until the following morning in Delhi – by which time his own report of the final breakdown had already reached Churchill, and indeed Roosevelt.[8]

None the less, the tone of the proceedings in London, as much as their substance, illuminates the difficulties that Cripps faced and helps explain his own readiness to quit India. Cripps's indignant first telegram of 10 April, as drafted with Spry and sent early morning Delhi time, lay before Cripps's colleagues on the India Committee; but its implied threat of resignation left them unmoved. They already felt under-informed, especially about how fully it was proposed to Indianize the Executive Council. Such understandable causes of annoyance fed less justifiable suspicions about Cripps's general fidelity to his brief.

Churchill's role became crucial. This, the fourteenth meeting of the committee, had begun as usual under Attlee's chairmanship. The latent apprehensions of its members did not prevent them from approving the Cripps–Johnson formula, which, hypothetically, could have been the key to an agreed settlement. It was at this stage that a telegram from Linlithgow arrived, asking for support against Cripps's suggestion that appropriate

8. With his customary acuity, Stokes seized on this point thirty years ago, as soon as Mansergh had published the relevant documents: 'Before this telegram arrived on 11 April, however, the talks had already broken down.' Stokes, 'Cripps in India', p. 431.

conventions could be agreed over the working of the Executive Council. The committee was reconvened at Number 10, with Churchill now in the chair. Anticipating 'public repercussions if Cripps did resign and all the telegrams were published', Amery had prepared 'a soothing message from the PM', only to find it rejected by him 'as too conciliatory to Cripps and expressing a confidence which he, Winston, no longer feels'.[9] A tight reading of the constitutional position was endorsed by the committee and any talk of conventions scotched. 'Moreover,' it was minuted, 'no such proposal had ever been made or, indeed, contemplated, in the discussions before the Lord Privy Seal had left this country.'[10]

This was disputable. Churchill might have known better had he attended previous meetings of the committee; but it now agreed this point and approved the Prime Minister's complementary telegrams to Linlithgow and Cripps, with copies to each other. These backed the Viceroy's view and told Cripps that he had no authority to negotiate. 'It was certainly agreed between us all that there were not to be negotiations but that you were to try and gain acceptance with possibly minor variations or elaborations of our great offer which has made so powerful an impression here and throughout the United States.'[11] Cripps's immediate colleagues in Delhi knew that the Prime Minister's imputation was false: 'not generous', as Coupland put it.[12]

By the time that Cripps received these discouraging communications, he knew that his mission had not succeeded anyway, and he had signed off accordingly. But it is a real question whether an emissary with stronger backing at home would have had a better hand to play all along. It was a source of strength that he alone in the British Government could come to India with clean hands, uncompromised by previous office. But it was a source of weakness that he had only been in the War Cabinet for a month and had not forged bonds of common experience and trust with his colleagues. His lack of friends at this juncture was not so much because he was personally untrustworthy: it was, above all, because of his lack of party connections to deliver him loyal support. Had he resigned, he would have resigned alone; the Labour Party owed him nothing. An Eden or a Bevin would not have faced repudiation in the way that Cripps did.

Yet none of this was fatal. Had Congress accepted the terms on offer on

9. Amery diary, 10 April 1942, in Barnes and Nicholson (eds.), *Empire at Bay*, p. 793.
10. Minutes, 14th meeting, 10 April 1942, in Mansergh, *TOP*, i, p. 720.
11. Churchill to RSC, 10 April 1942, in Mansergh, *TOP*, i, p. 722.
12. Coupland diary, 11 April 1942.

9 or 10 April, it is difficult to see how Churchill's concurrence could have been withheld. There is an unintentionally revealing passage in Amery's diary for 10 April, recording the first news of Congress's rejection.

That certainly gets Cripps out of a pretty awkward tangle for I don't think he would have liked facing his Congress friends with definite Cabinet instructions to make clear to them that there could be no nonsense about a convention but that if they came in it must be under the existing constitution and that if they differed from the Viceroy they could only resign.[13]

The irony is that this is almost word for word what Cripps had in fact been telling Nehru and Azad: a point that struck the constitutional expert, Coupland, as soon as he saw the relevant telegrams in Delhi.[14] So had Congress accepted this position, with whatever private hopes and reservations, there would have been no need for the sort of disentanglement that Amery envisaged.

The War Cabinet's growing suspicions about Cripps are now clearly documented; but so is the fact that those suspicions were largely misplaced. There is implicit confirmation of this point in later entries in Amery's diary, written with the benefit of subsequent debriefing from his own trustworthy private secretary, Frank Turnbull, as well as the returned Cripps. If Churchill came to think 'that our telegrams from here at the last moment helped to make Cripps more precise at his last meeting with the Congress leaders', this betrayed not only some chronological inexactitude but also a satisfaction that (irrespective of the actual reason) Cripps had faithfully represented the Cabinet's line. Indeed, Churchill so warmed to the theme that he now wondered 'whether the thing might have advanced further if at that stage of the discussions the Viceroy had invited the Party leaders to meet him and discuss both the composition of a future executive and the way he proposed to handle it'.[15] While there is copious evidence of Churchill's misgivings about the Cripps offer, of his readiness to abort American initiatives that exceeded it, and of his determination to keep Cripps himself on a short leash, there is no sign that a settlement of the kind that Cripps actually proposed would have been sabotaged in London. No more than Linlithgow did Churchill want to appear 'the bad boy'; rather more than Linlithgow,

13. Amery diary, 10 April 1942, in Barnes and Nicholson (eds.), *Empire at Bay*, p. 794.
14. Coupland diary, 10 April 1942
15. Amery diary, 14 May 1942, in Barnes and Nicholson (eds.), *Empire at Bay*, p. 813.

Churchill had an imagination that could be stirred by the possibilities of the situation.

It is true that there was one sensitive and ambiguous area where Cripps's colleagues found themselves ill-prepared for what emerged from the Delhi negotiations. Cripps had long differed from Churchill, Amery and Linlithgow over the extent to which the Executive Council should be Indianized. As soon as this became apparent, so Amery recorded, it 'undoubtedly frightened Winston and the Cabinet, for our idea when Cripps left was certainly not that of a completely clean sweep of the existing Executive'.[16] The problem was not that this was unthinkable – Amery himself subsequently pressed for similar measures – but that it had never been settled in advance. A great deal of latitude was implied in Cripps's draft of 'Instructions to the Viceroy'; and the discretion exercised by the Viceroy was crucial. But which Viceroy – Linlithgow or a successor chosen by a triumphant Cripps?

An agreed settlement necessarily meant inducing everyone to settle for less than they had originally demanded. This was Cripps's assigned task. There was little difference between what the Government had agreed to offer and what Cripps conveyed to Congress – except in tone and emphasis, natural enough in a subtle exercise in persuasion. Less formal than the Viceroy, to be sure, Cripps none the less bore himself as an emissary of the British Government. Indeed, it was Nehru's subsequent reproach that Cripps spoke throughout as 'the formal representative of the War Cabinet, in fact he was the War Cabinet speaking to us with a take it or leave it attitude'.[17]

'I certainly used the terms "National Government" and "Cabinet" but they were merely to illustrate my ideas on particular questions which I was discussing with my Congress friends,' was how Cripps put it in a press interview. 'What I sincerely asked the Congress to do was to accept the draft proposals as a basis for joining the Viceroy's council and then discuss with the Viceroy the ways and means by which the Council could function more as a Cabinet.'[18] Beyond this, as he also acknowledged, he dropped dark hints to Nehru about the Viceroy's tenure. Now Cripps's expertise in settling out of court had been lauded by those who originally commissioned him; Amery had heard that he had 'always been good at settlements and compromises'.[19] What art was it ever supposed that the great advocate would employ?

16. Amery to Linlithgow, 11 April 1942, in Mansergh, *TOP*, i, pp. 756–7.
17. Nehru to Evelyn Wood, 5 June 1942, in Gopal (ed.), *Nehru: Selected Works*, xii, p. 242.
18. Tahmankar interview, 4 June 1942, as amended by RSC.
19. Amery diary, 8 March 1942, in Barnes and Nicholson (eds.), *Empire at Bay*, p. 786.

The charge that Cripps exceeded his brief has often been made. The piquancy here is that it obviously suited not only Congress, especially Azad, but also the Viceroy to believe this. Linlithgow privately alleged that 'Cripps was crooked when up against it.'[20] True, Amery at one point wrote to the Viceroy, in explaining the lack of a *post mortem* on the Cripps Mission: 'Winston may, of course, have been influenced, in deciding to avoid Cabinet discussion, by a reluctance to bring up the question of how far Cripps went beyond his instructions.'[21] This was undoubtedly what Linlithgow wanted to hear; but Churchill's notable reticence does not need to be explained simply by his magnanimity towards an errant Cripps.

Churchill's feelings were nothing if not mixed, and theatrically modulated too. 'You have done everything in human power and your tenacity, perseverance and resourcefulness have proved how great was the British desire to reach a settlement,' he immediately assured Cripps on the night of 10–11 April, in a wholly different tone from his telegrams earlier that day.[22] Cripps, for his part, was likewise nothing amiss in cordiality. 'We are not depressed though sad at the result,' he cabled back. 'All good wishes. Cheerioh. Stafford.'[23] The text of Churchill's telegram to Cripps was immediately sent to Roosevelt, who, less impressed by what the British told him than by his own reports from Johnson, pleaded for Cripps to be kept in Delhi for a final effort. Churchill, still closeted with Harry Hopkins at 3 a.m. on the night of 11–12 April when he received Roosevelt's message, was in no mood to truckle further; and he seized on the fact that it was too late to prevent Cripps's departure – deep night at Chequers was already morning in Delhi – to brush aside the President's plea.[24]

It is clear that, spared the necessity of going through with the Cripps offer, what was now uppermost in the Prime Minister's mind was the effect upon American opinion of having made it. He could not repudiate the bearer of the offer without undermining this impression; their touching exchanges reflected this tactical imperative. In later years, however, Churchill, the spokesman of the English-speaking peoples, was intermittently subjected to the impulsive interventions of Churchill, the unrepentant imperialist. It was the latter who was tempted on one subsequent occasion to reproach Cripps for selling the pass in India. In the India debate in

20. Wavell diary, 19 October 1943, in Moon (ed.), *Wavell: journal*, p. 33.

21. Amery to Linlithgow, 6 May 1942, in Mansergh, *TOP*, ii, p. 43.

22. Churchill to RSC, 11 April 1942, in Mansergh, *TOP*, i, p. 739.

23. RSC to Churchill, 11 April 1942, in Mansergh, *TOP*, i, pp. 740–41.

24. Kimball, *Churchill and Roosevelt*, i, pp. 444–8; *FRUS*, 1942, i, pp. 631–5; Churchill, *Second World War*, iv, pp. 192–5; Moore, *Churchill, Cripps and India*, pp. 130–31.

December 1946, as Leader of the Opposition, he became heated over Cripps's role in the Labour Government's Cabinet Delegation and responded to one intervention with a gibe about 1942, 'and how we had to pull him up because – (Interruption.)' Immediately challenged by Cripps 'to disclose what passed between me and the Cabinet on that occasion', Churchill quickly retracted amid laughter.[25] He clearly sensed that it was not Cripps who would come out badly from such recriminations. By the time he came to write the relevant part of *The Second World War*, with Indian independence now a *fait accompli* over which the English-speaking peoples might all rejoice, the best face to put on things was a show of magnanimity – towards Nehru, and by extension towards Cripps too.

In the immediate aftermath of the Cripps Mission in 1942, it suited Churchill to laud the efforts of a colleague whose left-wing credentials were so useful in testifying to the good faith of the British Government. Admitting Cripps to the War Cabinet had already helped the Government; whether it would fulfil the hopes of the Left or the ambitions of Cripps himself remained to be seen. His popular standing in Britain remained high, with an approval rating of 69 per cent in March, when he went to India, 70 per cent in April when he returned, 71 per cent in July, and still 70 per cent in August 1942.[26] The pollsters' standard question (who was the preferred Prime Minister if anything should happen to Churchill) showed Cripps neck-and-neck with Eden in April 1942. Even in November 1942, when he was sacked from the War Cabinet, Cripps still had a rating of 24 per cent, against Eden's 39 per cent (as compared with Bevin on 4 per cent and Attlee on 3 per cent).[27]

Such findings were not lost on Cripps. The public opinion surveys undertaken by Mass-Observation, under the direction of Tom Harrisson, were passed on to Cripps (and may well have been financed by him). He referred to them in the course of discussions with political adherents, aware in September that, although his standing was in decline, he could still point to 'a steady 70% popularity'.[28] Such figures show that Cripps remained popular as Churchill's colleague, not how he would have fared as Churchill's rival. Indeed, the news that he had left the War Cabinet in November was to be regretted by more people than welcomed it – even though it was presented

25. 5 HC Debs., vol. 431, col. 1368 (12 December 1946).
26. Fielding, 'The Second World War and popular radicalism', Table 1, p. 43.
27. Cantril (ed.), *Public Opinion*, pp. 279–80.
28. Gordon Walker diary, 3 September 1942, in Pearce (ed.), *Gordon Walker: political diaries*, p. 110; cf. ibid., 1 October 1942, p. 114.

as a move by consent – coupled with comments that suggested acquiescence in a *fait accompli*: 'Well Churchill should know shouldn't he?' 'It's a little bit strange, but Churchill knows what he's doing.'[29] Indeed, the Prime Minister seems to have known what he was doing all along: in bringing Cripps into the Government at a moment of political weakness, in putting up with him while the crisis of the war was resolved, and in getting rid of him thereafter.

Cripps was a leader without a constituency. The Government's standing remained low, as shown by its loss of by-elections to independent candidates and the emergence of the idealistic left-wing political grouping, Common Wealth. Public opinion was apparently dissatisfied with the conduct of the war; and so was Cripps; but once he joined the War Cabinet himself, he was obviously implicated in the process of government and needed to show results. The Cripps Mission was an enigmatic beginning. Thereafter, Cripps needed to state his agenda and to mobilize potential supporters. In this he failed, inhibited by his notorious lack of political realism and political adroitness.

As a wartime leader of the Left, Cripps found a disjunction between his own strategy and that of his warmest supporters. Looking back, in the closing stages of the war, George Orwell admitted that he had been led to 'exaggerate the depth of the political crisis in 1942, the possibilities of Cripps as a popular leader and of Common Wealth as a revolutionary party', because for a couple of years he 'fell into the trap of assuming that "the war and the revolution are inseparable" '.[30] It is a revealing comment, suggesting how the Left projected onto Cripps an outlook that he did not share. Thus in the early summer of 1942 Orwell wrote that the people were as fed up as at the time of Dunkirk, 'with the difference that they now have, or are inclined to think they have, a potential leader in Stafford Cripps'.[31] What his hopeful adherents heard on meeting Cripps, however, was a flat affirmation that 'you can't fight total war and have a revolution on your hands at the same time'.[32] There was a gap in perceptions here, illustrated

29. 'Sir Stafford Cripps', 7 December 1942, Mass-Observation Archive, FR 1524. The sample were asked what they felt about Cripps leaving the War Cabinet: Good, 22 per cent (same for men and women); Bad, 29 per cent (35 per cent of men and 22 per cent of women respondents).
30. London Letter to the *Partisan Review*, Winter 1944–5 (probably written October 1944), in Davison (ed.), *Orwell: Complete Works*, xvi, p. 412.
31. London Letter to the *Partisan Review*, 8 May 1942, in Davison (ed.), *Orwell: Complete Works*, xiii, p. 302.
32. James Callaghan notes, June 1942, Callaghan papers in private possession; cf. Morgan, *Callaghan*, pp. 44–5.

in an exchange recorded by Orwell, who was 'slightly horrified' to hear Cripps mentioning that some people thought Germany might, within months, be out of the war: 'When I said that I should look on that as a disaster pure and simple (because if the war were won as easily as that there would have been no real upheaval here and the American millionaires would still be in situ) he appeared not to understand.'[33]

If the Left overestimated its own strength in 1942, Cripps neither shared this view nor pretended to do so. The rhetoric of a 'people's war', with an end to class distinctions, infused his speeches. But, like his earlier advocacy of a popular front, his position was based on pessimism about what the Left could achieve by itself, combined with optimism about the prospect of rallying centrist support for progressive policies. He baffled a group of trade unionists by telling them that the 'initiative in post-war politics was likely to come from the centre and not from the circumference', and citing the 'change of heart' that he detected among younger Tories to deplore a return to party politics.[34] He told Barrington-Ward that 'present parties will have to be ignored, broken up, recast'.[35]

Cripps had never been a good party man. Nor, it might be said, had Churchill; but each handled this matter in a very different way, in 1942 as in 1940. Cripps's dilemma may have been insoluble. Returning from Russia adamant about not rejoining the Labour Party,[36] he had climbed into the War Cabinet on a ladder of anti-party sentiment which it was hardly decent to kick away. 'For a man not in Office, lack of Party affiliation may be an advantage,' his rival Beaverbrook commented sanctimoniously; but in saying that 'in office it is a grave handicap' he spoke with the benefit of his own recent experience.[37] Cripps resented the way that the 1922 Committee (the organization of backbench Conservative MPs) enjoyed 'power of direct access to the P.M. – part of the price paid for his leadership of his party, which, as national leader, he had much better have forgone'.[38] But Churchill fully realized that the wartime Coalition was nothing if not a coalition of parties and that, in succeeding Chamberlain as Conservative leader, he was consolidating his own tenure on power. Cripps's argument, that he could

33. Orwell diary, 7 June 1942, reporting 2 June, in Davison (ed.), *Orwell: Complete Works*, xiii, p. 351. It is also worth noting that the only talk of defeating Germany in 1942 came from advocates of a bombing strategy, as will be seen in the next chapter.

34. James Callaghan notes, June 1942, Callaghan papers.

35. Barrington-Ward diary, 4 May 1942.

36. Gorodetsky, *Mission to Moscow*, pp. 264–5. Quoting Anthony Greenwood in Kuibyshev.

37. Beaverbrook to Paul Patterson, 29 September 1942, in Taylor, *Beaverbrook*, p. 538.

38. Barrington-Ward diary, 21 May 1942.

not rejoin the Labour Party 'because it would weaken my position as Leader of the House of Commons', was surely misguided.[39]

A memorandum by Spry explicitly addressed the general assumptions that Cripps had made in taking office in February 1942:

1. SC should enter and cooperate with Govt. The public wants not another government or an opposition but an improved government under WSC.
2. Hence, SC should support both WSC and govt.
3. Given that SC did not lead or have the support of a party, then, it was desirable he should, in a sense, have the personal cooperation of EB and a Conservative such as AE.[40]

Ernest Bevin and Anthony Eden were thus seen as the crucial allies, symmetrically flanking Cripps on the left and the right, in the Labour movement and in the Conservative hierarchy. In fact, the asymmetrical (and halting) way that Cripps's alliances developed is striking. He possibly tried but he certainly failed to win over Bevin, for whom Cripps had one great asset as a ministerial colleague: he was not Beaverbrook. But the low opinion of Cripps's political acumen that Bevin had formed in the 1930s was not modified by what he saw in 1942 – dismissing coalition-building overtures from others with the contemptuous retort: 'I am not Stafford Cripps.'[41]

Faute de mieux, Cripps looked right rather than left. He spoke warmly of working with two Conservative colleagues in the War Cabinet, not only Anthony Eden as Foreign Secretary but also Oliver Lyttelton as Minister of Production. Rather than any sort of cabal to replace the Prime Minister, this was exactly the same group of ministers to whom Churchill now looked, in a comment noted in Eden's diary: 'Cripps, Oliver and I he thought pretty powerful with himself.'[42] Admittedly, his long-term differences in outlook with the Prime Minister did not escape Cripps, even in these early months of amity. His table talk at a dinner of Conservative MPs in June was recorded by a quizzical Butler: 'He implied that in due course Churchill would be pushed aside, because he did not understand the home front. He did not deny that Churchill was the best for the strategic war

---

39. James Callaghan notes, June 1942, Callaghan papers.
40. Spry memorandum, 14 July 1942. Spry 45/4.
41. Dalton diary, 24 August 1942, in Pimlott (ed.), *Dalton: War Diary*, p. 480; cf. Gordon Walker diary, 4 March 1942, in Pearce (ed.), *Gordon Walker: political diaries*, p. 108, for IC's awareness of the need to cultivate Bevin.
42. Eden diary, 24 April 1942, in Eden, *Reckoning*, p. 326.

period.'[43] Cripps, entertaining hopes that the War Cabinet was now working better, agreed with Barrington-Ward that 'there is no question of unshipping Winston'.[44]

Cripps's scheme of priorities seems clear in retrospect, even if it seemed puzzling at the time to those who wanted to make a puzzle out of it. It needs to be remembered how scathingly the pre-war Cripps had unmasked the way that 'the traditional calls of patriotism are furbished up' to mislead the workers. 'The need for national unity is stressed,' he had scornfully suggested, 'and every available organization, political, religious and social, is drawn in to play its part in creating the psychology of war and in organizing the country upon a war basis.'[45] Little wonder that the young firebrand James Callaghan, who met his hero in the changed context of 1942, was disconcerted to find his message so simple: 'Cripps' reaction to any given problem can be gauged as soon as it is realized that he sincerely believes that "national unity" is necessary to carry us through the War.'[46] These were the stark imperatives that made him ready to work within the system, though not on a party basis.

Altogether, he was not the man – or no longer the man – the Left had taken him for. Though George Strauss remained Cripps's bagman, in office as in opposition, the third Labour MP expelled along with them in 1939, Aneurin Bevan, was now observed 'watching Cripps as if he were a fallen angel' in the House of Commons.[47] Bevan did not turn against Cripps; he simply became fearful for him; but other former comrades were more outspoken. 'I won't say – yet – that I feel that he is the lost leader,' Harold Laski put it, with an allusion to Browning that he knew would not be lost upon Isobel Cripps. 'But I will say that, for reasons I can't profess to grasp, he is helping Churchill to fight this war on principles of which the outcome seems to make certain the victory of reaction in Britain.'[48]

For the Left, it was never glad confident morning again. But the idea that Cripps had been suborned by a riband to stick on his coat, still less by a handful of silver, was hardly a subtle enough interpretation. 'I can't help

43. At a dinner of Conservative MPs, held in Cripps's honour at the Savoy Hotel, 17 June 1942, memo by Butler, July 1942, Trinity College, RAB G14.60.
44. Barrington-Ward diary, 25 June 1942.
45. Cripps, 'The political reactions of rearmament'.
46. James Callaghan notes, June 1942, Callaghan papers in private possession; partly quoted in Morgan, *Callaghan*, pp. 44–5.
47. Chuter Ede diary, 25 February 1942, in Jefferys (ed.), *Labour and the Wartime Coalition*, p. 58.
48. Laski to IC, 29 September 1942.

feeling a strong impression that Cripps has already been got at,' Orwell reflected in June. 'Not with money or anything of that kind of course, nor even by flattery and the sense of power, which in all probability he doesn't care about: but simply by responsibility, which automatically makes a man timid.'[49] Cripps's sense of duty was always easily activated; it consorted with his executive temperament to give him a taste for office; and he was hopeful of exerting real influence now that he was at last a highly-placed insider. 'He came into government on [the] understanding that he and Churchill were to run the war,' one confidant noted. 'And it went like this until C. went to India.'[50] The Cripps Mission was his first test. It should come as no surprise that, from first to last, its history shows him rallying to the task of supporting rather than displacing or replacing the Prime Minister.

If Congress had accepted the Cripps offer, it would have strengthened his hand at home and thus ensured that the offer would stick. Cripps's appreciation of this point could be reported in a pejorative way: 'I told Nehru that if they accepted my terms *I* should be such a Tremendous Figure in England that *I* could do everything.'[51] But Nehru well understood that Cripps's position in the War Cabinet was his own best guarantee.[52] Cripps had spoken frankly of 'the inferences which he hoped his Congress friends would draw' in a way that left a strong impression of his sincerity on Coupland: 'His success would make him the dominant person in Indian policy for 20 years. His failure would leave Indian nationalism without a friend in England of the front rank.'[53] The genuineness of Cripps's own effort to find a solution can hardly be doubted, nor his disappointment that Nehru was finally unable to bring off their daring exercise in partnership.

That the Cripps offer was the most that could have been squeezed out of the Churchill Government seems clear, if only from the qualms of the Prime Minister in living up to what had already been agreed. But was it enough to offer Congress? Obviously it fell short of Congress demands, as the Working

49. Orwell diary, 7 June 1942, reporting 2 June, in Davison (ed.), *Orwell: Complete Works*, xii, p. 351. *Tribune*, for which Orwell wrote, was warning Cripps to remember that he was 'put into office because he had become the spokesman of the people, and so he must look to them for his support', not play 'parlour politics' with the old party politicians. 'Stand fast, Cripps!', *Tribune*, 29 May 1942.

50. Gordon Walker diary, 3 September 1942, in Pearce (ed.), *Gordon Walker: political diaries*, p. 112.

51. Lionel Fielden to Edward Thompson, n.d. but 1942, quoted in Gupta, *Imperialism and the British Labour Movement*, p. 270n.

52. Johnson: 'N. said Cripps in govt wld be protection.' Spry diary, 8 April 1942.

53. Coupland diary, 26 March 1942.

Committee made clear in its formal resolution; and satirical references to responsibility for 'canteens' subsequently gave a derisory view of the proposed defence arrangements. Yet the first and most telling question that Nehru faced from the press after the breakdown was: 'Why did the Congress take a fortnight to reject the Cripps proposals?'[54]

The fact is that Congress was tortured by a terrible dilemma. Arguably, Cripps offered it an opportunity to use the war to claw back, through participation in central government, the authority that it had surrendered too impetuously, along with the seals of provincial office, in 1939. Instead, the political vacuum was filled by the 'Quit India' campaign, which Gandhi claimed to have produced as 'an answer to Cripps's failure'.[55] India's defence was left in the hands of the British Raj, excluding and embittering Congress, which thereby missed its best chance to sustain Indian unity through a common defence effort against Japanese aggression. On the Congress side, Rajagopalachari spoke out prominently along these lines: refusing to blame Cripps himself, urging rapprochement with the Muslim League, and arguing that for Britain to quit India at its moment of peril from Japanese invasion would constitute betrayal. But Rajaji's marginalization within Congress was rapidly and ruthlessly revealed. In 1948, he feelingly told Cripps: 'How I wish that you and I had been listened to six years ago instead of being distrusted.'[56]

By contrast, Cripps crawled back into Churchill's shadow and Nehru into Gandhi's. Their search for agreement had hinged on a presumed compatibility over the war crisis. For each of them, the prize was an agreed settlement leading to Indian independence; and the reason to clinch on these proposals – which were far from ideal, somewhat provisional, and hastily improvised – lay in the peremptory demands of the world war, which both recognized. Afterwards, however, Nehru attributed the failure of the Cripps Mission to the Government's refusal to entrust Congress with the power to fight invaders.[57] Cripps, conversely, left facing the problem of actually providing for Indian defence, regarded it as 'the central strategical question of the war'. It was thus Stafford Cripps, of all people, who now lectured Winston Churchill, of all people, that 'we must make up our minds whether we are going to try to hold India or not'.[58]

---

54. Press conference, 12 April 1942, in Gopal (ed.), *Nehru: Selected Works*, xii, p. 213.
55. Fischer, *Week with Gandhi*, p. 103.
56. Rajagopalachari to RSC, 19 May 1948, PRO, CAB 127/148. In 1946 Cripps noted Rajagopalachari's view that 'we might have settled it all then and much regrets that we didn't'. RSC diary, 13 April 1946.
57. Gopal (ed.), *Nehru: Selected Works*, xii, p. 262.
58. RSC to Churchill, 13 April 1942 (from Karachi), T. 563/2, Churchill papers, CHAR 20/73.

Azad remained 'convinced that we were within an ace of success', so he told Cripps later.[59] There seems little reason to doubt that Nehru, torn as he was, felt the same; it was from him that the cartoonist Shankar derived his image of the flying trapeze.[60] At the heart of the negotiations, Cripps and Nehru had stretched out towards each other until their fingers had almost touched. 'It surprises me how far we went in our desire for a settlement,' Nehru admitted.[61] In the process, each had inevitably revealed just how far he was prepared to go, thus compromising the formal negotiating stance of his own side by showing how much he was prepared to give up. Yet from the moment that a negotiated settlement slipped through their fingers, both sides ran for cover – not least Cripps and Nehru themselves – and a hairline crack of mutual credibility inexorably widened into a yawning chasm.

The difficulties on the Congress side had been well appreciated within the Crippery. On 10 April, as the bad news came through, Spry made some pencilled jottings, enumerating what he saw as the reasons for rejection. Of these, the chief was the failure of Congress to find consensus within itself, notably in the face of Gandhi's non-cooperation policy. Despite having withdrawn to Wardha, Gandhi undeniably cast a very long shadow. His loyal ally, Rajendra Prasad, President of Congress in 1939, was there to voice the fears of taking responsibility during the war, and the hopes that everything would be granted after it. Spry had no difficulty in appreciating the force of this 'post-dated cheque' argument, which was really the nationalist counterpart to the Viceroy's exasperated comment: 'Give me a single 1st rate British victory over the Japs and I will give you a settlement.'[62] Caught in its own quandaries, and including few experienced negotiators, the Congress Working Committee, in Spry's view, fatally lacked a capacity to compromise.

What Spry jotted down on the spot, almost certainly in conjunction with Cripps, reveals the essential sticking-points in the negotiations, not only for

59. Azad to RSC, 25 March 1946, PRO, CAB 127/119. Admittedly, this sits uneasily with his subsequent representation of Nehru as minimizing the differences with the British. Azad, *India Wins Freedom*, pp. 65ff.
60. See Hodson to Coupland, 8 May 1942, in Coupland, *Cripps Mission*, p. 246. 'Shankar, the cartoonist, told me the other day that on the Wednesday before the negotiations broke down Jawaharlal himself said to him, "in a few days' time you will be drawing war cartoons and backing up a 'National Government'. I think we are very near agreement." Apparently, at least for a short time Jawaharlal was animated by a vision of himself rousing and leading the country against the Japanese.'
61. Press statement, 15 April 1942, in Gopal (ed.), *Nehru: Selected Works*, xii, p. 234.
62. Marginalia on Amery to Linlithgow, 3 April 1942, in Mansergh, *TOP*, i, p. 632.

Congress but for Cripps. The great underlying issue was the lack of unity on the Indian side, with intractable and complex divisions, which simultaneously made it difficult to reach agreement on how self-government should be achieved, but rendered it impossible for Britain to privilege one single community. This was the frame within which any proposals had to be viewed. The official Congress response to Cripps on 10 April, nominally from Azad but in fact drafted by Nehru, was framed on altogether different assumptions. Spry summarized its essential points as a demand for an important change in the constitution and a government responsible only to the Indian parties; and, thinking this obviously unacceptable outside the ranks of Congress, briskly concluded, 'i.e. asked Cripps to set up a dictatorship'.[63]

These two points formed the gist of Cripps's combative reply, which he drafted himself, in his usual red ink, and sent back the same evening. Constitutional changes, as proposed by Azad and Nehru 'for the first time last night, nearly three weeks after you had received the proposals', were scouted as impractical. Secondly, their claim that there must be 'Cabinet Government with full power' was construed as meaning that Congress alone would accept office; and because it would be responsible to nobody but Congress, it 'would in fact constitute an absolute dictatorship of the majority'. This rather abstract constitutional point reflected the prevailing assumptions of the British Government. 'In a country such as India where communal divisions are still so deep,' Cripps wrote, 'it is generally recognized that simple majority Government of this kind is not possible.' In the final draft he strengthened this further by substituting the phrase, 'an irresponsible majority Government'.[64]

The exchanges of 10 April had thus already slipped into a polemical confrontation, voicing conflicting contentions that had not been heard previously, perhaps because they had been suppressed as long as they seemed susceptible of resolution within an overall agreement. But their sting had not been drawn and an obvious opening was created on each side for accusing the other of introducing factitious new issues. Cripps later reported to the War Cabinet that Congress had 'determined to find a reason for refusal and that, having discarded the earlier objections as valid causes, they had been driven to find this new reason'.[65] Congress, in turn, accused Cripps of putting forward 'an argument in your letter which at no time during our

63. (Spry), pencil memo, 'Some Reasons for Rejection', 10 April 1942.
64. RSC to Azad, 10 April 1942, in Mansergh, *TOP*, i, p. 733; drafts in PRO, CAB 127/70.
65. RSC report, in Mansergh, *TOP*, ii, p. 330.

talks was mentioned by you', which was clear evidence that 'unhappily even in this grave hour of peril the British Government is unable to give up its wrecking policy'.[66] Drawing attention to the interlinked problem of majority rule and communalism was itself read as a token of bad faith, given that there had been no reference to it throughout their talks and correspondence. 'The communal issue in any form was never discussed,' Nehru told his first press conference after the breakdown, and went on to reproach Cripps for 'continually thinking in regard to every matter in terms of Hindu and Muslim, which even Mr Jinnah does not do'.[67]

Cripps tried to have it both ways on leaving Delhi: worsting Congress yet adopting an air of pious magnanimity. 'Never mind whose fault it is,' he said. 'Let me take all the blame if that will help in uniting India for her own defence.'[68] In his broadcast to the Indian people, Cripps did not retreat from commending 'a single national government', a concept which he juxtaposed against 'the deep, communal divisions in India' to show the inappropriateness of Congress's insistence on its own domination.[69] The more he elaborated this point, however, the more deeply he offended those like Nehru who staked their political credibility on a denial of communalism. Every time Cripps opened his mouth, he offered further proof that his attitude was now 'anti-Congress, communal and reactionary'.[70]

After his broadcast in Delhi on 11 April, Cripps was off home the next morning. He arrived back in London on 21 April, looking well and sunburned, according to Amery, who met him at Hendon aerodrome. Cripps held a press conference the next day, under the auspices of the Ministry of Information, which was responsible for Government propaganda, especially in the USA.

Cripps sought to identify some net gain from the initiative. He took the line that it had established beyond doubt that Britain was unequivocally committed to Indian independence, and to a practicable procedure for achieving it in due course. He sought to play up Nehru's pro-war statements to suggest that Indian leaders were ready to 'extend themselves in order to

66. Azad to RSC, 11 April 1942, in Mansergh, *TOP*, i, pp. 743–5.

67. Nehru press conference, 12 April 1942, in Gopal (ed.), *Nehru: Selected Works*, xii, pp. 219–21.

68. RSC statement to the press, 11 April 1942.

69. RSC broadcast, 11 April 1942, in Mansergh, *TOP*, i, p. 755.

70. Nehru to Menon, 15 April 1942, in Gopal (ed.), *Nehru: Selected Works*, xii, p. 232. Conversely, Spry had written earlier: 'In fact Congress does not appeal to me. It is *fundamentally* reactionary – a merging of mill owner capitalism, reactionary Hinduism and a democratic façade.' Spry diary, 29 March 1942.

do anything they can to assist in an unofficial capacity in maximizing the defence of India'. Far from being gloomy, the picture was 'much more encouraging than it would have been if nothing had been done'. When, under questioning from journalists, Cripps was pressed to justify his phrase about the dictatorship of the majority, he argued that 'the question of the majority and the minority in India is not a question of a fluctuating majority and minority, one of which may be converted into the other, but it is a question of a communal minority and a communal majority neither of which can be converted . . .'[71] The point that Jinnah had tried to get across to Nehru's friend in 1939 had fully sunk home.

Their friendship was sinking too. Not only did Nehru insist that Cripps's visit had worsened the situation: he was led progressively into personal criticism of Cripps himself. A remark attributed to Cripps on leaving India, that Congress wanted everything or nothing, though almost certainly a product of misreporting, had soured the atmosphere. After Cripps's London press conference, which made it 'quite clear to us that those in authority in England live in a world of their own', Nehru was stung into increasingly forthright criticisms from which 'even a person like Sir Stafford Cripps' was not excepted.[72] In one speech Nehru came out in public with the sort of remark hitherto only vented in the fitful gusts of his private correspondence: 'In fact, Sir Stafford knew nothing about India.'[73] Once this had been said, there could have been few illusions left about the dilapidated state of their relationship, which had waxed and waned with the political freight it had been asked to carry.

Cripps continued to reiterate all the points that most annoyed Congress. His report to the House of Commons on 28 April was not a great parliamentary occasion; the House was no more than three-quarters full, and Churchill was absent. Cripps's speech had been drafted on the journey home and cleared with Amery, who thought the delivery 'skilful and straightforward', but with 'no touch of eloquence or breadth in it and his actual voice and manner are rather wooden'.[74] Cripps came out with the same assertion that 'nothing but good' would ensue; the same assumption of the role of

71. Press conference, 22 April 1942, in Mansergh, *TOP*, i, p. 815.

72. Press conference, 25 April 1942; interview 25 April 1942, in Gopal (ed.), *Nehru: Selected Works*, xii, pp. 238, 588.

73. Speech, 24 April 1942, in Gopal (ed.), *Nehru: Selected Works*, xii, p. 237. Hodson's comment, some two weeks later, that it was 'significant that Jawaharlal has studiously refrained from attacking Cripps personally', seems mistaken. Hodson to Coupland, 8 May 1942, in Coupland diary, p. 247.

74. Amery diary, 28 April 1942, in Barnes and Nicholson (eds.), *Empire at Bay*, p. 811.

arbitrator in Indian affairs; the same emphasis on the communal difficulty, this time backed with a citation from Gandhi. All that was new was the respectful tone adopted towards the Viceroy's Executive Council, whose current membership had not hitherto enjoyed Cripps's favour.[75] In its subfusc way, the speech made a good impression in showing that Cripps had done his best.[76] The American diplomats in the gallery thought so, as did George Orwell. 'No question that Cripps's speeches etc. have caused a lot of offence, i.e. in India,' Orwell judged. 'Outside India I doubt whether many people blame the British government for the breakdown.'[77] When Spry subsequently noted that the 'Indian mission confirmed, did not set back [Cripps's] reputation', he had special reason to feel pleased.[78] The negotiations might have failed; battles might have been lost in the East; but this was a war in which propaganda victories bulked large.

75. 5 HC Debs., vol. 379, cols. 826–43 (28 April 1942).   76. *FRUS*, 1942, i, pp. 646–7.
77. Orwell diary, 18 April 1942, in Davison (ed.), *Orwell: Complete Works*, xiii, p. 276; cf. ibid., pp. 283 and 305.
78. Spry memorandum, 14 July 1942.

5

Quasi-war

As Gandhi's biographer has written: 'Dislodging the imperial power was in large part a battle for the mind, both of Indians and the British rulers and electorate, and their foreign allies.'[1] No British politician appreciated this point more keenly than Cripps, who had said in 1939 that war made India 'a test question in the eyes of the world'.[2] Amery's opinion was that 'on the whole the after-effects of the mission may be good in India and the immediate effect excellent in America'.[3] This was a half-truth; the more fulsome Cripps's reception in the West, the worse the aftertaste in the East, starting sour and becoming bitter.

Gandhi's simple proposal for the British to quit India was gathering support in Congress, making the position of Rajagopalachari virtually impossible and that of Nehru extremely difficult. The drafts now before the Congress Working Committee were, as Nehru complained, so saturated in anti-British assumptions as to favour Japanese claims, while their language condemned the Cripps proposals in terms sharply questioned by the moderate, G. B. Pant: 'If the proposals were so bad why did we spend so much time over them?'[4] Some of these documents were secretly intercepted by the British authorities; others were seized at the end of May; extracts were published, sometimes covertly, as part of a concerted attempt to discredit Gandhi.[5]

Cripps saw the opportunity to redeem his failure in Delhi by a propaganda triumph. *En route* from Delhi to London, he telegraphed the text of the documents that were to appear in the thirty-page White Paper, published at the end of the month.[6] An American version, edited by Spry, was to appear

1. Brown, *Gandhi*, p. 387.   2. *The Times*, 27 October 1939.
3. Amery to Linlithgow, 6 May 1942, in Mansergh, *TOP*, ii, pp. 42–3.
4. Discussion, 27 April–1 May 1942, in Gopal (ed.), *Nehru: Selected Works*, xii, pp. 286–93, at p. 289.
5. French, *Liberty or Death*, pp. 149–54.
6. India (Lord Privy Seal's Mission) Cmd. 6350 (April 1942), 30pp.

in June.[7] Here was the Government's case: inevitably argued in the face of Congress, with Cripps as the appointed spokesman. He felt that he had a good story to tell, not only to his Cabinet colleagues but to the world; it was to improve in the telling; and it was aimed particularly at American opinion.

In this enterprise the Crippery was crucial. They had seen everything and discussed everything; now they were to show that they had forgotten nothing and forgiven nothing. David Owen vigorously propagated the Cripps line in London; Reginald Coupland, back in Oxford, provided the academic gravitas; but it was Graham Spry who was first and foremost in the fray.

It was his own idea. Over the Sea of Galilee, *en route* from Delhi to London, Spry came up with the proposal of going direct to the USA; it had obvious attractions for him in enabling him to see his wife and his infant son; and over the Sinai desert Cripps agreed to his making the necessary arrangements through the Cairo embassy.[8] This was a shrewd decision. Spry stayed in the USA for ten weeks, saw more than a hundred groups of Americans, publicized a telling account of the Cripps Mission, and in the process became his master's voice.

Spry began by talking to his own countrymen, with a broadcast on the CBC the night after his arrival in Canada. He described at length the tortuous journey he had just undertaken, marvelling that only thirteen days previously he had seen the sun rise in Karachi – one reminder that the Cripps Mission represented a dramatic leap in the scale of shuttle diplomacy from the pre-war days when Chamberlain's decision to take an aeroplane to Munich seemed so bold. Spry made the point that, until the last moment, the constitutional issue had not been raised and that everyone accepted that 'India could become as free as Canada' after the war. In countering 'suspicions and doubts' about the offer, he tendered a personal affirmation: 'these proposals of the British War Cabinet were conceived in sincerity, they were offered in sincerity, and if they had been accepted, they would have been executed in sincerity'.[9]

On reaching Washington, Spry cabled to Cripps, alerting him to the widespread view that 'your mission almost proved successful and at moment of success was sabotaged by War Cabinet and/or Viceroy'.[10] Spry impressed the State Department official with whom he had lengthy talks as 'a very

7. Spry (ed.), 'Cripps Mission to India', June 1942.   8. Spry memoirs, 84/9.
9. Spry, CBC broadcast, 26 April 1942, CBC archives 420426–1 D.
10. Spry to RSC, 13 May 1942, copy, Spry 45/8; cf. interview with Lachlan Currie, 9 May 1942, Spry 45/6.

intelligent and liberal minded person who, as a Canadian national, saw both the British and the American point of view'. Spry's task was twofold. First he needed to dispel suspicions about the role of Churchill, duly represented by Spry as a man who would never have dreamt of disabling the political career of his close personal friend, Sir Stafford, whose own heartfelt wish it had been to go to India. Secondly, Spry had to unmask Gandhi, and the four or five members of the Congress Working Committee who went along with him, as the cause of failure, with their reasoning that 'there was no political gain for the Indians to take over at this time'.[11]

This was what Cripps wanted the Americans to hear; and he knew that they had heard a somewhat different account from Colonel Johnson. If Cripps's reputation had been staked on achieving a settlement, so had Johnson's; each needed someone to blame for failure. They did not quarrel directly between themselves; but their accounts clashed in so far as Cripps blamed Gandhi and Johnson blamed Churchill. It was a view that Johnson had taken at an early stage, probably based on his frustration at awaiting approval from London of a revised defence formula.[12] He and Cripps had worked together in Delhi, in the hurly-burly of the final days of hectic diplomacy, which perhaps concealed some differences of nuance between them. For instance, Johnson talked not of a National but a Nationalist Government. More significantly, he may not have meant the same thing by a cabinet as those schooled in British constitutional conventions. After all, the Executive Council was a body of ministers (as Cripps later put it himself) not unlike the American Cabinet.[13] The whole point at issue, in effect, was whether the Indians had been offered a British or an American Cabinet. Certainly Johnson's grasp of the constitutional niceties did not impress his colleagues in the State Department.[14]

The broad-brush approach of his personal representative was well known to the President, who cheerfully affirmed that Johnson's 'heart is in the right place' in the course of an interview granted to Spry on 15 May. Nothing was said to impugn Johnson; but Spry used his half-hour with Roosevelt to reinforce the Cripps version, while the President intermittently stabbed at a figure of Hitler as a pin-cushion on his desk. Roosevelt naturally viewed India through American spectacles. His ready analogies from the thirteen states' epic struggle for independence, which had so taxed Churchill's

11. Conversation between Alling and Spry, 13 May 1942, in *FRUS*, 1942, i, pp. 651–3.
12. See Coupland diary, 8 April 1942, on rumours from 'high-placed Americans'.
13. Text of broadcast to the USA, 27 July 1942; cf. Patel, *Cripps Mission*, p. 98.
14. *FRUS*, 1942, i, pp. 631, 661–2.

patience, were developed 'with a rather delightful and almost boyish relish' for Spry's benefit. The President had one big question: 'Some people believe that the mission would have been successful if the instructions had not been changed during the later stages of the negotiations. Can you tell me if there is anything to that – were there any restrictions placed on Cripps's instructions?' Spry had his answer ready. He had telegraphed Cripps for guidance two days previously and now had a reply in his hand: 'Please convey to the President my personal assurance that throughout the Indian negotiations I was loyally supported by the War Cabinet, the Viceroy and Commander-in-Chief.'[15] This may well have been the right thing for a member of Churchill's War Cabinet to tell a foreign head of state whose support for the common war effort was crucial. Whether it did justice to the history of the Cripps Mission is another matter. In the White House, Spry duly supplied his own corroboration.

The Cripps–Spry version seems to have enjoyed some success in Washington in countering the rival Johnson version – even when the latter was presented in person. Johnson spent little more than a month in Delhi before returning to the more congenial climate of Washington, where he in turn briefed the State Department. The official minute of this meeting is defective in that it fails to convey the import or even sequence of the negotiations, beyond reporting Johnson's sweeping contention that the terms had been changed at the last moment because Cripps's authority had been rescinded. This was nothing new; Johnson was simply repeating verbally what he had cabled on 11 April. But the fact that he had got wind of Cripps's differences with his ministerial colleagues – thus challenging the sanitized Cripps–Spry pieties – did not mean that he could substantiate his own central allegation. Even if he were correct 'in believing that Churchill, the Viceroy and Wavell were pleased to see the Cripps Mission result in failure', concluded the State Department minute, Johnson had presented no sound evidence that it failed because of sabotage from London.[16] The battle for public opinion on this point, however, was far from over.

The position of Coupland was delicate; his reputation as Beit Professor at Oxford would give weight to anything he wrote, but equally might be compromised by overt partisanship. Cripps's first thought was that Coupland should write an article for *Life* magazine, with its wide circulation in the USA.[17] In the

15. Spry's note of interview with Roosevelt, 15 May 1942, in Mansergh, *TOP*, ii, pp. 89–92, at pp. 90–91; and see his report, Mansergh, *TOP*, ii, p. 473. Spry memoirs 84/9, p. 12.
16. Memorandum, 26 May 1942, *FRUS*, 1942, i, pp. 660–62 at 662.
17. Coupland diary, 11 April 1942.

event, his sixty-page pamphlet, *The Cripps Mission*, finished in May, was published by Oxford University Press. It is still a very good account, hardly to be dismissed merely as war propaganda; but naturally it argues a case. Potential American readers, from the President down, might have liked Coupland's notion that Cripps took with him a Declaration of Indian Independence – a point hitherto crucial but, once established, paradoxically neglected throughout negotiations that concentrated instead on interim arrangements.

Coupland offered a sophisticated justification of the quasi-cabinet concept that had become the crux of the dispute. Coupland suggested that 'it may be taken for granted' that the Viceroy would operate the relevant conventions.[18] Here it is surely reasonable to assume that Coupland shared Cripps's own robust sense of the political realities that would prevail, under this Viceroy or the next.[19] Indeed, when Coupland later reworked this material for an academic book, he squared his account with Cripps, using Spry as the intermediary. Cripps was by this point much more cagey about assertions that he had simply offered cabinet government *de facto*, with the implication that he had later backtracked. It was at his suggestion that Coupland's final text discriminated between the different nuances of the term 'convention'. Such amendments were now urged 'from the point of view of American opinion', which Spry was anxious should not be misled, since 'not the least of the results of the Mission was the education of at least American editorial opinion and, as I know, of the highest levels of the American government'.[20] As to the reason for breakdown, Coupland's measured view was that 'it may well have been Mr Gandhi's opinions, though he was not there to utter them, that at the last moment turned the scale'.[21] In private, he and David Owen had put it more pithily: 'Gandhi the wrecker'.[22] This was just what Cripps himself was telling his friends: 'Gandhi was anything but a saint and had determined to wreck the negotiations from the beginning.'[23]

Cripps was an active combatant in the propaganda war. D. V. Tahman-

18. Coupland, *Cripps Mission*, p. 55.

19. And therefore unnecessary to suppose that Coupland, whose diary shows him so close to Cripps's thinking, was specifically and successfully kept in the dark by Cripps about Linlithgow's prickly refusal to lay down new conventions in advance, as argued by Moore, *Churchill, Cripps and India*, pp. 126, 131.

20. Spry to Coupland, 26 February 1943, copy; commenting on the proofs of Coupland, *Indian Politics*, pp. 284–6.

21. Coupland, *Cripps Mission*, p. 61.   22. Barrington-Ward diary, 28 April 1942.

23. Gordon Walker diary, 25 April 1942, in Pearce (ed.), *Gordon Walker: political diaries*, p. 110.

kar, London correspondent of the United Press of India and later biographer of Vallabhbhai Patel, had been relaying Nehru's rejoinders to Cripps for several weeks, no doubt in hopes of provoking further controversy; and his hopes were granted when Cripps agreed to be interviewed on 4 June. The extensive revisions made before publication show the influence of David Owen, now firmly established on Cripps's own staff, as well as that of Frank Turnbull, back in the India Office, in seeking to cover every angle of possible objection and to pre-empt openings for Congress allegations. Turnbull told Cripps, 'I feel myself – increasingly as I watch Mr Gandhi's dilemma – that the "Mission" was a much greater success than it appeared to be.'[24]

Controversy focused on one passage, dealing with the final stage of the negotiations. Indications that the Congress Working Committee had accepted his proposals, so Cripps claimed, had reached him not only in a telephone call from 'a great friend of mine in Congress' but also 'through the press from another high authority on the Working Committee'. The former was J. C. Gupta, the lawyer with whom Cripps and Wilson had stayed in 1939; he had acted as a go-between in Delhi before returning home to Calcutta, and his own source for the optimistic news was Azad. The other 'high authority', quite transparently, was Rajagopalachari, whose exit from the Working Committee in the middle of Thursday, 9 April, had been widely reported. Cripps's interview continued: 'Then further consultations took place in which I understand Mr Gandhi was consulted and after some further delay Congress finally turned down my proposals.' This was attributed to Gandhi's views on non-violence. 'I understand and appreciate Jawaharlal's position,' Cripps added. 'His opposition to Fascism and Nazism is too fundamental to be obscured by mere national considerations; I am convinced of that.'[25]

The evidence is all for Cripps's sincerity in making this point; it is at one with what he privately said about the young left-wing Indians who were Nehru's constituency.[26] Yet this does not mean that Cripps was oblivious to the tactical effect of his words. If, however, he imagined that he could so easily divide Congress, still less isolate Gandhi, he was quickly shown his error. Nehru immediately contradicted Cripps's statement as 'entirely incorrect' and his allegation about the centrality of non-violence as 'also wholly incorrect'.[27] A couple of days later, Gandhi denied 'any interference or guidance'

24. Turnbull to RSC, 30 June 1942, PRO, CAB 127/80.
25. Final version, 18 June 1942, PRO, CAB 127/81, with text of 'the passage which has given rise to controversy' in telegraphese.
26. Orwell diary, 15 May 1942, in Davison (ed.), *Orwell: Complete Works*, xiii, p. 323.
27. Interview, 16 June 1942, in Gopal (ed.), *Nehru: Selected Works*, xii, p. 243.

in the deliberations of the Working Committee.[28] On this point at least, Rajagopalachari was to add his testimony in support of Gandhi. Cripps's interview thus widened his breach with Congress – not only on personal recriminations about the Cripps Mission but on future British policy too.

The message from Cripps that was flashed around the world was: 'We are not going to walk out of India – not that we want to remain there for imperialistic reasons – right in the middle of the war.'[29] This scorning of 'Quit India' came from the War Cabinet's reputedly most left-wing member and a supposed friend of Congress; its publication on the eve of a visit to Washington by Churchill was notably helpful to him, in substance, in impact, and in timing. It at least allowed him to evade the tiresome Indian question during a visit punctuated by the appalling news on 21 June that Tobruk had fallen. This was an even bigger blow than the fall of Singapore and brought rumours that the Government too might fall.[30]

Emerging at this critical moment as Churchill's staunch colleague, Cripps became Gandhi's declared enemy. He progressively shed the Savile Row elegance that had clothed their mutual antagonism, which now emerged increasingly naked. The passage in his interview which had annoyed Gandhi had originally contained a more explicit claim about the breakdown of negotiations. 'Long distance telephone calls were put through: the voice at the other end counselled for the final rejection of the proposals,' Cripps had claimed. Cripps may have suppressed this information for the moment to conceal its source, which was apparently a British intelligence report. This cannot be traced; and doubts over its authenticity are strengthened by the lack of response to Gandhi's subsequent challenge for the evidence to be published.[31] The legend of the long telephone call from Wardha took on a life of its own. Cripps eagerly accepted it because it explained how the personal intervention of Gandhi could have been brought to bear. By the time Cripps made his report to the War Cabinet in July, Gandhi's telephonic intervention was the key to an otherwise inexplicable change of front by Congress during that long, hot afternoon of Thursday, 9 April.[32] What

28. Gandhi article, 19 June 1942, in Gandhi, *Collected Works*, lxxvi, p. 235.
29. Compare Tahmankar's original text: 'We are not going to quit India – not that we want to hold on to it for imperialistic reasons though – just in the middle of the war.' Tahmankar interview, 4 June, PRO, CAB 127/81. Perhaps 'quit' was softened by Cripps in a vain attempt at palliation, but Gandhi was equally stung by 'walk out'.
30. See Gilbert, *Churchill*, vii, pp. 126–34; Gupta, *Indian National Movement*, p. 227.
31. See Fischer, *Life of Gandhi*, p. 359; Moore, *Churchill, Cripps and India*, p. 127n.
32. Report, in Mansergh, *TOP*, ii, p. 330. There is at least one phone call too many in this account. As first told to Tahmankar, 'the most optimistic point' was reached with the redrafting ('on the spot') of the Cripps–Johnson formula, which Cripps misdated to Thursday afternoon.

remains constant is not Cripps's circumstantial evidence but his determination to pin the blame personally on Gandhi and, as he put it to Lord Halifax in Washington, 'to make the Americans feel that Gandhi's resistance is against them as well as against us'.[33]

Cripps's broadcast to the USA on 27 July 1942 followed the same line. Prepared with advice from both Spry and Turnbull, the broadcast had the aim of exposing Gandhi by showing that 'Quit India' meant anarchy: a proposition not difficult to sustain from Gandhi's own incoherent utterances. Some of these quotations had been supplied to Spry by Turnbull at the India Office, and were used by Cripps to show Gandhi's hostility to the war waged by the United Nations against Japan. His responsibility for engineering the rejection of the Cripps offer was put in this light. 'Like a clever lawyer,' commented Nehru, 'Sir Stafford has picked out phrases from Mahatma Gandhi's statements without reference to their context and tried to prove the British imperialist case.' It was 'sad beyond measure' that, in a bad situation, Cripps should have made things worse and 'thus injured Indo-British relations more than any other Englishman could have done'.[34] Nehru's private opinion matched his public rhetoric. No longer did he simply identify distrust as the fundamental cause of the breakdown of talks: he identified the British policy as one of dividing Muslims and Hindus, and bitterly called the Cripps Mission a 'plant', devised to range world opinion against Congress.[35] This was the background to Nehru's platform gibe: 'I am happy that the negotiations failed and we were not caught in that snare.'[36]

As the Indian situation polarized, Nehru stood with Gandhi just as Cripps stood with Churchill. *Faute de mieux*, Congress was moving towards the Quit India policy, backed by civil disobedience. Its adoption by Congress on 8 August came as no surprise, given the fact that the key documents had

---

Since this actually took place on the evening of Wednesday, 8 April, it is odd that Cripps maintained that Gupta 'rang me up the same night'. In his report to the Cabinet, backed by proper documentation, this conversation with Gupta is said to have happened on the morning of Friday, 10 April, which is confirmed by Spry's diary. The first draft of Spry's reply to Fischer, citing 'a diary written as these events occurred', correctly dates the optimistic afternoon as that of 9 April, though including Gupta's phone call; oddly, his published text shifts most of this to 8 April, with the Gupta phone call the next day. See Spry, *Nation*, 14 November 1942, p. 503. That the incident actually took place is confirmed from Cripps's comments when he met Gupta again in 1946: RSC diary, 31 March, 13 April 1946.

33. RSC to Halifax, 8 July 1942, copy, PRO, CAB 127/80.

34. Press statement, 27 July 1942, in Gopal (ed.), *Nehru: Selected Works*, xii, 420–21.

35. Sir Edward Villiers, memorandum of talk with Nehru, 5 July 1942, PRO, CAB 127/143; cf. Mansergh, *TOP*, ii, p. 690.

36. Speech at Bombay, 5 August 1942, in Gopal (ed.), *Nehru: Selected Works*, xii, p. 430.

already been intercepted, and indeed disclosed to the press – a provocative step approved by neither Cripps nor Eden.[37] But in the War Cabinet Cripps fully supported appropriate counter-measures. Admittedly, when Churchill produced one of his crude stereotypes – 'Congress represents mainly the intelligentsia of non-fighting elements' – Cripps expostulated against this sort of government by whim.[38] Less bloodthirsty than some of his colleagues, he sought to turn Gandhi's own weapons of propaganda against him, devising ingenious tactics for outwitting the old man and rendering any hunger strike undertaken by him ineffective.[39] On the eve of the Congress meeting, Cripps proposed making a further broadcast to the Indian public, partly as 'a justification of my position in the face of a great deal of vilification in India'.[40] But the Viceroy, though full of praise for his American broadcast, argued that Cripps's stock was 'so low in this country both with Congress and with other parties that nothing he might say would carry any weight'.[41] Force of arms was the Viceroy's strategy and, with the War Cabinet's full backing, the pre-arranged response to the passage of the Quit India resolution was the arrest of the Congress leadership the next morning.

Cripps lost his Indian following as the price of his success with the Anglo-American public. He was now at one with the Labour Party in breaking with Congress, which also found itself facing sustained criticism in the American press.[42] Cripps added his own contribution in a long article, published in the *New York Times* on 23 August, which had gone through several drafts in his own hand. He renewed his accusation that Gandhi was responsible for a policy which was in itself impracticable but which would do 'the greatest harm to the Defence of India and to the cause of the Allied Nations'. In explaining the complexities of Indian politics, Cripps showed how far he had moved from Nehru, let alone Gandhi. The Muslim League, which 'upon any communal or religious issue speaks for the great majority of the Muslim population of 80 millions or more', was depicted as naturally opposed to Congress, 'which is predominantly Hindu though with some

37. Barrington-Ward diary, 5 August 1942.
38. This was a quotation from the War Cabinet paper, WP (42) 334; see RSC note, 3 August 1942, PRO, CAB 127/80.
39. Amery diary, 6, 7, 10 August 1942, in Barnes and Nicholson (eds.), *Empire at Bay*, pp. 824–5; Mansergh, *TOP*, ii, p. 629.
40. RSC to Amery, 3 August 1942, in Mansergh, *TOP*, ii, p. 540.
41. Linlithgow to Amery, 4 August 1942, in Mansergh, *TOP*, ii, p. 555; cf. ibid., p. 487. Barrington-Ward agreed to carry a long article, drafted by Cripps with Owen's help, in *The Times*; Barrington-Ward diary, 5 August 1942.
42. Rizvi, *Linlithgow and India*, p. 215; cf. Menon, *Transfer of Power*, p. 142.

Muslim members and which is controlled by the High Caste or Brahmin class'.

The offence that Cripps now gave to Congress was not so much because what he said was false but because it was true. But he had never said these things, of course, in the days when he had chosen to closet himself with these same Brahmins. Conversely, in March 1942 the Lord Privy Seal had snubbed the Viceroy's Executive Council; in August he lauded it. He made much of the fact that it had eleven out of fifteen Indian members. 'These men – most of them ardent nationalists, some of them former leaders of the Congress party itself, – are not mere mouthpieces of the British raj,' Cripps now maintained. 'They are today bravely conducting the Government of India in what they are convinced are the best interests of India herself.' There was a single obstacle to crossing the short bridge between 'Indian self government in its fullest form and the present highly Indianised Government'. This obstacle was 'the influence of Mr Gandhi and the Congress party,' Cripps asserted. 'They were offered full participation but they refused it.'

The security of India was now threatened both from without and within. As the immediate danger of invasion diminished, over fifty battalions of British troops were tied down in suppressing insurrection in India itself; the Viceroy called it the biggest rebellion since that of 1857. In a sense it showed how right Cripps had been – Nehru and Rajagopalachari, too – in trying so hard during the first week of April to avert such a prospect. Cripps was left protesting against some of the Viceroy's approved methods, like whipping. Characteristically, however, he laid 'great stress on what the outside world will say if the Congress leaders are detained indefinitely', especially if this meant that they were thereby denied the opportunity of calling off a doomed campaign. Cripps even suggested to Amery that the Viceroy might use 'some trusted person like Rajagopalachari', who was not in gaol, as a discreet intermediary.[43] 'We are fighting for *democracy* not for administrative improvement only,' he reminded Amery.[44]

In September Cripps produced a Note on India which gives an indication of his thinking. It was premised on a commitment to Indian self-determination after a war that seemed likely to be prolonged for at least a couple of years. 'The sole question is therefore how we can make India most

43. Amery to Linlithgow, 13 August 1942, in Mansergh, *TOP*, ii, p. 692; cf. ibid., p. 734; Amery diary, 13 August 1942, in Barnes and Nicholson (eds.), *Empire at Bay*, p. 827; cf. ibid. 9, 12 November 1942, pp. 841–2, for Cripps's renewal of the idea of approaching Rajagopalachari.
44. RSC to Amery, 7 September 1942, PRO, CAB 127/80.

useful or least embarrassing to the United Nations for the rest of the war,'
Cripps argued. His answer crossed Marx with Machiavelli. It was to by-pass
communal conflicts by instigating economic reforms, thus furthering the
interests of the masses against 'the Indian millowners, landlords and money
lenders, many of whom are the financial backers of Congress'. In this way,
'the struggle in India would no longer be between Indian and British upon
the nationalist basis, but between the classes in India upon an economic
basis'.[45] The seasoned riposte from the India Office was to doubt whether
class and communal identities could be discriminated so neatly, still less
manipulated so effectively. But Cripps won a more favourable, if no less
cynical, response from an unexpected quarter. The Prime Minister seized
on this aspect of Cripps's analysis and asked that 'these points should not
be excluded from any statements that may have to be made on Indian
policy'.[46]

It was in this context that one further set-piece controversy over the
Cripps Mission was played out in the autumn of 1942. The influential New
York magazine *The Nation* printed a long article, 'Why Cripps Failed',
which offered a dangerously plausible challenge to the fragile Anglo-
American consensus on India. The author, Louis Fischer, was a left-wing
journalist, whom Cripps had met in New York in 1940 and with whom at
that time he had much in common. Fischer's former enthusiasm for the
Soviet Union had meanwhile been supplanted by a strong sympathy for
Gandhi, whose biography he was later to write. Fischer had recently spent
a well-documented week at Wardha and had been the bearer of a letter from
Gandhi to Roosevelt (drafted by Nehru). Not only had Fischer talked with
the Congress leaders about the Cripps Mission, he had also been briefed by
his compatriot Johnson. It is hardly surprising that Fischer's article should
have blamed, not Nehru and Azad, certainly not Gandhi, nor primarily
Cripps himself, but Churchill.

Fischer's account depended on Cripps having made a promise on which
he had been forced to renege. Fischer rehearsed Azad's complaint that he
had been misled by Cripps's talk of a national government; and the fact that
this had never been denied by Cripps was given a sinister significance. This
correspondence had, of course, been published in a British White Paper, on
which Fischer drew; but he further alleged that unpublished documents
would bear out his case. In the meantime, he relied upon an interview with

---

45. RSC note, 2 September 1942, in Mansergh, *TOP*, ii, pp. 882, 883–4.
46. Churchill to RSC and Amery, 20 September 1942, in Mansergh, *TOP*, ii, p. 999; cf. ibid.,
pp. 943–6 (India Office, W.D. Croft).

an unnamed British General (Wavell?) to support his own inference that Cripps had gone further than he had been authorized; he used newspaper comment, especially from the *Statesman*, to support the contention that the diehards had exerted a disabling influence; and he wrapped it up with Johnson's anonymous but inimitable judgement: 'Cripps was bitched in the back.'[47]

Fischer's article was a stimulating exercise in contemporary history. Like Coupland's pamphlet, on which it also drew, it married evidence in the public domain with private information and intelligent conjecture. Two points remain salient. One is that its historical reading cannot, in fact, be sustained on the basis of the full documents now available – for reasons which have already been argued, both over Cripps's fidelity to his brief and Churchill's actual role. The other is that the polemical force driving Fischer's account obviously arose out of the immediate circumstances of its composition. It was Cripps's recent *New York Times* article that understandably provoked Fischer to speak out, chiding his old comrade for repeating 'ancient imperialist arguments' which sat awkwardly with his past utterances.[48]

This was a wounding attack. Invited to reply, Cripps handed over the task to Spry, who carefully checked his drafts with Coupland, whose own opinion of 'Fischer's calumny' they all seem to have shared.[49] The authority for Spry's refutation was the fact that he had been in Cripps's confidence throughout and had seen every document. He could therefore 'state with all definiteness that Cripps did not make, did not seek to make, to Indian political leaders any promise of National or Cabinet government with full powers in the war period, and received no instructions from London to withdraw such promise or concession'.[50] How, then, had contrary assertions gained ground? Spry claimed that 'the hounds of propaganda were unleashed' as early as 12 April – indeed, he might have put it a few days earlier – in elaborating their sabotage theory, which he had first heard in India, then throughout the United States, and which Fischer had cast 'into its classic mould'.[51]

In subsequent skirmishes over the small print, Fischer was forced into a

47. Fischer, 'Why Cripps Failed (1)', *Nation*, 19 September 1942, at pp. 230–31; cf. his sources in *Life of Gandhi*, p. 538.
48. Fischer, 'Why Cripps Failed (2)', *Nation*, 26 September 1942, pp. 258–9.
49. Coupland to Spry, 16 February 1943.
50. Spry, 'A British reply to Louis Fischer', *Nation*, 14 November 1942, p. 501.
51. ibid., p. 504.

covert retreat.[52] On his main thesis, however, he simply recapitulated, *forte*, that Cripps was 'stabbed in the back by Englishmen who differed from him'.[53] The real incompatibilities between the rival accounts centred on different readings of Gandhi's position. Once satisfied on the independence issue, so Fischer affirmed, Gandhi would not obstruct the war effort. Spry, by contrast, explained the breakdown of negotiations by identifying Gandhi's influence as a 'crucial aspect which Sir Stafford, for sound reasons, avoided stating'.[54]

There was, however, no reference in Spry's article, or in any of the drafts, to any telephone call from Gandhi: a specific allegation which Cripps seems by October to have discounted, though without altering his general contention that 'his influence and ideas' had been crucial.[55] Cripps's diary later records his telling Gandhi, when they met again four years later, 'that I had always put down the refusal of Congress to his action and influence and he told me that it was his influence but not his action'.[56] This was nicely put.

Amery was no doubt correct, two months after the Cripps Mission had failed, in writing of Churchill: 'For him, the main thing about it has been the good effect in America; for the rest, he isn't interested, really disliking the whole problem as much as ever before.'[57] Here some distinction needs to be made between Churchill's position and Cripps's; but not that of the familiar stereotypes. 'If Cripps had failed and remained the old Cripps,' Fischer wrote, 'the tragedy would have been much smaller than it is.' It was a tragedy that a man who was 'the possible alternative to Churchill and the hope of England' had attempted to justify the unjustifiable when he could have 'at least kept quiet and refrained from adopting all the threadbare, obsolete phrases about India which his diehard colleagues have been using

---

52. For example, pressed by Spry on the discrepancies in Azad's allegation of how he was misled 'in our very first talk with you', presumably on 25 March, Fischer subsequently shifted his ground – 'This was not a "talk"' – and blustered that the assurance must therefore have been offered in later 'talks'. Fischer, 'Gandhi, Cripps and Churchill', *Nation*, 5 December 1942, p. 619.

53. Fischer, ibid., p. 620.   54. Spry, 'A British reply', p. 504.

55. RSC interview with Dewett Mackenzie, *Manchester Guardian*, 24 October 1942: one source cited in the careful analysis by Mishra, *Cripps Mission*, p. 153.

56. RSC diary, 1 April 1946. When Fischer again met Gandhi (and indeed, briefly, Cripps) in Delhi at the end of June, he was given a rather more emphatic denial, even of having 'influenced, the negotiations'. Fischer, *Life of Gandhi*, p. 359.

57. Amery to Linlithgow, 10 June 1942, in Mansergh, *TOP*, ii, p. 198.

for decades'.[58] This was a common enough view at the time; but it does not do justice to the subtlety of the interplay between two men who both gave top priority to winning the war. Part of Cripps's achievement had been to overcome Churchill's lack of interest, his dislike for India, and to secure his acquiescence in the Cripps offer. Here was the risk that Cripps took. India stood to gain; so did Britain and the Allied war effort; and so, of course, did Cripps himself. If he could have produced agreement, his return from Delhi would have put his return from Moscow in the shade; and Churchill would have been trapped into acceptance, regardless of his own inner motives.

Unlike Churchill, however, Cripps only stood to gain personally from actually achieving a negotiated settlement. He remained a prominent figure in the War Cabinet but in a post to which he was not well suited. 'It seemed to me that Sir Stafford had every quality for leading the House,' Churchill wrote of his appointment, in either a misconceived or a sardonic comment.[59] Cripps was a good debater when it was a question of marshalling a case, pressing a point or making a telling response to a question; but his speeches lacked the emotional timbre to inspire affection; and he showed himself poor at reading the House and its moods. He had been away from it for the best part of two years; he had never liked its Smoking-Room culture nor thought that gossiping over a drink was the way to oil the wheels of politics. He made few efforts to change his style when handling the House in 1942 and was thought aloof, headmasterly and unsympathetic.

Crucially, Cripps became frustrated in his attempts to forge a strong working relationship with Churchill. Their lack of personal or social compatibility was the stuff of legend. Many of Churchill's *obiter dicta* about Cripps date from this period. 'Here we are,' Churchill supposedly tells the Eighth Army, 'surrounded by sand, not a blade of grass or a drop of water – how Cripps would love it.'[60] Again: 'He has all the virtues I dislike and none of the vices I admire.'[61] Harold Nicolson was not alone in guessing that Cripps found 'the atmosphere of Downing Street (with its late hours, casual talk, cigar smoke and endless whisky) most unpalatable, while Winston never regards with affection a man of such inhuman austerity as Cripps, and cannot work easily with people unless his sentiment as well as his respect is aroused'.[62] This might not have mattered if Cripps had occupied

58. Fischer, *Nation*, 26 September 1942, pp. 258–9.
59. Churchill, *Second World War*, iv, p. 70.
60. Burgess, *Cripps*, p. 177; another version in Calder, *People's War*, p. 271.
61. Davenport, *Memoirs*, p. 140.
62. Nicolson diary, 9 September 1942, in Nicolson (ed.), *Harold Nicolson: Diaries and Letters*, ii, p. 241. Churchill's doctor made the same point, also instancing Cripps: 'Winston, for his

a clearly subordinate role in the administration, as indeed he later did, fairly happily, as Minister of Aircraft Production. But as Leader of the House and a member of the War Cabinet he was full of pretensions to change the whole style of government, as a signal that the British people were as serious about the war as the Russian.

Temperamental differences, then, spilled over into policy differences. Personally less austere, by quite a wide margin, Churchill could not see the point of Cripps's austerity measures, which appalled the Prime Minister as a gratuitous resort to 'misery first'.[63] Little wonder that the coal crisis, which threatened the Coalition in the spring of 1942, saw them pitted against each other, with the first murmurs of resignation from Cripps. Dalton, the responsible minister as President of the Board of Trade, found Cripps an unexpectedly good ally in advocating comprehensive fuel rationing, which struck Cripps as 'a first-class occasion for a show-down with the P.M. on wartime Socialism'.[64] For him, it epitomized the altruistic majority view – Mass-Observation said that 70 per cent favoured the scheme[65] – as against small and selfish interests. Just as he naturally opted for a properly calculated plan for conserving fuel supplies over the next twelve months, so Churchill naturally found this approach unnecessarily vexatious, especially when it upset his Tory supporters on the backbenches. Dalton's diary conveys the tone: 'The P.M. says that last year they were told things would be very awkward in the winter, and yet they weren't. Why should it be any worse this time?'[66] Here was the unscientific, complacent mind-set of a Prime Minister reluctant to upset his own political supporters – just what the impatient Cripps could not bear.

If Cripps considered wartime austerity necessary, so too was a glimpse of the New Jerusalem. 'The present state of public morale is not good,' he claimed, and argued that 'a new spirit is needed throughout the national war effort'.[67] He pressed for a clear statement of war aims – by which was meant peace aims – in order to animate the war effort. 'The reward should

---

part, was slow to recognize the merits of anyone who was not congenial to him.' Moran, *Churchill*, p. 753.

63. Churchill to Cherwell, 10 March 1942, in Churchill, *Second World War*, iv, p. 756.

64. Dalton diary, 24 April 1942, in Pimlott (ed.), *Dalton: War Diary*, p. 417; 'good ally', Dalton diary, 31 May 1942, ibid., p. 450. For a lucid account of the coal crisis and its resolution under Conservative pressure, see Pimlott, *Dalton*, pp.351–9.

65. Calder, *People's War*, p. 283.

66. Dalton diary, 12 May 1942, in Pimlott (ed.), *Dalton: War Diary*, p. 433.

67. War Situation: immediate needs. Note by the Lord Privy Seal, 30 July 1942. PRO, CAB 127/67, copy in Spry 45/6.

be what we are fighting for and not what people can get *now*,' he argued.[68] Churchill resisted Cripps's suggestions for discussion of post-war policies, regarding this as a distraction from the war rather than as a means of raising morale in order to win it. By the autumn of 1942, the forthcoming Beveridge Report on social insurance, which came to be seen as the foundation document for the post-war welfare state, was looming as the focus of disagreement.

Above all, Cripps found it unprofitable to venture on to Churchill's own territory, in offering advice on how to run the war itself. In the light of military failures, the question was often asked, whether it was wise for the Prime Minister also to hold the post of Minister of Defence. By doing so, of course, Churchill not only had direct access to the chiefs of staff: he thereby excluded his colleagues in the War Cabinet. 'All I wanted was compliance with my wishes after reasonable discussion,' was how he put it later.[69] It all depended on one man: on his capacity, his stamina, his intuitions, his whims. 'The man simply will not listen to evidence,' was Cripps's complaint, as he found his schemes for rational decision-making stalled by a Prime Minister intent on playing for time.[70]

This was an intractable problem at the heart of government. As Spry warned Cripps, 'The aspect of the conduct of the war with which you are primarily concerned is, in fact, the Prime Minister's individual, almost personal direction of strategy.'[71] Cripps was not alone in suggesting that the war effort could be more efficiently planned by a collective directorate, still under Churchill, but unencumbered with operational responsibilities. Here lay an old dilemma: whether strategic decision-making should be separated from the responsibility for implementing the strategy. Churchill, with much experience on his side, saw this as the flaw in the Lord Privy Seal's blueprint, dismissing it as 'a planner's dream'.[72]

Such endemic causes of personal and political friction, however, did not

---

68. To Churchill, 21 September 1942, PRO, CAB 127/85. Cripps later argued this in a radio broadcast, 20 December 1942: 'We are not fighting this war because we like fighting, you are not working long hours and living sometimes in difficult and inconvenient circumstances just for the fun of practising austerity . . . Our reward – the reward of our fighting men – will be the new Britain that between us we must create after the war.' Bottome (ed.), *Our New Order – or Hitler's?*, pp. 28–9.

69. Churchill, *Second World War*, iv, p. 78.

70. Moran, *Churchill*, pp. 93–4, 201, which offers a surprisingly sympathetic view of Cripps's difficulties, as does (less surprisingly) Danchev and Todman (eds.), *Alanbrooke: War Diaries*, e.g. pp. 280–81, 450–51, 570.

71. Spry memorandum, 31 August 1942.

72. Churchill, *Second World War*, iv, pp. 497–500 at p. 498.

amount to a conflict of view on grand strategy or a direct challenge to Churchill's position. Eden was surely right when he pointed out to Cripps that his criticisms 'scarcely affected major issues of war or major decisions of policy on which we were all agreed'.[73] Churchill, with the luxury of hindsight, ruminated that, what with the humiliating fall of both Singapore and Tobruk, it was 'remarkable that I was not in this bleak lull dismissed from power, or confronted with demands for changes in my methods, which it was known I should never accept'.[74]

Churchill was right to sense the vulnerability of his position. True, his own approval rating, though it dipped to 78 per cent in July 1942, remained remarkably solid. But during the summer, after Tobruk, approval for the conduct of the war fell well below 50 per cent for several months.[75] It is striking, then, that Cripps did not, like Beaverbrook, convert his pro-Russian posture into a demand for a second front in the west, still less encourage popular agitation to project this as an alternative to Churchill's own policy. The scope, or temptation, for doing this was obvious. In July, when the Gallup Poll asked, 'Should the Allies try to invade Europe this year?', the response was 60 per cent Yes and only 12 per cent No.[76]

The name of Cripps hardly figures in histories of grand strategy. Perhaps that is a mark of his failure to identify himself with any distinctive option, at a moment when several intertwined arguments were coming to a head. It is worth establishing that alternative priorities enjoyed credible support. For it was not only the Russians who pressed for a second front: many Americans, from Roosevelt down, wanted an early engagement with the enemy in Europe, by land or sea. The difficulty, as the British chiefs of staff had little difficulty in showing, was that such operations were hardly feasible in 1942, whatever Stalin had been led to believe to the contrary.

If a second front were to be opened, it would need a single-minded concentration of Allied forces in Britain in order to launch a cross-Channel assault in 1943, as the American chief of staff, General Marshall, cogently argued. Churchill, however, already intent on extending operations in North Africa, bent his efforts to persuading Roosevelt that operations in this

73. Eden diary, 1 October 1942, in Eden, *Reckoning*, p. 342.

74. Churchill, *Second World War*, iv, p. 494.

75. Fielding, 'Second World War', Table 1, p. 43.

76. Gallup, *Gallup Poll*, i, p. 328; cf. response to the more general question in April, 'Would you favour an offensive operation this year?': 67 per cent Yes, 10 per cent No. To say that 'Cripps had returned from Moscow to lead the "second front" forces' is to misread the position. Gardner, *Spheres of Influence*, p. 121.

theatre, somewhat improbably, represented the best means of relieving the Russians – 'here is the true Second Front of 1942'.[77] Marshall, accompanied by Cripps's old friend Harry Hopkins, argued against such a diversion of effort in London in July 1942. But, given the President's urge for action against Hitler before the end of the year, and the well-founded military objections to premature invasion of France, the plan for Anglo-American landings in North Africa, later code-named 'Torch', was conditionally agreed. The condition specified was the occurrence of an imminent Russian collapse, which would itself rule out the (nominally preferred) alternative of an invasion of France in 1943. Notwithstanding, Churchill prevailed upon Roosevelt to sanction 'Torch' unconditionally at the end of July 1942, with operations planned to follow at the end of October.

There is no need to prove that 'Torch' was misconceived: only that there were other options which 'Torch' precluded and for which a powerful member of the War Cabinet might well have marshalled the arguments. In particular, the commitment to operations that were initially premised on a Russian collapse sits oddly with Cripps's well-known faith in the Red Army. Moreover, although he and Eden raised objections in the War Cabinet, it accepted a memorandum which plainly admitted that going ahead in North Africa would imply 'a defensive, encircling line of action for the continental European theatre, except as to air operations and blockade'.[78] When he met Stalin in August, Churchill sought to evade the implication that there could be no second front in 1943; and he subsequently offered air support in the Caucasus – the sort of aid Cripps had urged a year previously – as a means of assuaging Russian disappointment. Here, as over the expansive promises Beaverbrook had made about increased supplies to Russia, the delivery of effective British aid was in fact compromised by the diversion of the relevant resources to 'Torch'.[79] Churchill, with his bloody-minded support for Bomber Command, actually had no difficulty in swallowing the fact that the only means of engaging the enemy in western Europe in 1942–3 was through an air offensive. What about Cripps?

Sir Arthur ('Bomber') Harris had been appointed Commander-in-Chief of Bomber Command on 24 February 1942. On the following day he had been much perturbed when the new Lord Privy Seal, himself only days in

77. Churchill to Roosevelt, 8 July 1942, quoted in Howard, *Grand Strategy*, iv, p. xx: a lucid exposition on which this paragraph is based.
78. Chiefs of Staff memorandum for the War Cabinet, 24 July 1942, verbatim in Howard, *Grand Strategy*, pp. xxiii–xxiv; cf. Danchev and Todman, *Alanbrooke: War Diaries*, p. 285 (24 July 1942).
79. Howard, *Grand Strategy*, pp. 33–42.

office, said in the House that the bombing policy had been initiated at a time when it was the only initiative available to Britain, but that, with the entry of the USA and the USSR into the war, the policy was under review.[80] Was it justifiable to tie up so many scarce resources in expensive bombing raids? When Cripps was in Delhi, the desperate need for air reinforcements over the Indian Ocean was brought home to him. After a meeting with Cripps, Wavell told the Prime Minister that the Japanese success in sinking virtually undefended Indian warships 'gives us furiously to think' when 'we see that over 200 heavy bombers attacked one town in Germany'. Churchill later commented that any such diversion 'would seriously have deranged the main strategy of the war in Europe', by which he meant bombing, of course.[81] At this point Cripps supported Wavell, warning Churchill that 'it is a matter of the utmost immediate urgency to decide whether we are to allow the Eastern Fleet to be wiped out from the air bit by bit and then India to fall in order to maintain nightly bombing of Germany'.[82]

Historians have long recognized that the effects of bombing fell far short of the claims made at the time. Even the 'thousand-bomber raids' which Harris put together in May and June 1942 relied on ideal conditions – a clear night and a full moon over Cologne – to inflict serious damage; the RAF could not find Essen in the smog, the Krupp armaments works were left unscathed, and so many bombs dropped elsewhere in the Ruhr valley that the Germans remained unaware that Essen had been the target.[83] The best that could be said was that bombing had some success in diverting German efforts from other fronts and operations. Even here, the force of Churchill's contention that it was 'the only way in our power of helping Russia' is weakened by the fact that what Russia needed were direct strikes at the German air force – which the RAF was incapable of delivering.[84] Under Harris, operational feasibility rather than strategic desirability determined bombing targets, with a natural preference for large cities.[85] Lord Cherwell, Churchill's scientific adviser, produced his own statistics ('partly to save the Prime Minister the trouble of making arithmetical calculations') showing that 'on the average, 1 ton of bombs dropped on a built-up area

80. Webster and Frankland, *Strategic Air Offensive*, i, p. 329.

81. Churchill, *Second World War*, iv, p. 165, which quotes Wavell, 12 April 1942.

82. RSC to Churchill, 13 April 1942, Churchill papers, CHAR 20/72 ff. 89–90.

83. Webster and Frankland, *Strategic Air Offensive*, i, pp. 407, 411, 415, 485–7.

84. Churchill, 16 April 1942, in Churchill, *Second World War*, iv, p. 165; cf. Webster and Frankland, *Strategic Air Offensive*, i, pp, 351–2, 480–81.

85. Webster and Frankland, *Strategic Air Offensive*, i, p. 345; cf. ibid., p. 464.

demolishes 20–40 dwellings and turns 100–200 people out of house and home'.[86]

The fallacious assumptions behind Cherwell's calculations are fully apparent in hindsight; but they were also discernible at the time. Another eminent scientist, Sir Henry Tizard, exposed many of them in a memorandum of 20 April 1942.[87] Thus at the very time that Cripps returned from India the argument about strategic bombing was in full spate, with an opportunity for a scientifically trained member of the War Cabinet to deploy well-found objections to a policy that denuded India of air cover while failing to assist the Red Army. The Harris policy, moreover, was a surrogate for a real second front in Europe – the more so once a second front was precluded by giving priority to North Africa, thus in turn enhancing the significance of the campaign of the Eighth Army in the western desert of Egypt around El Alamein.

The point is that, if Cripps had wished to mount a full-scale challenge to Churchill's conception of grand strategy, the opportunity was surely there between April and July 1942.

He did not seize it. Perhaps Cripps was impressed by the way that Bomber Harris 'laid on' the thousand-bomber raids at this juncture. They were a sort of Cripps Mission of the air, with failure to achieve the ostensible objective compensated by a subsequent propaganda triumph at home which impressed the Americans. Perhaps Cripps was inattentive to the sleight of hand whereby the commitment to 'Torch' eclipsed other options, notably a second front, and left bombing as the British priority.[88] At any rate, when Harris prepared a paper for the War Cabinet, for circulation at the end of August 1942, it was completely redrafted by Cripps himself, as he put it, 'in order to get it the serious consideration you desire and it deserves'.[89]

If we need evidence of Cripps's conversion to the Churchill–Harris strategy, it is here. What Harris had written was characteristically blunt. 'In

---

86. Cherwell minute, 30 March 1942, Webster and Frankland, *Strategic Air Offensive*, i, pp. 331–2, cf. ibid., p. 334.

87. ibid., pp. 333–5.

88. See Verrier, *Bomber Offensive*, pp. 98–9, which persuasively argues (against Webster and Frankland, *Strategic Air Offensive*, i, pp. 342–3) that Churchill in effect supported rather than rejected Harris's strategy. Churchill cleverly paid lip-service to the arguments for a change in priorities (much like Cripps's House of Commons speech in February 1942) but then endorsed bombing as 'second only' to an invasion – which he knew would not happen. See Churchill's memorandum, 21 July 1942, Churchill, *Second World War*, iv, pp. 781–4, contrast pars. 6 and 7.

89. RSC to Harris, 31 August 1942, copy.

the final issue this War will be decided by Air,' he began – a point reiterated throughout with what can truly be called an offensive spirit. 'The Generals and the Admirals, ours and the U.S., have with unvarying consistency and unanimity been proved to be wrong, and utterly wrong, in every prophecy and pronouncement they have made about the air during the past quarter of a century,' Harris concluded, spoiling his case, as usual, by unnecessarily antagonizing other forces.[90] What Cripps did was to take Harris's rebarbative and repetitive rant, straggling over four closely typed pages of foolscap, and reduce it to a forensic exposition of the case for air power in twenty-eight cogent paragraphs. Of these, Harris adopted twenty-seven as his own in the final draft. It was Cripps who now closed the possibility of an early second front, even if Germany were exhausted on the eastern front, by citing British failures in North Africa against Rommel's deployment of mechanized armament. 'In the last analysis therefore,' Cripps argued, 'the one way in which Germany can be defeated is by air attack.'[91]

Cripps thus pressed his gifts for advocacy to the verge of ventriloquism. 'I cannot thank you enough for the time and trouble you have given to expressing on paper the ideas which I put before you,' Harris told him; 'moreover in a manner which, with your experience and in your position, you deem to be the most likely to secure the desired result.'[92] He was properly appreciative of the fact that he now had the personal backing not only of the Prime Minister but also of the man widely regarded as his greatest rival.

If Cripps had become, in all essentials, the captive of the Churchillian approach to grand strategy, it was of his own volition. There is some piquancy in the fact that, as Leader of the House, it was Cripps's job to meet, divert and deflect post-Tobruk criticism of the Prime Minister (not always very effectively). When a no-confidence motion was put before the House in July 1942, Aneurin Bevan's barb against Churchill was 'that he fights debates like a war and the war like a debate'; and he might well have given a warning to his old political comrade, as Lloyd George had to Churchill in the Norway debate, not to act as an air-raid shelter for a beleaguered Prime Minister.[93]

Far from mounting an effective bid to replace Churchill, Cripps found himself increasingly marginalized during the summer of 1942. The diary

90. Harris, first draft, 28 August 1942; cf. Messenger, '*Bomber*' *Harris*, pp. 65, 83.
91. RSC draft, 31 August 1942, repeated Harris final draft, 3 September 1942.
92. Harris to RSC, 3 September 1942.
93. See Foot, *Bevan*, i, pp. 371–7.

kept by Barrington-Ward is a revealing source since Cripps used him as a confidant: partly to keep *The Times* on his side, no doubt, but mainly as a way of letting off steam. 'Most unhappy about the Govt.,' was the story in July. 'Winston has not seen him (except, I suppose, in Cabinet) for 7 or 8 weeks – the leader of the House! – and listens to nothing or no one but his immediate cronies, among whom the Beaver is prominent again.'[94]

Churchill, however, was right to suggest that, when facing the July vote of censure, which was defeated by 475 to 25, there had been 'not a whisper of intrigue' within the Government.[95] In fact, direct evidence that Cripps thought himself capable of overthrowing Churchill is lacking, though malicious Cripps-watchers, like Dalton, were ready to credit the anecdotes that reached them.[96] What Cripps is reliably documented as reiterating is that they might now be better off without Churchill; that the practicable alternative to him was Eden; that he (Cripps) could work as right-hand man to Eden; that Eden would not act himself to bring about such a change; that Beaverbrook could be vetoed as a War Cabinet member (so long as Cripps remained Leader of the House) but remained the evil genius; and that Churchill would probably carry on regardless, Cripps or no Cripps – with a mutual preference for the latter.[97]

The memorandum that the faithful Spry presented to Cripps at the beginning of September encapsulated the problem. 'You are the second or third person in the War Cabinet to whom this country looks for leadership', Spry bluntly stated. Since the public wanted Cripps 'to be a partner and not a rival of the Prime Minister', Spry argued against a resignation that would signal rivalry, if only because the ensuing political crisis would probably fail to produce the desired changes in the structure of government. 'In sum,' Spry concluded, 'cannot the changes you believe essential be achieved without the damage which a political crisis will cause?'[98] There is every sign that Cripps accepted this analysis. 'His complete objectivity about his own position was

94. Barrington-Ward diary, 13 July 1942.
95. Churchill, *Second World War*, iv, p. 351.
96. For example, Dalton diary, 24 August 1942, in Pimlott (ed.), *Dalton: War Diary*, pp. 479–80. For an interpretation premised on Cripps's disloyalty see Jefferys, *Churchill Coalition*, esp. pp. 99–105.
97. Elvin diary, 4 September 1942 and notes; Gordon Walker diary, 3 September and 1 October 1942, in Pearce (ed.), *Gordon Walker: political diaries*, pp. 110–16, and Gordon Walker to RSC, 13 October 1942; Eden diary, 2 October 1942, in Eden, *Reckoning*, pp. 342–3. Cripps alluded to his veto on Beaverbrook's re-entry to the War Cabinet in 1942, and Churchill implicitly accepted that this had been the case, in a subsequent exchange of letters, both dated 1 October 1943, Churchill papers, CHAR 20/95B, f. 230, and 20/94B, ff. 138–9.
98. Spry memorandum, 1 September 1942. Spry 45/4.

almost shocking,' noted his old political sympathizer, Lionel Elvin.[99] Cripps had neither the will to topple the Prime Minister nor the power to shackle him with the sort of 'thinking cabinet' that he thought indispensable and Churchill thought intolerable.

Cripps's growing resolve to resign was thus the product of despair rather than hope; and it was only thwarted by the exigencies of the war situation. By September, 'more and more left out', Cripps confided to Barrington-Ward that he felt he could go on no longer:

he could not decently resign if a catastrophe came. Better for him to go out sooner, even into possible oblivion: Winston's attitude to him is, he thinks (rightly), determined by his sense of the power factor. Cripps had value and bargaining strength when he joined the Govt. in the Spring. But he has not party support. Winston may feel he can safely unship him now ... Cripps is not, I think, without political ambition – in fact, I'm sure he isn't – but ambition of a praiseworthy kind and answerable to conscience.[100]

This nicely captures Cripps's feelings at the juncture when he decided that there was no future for him in the Government. Only a couple of days previously, as Leader of the House, he had upset fellow MPs by his 'priggish sermon', accusing them of preferring their lunch to the debate – a maladroit, gratuitous and unwise act, but hardly a sign that he was mobilizing supporters for a coup.[101] Cripps had summarized his criticism of the conduct of the war in a long memorandum, which the Prime Minister had been in no hurry to answer, least of all favourably. Cripps put his finger on the real difficulty between them in offering his resignation. 'As you have stated,' he conceded to the Prime Minister, 'if you are to run the war, you must run it in your own way.'[102] This was, almost word for word, what Churchill repeated when the matter was discussed on 30 September, with Cripps hauled from his bed for 'a firm but friendly talk' into the small hours.[103]

Hence the final showdown, the following night. Cripps had not gone to bed this time when the summons came to Downing Street. Attlee and Eden were also present, begging him to consider the effect of his resignation while

99. Elvin diary, 4 September 1942.

100. Barrington-Ward diary, 11 September 1942. Some of these entries are used in McLachlan, *In the Chair*, pp. 200–202.

101. Dalton diary, 8 September 1942, in Pimlott (ed.), *Dalton: War Diary*, p. 490; cf. Nicolson diary, 9 September 1942, in Nicolson (ed.), *Harold Nicolson: Diaries and Letters*, ii, p. 241.

102. RSC to Churchill, 21 September 1942, PRO, CAB 127/85.

103. Barrington-Ward diary, 1 October 1942.

'Torch' remained in doubt. Eden played an emollient role, not least in disabusing Churchill of the idea that this was a 'Machiavellian political plot'.[104] Churchill's suspicions were not unreasonable. His friend Lloyd George's maxim was that there are no friendships at the top, and Churchill had been at the top for a very long time. It should be remembered that he was both a veteran and a victim of the political crises that had besieged the British Government during the First World War; his depiction of the lengths to which the normally imperturbable Asquith had been driven – 'the convulsive struggles of a man of action and ambition at death-grips with events'[105] – provides an insight into the combination of bloody-mindedness and tactical adroitness he felt natural to the situation. When he had delicately hinted, in reply to Cripps's resignation letter, that 'no one knows better than you the controversial significance of all that you write', the Prime Minister had been shaping up for a bruising public encounter.[106]

What Churchill initially found hard to credit was that Cripps was not a usurper of Lloyd George's mettle. 'The trouble is,' Churchill had confided to an equally baffled Stalin, 'his chest is a cage in which two squirrels are at war, his conscience and his career.'[107] Attlee's chosen biographer likewise writes of Cripps's 'clear intention of replacing Churchill as prime minister' at this point.[108] It was, in fact, as difficult for politicians at the time as for subsequent political historians to accept that Cripps was not simply using the threat of resignation as a personal bid for power. It is telling that Asquith's daughter, Violet Bonham Carter – surely the first person who would have sniffed out a conspiracy on the Lloyd-Georgian paradigm – could remain personally loyal to both Churchill and the Crippses; just as it is piquant that Asquith's most elegant biographer should remark on Cripps's 'surprisingly good-tempered dispute with Churchill'.[109] Nicolson's *aperçu*, 'that Cripps, who in his way is a man of great innocence and narrow vision, might be seriously unaware that his resignation would shake Winston very severely', is fairly close the mark.[110]

This was hardly a *putsch* in the making. Even David Owen, the most

104. Eden diary, 1 October 1942, in Eden, *Reckoning*, p. 342.

105. Churchill, *Great Contemporaries*, p. 148.

106. Churchill to RSC, 22 September 1942, in Churchill, *Second World War*, iv, p. 500.

107. Presumably this was during Churchill's visit to Moscow in August 1942; quoted in Moran, *Churchill*, p. 94.

108. Harris, *Attlee*, p. 206.

109. Jenkins, 'Stafford Cripps', p. 97; and see Bonham Carter letters to IC, esp. 27 November 1942.

110. Nicolson diary, 9 September 1942, in Nicolson (ed.), *Harold Nicolson: Diaries and Letters*, ii, p. 241.

combative member of the Crippery, did not report his boss's views in such terms: 'Cripps has no intention of leading a campaign against the P.M. but simply wants to dissociate himself from the P.M.'s methods of running the war. He agrees that if the P.M. is to run the war he must do it in his own way but he doesn't want to be official apologist – as he was today – for policies to which he is opposed.'[111] Thus, when he faced Churchill on 1–2 October, Cripps proved amenable to the suggestion that he might take another official post, outside the War Cabinet, on an administrative basis, perhaps as head of a mission to the USA or – a more attractive option – at the Ministry of Aircraft Production (MAP).

Moreover, Cripps was ready to postpone his resignation. This was a course urged on him by Eden, as the latter recorded in his diary: 'I told him that national interest was the only thing he could consider, that this was not the moment to rock the boat. Later, if "Torch" failed, we were all sunk, if it succeeded, he was free to act as he wished.'[112] That such a proposition could have been advanced by a colleague who knew him well can be seen as a remarkable testimony to Cripps's impressive high-mindedness, to his breathtaking unworldliness, and to his astounding political naivety.

Tails, Cripps would lose, along with the rest of the War Cabinet; heads, the Prime Minister would win anyway – and could then dispense with any awkward critic. This somewhat asymmetrical bargain naturally won Churchill's respect for Cripps's patriotism if not for his political trenchancy. Their final meeting was the acme of cordiality.

Very friendly talk. Winston said he now saw it was a genuine personal difficulty and not the desire for a political coup which actuated Cripps. 'You are an honest man. If you had been Ll.G. you would have resigned on the issue of a "second front".'[113]

This account is admittedly at second hand, from Cripps via Barrington-Ward. Churchill's version (at third hand) is more graphic, but compatible: 'I ordered him to remain silent until the battle had been fought and won. He gave me his word. Of course, he will have to go.'[114]

At virtually every level, Churchill had grasped the politics of the confrontation with a shrewdness and robustness that Cripps could not match. Events duly unfolded so as to vindicate the Prime Minister's self-confidence.

111. Cairncross diary, 2 October 1942, copy in Cripps papers. 'David Owen drew me aside and we went for a walk to Westminster while he told me of the threatened political crisis,' wrote Cairncross, a trusted sympathizer who later worked under Cripps at MAP.
112. Eden diary, 1 October 1942, in Eden, *Reckoning*, p. 343.
113. Barrington-Ward diary, 2 October 1942. 114. Davenport, *Memoirs*, p. 139.

A successful outcome in North Africa was hardly in serious doubt by this stage. A week before he accepted Cripps's deferred resignation, Churchill was anticipating 'a victorious battle' at El Alamein.[115] The significance of these operations, moreover, was to be seized upon by British propaganda so as create an impact wholly disproportionate to the military achievement.

This too was a form of quasi-war. 'What the public really want is victory,' Spry had advised his master;[116] but by the time victory came Cripps was, through his own actions, in no position to benefit from it personally. In early November, news of the success of 'Torch' came within days of that of the victory under Montgomery at El Alamein. In the House of Commons the Lord Privy Seal associated himself with the many generous tributes to the Prime Minister's 'long and arduous and, indeed, brilliant contribution to our victories'. Indeed, Cripps went beyond anything he need have said in claiming that, contrary to criticisms that had earlier been aired, El Alamein 'has now demonstrated to the country and the House that the inactivity was only apparent and that the long and trying months of waiting through the summer were, in fact, months of most active preparation, in which both we and our American Allies were very fully engaged'.[117]

Compared with what was happening on the eastern front, where the German army was fought to a standstill by the Russians at Stalingrad, El Alamein was a sideshow in the World War. Even from a British imperial strategic standpoint, it hardly had the significance of the halting of the Japanese advance in Burma by the monsoon, or the final removal of the threat of invasion to India by the American naval victory at Midway in the Pacific. But El Alamein was the first great victory that the British could claim after three years of hostilities and a manifest exoneration of Churchill's own North African strategy. The fact that this was also Cripps's preferred strategy was neither here nor there. Approval of the Government's conduct of the war leapt from 41 per cent in September to 75 per cent in November; and while Churchill's approval rating climbed to over 90 per cent, Cripps's declined to 51 per cent.[118] What brute events showed was that, with all his faults, Churchill should be left to run the war in his own way.

Churchill hailed El Alamein as 'the end of the beginning', but for Cripps's wartime career, it was more speedily terminal. 'Winston has profited by the victories to revive the issue raised by Cripps in the October correspondence,'

115. Churchill to Alexander, 25 September 1942, in Howard, *Grand Strategy*, p. 67
116. Spry memorandum, 14 July 1942.
117. 5 HC Debs., vol. 385, col. 452 (18 November 1942).
118. Fielding, 'Second World War', Table 1, p. 43.

Barrington-Ward noted on 20 November. 'Very friendly, of course, but it comes to this: that Cripps must either leave the War Cabinet and take the Ministry of Aircraft Production or resign.'[119] Resignation at this moment would have been truly pointless, whereas the appropriateness of Cripps's technocratic skills for managing a military supply department had been canvassed ever since his return from Moscow.

Cripps's nine months in the War Cabinet thus ended with demotion but not open discord. Though at the time Bevan called it 'political assassination', Michael Foot seems nearer the mark in preferring 'anaesthetization'.[120] That Cripps was still a major public figure was attested by his nomination by students of Aberdeen University for its honorific Rectorship – an election in which the other two high-profile candidates, who both withdrew in Cripps's favour, were the left-of-centre author J. B. Priestley and the glamorous sailor Lord Louis Mountbatten.

Cordiality was the keynote, now that the Prime Minister could call the shots. Cripps reciprocated, sending Churchill birthday greetings a week after the reconstruction of the Government: 'However much we may differ in outlook on certain matters, it has been a great joy to me to witness your tireless work for victory.'[121] The evidence is that, at a personal level, there was more magnanimity than malice in their subsequent wartime relations. The Prime Minister repeatedly showed himself solicitous that the demands of MAP should not induce overwork by its conscientious minister. Indeed, he later described Cripps's behaviour to his biographer Estorick as 'a magnificent act of patriotism and loyalty' and, in *The Second World War*, reiterated that Cripps's 'patriotism ruled his conduct' – hardly the barbed or vitriolic comments he would have reserved for a rival who had tried and failed to oust him.[122]

At the time, the bland official announcement of the Government reconstruction left the public bemused. Cripps was replaced in the War Cabinet by Herbert Morrison and as Leader of the House by Eden, thus strengthening the grip of party hierarchy within the Coalition. Cripps's move was the big news, received with some bafflement by the public. 'I frankly don't understand,' was one Mass-Observation response. 'Cripps has always been a square peg in a round hole it seems.'[123] Cripps himself was of much the same mind. 'I never seem able to team up with anyone,' he privately

119. Barrington-Ward diary, 20 November 1942.   120. Foot, *Bevan*, i, pp. 401–2.
121. RSC to Churchill, 29 November 1942, in Gilbert, *Churchill*, vii, p. 267.
122. See Churchill papers, CHUR, for MAP letters; Estorick, pp. 317–18. Churchill, *Second World War*, iv, p. 501.
123. 'Sir Stafford Cripps', 7 December 1942, Mass-Observation Archive, FR 1524.

admitted.[124] Unsurprisingly, Dalton reacted with unconcealed relish to his colleague's demise. 'Nearly all Cripps's "mystique" is now gone, and he has missed all his chances – never really very good – of resigning with credit,' he wrote. 'He has, I think, been very skilfully played by the P.M.'[125]

It is undeniable that Cripps paid a heavy price for pitting himself against Churchill's superior insight into both war strategy and political tactics. Throughout their relationship as ministers in 1942, their common commitment to securing victory in the war had masked a tension over both means and ends. Cripps's vision of a people's war – rather than an imperialist war – left Churchill unmoved, as he used his hour of triumph to make clear. On 10 November Churchill proclaimed his own unrepentant and provocative statement of war aims: 'I have not become the King's First Minister in order to preside over the liquidation of the British Empire.'[126]

It immediately became a widely quoted remark, not least in India. Cripps was not the only minister to find this speech embarrassing; but he was the most prominent, given his known views; and it was a sharp signal of his own declining influence.[127] It was, too, a propaganda gift in the continuing recriminations over the Cripps Mission. Louis Fischer duly quoted it as his exit line in his controversy with Graham Spry, adding only: 'That is really why Cripps failed.'[128] If the tone was repugnant to Cripps, however, the substance of the policy that the Churchill Government followed in India was accepted by him, if only because he saw little prospect of a successful alternative. 'Only practical aim is to split Congress,' was his private view. 'No other way of getting any Indian settlement.'[129] He was to remain a member of the India Committee until the end of the Coalition Government in 1945, seeking to temper the erratic atavistic impulses of the Prime Minister while, rather to their mutual surprise, discovering common ground with Amery as Secretary of State. Together they watched for any opportunity to develop a more constructive policy.

Once he was outside Churchill's War Cabinet, Cripps's position became

124. Gordon Walker diary, 1 October 1942, in Pearce (ed.), *Gordon Walker: political diaries*, p. 116.
125. Dalton diary, 21–22 November 1942, in Pimlott (ed.), *Dalton: War Diary*, p. 522; cf. ibid., 8 November 1942, p. 515. Pimlott, *Dalton*, p. 371, implies an unwarrantably harsh view of Cripps's motives in simply stating that he did not resign earlier, without indicating why he was persuaded not to do so.
126. Gilbert, *Churchill*, vii, p. 254.
127. cf. Amery to RSC, 18 November 1942, PRO, CAB 127/80.
128. Fischer, *Nation*, 5 December 1942.
129. Gordon Walker diary, 1 October 1942, in Pearce (ed.), *Gordon Walker: political diaries*, p. 113.

less conspicuous. Nehru, of course, was now leading an even more incon-
spicuous life, following the round-up of the Congress leadership for their
support of 'Quit India'. In his prison diary Nehru expostulated, after hearing
of Churchill's non-liquidation doctrine: 'How can even Stafford Cripps
bow down to this?'[130] Further reflection simply confirmed his sense of
disillusionment. 'Stafford Cripps?' he wrote in 1943. 'A total failure – How
badly he came out of last year's negotiations and after.'[131]

From the point of view of personal advantage, Cripps came badly out of
almost everything he touched in 1942. One effect of the Cripps Mission was to
lose its author some old friendships in India, when the tragedy in Delhi was
succeeded by a propaganda triumph in the West. It was not, however, a triumph
that redounded to his own benefit, however much it helped the war effort.

The chief beneficiary, here as elsewhere, turned out to be Winston
Churchill, to whose domination of wartime politics Cripps provided the only
plausible challenge. Theirs was a working partnership that never worked. It
was a clash of temperament and style between two strong personalities,
each deriding the methods characteristic of the other. Yet if Cripps could
not work with Churchill, he was finally not prepared to work against him.
This was a cause as much as an effect of Cripps's failure to mobilize support,
either at a popular level, or through party support, or within the governing
elite. The Lord Privy Seal, in his tiresome way, might present the Prime
Minister with administrative blueprints; but if Churchill doggedly insisted
on his own idiosyncratic procedures, the verdict would rest with ultimate
military success, in which his confidence turned out not to be misplaced.

As a threat to the Prime Minister, Cripps was much overrated, not only
by the Left and his own cronies but by paranoid rivals too. The fact is that
he lacked not only political finesse but a sufficiently distinctive agenda.
There was a large area of substantive agreement with Churchill – not least
on resistance to a second front in Europe, on readiness for a ruthless
bombing campaign and on support for a North African strategy (which
brought the victory that Churchill needed). Above all, Cripps rallied to
Churchill on crucial, simple issues that really mattered in 1942: determination to wage war on a world scale, at all costs; the consequent need to
sustain national unity, at any price; a projection of the British case to
American opinion, to sustain the Grand Alliance. All of this had an important impact on wartime politics in Britain – and in India too, as Cripps was
never allowed to forget.

130. Nehru diary, 13 November 1942, in Gopal (ed.), *Nehru: Selected Works*, xii, p. 29.
131. Nehru diary, 17 December 1943, in Gopal (ed.), *Nehru: Selected Works*, xiii, p. 311.

ENTR'ACTE
1943–5

Bomber Cripps

Cripps's period as Minister of Aircraft Production, from 22 November 1942 until 23 May 1945, when the wartime Coalition ended, saw the realization of his talents as an executive minister. The fascination with aircraft that he had displayed as a twenty-year-old amateur engineer, the administrative capacity that he had applied to munitions production during the First World War, the priority of sustaining morale on war work that he had enjoined on his return from Russia – all these informed Cripps's role at MAP.

The job of MAP was to supply the RAF, which in turn provided the chief means of hitting Germany until a second front could be opened. Cripps took an uncompromising view on the need to intensify the Allied offensive through strategic bombing. 'The more we and our American and Russian allies can destroy from the air the industrial and transport facilities of the Axis, the weaker will become their resistance,' he declared in a peak-time BBC broadcast. 'The heavier our air attack, the lighter will be the total of our casualties.'[1] It might be thought that this was what a minister in his position had to say in public; it has often been suggested that in private Cripps expressed or encouraged doubts about this policy.

The Cripps papers show that, in fact, he had put the point even more vehemently behind closed doors. As has been seen, he supported Bomber Harris's strategy: more than that, Cripps also honed his rhetoric. In 1942 Harris had wanted to tell the War Cabinet: 'Either we bomb Germany "soft" and staggering or we lose the war.' What Cripps had helpfully advised him to say instead was that 'it would be possible in the next few months to raze substantially to the ground 30–40 of the principal German cities, and it is suggested that the effect upon German morale and German production

1. Broadcast after the 9 o'clock news, 9 July 1943.

of doing so would be fatal'.[2] In supporting this strategy, Cripps spoke not only for Harris but for most British people at the time. Opinion polls showed serious opposition to strategic bombing at less than 10 per cent.[3] Nor was the Minister of Aircraft Production inhibited by his Christian scruples.

Indeed, the phrase 'God is my co-pilot' came to be associated with Cripps. This was the title of a newsworthy book (which, characteristically, he had not read) by Robert Lee Scott, a pilot in Bomber Command. Prompted by it, Cripps gave attention to the moral dilemma in waging war by admittedly terrible means against an incontrovertibly evil menace. Repudiating 'an eye for an eye and a tooth for a tooth' as the relic of a 'nationalist religion', he none the less recognized a continuity between the Old and New Testaments through an everyday relationship of God to man; and it followed that 'God is to be regarded as our co-worker in everything that we do'.[4] Though the tenor of Cripps's remarks was apparently insufficiently bloodthirsty for some senior officers in Bomber Command, it surely lived up to the conventional Old Testament standard. Consistent with his lifelong belief that Christianity was a seven-day-a-week religion, he stopped short only of claiming God's active sanction. 'To say therefore that he is the co-pilot of a bomber is not to suggest that he approves of bombing,' he concluded; 'it is only to express the essential Christian belief that God is omnipresent and is profoundly concerned with our every thought and action.'[5]

Cripps certainly needed all the co-workers he could get. He was responsible for a huge industry, employing over a million and a half workers, directly or indirectly. Among the private firms that engaged in massive expansion was the Bristol Aeroplane Company at Filton, many of whose workers lived and voted in Bristol East – as Cripps showed himself well aware, not least in subsequently resisting a rapid rundown of aircraft factories in the closing stages of the war.[6]

Assessing British aircraft production during the Second World War is by

2. Harris first draft, 28 August 1942; RSC draft, 31 August 1942, repeated Harris final draft, 3 September 1942.
3. Cantril (ed.), *Public Opinion*, p. 1069.
4. 'God is my co-pilot', address to Bomber Command, 8 December 1944, p. 21; reprinted in Cripps, *Towards Christian Democracy*, pp. 82–90.
5. 'God is my co-pilot', address to Bomber Command, 8 December 1944, p. 21. See Collins, *Faith under Fire*, p. 89, for an account (somewhat improved in retrospect?) of the reception of Cripps's address at High Wycombe, with him routing opposition from senior officers present.
6. cf. Edgerton, *England and the Aeroplane*, p. 72; Dalton diary, 14 September 1943, in Pimlott (ed.), *Dalton: War Diary*, p. 638. For a good account of Cripps at MAP see Burgess, *Cripps*, ch. 14.

no means easy. In the fourth quarter of 1942, when Cripps took over, monthly output for the first time exceeded 2,000 aircraft and never subsequently fell below this figure until the end of 1944, when, with British troops at last fighting on the ground in northern Europe, resources were transferred elsewhere.[7]

Early post-war histories lauded a great achievement. More recently, however, iconoclastic claims that British productivity was far outstripped by that in the USA, and was even markedly inferior to that achieved in Germany, have received much attention, though also effective rebuttal.[8] Of course it is true that British productivity was held back by relatively small production runs, especially in comparison with the USA, as Cripps was acutely conscious. Moreover, every modification designed to increase the efficiency of the product entailed at least a temporary decrease in the efficiency of production through the disruption caused.[9] Often, then, the best was the enemy of the good under war conditions.

Cripps's task was actually to maximize production itself – in short order. The priority here, by 1942, was production of bombers. The first heavy bomber was only delivered in May 1940; monthly production was still only in double figures until March 1942. Yet Churchill regarded bombers as crucial to British strategy, and Cripps agreed. In November 1942, when Cripps went to MAP, 220 heavy bombers were produced. The monthly figures subsequently averaged 385 throughout 1943 and 458 throughout 1944.[10] The rate of production, where it mattered, was thus doubled under Cripps.

These figures, however, fell well short of the official target. A major reason for this was that, since the days when Beaverbrook had been at MAP – anarchically improvising his way through the Battle of Britain – the production target had been set at progressively fantastic levels. This had been done deliberately, on the principle of the carrot, supposing that, even if it could never be reached, it would spur on production. Cripps took the opposite view. So did Sir Wilfrid Freeman, who had returned to MAP as its new chief executive in October 1942, having experienced his own

7. Postan, *British War Production*, Table 41, p. 310, and App. 4, p. 485.
8. See Barnett, *Audit of War*, p. 146. Barnett's statistics turn out to be technically inaccurate and in any case seek to measure productivity by structure-weight – a perverse indicator of efficiency for machines where lightness was at a premium. See Edgerton, *England and the Aeroplane*, pp. 79–81; *idem*, 'The prophet militant and industrial', pp. 373–4.
9. Cairncross, 'How British aircraft production was planned in the Second World War', pp. 352–3.
10. Calculated from Postan, *War Production*, App. 4, p. 485; cf. ibid., pp. 125–6.

frustrations in previously working under Beaverbrook. Their objection to the carrot was partly psychological; as Cripps put it, 'if dangled too long it loses its effect altogether'.[11] It was, moreover, the negation of planning in that an unachievable target misallocated resources that were pre-empted but not used. Waste thus entailed inefficiency. 'Far from exceeding its scheduled programme,' Freeman wrote, 'each firm will fail.'[12] A 'realistic' programme was put into place in January 1943 and subsequently subjected to conservative revisions. None of this made as uplifting a story as the one that Beaverbrook had told.

The record of Cripps's performance at MAP is further complicated by the attendant polemics, politics and personalities. The new minister's regime was inevitably contrasted with that of his legendary predecessor (whose return to the Government in October 1943 Cripps was now unable to block); and the legend was equally inevitably burnished in the pages of Beaverbrook's newspapers. Press criticism, moreover, re-acquired a sharper edge as the party truce began to fray. Cripps engaged upon a taxing round of factory visits, clocking up more than a hundred in his first seven months in office, at a rate of one every two days, weekends included. Numerous photographs show Stafford, with Isobel usually at his side, striding through vast aircraft factories or addressing the workers from makeshift podiums. 'The feeling of Partnership is a very great inspiration,' ran a typical exhortation.[13] These visits may not have been advertised in advance but they were certainly well publicized after they had taken place. One complaint by a Tory MP alleged that workers 'had been "stood off" because of a "secret" visit by Sir Stafford Cripps the next day'.[14]

Cripps's major initiative concerned Joint Production Consultative Committees (JPCC). These were to be set up in factories responsible to MAP, with representation from management and unions. Cripps made a point of sitting in on their meetings during his factory visits and heard for himself how they were regarded, as their minutes show: 'Mrs Mills said that very often she felt out of her depth when dealing with such matters as those placed before this Committee, but Sir Stafford said that he was very pleased to know that a woman had been elected as this was the weakness with many

11. RSC minute, 12 December 1942, in Postan, *British War Production*, p. 306.

12. Freeman in February 1943, in Furse, *Freeman*, p. 267; cf. Cairncross, 'How British aircraft production was planned in the Second World War', pp. 348–9.

13. Bristol Aeroplane Company, notes on visit of Sir Stafford and Lady Cripps, speech in the south canteen, Banwell aircraft factory, 7 August 1943.

14. J. H. Davies, Conservative MP for Heywood and Radcliffe, *Liverpool Evening Express*, 28 June 1943.

other such Committees.'[15] When one employees' representative stated that 'the only fault with the Committee was that often they met but found nothing whatever to discuss', Cripps's reply, that 'this was an extremely good fault', may have been thought rather evasive.[16] He fielded requests for overtime to be worked on Sundays by briskly reminding the JPCC that 'double time was not paid as an incentive to the employees to work on Sunday, but rather as deterrent to the employer'.[17]

Cripps's own priority was clearly to increase production by eliminating friction, imposing reciprocal obligations on both sides of industry. 'A democracy at war must have the efficiency of a disciplined machine within a living body,' he proclaimed; and, while acknowledging the existence of grievances, he said that 'none of these to-day justify a strike in the factories any more than they would justify a mutiny in a ship or at the front'.[18] But what Cripps demanded of the employers was, of course, no less exacting.

In general, and increasingly, Cripps's critics were on the right, his allies on the left. In an era when socialism was identified with statist solutions, the command economy of wartime was seized upon as a model for the future rather than simply as a present expedient. Cripps argued that the war had 'developed for us many mechanisms for political and economic co-operation, many controls and much machinery of planning', which could be quickly and easily adapted to the needs of peace.[19] His naive enthusiasm for *dirigiste* methods – 'there's no limit in theory, is there,' he asked, 'to central planning?' – immediately struck his officials.[20] One of them, the economist Alec Cairncross, himself educated in the concepts of risk and uncertainty, found that the new minister was still very much the physical scientist, making determinate calculations: 'Cripps thought that there was a factor that could be applied and that whatever the route by which one arrived at the factor it was fixed and communicable.'[21]

It is easy to see, therefore, how Cripps manifested a confidence in planning that in turn carried a political freight. In March 1943 there was controversy when he used his powers under Defence Regulation 78 against the Belfast

15. Bristol Aeroplane Company, notes on visit of Sir Stafford and Lady Cripps, Rodney works JPCC, 7 August 1943.
16. ibid., Weston aircraft factory JPCC, 7 August 1943.
17. ibid., Rodney works JPCC, 7 August 1943.
18. RSC speech at Hull, *Morning Advertiser*, 5 April 1943.
19. *Shall the Spell be Broken?*, p. 15.
20. Cairncross diary, 10 December 1942, copy in Cripps papers.
21. ibid., and see Toye, *The Labour Party and the Planned Economy*, ch. 5, which offers a lucid analysis of Cripps's changing views on planning.

firm of Short Brothers. Since the firm refused to switch production from its own unsatisfactory Stirling bomber to Avro's Lancaster, the most successful heavy bomber of the war, it was taken into public ownership.[22] The *Daily Mirror*, sympathetic to Labour, hailed this move as 'an unexpected trump card played by Sir Stafford in a battle with industrialists and Tory MPs which has been proceeding behind the scenes for some weeks'.[23] Conversely, the Conservative *Daily Telegraph* struck a monitory note: 'A precedent has in fact been established by the case of Short Brothers for socialising legitimate private enterprise by the back door.'[24] Beaverbrook's *Evening Standard* contented itself with a teasing parliamentary report. 'Sir Stafford Cripps is having a new experience. He is being cheered by the Socialists, who once expelled him from their party.'[25]

Like it or not, Cripps found that his policies became politically charged, especially since he himself projected them in a high-profile way. In the rapidly expanded aircraft industry, with its commensurate increase in trade-union membership, the shop stewards' movement was dominated by Communists. It may have been only prudent for a minister concerned with raising production to signal strong support for aid to Russia. Just as Isobel Cripps's United Aid to China Fund attracted much publicity, so Stafford's appearances at events like the Red Army Parade in Sheffield in February 1943 were prominently reported.[26] The Communists, to be sure, kept their distance from him; for example, the *Daily Worker* prominently reported allegations by shop stewards of 'window-dressing' (allegedly giving an appearance of unusual activity during a Cripps visit).[27] Still, the fact that Cripps, in speeches in aircraft factory canteens, addressed the workers as 'comrades' was bound to provoke comment.[28]

It was this brand of ideological octane that fuelled an early conflagration within MAP. In Freeman, Cripps found an outstandingly capable administrator whose career as a senior RAF officer had been blighted by the personal scandal of his divorce. There was a volatile tension between Freeman's overwrought self-awareness and his upright, uptight principles as a former

22. Edgerton, *England and the Aeroplane*, pp. 72–3, 78–9.
23. Political correspondent, *Daily Mirror*, 24 March 1943.
24. Leader, *Daily Telegraph*, 1 April 1943.   25. *Evening Standard*, 31 March 1943.
26. *Sheffield Telegraph and Independent*, 22 February 1943.
27. *Daily Worker*, 25 October 1943.
28. For example *Daily Mirror*, 11 February 1943, *Evening Standard*, 24 March 1943; cf. Maurice Edelman, 'Cripps visits an aircraft factory', *Picture Post*, 17 April 1943, and Bristol Aeroplane Company, notes on visit of Sir Stafford and Lady Cripps, speech in the Filton aircraft factory canteen, 9 August 1943.

serving officer, worried about his minister's apparent political agenda. 'I'm fundamentally opposed to much of what he is doing and it's obvious that as his chief executive I either work for him or against him,' Freeman told his new wife. 'My conscience will not let me work with him neither, from a different angle, allow me to work against him behind his back.'[29]

In the middle of February 1943 Cripps and Freeman thus found themselves at loggerheads. What is really significant is how speedily this potential crisis was defused. Freeman's account of the interview at which he had intended to offer his resignation is worth quoting to show how they became reconciled.

I had an hour with the Minister this evening and I have promised to hold my hand for 24 hours. In a nutshell he says he would sooner go than I should. If he goes he will do so as a martyr and Labour will kick up hell and I told him so. He told me that if I went the effect was likely to be worse and that his [Cripps's] position would become impossible.

His point of view is that the newspapers egged on by Beaverbrook are purposely misrepresenting him and of course that's true.[30]

Within a matter of days, Freeman was conceding that 'in so many ways he is easily the best Minister I've ever had'.[31]

Cripps's remarkable ability, through personal contact, to win the confidence of initially sceptical subordinates is testified time and again. One of his later Treasury officials stated that 'until he had known Stafford he had not realized what management and leadership of a Department could be'.[32] With Freeman, we can see that Cripps succeeded partly through his own disarming emollience and charm in private conversation; partly through his ability to inspire a mutual recognition of a common duty going beyond mere public platitudes; partly through his unpretentious display of an unrivalled grasp of the actual business in hand – and partly through opportunely invoking the name of a mutual antagonist. This latter ploy shows Cripps displaying a political adroitness that he had belatedly learnt on the job, in high office, rather than through an apprenticeship. Hardly an easy man to please, Freeman came to appreciate working – or overworking – for Cripps, whom he plied with thanks for 'your inspiration, your unfailing support and your generous consideration for a somewhat difficult and troublesome

29. Freeman to E. Freeman, 12 February 1943, copies courtesy of A. W. Furse.
30. ibid.   31. Freeman to E. Freeman, 15 February 1943.
32. Quoted (in the third person) in Schuster, 'Richard Stafford Cripps', p. 22.

subordinate'.[33] From unpromising beginnings, then, this blossomed into a uniquely rewarding experience for Freeman. He told Isobel Cripps 'that of all the men that I have worked for only Stafford really counted. The rest seemed puny compared to him.'[34]

Cripps and consensus

The end of the beginning of the war spelt the beginning of the end for the Coalition. Churchill was henceforth unchallenged in his direction of the war; conversely, his Government was increasingly challenged over its post-war plans. The publication of the Beveridge Report on social security at the end of 1942 would, in any event, have been likely to provoke political differences over the scale, kind and priority of post-war commitments to build what was coming to be called a 'welfare state': what El Alamein did was to relieve tension about military strategy and thus create the space for political controversy about reconstruction, for which the Beveridge Plan became both the blueprint and the symbol. Cripps had already signalled his restiveness over the Government's negative response here, though, as with the second front, he made no move to exploit a potentially popular issue for his own ends. A cartoon by Low showed Beveridge wheeling his plans through a door marked 'Inner Cabinet, where things are decided', while Cripps briskly walked out of it. Two black-coated figures labelled 'Anti-Plan' watch; one makes the worried comment, 'Look what's going in!', while the other responds with a broad smile, 'But look who's coming out!'[35]

An explicit guide to Cripps's thinking about post-war reconstruction is provided by his rectorial address at Aberdeen University, published under the title *Shall the Spell be Broken?* (1943) Would the disappointment of wartime hopes for a better world – what Churchill had, after the First World War, called the 'Broken Spell' – yet again take place? Cripps sharply repudiated cynical comments that an unspecified 'they' would never implement promises for a new Britain, saying that this was 'not the language of democracy, or even of the class struggle!'[36] Unusual among his writings for its reflective nature and its range of literary references, the address looked

---

33. Freeman to RSC, 17 March 1945. As he admitted in another letter, 'in most ways I am a difficult person to work with'. Freeman to RSC, Christmas Day 1944.
34. Freeman to IC, 27 May 1952.
35. *Manchester Guardian*, 25 November 1942; reproduced in Pimlott (ed.), *Dalton: War Diary*, p. 523.
36. *Shall the Spell be Broken?*, p. 4.

to history for a more sophisticated reading of the situation. 'Do not allow others to lead you astray by facile explanations dealing with the deceitfulness of politicians or the trickery of the ruling class,' Cripps warned. 'The problem is not as simple as that.'[37] Before the war, of course, this had been exactly his own line against the sham of bourgeois democracy.

With hindsight, Cripps already emerges as a key figure in the forging of a post-war political consensus, identified with the doctrines of Beveridge and Keynes.[38] The political process through which this came about, however, was hardly that which he envisaged at the time, since Cripps looked for a consensus achieved directly through intra-party agreement, not a consensus produced indirectly as the result of party competition. When he looked back to the example of the First World War, claiming that it had been 'vital that all the progressive forces should come together on a common platform to defeat reaction', he immediately added, by way of warning, that 'their ideological differences prevented them from securing common action'.[39] The implication here is inescapably that Cripps's notion of a progressive consensus crossed party lines and therefore could best be mobilized through cross-party cooperation – just as he had argued in his pre-war popular front days.

There was a clear religious dimension to this hope of mobilizing the forces of good against evil. 'As I view religion,' Cripps affirmed from the pulpit of St Martin-in-the-Fields, 'it is as much concerned with the insult offered by the slums to God and to man as it is with the praise of God in the churches and chapels.'[40] He took literally the rhetoric of the war propaganda that he had himself helped to generate. 'Twice we have vindicated with enormous effort and great losses amongst our people the principles upon which we believe world society must be built,' he claimed later. The principles themselves were 'the simple expression of the most profound religious beliefs in which we have been brought up'; their implementation was a question of 'moral and spiritual force'.[41]

In his last days in the War Cabinet, Cripps had made a widely reported plea in the Commons for national solidarity. While warning the Left that

37. ibid., p. 12.
38. The seminal study of this process remains Addison, *Road to 1945*. Where Brooke, *Labour's War*, justifiably modifies this account is through his lucid exploration of a process of negotiation in which Labour's own distinctive ideas survived. A lot depends on whether 'post-war consensus' simply means agreement – or agreement to differ within given (and newly established) parameters.
39. *Shall the Spell be Broken?*, p. 13.   40. *News Chronicle*, 14 November 1942.
41. Notes for speech at Gresford, 7 August 1948.

they 'must hold themselves back for the purposes of maintaining unity', he correspondingly asked the Right 'to hurry their steps forward in some degree'. This he commended as 'a democratic way of solving that problem', via a compromise, with 'the one side retarding their advance, and the other quickening their steps, so that the two may march abreast'.[42] The difficulty of maintaining such a delicate balance is shown by the fact that some Conservatives swiftly seized on a supposed 'Cripps rule', whereby no controversial legislation should be introduced in wartime.[43] Cripps's own emphasis was on the dynamism of a process that the progressive forces might capture, and thus 'travel a very considerable way along the road of post-war reconstruction, thereby ensuring a greater degree of stability in the period immediately following the armistice'.[44]

What shines through is his overriding commitment to democracy and his faith in the growing political maturity of the electorate. 'We now approach once again one of those critical periods of hope which occur in every great war, as the prospect of ultimate victory begins to loom on the horizon,' he affirmed.[45] There were thus two lessons to learn from past experience, especially that of the First World War. 'The progressive forces failed to strike while the iron was hot,' he warned. 'The time to get agreement on post-war plans is during the war when the atmosphere of cooperation is strong.' Secondly, 'they underestimated the support they would win from the people – the common men and women of the country – for a bold programme of change'.[46]

Not for the first time, Cripps overestimated the prospects for constructive political cooperation among the likeminded, and underestimated the resistance generated by party loyalties. He remained famously a man of no party. So long as hostilities continued, the war allowed Cripps to hold high ministerial office while maintaining his nominal independence – for longer than would otherwise have been the case. This was lucky for him since it left him free to drift back to the Labour Party in his own time.

Cripps was right to think that the winter of 1942–3 represented a moment of polarization around the issue of post-war reconstruction. He was wrong, however, to think that this would precipitate a new kind of politics (or substitute for politics). True, there was more talk of social Christianity, but this fed into existing debates and processes. Reconstruction did not produce

42. 5 HC Debs., vol. 385, col. 461 (18 November 1942); *Daily Mail*, 20 November 1942.
43. *Daily Herald*, 11 February 1943, admonishing Cripps for giving the *Sunday Times* ground for criticizing the Catering Wages Bill.
44. 5 HC Debs., vol. 385, col. 461 (18 November 1942).
45. *Shall the Spell be Broken?*, p. 12.   46. ibid., p. 13.

27. Austerity lunch in the staff canteen, 1947.

28. Not everyone's cup of tea: at the Treasury, 1949.

29. *(Left)* No intention of devaluing the pound, July 1949.

30. *(Below)* Into the television age.

31. *(Right)* Cripps arrives at 11 Downing Street, 1947.

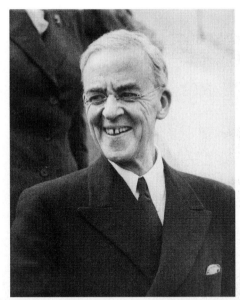

32. False dawn: return from Switzerland, August 1949.

33. Washington, DC, September, 1949: with Ernest Bevin and Sir Oliver Franks, British ambassador (at back).

34. Devaluation crisis, 1949: Cripps leads Harold Wilson into a cabinet meeting.

35. Last victory: after the poll in Bristol, General Election of February 1950.

36. Last budget: Isobel and Stafford outside 11 Downing Street, April 1950.

37. The strain shows, May 1950.

38. The invalid: flanked by Isobel and Peggy Cripps in Zurich, August 1951.

39. Peggy's marriage to Joe Appiah in 1952, with support from Isobel Cripps (left)
and John Cripps (right).

a stark new fissure between progressives and reactionaries but served to reanimate an old party conflict (essentially between Labour and Conservative).

In practice, Cripps usually cooperated with Labour ministers on post-war planning issues. Not only did he rekindle the cordiality between himself and Attlee and Morrison that they had enjoyed in the early 1930s, he also made some inroads on the prejudice against him held by Dalton – and also Bevin – as a result of Cripps's pre-war postures and gestures. (One difficulty with Bevin, responsible for finding manpower as Minister of Labour, stemmed from MAP's claims for skilled labour; once this problem eased, by 1944, so did the conflict between the two ministers.)[47] Conversely, Cripps found increasingly that the progressive Conservatives, on whom he had staked so much faith in 1942, were correspondingly drifting back to their own partisan allegiance.

It thus seemed to depend, *faute de mieux*, on Labour as to whether the spell would be broken. By the end of 1944, it had become clear that Cripps would rejoin the Labour Party – 'if they will have me', as he put it, while still making clear his preference for 'a coalition of the Left'.[48] The prodigal son, when he finally came home, was much changed from the left-wing maverick of pre-war days, as even those responsible for his expulsion well appreciated. At one committee contemplating public ownership of the light metal industry, Dalton mordantly noted Cripps's opposition to the proposal. 'I say that I am much struck by this most impressive presentation of the anti-Socialist case,' Dalton recorded. 'He doesn't think this at all funny!'[49] Nationalization no longer seemed necessary, so Cripps now professed, since 'we have learned in the war that we CAN control industry'.[50] In short, with his scorn for utopian panaceas and his exhortations for realism, Cripps now appeared as the epitome of responsibility.

Two technical difficulties stood in the way of reconciliation with Labour. One was that the local party in Bristol East, already tainted by association with its errant member, had itself suffered expulsion in 1943 after leading members had supported the candidature of the former ILP activist Jennie Lee (married to Aneurin Bevan) in a by-election in a neighbouring Bristol seat.[51]

47. Bullock, *Bevin*, ii, pp. 250–52; and generally on reconstruction arguments see Brooke, *Labour's War*, pp. 219–30.
48. Barrington-Ward diary, 13 September, 3 October 1944.
49. Dalton diary, 7 March 1945, in Pimlott (ed.), *Dalton: War Diary*, p. 841.
50. Acland diary, 12 October 1944, quoted in Addison, *Road to 1945*, p. 262.
51. Burgess, *Cripps*, pp. 188–9, and Hollis, *Jennie Lee*, pp. 103–7. Correspondence in the Cripps papers shows that Lee colluded with Cripps to avoid implicating him in her campaign, while he used his independent status to avoid endorsing her Conservative opponent.

The other difficulty was that Cripps had at various times offered assurances that, having entered the Government as an independent, he would tender his resignation if he rejoined Labour. These might have been substantial points in another context – if the NEC had been determined not to have the rebels back, or if Attlee had not been ready to accept Cripps as one of his quota of Labour ministers, or if Churchill had simply wanted to be rid of Cripps. As it was, Attlee worked to heal the breach within the party organization, while Churchill responded benignly when he received Cripps's formal offer of resignation just before Christmas 1944:

My dear Stafford,
I have always considered you a Socialist and as belonging to the Socialist representation in the Government. Your decision to re-establish your formal position as a member of the Labour Party raises no question affecting the balance in the Government, except of course that you will henceforward count as a Socialist instead of something even worse. The happy relations prevailing between us all, especially when things go a bit wrong, makes it all the more essential that you should lend your gifts and energies to the highly-complicated war task of which you have so fine a grip.[52]

That Cripps would occupy high office in a Labour Government was fully expected by the time of the 1945 General Election: what was less widely expected was that there would be a Labour Government. This was an age of innocence in which there was little experience to inspire trust in opinion polls (still less subsequent distrust), so the fact that Gallup had been reporting a Labour lead of 15 per cent since the middle of 1943, and touching 20 per cent at the beginning of 1945, was not fully appreciated. Moreover, it was relatively late in the day that the Labour leadership made clear that it would withdraw from the Coalition following victory in Europe (VE Day was 8 May 1945) rather than dally with Churchill's repeated entreaties to keep his wartime Government in office until victory had also been secured over Japan, which was currently expected to take up to eighteen months. This was a strategy which might have been supposed to appeal to Cripps, with his longstanding susceptibility to the charms of a government of national unity; but the evidence is that, when the NEC voted for immediate withdrawal on 20 May, it was Attlee, Bevin and Dalton who had opposed

52. Churchill to RSC, 22 December 1944; cf. NEC minutes, elections sub-committee, 14 November 1944; organization sub-committee, 21 February 1945 (reference courtesy of Richard Toye).

the move.[53] Everyone concerned had come a long way since the fraught meetings of the NEC in 1939 that had resulted in Cripps's expulsion.

Along with the other Labour ministers, Cripps left office on 23 May. Since Churchill had set polling day for 6 July, there ensued a relatively short but vigorous campaign, in which Cripps took a prominent part. There was nothing austere about his election address, which excited some comment. On its front page, under the bold headline 'THE MAN', it quoted the words of Mark Antony on Brutus:

> His life was gentle, and the elements
> So mix'd in him that Nature might stand up
> And say, 'This was a man'.

Below this was a photograph of Stalin watching Cripps sign the Anglo-Russian agreement of July 1941; and any suspicion that the ex-ambassador or his wife might have been embarrassed by the extravagance of this document is dispelled by the fact that the proof copy is carefully amended in Isobel Cripps's handwriting.[54]

Cripps revealed an unsuspected relish for his return to partisan commitment. Precisely because he had been a strong supporter of the wartime coalition, he showed himself jealous of its credentials, watchful that the Conservatives should not appropriate them. 'We won the war very largely because of careful planning of our war organisation and our war production,' ran a typical Cripps speech, claiming that this was how the twin problems of output and unemployment had been solved.[55] The contrast with the Conservatives' pre-war record spoke for itself (or might have, if Cripps had not gone on to link it explicitly with their continuing attachment to unfettered private enterprise). 'The Labour Party says that the comfort, the happiness, and the welfare of our people are the A1 priorities,' he declared. 'We do not want to control people but things; we want to control finance, land, factories, raw materials, prices – all those things that have been controlled during the war with such remarkable success.'[56]

With the return to party politics, Cripps's provocative record was no longer forgiven or forgotten by his opponents. His pre-war appeal for

53. See Morgan, *Labour in Power*, pp. 34-6; King, *British Political Opinion*, p. 2. Cripps, of course, was not a member of the NEC.
54. 'And say to all the world' is the usual reading (*Julius Caesar*, V, iii). The address received mildly satirical analysis in McCallum and Readman, *General Election of 1945*, pp. 113-14.
55. RSC speech at Newcastle, *Newcastle Journal*, 16 June 1945.
56. RSC speech at Glasgow, *Glasgow Herald*, 13 June 1945.

workers to refuse to make armaments was duly dredged up by one Conservative candidate, and provoked Cripps's unwise riposte that this had been a ploy to replace Chamberlain, as though it simply anticipated the latter's (fortunate) replacement by Churchill in 1940 (whereas the fact was that Baldwin had been Prime Minister at the time).[57] Moreover, the tenor of Churchill's reaction is significant, as he privately goaded Eden into joining the fray: 'This demolishes the last vestige of a stool upon which he can stand and proves him a liar never at a loss for corroborative detail.'[58] This controversy was not pursued; but it shows Churchill already in the mood to unleash bitter recriminations upon old colleagues, as his warning of a 'Gestapo' if Labour were returned notoriously demonstrated. Cripps's response here was that 'it was a great pity that Mr Churchill should step down so low off the platform of public esteem that he had rightly earned during the war'.[59]

With Labour's landslide victory, once the votes had been counted at the end of July 1945, Cripps was immediately seen as one of the half-dozen most prominent members of the new Cabinet. The *Daily Herald* judged that his 'clear expositions of economic issues have contributed notably to Labour's success at the polls'.[60] He emerged as both spokesman and executor of an approach to economic policy that attempted to turn the experience of wartime to good account in confronting the hardly less daunting problems of peace.

Cripps thus became one of the Big Five in the Government, along with Attlee himself, Morrison, Bevin and Dalton. They found a common purpose in working together as ministers, taxed with finding pragmatic solutions to pressing problems. The experience brought out in Cripps a sort of collegiality notably lacking in his pre-war career. True, his capacity for teamwork had been nourished under conditions that identified him as the captain of the team, whether leading the Crippery in India or heading the command structure of MAP. Cripps's maturity as a politician came with office, whereas opposition had merely fostered his waywardness. His later perspective is surely expressed in a passage of Estorick's: 'From the *practice* of statesmanship and acceptance of the responsibilities of Government he had become the 'planner of the new order of social democracy'.[61]

---

57. For the key statements, see *Western Daily Press*, 15 June 1945.
58. Churchill to Eden, 14 June 1945, Churchill papers, CHAR 20/194B, f. 128.
59. RSC speech at Huddersfield, *Huddersfield Weekly Examiner*, 23 June 1945.
60. Leader, *Daily Herald*, 28 July 1945.   61. Estorick, p. 361 (italics in original).

End of empire

It might seem that, during his first eighteen months in office under Attlee, a disproportionate amount of the time of the President of the Board of Trade was consumed by India. Most biographies of Cripps treat this as a sideshow: a distracting episode dutifully recounted in a few pages stuck in the middle, or at the end, of a chapter otherwise devoted to the theme of post-war economic policy.[62] Such treatment not only fails to do justice to the events that brought independence and partition to the Indian subcontinent – hardly an unimportant topic – but, in the process, leaves many misleading impressions about Cripps's role unchallenged.

The wartime Coalition had embodied and articulated substantial agreement about Britain's world role; Labour leaders, notably Attlee and his Foreign Secretary Bevin, shared Churchill's outlook on many issues; so it is hardly surprising that there should have been a large area of continuity in the overseas policy of the post-war Labour Government. A post-war Churchill Government would probably have taken broadly the same line in a world where, even if Britons could not forget that they had won the war, they had to remember that Britain's straitened circumstances now imposed harsh constraints on the options available. Yet there is little sign that Churchill was ready to quit India.

A full measure of independence, with the new republics of India and Pakistan choosing to remain members of the Commonwealth, was only implemented once Labour came to power. It may now appear naive to hail the Attlee Government as the executors of a plan, as highminded as it was farsighted, to give justice to the Indian subcontinent; and the trauma of its partition in 1947 remains contentious as well as painful. Even so, it is surely plain that the election of a Labour Government did make a crucial difference to the way in which Indian independence was achieved – not least because it gave a central role to Stafford Cripps rather than Winston Churchill. In 1942, as emissary and servant of the War Cabinet, Cripps had made full use of the contacts he had made in India in 1939 as a private individual; and in 1946 he made his third and longest visit, this time with real power in his hands, clearly hoping to benefit from the lessons of hard-won experience.

Leaving London in March 1946, Cripps went as one of three Cabinet Ministers charged with seeking agreement on the transfer of power from

62. For example, Estorick in 'Britain's economic controller', Cooke in 'Building the new Britain: India again', Bryant in 'Another industrial revolution'.

Britain to an independent government. The idea of sending out a representative of the Cabinet came from Attlee, though he did not initially have Cripps in mind. It was Cripps, however, who promptly seized the initiative and made his own appointment seem inevitable, and Cripps who then drafted the Directive which defined the Cabinet Delegation's task. In these, as in other ways, the story of the Cabinet Delegation of 1946 was to replicate that of the Cripps Mission of 1942. Indeed, in February 1946 Cripps prepared himself by asking his private secretary to collect all his telegrams and personal files from 1942, laying particular emphasis on having verbatim reports of his press conferences.[63] He knew that he was returning to India as a man with a record – of failure. His determination to redeem the failure of the Cripps Mission not only gave him a motive for joining the Cabinet Delegation but suggested a strategy for its operation.

Cripps was seen as the man in charge, and not just by Linlithgow's successor as Viceroy, Lord Wavell, who, for all his other reservations, readily conceded that Cripps was 'much the ablest of the party'.[64] From the outset, it was Cripps who attracted most public attention, if only because he was already the most famous minister in the Cabinet Delegation. The day after its appointment was announced, a Giles cartoon showed him striding into Delhi, his colleagues far in the background, and with Gandhi at Cripps's elbow, saying: 'Before we get down to business, Stafford, I suppose you couldn't let me have a couple of clothing coupons?' Another cartoon, turning the Indian motif to the problems that he was leaving behind, depicted a turbaned Cripps trying to charm a snake, representing the British Public, by playing on a pipe labelled 'Austerity'. The *Daily Mail* pocket cartoon simply showed Gandhi and Cripps, with the caption: 'Quite frankly, I've forgotten more about sheer bleak austerity than you ever knew.'[65]

The Cabinet Delegation is well chronicled. A whole volume of Mansergh's *Transfer of Power* is devoted to it, and the secretary to the mission, Frank Turnbull of the India Office, who had acted in a similar capacity in 1942, this time kept his own diary. Moreover, Wavell, an exceptionally literate soldier, left an account in his journal which, sympathetically edited by Penderel Moon, has rightly recruited many readers' solicitude for the difficulties of the penultimate Viceroy, whose record had so often previously

63. Cripps note for PS, 17 February 1946, PRO, CAB 127/72.
64. Wavell diary, 1 July 1946, in Moon (ed.), *Wavell: journal*, p. 310.
65. *Daily Express*, 21 February 1946; *News of the World*, 24 February 1946; *Daily Mail*, 21 February 1946.

been eclipsed by that of his charismatic successor, Mountbatten. Furthermore, the diary kept meticulously by the First Lord of the Admiralty, Albert Alexander (and subsequently made accessible in the Churchill Archives Centre) also manifests a strong sympathy for the straightforward decency shown by Wavell, latterly his frequent and convivial host, who reciprocated this growing warmth, calling the First Lord 'the very best type of British Labour, the best we breed'.[66] Since, in the internal politics of the Delegation, Wavell and Alexander tended to side together, it is hardly surprising that historians who have been able to draw on both their diaries have found it easy to see their viewpoint.

But Cripps too kept a diary. He did so in much the same way as when first in Moscow, writing letters home which he intended to be typed up in diary form for later perusal. Isobel Cripps duly read Attlee some of the early instalments ('which he liked') on visits to 10 Downing Street.[67] It was a further stage of her emergence into a public role, when 'for the first time (in a way) I am having to see a variety of things *thro'*, a very different affair to "dabbling"!! as you know.'[68]

Cripps's Indian diary comprises some eighty pages of war-economy standard paper, based on the record which Stafford kept in his characteristic red ink, usually very early in the morning with often a postscript later in the day. An intimate account, the diary does not replicate the official record of interviews or correspondence that is otherwise available. Since this source has never previously been available for citation, the only previous reference to it in print is deliberately obscure.[69] Now that it is accessible, Cripps's Indian diary thus gives a unique opportunity for a fresh look at the Cabinet Delegation. It is an inevitably partisan document as much as any of the others, and possesses no privileged status over them; but it does give Cripps's personal impressions with candour and insight – not least about himself.

66. Wavell diary, 1 July 1946, in Moon (ed.), *Wavell: journal*, p. 310.
67. IC to RSC, 10 April 1946.
68. ibid., 25 March 1946. It was during Stafford's absence that Isobel was offered the GBE. 'Changing from Lady as your wife to Dame on my own!! is rather a frightening idea,' she at once told Stafford. 'It will make it more difficult to hide in your shadow!!!' (IC to RSC, 20 May 1946). To accept or not to accept? The answer quickly became obvious: 'I think really Clem would feel it almost an insult if I did refuse' (IC to RSC, 21 May 1946).
69. Hodson, *Great Divide*, quotes four short comments from this copy, cited as from private letters to Isobel Cripps, who evidently repented at a late stage of her decision to let Hodson see it. See IC's notes, 17 June 1966 and Spry to IC, 7 September 1968. The diary as cited here comprises the typescript copy, checked where possible against the surviving letters written to Isobel, 9–31 May, until she flew out to join Stafford, and those subsequently written to Diana and Peggy.

'He indulged in no luxuries and did without many things that most of us would regard as necessities.' Thus Cripps on Gandhi after his death – a connoisseur's appreciation. 'He never took the view that he must divorce his religion from his everyday life,' Cripps continued. 'Religion was his life and his life was religion.'[70] Some glaring similarities between the two men were often noted at the time. One review of Strauss's biography of Cripps was headlined 'The English Gandhi'.[71] Some supposed parallels were merely provocative or superficial. But even where substantial affinities existed, it is not axiomatic they led to a genuine meeting of minds or helped produce the best political outcome for the Indian people in finally unravelling the British Raj.

Whether Cripps and Gandhi were well suited to negotiate with each other is thus a difficult question. Each had a strong political instinct, to which their discourse gave inadequate play. They shared an obvious weakness for vague, ambiguous but uplifting rhetoric; on another level, they were each inclined to employ – and to admire – the nicely judged stratagems of the clever lawyer. But such mutual susceptibilities conspired to close their eyes to a dimension of political realism, itself arguably more lacking in 1946 than either good feeling or good drafting.

When India became a republic in 1950, Cripps acceded to requests for a personal message, which was widely used in the Indian media. Looking back to the period of the Cabinet Delegation, he spoke of hardly expecting then 'that it would be possible to accomplish so great a task as the new constitution in so short a time', and paid tribute to the Indian leaders who had made it possible. 'The greatest of those leaders was Gandhiji,' he claimed, calling him 'the Prophet who gave his work and life to accomplish this very end'.[72] No doubt this was exactly the right thing to say on Republic Day about a man now revered as a national martyr. It was, however, an adroitly edited claim, more faithful to Cripps's longstanding view of the Mahatma's pure intentions than to his own experience of the actual consequences of Gandhi's political impact in 1946–7.

---

70. RSC text, service of intercession, Westminster Abbey, 17 February 1948.
71. 'An MP I know who would rather say a smart thing than utter a considered judgment described Sir Stafford Cripps to me the other day as an "English Gandhi", and in saying so he had no intention of flattering the Minister of Aircraft Production.' Emrys Jones review, *Daily Mail*, 9 February 1943.
72. RSC manuscript message, December 1949, to be used also by BBC, etc., PRO, CAB 127/ 113; published *Times of India*, 26 January 1950.

PART FIVE

CRIPPS VERSUS GANDHI
1946–7

"Before we get down to business, Stafford, I suppose you couldn't let me have a couple of clothing coupons ?"

I

India Revisited

> There's no discouragement
> Shall make him once relent
> His first avowed intent
> To be a pilgrim.

Bunyan's hymn was to be sung at Cripps's funeral; its words can readily be applied to his final Indian pilgrimage. It is not the case that he had forgotten nothing and forgiven nothing since his mission to India in 1942. It had been embarrassing that the author of the Cripps offer should no longer be *persona grata* with his old friends in Congress, at least so long as the war lasted and they remained in gaol; but Cripps kept up contacts with the India League in London, headed by Nehru's confidant, Krishna Menon. Above all, it was frustrating that Cripps's continued membership of the India Committee, which lasted throughout his service in the Churchill Government, was subject to one tiresome, if intermittently erratic, constraint: the Prime Minister's prejudices. This became, however, the making of a bond between himself and the committee's other relatively enlightened members. Unexpectedly, Cripps did not find his closest ally in Attlee, whose suspicions of what he once termed the 'totalitarian dictatorship' of Congress had set solid since its rejection of the Cripps offer.[1] It was the alliance between Cripps and the beleaguered Secretary of State, Leo Amery, that came to provide the best openings for any constructive moves in wartime Indian policy.

The Amery–Cripps axis was based on their common appreciation of the urgent need for Indianization of a government that was soon to be granted independence anyway. When Amery argued in 1944 that 'the Viceroy's Council was ceasing to be a small Council of expert officials and was becoming something much more like a Cabinet, overwhelmingly Indian', he was (unavailingly) seeking to persuade Churchill of a proposition that

1. See Moore, *Escape from Empire*, pp. 5, 16.

Cripps had, equally unavailingly, pressed in Delhi two years previously.[2] Likewise, when the taciturn Wavell had been appointed Viceroy in 1943, he had quickly revealed a more flexible approach than his stance as Commander-in-Chief at the time of the Cripps Mission might have suggested. If this change owed much to his soldier's realism, his strategic shrewdness and his lack of viceregal vanity, these are qualities that have subsequently made him seem an attractive figure – though often at the expense of the very man from whom he had learnt some of his new wisdom. 'Wavell's idea is to renew the Cripps offer as regards the interim period,' Amery noted.[3] Though such initiatives were stalled under Churchill, Cripps must have felt some rueful sense of personal vindication.

What the new Viceroy wanted was a fully Indianized interim government. Quite unlike Linlithgow, Wavell persistently sought authority to take action during the war, using its imperatives to forge some kind of unity, which might last into the peace and thus facilitate agreement over the final transfer of power. What Amery suddenly came up with – Cripps called it 'startling' – was a plan to pick up the other end of the stick. At the end of 1944 he proposed 'the inversion of the Cripps offer, viz. give India freedom from Whitehall first and let her work out her permanent constitution at leisure – a superficially daring but really cautious and practical policy'.[4] Of these two approaches, Cripps naturally found Wavell's closer to his own thinking: Indian freedom, yes; but democratization first.

The Viceroy's recall for consultation in London in the spring of 1945 gave him his opportunity to argue his case, partly thanks to Cripps, who lent a sympathetic ear to the proposals for rapid Indianization. Here was an ally of whom Wavell had previously been dismissive, on the grounds that 'Cripps won't stand up to Churchill'.[5] With the end of the war in sight, however, Cripps showed himself ready to join Amery in resignation, along with Wavell, if all initiatives were blocked by Churchill.[6] Cripps was by now busy producing alternative drafts for the India Committee, just as in 1942, and he provided Amery with his sole support, with even Attlee sometimes against them. A letter from Amery captures the spirit of his relations with Cripps at this time: 'I am by no means sure that your old pal Gandhi is not right about "Quit India", on the understanding that it is not

2. WM (44) 2, 6 January 1944, RSC present, in Mansergh, *TOP*, iv, p. 606.
3. Amery diary, 10 September 1943, in Barnes and Nicholson (eds.), *Empire at Bay*, p. 938.
4. Amery diary, 28 December 1944, ibid., p. 1023; Wavell diary, 20 January 1945, in Moon (ed.), *Wavell: journal*, p. 111; and see Louis, *In the Name of God, Go!*, pp. 174ff.
5. Wavell to Amery, 28 August 1944, in Mansergh, *TOP*, iv, p. 1228.
6. Amery diary, 19 January 1945, in Barnes and Nicholson (eds.), *Empire at Bay*, p. 1026.

the Englishman, official or unofficial, civil or military, who should quit, but that sinister figure, the Secretary of State!'[7]

Wavell's visit was not entirely happy. Having been brought all the way home, he was surprised at participating so little in the discussions of the India Committee; as he put it, 'of being treated as an Untouchable in the presence of Brahmins'.[8] Yet when actually permitted to join in, Wavell found himself working amicably alongside Cripps, whose instantaneous grasp of problems and versatile capacity for adroit conciliation he came to appreciate. Amery records how Cripps dealt with one unhelpful amendment, which narrowly stipulated the Viceroy's freedom of action, 'by judiciously pretending to be in favour of it' in order to draw its sting, and subsequently ensuring that his draft became 'even more vague' on the crucial point.[9] Such tactical alertness, quickness of mind and ability to exploit ambiguity had not always elicited warm approval from Amery, but he was grateful enough now to the 'ever useful Cripps', reflecting: 'It is an odd thing to think of Cripps and myself as the two main collaborators in this business.'[10]

All told, Cripps could look with some satisfaction on the extent to which variations on the Cripps offer had become the common currency in British politics by the end of the war. Cripps, Amery and Wavell did not get everything they wanted. But when Wavell noted at one point that 'we agreed that if we three stood pat on this, it would be difficult for the India Committee or Cabinet to override us', he correctly sensed the strength of their united front.[11] It was this that enabled Amery to convey an indirect warning to Churchill of 'the seriousness of the position that would follow if Wavell were turned down and he, Cripps and myself resigned'.[12] It was Churchill's wish to renege on the Cripps offer that still blocked progress. 'Winston frankly takes the view that we made the offer when in a hole and can disavow it because it was not accepted at the time,' Amery grimly recorded.[13]

Though Wavell's low opinion of politicians was reinforced by his experiences in London, as elsewhere, he showed himself quite ready to play a political hand himself when necessary. The final decision on his proposals was not taken until the end of May, when the Coalition Government had been replaced by a purely Conservative Government pending the British

7. Amery to RSC, 18 February 1945, PRO, CAB 127/80.
8. Wavell diary, 26 April 1945, in Moon (ed.), *Wavell: journal*, p. 127.
9. Amery diary, 10 April 1945, in Barnes and Nicholson (eds.), *Empire at Bay*, p. 1036.
10. Amery diary, 12 April 1945, ibid., p. 1036; cf. ibid, 14 May 1945, p. 1041.
11. Wavell diary, 23–25 April 1945, in Moon (ed.), *Wavell: journal*, p. 126.
12. Amery diary, 26 April 1945, in Barnes and Nicholson (eds.), *Empire at Bay*, p. 1038.
13. Amery diary, 30 April 1945, ibid., p. 1040.

General Election. Now it was Wavell's turn to convey (through Amery) a further indirect warning to Churchill: 'that P.M. could not expect me to return to India empty-handed, and that surely it would be unfortunate if from an electioneering point of view India came into party politics, which could hardly be avoided if I was turned down since Attlee, Cripps and Bevin all knew of the proposals'.[14]

Even before Churchill himself lost office, then, his veto was effectively countered by threats of resignation which, in a pre-election atmosphere, proved irresistible. If it had been the resignation of Cripps alone that Churchill had had to face in early 1945, the loss could no doubt have been borne; and that of Amery and Cripps, along with Wavell, could perhaps have been survived by the Coalition. But the resignation of Wavell, backed by Amery, and with Cripps now out of office but in possession of compromising information, was not something that a Conservative Government could countenance at the outset of the General Election campaign. Relying on Cripps's forbearance under such conditions, with memories of 1942 to animate both men, was hardly the course of prudence for Churchill. He backed down.

'The climax of my visit was an extraordinary one,' Wavell recorded on 31 May. 'At the meeting of the Cabinet at 10.30 p.m. the P.M. made just as forcible an address in favour of my proposals as he had made in their damnation this morning.'[15] Essentially, the Viceroy was belatedly authorized to begin immediate negotiations with the Indian parties about the formation of an interim government. But first the leaders of the major party had to be sprung from gaol, whether by granting them parole or, as Cripps urged, unconditionally.

'The release of the Working Committee I believe was due to Labour and to a large extent your personal influence,' a Congress friend later flatteringly assured Cripps.[16] Certainly the decision to release the Congress detainees in mid-June 1945 afforded him a peculiar satisfaction. Campaigning in Edinburgh, Cripps expressed his delight: 'These releases will mark the end of one of the sad chapters of our relationship with India and will provide the opportunity for that vigorous India leadership which alone can solve India's problems of reconstruction.'[17] He saw this step as justifying his participation in the process of government and discharging a burden of

14. Wavell diary, 30 May 1945, in Moon (ed.), *Wavell: journal*, p. 134.
15. Wavell diary, 31 May 1945 ibid., p. 135.
16. J. C. Gupta to RSC, 25 July 1945, PRO, CAB 127/130.
17. RSC speech at Edinburgh, 14 June 1945, TS handout.

embarrassment, if not guilt, towards some old comrades. Cripps fired off a telegram of congratulations to Jawaharlal Nehru.

Labour's new Secretary of State for India was Lord Pethick-Lawrence. A gentle and manifestly well-meaning intellectual, much influenced by his wife, Emmeline, who had long been a member of the India Conciliation Group, he was only slightly younger than Gandhi, whose idealism Pethick-Lawrence effusively admired. He stood belatedly at the summit of his career, with no ambition save to do the right thing, and was thus the ideal minister so long as India needed nothing more than the implementation of an agreed plan and the reciprocation of inchoate professions of goodwill.

That the task was rather less tractable soon became apparent. By the time Labour took office, Wavell had already failed in his attempt to reach agreement with the Indian party leaders. Their conference at Simla had shown that, while Congress was prepared to concede parity of numbers between Hindu and Muslim members of an interim government, Jinnah's insistence that all the Muslims should be nominated by the Muslim League was now the sticking point. It was a token of the increasing bitterness of the communal divide as well as the keen struggle for position among the political elite.

The policy of the Attlee Government was to revive the Cripps offer. Cripps had said as much himself in the wake of the Simla breakdown, in a widely reported speech which attributed the failure to agree on sharing power in an interim government to the implications that this would have for constitution-making in a free India. New elections were therefore the key to progress.[18] As an inevitably powerful member of the Labour Government's India (and Burma) Committee, Cripps was well placed to argue this case. He was helped by the fact that the making of a post-war constitution suddenly became a much more urgent task than anyone had anticipated. Arguably, this had not been an immediate problem so long as the war in Asia was expected to last another year or more; but the speedy Japanese surrender after Hiroshima and Nagasaki created a new situation.

Pushed to act quickly, Pethick-Lawrence advocated that 'the Cabinet should now proceed to implement the long-term proposals in the Cripps Declaration'.[19] One issue was whether to base the formation of a single constituent assembly upon the results of provincial elections, as Cripps

18. Statement published 16 July 1945, in Mansergh, *TOP*, vi, p. 21n.
19. CP (45) 121, Pethick-Lawrence memorandum, 18 August 1945, in Mansergh, *TOP*, vi, p. 87.

urged, or whether to heed the Viceroy's warnings that this would simply result in a boycott by the Muslim League, which was insisting on prior recognition of Pakistan. Wavell was ready to envisage the shape that such an entity might take, provided it were confined to territory with a Muslim majority; but, on returning to London to meet the new India Committee at the end of August, he found that Cripps – 'mainly I think for reasons of personal prestige' – went no further than the original Cripps offer, which allowed secession from an Indian union by individual provinces.[20] Cripps's own drafts continued to draw attention to 'the method suggested in the offer of 1942' as the best way of forming a constituent assembly.[21] Wavell got his way, and with less difficulty than under the Churchill Government, but in the process mutual confidence between him and Cripps was shaken. After an obviously uncongenial dinner together, Wavell concluded that, under pressure from the Labour Party, 'they are obviously bent on handing over India to their Congress friends as soon as possible'.[22]

Yet in Congress eyes, British policy had changed all too little by the end of 1945. The Viceroy's announcement about the form of any constitution-making body – keeping his options open until after the forthcoming provincial elections – was received as yet another piece of British procrastination. Moreover, the attempt to prosecute former members of the Indian National Army, who had collaborated with the Japanese, was a clumsy piece of provocation. Aware of a deteriorating situation, Cripps continued to press, with limited success, for conciliatory gestures: a meeting between the Viceroy and Gandhi (which Wavell resisted); a parliamentary tour of India (which led to the dispatch of two peers and eight backbench MPs at the end of the year); an invitation to Nehru and Jinnah to visit London (which was vetoed by Attlee). It was in this context that Attlee appeased Cripps in November by producing the germ of the idea that became the Cabinet Delegation. In so far as this opened the way to a complete reappraisal of the Indian situation, the implication was that the Cripps offer would lapse. Instead of a unitary constitution for Indian independence, the possible alternative of partition was now officially contemplated.[23]

As yet, Cripps was not the prospective emissary. Attlee's first thought was simply to send the retired Labour Cabinet minister, Tom Johnston, apparently on the strength of his negotiating skills; but the Prime Minister

20. Wavell diary, 29 August 1945, in Moon (ed.), *Wavell: journal*, p. 167.
21. RSC memorandum, 3 September 1945, in Mansergh, *TOP*, vi, p. 203.
22. Wavell diary, 4 September 1945, in Moon (ed.), *Wavell: journal*, p. 169.
23. Moore, *Escape from Empire*, pp. 31–45.

was disabused of this notion by an increasingly cosy alliance between Cripps and Pethick-Lawrence, whose transparent alternative ploy was to suggest a two-man mission, recruited from the Cabinet itself, and thus able to face down Wavell if necessary. Perhaps to counterbalance their all-too-obvious Congress sympathies, by the middle of January 1946 the agreed plan was for a third minister to be added.

Cripps had already been busy in mending his fences with Congress. His open citation of the opinions of the journalist Shiva Rao and of the industrial magnate G. B. Birla, both of them old acquaintances who were currently in London, had inflated the impression of his special access to Congress. Cripps did nothing to play this down. Taking advantage of Gandhi's ecumenism, Cripps sent him Christmas greetings which Gandhi reciprocated with a generally conciliatory letter. Cripps made a point of showing this 'very friendly response' to Pethick-Lawrence. 'I am hoping that this time there is determination to do the right thing in terms of Indian thought,' Gandhi had written, perhaps in a more minatory spirit than his recipients appreciated.[24] Some of Cripps's Indian mailbag had been introduced into the official proceedings of the India Committee, notably the letters that Rao sent on his return to Delhi. But a few letters which Cripps conspiratorially showed to Pethick-Lawrence – 'It is *not* for circulation in your Dept.!'[25] – were reserved for the two of them.

This special treatment applied particularly to Cripps's communications from Nehru. Their friendship had been the pivot of the 1942 negotiations, apparently enhancing the chances of a successful agreement. Cripps had spoken publicly as though this episode were something to build upon. 'Though my mission in 1942 brought no immediate success in its train, I hope and believe that I still have many friends in India who know that I have done my best to advance the realisation of Indian self-government,' he claimed. 'To all those friends I would most earnestly appeal for co-operation in a new joint effort of Indians and British, as equals, determined to find a way out of our difficulties.'[26] Fine sentiments, no doubt; but could they bear such weight, after everything that had happened since 1942?

The telegram that Cripps had sent Nehru in June 1945 had likewise expressed hopes of a new era of cooperation.[27] In 1949, Estorick, writing

24. Gandhi to RSC, 12 January 1946, PRO, CAB 127/128; enc. with RSC to Pethick-Lawrence, 24 January 1946, Trinity College, P-L5 f. 65.
25. RSC to Pethick-Lawrence, 19 December 1945, Trinity College, P-L5 f. 63.
26. RSC speech at Edinburgh, 14 June 1945, TS handout.
27. RSC to Nehru, 18 June 1945, Nehru catalogue, p. 100.

in Cripps's lifetime and with Cripps's approval, printed the full text of the reply from Nehru, who had meanwhile taken office as India's first Prime Minister.

Dear Stafford,

It was good of you and your wife to send me a message of greeting on my discharge from prison. I appreciated it very much. I am ashamed that I should have delayed in thanking you for it. I was overwhelmed with messages from friends and, at the same time, had no rest anywhere.[28]

The letter continued with more excuses, but also with some ambiguously veiled remarks, over which Estorick did not linger, instead glossing Nehru's concluding reference to 'old problems in new shapes' with the blandly benign comment: 'Yes, that was it.'[29] Fifty years later, there is rather more that needs saying about how things stood between Cripps and Nehru in 1945–6.

The impression that the two men simply picked up an old friendship, after a thousand days spent respectively in His Majesty's Government and in one of His Imperial Majesty's prisons, is not only psychologically improbable but demonstrably untrue. Krishna Menon had evidently reported from London that Cripps was somewhat hurt at receiving no acknowledgement of his cable for ten weeks, and it was as a result of this prodding that Nehru was eventually induced to send his 'brief reply by air letter'. As he explained to Menon, 'I have not yet got over Stafford Cripps' behaviour just after his visit to Delhi in 1942.' The propaganda battle over the Cripps Mission had left deep scars. Cripps's reiterated statements after leaving Delhi 'meant of course that either he or I was a liar', as Nehru put it, reinforcing his sense of Cripps's irritating condescension. Even though Churchill may have been most responsible for the failure of the Cripps Mission, 'Cripps proved that he was not capable of handling a difficult situation satisfactorily', showing that 'something more than self-righteousness is necessary to understand and deal with a difficult problem'.[30]

Hence the barbs concealed in a missive that was not signed, 'Yours, Jawaharlal', as in the past, but now: 'Yours very sincerely, Jawaharlal Nehru'. He did not just invoke his need for the air of the mountains of

28. Nehru to RSC, 4 September 1945, PRO, CAB 127/143, quoted Estorick, p. 337 (misdated 9 September 1945).
29. Estorick, p. 337.
30. Nehru to Menon, 3 September 1945, in Gopal (ed.), *Nehru: Selected Works*, xiv, p. 81.

Kashmir to explain his tardiness as a correspondent but went on to ruminate: 'After a long period in prison, both the body and mind require adjustment to the new environment, especially the mind.' He warned that 'much adjustment and adaptation are necessary', adding enigmatically: 'I suppose that will happen gradually.'[31]

Isobel Cripps, with her more intimate touch as a correspondent, was enlisted to help repair the breach with Nehru, sending 'a little note to tell you what a deep pleasure it was to Stafford – & to me too – when your letter came today'.[32] Stafford's own letter, enclosed with it, though evidently friendly and personal in tone, provoked Nehru's private comment that 'I wish there was some psychological understanding of the Indian problem'.[33] This time he sent back a more substantial reply, once more resuming their more intimate forms of address, but still infused with his own sense of frustration. He dwelt on 'the powerful psychological factors which influence us tremendously' and which meant that 'with all the good will in the world we fall out and have wars and hatred and passion in place of peace and sweet reason'. He now told Cripps more plainly: 'And so somehow India and England drift further apart – they were far enough – till it becomes frightfully difficult for either to have any real conception of the other, much less understanding.'[34]

When Cripps reported the gist of this correspondence to the India Committee, he admitted that he had been inclined to interpret it as ending relations. He yielded, however, to the view of Amrit Kaur, one of Gandhi's confidants and currently visiting London, that the letter was a *cri de cœur* from Nehru, who might yet be amenable to suitable courting.[35] The following day Cripps tried again, in more apologetic vein at a personal level, but making a strong claim on behalf of the Government: 'We believe that we had arrived at a really important decision when we expressed our intention to go ahead with the constitution making for India without any reservations as to agreement in India.' He pleaded with Nehru to wait until the election results were in, then to test 'the reality of our intentions'.[36]

31. Nehru to RSC, 4 September 1945, PRO, CAB 127/143.
32. IC to Nehru, 17 September 1945, manuscript copy, PRO, CAB 127/143; Indira Gandhi to IC, 13 October 1945.
33. Nehru to Menon, 30 October 1945, in Gopal (ed.), *Nehru: Selected Works*, xiv, p. 113. Cripps's original letter seems to be lost.
34. Nehru to RSC, 1 November 1945, PRO, CAB 127/143; cf. Mansergh, *TOP*, vi, p. 503n.: 'not traced in the India Office records'.
35. India Committee minutes, 19 November 1945, in Mansergh, *TOP*, vi, pp. 501–6.
36. RSC to Nehru, 20 November 1945, copy.

Cripps was rewarded, in December 1945, by the first sign that Nehru was at last ready to reciprocate the expressions of good faith that Cripps had been evincing for the last six months. 'I think I have some realisation of your wish to see India free, also of your difficulties,' Nehru now wrote, and added, with a new frankness: 'Many of the things that have been said and done during the past few years have hurt me and dull pain endures, but at no time did I doubt that you had the cause of India at heart.' He went on to paint a bleak picture of the desperate mood that now prevailed in India, making it difficult for individuals to influence, let alone control, the powerful forces of nationalism that had been unleashed.

Even so, Nehru professed new optimism, however qualified. 'I can have faith in an individual but not in a machine, and it appears that the machine counts in the long run,' he told Cripps. 'It is your presence in the British Govt that gives me some hope.'[37] Cripps clutched at this straw. He responded warmly to Nehru, acknowledging the 'impersonality of the chain of events', but maintaining that 'there is not the slightest doubt that personal contacts and reactions have the most profound influence upon the direction of these impersonal trends'. Having reported the correspondence to the India Committee, Cripps seized his chance to pose a series of questions to Nehru: 'How do you yourself picture matters developing after the elections? or may I put it in this way. Look at the matter quite objectively, if you were in the Viceroy's place what line of action would you lay down to be followed after the election?'[38]

The result was a long analysis of the Indian political situation, written by Nehru at the end of January 1946. It was, Cripps said, 'exactly what I wanted' and he duly passed it on, in a cyclostyled copy running to six pages of foolscap, to Pethick Lawrence.[39] Cripps had other sources: there were Rao's letters and later those of Agatha Harrison, following her arrival in Delhi in December; there were two perceptive reports prepared for Cripps by tough-minded experts on Indian politics (Freda Martin and Penderel Moon). All these helped him to come to terms with a situation where the tightly ordered procedure for constitution-making envisaged in the Cripps offer was being overtaken by events.

What Cripps was told on all sides was that India was on the move again.

37. Nehru to RSC, 3 December 1945, PRO, CAB 127/143.

38. RSC to Nehru, 12 December 1945, copy, PRO, CAB 127/143. Mansergh, TOP, vi, p. 851n. says 'unable to trace'.

39. Nehru to RSC, 27 January 1946; orig. PRO, CAB 127/143; printed in Mansergh, TOP, vi, pp. 851–9; Gopal (ed.), Nehru: Selected Works, xiv, pp. 138–47. RSC to Nehru, 10 February 1946, PRO, CAB 127/143, Mansergh, TOP, vi, p. 1107 n.1 says 'unable to trace'.

The political stagnation of the war years had been replaced by an impatient mood of change, potentially violent in expression. While the INA prosecutions showed how out of touch the British authorities now were, the tide of nationalism in Indonesia spelled out a further warning for them. But the problems in transferring power to a successor regime had also been exacerbated by the inexorably widening communal gulf, which dominated the provincial elections that were currently under way.

While Congress was bound to do well – estimates agreed in correctly predicting its victory in up to eight provinces – this represented a recovery of ground lost since 1937: a rehabilitation after its unfulfilling experiences during the war, when its opponents had been left a clear field. What was new was the force of Muslim militancy, fuelling the widespread advance of the Muslim League. This simultaneously made Congress's claim to represent non-Hindus 'little more than a debating point', as Cripps was now informed, while it opened, for the first time, the prospect of electoral legitimation for Jinnah's demands. But whereas Rao had for months consistently predicted, albeit against his inclinations, that the League might take Bengal and possibly Sind, though not the Punjab, as late as the end of January Nehru was stubbornly denying any such possibility.[40]

Even in 1939, Cripps had not visited India with an innocent mind, but one that had already been deeply influenced by Nehru; and the same was true in 1946. To some extent this may have been *faute de mieux* – 'I only wish Jinnah would write me a similar well argued letter'[41] – but the fact that Cripps was strongly predisposed to see things from Nehru's point of view was the reason that he had elicited Nehru's long letter in the first place.

What it revealed was rigidity of the Congress mindset. Nehru blamed a century of British rule for preventing 'the internal forces from establishing an equilibrium among themselves' and accordingly called the introduction of separate electorates 'the seed of the poisonous tree that has grown now to poison all our national life and prevent progress'. The political backwardness of the Muslims was taken for granted; the success of League organization explained as 'strikingly similar to the Nazi technique'; the cry for Pakistan dismissed as 'a sentimental slogan which they have got used to'. Talk of direct action could thus be dismissed – 'I do not think there is

---

40. See Rao to RSC, 15 October, 20 November, 15 December 1945, 30 January, 27 February 1946, PRO, CAB 127/147, partly reprinted in Mansergh, *TOP*, vi, pp. 564–5, 704–5; Harrison to RSC, esp. 2, 27 February, 6 March 1946, in Cripps papers; reports by Freda Martin, November 1945, and E. P. Moon, December 1945, both via J. McL. Short, PRO, CAB 127/150, printed in Mansergh, *TOP*, vi, pp. 766–75; Nehru in Mansergh, *TOP*, vi, p. 854.
41. RSC to Rao, 10 February 1946, copy, PRO, CAB 127/147.

much in Jinnah's threat' – and the imposition of a unitary constitution based on majority voting was urged despite the Muslim League's bluff about resistance. 'There may be some petty riots in some cities,' Nehru conceded.[42]

Looking backward on the historical record, Nehru's strictures on British agency may be unduly flattering to the talent for manipulation allegedly displayed by generations of predominantly dull Viceroys. Looking forward to our own times, when the authenticity of Islamic nationalism as a potent historical force can hardly be doubted, other questions arise. If Cripps was insufficiently alert to the growing power of the Muslim League, the source is not difficult to discern. At a personal level, the message of Nehru's letter was that 'the problem is not one so much of logical analysis as of psychological appreciation' – something he found 'wholly lacking in statements and speeches made in London'. That he saw this as Cripps's own deficiency was tactfully concealed behind a generalized appeal to address this 'emotional and psychological' crux of the problem through an exercise of imagination and sympathy.[43] Both Cripps and Pethick-Lawrence took this cue from Nehru as licensing a display of rhetorical empathy with Congress's aspirations which subsequently struck the Viceroy as cloying.

By February 1946 Cripps's attention was firmly focused on India. The Cabinet had agreed to appoint A. V. Alexander as the third member of its Delegation. With a long career in the Co-operative Movement behind him, Albert Alexander had served since 1940 as First Lord of the Admiralty, and was as happy singing 'Rule Britannia' around the piano as 'The Red Flag'. Like Bevin, his instincts were to maintain British power rather than give it away, but in India, about which he hitherto knew little, he started with the conventional pro-Congress sentiments of his party. He joined a Delegation on which Cripps and Pethick-Lawrence had already set their stamp and in which they made all the running. The three of them set to work together for the first time during a weekend with Attlee at Chequers at the end of February.

'I am afraid that Cripps will be the operative element,' Wavell had noted, 'and I think he is sold to the Congress point of view, and I don't think he is quite straight in his methods.'[44] He would not have been reassured to have known that Cripps had already secured a subtle downgrading of the Viceroy's role in the official announcement; and Wavell's correspondence with Pethick-Lawrence shows him clearly suspicious that Cripps intended

42. Mansergh, *TOP*, vi, pp. 852–3, 856, 857.   43. Mansergh, *TOP*, vi, pp. 856, 858.
44. Wavell diary, 11 February 1946, in Moon (ed.), *Wavell: journal*, p. 211.

the Viceroy to be a 'a lay figure' in the negotiations – both of them in different ways mindful of the Cripps Mission in 1942. It was settled that while the Delegation should act as a team with the Viceroy, its members should be free to pursue informal contacts.

The Chequers weekend was dominated by Cripps. His view prevailed that 'the Mission should start with an open mind and see as many people as possible', rather than the alternative, which Wavell favoured, of a brisker approach with a predetermined agenda. 'Cripps has a mind which crystallizes very hard,' was how Pethick-Lawrence justified the strategy to Wavell, 'and he feels I think that he would rather have a period in which to soak himself in every aspect of the matter before we take our decisions.'[45] Cripps had also produced a draft Directive which specified that, if agreement were reached in Delhi, 'the Government will be prepared to implement the arrangement so come to'.[46] This would have amounted to plenipotentiary powers; and while the final draft was rather more cautious in its wording, in line with what Attlee had already told the House of Commons, the fact is that Cripps and his colleagues were virtually given *carte blanche* as to how the transfer of power was to be achieved.

The decision to send the Cabinet Delegation had been announced on 19 February 1946, taking many MPs by surprise. Security had been tight; even Pethick-Lawrence's clothing coupons for tropical kit had been issued anonymously.[47] The initiative was widely welcomed. The *Manchester Guardian* called it 'a stroke of courage and imagination'.[48] News of mutiny in the Indian navy, and of riots in Bombay, reinforced a sense of urgency.

Maulana Azad, still President of Congress, made a conciliatory statement about the Delegation, and specifically welcomed the presence of Cripps, whose selection had created some adverse comment in India. Nehru too spoke in optimistic, if characteristically barbed, tones about the prospects of agreement. Privately, he assured Cripps of his readiness to meet him but challenged him on one crucial and familiar point of terminology: 'I find a strange reluctance to use the word "independence" with all that it conveys.'[49] The Chequers meeting had already determined this point and, once the King had been squared, the British Government finally produced an unequivocally satisfactory answer. When Attlee spoke in the India debate on 15 March,

45. Record of discussion, 24 February 1946, in Mansergh, *TOP*, vi, p. 1058; Pethick-Lawrence to Wavell, 1 March 1946, in Mansergh, *TOP*, vi, p. 1090.
46. Record of discussion, 24 February 1946, App. 1, RSC draft, in Mansergh, *TOP*, vi, p. 1061.
47. Turnbull to Blaker, 31 January 1946, PRO, CAB 127/96.
48. Leader, *Manchester Guardian*, 20 February 1946.
49. Nehru to RSC, 5 March 1946, in Mansergh, *TOP*, vi, p. 1108.

he affirmed that membership of the Commonwealth was the desired option; but that if India 'elects for independence, she has a right, in our view, to do so'.[50] Cripps happily repeated these assurances on arrival in Delhi: 'We want to give independence to India as quickly and as smoothly as we can.'[51]

50. *News Chronicle*, 16 March 1946.
51. Press conference, 1 April 1946, PRO, CAB 127/98.

2

The Search for Agreement

The ministers left Britain on 19 March 1946. The question was raised as to how Cripps could be spared. One letter in the *Daily Telegraph* tried to have it both ways in bewailing the fact that the Board of Trade would be left 'rudderless' while claiming that it would be a benefit that 'the voice of austerity may be less heard in the land'.[1]

Alexander, with his defence responsibilities as First Lord, flew separately, while Cripps had four days to impress his ideas upon Pethick-Lawrence. *En route*, Tunis provided an oasis of calm and French hospitality. Turnbull found his spirits raised by the constant flow of aperitifs – 'Cripps of course refused every time' – and did his best, along with George Blaker, Cripps's private secretary from the Board of Trade, to make amends. For Cripps himself, 'no hurry, no meetings and no papers to read' provided a sufficient respite.[2] Only at Karachi was the party reunited, with Turnbull given the 'very sticky' assignment of winkling Alexander out of his comfortable Dakota so that the entire Delegation could arrive together in Delhi on 24 March.[3] On landing, press reports had everyone acting in character. 'Come on, Cripps,' said Alexander, tugging at his sleeve, 'let's go and get some beer.' 'Not for me,' was the reply. Pethick-Lawrence emerged wearing an enormous topee of the missionary type. Cripps was complimented on having put on weight since 1942. 'I have been eating recently a great deal of cauliflower,' he responded, to general laughter. 'Yes and many carrots.'[4]

Cripps took pains with media presentation throughout. The efforts of A. H. Joyce, the publicity adviser to the Delegation, seem to have been largely redundant. It was Cripps rather than Pethick-Lawrence who took most of the press conferences, on a variety of bland pretexts which certainly

1. Francis Angell, *Daily Telegraph*, 21 February 1946.
2. Turnbull diary, 20 March 1946; RSC diary, 22 March 1946.
3. Turnbull diary, 23 March 1946.
4. Robin Duff and James Cameron, *Daily Express*, 25 March 1946.

did not fool Alexander, who felt some sensitivity about his 'silent man' status.[5] Cripps found the journalists more friendly than in 1942 and after one early press conference commented in his diary that 'I think we all enjoyed ourselves!!'[6] His plea on this occasion was that differences of view should not be 'hotted up' so as to prejudice the chances of a settlement. He explained that the Delegation's plan was 'to meet informally a great number of people of different views and different opinions, many of whom are old personal friends of ours with whom we want to renew our acquaintance not on formal terms but on those of pleasing friendship and informality to which some of us have been accustomed in the past'.[7]

This informality extended to relations with the press. In line with his normal practice, Cripps gave sympathetic journalists access for off-the-record briefings. Robin Duff and James Cameron of the *Daily Express* and Norman Cliff of the *News Chronicle* were specially favoured; so was Peter Stursberg of the *Daily Herald*, who, conscious that he was writing for Labour's official mouthpiece, did not allow his personal impression of Cripps as a cold man to percolate into print. Blaker, as the protective private secretary, became concerned about drawing the line, as more requests for interviews poured in, so as to protect Cripps from doing too much himself.

The Delegation occupied its own house at 2 Willingdon Crescent, half a mile from its offices in an air-conditioned wing of the Viceregal Lodge. Cripps had initially shown himself reluctant to stay even for a couple of nights at the Lodge on arrival, no doubt still mindful of Linlithgow's brooding aura, and Pethick-Lawrence had to avert such a snub. 'I think it is very important to maintain close relations with Wavell,' he pleaded. 'We shall want in the first week to bring him round to an approach to the problem which differs a good deal from what he has been contemplating.'[8] Despite appearances – his single eye and taciturnity were famously forbidding – the pragmatic Wavell proved accommodating and Cripps wrote of 'a preliminary chat with the Viceroy last night which seemed successful since there was no great divergence of opinion'.[9] Still, the move to their own house came as a relief from 'the grandeur of the proceedings and all the formality'.[10]

Cripps staked a good deal on employing an informal approach. A letter of welcome from Azad, reflecting on their experience in 1942, made the

5. Alexander diary, 12 April 1946.   6. RSC diary, 1 April 1946.
7. Report of press conference, 1 April 1946, PRO, CAB 127/98.
8. Pethick-Lawrence to RSC, 27 February 1946, Mansergh, *TOP*, vi, p. 1075.
9. RSC diary, 25 March 1946.   10. ibid., 26 March 1946.

point: 'Looking back on the negotiations it seems to me that the chief reason for failure lay in the formal and official manner in which they were carried out.'[11] Cripps's methods in 1946, much criticized at the time and subsequently, have to be understood as a determination to avoid making the same mistake, even if this led him to make the opposite mistake. In 1942, of course, he had exploited informal contacts with Congress, notably through Shiva Rao, Rajagopalachari and J. C. Gupta, all of whom he soon met again in 1946. Above all, since he attributed the failure of the Cripps Mission to Gandhi, this time Cripps went to great lengths to win him round, both directly and indirectly. Horace Alexander and Agatha Harrison of the ICG, who became part of the Mahatma's entourage in Delhi, were conscripted by Cripps as helpers. He had already shown himself responsive to Harrison's advice on how to heal his rift with Congress, stemming from the aftermath of the Cripps mission, and he now relied upon her to facilitate informal social engagements with Congress leaders.

Cripps likewise tried to establish an equally effective network with the Muslim League and the Sikhs. This was the task assigned to two young personal assistants, Major Woodrow Wyatt and Major John McLaughlin Short. Wyatt was an ebullient Labour MP, whose political career was to describe a long arc from the *Tribune* left to the Thatcherite right, and whose recent experience as a member of the parliamentary delegation to India made him a well-connected aide for Cripps. Though he also cultivated links with Congress, Wyatt's main job was to keep open the line to the Muslim League. Short, currently working for the Ministry of Information, was an expert on the Punjab who had met Cripps in 1942 and who bombarded him with memoranda throughout the winter of 1945-6, educating him on the Pakistan issue. As eccentric in his methods as he was idiosyncratic in expression, Short was difficult to pin down, but his main job was to talk to the Sikhs. Cripps thought that both were 'doing first class work' – 'Their unorthodoxy makes them acceptable where the orthodox would be without hope!'[12]

'The two Majors' relished their work. Their doings weave a busy sub-plot through the pages of Cripps's diary, mainly Rosencrantz and Guildenstern, with touches of Trinculo and Caliban, finding a brave new world amid the luxury of the Imperial Hotel. The bills they ran up during April created embarrassment for Blaker and Turnbull, conscious that the Treasury had only allowed the Delegation itself an entertainment allowance of £50 per month, a rate which Wyatt and Short comfortably exceeded on their own

11. Azad to RSC, 25 March 1946, PRO, CAB 127/119.   12. RSC diary, 7 April 1946.

account. 'You will probably agree,' Blaker remonstrated, 'that we cannot ask [the taxpayer] to pay for your smokes and drinks!' But the remonstrance fell on three pairs of deaf ears. When Turnbull raised the matter with Cripps, he was simply told to inform the Treasury that the President of the Board of Trade was 'definitely of opinion that entertaining on the scale which Major Wyatt and Major Short have been giving is essential for the discharge of the functions which he wishes them to perform.' At the end of the next month, Short had run up a total of £477 on expenses. The wine bill alone, at £388, would be of the order of £5,000 at today's prices.[13] If the performance continued unabated, it was with Cripps's full approval. 'He never told me that I drank too much, though I drank a lot then,' Wyatt later recalled.[14]

Uncensorious, intent on success, and ready to pay a high price for it, Cripps thought that he was getting good value. Within days of arrival in Delhi, he had opened up personal lines of communication with both Congress and the League. The advice he had received from his Australian friend R. G. Casey, now Governor of Bengal, reinforced Cripps's hunch that the way forward was to 'have a chat', and engender warmth and cordiality, rather than restrict contact to formal meetings.[15] It was Casey who recommended Sudhir Ghosh, whose role as 'Gandhi's emissary' offered him eagerly exploited opportunities to inflate his own position. The youthful Ghosh, Cambridge-educated and purposefully ingratiating, was now an employee of the Tata conglomerate, which seemed happy to finance his apprenticeship as a spin doctor. Already known to Wyatt, whose talents were not dissimilar, Ghosh used him to send a warning to Cripps: 'When Sir Stafford came to India in 1942, the old man described his offer as a "post-dated cheque" and that was the end of it. So beware of the old man.'[16] Ghosh presented himself as a man uniquely suited to avoid the pitfalls of undue formality on this mission and, according to his own account, 'Cripps at first sight adopted me as someone he had known for ever.'[17]

Their initial encounter was on 28 March, the first day of official meetings, which were interrupted, not for the last time, by a sudden visit from Ghosh. After hearing his story, Cripps commissioned Ghosh to go and summon Gandhi, who was currently living near Poona:

13. See correspondence, esp. Blaker to Wyatt and Short, 2 May 1946, Turnbull to R. S. Brown, 6 May 1946, Turnbull to Short, 29 May 1946, PRO, CAB 127/150.
14. Wyatt, *Confessions*, p. 141.
15. Casey to RSC, 23 December 1945, PRO, CAB 127/122.
16. Ghosh to Wyatt, 1 March 1946, PRO, CAB 127/129.
17. Ghosh, *Ghandhi's Emissary*, p. 13.

... the old man was upset at the (very unfortunate) way he had been handled over these meetings. So I wrote him a nice personal letter which S. G. thinks will put matters right and he takes it back with him to-night. I hope Ghandiji [sic] will come up on Sunday in time for Agatha's special quaker service which I am going to.[18]

The next day's instalment made an even better story. Ghosh was not called for his early morning flight, which he therefore missed, only to find that the plane then crashed, killing all passengers. 'It really looks as if there were divine intervention to save him,' wrote Cripps, 'as his visit and messages are of the utmost importance.'[19]

Primed by the dramatic way in which Ghosh had been spared, Gandhi and Cripps were united in seeing it as providential that they should meet. Cripps had drawn the conclusion from his early conversations that 'the one effective way of settling the matter was to get Jinnah and Gandhi to agree'. This was easier said than done, but he made sure that his first courtesy call ('and so a great compliment') was upon Jinnah.[20] Cripps found Jinnah reasonable. 'To use the common language, he had got rid of his inferiority complex.' He assured Cripps that he was ready to meet Gandhi. 'I suggested that if they got stuck,' Cripps recorded, 'I might perhaps help as a friend of both – unofficially.'[21] Cripps clearly hoped that his inevitably well-publicized first visit to Gandhi would be perceived as a further step in mutual conciliation rather than as any kind of snub to the Muslim League.

'Gandhi Chooses to Live with "Untouchables"' was the *Daily Herald* headline. Gandhi arrived in Delhi on an officially commissioned special train (towards the cost of which Ghosh was duly sent to press the third-class fare upon the Viceroy's secretary) and on arrival took up residence in the Harijan sweepers' quarter, where a camp had been set up. The simplicity of the Mahatma's hut was juxtaposed with the installation of electricity, loudspeakers and telephones.[22] Here Cripps had his initial informal meeting with Gandhi on 31 March, first joining over 3,000 people for prayers before retreating, shoeless, to the hut for forty minutes of private talk. Cripps then whisked Gandhi off in the official car to meet Pethick-Lawrence. 'We both asked him to act as our adviser with all frankness and this he promised to

18. RSC diary, 28 March 1946.
19. ibid., 29 March 1946. Ghosh's memoirs have often provoked charges as to their unreliability but it should be noted that Cripps corroborates the colourful account in *Gandhi's Emissary*, pp. 82–8.
20. RSC diary, 30 March 1946.
21. ibid., 31 March 1946 (entries generally refer to the previous day).
22. *Daily Herald*, 1 April 1946.

do and to help as best he could,' Cripps recorded in his diary. 'Old Gandhi seemed physically very fit,' he concluded. 'I am really fond of the old man though he is no child at negotiation! He's got an unassailable position in the country and knows it . . .'[23]

It is obvious that Cripps hoped for more than spiritual uplift from Gandhi. It was his proven ability to thwart a settlement that made his position pivotal and thus made efforts to propitiate him worthwhile. The alternative strategy was to keep the old man at arm's length – as the Viceroy clearly wished – and to rely on Azad's diffuse professions of goodwill or Nehru's subtle exercise of authority in carrying Congress. But Cripps felt that he had tried this in 1942, only to be disappointed. Believing that the Muslim League was bluffing about the irreducibility of its demand for an independent Pakistan, Cripps thought that Congress could be induced to acquiesce in an acceptable compromise if only Gandhi did not feel his *amour propre* slighted in the process. No trouble was to be spared in courting the old man. Wavell confessed himself 'frankly horrified at the deference shown to Gandhi' during his first official meeting with the Delegation on 3 April, when a delay in supplying him with a glass of water meant that 'Cripps hustled off himself to see about it.'[24]

The programme of official interviews was as exhausting as it was exhaustive. The three ministers sat alongside the Viceroy, day by day, through a series of over 400 interviews that lasted from 26 March until 17 April. Though an official record was kept throughout, under Turnbull's direction, Cripps sat busily writing his own notes, as indeed did Alexander. All accounts agree that Cripps showed formidable skills in cross-examination, for example grilling the Muslim League representatives as to what, in practice, they meant by Pakistan.

The process may have had some educative value, certainly for Alexander, possibly for Pethick-Lawrence, though hardly for Wavell. For Cripps the real work was behind the scenes, especially with his friends in Congress. 'We had some intensely interesting talks and I ended up with a long talk with Jawaharlal in the garden,' he wrote after a reception given for the Working Committee. 'I think the whole atmosphere was most promising and there did not seem to be any suspicions about us as there were last time.'[25] Wavell, however, had a more jaundiced view of the 'hole-and-corner'

23. RSC diary, 1 April 1946; suspension marks in original.
24. Wavell diary, 3 April 1946, in Moon (ed.), *Wavell: journal*, p. 236.
25. RSC diary, 13 April 1946.

methods adopted by 'Cripps and his minions (Wyatt and Short)'.[26] On the surface, relations with the Viceroy remained harmonious, and even friendly, but Cripps was somewhat naive in supposing that 'we have, I think, quite got over the slight suspicions that were in his mind when we came out'.[27]

Press reports in the middle of April began to speak increasingly of a deadlock. Backed by the final election returns, showing that the League had won around 90 per cent of the Muslim vote, thus matching Congress success elsewhere, Jinnah was becoming increasingly intransigent in his public demands for Pakistan. Stursberg's reports in the *Daily Herald*, citing 'the highest sources', none the less stressed that 'the mission has no intention of returning to London without having achieved its avowed purpose to hand over India to the Indians'.[28] This chimed with what Cripps wrote in his diary: 'We can't leave this country without a settlement of some kind. If we did there would be bloodshed and chaos within a few weeks.'[29]

Cripps was becoming restive, impatient and fearful. He wrote to Pethick-Lawrence: 'I have the feeling that all this interviewing is dragging out the time for a settlement to a rather dangerous extent and that unless we are careful we shall lose the initiative which might at this stage be disastrous.' The time had come to lay down a timetable and to make hard choices, especially about Pakistan. Cripps accordingly enclosed a long memorandum in his own hand – 'A v. valuable MS', as Pethick-Lawrence called it – which formed the Delegation's agenda at an important meeting on 10 April.[30] It was a statement, to be put to the parties, posing two alternatives: either Scheme A for union or Scheme B for partition. Scheme A suggested the most flexible form of union, while Scheme B stipulated the possible extent of an independent Pakistan in rigorous terms. If Jinnah's 'two-nation theory' justified Muslim separation, Cripps argued, it would be 'wholly inconsistent with this theory if non-Muslim majority areas should be added to Pakistan'.[31]

Cripps was clearly intent on telling both sides that neither could have everything it claimed. Jinnah might champion the Muslim minority in India as a whole, but a Scheme B Pakistan could only offer salvation to Muslims in those parts of northern India where Muslims were already relatively

26. Wavell diary, 15, 24 April 1946, in Moon (ed.), *Wavell: journal*, pp. 245, 251.
27. RSC diary, 17 April 1946.   28. *Daily Herald*, 12 April 1946.
29. RSC diary, 7 April 1946.
30. RSC to Pethick-Lawrence, and Pethick-Lawrence note, with RSC memorandum, n.d. but 9–10 April 1946, PRO, CAB 127/98.
31. RSC memorandum, n.d but drafted for meeting on 10 April 1946, in Mansergh, *TOP*, vii. at p. 179.

secure in their majority status. Faced with an agonizing choice, could he be tempted into some form of federation under Scheme A? Cripps's information was that Vallabhbhai Patel, the strong man of Congress, stood for the hard line on a unitary solution in which the Hindu majority would naturally prevail. Could he be persuaded by Gandhi to offer the olive branch of Scheme A, so as to avert partition? But before the Indians could be confronted with a delicately poised choice, the British Government had to face its own moment of truth. Cripps's negotiating strategy demanded that Scheme B be specified in a form unattractive to the Muslim League; but Pakistan's consequent economic and strategic weakness also made Scheme B an unattractive option from the point of view of British defence interests in the region, which were supposed to be safeguarded by any Indian settlement. The Cabinet and the Chiefs of Staff in London therefore had to be won over. Attlee cabled back that even Scheme B was 'better than no agreement at all as this would lead to widespread chaos'.[32]

'Crucial Week in India: attempt to bring parties closer,' *The Times* reported on 15 April. On the same day, Cripps received a private letter from Azad, who knew that the Delegation's plan was to put a proposal to both parties and then to leave them to chew it over while the Cabinet ministers left Delhi for a break in Kashmir over Easter. Azad suggested that he should himself first receive an informal briefing, so as to anticipate likely objections from Jinnah and put Cripps 'in possession of the Congress attitude and the modifications or concessions it would accept in order to win the cooperation of the League'.[33] Cripps at once went to see Azad, reassuring him that no 'cut and dried' scheme was envisaged. 'He was as usual very friendly and co-operative and again said he would do his best to get the Congress Working Committee to accept any reasonable solution,' Cripps noted.[34]

Any hopes that the League would enter into informal negotiations with Congress were promptly dashed by Jinnah. Twenty minutes of 'photographing and cinematographing a fake meeting' did not help his official interview with the Delegation to get off to a good start on 16 April. 'I am afraid it yielded no useful results,' admitted the usually indomitable Cripps.[35] Although he had subjected Jinnah to 'a pretty severe cross-examination', by Alexander's reckoning, the tone of the meeting had been set, much to the Viceroy's chagrin, by the Secretary of State's insistence on the 'velvet glove', which in his hands was liable to become a woolly glove of unravelling

32. Attlee to Delegation, 13 April 1946, in Mansergh, *TOP*, vii, p. 260.
33. Azad to RSC, 15 April 1946, PRO, CAB 127/119.
34. RSC diary, 16 April 1946.   35. ibid.

platitudes.[36] None the less, Pethick-Lawrence struck Cripps as 'admirable in his friendliness and persuasiveness', and the ministers seem to have been agreed in relying on personal appeals to Jinnah rather than a sterner confrontation with him. Cripps accordingly solicited his colleagues' approval for 'a supreme and prolonged effort to persuade him to be more forthcoming'.

This is the really critical time and I feel personally that I must leave no stone unturned to get a favourable result for the future of 400 million people hangs in the balance in the next few days. May God give us wisdom to do what is right. I have never felt a heavier responsibility on my shoulders than just at this moment. I still feel we *must* succeed somehow. That is our duty and our debt to India . . .[37]

Cripps's awareness that general opinion was now pessimistic simply reinforced his determination not to 'give up hope till the last minute and anyway until I have seen J. and G. personally and at length'.[38] He spared himself no effort. On 17 April he spent a long evening with Jinnah, not getting home until nearly one o'clock, only to rise at 5.45 a.m. for a meeting at Gandhi's camp in the sweepers' colony.

Jinnah seemed to be locked into a posture of total inflexibility. 'He isn't quite big enough to take the plunge, though he realises the immense dangers if there is no agreement,' thought Cripps. 'I told him that his attitude tended to throw us into the arms of Congress and appealed to him to make some advance to a compromise – but I could not get anything out of him.' Neither Scheme A nor Scheme B was regarded as any basis for negotiation with Congress. If only by comparison, Gandhi appeared more forthcoming. 'As always he was charming and wanted to be helpful,' Cripps noted; and he seized on the suggestion that if anyone were to meet Jinnah, it should be Nehru.[39]

This at least was welcome news. Although no such meeting came off, the fact that Gandhi himself nominated Nehru as the Congress spokesman absolved Cripps from any reproach of going behind the old man's back in seeking out Nehru himself; but seek him out Cripps certainly now did. Moreover, it should be remembered that throughout the visit of the Cabinet Delegation, a contest was taking place for the presidency of Congress, which was a key factor in settling who would shortly become Prime Minister. In

36. Alexander diary, 16 April 1946; Wavell diary, 16 April 1946, in Moon (ed.), *Wavell: journal*, p. 246.
37. RSC diary, 16 April 1946; suspension marks in original.   38. ibid., 17 April 1946.
39. ibid., 18 April 1946.

declaring to Cripps that 'the real man to consult was Jawaharlal', rather than Azad or Patel, Gandhi had given a highly significant indication of his own preference, which turned out, as usual, to clinch the matter.[40] What weighed with Gandhi was, above all, Nehru's qualifications as a sophisticated negotiator who could stand on level terms with any British opposite number. In effect, Nehru was chosen because he was a match for Cripps.

Cripps heard what he wanted to hear from both Jinnah and Gandhi in one further respect: that, although the parties were fearful of themselves being seen to offer the necessary concessions, a compromise solution that was imposed by the British would actually be accepted on both sides. At the Delegation's meeting with Wavell on 18 April, Cripps opportunely tabled his own proposal for an award.

The way this was done, and the impression it made, illustrate Cripps's methods and Cripps's dominance. Pethick-Lawrence later retailed (and perhaps improved) the story:

Then came the time for the Mission to prepare its most important memorandum setting forth its views. One by one the complicated points had been decided in consultation with the Viceroy (Lord Wavell). One of us was then required to make out of them a comprehensive document. Cripps volunteered. In one hour he brought to me the finished work – some three thousand words written out in his own neat handwriting, in his usual red ink, covering ten closely packed foolscap pages.[41]

Certainly there survives a hand-written version (in red ink) of this long and complex document.[42] It is also the case that it was tabled only a couple of hours after Cripps had left Gandhi, following his late night with Jinnah. It is possible that, before Cripps saw either of them, an earlier draft had been produced, which was read by his fellow ministers overnight and then rewritten in a couple of hours the next morning. There is no evidence that the document was shown in advance to either Jinnah or Gandhi. Cripps's diary, however, does hint that, when he went on from the Viceregal Lodge to meet Nehru for lunch, he was more open: 'We discussed the merits of various compromises and it didn't look as if the Working Committee were going to give very much either!'[43]

40. ibid. and see French, *Liberty or Death*, pp. 262–3.
41. Pethick-Lawrence, tribute to Cripps, BBC transcript as recorded, 22 April 1952.
42. Memorandum, 18 April 1946, PRO, CAB 127/99; printed in Mansergh, *TOP*, vii, pp. 303–10. Moore comments: 'It is not clear whether or when Cripps showed or disclosed the contents of his draft to the Congress leaders.' Moore, *Escape from Empire*, p. 92.
43. RSC diary, 18 April 1946.

Cripps's own attempt to square the circle, it quickly emerged, was not acceptable to Congress. Admittedly, his draft award rejected partition as impracticable, on the ground that if Pakistan were to be extensive enough to be viable, its claim to non-Muslim areas would be unjustifiable. Cripps proposed instead to accommodate the Muslim demand for some kind of self-government by means of a three-tier structure, in which provinces could opt for grouping into Hindustan or Pakistan at an intermediate level below that of a Union of All India, which would be responsible for certain common functions, including defence.

Here, it might seem, was the only chance of weaning the Muslim League from the Pakistan option. The underlying problem was that Congress found the notion of grouping repugnant, and therefore refused to grant it the sort of legitimacy necessary to entice the League into such constitutional arrangements. Since it would only participate if it were persuaded to trust Congress, their mutual perceptions became the real issue at every stage. As Cripps told Nehru, in reference to a possible interim government: 'If there was confidence and goodwill, it would work anyway; if there wasn't, it wouldn't – and he more or less agreed.'[44] Everything in the end turned on trust or its absence; but not, as in 1942, mistrust of the Viceroy so much as mistrust between Congress and the League.

As communal tension rose, press comment suggested a total impasse at Easter 1946. In Britain, Conservative newspapers struck a bitter note. 'Indian leadership has failed dismally to bridge the ever-widening gulf between Muslims and Hindus,' wrote the *Observer* correspondent. 'The great Congress hoax of India's "oneness" has been exposed, as Mr Jinnah always maintained it would be, as a pure myth.'[45] 'It May Be A Long Job' read the *Daily Herald*'s headline, loyally seeking to make the best of it.[46] The ministers left Delhi for their holiday, knowing that no progress would be made in their absence – and perhaps not after their return either.

Five days amid the mountains of Kashmir gave Cripps an opportunity to relax, of which he took full advantage. He was tired, of course, and had been working hard; but no more so, perhaps, than had he simply been in England. Indeed his private secretary, George Blaker, set about reassuring Isobel Cripps on just this point. Cripps preferred heat to cold; the sun was welcome and with it a profuse abundance of exotic fruit. He was enjoying his early morning rides, especially since the Viceroy's stables had provided mounts that were not too temperamental for him. An afternoon swim in

44. ibid.   45. *Observer*, 21 April 1946.   46. *Daily Herald*, 25 April 1946.

the Viceroy's pool formed another welcome break. Most important, Blaker judged, 'is that life is lived at a much lower pressure than in London', with less paperwork to deal with than at the Board of Trade, meaning that both of them were actually working shorter hours under less oppressive conditions.[47] So far, so good; and it got better before it got worse.

The ministers were guests of the Maharajah at his guest house near Srinagar; the gardens were beautiful, the weather cool, the streams refreshing. Stafford wrote long and sentimental descriptions for Isobel:

In the evening light it was a quite unforgettable sight. I had to wander off alone, it was too beautiful to share with anyone but you – it was that beauty which makes one happily sad – a deep sadness for humanity, an overwhelming sense of the smallness of man and his inability to cope with life . . .

I feel I don't want to talk to anyone but just to sit still with the memory of what I have seen. Somehow it seems peculiarly appropriate that this should be eastertide and somehow this and easter and our job all seem fitted in together – I am not sure how but I am certain that they are. This is perhaps God's answer to my and your prayers for guidance and out of this experience will come wisdom to deal with what is so intensely difficult a problem. I am sure that beauty and peace give wisdom and perhaps in the next 3 days God will give his guidance.[48]

Cripps took the opportunity for a couple of days fishing and caught a good number of trout his first time out but nothing worth keeping on a subsequent day. Alexander preferred billiards and was much impressed by the aptitude shown for the game by Pethick-Lawrence, who triumphed in a game of snooker despite conceding a handicap of 21 points. But two evenings were pre-empted for consideration of Cripps's latest plan, based on a complex scheme put forward several days earlier by Nawab Gurmani from the Punjab, 'trying to meet both sides by arranging for a limited sort of Pakistan by election', though without the sort of legislature to which Congress objected.[49] Cripps was pleased, moreover, at the atmosphere that had been created: 'I think we have got the whole party onto a friendly happy basis – all Christian names! and enough jokes and humour to keep them laughing.'[50]

The heat was now on, in every sense. On returning to Delhi, temperatures steadily soared to around 40°C. Jinnah was wary of the new plan when Cripps put it to him. 'However I went on and on (like casting a fly over a

47. Blaker to IC, 15 April 1946.   48. RSC diary, Good Friday, 20 April 1946.
49. Alexander diary, 22 April 1946.   50. RSC diary, Easter Monday, 22 April 1946.

fish that won't take),' Cripps wrote, though clearly finding him as difficult to play as any Kashmir trout.[51] This proved not to be crucial since, as Cripps admitted the following day, 'Jawaharlal turned it down flat! So that was that.'[52] No sooner was one scheme rejected by one party than Cripps tried an alternative on the other side; dining privately with Jinnah one night, Cripps detected the first signs of concession towards the idea of a federal centre. 'The plot thickens!' he wrote as he pondered his tactics, deciding what to say and to whom to say it.[53]

At last there came a corresponding sign from Congress of a willingness to engage in face-to-face talks. Much oppressed by the Delhi heat, Azad pined for escape to another Simla conference; he determined to ignore his evidently divided Working Committee in seeking out Cripps on 26 April. Azad said to him – none of this was on paper – that he was confident that Congress would, after all, enter negotiations on the basis of a federal three-tier approach; Jinnah could be told as much. Little wonder that Cripps lauded Azad as 'most forthcoming and helpful though I am not sure how far he can carry his Working Committee with him'. The precariousness of the position was patent: 'He didn't want me to say anything to Gandhi or Jawaharlal about this as he said it would make it more difficult for him to put it across to his Working Committee.'[54] Cripps reported back to his colleagues and, despite the Viceroy's growing wish 'to stop all this to-ing and fro-ing by Cripps', secured their approval.[55] Cripps respected Azad's confidences when he met Gandhi but 'had a very nice and friendly chat and I was regaled with hot water and honey – a good drink!' Finally Cripps played on Jinnah's fear of being held responsible for a breakdown to bring him into line.[56]

The upshot of Cripps's efforts was thus an agreement, if only an agreement to leave Delhi for the first face-to-face negotiations between the parties since the breakdown of the 1945 Simla conference. 'This important move, at a time when negotiations were threatened with deadlock,' reported the *Sunday Times*, 'is a major triumph for Sir Stafford Cripps.'[57] The Delegation's invitations to a second Simla conference specified its agenda: to consider a constitution for a union government, as Congress wished, balanced with the creation of two groups of Hindu and Muslim provinces, respectively – the essential concession to win Jinnah's acceptance.[58] Uneasily

51. ibid., 24 April 1946. 52. ibid., 26 April 1946. 53. ibid. 54. ibid.
55. Meeting, 26 April 1946, in Mansergh, *TOP*, vii, pp. 345–6; Wavell diary, 26 April 1946, in Moon (ed.), *Wavell: journal*, p. 253.
56. RSC diary, 26 April 1946. 57. *Sunday Times*, 28 April 1946.
58. Invitations to Azad and Jinnah, 27 April 1946, in Mansergh, *TOP*, vii, p. 352.

conscious that he had offered assurances that went beyond what the Working Committee was ready to sanction, Azad sent a letter to Pethick-Lawrence maintaining that Congress had never accepted this sort of Hindu/Muslim distinction; and the Delegation quickly concocted an emollient clarification.[59]

There followed an episode – part high politics, part low escapade – which illuminates many of the personal relationships at stake and explains some subsequent conflicts in testimony. It should be noted that, only the previous day, Azad had been induced by Gandhi to stand aside as President of Congress and to nominate as his successor not Patel, the self-appointed hammer of the Muslims, but Nehru. This move made Jinnah's participation in the tripartite talks easier for Cripps to secure. The Muslim League Working Committee seemed friendly when they attended a reception given for them by the ministers, who felt fortunate, for once, over its timing. In fact the last difficulty to be overcome before the Simla conference could meet came from quite another quarter. Gandhi was alarmed at the conditions which Congress was apparently being asked to accept, or so Ghosh warned when he turned up at 2 Willingdon Crescent after Sunday lunch on 28 April.

Cripps's energetic response was characteristic. He failed, however, to conscript an increasingly sceptical Alexander, who decided to go to church that evening rather than join the conspiratorial manoeuvres that Cripps confided to his diary.

So we had to arrange to see the old man without the Press getting to know as otherwise it might have adversely affected Jinnah and made him think there was some frame-up. So we arranged for the old man to take his walk in the Viceroy's park and garden and 'meet' us on our way back from bathing. We went and bathed and at about 6.50 went and sat in the round sunken garden (Pethick and I) and George [Blaker] did the scout outside.

Frank Turnbull was also at hand, and just as well, since he had to intervene in the nick of time so that the police did not stop Gandhi from entering the Viceregal grounds.[60] Cripps was in his element.

It was a lovely evening, first with the birds (flocks and flocks of green parroqueets) flighting home and then as it got darker the bats of all sorts and sizes. A storm was brewing up, with gusts of warm air. Gradually it became quite dark and then I heard

59. Mansergh, *TOP*, vii, p. 356.   60. Turnbull diary, 28 April 1946.

the old man coming and went out and met him and took him on my arm and led him down to our seat where we talked and smoothed matters out. Then we left him to go out one way and we walked off in the other direction and home. A most successful operation completely undiscovered![61]

Cripps had one further assignment before bed. Azad called to admit that he had not shown the Working Committee his first reply to the invitation to Simla; nor, therefore, could he show them the Delegation's subsequent response to him on the proposed agenda without revealing his earlier omission. Cripps simply observed in his diary that 'he had got himself into a bit of a jam out of which we will get him this morning!' Since Azad had now made a clean breast of it to the understanding Cripps, a further official letter, discreetly framed, could no doubt be concocted to cover the misdemeanour. 'Fortunately,' concluded Cripps, 'they feel they can send for me and ask me about these matters and so we can get them ironed out.'[62]

Alas, Cripps's congratulatory tone was premature. His interventions had solved one problem, only to exacerbate another. His own unguarded references at the round pool to a correspondence with Azad had alerted Gandhi to its very existence – letters which Azad then solemnly told the Mahatma he had never written. Gandhi was naturally upset at this discrepancy. 'You do not understand how uneasy I feel,' he wrote to Cripps (unusually, in his own shaky handwriting). 'Something is wrong.'[63] If he did not say what, Ghosh and Rajagopalachari were ready to be more explicit.

Cripps now determined to reveal all – whatever the embarrassment to Azad, since, as he told him, 'I could not leave Gandhi thinking that I had purposely withheld information from him, while pretending to be frank.' So a further early-morning call on Gandhi was necessary, which 'cleared the whole matter up as far as I am concerned in particular'.[64]

Cripps acceded, moreover, to Gandhi's request to be shown the correspondence with Azad. Blaker was simply informed in a cryptic note that Gandhi had been squared – Cripps drew a little square to make the point – and was sent over with the actual letters that had passed. Cripps rationalized this disclosure of official business on the ground that a copy of Azad's first reply to Pethick-Lawrence had reached Cripps independently, along with a covering letter that had a personal status.[65] This letter from Azad has survived in Cripps's papers. It is handwritten – *by Nehru*, as Cripps must

61. RSC diary, 29 April 1946.   62. ibid.
63. Gandhi to RSC, 29 April 1946, PRO, CAB 127/128.   64. RSC diary, 30 April 1946.
65. ibid.

immediately have recognized, though signed by Azad.[66] By the same token, it must also have dawned on Cripps that, if Azad had been acting behind the back of Gandhi and the Working Committee, so too had Nehru, at least to the extent of trying to cover up for his friend.

Not the least revelation for Gandhi, for whom Nehru had often acted as amanuensis, must have been this demonstration of his protégé's complicity in the process. Little wonder that Nehru was out of sorts and, displacing his embarrassment, lost his temper with Ghosh as the perpetrator of the whole nuisance. 'I am afraid the old man will not easily forgive Azad,' Cripps noted, 'but it is better to have it all out now rather than let it poison the whole situation at a critical moment.'[67]

The effect was more serious than Cripps realized, not least for himself. This petty chicanery, mainly on Azad's part, served to impair trust, which was already in short supply and which Cripps could not afford to squander. Gandhi was encouraged in his recurrent notion that some kind of underhand compromise was being hatched – even by Azad and Nehru – and that only his own vigilance could avert a betrayal of his life work. Moreover, Azad's dissimulations polluted the channels of communication, confirming Wavell in his suspicion that 'Cripps has been saying different things to different people'. Overburdened as Viceroy, out of touch with the need to finesse Azad out of his self-inflicted difficulties – 'I don't know how or whether it got straightened out' – Wavell was understandably subject to misconceptions, which in turn recycled pejorative allegations from 1942.[68] These were none the less important at the time and, through his journal, have fed many subsequent historical strictures on Cripps.

Simla was the Viceroy's summer residence, almost due north of Delhi in the foothills of the Himalayas. A straggle of well-appointed chalets, set amid bountiful English-style gardens, clung to a ridge at over 2,000 metres. On arrival on 1 May, Cripps was given a comfortable suite in the rambling Viceregal Lodge, with striking views over the hills to the Himalayas beyond.

---

66. Azad to RSC, 27 April 1946, PRO, CAB 127/106, enclosing his letter to Pethick-Lawrence as printed in Mansergh, *TOP*, vii, p. 353.

67. RSC diary, 30 April 1946; and RSC to Blaker, 29 April 1946, PRO, CAB 127/106. This account is broadly in accord with Ghosh, *Gandhi's Emissary*, p. 105, except that the exchange of letters which Cripps handed over did not contain a statement by Azad that he was confident of carrying the Working Committee; that had been given verbally to Cripps and reported by him at the Delegation's meeting on 26 April, in Mansergh, *TOP*, vii, pp. 345–6. Also Ghosh confuses the meeting at the round pool with that at which Cripps made his final confession.

68. Wavell diary, 28, 29 April 1946, in Moon (ed.), *Wavell: journal*, pp. 253–4.

Here was an attractive refuge from baking Delhi for the twelve official participants in the tripartite talks: four each from Congress and the Muslim League, three ministers plus the Viceroy. Their seclusion was part of the plan. Journalists, denied any hard news, competed in their evocative word-pictures and speculated, with increasing tetchiness, on the hopes of a settlement. 'India, frustrated by seven weeks' inconclusive comings and goings,' reported James Cameron, 'is now beginning to chafe at the complete screen of secrecy let down on the talks.'[69]

Gandhi orbited the conference, eccentrically. He was not an official delegate but he had been officially invited and accommodated, along with his fifteen attendants. No sooner had they all settled in than all fifteen, with the exception of Ghosh and Rajkumari Amrit Kaur, who in any case had her own house at Simla, were told to return to Delhi, so that the Mahatma could follow his own precept of relying on God. Or so Cripps was to be told by Gandhi's physician, with whom Cripps came to form a close bond as an indirect result of his own too strenuous exertions. Since only four official cars were permitted to use the narrow roads, Cripps had faced his old dilemma of whether to use a rickshaw, 'as I hate the idea of being dragged about by human beings', or to walk considerable distances between meetings.[70] Cripps found that Gandhi's house was a fifty minutes' walk each way when he paid a visit before breakfast on 3 May; and at this altitude the effort laid him low. Unusually, Gandhi wrote in his own hand.

Dear Sir Stafford,

I have just heard from Sudhir that after you went away from me, you took suddenly ill and that you were bed-ridden. I do hope however you will be quite well tomorrow morning. May Raj Kumari send you curds & fruit? Will you let Dr Dinshah Mehta see you?

With all good wishes,

Yours sincerely,

M. K. Gandhi[71]

Dr Mehta could hardly believe his luck in ministering to two such eminent valetudinarians, both testifying their faith in his Nature Cure Clinic. Cripps's strictly temporary collapse – for a few minutes he had felt that he might faint – was seized on by Mehta as an excuse to stay in Simla himself and proffer his services for a couple of hours every day. Cripps's own fortitude

69. *Daily Express*, 6 May 1946.   70. RSC diary, 1 May 1946.
71. Gandhi to RSC, 3 May 1946.

ensured that he pulled himself together, despite his morning setback, for two long meetings of the Delegation later on 3 May, aware that Alexander had had to miss a session when similarly afflicted the day before. 'I cut out lunch and had only orange juice and am doing the same for dinner,' Cripps recorded, adding that 'Albert is up and better again today' – having responded to a less rigorous regime.[72] Cripps remained under Mehta's care, one way or another, for the rest of his time in India, happily forgoing dinner most nights in favour of under-water massage from the doctor in a hot tub.

Simla provided a curious interlude. This was the first meeting between the parties since the end of the war; it offered their last chance for agreement; and all the while the Delegation – mainly Cripps, as usual – was hard at work drafting a settlement to be imposed if and when the long-heralded breakdown occurred. The signs were never good. Jinnah made a point of arriving late; his clothes got lost in transit; he refused to shake hands with Azad. Congress's other Muslim representative, the gigantic Ghaffar Khan, 'the frontier Gandhi', spoke no English; his role was to bulk uncomprehendingly large as a symbol of Congress's hold on the North-West Frontier Province, within the territory claimed for Pakistan. Nehru thus did most of the talking for Congress, if only as interpreter. The brooding Patel, so recently slighted in his political ambitions, was hardly an encouraging influence as Congress's fourth representative.

Moreover, Gandhi promptly proposed to fill his recently liberated accommodation with the members of the Congress delegation, perhaps with the intention of keeping a close eye on Azad, who resisted the plan. Sharing the same voluble doctor with Gandhi, Cripps was accordingly enlightened by this new source of *aperçus*, though he remained concerned that, with Patel having moved in, 'Gandhi gets his mind poisoned all the time'.[73]

The talks provided moments of optimism. When, on 6 May, Jinnah offered to come into a union if Congress would accept grouping – the essence of any conceivable bargain – Cripps's spirits rose. Nehru's response was encouraging. 'The atmosphere, except for Vallabhbhai Patel's scowls, was good and helpful,' Cripps noted. 'Patel is just anxious to break the thing up and doesn't want anything but a Congress dictatorship with himself as dictator!' Cripps, ever more convinced that the way to outflank the Congress hardliners was to enlist Gandhi's influence, accordingly arranged for him to meet the Viceroy and the Delegation that evening. The stratagem backfired. Gandhi was in his uncompromising mood – 'we must choose

72. RSC diary, 3 May 1946; cf. Alexander diary, 2 May 1946; Blaker to IC, 6 May 1946.
73. RSC diary, 7 May 1946; cf. ibid., 5–6 May 1946.

between the two parties and then hand the matter over to one or the other of them to do entirely in their own way' – a course which he followed to the logical conclusion of calling the three-tier plan worse than Pakistan. In sparring with Cripps, however, Gandhi did throw out the challenge for him to come up with a workable scheme; and this, despite everything, Cripps set about doing. 'The *only* chance now of getting anything agreed is the old man.'[74]

Cripps showed himself characteristically adroit in drafting a nicely balanced compromise. In effect the Muslim League was asked to work within the framework of an All-India Union Government, while Congress was asked to accept Hindu–Muslim parity within it and the legitimacy of provinces entering groups, which might set up their own legislatures and executives.[75] Having cleared his draft with his colleagues, while the Viceroy saw Jinnah on the evening of 7 May, Cripps met Gandhi and 'we went through it word by word and line by line.' Cripps thought that he had 'convinced him that it was fair' and wrote that the meeting was 'wholly successful I think and as he left he said he went with a light heart'. Cripps accepted not only Gandhi's minor drafting amendments but his advice on postponing formal meetings for twenty-four hours.

He was most helpful and charming in every way and I hope that he will not change his mind. I regard this as a most vital interview and one that *may* be decisive. I prayed hard for guidance before it and I am sure that I got all that I asked for. I felt more in harmony with him than ever before.[76]

Cripps did not conceal his jubilation from his colleagues. The putative deal would clearly put Jinnah under overwhelming pressure to acquiesce. Wavell had qualms about whether this was fair to the Muslims, which nourished his own doubts about this whole style of negotiation. Unaware of the Viceroy's private opinion – 'I do not quite trust Cripps and wholly mistrust Gandhi' – Cripps may have been guilty of some complacency: 'I must say that we really have been an excellent team!'[77] But when, on 8 May, he wrote in his diary that 'I am happy and pleased tonight', he had prudently added that 'the mercury may fall again tomorrow'.[78] In the event, he did not even have to wait for the morning since Ghosh visited Cripps just after

74. ibid.; cf. Wavell diary, 6 May 1946, in Moon (ed.), *Wavell: journal*, p. 258.
75. 'Suggested points for agreement', 7 May 1946, in Mansergh, *TOP*, vii, pp. 452–3.
76. RSC diary, 8 May 1946.
77. Wavell diary, 7 May 1946, in Moon (ed.), *Wavell: journal*, p. 261; RSC diary, 9 May 1946.
78. RSC diary, 8 May 1946.

he had gone to bed, bearing a letter with the fairly predictable caveats that Gandhi wished to enter having talked with the four Congress delegates. They could not be bound by the proposed constitutional arrangements for grouping and, above all, could not accept parity with the Muslims. Gandhi reiterated: 'This is really worse than Pakistan.'[79]

'The barometer goes on rushing up and down!' Cripps commented in his diary, as each day's prognostications were successively confounded. Having gently parried Gandhi's contentions, Cripps decided to work on Azad and Nehru, closing the gap by inches – much as in 1942, as all of them must have been well aware. This was negotiation by attrition. Cripps's tactics consisted of patient informal conciliation to outflank the formal gestures of confrontation. 'Each time they break away and write letters saying they can't do this or that, we draw them back again!'[80] Wyatt brought back encouraging news 'of the changed atmosphere in Gandhi's entourage and in his own mind'. It seemed that he was, after all, prepared to see Congress accept Cripps's proposal, provided two points were met. First, that Congress should remain free to argue against grouping upon entering a constituent assembly. Secondly, that though parity was unacceptable as a principle, if the issue were left specifically to Nehru and Jinnah, then something practically amounting to parity might emerge, which 'would then be an entirely different matter as it would have been done without outside pressure'.[81]

The fact that Cripps had this information may explain why he took a more hopeful view than Wavell of what happened next. At the conference on Thursday, 9 May, Alexander was cheered by 'a sudden dramatic turn' in the proceedings, producing 'feelings of greater optimism than we had experienced at any time since we had been in India'.[82] Nehru had proposed talks between the two parties, along with an umpire to adjudicate on differences. If Jinnah's slighting riposte, that he was ready to meet any *Hindu* member of Congress, was intended to provoke uproar and breakdown, it failed. Azad magnanimously did not rise to the insult; the restraint on the Congress side was notable; after a silence, Nehru simply suggested an adjournment while he talked with Jinnah. The two withdrew for forty minutes while most of the rest spilled out into the gardens, though Alexander took his chance to try to soften up Patel, who remained indoors. The upshot was an adjournment for two days, to allow Jinnah and Nehru to get down

79. Gandhi to RSC, 8 May 1946, PRO, CAB 127/128, printed in Mansergh, *TOP*, vii, pp. 465–6.
80. RSC diary, 9 May 1946.
81. Wyatt report on meeting with Gandhi, 9 May, PRO, CAB 127/99.
82. Alexander diary, 9 May 1946.

to business – which, of course, is exactly what Gandhi had suggested. 'This is a tremendous [advance] and we are all crossing our fingers and holding our breaths hoping that they may work out some plan of some kind,' Cripps noted. 'It is far the most hopeful thing so far and arises I think we can say from our patient persistence.'[83]

The proposed Jinnah–Nehru summit talks gave the press its most positive news. 'This can only be considered a hopeful sign,' wrote James Cameron in the *Daily Express*; Norman Cliff reported 'solid progress' in the *News Chronicle*; 'More hope for India talks' read the *Daily Mail*'s headline.[84] The crucial point was that the leading Indian politicians themselves – facilitated by British mediation but at last free of British tutelage – were getting to grips with the problems of resolving their own fate. Had some form of compromise between Congress and the Muslim League ultimately flowed from these exchanges, the vision of Indian unity through non-violence might not have perished through a deficiency in the political skills necessary to implement it.

It was a moment which we know, over half a century later, to have been delusive in its hopes. For Cripps personally, his negotiating tactics were not to be vindicated by success but branded with failure. There is thus some pathos – partly, but surely not wholly, of a comic order – in the record that Cripps kept in his diary at this juncture.

I had a long talk with Gandhi this evening about the developments which had taken place and which he said were due to my talk with Azad and Nehru this morning. I said I was sure it was really due to him which made him remark 'We mustn't become a mutual admiration society!' He is a great dear and I am really fond of him – though sometimes he is difficult to understand because of the way his mind works. He appears to be quite irrational but that is because he acts sometimes inspirationally . . .

I also talked tentatively about the Interim Government and impressed upon him that the only thing that mattered was mutual confidence. If that was absent, we should never make a job of it – if it was present we need not worry about precise stipulations as to how it should be carried on.[85]

On Friday, 10 May, as planned, the full Simla conference did not meet. But nor did Nehru and Jinnah. Why not?

'I felt inordinately proud of my friendship with you yesterday afternoon,'

83. RSC diary, 9 May 1946.
84. *Daily Express*, 10 May 1946; *News Chronicle*, 10 May 1946; *Daily Mail*, 10 May 1946.
85. RSC diary, 9 May 1946.

Cripps had written to Nehru that morning, telling him: 'I pray that success may come to your labours and that you two may be hailed as the Saviours of India . . .'[86] Nehru, more guarded from the outset, sent a workmanlike response; but it was the second letter he wrote to Cripps later in the day that apprised him of a deteriorating situation.

Cripps's attempts to represent what he was told by Nehru as indicating a personal squabble between Jinnah and Azad have too readily been accepted by historians who lacked access to the original sources.[87] The text of Nehru's second letter to Cripps, however, warning of 'another difficulty which threatens to come in the way completely', points to the real difficulty. It was hardly news that Azad's presence was unwelcome to the Muslim League. The new point, feeding on old resentments about how Muslims had been excluded from provincial power after 1937, was that Jinnah now sought to make it a principle that Congress should not choose any Muslim representatives. Faced with this demand, and responding to Congress feeling, Nehru's posture changed from one of negotiation and flexibility to one of equally principled defiance. He now told Cripps:

We simply cannot agree to this, even temporarily, for it means a negation of what we have stood for all these long years. It would be a dishonourable act on our part which is bound to be deeply resented. It would result in those injuries of the spirit which are so hard to heal.[88]

Here was a sinister portent of a dispute that returned to dog subsequent negotiations; and in fact Cripps's reaction betrays an apparent obliviousness on his part to the fact that Congress and the League were engaged in a broader and finally intractable struggle for representative legitimacy. Soon enough it became apparent that no proper talks were going to materialize. Nehru's position was that both sides had agreed to accept arbitration, necessarily accepting thereby the final decision of an umpire; and he saw no objection to any of the names of potential umpires suggested by Cripps. Jinnah's position, by contrast, was that Congress first had to accept group-

86. RSC to Nehru, 10 May 1946, in Gopal, *Nehru*, i, p. 318; copy, PRO, CAB 127/143.
87. See RSC diary, 10 May 1946, evidently passed on to Pethick-Lawrence; see Pethick-Lawrence to Attlee, 10 May 1946, as quoted in Gopal (ed.), *Nehru: Selected Works*, xv, p. 162n.; cf. Moore, *Escape from Empire*, p. 103 supports a personal interpretation.
88. Nehru to RSC, 10 May 1946 (Second letter); and see Nehru to RSC, 11 May 1946, enc. Jinnah to Nehru, same date, PRO, CAB 127/143; the correspondence of 11 May is printed in Gopal (ed.), *Nehru: Selected Works*, xv, pp. 162–3; the editors evidently also knew of one letter to Cripps of 10 May, but not of a second.

ing: otherwise the Muslim League's essential demand for recognition would itself be subject to arbitration.[89] The result was impasse. 'The situation has gone bad on us!' Cripps admitted. 'Jawaharlal in his talk with Jinnah found that Jinnah had gone back upon the whole situation and we are now at the beginning again – so nothing came of them.'[90]

When official proceedings resumed on Saturday, 11 May, Jinnah returned to his fundamental worry: that Congress had not yet supplied the premise for any process of arbitration since it was still equivocal on grouping; and he reiterated that 'if the Congress would agree to Groups of Provinces as desired by the Muslim League he would seriously consider a Union'.[91] Cripps was largely responsible for prolonging the proceedings beyond this point of obvious deadlock, apparently unable to restrain himself from making long interjections in the already unprofitable wrangle that developed between Jinnah and Nehru.

Cripps now put the odds as 100 to 1 on disappointment, despite not giving up on his own efforts to leave no stone unturned. 'It will be tragic but it cannot be helped,' he wrote with resignation, 'and we must assume that that is how the matter is intended to turn out by the higher powers in their own inscrutable judgement!'[92] A further meeting on Sunday, 12 May was little more than a formality. As the delegates gathered that evening, so did a storm which had been threatening all afternoon. Following the confrontation of the previous day, there was what Turnbull called 'a general air of inability to agree and hopelessness.'[93] The *Daily Mail*'s headline captured the mood: 'Simla ends in fiasco – and a thunderstorm'. The next day, on the eve of departure, Cripps took his chance to get out again for the first time since his upset. 'I walked back up the hill very slowly like an old, old man,' he told Isobel.[94]

89. Gopal (ed.), *Nehru. Selected Works*, xv, p. 163; Moore, *Escape from India*, pp. 103-4.
90. RSC diary, 11 May 1946
91. Sixth meeting, 11 May 1946, in Mansergh, *TOP*, vii. p. 508.
92. RSC diary, 11 May 1946.   93. Turnbull diary, 11 May 1946.
94. RSC to IC, 13 May 1946.

3

Attempting the Impossible

In so far as Cripps did not attribute the outcome of the Simla conference to God, he attributed it to Jinnah. In the conference's final stages, Cripps struck Wavell as deplorably partisan in seeking to pin the blame upon the Muslim League. Both he and Alexander thought that the chances for acceptance of the Delegation's own solution, on which work had steadily been proceeding, had been prejudiced.[1] Cripps, who was in charge of drafting their forthcoming Statement, did not agree.

I have been thinking a good deal today about the situation and whether we could have done or achieved anything else and I am satisfied that less patience would not have got us so far as we have got and that more patience would only have exasperated everyone. I think the 8 weeks we have spent here have exhausted people's patience and they really want us to say and do something – though of course they all want different things said. We are bound to get a chorus of abuse from all sides when we put our statement out but I hope that despite that the people will settle down to get on with the job.

I've read our statement through time and again and I am pretty satisfied that it is the fairest and justest things that we can do.[2]

Cripps's more constructive assessment to some extent reflected his own resiliently optimistic temperament; but it also drew on his closer knowledge of the Congress position, reinforced by reports from the two Majors. Cripps thus returned undaunted to the furnace of Delhi, where temperatures of up to 45°C had been recorded; and personally he seems to have preferred the heat to the thin air of Simla. He made the journey by air, while a special train brought back the press correspondents in first-class carriages, with

1. Alexander diary, 11 May 1946; Wavell diary, 11 May 1946, in Moon (ed.), *Wavell: journal*, p. 265.
2. RSC diary, 13 May 1946.

'the most important man in India', as Norman Cliff called him, in an even more special third-class coach at the rear, greeted by crowds at every stop.[3]

Cripps undoubtedly wanted Gandhi to remain involved in the negotiations and chafed at his colleagues' veto on the idea that the two of them should go over the draft of the official Statement before it was finalized.

I think that more than ever he holds the key to the situation. It is very doubtful whether Congress will ever acquiesce in our statement and its suggestions. Gandhi alone can persuade them to do it and I believe we could have got his support if we had trusted him and consulted him first. I see the dangers but I would have taken the risk . . .

The really critical situation has been reached because if Congress turn it down and refuse to come into an interim Government, it will be impossible for us to carry on in the existing state of tension without wholesale suppression which will in effect mean war. My own view is that we *must* at all costs come to an accommodation with Congress. We can get through I believe without the League if we have Congress with us but not without Congress even if we have the League.[4]

Cripps saw here the potential for a split in the Delegation. Wavell and Alexander, after golfing together in Simla, had taken to dining together in the air-conditioned luxury of the Viceregal Lodge, and were plainly hostile to further 'appeasement' of Congress. Indeed Wavell was now talking of resignation if there were concessions: Cripps if there were not. On 15 May, however, when Pethick-Lawrence joined Cripps in threatening to resign, this implied threat was directed against the Cabinet in London and they were supported not only by Alexander but by the Viceroy.

The issue concerned the references to Indian independence in the final draft of the long-awaited, much-revised Statement. In drafting it, Cripps had seized on Attlee's 'historic words' in the House of Commons, committing his Government unequivocally to offering 'independence', by implication as an alternative to Commonwealth membership. The Statement concluded with the hope 'that the new independent India may choose to be a member of the British Commonwealth' and throughout made frequent and unvarnished use of the term independence, appreciating that its introduction had dispelled longstanding suspicions which its subsequent qualification would simply rekindle with renewed force. Yet Attlee had proposed just such prudential amendments, reflecting the wholly different imperatives of British party politics, knowing Churchill's predilections as Leader of the Opposition.

3. Norman Cliff, *News Chronicle*, 15 May 1946.   4. RSC diary, 14 May 1946.

Attlee confessed himself reluctant to 'give ammunition to critics of the Government here' but gave way to the united expertise of the Delegation and Viceroy, backed by their refusal otherwise to take responsibility for the Statement.[5] It was a crisis in London–Delhi perceptions not unlike that of 1942; but this time Cripps had better cards in his hand, as well as access to a modern teleprinter, and the exchanges hardly show Attlee getting his own way.[6]

The Statement was published on Thursday, 16 May, 'our D-Day', as Cripps called it. Four hours before publication he solicitously read it over to Gandhi. Cripps had made the media arrangements himself, displaying to Alexander a 'clear intention to shut me out of it',[7] which averted possible offence to Congress. 'It will make a tremendous difference what appears in the Press in the next couple of days,' Cripps wrote, fortified in his judgement that Simla, and the lack of public recrimination after it, had improved the chances of a settlement rather than the reverse.[8] He was pleased with 'a most successful Press Conference' held by the ministers and judged it 'remarkable for the very serious-minded atmosphere and the complete lack of any cynicism in the questions'.[9] Turnbull, a more objective observer, thought that Pethick-Lawrence was 'not so slick but goes over better than Stafford who always produces the effect of an intellectual game'.[10] When the Secretary of State suddenly said 'Thank you', and the conference ended, Alexander, waiting his own turn on the platform, was left literally speechless. He quietly pointed out afterwards that 'there was no need to boost the other two members of the Delegation all the time'.[11]

The Statement, simultaneously published as a White Paper in London, was essentially Cripps's attempt to build on the measure of agreement revealed at Simla and to erect this into a system of government. At its heart was the historic compromise necessary to secure political acceptance: an All-India Union sufficiently strong to appease Congress, balanced against a system of provincial grouping with sufficient legitimacy to win the acquiescence of the Muslim League. In drafting and redrafting it, Cripps had walked on eggshells around Gandhi's susceptibilities so that he might have no

5. Draft Statement, in Mansergh, *TOP*, vii, p. 528ff. at p. 537 (p. 591 in final text); Attlee to Delegation, 15 May 1946, Mansergh, *TOP*, vii, p. 562.
6. cf. Kenneth Harris: 'The exchange of dispatches between Attlee and the Cabinet mission indicates quite clearly that it was he who was in charge of Indian policy.' Harris, *Attlee*, p. 368; and see above, 'Tragedy in Delhi', p. 308.
7. Alexander diary, 15 May 1946.   8. RSC diary, 16 May 1946.
9. ibid., 18 May 1946.   10. Turnbull diary, 17 May 1946.
11. Alexander diary, 17 May 1946.

excuse for branding this scheme as 'worse than Pakistan'. The name Pakistan was not used and a dichotomous 'vivisection' of India was avoided by proposing three groups – in essence, today's Pakistan, today's Bangladesh, and today's Republic of India. These were not to be constituted on an explicitly communal basis but through the consent of the provinces. 'A United India', the *Manchester Guardian*'s headline called it, adding: 'Pakistan Claim Rejected'.[12] The chances of a settlement and the possibility of forming an interim government suddenly appeared closer, with friends in Congress like Rajagopalachari signalling their approval.[13]

In a remark almost as widely quoted as that about 'a postdated cheque' in 1942, Gandhi abandoned banking metaphors in favour of horticulture: the proposals contained 'a seed to convert this land of sorrow into one without sorrow and suffering'. What attracted less attention at the time was his assertion that, since the constituent assembly was necessarily a sovereign body, it was open to it to vary any of the provisions in the Statement, notably on grouping.[14] After joining Pethick-Lawrence in spending several hours with Gandhi, Cripps was privately cautious: 'I gather there is a battle going on in Congress as to whether they will accept the Statement or not and if he finally comes down firmly on our side, we shall win – but not otherwise I fear.'[15]

What now consumed Gandhi's attention was the small print of the Statement, which could, with the requisite ingenuity, be construed as providing an escape clause from the acceptance of grouping. Yet what Congress really had to understand was not the relationship of the procedure specified in paragraph 15 of the Statement to that laid down in paragraph 19: it was the political reality of striking a bargain with the Muslim League. And what that meant was – rather than outwitting the discredited and obsolescent British Raj – offering their fellow Indian citizens a *quid pro quo* that they could decently accept.

It was this kind of problem that Cripps and Gandhi, however often they met, failed to resolve. It simply slipped between the other levels at which their exchanges took place. 'This morning at 6.30 a.m. Gandhi came again and we had two hours with him,' Cripps recorded on Sunday, 19 May. 'A very happy atmosphere but he is very pernickety about a number of points

12. *Manchester Guardian*, 17 May 1946.
13. 'By this decision Britain has discharged her duty and has put the scaffolding safely and well for the construction.' Rajagopalachari to Wyatt, 18 May 1946, copy, PRO, CAB 127/106.
14. Gandhi statement, 17 May 1946, in Mansergh, *TOP* vii, pp. 613–15.
15. RSC diary, 18 May 1946.

and the only thing to do is to listen and argue them out patiently.'[16] Others were less indulgent, coming to share the Viceroy's patent scepticism. 'I smell trouble,' Turnbull now admitted. 'The nasty old man has grasped that he can get what he asks for & so goes on asking for more & more.'[17]

On 20 May the Delegation sat with the Viceroy, considering a letter from Gandhi. It was again concerned with whether Congress could seek to repudiate grouping; but it leapfrogged from the legality of doing so to 'the honourableness of opposition to grouping'.[18] What was ignored, as usual, was the political implication, if the Muslim League concluded that Congress had no intention of keeping its side of an implicit bargain. Cripps had produced a lengthy draft reply, arguing every point with Gandhi ('You will appreciate from Sec. 16 of the Statement the reason for our making the recommendations in paragraph 15').[19] Alexander, his patience wearing thin, had produced a shorter, more robust riposte. The meeting was already becoming acrimonious, with Cripps making what Wavell called 'a heated reply' to his warnings about being drawn into argument by Gandhi.[20]

What happened next was dramatic. Here is Cripps's version.

Then just as we were considering answering Gandhi's first letter we got a second one purporting to set out a whole lot of points gone over in our talks and representing wholly wrongly what we had said or promised. That made the Viceroy and Albert go completely off the deep end and decided the Mission that in future we must all see him together or none of us. It is a very serious matter as it means I can't see the Old Man and keep him on our side. I fear we shall lose him in consequence.[21]

Unlike 1942, when similar discrepancies had emerged about his assurances to Congress, Cripps was not without a witness; no one doubted Pethick-Lawrence's veracity nor mistook his indignation at being misrepresented – indeed it was his idea to restrict any future contact to recorded interviews with all three ministers.[22] 'I have never seen three men taken more aback by this revelation of G. in his true colours,' noted the Viceroy, who took special care to observe Cripps's reaction – 'shaken to the core' and 'quite *ahuri*'.[23] Turnbull, impressed with the impact of Gandhi's 'corking

16. ibid, 19 May 1946.   17. Turnbull diary, 19 May 1946.
18. Gandhi to Pethick-Lawrence, 19 May 1946, in Mansergh, *TOP*, vii, p. 622.
19. RSC draft, in Mansergh, *TOP*, vii, p. 634.
20. Wavell diary, 20 May 1946, in Moon (ed.), *Wavell: journal*, p. 274.
21. *RSC* diary, 20 May 1946.   22. Alexander diary, 20 May 1946.
23. 'Outraged' would capture the sense. Wavell diary, 20 May 1946, in Moon (ed.), *Wavell: journal*, p. 274.

letter', noted: 'Even S. C.'s optimism & confidence was markedly halted.'[24]

Cripps sought to compose himself. While the meeting adjourned until the afternoon, he produced a further point-by-point response to Gandhi. This was shown to Alexander when he was waylaid by his fellow-ministers, intent on winning him over. Of course they sympathized with his John Bull indignation, they told him, 'but if there were a complete breakdown where did we go from there?' A reconquest of India? Scuttle? Cripps deftly incorporated into the new draft most of Alexander's suggestions ('meeting my point handsomely'), and thus restored the ministerial common front on dealing with Gandhi.[25] 'We are answering his letters rather brusquely but politely but I am very concerned as to the consequences,' wrote a worried Cripps that night in his diary. 'So far he has been with us publicly but he is quite likely to turn right round or to walk off, both of which will be very serious in their effect upon Congress.'[26]

The next morning Cripps was absent, confined to bed. Alexander, who was living in the same house, wrote of a return of Cripps's stomach trouble but added: 'undoubtedly he had also received a very severe shock from the line taken by Mr Gandhi in his letters'.[27] Cripps had in fact been under Dr Mehta's care for the past three days with a recurrence of his colitis. Even his daily ride in the Viceregal park had been abandoned while Cripps submitted to an intensive diet, 'as the Doctor wants to change my intestinal flora!'[28] It was Mehta who stayed up all night with him following his attack on 20-21 May and he continued to enjoy Cripps's confidence.

Turnbull, concerned that Cripps was 'quite seriously ill', was relieved the next day when Colonel Williamson, the official Surgeon to the Viceroy – 'skilfully', as Turnbull chose to put it – arranged for Cripps to be admitted to the Willingdon Nursing Home, 'on ground suspicion of amoebic dysentery'.[29] But this diagnosis was highly problematic. When a sample of Cripps's stool was sent for examination at 3 a.m., Williamson raised the possibility of amoebic infection, but Mehta's clinical notes record that 'the report does not indicate any infection', while adding: 'as it was examined hurriedly a fresh sample to be sent today if diarrhoea persists'.[30] The cultural report in due course confirmed that the sample was negative for the dysentery group

24. Turnbull diary, 20 May 1946.
25. Alexander diary, 20 May 1946; cf. RSC manuscript, 'read out at meeting of Mission, 20.5.46', PRO, CAB 127/100.   26. RSC diary, 20 May 1946.
27. Alexander diary, 21 May 1946.   28. RSC diary, 19 May 1946.
29. Turnbull diary, 21 May 1946.   30. Mehta notes, 6 a.m., 21 May 1946.

of organisms.[31] Even in the first newspaper reports of Cripps's illness it was attributed to the effects of overstrain, exacerbated by the heat of Delhi and the altitude of Simla; and the well-informed Cliff at once correctly reported 'exhaustion through overwork and a recurrence of colitis'.[32]

The Viceroy must have been practically the only person in New Delhi left with the idea that this was simply a case of 'dysentery'.[33] But his Surgeon, from whom this information no doubt derived, as well as pursuing a cautious diagnostic procedure, had provided a convenient cover story that served more than one end. Not only did it have the immediate effect of persuading Cripps to enter hospital, against his inclinations but arguably for his own good, safely away from the work of the Cabinet Delegation; the investigation also, by putting him into hospital, brought him, willy-nilly, under the aegis of western medicine. Cripps's private secretary, George Blaker, had the delicate task of coordinating visits from Cripps's two rival physicians: Gandhi's doctor, with his reliance on natural therapies, and the Viceroy's doctor, backed by the canon of orthodox imperial medicine. In practice, both seem to have acquitted themselves in the finest medical tradition, subordinating other considerations to the interests of their patient, on whose need for seclusion they were agreed. Mehta's diagnosis was 'nervous exhaustion and aggravation of his chronic susceptibilities', much as he had been saying since the beginning of the month, with the recommendation of 'complete rest for at least a week' as the essential first step.'[34]

The fact that this was not Cripps's first breakdown was often mentioned in press reports: a worrying state of affairs, especially in the unrelenting heat of Delhi. Cripps had driven himself hard, living off his reserves of nervous energy as he chased the elusive prospect of agreement, persuading himself each day that one more arduous session with Gandhi would do the trick. With so much invested in this process, and used to getting his own way, Cripps was vulnerable to the sort of rebuff he received on 20 May, when his overstretched body rebelled.

The need for Isobel Cripps to come out to Delhi as soon as possible was quickly recognized – or belatedly recognized, as she saw it. For Isobel had not accompanied Stafford in the first place only because Attlee's nervousness over the position of other wives had ruled it out; and she had been trying

31. Provincial Laboratory, New Delhi, report by Medical Supt. W. N. Home on sample of 21 May, dated 23 May 1946.

32. News Chronicle, 22 May 1946; cf. The Times and Daily Telegraph, 22 May 1946.

33. Wavell diary, 21 May 1946, in Moon (ed.), Wavell: journal, p. 275.

34. Mehta's clinical notes, 21 May 1946; Blaker to IC, 21, 23 May 1946 and 29 September 1976.

for weeks to find a way around this. In April she had made a determined effort to try and join him, approaching the Prime Minister herself, and going so far as to forward a letter from Harrison pleading that Isobel's social skills were sorely needed to humanize the official contacts of the Cabinet Delegation. At that stage, Stafford had obviously felt awkward in broaching the suggestion, caught between Isobel's reproaches and his own sensitivity to his colleagues' feelings. Their reaction – 'Albert at once said he would get into trouble with Esther if you came!' – was a signal that he would be letting the team down.[35] But Stafford's breakdown now out-trumped Esther, and Isobel prepared to fly out, if only to accompany her husband on a recuperative voyage home again.

Cripps attended no official meetings from 21 May until 3 June. He was missed by everyone. Even the Viceroy noted the loss of 'our chief drafter' and Alexander, despite their disagreements, called it 'a great loss to the delegation to be without his fertile suggestions as regards courses of action'.[36] Turnbull, charged with reducing the Delegation's discussions to a business-like set of minutes, noticed the difference: 'Meetings waffle a bit without S. C.'.[37] Pethick-Lawrence sent a personal message to the Willingdon: 'Give your fine body a chance to catch up with your eagle mind.'[38]

'I have greater faith than ever in my Doctor who has been a darling,' Stafford told Isobel after a few days, as his condition began to improve.[39] He evidently benefited from Mehta's prescribed regime which soon had him ingesting doses of buttermilk virtually every hour, up to six pints a day. Increasingly restive – 'I am just beginning to feel alive again & so a bit bored!'[40] – Cripps brooded on the political situation.

While Cripps was ill, he had been sent a personal letter by Gandhi, enclosing an advance copy of his public response to the Cabinet Delegation's State-ment. It larded a compliment to 'the best document the British Government could have produced in the circumstances' with the characteristic reflection that 'what is best from the British standpoint' might, from the Indian, 'possibly be harmful'.[41] Cripps, after a week away from official business,

35. RSC to IC, 18 April 1946; and official telegram, same date; cf. IC to Attlee, 15 April, 1946, enc. Harrison to IC, 6 April 1946, and Attlee to IC, n.d., and IC to RSC, 19 April 1946
36. Alexander diary, 22 May 1946.   37. Turnbull diary, 22 May 1946 (misdated 21 May).
38. Pethick-Lawrence to RSC, 22 May 1946.   39. RSC to IC, 25 May 1946.   40. ibid.
41. Gandhi to RSC, 20 May 1946, enc. analysis, PRO, CAB 127/128; incorrectly dated 21 May in Gandhi, *Collected Works*, lxxxiv, p. 181; text of statement in Mansergh, *TOP*, vii, pp. 646-9.

turned to composing 'a very private letter to the Old Man', almost Gladstonian in its providential overtones.[42]

I have naturally wondered why it was just at this critical time that I should have been withdrawn; but no doubt there must be some purpose in it. I have of course done a good deal of thinking since I have been here and perhaps that was why I was withdrawn from the more active work.

Cripps expatiated on how much he had relied upon Gandhi over the previous couple of months and tried to shake his insistence that independence would be a farce unless Britain simply quit India, leaving no troops to maintain peace and order, and with no provision that a constitution should first be made.[43] 'The key to the whole matter is surely *Trust*,' Cripps beseeched Gandhi. Surely any interim period was of little consequence provided British sincerity were believed? Surely power-sharing 'in a spirit of full and frank cooperation' was possible until the formal transfer of power took place under a new constitution?

I feel that the moment has come for the supreme act of Faith or Trust on all sides. It will be an act of great statesmanship in which we who have been so opposed & hostile in the past agree to act together in order that we may avoid the ghastly horrors for the Indian People that otherwise will so surely come.

I am certain that there is no other basis for a non-violent Transition – which will truly be the greatest event in world history – than Trust and cooperation. I also believe that you, my dear friend, can do more in this direction than any other man in the world.[44]

Gandhi's all-or-nothing utterances had often served a prophetic function, asserting an ethic of ultimate ends as he simply insisted on doing what seemed right, regardless of the consequences. Naked, he had challenged the panoply of British imperialism, with courage and with guile, and left the British to face the consequences. But an ethic of responsibility, accepting second-best solutions for fear of worse, was perhaps what Indian politicians needed on the threshold of independence. In this respect, Nehru showed the necessary discernment, Patel the necessary ruthlessness – but they did not show them soon enough, through deference to Gandhi.

Gandhi's own distinctive approach was different. 'Whatever we get, will

42. RSC to IC, 26 May 1946.   43. cf. Gandhi, 20 May, in Mansergh, *TOP*, vii, p. 636.
44. RSC to Gandhi, 26 May 1946, original manuscript as sent, PRO, CAB 127/128.

be our deserts, not a gift from across the seas,' he said, in a statement sent to Cripps.[45] His message had a strong tincture of fatalism. As Penderel Moon later put it: 'Following the promptings of an inner voice he was all too often careless of consequences – until they overtook him.'[46] Pethick-Lawrence confided at the time that 'he was coming to believe Gandhi did not care whether 2 or 3 million people died & would rather that they should than that he should compromise'.[47] Pethick-Lawrence came to this view sadly, ruefully, and still not despairingly; but it was Gandhi's incapacity to abide any imperfect solution that now struck him as fatal when seeking a negotiated settlement.[48] Gandhi's sincerity need not be impugned; but nor is there reason to doubt either Cripps's sincerity or his political judgement in appealing for a non-violent, political solution, now that his own efforts had affirmed that the British at least were ready for Indian independence. 'I know that you will not mind my pouring out my heart to you from my sickbed in this way,' he told Gandhi, 'but sickness often makes us more sensitive than we usually are and perhaps that is another reason why I have been sent here.'[49]

Gandhi's reply to this 'touching letter' was a masterpiece. He wrote through Amrit Kaur, whom he often used as amanuensis, apparently copying from an inimitably original draft. 'I entirely agree with you that the State Paper demands & commands trust,' he told Cripps. 'Yet it, like everything coming from the British, creates nothing but distrust.' He knew, of course, that Cripps was the author of the Statement, so this was a wounding snub – 'Trust put on is worse than useless.' Above all, Cripps found his own manuscript returned to him, in a neat finesse on the personal status with which he had sought to endow it: 'I am returning your letter as it is marked "very confidential". However, I see nothing in it which the world may not see, if it is curious.'[50] Thus Gandhi literally threw Cripps's appeal back in his own face.

Cripps was back at 2 Willingdon Crescent by the end of May. Pethick-Lawrence wrote to Isobel Cripps that 'he is looking quite a different man

45. 'Vital Defects', 26 May 1946, PRO, CAB 127/128.
46. On Gandhi's mindset, see Moon, *Divide and Quit*, pp. 54–5.
47. Turnbull diary, 24 May 1946. When Alexander went off to Ceylon to inspect the fleet, Turnbull found it 'rather pleasant' alone in the house with Pethick-Lawrence, who started gossiping more freely (28 May). The Secretary of State was more discreet in communicating with the Prime Minister; see Pethick-Lawrence to Attlee, 26 May 1946, Attlee papers.
48. See Brittain, *Pethick-Lawrence*, p. 171.
49. RSC to Gandhi, 26 May 1946, original manuscript as sent, PRO, CAB 127/128.
50. Gandhi to RSC, 27 May 1946, PRO, CAB 127/128; the text is somewhat garbled in Gandhi, *Collected Works*, lxxxiv, pp. 216–17.

from what he did when he went into hospital a week ago. I was really relieved to find him so greatly recovered.'[51] Though he quickly picked up his work, it must be doubtful whether he was fully restored to health and Dr Mehta remained concerned lest his treatment not be followed through.

On 8 June Isobel arrived, much to Stafford's excitement, and she at once became fully involved in his life, despite herself suffering a bout of illness. Arrangements were made for her to meet Jinnah.[52] Within days of her arrival she had seen Gandhi, who later wrote to Stafford: 'I have come to know you & of you more through your good wife than through anyone else.'[53] She liked to attend the prayer meetings at the Harijan colony; Louis Fischer found her there, seeing Gandhi, on the evening of 25 June.[54] Especially since she seems to have been initially distrustful of Ghosh,[55] Isobel's own role as a further go-between should not be overlooked. The plan was for her and Stafford to sail home from Bombay in the middle of June, by which time it was expected to be clear whether or not the Statement of 16 May had found acceptance.

In Cripps's absence, Wavell had initially made good progress towards the formation of an interim government, which Congress wanted settled before they would give a decision on the constitutional proposals. As so often, there were echoes of 1942; though this time with the difference that meetings between the Viceroy and Nehru inspired a degree of mutual confidence, not least in Wavell's readiness to observe a convention of non-interference; and in fact Congress was already satisfied on this point.[56] This was not known to the Delegation, however, at Cripps's first meeting since his illness, on 3 June, with the result that it inauspiciously ended in a row. Cripps continued to hold that a written convention – he had helpfully written it himself – was needed; Pethick-Lawrence, becoming heated in support, at one point expostulated that 'the Viceroy really should not think him such a blithering idiot or such a paltroon as he seemed to do!'[57] Afterwards Wavell shared with Alexander his suspicion that Cripps might have promised Congress such a statement, and Alexander in turn, over dinner that night, 'said that Cripps was quite capable of making out at home, if the scheme failed, that it was because he, Alexander, had backed

51. Pethick-Lawrence to IC, 28 May 1946.
52. Jinnah to RSC, 7 June 1946, PRO, CAB 127/136.
53. Gandhi to RSC, 7 August 1946, PRO, CAB 127/128.
54. Fischer, Life of Gandhi, p. 421. It was earlier the same day that the official Congress reply to the Cabinet Delegation had been sent.
55. Wavell diary, 13 June 1946, in Moon (ed.), Wavell: journal, p. 293.
56. Moore, Escape from Empire, pp. 115–19.   57. Alexander diary, 3 June 1946.

the Viceroy in being intransigent'.[58] The circumspect view recorded by Cripps, however, that 'I hope the need to resolve the trouble may not arise', was borne out by events.[59]

The real trouble arose on other issues. The Muslim League was edging, with frustrating slowness, towards acceptance of the Statement; Congress swaying, with frustrating indecisiveness, between acceptance and rejection. Cripps wrote that 'it is very tense and exciting for these next few days to see how things develop – when one remembers that the future of this great continent of 400 millions depends upon it for its future'.[60] His colleague Alexander, just off for another game of billiards at the Roshanara Club, was more forthright, observing ('jovially', as Turnbull recorded): 'Truth is they are all B—-rs.'[61]

Jinnah now held the key. He had been playing a hard tactical game all along, never disclosing his bottom line even to his own awed followers. Was it irreducibly a demand for an independent Islamic state based on severance of the Muslim-majority provinces? If so, no real negotiation was possible. Cripps's guiding insight was to sense that 'Pakistan', that elastic concept, might itself be a negotiating ploy allowing Jinnah to settle for something less – but something he himself valued more – in entrenching the Muslims' position throughout India, notably in provinces where they would always be a minority and thus most vulnerable. 'The Mission's plan in fact was a way forward for Pakistan,' one historian has argued, 'at least the Pakistan Jinnah was after.'[62]

Thus Jinnah had to educate the League into accepting the Delegation's Statement, which rejected Pakistan in favour of Indian unity. Once it did so on 6 June, and by a large majority, Cripps thought that it made it easier to persuade Congress too. 'I think Jinnah has been very good and helpful in the way he has put it across to the League – though from his speeches one might imagine that the Cabinet Mission were halfwits and not his best friends!' Cripps wrote, pleading indulgence of Jinnah's tactics: 'That was I think to get the majority with him!'[63] The League's demand for parity in an interim government now became crucial. Cripps, still confident that he might soon be free to depart, thought that this issue '*must* be overcome but I hope it won't mean missing our boat!'[64]

Gandhi had joined the Congress Working Committee in withdrawing

58. Wavell diary, 3 June 1946, in Moon (ed.), *Wavell: journal*, p. 287.
59. RSC diary, 3 June, 1946.   60. ibid., 4 June 1946.   61. Turnbull diary, 4 June 1946.
62. Jalal, *Sole Spokesman*, p. 201. The arguments of this challenging book marry nicely with my account of Cripps's perspective.
63. RSC diary, 6 June 1946.   64. ibid., 9 June 1946.

from Delhi into the northern hills and only returned on Sunday, 9 June for further deliberations. Cripps was kept informed of Gandhi's fluctuating views through Horace Alexander and Agatha Harrison. But the suggestion that the Delegation should arrange a privileged preparatory meeting with the Mahatma was resisted not only by Alexander but Pethick-Lawrence and Cripps too. A new wariness was natural in view of recent correspondence. A report that the Working Committee was favourable on the interim government was brought on Sunday evening by Ghosh. 'Unfortunately that proved too optimistic,' Cripps noted later, 'largely because of the attitude of the Old Man!'[65] Dr Mehta, commuting between treatment of Stafford and Isobel Cripps in the mornings and of Gandhi in the afternoons, confirmed that parity would constitute the breaking-point.

On the evening of 10 June Ghosh and Harrison visited the Delegation. Their message, Alexander recorded, was that 'Mr Gandhi was feeling neglected and somewhat hurt that he was not being contacted' and, after they had gone, the ministers debated what to do about it. When Pethick-Lawrence and Cripps said that there was no way out except by seeing Gandhi, Alexander invoked their experience of 18–20 May and warned that unless the whole Delegation were formally involved, he would have to consider leaving for home.[66] They parted for bed on this discordant note. Cripps, while admitting that it was a 'pretty black' moment, bounced back as usual, noting the next day that 'we all thought it out during the night - at least, I did! – and I came to the conclusion that we must do two things today'. The plan was for Wavell to see Jinnah and Nehru together, building on his success so far, with a view to reaching agreement on the personnel of an interim government that would in practice embody parity, while not conceding it as a principle. Secondly, Pethick-Lawrence alone would be sent to see Gandhi. If both initiatives failed, Cripps would demand 'to have a shot at it myself'.[67] Meanwhile it is evident that Isobel Cripps visited Gandhi on 11 June and revealed Stafford's increasingly anxious state of mind.[68] In his diary that morning he wrote:

Dr Mehta and others tell me that all hope now resides in me! which is embarrassing particularly as my colleagues at the moment seem to take the view that I must not talk to anyone on either side!

65. ibid., 11 June 1946.
66. Alexander diary, 10 June 1946. Ghosh, *Gandhi's Emissary*, p. 155, represents his visit as having arisen at the instigation of Pethick-Lawrence.
67. RSC diary, 11 June 1946
68. See Gandhi to RSC, 13 June 1946: 'I met your good wife the day before.'

I am afraid my ideas on how to negotiate with these people many of whom I now know intimately are different from some of theirs.

The Viceroy and First Lord particularly seem terrified lest I should give something away and don't understand the need for frank and free *personal* talks – as against formal interviews – for getting this sort of business through. Fortunately they didn't take this view earlier when I was having the long talks to get the Simla meeting arranged or it would never have come off and we should have been back in England having failed long ago!![69]

In the end, the Delegation's plan for a coalition government did not come off; its constitutional scheme failed to be implemented; partition and bloodshed duly ensued. It has therefore been easy to dismiss Cripps's efforts as a misguided determination, driven by personal vanity, to prolong the misery. His own view, however, deserves to be considered.

I feel that with all the longing for a settlement that there is throughout this country, except for a handful of extremists who want a revolution, we must somehow get through.[70]

Wavell, with his single but unillusioned eye, observed the politicians' frailties, which he conveyed tellingly in his journal. Admittedly, his own take-it-or-leave-it approach had notched up some success to date, before it too failed in the end. Yet Cripps's claim to have employed a consistent strategic approach to the conduct of business deserves to be considered, as does the question of whether failure was due to the methods adopted or to ultimately irreconcilable differences between the Indian parties. Where Cripps can be faulted is in having made Gandhi more central to the actual process of negotiation than might otherwise have been the case. But here, of course, Cripps could plead the excuse that he had been burned by experience. Like Pethick-Lawrence, he now banked on the hunch that 'Gandhi in his own peculiar way is at the moment fighting three-quarters on our side.'[71]

Memories of the Cripps Mission were never far away. As the deadlock persisted on 11 June, a phone call came through – it was Birla this time – 'it looked as if there might be a breakdown now in just the same way as there had been in 1942'. [72] Gandhi was reported as saying: 'If the negotiations

69. RSC diary, 11 June 1946.   70. ibid., 12 June 1946.
71. Pethick-Lawrence to E. Pethick-Lawrence, 12 June 1946, in Brittain, *Pethick-Lawrence*, p. 170.
72. Blaker to RSC, 11 June 1946, PRO, CAB 127/100.

break down it is God's will.'[73] Cripps, less quietist in his religion, summoned all his resources.

We are right in the thick of the last lap. Yesterday morning [11 June] it looked black so I bestirred myself to try and rally the sinking spirits!! It's most disconcerting but when these dark spots occur I feel a definite cheerfulness and vigour which I think comes from the knowledge of inner help and the support of all my family and friends![74]

Anxious to get home as soon as possible but determined to stay as long as necessary, Cripps found himself still enmeshed in 'a hectic rush of negotiation'. Since it was Nehru alone who had accepted the invitation for talks about an interim government, it was Nehru alone who met the Viceroy, while Cripps raced off to persuade Jinnah to join them – with apparent success one day, only to find on the morrow that Jinnah had reneged: 'He apologised for misleading me and putting me in an awkward position and said that he had been very overwrought and nervy and had perhaps not made clear enough what his position was.'[75] The upshot was that Nehru and Jinnah negotiated separately with the Viceroy. Cripps's renewed activity did not go unreported. Stursberg wrote in the *Daily Herald*: 'He always shows up best in a crisis – and there is no doubt about this being the crisis of the negotiations.'[76]

The crisis centred on the formation of an interim government. Wavell's transparency about his intentions had helped him to secure agreement for participation under the existing conventions; but his lack of finesse in playing his hand was now a handicap in the keen bargaining, and bluffing too, that took place over personnel. For the first time in six weeks, Cripps dined out. Over a cordial dinner at Shiva Rao's with Nehru – 'Jawaharlal was his dear and charming self and in very good form' – Cripps received new information. Nehru gave him to understand that agreement on an interim government was unlikely; 'but he clearly contemplated we should go ahead with the constituent assembly and perhaps ask the Muslim League to form a Government'. Nehru thought that no communal trouble was imminent. 'I definitely asked him what his advice was,' Cripps recorded, 'and it was to go ahead with our scheme even if there were a refusal by Congress.'[77] Here was a new twist: possibly a more hopeful one. The indication that Congress could still contemplate accepting the constitutional scheme, even if it rejected the government posts currently on offer, came as news to Cripps. It was not,

73. *Manchester Guardian*, 12 June 1946.   74. RSC diary, 12 June 1946.
75. ibid., 13 June 1946.   76. *Daily Herald*, 14 June 1946.   77. RSC diary, 13 June 1946.

contrary to later allegations, an idea that he had to introduce into the slow-witted heads of Nehru or Patel.

In another respect, too, Cripps has been misrepresented. The notion of the Muslim League forming a government was a familiar Gandhian ploy, mentioned by Nehru to Cripps as 'perhaps' what ought to happen. It was not seen by either of them as an ineluctable consequence of failure to reach agreement on Wavell's terms, still less as an appalling consequence which had to be averted by means of an underhand stratagem.[78] Indeed Gandhi repeated the same advice in a letter to Wavell on 13 June,[79] and again in one to Cripps. This letter, and Cripps's reply, show the incompatibility of two mindsets. Gandhi told Cripps: 'You are handling the most difficult task of your life', and urged courage in making a stark choice. 'You will have to choose between the two, the Muslim League & the Congress, both your creations,' he enjoined. 'Every day you pass here coquetting now with the Congress, now with the League & again with the Congress, wearing yourself away, will not do.' In advising Cripps to catch his boat and 'take your poor wife with you to England', Gandhi's stance was that of the prophet: 'Stick to your dates even though the heavens may fall.'[80]

Ruat coelum was not Cripps's motto in 1946. He called this 'a most ridiculous letter from the Old Man', over which he 'laughed heartily' with its bearer, the ubiquitous Ghosh, whose mirth may well have been put on for the occasion.[81] 'I am afraid you like some others of us are feeling somewhat impatient!' Cripps replied to Gandhi. 'But I always remember you advised me to show "infinite patience" in dealing with these difficult matters.'[82] More than ever, he was resolved to keep trying; far from taking his poor wife home, their passage to England was now cancelled. It may be a moot point whether Cripps was displaying more patience or impatience, as he watched the Viceroy juggling the portfolios in the proposed coalition. What Wavell had offered, and to whom, and whether the offer could be varied, and if so, how – these intricate questions, replete with mutual recrimination and suspicion, continued to go round and round.

78. Thus Hodson, *Great Divide*, p. 159, is surely wrong to make this suggestion – all the more so since he had the benefit of Cripps's diary, which he paraphrases in a misleading way at this point.

79. Gandhi to Wavell, 13 June 1946, in Mansergh, *TOP*, vii, p. 910.

80. Gandhi to RSC, 13 June, 1946, PRO, CAB 127/128; with variations in Gandhi, *Collected Works*, lxxxvi, pp. 330–31.

81. RSC diary, 13 June 1946; cf. Wavell diary, 13 June 1946, in Moon (ed.), *Wavell: journal* p. 293.

82. RSC to Gandhi, 13 June 1946, copy, PRO, CAB 127/128.

Given that there were to be five Muslim League and two minority ministers, in the end the dispute was whether there would be six Congress Hindus (including one from the Scheduled Castes) or seven. It was, Cripps acknowledged, 'a complete impasse, although it was only about one person out of 14!' When the Viceroy reported the position to the ministers, Cripps alone favoured proposing seven Hindus; knowing Jinnah's position, Wavell persuaded the others not to budge from six. Cripps, advised by Rajagopalachari on Congress's bottom line, judged that 'they were almost bound to reject it and if they did they wouldn't play on the constitution-making scheme either'.[83] On 16 June, therefore, a second Statement was to be issued, exactly a month after the first. Drafted by Cripps, it announced that invitations to serve in a coalition government had gone out to fourteen named individuals. These comprised six Congress Hindus, five Muslim League members and three from the minorities.

Cripps still wanted to square Gandhi first, as Rajagopalachari urged. 'It is unfortunate that my colleagues seem afraid of my seeing Gandhi alone in case I let them down!' Cripps had noted.[84] The second best was for an interview to take place with Pethick-Lawrence; and, in the hours before the publication of the 16 June Statement, Cripps finally got his way on this suggestion. At 1.30 p.m., in the heat of the day, only half an hour before the Working Committee was due to meet, Gandhi duly appeared at 2 Willingdon Crescent, 'with a wet cloth on his head & very few clothes'.[85] In the house at the time, virtually behind the arras, Cripps considered this interview 'an unqualified success'. His spirits were further raised when he was later told that Gandhi 'prevented Patel from carrying the rejection of the proposals by storm and got the Working Committee thinking and discussing the matter on its merits'.[86] From whom did Cripps learn this? What remains obscure is the putative role of Dr Mehta, who left a highly circumstantial testimony to his efforts at this juncture 'to act as a uniting factor between the two great souls – Sir Stafford and Mahatma Gandhi', whose successive hot-tub massages were his daily chore.[87] With Mehta briefing him by phone, and Rajagopalachari in person, it was evident that Cripps was now thick with Congress – so much so that Wavell and Alexander sought to keep Jinnah reassured that policy remained set.

'Hand-over to Fourteen Indians on June 26' ran the *Daily Herald*'s banner headline over Stursberg's report: 'Gandhi has spoken – I heard him

83. RSC diary, 16 June 1946.   84. ibid., 14 June 1946.
85. Turnbull diary, 16 June 1946.   86. RSC diary, 17 June 1946.
87. See Mehta's memorandum, 11 April 1953.

– but the saintly old man on whom so much depends did not commit himself.'[88] For a couple of days, press reports were full of optimism, only to be confounded yet again by events.

The next move – 'Gandhi has raised a new hare' – came to Cripps as a last-minute upset: the proposal to substitute a Muslim for a Hindu as one of the Congress representatives in order to affirm its non-communal character. This was an admirable principle; its effect otherwise. 'Of course he must know – as we pointed out – that this would be like a red rag to Jinnah and would make a settlement out of the question,' Cripps wrote, relying now on the ability of Rajaji and others to 'to suppress this idea'.[89] The debates over the next couple of days began to realize Cripps's worst dreams, as the potency of Gandhi's influence was felt and those who had favoured compromise appeared to buckle. 'Nehru who had opposed Gandhi yesterday gave in to him to-day and went round to his side – most disappointingly through, I fear, weakness,' Cripps wrote on 18 June, with memories of 1942 resurfacing.

It really is rather maddening that after these three months the whole scheme long and short term looks like being broken down by a completely new stunt idea introduced by Gandhi, and apparently the Working Committee haven't the guts to disagree with him! He is an unaccountable person and when he gets these ideas in his head is as stubborn as an ox because he is convinced that he is right and no arguments will move him.[90]

For Cripps the issue was not one of principle but one of tactics; for Gandhi perhaps both. 'The real thing seems to me to be that he is much more interested in the philosophical and historical background of it all,' Cripps reflected, 'with an inclination, which is natural, to dwell on his own past struggles for independence, and is not so interested in the practical problems of government and of the present Indian situation.'[91]

Everything was now up in the air. For Cripps, the good and bad news continued to alternate, just as the good and bad men in this drama subtly switched roles. The crucial figure was Vallabhbhai Patel, hitherto invariably depicted as a sulking, brooding, scowling Hindu nationalist, resentful of Nehru's access to the British elite. Yet, as both men came to sense, Patel's hard-nosed realism made him in some respects a better ally for Cripps in the

88. *Daily Herald*, 17 June 1946.   89. RSC diary, 17 June 1946.
90. ibid., 18 June 1946.   91. ibid., 19 June 1946.

last resort than did Nehru's unpredictable impetuosity, let alone Gandhi's unbending moralism. As Mountbatten later wrote after meeting Patel himself: 'He is apparently very fond of Sir Stafford Cripps.'[92]

On 19 June Cripps listened to an account from Rajagopalachari of 'an epic struggle' in which he and Azad, reinforced by Patel, had led the Working Committee in rejecting Gandhi's arguments. Was this, Cripps reflected, to be the moment of truth when the politicians asserted themselves against the moralists?

I felt – and said – in 1942 that the only way we should get an agreement was if the Congress would divorce themselves from Gandhi and that has again proved to be the position though this time *we hope* that it will stick and will not be reversed as it was in 1942. I feel that now Congress are embarking on a constructive share of the Government and are no longer to be oppositional, this divorce was almost inevitable though its repercussions, if it persists, may be difficult and dangerous.[93]

Cripps may have exaggerated his own consistency here, for he had hitherto reversed his 1942 strategy, that of trying to split Congress from Gandhi, by instead courting the old man as the means to win over Congress. But Cripps's insight about the necessary shift of perception was surely sound. As Gandhi's biographer has put it: 'His skills and dreams had suited Congressmen while their primary objective was to agitate for independence and to spread the ideal of a new nation. Now they were involved in the endgame of an imperial raj, and facing real problems of government, and the leadership naturally fell into the hands of those who had the skill suited to the times.'[94] It was this sort of premium on pragmatism that made the tough-minded Patel an ally of Cripps rather than an opponent. But the trouble was that this transfer of power within Congress was not accomplished until the following year.

Meanwhile, Gandhi was not easily set aside. Some of those who had screwed up their courage to oppose him on 18 June then left Delhi. Nehru was absent, having made a dramatic flight to intervene in the crisis in Kashmir over the imprisonment of his supporter, Sheikh Abdullah. So by 20 June, Azad found himself beleaguered within the depleted Working Committee, in face of Gandhi's tirelessly renewed assaults. That morning, a meeting of the Delegation was interrupted by Wyatt with an appeal from Rajagopalachari for intervention to save the situation. Cripps promptly

92. Interview notes, 25 March 1947, in Mansergh, *TOP*, x, p. 17.
93. RSC diary, 19 June 1946.   94. Brown, *Gandhi*, p. 374.

volunteered his services: to go and see Azad and, if asked, Gandhi too. Despite the firm protests of Alexander, who was supported by Wavell, Cripps got his way. Finding Azad exhausted after three days of argument, Cripps took up the suggestion that he should next see Gandhi, though prudently first calling back at 2 Willingdon Crescent to put his colleagues in the picture.

Cripps had not seen Gandhi for a month: first because of his illness, then because of Gandhi's absence from Delhi, next through Cripps's own choice, and finally because of his colleagues' veto. Meeting him again at the Harijan colony, Cripps found their talk 'interesting but I fear wholly unproductive'. Having put every argument against breaking over the interim government, Cripps admitted that 'as he thinks it definitely a good thing to break it didn't cut any ice'. All that Cripps was offered was an invitation to address the Working Committee, which he saw would cast himself as the Christian in a gladiatorial arena where Gandhi was lionized. Cripps declined. 'It's disappointing after all the hopes raised – as it was in 1942!' Cripps concluded. 'But we must plug on doing our best though we can't stay here for ever.'[95]

Congress was now clearly ready to reject the plan of 16 June for a coalition Cabinet, and with it, so the Delegation assumed, the Statement of 16 May, providing for a constitution-making body. 'Now will come the difficulty of what next?' Cripps noted, darkly. 'And that I have always felt was more likely to split the Mission than anything else.'[96] When he met his colleagues on 21 June, he appreciated how far his vain efforts at conciliation the previous day had alienated Wavell and Alexander. The two of them were now united in opposing Cripps's suggestion that Jinnah be asked to form a government, which they saw as a ploy, in which, according to Wavell, 'Cripps showed his Congress bias strongly'.[97] Alexander recorded: 'Sir Stafford Cripps expressed the view that if Mr Jinnah broke down we should then go back to Congress and see if they could not be persuaded to accept the Statement of May 16 and form a Government.'[98] Cripps was threatening to take this to the Cabinet, backed with the threat of his resignation; so his comment that 'it looks as if we may have some difficulties' was a considerable understatement.[99]

Congress's rejection of the government posts was sealed when Patel

95. RSC diary, 20 June 1946; cf. Alexander diary, 20 June 1946, and Wavell diary, 20 June 1946, in Moon (ed.), *Wavell: journal*, p. 298.
96. RSC diary, 20 June 1946.
97. Wavell diary, 21 June 1946, in Moon (ed.), *Wavell: journal*, p. 299.
98. Alexander diary, 21 June 1946.   99. RSC diary, 21 June 1946.

decided that it was impossible for the Working Committee to repudiate Gandhi on such an issue. Partly because of Nehru's absence in Kashmir, Patel had become the pivotal figure. As such, it was clearly advantageous that he be seen face-to-face by the Delegation and, in Ghosh's typically clandestine way, a meeting was engineered on the morning of 23 June with Pethick-Lawrence.[100] He reported back to his fellow ministers that, when he pointed out, in reproach to Congress, that the Muslim League had accepted the Statement of 16 May, Patel made the 'astonishing reply', as Alexander recorded it: 'But so had the Congress.'[101] Wavell too was surprised at this new development and later confided: 'I am afraid that I would not put it past Cripps to have suggested to Congress in one of his many talks that they would put themselves in a better tactical position if they did so.'[102]

Such suspicions, though predictable by this point and from this quarter, seem to have been ill-founded. Though Patel represented his own potent intention as an actual decision of the Working Committee, he knew that his reading of the position was shared by Nehru and Azad. Moreover, Cripps's diary not only shows that such a possibility had long been entertained by Congress, independent of any suggestion from him, but also shows him curiously obtuse as to what transpired on 23 June. The diary simply states that 'this morning Pethick saw Vallabhbhai Patel but with no result at all'. What is notable is not just Cripps's apparent lack of surprise but his apparent lack of awareness of the significance of what Patel had said. Cripps wrote: 'We feel that having put forward our scheme of June 16th we can't go back on it and start negotiations all over again and also that as the Muslim League have accepted the Constituent Assembly scheme of May 16th and Congress have not there is no logical reason for preferring the latter to the former.'[103]

At this point Cripps envisaged complete breakdown and an early return home for consultation. The contention over the interim government had now spilled over into the press, mainly through Jinnah's agency, thus exacerbating tension.

We feel we have done all that we could but this unfortunate communal issue being imported with wide publicity into the discussions at this last moment has made it

---

100. Ghosh, *Gandhi's Emissary*, pp. 167ff., cf. Moore's caveat 'not wholly reliable'. *Escape from Empire*, p. 132n.192.

101. Alexander diary, 23 June 1946; official record, in Mansergh, *TOP*, vii, p. 1010.

102. Wavell diary, 23–24 June 1946, in Moon (ed.), *Wavell*: pp. 300, 302.

103. RSC diary, 23 June 1946.

well nigh impossible for Congress to arrive at the accommodation that we might otherwise have achieved.

It is no good blaming anyone for it – it arises from the long and deep communal division and perhaps it was too much to expect that we should be able to overcome it.[104]

The last scene in this drama was as histrionic as any that had gone before. As Congress, having rejected places in the interim government, moved towards its formal acceptance, subject to qualifications, of the Statement of 16 May, Gandhi again broke loose. He seized on the nomination forms prepared by the authorities for elections to the constituent assembly, stipulating adherence to the long-disputed paragraph 19, requiring attendance at sectional meetings to consider grouping of provinces. Cripps, the draftsman, called this 'a completely new accusation by the Old Man arising out of a perfectly harmless paragraph in the Governors' instructions' and blamed the messenger, Amrit Kaur, who had been sent to raise the issue, for 'instilling poisonous accusations against us into his mind'.[105]

A further cause of disturbance contributed to Gandhi's increasing agitation. He had only just become aware of the fact that Azad had assured the Viceroy that Congress would not prejudice his formation of an interim government through insistence on nominating a Muslim. Unsurprisingly, this came to the old man as a further example of Azad's untrustworthiness; equally unsurprisingly, it came to him through Ghosh. The latter, however, seems to have kept the information from Cripps when he saw him on the evening of 23 June, with a message this time from Patel. If Cripps would go with him to see Gandhi, Patel was said to be confident that the Working Committee would accept the 16 May Statement. With Ghosh closeted with the ministers in one room, when Rajagopalachari also arrived he had to be put in another room, continuing the discussions until midnight. What was eventually settled was that all three ministers should see Gandhi with Patel.

The interview with Gandhi took place early the next morning. Alexander, 'roused from my wet and sticky bed at 6 o'clock', prepared for the worst and duly found that 'Gandhi who was enjoying his weekly 24 hours of silence, had removed all but his loin cloth and then sat right up in a divan chair, with his legs crossed, nodding and waggling his head as the case might be!'[106] Cripps did much of the talking, while Gandhi laboriously scrawled his comments on small pieces of paper, to be read out by the attendant Ghosh. The proceedings left Cripps apprehensive. 'I really believe that at

104. ibid.   105. ibid., 24 June 1946.   106. Alexander diary, 24 June 1946.

77 he is not able always to take things in,' he wrote afterwards, 'and consequently he sticks to what is in his mind and so muddles it – with alas disastrous results to everybody.'[107] It was Patel who struck everyone as the man of business. After seeing him, Cripps knew what he wanted from Congress – or at least what he could get 'Much optimism by Stafford that Congress will now accept the long & refuse the short term,' noted Turnbull. 'He has I suspect prompted them to do it, in order to get the M/L on the spot & a Congress interim Govt formed.'[108]

At Gandhi's request, it was arranged that he should attend a formal interview that evening. At the ministers' insistence ('so that he may not misrepresent what we say', as Cripps put it), Patel was asked to come too.[109] Nehru had now returned from Kashmir, he joined Stafford and Isobel Cripps for an hour's gossip but struck them as 'very tired and nervy and most indecisive in some ways'.[110] Cripps was now relying instead on Patel. At 8 p.m. on 24 June, ten minutes after the end of Gandhi's period of silence, he came with Patel to the Viceroy's Lodge. 'A lot of rather distasteful heartiness,' noted Turnbull, aware of the Viceroy's jaundiced view of this 'deplorable affair'.[111]

The atmosphere was false for many reasons, not least the fact that earlier in the day Pethick-Lawrence, at Cripps's instigation, had pressed Wavell to appoint a high-level political adviser to his staff – a clear aspersion on his own competence. It is not surprising that Wavell thought Cripps and Pethick-Lawrence 'dishonest' in the assurances they gave Gandhi about grouping. They certainly dissimulated a goodwill towards him that they no longer genuinely shared. The strategy, as Cripps described it, was to 'let the Old Man talk all the time', to bear with his 'long references to his S. African experiences', and generally to humour him. 'Patel seemed to be with us practically throughout the interview,' Cripps noted pointedly, 'and we thought it had gone off pretty well and at any rate nothing had come up of any real importance to prevent them accepting the long-term scheme.'[112]

That night Cripps had resolved to sit up until midnight, so that there should be someone to receive Congress's answer, however late it came. Instead, after a late supper, he received a letter from Gandhi. 'I read it

107. RSC diary, 24 June 1946; cf. Ghosh, *Gandhi's Emissary*, pp. 171–4.
108. Turnbull diary, 24 June 1946.   109. RSC diary, 24 June 1946.
110. ibid., 25 June 1946.
111. Turnbull diary, 24 June 1946; Wavell diary, 24 June 1946, in Moon (ed.), *Wavell: journal*, p. 303.
112. RSC diary, 25 June 1946.

and couldn't make head or tail of it except that he was going to advise the Congress to reject the whole thing,' Cripps wrote.[113] The letter certainly showed signs of agitation. 'My whole heart goes out to you and Lady Cripps and I would far rather not write this note,' it began. The language was metaphorical: the light in the darkness had vanished, leaving a vacuum. 'I must not act against my instinct,' Gandhi claimed, acknowledging that he 'had nothing tangible to prove that there were danger signals'.[114]

As Cripps sat writing his diary on the morning of 25 June, the Congress Working Committee was sitting. It was a scenario with which he was all too familiar; the final passage he wrote catches the moment.

It really is the most devastating way of conducting negotiations. Twice we have had complete agreement with the working Committee, once about 5 days ago on the whole thing and yesterday on the long term proposals alone. (I have just been called to the telephone (10 a.m.) to receive a message from the Maulana that 'They have accepted the long term proposals' and the letter was being typed and would be with us in an hour.)

I only hope that they have not filled it up with qualifications and reservations so that it really amounts to a rejection!!

We shall see later.[115]

Gandhi had thus been overruled and Congress's ostensible acceptance secured in the end. But Cripps was right to wonder whether the scheme would not be rendered nugatory by Congress's insistence on holding to its own interpretation of the provisions on grouping. Both he and Pethick-Lawrence had refrained from pressing the point in the final interview with Gandhi, so they subsequently explained to the Viceroy, because 'it might have kept the Congress from agreeing to the long-term plan'. In asking his colleagues to 'bear in mind that a lot of this trouble about the sections and grouping was due to Mr Gandhi personally', Cripps disclosed his own view: 'The Working Committee were not so keen about it but they could not throw Mr Gandhi over completely.'[116] That it was essentially a political decision is underlined by the fact that all three politicians, including Alexander, agreed to this fudge, leaving the Viceroy alone in wishing for immediate clarification.

113. ibid.   114. Gandhi to RSC, 24 June 1946, in Mansergh, TOP, vii, pp. 1029–30.
115. RSC diary, 25 June 1946.
116. Meeting, 25 June 1946, in Mansergh, TOP, vii, pp. 1042–3.

The door was now open for Congress to be invited, after all, into an interim government, which was undoubtedly what Cripps wanted. Everything turned on paragraph 8 of the 16 June Statement: drafted by Cripps, little noticed at the time, but now the point at issue. It covered the possibility of one or both parties rejecting the Viceroy's invitations to serve in the proposed coalition government. Cripps had undoubtedly intended the paragraph to mean that the Viceroy would nevertheless himself put together an interim government, 'as representative as possible of those willing to accept the Statement of May 16th'.[117] This meant that accepting the Statement (which Congress had not yet done) became the passport to power in an interim government (which Congress clearly wanted). Wavell thought it evidence of sharp practice on Cripps's part that he apparently told him, 'with some satisfaction, that it was Paragraph 8 which had brought about the Congress acceptance of May 16 Statement'.[118]

The Viceroy felt that he had been outmanoeuvred and put into a false position via-à-vis the Muslim League. In an encounter with Jinnah, hours after receiving the Congress reply, a new bitterness was disclosed. Scorning the Congress move as insincere, Jinnah found himself upbraided by Pethick-Lawrence for the 'devastating effect' on the negotiations of his press leaks. Inflamed, Jinnah then interpreted paragraph 8 to mean that the interim government should consist only of those who had not declined the invitations to serve in the coalition. No, said Cripps: it was clear that 'the fresh negotiations for an Interim Government must be on a new basis'.[119] Jinnah went straight back to his Working Committee and obtained a vote to accept the posts on offer in the coalition – posts that were no longer on offer in a coalition-that-never-was. The main effect of these manoeuvres was to exploit the Viceroy's embarrassment over unresolved problems with which the Delegation left him.

'General air of end of term,' wrote Turnbull, voicing relief at 2 Willingdon Crescent over their now imminent departure. On the penultimate evening in Delhi, Alexander was to be found at the piano after dinner – 'at first decorous' – but once the Viceroy, Pethick-Lawrence and Cripps had gone, a 'somewhat uproarious party' went on until 1 a.m.[120] More to Cripps's taste was the quiet dinner that he and Pethick-Lawrence held the next night for 'the Trinity': Agatha Harrison, Horace Alexander and Sudhir Ghosh.

117. Statement 16 June 1946, par. 8, in Mansergh, *TOP*, vii, p. 955.
118. Wavell diary, 1 July 1946, in Moon (ed.), *Wavell: journal*, pp. 313–14.
119. Meeting, 25 June 1946, in Mansergh, *TOP*, vii, pp. 1046–7.
120. Turnbull diary, 27 June 1946.

At it, according to Ghosh, Ghosh's praises were sung by Cripps; and it is certainly true that the next day a request for special facilities for him to go to London as an unofficial envoy was put to Wavell, who, however, declined to expedite the career of this 'snake in the grass'.[121]

Wavell saw the ministers leave with mixed feelings. He had developed a mutual friendship and respect for Alexander; with Pethick-Lawrence, he recorded parting 'on quite friendly but not cordial terms'. Wavell added: 'I did not see Cripps.'[122] Rather than lavish his effusiveness upon a Viceroy whom he was now determined to remove, Cripps reserved it for Pethick-Lawrence, with a three-page letter in an unrelievedly gushing style: not only lauding 'courtesy, fairness and deep sincerity' but inviting satisfaction at 'the contribution that you have made to World History'.[123]

'Success of a Mission', loyal readers of the *Daily Herald* were blandly assured. 'The successful conclusion of the Indian talks is more than just a diplomatic triumph for Labour Party policy,' wrote its correspondent, Peter Stursberg. 'It is the first great victory of the peace and a sign that there are still men of good will on earth.' Stursberg was privately more sceptical; but he had been hand-fed by the ministers for weeks, and this glowing account depicted the complementary virtues of each, but especially 'the "heavenly spark" of Sir Stafford Cripps's unfaltering zeal'. It had been of 'inestimable value' that Gandhi had been kept in the picture throughout. 'Sir Stafford must be given credit mostly for this,' Stursberg claimed. 'Perhaps it is because they are both vegetarians, but he seemed best able to understand the mysteries of the Mahatma's mind.'[124]

The fact is that mutual comprehension, even between herbivores, actually remained somewhat imperfect, as other journalists well appreciated. Cliff, the foreign editor of the *News Chronicle*, had been in India throughout the period of the Delegation's visit and remained supportive. His final assessment was that, despite the breakdown of negotiations at Simla, 'the gap between the parties had been narrowed and it was a brilliant act of statesmanship to plan a well-balanced bridge between the nearest points of agreement'. It was 'a big accomplishment that three months ago it appeared a complete impossibility' to have secured agreement for the constitutional scheme; but, Cliff added guardedly, 'whether Congress intend to work it in

121. Ghosh, *Gandhi's Emissary*, p. 176; Wavell diary, 28 June 1946, in Moon (ed.), *Wavell: journal*, p. 309.

122. Wavell diary, 29 June 1946, ibid., p. 309; cf. ibid., 1 July 1946, p. 314.

123. RSC to Pethick-Lawrence, 29 June 1946, Trinity College, P-L5; printed in full in Brittain, *Pethick-Lawrence*, pp. 176–7.

124. *Daily Herald*, 27 June 1946; interview with Peter Stursberg.

the spirit in which it was conceived or to interpret it in a sense that will wreck its foundations, time alone will reveal'.[125]

In writing this, Cliff was drawing on a long off-the-record talk with Gandhi, whose allusions to his 'indefinable misgivings' about the constituent assembly were far from reassuring. Though unable to quote directly, Cliff published this perceptive assessment of 'the First and Greatest Indian':

Every issue is judged by him from his absolute standard, and nothing that falls short of it has any hope of acceptance. Any other politician may be willing to make some small compromise with principle or even with truth to gain what he conceives to be the large goal. Not so Gandhi.[126]

Cliff, moreover, sent the original full interview notes to Cripps, who took up some of the points raised. What particularly stung him was Gandhi's talk of a gap between himself and the ministers. 'They did their best, but after hours of discussion they couldn't understand my position or I theirs,' Gandhi told Cliff. 'Towards the end I think they gave up trying to understand.'[127] Cripps later wrote personally to Gandhi to refute this. He argued yet again that simply to devolve the task upon Congress was 'an almost impracticable solution'; that the possibly best method, at some other time or place, had to yield to the immediate need for a second-best solution, here and now, through cooperation.[128]

Such cooperation was not to be forthcoming, thus exposing the fragility of what the Cabinet Delegation had achieved. On leaving Delhi, Turnbull observed that Pethick-Lawrence was 'really quite played out & under no delusion that we have achieved necessarily very much'.[129] The constitutional arrangements, over which Cripps had laboured so long, were never to be implemented, basically because Congress failed to evince its willingness to accept the provisions on grouping. Yet this was not really a matter of untidy drafting nor legalistic interpretation, with the British Government in the position of negligent or treacherous arbitrators. If the Delegation did nothing else, it served to demonstrate that Britain intended to quit India and that the transfer of power was no longer a question of whether but of when and how and to whom.

125. *News Chronicle*, 5 July 1946.
126. See undated clipping, 'The remarkable Mr Gandhi', based on notes by Norman Cliff, 29 June 1946, PRO, CAB 127/128.
127. Notes by Norman Cliff, 29 June 1946, PRO, CAB 127/128.
128. RSC to Gandhi, 20 July 1946, copy, PRO, CAB 127/128.
129. Turnbull diary, 29 June 1946.

'The real obstacle on the way,' Ghosh advised Cripps at one point, 'is this extraordinary sense of moral responsibility which our British friends feel for everyone else.'[130] It was the last relic of imperialism. It made it difficult for highminded anti-imperialists like Cripps and Pethick-Lawrence actually to hand over this kind of responsibility along with the political kind. Quitting India was in this sense a state of mind.

The fact that the crux of the whole issue now lay within the ambit of Indian politics was, however, recognized by Cripps; as he put it later, 'it was for India to face and force its way through these difficulties'.[131] By 1946 the British politicians on the Cabinet Delegation possessed some residual prestige, a certain amount of influence, but visibly waning authority. The Muslim League, despite its commitment to Pakistan, had been induced by them into a constitutional scheme providing for a united India – on certain conditions, the most important of which was a recognition of grouping. Cripps trusted Congress, one way or another, to make good that inducement; the League soon concluded that the behaviour of the Congress leaders left it with no basis for such trust, and thus with no reason to compromise its own aim of Pakistan. It was now beyond the power of the British Government to secure compliance through an exercise of coercive authority – or through the Cabinet Delegation's mixture of paternalism, goodwill, ingenuity, pragmatism and bluff. 'The British,' as Gandhi said, 'imagining that they can bring the League and Congress together, are attempting the impossible.'[132] Cripps had realized that this would be astoundingly difficult: it was Gandhi himself who finally made it impossible.

130. Ghosh to RSC, 6 June 1946, received 12 June 1946, PRO, CAB 127/106; cf. Ghosh, *Gandhi's Emissary*, pp. 153–4.
131. RSC manuscript message for the *Times of India*, December 1949, PRO, CAB 127/113.
132. Note by Norman Cliff, 29 June 1946, PRO, CAB 127/128.

4

Quitting India

The nub of the Indian difficulty was a persistent lack of mutual trust, whether over an interim government or over a constitution-making assembly. The Cabinet Delegation could congratulate itself (and sometimes did) on having dispelled some of the distrust over British motives. It is true that the sincerity of the Labour Government's declared intention to leave India had been generally accepted by the summer of 1946, though there were lingering doubts about when it would do so. The Muslim League in effect counted on the British staying for as long as it took to secure agreement, which in practice meant satisfying Jinnah over Pakistan; and it was the setting of a date for British withdrawal that finally vitiated this strategy, undercutting the League's bargaining stance. Likewise, Congress, inured as it was to the inadequate fulfilment of Government promises over the years, was slow to wake up to the fact that this time the British were serious when they said that Dominion status would make India as independent as Canada. Even after the date for this transition had been advanced to 15 August 1947, Nehru found it hard to take in the fact that he would then be Prime Minister of an India that the British had finally quit.[1]

This consummation, so long awaited and so often heralded, in the end came quickly, little more than thirteen months after Cripps left Delhi for the last time. It was what he wanted and, to a greater extent than has generally been recognized, it was a result of his efforts. But it was not a smooth process, still less a consensual advance along the lines envisaged by the Cabinet Delegation, which was premised on an historic compromise.

If the price of a united India, for Congress, was a federal India, the price of a federal India, for the League, was a united India. Perhaps in the end neither side was prepared to pay the price. For most of the Congress leadership, Indian unity meant inheriting the strong centralism of the British Raj: maybe as a means to an end, in implementing a statist vision of

1. Gopal, *Nehru*, i, p. 356.

socialism, maybe as an end in itself. Giving the provinces any kind of blocking power had little appeal; legitimating their power through grouping even less. And even within a province like Bengal, with its delicately balanced communal politics, partition in the end seemed a more effective route to concentrating power in Congress hands.[2] Conversely, it may be that for the Muslim League, whatever Jinnah's own inclinations, Pakistan was a genie that could never be put back in its bottle.

The highway to independence might now be open. But this had the effect of relieving one traffic jam, only to move it to the next blackspot along the road, where the parting of the ways between Congress and the Muslim League created gridlock. Cripps may appear as a well-meaning policeman, waving his arms energetically but to little effect. True, a bit of give-and-take might indeed have been the rational way out of this jam, but the reality was better represented in the streetwise perspective of Patel, who saw only 'the demand for "give" on one side and "take" on the other', leading him to the conclusion: 'Conciliation and compromise can only be achieved when the desire is mutual but if there is only one-way traffic, only either surrender or a firm stand can bring about the close of this sorry episode.'[3] For months on end, Congress and the League each stood their ground: suspicious, truculent, bloody-minded, thwarted, stalled.

For the first six months after the Cabinet Delegation's return home, little was achieved. Cripps was ill in the summer and thereafter was largely preoccupied with running the Board of Trade. But with Pethick-Lawrence now a spent force at the India Office and the Viceroy increasingly mistrusted by the British Government, Attlee needed other advisers. In practice, that again meant Cripps.

Cripps knew perfectly well that Congress's acceptance of his constitutional scheme (the Statement of 16 May) had been hedged about with potentially disabling reservations, notably over grouping of provinces. Gandhi's susceptibilities had been appeased on this point. Cripps and Pethick-Lawrence – and Alexander too, it should not be forgotten – had refrained from exposing this ambiguity, treating it as a practical problem to be resolved by the increasing momentum of an actual transfer of power. Behind the shifting legalistic quibbles lay one stubborn political imperative. For if Congress were not prepared to make a reality of grouping, there was no reason for the League to accept the quid pro quo, an Indian Union. The political calculation was that this inescapable reality would evoke a

2. These are arguments well stated in Chatterji, *Bengal Divided*.
3. Patel to Arthur Henderson, 16 April 1947, in Mansergh, *TOP*, x, p. 268.

corresponding realism on the part of enough Indian politicians in securing the best compromise available. It is difficult to improve upon R. J. Moore's judicious summary of the options available: 'Congress might conciliate the League by accommodating the Pakistan idea at a sub-national level. If it failed to do so then the League must either give the idea up, or pursue it down the dangerous ways of separatism.'[4]

If one reads only the Viceroy's journal, of course, the cause of all subsequent difficulties can be explained by 'the dishonesty of Cripps and P. L. in instigating Congress to make such an acceptance' and by reiterated references to 'the duplicity of Cripps'. Wavell put the essential point, albeit in a prejudicial way: 'I don't believe that by his code he thought he was doing anything dishonest, he was merely being clever.'[5] In so far as Cripps is not indicted for being ingenuous, he is thus indicted for being disingenuous. The issue is how far political finesse – a face-saving formula here, an adroit form of words there – could be justified in brokering a messy compromise from which each side naturally hoped to gain different advantages. Like early steps in any peace process, the Cabinet Delegation's scheme did not tie up all the historically generated loose ends at once, but opened the way to incremental cooperation in creating, building and sustaining trust.

'We made it quite clear,' Cripps told the House of Commons, 'that it was an essential feature of the scheme that the provinces should go into sections though, if groups were formed, they could afterwards opt out of those groups.' But what about the possibility that a (Congress-controlled) province like Assam might find itself ensnared within a group where the superior numbers of (League-dominated) Bengal might manipulate the constitution so as to prevent Assam from opting out? 'I do not myself see how such a thing would be possible,' was Cripps's response, 'but if anything of that kind were to be attempted it would be a clear breach of the basic understanding of the scheme.' In saying this, so the Viceroy's secretary later claimed, 'Sir Stafford Cripps sailed very near the wind'.[6] But Cripps's own manuscript notes – saying that this 'would be a justifiable basis for any province to refuse to cooperate and indeed to indulge in passive resistance!' – show that he was intent on coaxing Congress into acceptance of grouping.[7] However tactfully his words were chosen, or however carefully vetted, they plainly

4. Moore, *Escape from Empire*, p. 143.
5. Wavell diary, 29 July, 30 October 1946, in Moon (ed.), *Wavell: journal*, pp. 324, 367, cf. ibid., 4 November 1946, p. 370.
6. Abell to Mountbatten, 27 April 1947, in Mansergh, *TOP*, x, pp. 458–9.
7. RSC notes for House of Commons speech, 18 July 1946.

affirmed that Congress ought to accept grouping in good faith, relying on the reciprocal good faith of the League in not abusing such provisions. The assumption that, in a free India, Indians would not be irreconcilably divided on communal lines was, after all, fundamental to the whole Congress position.

The fragility of such assumptions was exposed by the train of events in India. When Nehru assumed office as President of Congress in July 1946, Cripps wrote to him with an analogy from his own experience.

It reminded me a bit of the times when I was a left-wing rebel in the Labour Party and though we had great nominal support in the country we could never get many votes when it came to challenging the Executive at the Party conference. I hope the same result will come that the left-wing will be incorporated in the active and constructive work of Congress when they take over the reins of Government.[8]

In the long run, Nehru may have captured the left for the cause of good government in India, but for the moment his instinct was to consolidate his support, and to protect his flank, through radical rhetoric which showed that he was no flunkey of British constitutionalism. At a press conference on 10 July he spoke of grouping in contemptuous terms, which Jinnah seized upon as a sufficient excuse to repudiate the Statement of 16 May – a constitutional procedure in which his faith was already precarious. Instead, the League now resolved to achieve Pakistan by other means, and 16 August was declared Direct Action Day.

The result was the outbreak of communal violence in Calcutta, of a kind long feared and on a scale that horrified everyone, with deaths measured in thousands. Continued bloodshed now provided a sour and sombre commentary on the constitutionalism professed by Nehru and the goodwill preached by Gandhi. 'All this savagery is doing the whole of India permanent moral injury,' wrote Ghosh. 'We have been dragged down to the level of beasts.'[9]

Cripps did not give up. As he put it at the end of 1946, 'the experience of recent months showed that the dangers in the event of there being no settlement had been underestimated rather than overestimated'.[10] He clung to the view that 'there would be a settlement between the Congress and the Muslims, that there was a widespread demand for such a settlement and

8. RSC to Nehru, 8 July 1946, copy, PRO, CAB 127/143.
9. Ghosh to RSC, 5 November 1946, PRO, CAB 127/129.
10. RSC at London talks, 4 December 1946, in Mansergh, *TOP*, ix, p. 262.

that the Congress in their hearts knew that they could not achieve their purpose without a settlement'.[11] Likewise, he rejected the 'breakdown plan' proposed by Wavell, providing for a phased withdrawal by the British towards their strongholds in the north. He thought that this exceeded any military contingency. 'The Viceroy's plan was a political plan and seemed to him to invite disaster,' Cripps was minuted as saying. 'Civil war would come upon us at once.'[12] His alternative, which became the Government's, was to press ahead with a transfer of power: by consensus if possible, but with Congress alone if necessary.

Cripps's stance meant that he was often seen as pro-Congress. As Wavell put it, 'Jinnah and the League are entirely convinced that the Congress has completely got the ear of His Majesty's Government or at least of Cripps, and that it is no use any longer expecting justice to the Muslims from His Majesty's Government.'[13] One reason for this perception lay in the activities of Sudhir Ghosh, who had been in London for a couple of months as an unofficial envoy, with Cripps's complicity; and the Viceroy had grounds for thinking that this channel of communication to the Congress leadership undermined his own position. Ghosh had given the impression 'that he is negotiating with Ministers behind the back of the Viceroy,' Attlee told Cripps, stipulating that 'in future he must send anything he wants to say in writing'.[14] Pethick-Lawrence increasingly sympathized with Wavell, but Cripps persisted in trusting Ghosh, not least because this enabled him to keep open a direct line to Patel.[15]

Cripps had welcomed the formation of an interim government under Nehru in September, pending further efforts to bring in the Muslim League. He now sent a personal letter to Nehru – as he had in Delhi in April 1942 and in Simla in May 1946 – making an impassioned appeal for 'supreme statesmanship' on the grounds that 'only you can solve the problem at this stage'. He asked Congress to show 'the statesmanship and magnanimity to act the part of the strong man and give way to the weak'.[16] Nehru's response was firm: 'The Interim Govt can either function as a Govt or not at all. There is no middle position.'[17] It was the familiar problem of how far to go

11. Discussion with Pethick-Lawrence, 27 September 1946, in Mansergh, *TOP*, viii, p. 614.
12. Meeting of ministers and officials at Downing Street, 23 September 1946, in Mansergh, *TOP*, viii, p. 570.
13. Wavell to Pethick-Lawrence, 22 November 1946, in Mansergh, *TOP*, ix, pp. 138–9.
14. Attlee to RSC, 7 September 1946, PRO, CAB 127/85.
15. RSC to Patel, 23 September 1946, Das (ed.), *Patel's Correspondence*, iii, p. 301.
16. RSC to Nehru, 16 September 1946, in Gopal, *Nehru*, i, p. 334.
17. Nehru to RSC, 20 September 1946, PRO, CAB 127/143.

in conciliating the League: in particular, whether to condone Jinnah's claim to nominate all the Muslim members of the interim government.

Ghosh's account of what happened next framed the perspective in which Cripps viewed events. Ghosh was still in London when he read that Wavell had begun his own negotiations with the Muslim League, seeking to include it within the interim government. Ghosh writes in his memoirs of going at once to Cripps, and of being assured by him that the Viceroy was under instructions 'that Nehru must be treated as a real Prime Minister and the responsibility of bringing the Muslim League into the Government was his'. He writes, too, of deciding to return to Delhi and of apprising Nehru of Cripps's assurance that the British Government would back him rather than the Viceroy – only to be told by Nehru that, in a moment of exasperation at being nagged to hold talks with Jinnah, he had told Wavell to do it himself – which the Viceroy had taken literally.[18] On this showing, Nehru's famous temper had sold the pass.

This might be dismissed as a heavily retrospective gibe against Nehru but for the fact that an unpublished letter from Ghosh survives, showing that Cripps was fed the same story at the time. In this letter, Ghosh reported arguing with Gandhi, Patel and Nehru that the inclusion of a Congress Muslim was not a vital matter – 'if this one concession was made to the Muslims they would have accepted Nehru's leadership in the Cabinet and Nehru would have become the real Prime Minister of India'. So Nehru's obduracy and pique were held responsible for preventing a historic deal from being struck between the Indian parties themselves. 'Such a settlement would have made the Viceroy almost an unnecessary institution,' Ghosh told Cripps. 'Jawaharlal missed this opportunity.'[19]

As it was, it had been left to Wavell to bring Muslim League ministers into the interim government. They were imposed on a protesting Nehru, whose leadership they did not acknowledge, with the result that the government never functioned as a proper coalition. The prospects of agreement over procedure in the forthcoming constitutional assembly were further diminished. It was Cripps who was now busy drafting a contingency plan to be sent to the Viceroy.[20] At this point he received further information via Ghosh – 'This is virtually a letter from Nehru to you' – suggesting that the only way to redeem the situation was to get Nehru to London for a brief

18. Ghosh, *Gandhi's Emissary*, pp. 24–6.
19. Ghosh to RSC, 15 October 1946; this is the letter which could not be traced in Mansergh, *TOP*, ix, p. 25n.
20. Mansergh, *TOP*, ix, pp. 114–16, 19–21 November 1946.

visit in which he could have a personal meeting with Attlee, Cripps and Pethick-Lawrence.[21] With deadlock looming, the idea of summoning a conference in London thus seems to have come from Nehru. Why, then, did it need an appeal from Attlee to secure Nehru's attendance? The reason, as Cripps must have appreciated when drafting Attlee's message for him, lay in Nehru's rivalry with Patel, who declined the invitation. Before taking the risk of attending, therefore, Nehru needed not only further cajolery from Ghosh but, to protect his position, the written reassurance that the conference implied 'no intention of abandoning either the decisions of the Assembly to meet or the plan put forward by the Cabinet Delegation'.[22] This was the plan, it should be remembered, that had been accepted only nominally by Congress in June and repudiated totally by the League since August. Such was the task facing the London conference, for which the members of the Cabinet Delegation were once more mobilized.

The conference was convened for 4 December 1946. Wavell flew in the previous day and immediately handed Attlee, Pethick-Lawrence and Alexander a paper which he had prepared. It said that the short-term priority was to get back to the Cabinet Delegation's conception of the constituent assembly; and the long-term priority was a plan for withdrawal. Cripps was the only Government representative absent. It was on the following day that he first read the paper submitted by the Viceroy – whom he surprised by saying that he agreed with it. On strategic objectives, Cripps and Wavell were actually united by their realism, only divided by the difference between a politician's tactics and a soldier's.

Wavell then watched during the first session while Cripps and Nehru engaged in a fruitless duel – 'it got us nowhere' – on the interpretation of the 16 May Statement over compulsory grouping.[23] Cripps could not dent Nehru's confidence 'that the Muslims would come in anyhow, sooner or later, provided that they felt that the Constituent Assembly was going ahead in any case'. Cripps affirmed that the League's interpretation was in fact that intended by the Cabinet Delegation; but claimed that 'this dispute was rather artificial' since, in practice, the forming of the groups and any

21. Ghosh to RSC, 18 November 1946, PRO, CAB 127/129; air mail in three days at this time. 'Last night Jawaharlal talked at some length about you and your health,' Ghosh wrote a few days later, adding: 'you are very much in his thoughts.' Ghosh to RSC, 21 November 1946, PRO, CAB 127/129.
22. Prime Minister to Nehru, 27 November 1946 (drafted by Cripps), in Mansergh, *TOP*, ix, pp. 186–7. Ghosh to RSC, 30 November 1946, PRO, CAB 127/129: 'So Jawaharlal is going. I did all I could to get him to go.'
23. Wavell diary, 5 December 1946, in Moon (ed.), *Wavell: journal*, pp. 390–91.

opting-out from them by dissident provinces would be contemporaneous, after provincial elections. An obligation to enter into groups in the first place, however, was 'an essential part of the compromise the Mission had evolved'. Cripps suggested that this was 'a small price to pay for Muslim cooperation in the Constituent Assembly', to which Nehru responded that 'no price was too high for real cooperation from the Muslims, provided it was real'.[24] The following day Cripps reported to his colleagues that he had subsequently had a private conversation with Nehru – they evidently met socially – and Nehru had said that he could not get Congress support for compromise on this point.[25]

Cripps's prime objective remained an agreed settlement between the Indian parties. It would be up to them to live with each other after the British had gone. As he reminded Jinnah and Liaquat Ali Khan: 'we had no responsibility for the future constitution of India, and we could not police the procedure'.[26] Cripps had often reminded his own colleagues that 'Congress had always adopted the line that the Muslims could not be compelled to come into an all-India constitution'.[27] On the final day of the conference Cripps again 'asked whether Pandit Nehru would not be prepared to take a risk in the interests of agreement, which would surely be worthwhile'. Conversely, to the Muslim League he had 'emphasised the importance of having something which could be held out to the other side as affording some prospect of an accord being brought about'.[28] At the end of three days of discussions, however, the position was much the same as Cripps had stated it at the beginning: 'It looked as if it had got beyond the possibilities of compromise.'[29] The implication was that the British Government had to act – not to perpetuate its crumbling power but to divest itself of its historic obligations.

Cripps put the cardinal point to his colleagues in bald terms on 5 December:

there was a strong case for a declaration now that we would only stay a year or 18 months in India. We should have to hand over to a government set up by the Constituent Assembly. The Congress wanted Muslim cooperation and would very likely produce a constitution which was quite fair to them.[30]

24. 4 December 1946, in Mansergh,*TOP*, ix, pp. 257–9.   25. Mansergh,*TOP*, ix, p. 274.
26. 4 December 1946, in Mansergh,*TOP*, ix, p. 264.
27. Meeting of ministers and officials at Downing Street, 23 September 1946, in Mansergh, *TOP*, viii, pp. 571–2.
28. 6 December 1946, in Mansergh, *TOP*, ix, pp. 291, 293.
29. 4 December 1946, in Mansergh, *TOP*, ix, p. 254.
30. 5 December 1946, in Mansergh, *TOP*, ix, p. 276.

Nehru might want this, Pethick-Lawrence admitted, but could he persuade the more communal elements in Congress? Wavell bluntly said that there was no chance of Congress showing generosity. 'If the constitution did not conform to our requirements,' Cripps declared, 'we should have to hand over piecemeal to such authorities as we thought best at the time.'[31] This was the line – after the amalgamation of drafts from Cripps, Wavell and Alexander – that emerged in the official statement at the end of the conference: 'His Majesty's Government could not of course contemplate – as the Congress have stated they would not contemplate – forcing such a Constitution upon any unwilling part of the country.'[32] The logic was that, in the absence of agreement, a British withdrawal implied partition; and Cripps's proposal of setting a date for withdrawal now lay on the table.

The impasse was finally broken when Attlee announced a striking move: the appointment of Admiral Lord Mountbatten as the last Viceroy. The fact that the historiography of the transfer of power has long been dominated by accounts designed to celebrate his role has naturally provoked revisionist attempts to denigrate it. But the most striking effect of the Mountbatten version is its complicity with accounts that conspire in mutual admiration between himself, Nehru and Attlee – notably at the expense of giving Cripps his due. This is not how it appeared at the time; and the events that inaugurated the Mountbatten viceroyalty need to be seen in a rather different perspective.

The constituent assembly met at last in December 1946 but was boycotted by the Muslim League. In the India debate in the Commons on 12 December Cripps was the most prominent participant on the Government side. This was partly because Churchill was led into ill-advised recriminations about what had happened in 1942. 'India: Churchill Attacks Cripps' was one front-page banner headline. Deploring Cripps's influence over the Cabinet Delegation, Churchill offered the barbed comment: 'No one more than he has taken responsibility in this matter, because neither of his colleagues could compare with him in that acuteness and energy of mind with which he devotes himself to so many topics injurious to the strength and welfare of the State.'[33]

Behind the scenes, it was Cripps's role in formulating Government policy

31. 5 December 1946, in Mansergh, *TOP*, ix, p. 279.
32. Statement, 6 December 1946, in Mansergh, *TOP*, ix, p. 296.
33. 5 HC Debs., vol. 431, col. 1369 (12 December 1946); *Daily Graphic*, 13 December 1946.

at this stage that struck informed observers. 'Cripps is of course the directing brain,' Wavell wrote acidly after a series of frustrating encounters with the India Committee.[34] As Lord Listowel, at this time the committee's most junior member, later testified, Cripps 'played a more important part than Attlee in the policy decisions leading up to the transfer', even though the received view has long been to the contrary.[35] Dalton's diary confirms that it was Cripps, and only belatedly Attlee, who seized the initiative: 'Cripps is much the best man on this Committee, and alone seems to keep his mind fresh and keen and constantly on the essential points.'[36] In particular, the opinion expressed in Sudhir Ghosh's memoirs, that Cripps was 'the brain behind all that the Labour Government was doing regarding India', has been generally discounted as emanating from a tainted source.[37]

Ghosh's account of the replacement of Wavell by Mountbatten, published twenty years later, has admittedly met damaging criticism. According to Ghosh, during the London conference, Nehru and Mountbatten were brought together for dinner by Cripps, who realized that a new Viceroy was needed, and one who commanded Congress approval. Indeed, so the story continued, Stafford's notion of filling this post himself had only been abandoned on hearing from Isobel Cripps, newly returned from Delhi, that this would be a mistake. Hence Ghosh's alleged dinner for three, creating an instant rapport between the two guests, and eliciting a promise from the host to wave his magic wand! Hence too a letter some weeks later from Cripps to Ghosh, darkly alluding to 'the two suggestions I made to Jawaharlal'.[38] There is undoubtedly much self-aggrandisement in this account by the oleaginous Ghosh. Worse, the actual dates make his exact sequence of events impossible – a recurrent problem in his memoirs. Such justifiable criticism of the circumstantial detail has led to a dismissal of the whole story as false.[39]

Yet Isobel Cripps's papers suggest that, despite everything, Ghosh was essentially correct. She had undertaken a long-planned visit to China in the autumn of 1946 as part of her charitable activities, accompanied by Peggy Cripps. Incidentally, it is notable that they were received as guests not only

34. Wavell diary, 20 December 1946, in Moon (ed.), *Wavell: journal*, p. 398.

35. Listowel to IC, 5 October 1978, copy. Moore, *Escape from Empire*, esp. pp. 348–50, is a lonely but authoritative voice in support; and Jenkins, 'Stafford Cripps', p. 100, shows a good intuition in reaching the same judgement.

36. Dalton diary, 20 December 1946, in Dalton, *High Tide and After*, pp. 171–2.

37. Ghosh, *Gandhi's Emissary*, p. 44.   38. ibid., pp. 44–8.

39. Hodson, *Great Divide*, pp. 190–91, citing TLS, 27 July 1967, p. 672; cf. Moore, *Escape from Empire*, pp. 203–4.

by Madame Chiang Kai-shek in the then Nationalist capital of Nanking but also by Madame Mao in the territory controlled by the Communist insurgents.[40] Isobel kept the telegram she received in Nanking from Stafford's office in London: 'SUDHIR TELEGRAPHED THAT JAWAHARLAL WOULD LIKE HER TO STAY WITH HIM IN NEW DELHI.' On Stafford's advice that this might be 'useful', she accepted, even though it meant declining an offer from the Wavells, who were understandably sensitive to the implications for political neutrality. ('Of course, we quite understand you would enjoy staying with an old friend, especially one as interesting as Pandit Nehru,' wrote Eugénie Wavell. 'Whether your visit will be helpful, as you hope, or the reverse, time may prove.')[41] Whether the Wavells were equally sensitive to the implications for their own tenure of the Viceregal Lodge is unlikely.

Doubtless buoyed up by fresh memories of the fulsome Chinese street signs – 'Lady Kalyps is our deliverer' – the embarrassing guest arrived in Delhi only a day after her host had returned from the London conference. At the Nehru residence, 17 York Road, she was made welcome in a happy household – 'much laughter and teasing of Jawaharlal, most of all by Padmaja Naidu'.[42] But, after talking with him, Isobel told Stafford: 'At this moment I have a deep inner feeling that you and Jawaharlal are not "reaching" each other to the extent you should.'[43] Much of the trouble was put down to the total antipathy between Nehru and Wavell. She recorded Nehru's own reminiscence of the troubled interview with the Viceroy over the composition of the interim government:

Nehru asked the Viceroy to leave things without interfering because if the Muslim League came in his Government would then be functioning as a Cabinet.

The Viceroy wanted to invite Jinnah to come into the Government himself and in the end Nehru said 'I do not agree but if you say you will do it, I cannot stop you.' The Viceroy (seemingly misunderstanding) then published that Nehru had agreed to Jinnah being asked. This needless to say very much irritated Nehru.[44]

Disaffection with Wavell pervades Isobel Cripps's record of her stay. She was busy on Stafford's behalf, seeing an impressive list of political figures, usually accompanied by Ghosh. But it was only when he left

40. Appiah, *Attic*, pp. 72–4.
41. RSC to IC, telegram, 15 November 1946; cf. Nehru to IC, 10 November; Eugénie Wavell to IC, 5 December 1946.
42. Review of a week in New Delhi by IC, 9–16 December 1946; Appiah, *Attic*, pp. 75–6.
43. IC note, 10 December 1946.   44. ibid., 16 December 1946.

the room for a moment that Rajagopalachari was emboldened to ask outright: 'Lady Cripps, is there any chance of changing the Viceroy?' She gave no direct reply. In conversation with Ghosh, however, she raised the issue herself and later passed on his response to Stafford: 'that there was no one but you who could carry this thing through'.[45] There is other evidence that the possibility of Cripps going out to Delhi himself had been mooted - Major 'Billy' Short had argued against it at the end of November by telling Cripps: 'You are our key-man to the situation in London today.'[46] It should be remembered that Isobel had no means of direct contact with Stafford while in Delhi – she could hardly have asked the Viceregal Lodge to provide a secure line to London to check on this rather delicate point. But her note shows that the matter had evidently been discussed between them:

As we both know neither of us want to shoulder this burden but we also know what we have always questioned whether it might have to be. I want you to go on turning over in your mind whether if you were faced with taking the job for a year with the understanding that because of your special knowledge and position of confidence you have built up here through personal relationships, you might make a unique contribution in this crisis?[47]

By the time that Isobel wrote this for Stafford, let alone by the time he received it, it is likely that he had already relinquished the idea of becoming Viceroy himself – but only to seize on an alternative candidate.

The evidence for this is inferential, not direct; but it is strong. We know that Cripps had met Nehru in London the previous week for private conversation, as he had told his colleagues. We know that the idea of appointing Mountbatten had been mentioned several months previously by Cripps.[48] We know that the possibility of Nehru meeting Mountbatten during the London conference was aired (though we do not know if this resulted in dinner for three).[49] We do know that, in 1942, Cripps had confided to Nehru his plan for getting rid of Linlithgow; and we know that, in late 1946, he was equally determined to get rid of Wavell – and better

45. ibid., 10 December 1946. Ghosh later gave another version: that he advised against and conveyed this to Cripps in a letter sent back with Isobel (Ghosh, *Gandhi's Emissary*, p. 45). But the surviving letter contains nothing on this point: Ghosh to RSC, 11 December 1946.
46. Short to RSC, 28 November 1946, in Mansergh, *TOP*, ix, p. 208.
47. IC note, 10 December 1946.
48. RSC to Moon and Short at the end of June 1946; Moon (ed.), *Wavell: journal*, p. 458n.
49. Moore, *Escape from Empire*, p. 216.

able to do so. We know that the need to 'find a man with a much bigger personality' had been urged upon him by Ghosh and we know, too, that many of the otherwise implausible allegations in Ghosh's account can now be corroborated.[50] It seems reasonable, therefore, to infer that when Cripps wrote to Ghosh of 'the two suggestions I made to Jawaharlal', he was indeed alluding to his private proposal on 4 or 5 December that Wavell be replaced by Mountbatten.[51]

Attlee proposed this to the King on 17 December and to Mountbatten himself the next day. The India Committee had meanwhile been discussing future policy – in the inhibiting presence of Wavell, who had no idea that he was not to implement the policy himself – and by 20 December had firmly replaced Wavell's draft with one by Cripps. This included a statement of the Government's 'intention to recommend Parliament to hand over power in India by March 31st 1948', in the hope that some constitutional arrangement would meanwhile be made.[52] This clearly embodied Cripps's line, suggested two weeks previously at the end of the London conference, and it became the core of the Cabinet paper, 'Indian Policy: memorandum by the Prime Minister'.[53] This document was to be published by the Government on 20 February 1947 after further minor emendation, notably of the transfer date, which was finally settled as June 1948. Here was the ticket for a Viceroy determined on a swift transfer of power.[54]

Cripps did everything he could to ensure Mountbatten's success. They shared an upper-class self-confidence, simultaneously part of the establishment and insouciant of conventional stuffiness; both were reliant on personal charm in breaking down barriers and cutting through red tape; they were not old friends but they had common enemies, like Lord Beaverbrook. Above all, Cripps believed that he had found in Mountbatten the ideal agent for his own policy. It was not, contrary to his later claims, Mountbatten who imposed a deadline for the transfer of power; he tinkered with the date itself. In coaxing him to accept the appointment – Attlee had asked him to 'have a talk with Dicky'[55] – Cripps made a quixotic offer to go out as a

50. Ghosh to RSC, 5 November 1946, PRO, CAB 127/129.
51. RSC to Ghosh, 27 January 1947, Ghosh, *Gandhi's Emissary*, pp. 46–7; we now know, too, that this is a reply to Ghosh's letter to RSC, 19 January 1947, which survives in the Cripps papers.
52. Draft statement, 20 December 1946, in Mansergh,*TOP*, ix, pp. 393–4.
53. CP (46) 456, 24 December 1946, in Mansergh,*TOP*, ix, pp. 400–401.
54. This point is agreed by those who have studied the Cabinet papers: Harris, *Attlee*, pp. 374–5; Moore, *Escape from Empire*, pp. 200–201, 208–9, 221–3; cf. Hodson's contention that Mountbatten 'wrote his own ticket', *Great Divide*, pp. 193–9, at p. 199.
55. Attlee to RSC, 27 December 1946, PRO, CAB 127/85.

member of the new Viceroy's staff. Mountbatten graciously declined, telling the King: 'I don't want to be ham-strung by having to bring out a third version of the Cripps offer!!!'[56] Instead he suggested that Cripps take the India Office; but Attlee demurred, intent now on adopting an active role himself, ultimately with the pliant Lord Listowel, previously Under-Secretary, as Secretary of State.

Mountbatten also liked to reminisce about having secured 'plenipotentiary powers' as Viceroy. He recalled putting this demand to Attlee and Cripps in an interview where no notes were taken: 'But Cripps nodded his head and Attlee replied, "All right, you've got the powers and the job."' Listowel, who knew them all, thought it rang true that 'Cripps was the first to indicate agreement and that Attlee took his cue from him'.[57] Mountbatten no more possessed 'plenipotentiary powers' in any legal sense than Cripps did in 1942; but it is likely that some assurance was sought of the need for latitude on the part of the Viceroy and for confidence on the part of the Government – which Cripps would have been the last to deny.

When it came to the endgame in India, Cripps thus put all his chips on Mountbatten. Wavell, now back in Delhi, proved less easy to dislodge than anticipated; he refused a request that he fly home again, in effect so as to be sacked in person; whereupon an irritated Cripps drafted a reply, dismissing the old Viceroy by telegram. This Attlee did at the end of January. Then he sent the new Viceroy a directive ('which Stafford has produced rather at short notice') setting out his terms of reference.[58]

It was not until 20 February that the Government was ready to announce its policy and the change of Viceroy – the news for which Nehru had been waiting. 'We had felt anxiety lest you should think Stafford's promises were not going to be able to be redeemed,' Isobel Cripps wrote to him, with a redundantly warm commendation of the new Viceroy: 'he and Stafford have close links and confidence in each other'.[59] Isobel and Stafford were to see a good deal of Dickie and Edwina Mountbatten in the month before the latter pair left for India. 'We did so enjoy our evening with you,' Edwina wrote to Isobel, 'and your husband's (may I call him Stafford?) masterly and riveting tale.'[60] Confidential notes on the leading figures in Indian politics were duly passed over and introductions made.

56. Mountbatten to the King, 4 January 1947, in Mansergh, *TOP*, ix, p. 453.
57. Mountbatten, 'Reflections on the transfer of power', p. 9; Listowel, 'Whitehall dimension', p. 23; cf. Hodson, *Great Divide*, pp. 201-2, Ziegler, *Mountbatten*, pp. 355-6.
58. Attlee to Mountbatten, 8 February 1947, in Mansergh, *TOP*, ix, p. 652.
59. IC to Nehru, MS copy, 23 February 1947.   60. EM to IC, 4 March 1947.

'It has been a great privilege and joy to work with you,' Cripps told Mountbatten on his departure, 'and you know how passionately I desire your success for the sake of India's future.'[61] This was, of course, now Mountbatten's chance to find a path to Indian independence; there was, as he had made clear at the outset, to be no third version of the Cripps offer. Equally, there was to be no united India either.

Cripps's personal involvement, though henceforth more intermittent, did not cease. He received, at Mountbatten's request, one of five copies of the Viceroy's personal reports (the others went to the King, the Prime Minister, the Secretary of State for India and Albert Alexander). He continued to act as a useful member of the India Committee, as an indispensable support to Attlee in Cabinet, and as a lucid defender of the Government's India policy in debate. Cripps recognized, however, that the initiative had passed out of his hands – and would quickly pass out of those of the new Viceroy too. 'It must be obvious I think to anyone who objectively studies the present situation that there is really only one way in which all these difficulties can be overcome and that is by the cooperation of the Indian Parties,' Cripps told the House of Commons in March 1947. 'It is their problem and for it they alone can find the solution.'[62]

At this stage, on the eve of Mountbatten's arrival in India, Cripps still hoped that it might be possible for Congress to get Jinnah to join an All-India Union by itself accepting the implication of the procedure on grouping, especially in Bengal. His final differences with Patel, as seen in the Viceroy's correspondence and via Ghosh, turned on this point, with Cripps claiming: 'We are determined to be impartial.'[63] In the absence of agreement between the Indian parties, there would be no constitutional successor to the British Raj; the logic was, as Cripps had foreseen at the London conference, that power would have to be transferred 'piecemeal to such authorities as we thought best at the time'. Pro-Congress as he had always been, and always been perceived, Cripps none the less refused to accept Congress's claim to the whole of India, regardless of the Muslim League. Gandhi still maintained to the new Viceroy that he 'considered it wicked of Sir Stafford Cripps not to have recommended the turning over of para-

61. RSC to Mountbatten, 19 March 1947, in Ziegler, *Mountbatten*, p. 362.
62. RSC notes for his speech, 5 March 1947; 5 HC Debs., vol 434, cols. 494–512 (5 March 1947).
63. Ghosh to Patel, 14 March 1947, quoted Moore, *Escape from Empire*, p. 222; cf. Ziegler, *Mountbatten*, p. 374 and Mansergh, *TOP*, x, pp. 446–7, 519–20.

mountcy to the Central Government representing the sovereignty of the Indian nation'.[64]

The conclusion that some form of partition was inevitable, however, was fast becoming irresistible. This was, in effect, now accepted by Congress – but only on the basis that there would in turn be a partition of the two disputed provinces, Bengal and the Punjab. On this point Patel and Nehru were agreed, leaving Gandhi virtually isolated. Chastened by his first-hand experience of communal violence in Bengal and Bihar, which he played a morally admirable part in tempering through his own presence, Gandhi found that the merits of the Cabinet Delegation scheme retrospectively grew upon him – too late, of course.[65] By May, everyone else realized that a new plan was needed. As Listowel put it to the India Committee: 'We are, I think, bound, now that the Cabinet Mission's scheme is virtually abandoned, to adhere to the broad principles of the Cripps Offer.'[66] That would have meant, as in 1942, envisaging autonomous decisions on accession to an Indian union, province by province.

Mountbatten had drawn up his own plan. A key provision throughout was for the transfer of power on the basis of Dominion status – in effect, offering Congress the prospect of a quick solution while offering the British the prospect of continued membership of the Commonwealth by their successors. Mountbatten faced a sudden breakdown of his otherwise good understanding with Nehru over the first version of his proposals, which Nehru saw as a recipe for the balkanization of India. Instead, Mountbatten turned to a revised plan, hastily produced by his Reforms Commissioner, V. P. Menon, acknowledged as a close ally of Patel. The new package deftly combined Dominion status, a quick handover to two central governments in India and Pakistan, and the option of partition for Bengal and the Punjab. The difficulty here was that, no sooner had the Cabinet in London been asked to approve his first plan, than they were asked by Mountbatten to approve his second.

Faced with crisis and confusion, the India Committee proposed top-level consultation with the Viceroy. One alternative was for a couple of Cabinet ministers to go to Delhi – perhaps Attlee himself, accompanied by Cripps (on what would have been his third mission). The other alternative, more congenial to Mountbatten, was that he should himself fly home, which Attlee asked him to do. Mountbatten was thus back in London for ten days

64. Record of interview, 4 April 1947, Mansergh, *TOP*, x, p. 121.
65. Brown, *Gandhi*, p. 371. Mansergh, *TOP*, xi, p. 4.
66. Listowel memorandum, 17 May 1947, in Mansergh, *TOP*, x, p. 877.

at the end of May. The fact that he so readily secured the Cabinet's agreement to his revised plan can be attributed to the unwavering support, not only of the Prime Minister and Secretary of State for India but also of Cripps, whom Mountbatten made a point of seeing individually.

Back in Delhi, Mountbatten was able to secure the acquiescence of the Indian parties, thus exploiting the blend of confidence and latitude that Cripps had sorely needed in 1942. 'Magnificent,' he wrote to the Viceroy. 'We have been thinking of you hour by hour, and what you have accomplished has exceeded even our expectations and hopes.'[67] Meanwhile in London it was, yet again, Cripps who had charge of drafting many of the essential documents for the transfer of power. The necessary legislation had to be prepared at breakneck speed, to keep in kilter with the accelerated timetable to which Mountbatten was now working.

Finally set for 15 August 1947, independence was to be gravely marred, of course, by the trauma of the communal violence that accompanied partition, in which up to a million people died.[68] In this respect, it was an appalling outcome, misjudged to some extent by everyone concerned. Maybe different measures on the ground could have given more protection to the victims and saved some lives; but it is difficult to resist the conclusion that the Punjab massacres were unavoidable, given partition.[69] When Cripps had talked with Pethick-Lawrence, justifying their shoddy, second-best compromises as a means of avoiding partition itself, the scale of bloodshed that they envisaged as the stark alternative had been of the order of two or three million. This was what Cripps had striven to avoid in the middle of 1946; this was what he subsequently sought to mitigate.

Cripps persisted in regarding the coming of Indian independence with some pride. Geopolitically, it can be argued that Britain's escape from empire was a prudent, if improvised and imperfect, response to the realities of its declining power in the world, one jump ahead of necessity. Ideologically, however, the Labour ministers who nerved themselves to defend a policy that their opponents denounced as 'scuttle' showed an understandable wish to represent it in more positive and persuasive terms. Cripps's own longstanding commitment surely licensed him to put this more benign gloss on the process. 'It has largely been British people who by precept and

67. RSC to Moutbatten, 6 June 1947, in Ziegler, *Mountbatten*, p. 391.
68. French's estimate, *Liberty or Death*, p. 349; cf. Ziegler, *Mountbatten*, p. 437, plumping for Moon's estimate at the lower end of a range from 200,000 to 1 million, and Roberts, 'Mountbatten' in *Eminent Churchillians*, pp. 128–32, challenging this as too low.
69. Moore, *Escape from Empire*, p. 331, endorsing Moon, *Divide and Quit*, p. 275.

example inspired the Indians to desire to institute their own self-governing Democracy,' he had told the Commons in March 1947.[70] Four months later, he moved the third reading of the Independence Bill with the words: 'By passing this Bill we shall be firmly and finally establishing our honesty of democratic purpose.'[71]

This accelerated legislation needed agreement from all parties, in India and Britain alike. Cripps had supported Mountbatten in showing an advance draft of the Bill to Nehru, for whom he wrote a personal letter, to be used at the Viceroy's discretion in winning assent.[72] Mountbatten's own charm sufficed on this point, just as it had proved efficacious in gaining cooperation at Westminster from the Opposition. To cover their political nakedness, and to keep Churchill quiet, the Conservatives clutched at the fact that the measure provided for Dominion status within the British Commonwealth. But despite their objections, which Attlee faced down, the title was simply 'Indian Independence Bill', as Cripps had wished.

The final step in the settlement to concern Cripps was in reconciling independence for India and Pakistan with their continued membership of a redefined Commonwealth. This was achieved at the Commonwealth conference in London, April 1949. No longer 'British', nor accepting the monarchy as more than a symbol of unity, the Commonwealth took shape as a post-imperial association of free nations which could accommodate the Republic of India. No longer a subversive, radical notion, this was widely celebrated as a consensual, whiggish outcome. Like Mountbatten, Attlee privately acknowledged how much his own publicly lauded achievements owed to Cripps: 'Quite apart from all the work you have done during these years on the Indian problem I am most conscious and appreciative of all you did at the Conference to bring about the successful result.'[73]

From Claridge's, the Indian Prime Minister sent a handwritten note to the British Chancellor of the Exchequer.

70. RSC notes for speech in House of Commons, 5 March 1947; 5 HC Debs., vol. 434, cols. 494–512 (5 March 1947); full manuscript of text all in Cripps's hand. For comment on 'how Labour ministers transformed the political alternative they had hitherto construed as defeat into a moral and political triumph', see Singh, *Origins of Partition*, p. 208; cf. ibid., pp. 213–14 on Cripps's speech; and a similarly cynical view is taken in Owen, ' "Responsibility without power" '.

71. *Daily Mail*, 16 July 1947.   72. Mansergh, *TOP*, xi, pp. 475–6, 815–16.

73. Attlee to RSC, 30 April 1949, PRO, CAB 127/85; Mountbatten to RSC, 28 April 1949, PRO, CAB 127/139.

My dear Stafford,

Vallabhbhai Patel has asked me to convey to you his regards and gratitude for your understanding and sympathy with our point of view and your assistance in achieving this final result. To which may I add my own gratitude?

My love to you and Isobel.

Ever yours,

Jawaharlal.[74]

Stafford Cripps never fulfilled his ambition to visit a free India. Soon after his death, Isobel received an invitation to stay with Jawaharlal Nehru and made his generous hospitality the core of her own four-month journey to Pakistan, India and Ceylon in 1952–3. Received with courtesy and respect as Stafford's widow by an impressively wide range of his old friends, now often installed in high office themselves, she had little reason to suspect that, half a century later, the name of Cripps would no longer retain its axiomatic link with the story of Indian independence.

74. Nehru to RSC, 27 April 1949. In an official letter, on his return to Delhi, he explained that his main difficulty now stemmed from his friendly reception in London: 'The fact that even Winston Churchill should fall into line raises further suspicion. Such is the world.' Nehru to RSC, 8 May 1949.

PART SIX

'AUSTERITY CRIPPS'

1947–52

THE HORROR OF GREAT HEIGHTS

Cripps's moment

Cripps is best remembered for his efforts to rebuild the British economy after the Second World War. There was a relatively smooth trajectory to the final phase of his career. The Board of Trade, its responsibilities for industrial production enhanced by wartime controls, was an obvious place for him to go in 1945. His appointment two years later to the newly established Ministry of Economic Affairs extended the range of his brief but did not significantly change its nature; and Cripps's move to the Treasury in November 1947 again proved to be an augmentation of an existing role rather than a change of direction. Combining the posts of Chancellor of the Exchequer and Minister of Economic Affairs, Cripps occupied a position of unique dominance over virtually all aspects of British economic policy. How this came about can only be understood in terms of the overlapping crises that successively transformed his position.

Cripps initially worked fairly happily under Attlee's premiership. True, when the call from Buckingham Palace came in 1945, Morrison had again tried to assert his own claims, on the argument that the Labour Party first needed to elect its own leader in a new Parliament. Bevin, with his deepseated antipathy for Morrison, had no time for this; Attlee went to the Palace. This was the last occasion on which Cripps supported Morrison's claims, subsequently finding him unimpressive in fulfilling his responsibilities as economic co-ordinator. Instead, with Dalton installed at the Treasury, Cripps made common cause with him on a range of problems, domestic and international. As Dalton, formerly Cripps's arch-critic, later happily acknowledged, 'during this period we were colleagues in the Labour Government and worked closely together, generally in harmony and agreement, often giving each other mutual support in the Cabinet and outside'.[1]

1. Dalton, *Fateful Years*, p. 149.

Cripps was always good in a crisis – one reason why 1947 saw him riding high. In the fuel crisis that caught the Government unprepared in February, he kept his nerve and, though the 'Cripps plan' that he produced proved unable to cope with the worst winter of the century, he was one of the few ministers to emerge with an enhanced reputation. The same could not be said of Emanuel Shinwell, the Minister of Fuel and Power, who was soon replaced by his manifestly more capable deputy, Hugh Gaitskell, who thus gained his first chance to observe Cripps at close quarters.

Cripps's ability to exert an executive grip on immediate problems was badly needed by the Government, the more so when the fuel crisis was succeeded by a sterling crisis. The trouble was that the large North American loan, which had been granted at the end of the war, was rapidly being exhausted, as Dalton sought to warn his Cabinet colleagues in the middle of March 1947.[2] This looming crisis was the background to Cripps's moves in the following month, insisting that the Government display a more urgent approach to the economy. 'Unless we can get our planning done right, we shall be sunk,' he told Dalton.[3] His proposed solution, which he attempted to urge on Attlee, hinged on moving Bevin from the Foreign Office to take over Morrison's planning responsibilities. Though nothing came of this, the idea that Dalton and Cripps should work together to galvanize the Government – and perhaps to reconstruct it – did not go away; and nor did the sterling problem.

It was the commitment, under the North American loan agreement, to make sterling convertible with the dollar in July 1947 that precipitated the final crisis, which exposed the fragility of the Attlee Government as never before. The immediate effect of giving holders of sterling the option to buy dollars was a haemorrhage of the British reserves, which was exacerbated by the vacillations of the Cabinet and ended only by the suspension of convertibility in August. Dalton's diary, which shows him relying increasingly on Cripps in advocating sterner measures, is the key source for the plot which the two of them launched in the autumn.

In September 1947 Cripps pointedly assured a restive and frustrated adviser that 'things are going to change'.[4] Attlee's unimpressive handling of the convertibility crisis, combined with Morrison's continuing inadequacies, prompted Cripps into a new proposal: to replace Attlee with Bevin, on the understanding that the new Prime Minister would in turn replace Morrison

2. For the definitive study of the convertibility crisis see Cairncross, *Years of Recovery*, ch. 6, a work to which I am elsewhere indebted.
3. Dalton, *Fateful Years*, p. 236.　　4. Plowden, *Industrialist in the Treasury*, p. 18.

with Cripps as planning supremo. Since at least 1935 Cripps had considered Morrison to be, in principle, the person best fitted to lead the Labour Party, while, in practice, lending support to Attlee as the incumbent. Now he switched to Bevin as the only way to face down adverse events.

Instead, Attlee unexpectedly faced down Cripps. He could only do so, of course, knowing that he continued to enjoy Bevin's loyal support. The encounter between Cripps and Attlee on 9 September was wholly characteristic of each and has become legendary. Who but Cripps, having failed to mobilize sufficient support from key colleagues, would have gone alone with an open demand for the Prime Minister's resignation? 'S.C. at least has courage and clarity,' wrote a rather awed Dalton.[5] Who but Attlee, having behaved for weeks in a manner that bore out his mouselike caricature, would have summoned the inner reserves not only to stand his ground but, in effect, to buy Cripps off? 'Why shouldn't *you* take on the job, and become Minister of Production?' Attlee said, thus proffering the very planning responsibilities that Cripps had hoped to acquire under Bevin – but instead to be exercised under Attlee himself.[6]

Cripps thus succeeded to Morrison's previous role, with the new title of Minister of Economic Affairs; and relations between the two men were subsequently cooler. Yet the effect of the abortive 'Cripps putsch' was, curiously, to cement relations between the rest of the Big Five. The Prime Minister in particular knew that he had kept his own job because of the steadfast support of Bevin, on whom Attlee's inimitable comment, offered in later years, is not simply retrospective sentimentality: 'Like Stafford he was a tremendous egotist – Ernest having the egotism of the artist, Stafford the egotism of the altruist, and Stafford thought well enough of Ernest to suggest to him that he would make a better Prime Minister than I would in 1947.'[7] Yet thanks to a combination of Attlee's extraordinary capacity for not bearing a grudge with Cripps's extraordinary propensity for rethinking his position, the two men never got on better than after this botched political assassination attempt.

Cripps's rise was not yet concluded. His peculiar unworldliness licensed

5. See Pimlott, *Dalton*, pp. 510–13, at 511, for an excellent narrative of this incident, based on Dalton's diary; and Donoughue and Jones, *Morrison*, pp. 414–25, for a good account from Morrison's perspective.

6. See Dalton, *Fateful Years*, pp. 240–47, at p. 245. For an invaluable guide to the administrative structure see Alford, Lowe and Rollings, *Economic Planning, 1943–1951*.

7. Williams, *A Prime Minister Remembers*, p. 150. According to Dalton, Cripps continued for some time to think that 'it would be a disaster if he led us in the next election'. Dalton diary, 11 September 1948, in Pimlott (ed.), *Dalton: Political Diary*, p. 439.

him to prosper from manoeuvres that in any other politician – especially in the streetwise Morrison – would naturally have been attributed to ruthless ambition.[8] As Minister of Economic Affairs Cripps found himself with his hands on many of the levers of power; the notion was that he should control the 'real economy', leaving Dalton as Chancellor with responsibility for financial policy. One authoritative judgement is that 'for a while it looked as though economic policy was to be dominated by a ministry other than the Treasury'.[9] The inherent stability of this division of functions, however, was not to be tested for long, since only six weeks after Cripps took over Economic Affairs he was also to take over the Treasury. After a trivial and inadvertent leak to a journalist of some of the measures in his emergency Budget, Dalton suddenly resigned on 13 November and Cripps was immediately chosen to succeed him.

With Morrison already marginalized within the Big Five, the departure of Dalton in effect created a Big Three of Attlee, Bevin, Cripps – a new ABC for the Labour Government. Gaitskell, one of Dalton's protégés, was among the ministers dining with Cripps on the evening of his appointment, but evidently before Cripps was at liberty to confide his news to them. 'Cripps showed no remorse and I could not help feeling that he had now satisfied one more ambition by becoming Chancellor,' Gaitskell recorded with hindsight. 'He said to us recently "I cannot really do this job, you see, unless I am P.M."'[10]

A Cripps premiership, of course, was not to be. The evidence that Stafford seriously wanted or expected to become Prime Minister is not very strong, though there are indications that Isobel hankered after the possibility (consistent with her role in inspiring Eric Estorick to produce another biography in the years 1947 to 1949). Yet Cripps already had the substance of power in these years, as an unprecedentedly powerful minister who virtually overshadowed the Prime Minister himself in domestic policy, just as Ernest Bevin did in foreign policy. By the time he left office, a dying man, in October 1950, Cripps arguably wielded more power at the Treasury than anyone since Lloyd George; moreover, he arguably exerted more influence over Treasury policy than anyone since Gladstone. This was Cripps's moment.

The speech that he gave in commending his third and last Budget to the

8. A point well taken in Donoughue and Jones, *Morrison*, p. 419.
9. Tomlinson, *Democratic Socialism*, p. 226.
10. Gaitskell diary, 14 November 1947, in Williams (ed.), *Gaitskell: Diary*, p. 46. There is a minor puzzle here: since Gaitskell makes it clear that none of those present yet knew of Dalton's resignation, for exactly what could Cripps have been expected to display remorse?

House of Commons in April 1950 has understandably acquired the status of his final testament. In it he met the charge that the Government had betrayed the promises about planning on which it had been elected. It was specifically *democratic* planning that he defended and expounded. Since this had to be 'accomplished by agreement, persuasion, consultation and other democratic methods', it could not ensure that rigid targets were achieved. Instead, Cripps suggested that 'the Budget itself can be described as the most important control and as the most powerful instrument for influencing economic policy which is available to the Government'.[11]

There is some justice in calling this statement 'a requiem for economic planning as he had once conceived it'.[12] But whether the Budget itself constituted 'planning' – or merely a surrogate for planning – is partly a matter of semantics or at least of rhetoric. Cripps's substantive claim for the role of fiscal policy was that, by mopping up excess purchasing power in the British economy, it had enabled the maintenance of full employment to consort with the stimulation of exports. Thus domestic consumption had been kept in check so as to permit export-led growth through satisfying pent-up international demand for British goods. He thus justified the 'simple and clear' essentials of the function of the Budget:

It is our unquestionable duty to avoid the twin evils of inflation and deflation. This we can only do by maintaining a balance between the amount of goods and services which the nation seeks to buy and the amount which can be produced when the labour force is, as at present, fully employed. Excessive demand produces inflation and inadequate demand results in deflation. The fiscal policy of the Government is the most important single instrument for maintaining that balance . . .[13]

This was not the traditional Treasury doctrine, handed down from Gladstone's time. The canons of sound finance, as upheld throughout the first forty years of the twentieth century, had simply asserted that the Budget should be balanced annually, meaning that revenue should cover current expenditure for that particular year ('above the line', as the jargon had it). Capital items were naturally accounted for separately ('below the line') and could legitimately be funded through public loans, secured by the assets

11. 5 HC Debs., vol. 474, cols. 39–40 (18 April 1950).
12. Cairncross, *Years of Recovery*, p. 332. For a more nuanced discussion of the rhetoric see Francis, *Ideas and Policies*, pp. 36ff. Richard Toye's book on Labour and planning, *The Labour Party and the Planned Economy*, gives this contested concept the proper historical atttention it deserves.
13. 5 HC Debs., vol. 474, col. 62 (18 April 1950).

they represented.[14] Thus the Budget had simply been the Government's own housekeeping: whereas what Cripps declared in 1950 was that it now served as the prime instrument for regulating demand in the economy as a whole. This macroeconomic role was the novelty. It meant that Government was claiming competence – and accepting liability – for managing the economy, and in particular for achieving a trade-off between employment and inflation.

Such was the 'post-war consensus', which was only to be abandoned after the Thatcher Government came to power in 1979. For thirty years, both Labour and Conservative Governments operated within the constraints of this consensus – not simply agreeing, of course, but *agreeing to disagree* on what trade-off was appropriate at particular times and under particular circumstances. Both, in practice, accepted a common macroeconomic assumption about the nature of the 'Budget judgement' and the primacy of fiscal policy. In the process, Cripps's 1950 statement was enshrined as the *locus classicus*.[15]

It must be acknowledged that Cripps's championship of consensus failed to make headlines at the time. When he had finished, after nearly two and a half hours, an admiring Anthony Eden replied urbanely for the Opposition: 'I conclude by saying to the Chancellor what he knows, that his performance was of a lucidity which we always associate with him.'[16] In the press, however, there were less flattering comments on Cripps's decision to give 'a rather donnish lecture on economics and democracy'.[17] Several newspapers pointed out that a number of MPs seemed to be asleep. The Budget was judged dull, the speech over-long.

This is indicative of some limitations on Cripps's own part: some failure, albeit one measured by the most ambitious kind of comparison. When Gladstone established the canons of sound finance that prevailed for at least

---

14. It was no more expected that the industries nationalized by the Attlee Government should be paid for out of current taxes than that privatization of public assets (denationalization) would yield windfall revenue to the Exchequer – exactly the opposite of the practice, adopted in the 1980s, of measuring the Budget balance by the Public Sector Borrowing Requirement. See Clarke, *Keynesian Revolution and its Economic Consequences*, pp. 193–4.

15. See, for example, the way it was cited by the Permanent Secretary to the Treasury in Cripps's time, Sir Edward Bridges, in his quasi-official departmental handbook, *Treasury*, p. 93. As Samuel Brittan put it, in the 1964 edition of an influential book: 'Thus was born what later came to be called the Butskellite doctrine, now rather out of fashion.' *Treasury under the Tories*, p. 50. In a subsequent edition, explicitly acknowledging the 'monetarist' challenge, he wrote that the doctrine 'has, with varying accretions, governed economic policy ever since'. Brittan, *Steering the Economy*, p. 70.

16. 5 HC Debs., vol. 474, col. 90 (18 April 1950).   17. *Yorkshire Post*, 14 March 1950.

two generations, he did so by conquering public opinion as well as by exhibiting a mastery of Treasury business. And when Thatcher overthrew the policies of consensus, despite the incoherence of her supposed 'monetarist' alternative, she was notably successful in projecting her own personality (improbably, as a housewife) as one means of remoulding the common-sense assumptions of a later era. By contrast, some disjunction between Cripps's undoubted ministerial effectiveness and his public image was a problem that he failed to address adequately himself but one that can hardly be ignored in assessing his career.

'Such fun'

As a minister, Cripps earned widespread respect, albeit often grudgingly conceded. 'He is respected, but not generally liked,' was the refrain. 'They say he is a bit cold.'[18] Such comments were commonplace and not only from hostile sources; this example is taken from a generally well-disposed magazine article, published at the peak of Cripps's prestige as Chancellor, amid speculation that he might soon be Prime Minister. Even before the end of the war, the veteran Liberal journalist A. G. Gardiner had written that the only contemporary politician who could bear comparison with Churchill was Cripps: 'in gifts and character alike, he stands out from the general stature of the House'.[19] The *Scotsman*, publishing a profile of Cripps as Chancellor, concluded likewise: 'That he stands head and shoulders above his present Ministerial colleagues in education, brain-power, and intellectual equipment is obvious.' Yet this appeared under the headline: 'Great Gifts but Not the Human Touch'.[20] In his widely read column in the *Evening Standard*, W. J. Brown, MP gave a view of Cripps reflecting the mutual antipathy between him and the Opposition benches, conceding that 'he impresses by his cold competence', but calling him 'a disembodied Brain, which functions with enormous efficiency, but no warmth whatsoever'.[21]

That such perceptions gained general currency is itself important; but it is also important to recognize their selective nature. For example, Cripps's strong support for the performing arts is little noticed. Thus it may seem surprising to find the ballerina Margot Fonteyn writing from New York in 1949, on behalf of the Sadler's Wells company, to tell the Chancellor of the

18. Claud Morris, 'Exploding the Cripps myth', *John Bull*, 4 December 1948.
19. A. G. Gardiner, 'The human question mark of politics', *John Bull*, 20 January 1945.
20. *Scotsman*, 6 April 1948.   21. W. J. Brown, *Evening Standard*, 19 March 1946.

Exchequer 'what a pleasure it has been to have our miraculous success here capped by such a charming letter from you'.[22] Likewise, it might not be expected that difficulties over the status of the piano recitals given by Myra Hess in the National Gallery should only have been resolved by Keynes, in his role as first chairman of the Arts Council in 1946, following sustained personal intervention by Stafford and Isobel Cripps.[23] Again, their patronage of the film-maker Filippo del Giudice – his flamboyant lifestyle apparently little inhibited by rationing – may seem as incongruous as his own salute to Cripps: 'Your example is guiding inspiration for me in my modest work!'[24]

The popular images that stuck were those that confirmed and reinforced a two-dimensional stereotype, rather than those suggesting a wider range of human sympathies. 'But for me and the many others who worked in a small circle with him,' John Henry Woods attested, 'there is so much more.'[25] Permanent Secretary at the Board of Trade, Woods was as administratively formidable as he was socially convivial. By the time that Cripps had to leave for India in 1946, only eight months into his new post, his correspondence with 'My dear John Henry' leaves no doubt about the good relationship they had established. 'As we lazed at Tunis,' Cripps wrote *en route*, 'we constantly thought of you all toiling away and thereby increased the restfulness of our own state.'[26] During the three months that Cripps was absent, Woods might apologize for troubling the distant but hard-pressed president with queries but was trusted implicitly to handle departmental business. Telling Cripps that 'you will be amused to hear that I have been read somewhat of a lecture by my doctor, have been cut off all alcohol, and am very nearly down to your sort of diet', he was plainly on easy terms with a minister whom he respected.[27]

Woods later wrote: 'Nobody I ever worked with, and I have worked with many good men, so fully created round him a sense of partnership in a high and happy venture – and, perhaps oddly, I felt it most when I was disagreeing with him.'[28] It was, Woods told Cripps after his resignation from office, never a matter of whether his officials had agreed with him: 'You always listened to us with such care, and courtesy, and attention (do you remember Belloc's poem about "Courtesy"?); and, still more, you have demonstrated to all those who have worked closely with you and under you, an absolute

22. Margot Fonteyn to RSC, 21 October 1949.
23. See IC to RSC, 5 April 1946, and Myra Hess folder in the Cripps archive.
24. F. del Giudice to RSC, 7 April 1949.   25. J. H. Woods to IC, 23 April 1952.
26. RSC to J. H. Woods, 24 March 1946, PRO, BT 91/1.
27. J. H. Woods to RSC, 29 May 1946, PRO, BT 91/1.
28. J. H. Woods to IC, 23 April 1952.

integrity of spirit and purpose to which weaker vessels cannot but respond.'[29]
The demonstrable fact that Cripps evoked warmer feelings, albeit slowly
maturing sentiments among close colleagues with whom he enjoyed direct
personal contact, suggests that their impressions too need to be retrieved
and to be weighed.

It is lucky that a number of them kept diaries since Cripps did not do so
himself after his return from India in June 1946. For personal insights on
him as a pillar of the Labour Government we can turn not only to the diary
of Hugh Dalton, Cripps's predecessor as Chancellor of the Exchequer, but
to that of Hugh Gaitskell, who later succeeded Cripps. Dalton, of course,
was of Cripps's generation, while Gaitskell was nearly twenty years younger;
both 'big Hugh' and 'little Hugh' served as ministerial colleagues of a man
whom they came to admire but whose foibles are none the less faithfully
recorded by them with a mixture of tolerance, awe, affection and exasperation. Gaitskell, loyal to his longstanding ties with Dalton, initially looked
askance at the man who had displaced him, but yielded to the force of his
own observations as the new Minister of Fuel and Power.

Naturally in my present job I see a good deal of Cripps. The more I see the more
impressed I am. He has really the most amazingly keen intelligence ... Cripps
without the slightest difficulty gave the most lucid and detailed account of the
problem, which he began by saying, 'The Minister of Fuel of course knows much
more about this than I do.' I sat there just gaping with admiration ... You feel with
Cripps that almost nothing is politically impossible. He sails on simply concerned
with what is the best solution from every other point of view and ignoring all the
rocks which lie ahead ...

Remarking Cripps's intelligence and resolution, of course, only under-
lines what was widely perceived; but it was 'patience and, despite what
other people say, kindliness' that Gaitskell also emphasized, writing: 'He is
a thoroughly nice person to work for. He never loses his temper despite the
colossal strain upon him.'[30]

A different professional perspective influenced the observations of Sir
Raymond Streat, the adroit, pragmatic and long-serving chairman of the
Cotton Board. His diary sets out to give an account, as full as it is discerning,
of industrial policy at the Board of Trade; but the personal impact that

29. Woods to RSC, October 1950. I think there is room to doubt the oddly dissonant remark,
attributed to Woods via Estorick, in Burgess, *Cripps*, p. 222.
30. Gaitskell diary, 16 February. 1948, in Williams (ed.), *Gaitskell: Diary*, pp. 55–6.

Cripps made constitutes an encroaching theme. Streat began apprehensive, now that the cotton bosses were saddled with a minister whose fearsome reputation had preceded him. 'Can I conscientiously work for a conscientious socialist or ought I to resign?' Streat asked himself before they had met.[31] The echo of Sir Wilfrid Freeman at MAP is unmistakable. First contacts proved only slightly less alarming: 'slim and quiet: unpretentious but "on the job" in his allotted station and function; pleasant: quick of word and eye: flickers were discernible of a tendency to adopt a certain idea or method and to rank it in his mind as of equal importance to an objective and to be obstinate in holding to it.'[32] It made a favourable impression to see him 'hatless and unostentatious on the pavement outside the building waiting for his wife' while Streat and his companion sped away with their driver.[33]

Cripps wrought no overnight miracle. 'His fanatical theoristic mind is determined to alter the balance of influence and power in our society,' Streat ruminated, concluding: 'I think he will have to be fought.'[34] Even a chance encounter in the men's urinal – often a great leveller in politics – failed to breach Streat's Lancashire scepticism. 'Ran into Stafford Cripps in the wash room. "How's my old friend?" he said, all geniality. Really, "old friend" is absurd.'[35] Yet, within a few months, such spontaneous civilities – 'Stafford greeted me in friendly fashion' – were being reciprocated by his new friend Raymond.[36] As so often, face-to-face meetings over a period of time served to thaw an initial chill and to dispel *a priori* assumptions. 'I then said to Stafford,' Streat confides by 1948, 'that I thought he would acknowledge that he personally was in receipt of a remarkable degree of confidence and support from the business men, notwithstanding that so many were of another party colour.' Streat records too the response to one plea for sympathetic treatment: 'Characteristic of his innate niceness was his reply, "You may be sure, Raymond, that I will try." '[37]

There is understandably a close focus on economic ideas in the diaries of two former Oxford economists who worked with Cripps as officials: James Meade, who had played a crucial role in the formulation of Keynes's theory of effective demand, and Robert Hall, who emerged as the staunchest

---

31. Streat diary, 29 July 1945, in Dupree, *Lancashire and Whitehall*, p.267.
32. Streat diary, 2 August 1945, ibid., p.268.   33. Streat diary, 2 August 1945, ibid., p.271.
34. Streat diary, 19 September 1945, ibid., p.290.
35. Streat diary, 30 January 1946, ibid., p.326.
36. Streat diary, 26 September 1946, ibid., p.368.
37. Streat diary, 14 November 1948, ibid., p.473. 'The dominating mind in it all has been that of Stafford Cripps.' Streat diary, 7 January 1949, ibid., p.477.

guardian of Keynesian ideas in post-war Whitehall. Successively occupying the post of Director of the Economic Section of the Cabinet Office, each of them was a cogent advocate of the Keynesian revolution in economic policy, but each was likewise a rigorous and dispassionate judge of what it had actually achieved. To their contemporary records, moreover, one can add a couple of unusually revealing memoirs of the period: by Douglas Jay, who became Economic Secretary to the Treasury under Cripps, and by Edwin Plowden, whom Cripps recruited as head of the Central Economic Planning Staff in May 1947 and took with him to the Treasury that November. All told, then, there is a richer cache of personal evidence than might be suspected, yielding insights that are much needed in complementing the dry public records. Furthermore, these sources emanate particularly from a group clustered around Cripps by virtue of the basically Keynesian economic expertise – only recently adumbrated, even more recently acknowledged – that they felt they could offer him.

During the course of 1947, Gaitskell, Meade, Jay and Plowden were each at some point aged forty, and Hall was only a few years older; whereas Cripps was fifty-eight when he became Chancellor. The difference of genera-tion, implying different formative experiences and differential receptiveness to novelty, is worth noting in the context of Keynes's dictum that 'in the field of economic and political philosophy there are not many who are influenced by new theories after they are twenty-five or thirty years of age'.[38] This would set an upper age-limit exceeded only by Hall at the time of the publication of the *General Theory* in 1936. The book's impact upon these younger economists was profound: whether hot-off-the-press for Jay, or for Gaitskell as a delayed-action fuse, or for Meade – with his seminal role in specifying the multiplier – as a long-anticipated revelation. Conversely, the implication is that the cohort of young Keynesians who sought to advise Cripps were faced with teaching an old dog new tricks.[39]

The sheer age-gap, too, obviously influenced the terms of their personal dealings with Cripps. Though this was hardly another Kindergarten, none stood on a par with him; and he was always at his best when he was the boss – tolerant, appreciative, informal, even playful in his treatment of subordinates: but the boss none the less. If no apple-pie beds are recorded,

38. Keynes, *General Theory*, pp. 383-4.
39. A metaphor put to good use in Peden, 'Old dogs and new tricks: the British Treasury and Keynesian economics in the 1940s and 1950s', Furner and Supple, *State and Economic Knowledge*, ch. 7; and see the work of Sir Alec Cairncross, who had himself studied under Keynes and first worked under Cripps at MAP: not only *Years of Recovery* but also Cairncross and Watts, *Economic Section*.

there are abundant signs that younger colleagues responded not only to his authority but to his own well-attested charm. Plowden called Cripps 'a tremendously kind and generous man, not without a pleasant sense of humour'.[40] Woods recorded Plowden's lament after Cripps's demise: 'John Henry, why is everything so beastly? When Stafford was here it was such fun.'[41]

These effects were not accidental. Spontaneity was reinforced by assiduity. Cripps took pains to communicate his sense of a common endeavour, addressing open meetings of all his staff at the Treasury; and his custom of writing solicitously, usually in his own familiar red ink, to those who directly worked with him was warmly appreciated, especially by those who realized how busy he was.

My dear Chancellor,
Thank you very much for your very kind – too kind – letter. Judy too is most grateful and said when she read your letter – How very nice, the Chancellor never forgets the wives.[42]

Cripps's belief in the emollient influence of social contact was nowhere better seen than in his efforts to encourage good relations between the ministers with whom he worked as Chancellor. The convivial dinners that he organized – and paid for – notably spanned the conventional left–right divisions. 'I must say that Stafford is showing much more political acumen that I expected,' Gaitskell recorded after one dinner, adding: 'I could not help feeling that Stafford was surveying his future Cabinet.'[43] When nationalization was discussed, it was notable that 'Stafford did not take sides but kept on saying, "All I say is we must remember it is an experiment." '[44] Jay, who was one of the two junior Treasury ministers, conveys a vivid impression of how Aneurin Bevan, the champion of the left in the Cabinet as Minister of Health, was licensed to tease and amuse: 'But Bevan would always stop dead when Cripps, usually putting a hand on his arm, told him to be quiet, as serious economic debate was now to begin.'[45] For

40. Plowden, *Industrialist in the Treasury*, p. 19.   41. Woods to IC, 23 April 1952.
42. Leslie Rowan to RSC, 10 June (1949).
43. Gaitskell diary, 23 April 1948, in Williams (ed.), *Gaitskell: Diary*, pp. 61–2.
44. Gaitskell diary, 18 June 1948, in Williams (ed.), *Gaitskell: Diary*, p. 72.
45. Jay, *Change and Fortune*, p. 179; cf. ibid., p. 174. Jay was Economic Secretary from December 1947 to March 1950, when he became Financial Secretary in succession to William Glenvil Hall. He actually attended these dinners, unlike Michael Foot, who brushes aside evidence that Cripps had any kind of avuncular hold over his hero (and supposes the dinners to have been instituted in 1949). See Foot, *Bevan*, ii, pp. 38–9, 290, 294; and for a more plausible view of the Cripps–Bevan relationship, Campbell, *Bevan*, pp. 188–9. For reports of

Gaitskell, as his diary makes clear, this was a forum that enabled him, unexpectedly, to appreciate the wit and warmth of Bevan – thus encouraging the rising figures of the next generation to establish the kind of rapport and goodwill that the Labour Party sadly missed during the next decade.

Two letters in the Cripps papers, written within days of each other, hint at these lost chances.

My dear Stafford [Bevan wrote]

I think when the history of these times comes to be written, your work in 1948 will will be seen to be one of the most splendid achievments in the story. I am most happy to believe that my association in the task has been helpful, and I hope that our future collaboration will be equally amiable and fruitful.[46]

My dear Stafford [Gaitskell wrote]

I have been at times fairly depressed during the past year – but never after seeing you. That is a part, though a precious part of what your leadership has meant to me. I hope people realise (I think they do) what you have done for the Party and the Nation.[47]

Cripps both fostered and relished teamwork within a team that he could inspire. He knew that he was good at getting people to work together and built his working day around a purposeful projection of his own influence. As Chancellor he began every day (except Sunday) with a 'morning meeting' at 9.30 a.m. sharp in his room in the Treasury building in Great George Street, where he chose to work (rather than in his official residence at 11 Downing Street as Dalton had done). Nobody could turn up late with impunity. Present were the two junior ministers, William Glenvil Hall as Financial Secretary and Douglas Jay as Economic Secretary. The Permanent Secretary to the Treasury, Sir Edward Bridges, the grand panjandrum of Whitehall, would be there (and on time, too, even if he had had to run the length of Great George Street, as deeply etched memories affirm). Immediately below Bridges in rank were four Second Secretaries, of whom Leslie Rowan was closest to Cripps; but it was Sir William Eady and Sir Bernard Gilbert who usually turned up to represent the old guard of the pre-Keynesian Treasury, counterbalancing the influence of the two younger planners, Hall and Plowden. The complement was made up by Clem Leslie, originally a close aide of Morrison but now established as press officer in

---

these dinners from October 1947 onwards see Williams (ed.), *Gaitskell: Diary*, pp. 36, 49, 61–2, 72, 98, 104, 108, 111, 116, 131, 158.

46. Bevan to RSC, 24 December 1948.   47. Gaitskell to RSC, 30 December 1948.

the Treasury. These were essentially informal sessions, useful either for brainstorming or fire-fighting.[48]

The morning meeting was not the beginning of Cripps's day, as those attending it became well aware, if only from the fact that he invariably seemed so well prepared. 'That's what he does when he gets up at four in the morning,' was one whispered comment.[49] His spartan regime was now notorious. Stafford was generally reported to rise at 4 a.m. and to get down to work at once, breaking at 7 a.m. for a half-hour walk with Isobel, followed by a cold bath. Then there was breakfast of yogurt, fruit, toast and marmalade, before he left Downing Street for his office an hour before the first meeting. The day unfolded relentlessly – 'a Marathon of work', as one journalist put it, or in Streat's words, after a visit to Great George Street: 'The Cripps treadmill of duty was turning with its ceaseless revolutions, uninterruptedly, sixteen or eighteen hours a day.'[50]

Cripps's relations with his officials can surely be glimpsed in extracts from his postbag at Christmas 1949; the conventions of the season of goodwill are hardly enough to explain, or explain away, the tone of the exchanges. Bridges wrote that 'we all rejoice greatly in the privilege and the fun of working for you: and we thank you greatly for all the joy and satisfaction in our work that comes from working with you'.[51] Likewise the two advisers on whom Cripps relied most heavily. Plowden wrote: 'All of us who work with you think of it as a privilege.'[52] Hall wrote: 'Perhaps you will allow me to say how much I have appreciated working with you, whose ability and integrity are so outstanding among all those I have known: and yet somehow I have never felt any diffidence in saying what I think.'[53] It was in this context that crucial issues in economic policy were defined, deliberated and determined.

48. Jay, *Change and Fortune*, p. 173; Plowden, *Industrialist in the Treasury*, p. 20; and see Peden, *Treasury*, pp. 364–72, on Treasury organization and personnel.
49. Strachey recorded in Gaitskell's diary at a similar meeting. Gaitskell diary, 16 February 1948, in Williams (ed.), *Gaitskell: Diary*, p. 56.
50. Streat diary, 14 November 1948, in Dupree, *Lancashire and Whitehall*, p. 473.
51. Bridges to RSC, Boxing Day, 1949. Head of the home civil service since 1945, Bridges initially managed to combine his role with that of Cabinet Secretary.
52. Plowden to RSC, 23 December 1949.   53. Hall to RSC, 3 January 1950.

From Marx to Keynes

As Plowden put it to Cripps, 'during the period of your Chancellorship there has taken place a revolution in political-economic thinking and practice'.[54] This is a high claim. What can be said of its intellectual and ideological implications, once the rhetoric is examined? And how far does Cripps emerge as the active and conscious agent of change, once the evidence of his chancellorship is explored?

Writing in his diary just after the Labour Government took office, James Meade offered an influential view of what was at stake.

In internal policy there is already a conflict between the different main meanings that may be given to the idea of Socialist economic planning. Broadly speaking, there are on the one hand those (led by Cripps at the Board of Trade) who believe in the quantitative planning of the economy commodity by commodity. Such a Gosplan could not, in my opinion, be carried out without socialising all or most industries (which is expressly not the policy of the Labour Party) and, possibly, without losing freedom of choice of consumers and workers as to what they will consume and what they will work at.[55]

What Meade supported, by contrast, was 'the Liberal-Socialist solution', permitting greater market flexibility while reserving to Government the management of aggregate demand. His own schemes for regulating demand by fiscal means, notably through varying the rate of National Insurance contributions, had invoked the metaphor of thermostatic control; and this debate became characterized as one between 'Gosplanners' and 'Thermostatters'. These are terms of art, of course, circulating within an intimate and sophisticated coterie; no Soviet-style 'Gosplan' was envisaged by the protagonists of a *dirigiste* model, even though some of them defiantly accepted this pejorative terminology; and such a stylization of the two camps, with its intellectual clarity, is not literally faithful to the political actuality. In particular, Meade was wrong to suppose that, in bidding to absorb the Economic Section into the Board of Trade, Cripps showed that 'he thinks of all this in terms of planning the real resources of the community in the sense of deciding how many pairs of

54. Plowden to RSC, 20 November 1950.
55. Meade diary, 26 August 1945, in Howson and Moggridge (eds.), *Meade: Collected Papers*, iv, pp. 114–15.

boots, how many shirts, how many bicycles, etc., etc. shall be produced'.[56]

It remains profitable, none the less, to think of Cripps moving after 1945 towards a Thermostatic conception. If he had not started as a Gosplanner in 1945, his own public utterances, not for the first time, had left him liable to be misconstrued. In thanking the electors who had just returned him to Parliament, Cripps said: 'you must have patience to give your new team a chance to lay the foundations for that tremendous job that we are going to carry through – the transformation of this country from a capitalist into a Socialist country'.[57] He was certainly not the only Labour MP to retain the rhetoric of transformative socialism long after it had been effectively superseded by the reality of incremental reformism. At the beginning of 1946, Meade was still prone to glimpse a Gosplanner's cloven hoof every time Cripps put a foot forward; but he also happily noted that Cripps favoured the inclusion in the National Insurance Bill of 'a clause giving the Chancellor power to introduce a scheme for varying national insurance contributions at a later stage'.[58] Though this measure was never implemented, its symbolism as the aboriginal Thermostatic proposal was indeed significant.

It was, however, after 1947, once Robert Hall had succeeded James Meade as Director of the Economic Section, that Cripps's distinctive contribution was made. As Chancellor of the Exchequer, he simultaneously held the post of Minister of Economic Affairs, and was advised on economic policy by three separate staffs. As well as the established Treasury mandarins (under Bridges), Cripps had taken over the Economic Section (under Hall) from the control of Morrison; and he had, too, the new Central Economic Planning Staff (under Plowden), which had also briefly been part of Morrison's ramshackle Whitehall fiefdom.

Cripps, as usual, won golden opinions from those closest to him. From the moment he knew that he was to be Minister of Economic Affairs he began to repose great confidence in the advice not only of Plowden but also of Hall, who warmly reciprocated: 'He is really a very able man; he sees all the points and remembers relevant things which he has met before.' Cripps struck Hall from the first as 'a realist and able to understand a problem extremely quickly'.[59] Since Plowden likewise considered Cripps to have 'the

56. ibid., p. 115; see Tomlinson, *Democratic Socialism*, pp. 139–40, and Toye's persuasive analysis in *The Labour Party and the Planned Economy*, ch. 8.
57. RSC speech at Bristol, *Bristol Evening World*, 27 July 1945.
58. Meade diary, 13 January 1946, in Howson and Moggridge (eds.), *Meade: Collected Papers*, iv, p. 194; cf. ibid., 27 January 1946, p. 202, on planning.
59. Hall diary, 24, 30 September 1947, in Cairncross (ed.), *Hall: Diaries*, pp. 7–8.

clearest and most incisive mind that I have ever dealt with', a basis of trust, sustained by mutual admiration, was soon established.[60] 'The more I see of S.C.,' Hall was soon writing, 'the more highly I think of him – he is anxious to tell the truth, he is a man who is completely fair in his outlook, and completely bold if he is convinced that a particular course is right.'[61]

Once Cripps had reached his own conclusions, his views were projected with a distinctive mien of conviction. Gaitskell was surely right to sense that this was not purely intellectual in origin but manifested a black-and-white moral certainty, in keeping with Cripps's Christian tenets, as well as a self-belief that was perhaps innate but had certainly been fortified by his privileged upbringing. Intelligence, then, was not enough to explain Cripps's ascendancy.

The second great quality that he has is courage which is closely combined in his case with superb self confidence. As Plowden said to me the other day, 'When he has made up his mind he is absolutely certain he is right and therefore completely indifferent to any criticisms or objections or arguments.' This is where he differs from most politicians. Most of us, I think, are cowards in the sense that we are always counting the political difficulties and probably tending to exaggerate them . . . the courage is not obvious as courage; one does not feel that there is a great moral struggle because of this great confidence. Perhaps it is something to do with his religion . . . And of course you can always get a decision out of him. No man was ever less frightened of taking responsibility.[62]

That Cripps had the nerve to preside over a major shift in policy is hardly in doubt. That he had the intellectual resources to grapple with complex and arcane issues is hardly more in question. Still, it surely deserves comment, given his former political views, that he took up a position that was so radically different. His new doctrine affirmed that high levels of employment and low levels of inflation could be reconciled through maximizing output – and all within an economy that, despite now having a large public sector, was still postulated on market decisions, on the price mechanism, and on substantial private ownership of the means of production, distribution and exchange.

For an old Marxist, here was the completion of an ideological revolution. Writing in 1949, Estorick can be taken to represent Cripps's own view of

---

60. Plowden, *Industrialist in the Treasury*, p. 19.
61. Hall diary, March 1948, in Cairncross (ed.), *Hall: Diaries*, p. 19.
62. Gaitskell diary, 16 Febuary 1948, in Williams (ed.), *Gaitskell: Diaries*, p. 56.

the matter. 'His challenge to the Tories to-day is not the challenge he made in 1931 of "Socialism versus Capitalism",' Estorick explained. 'His challenge is that it is necessary to control capitalism in the nation's interests; also that it is the most patriotic way of blocking the road to Communism, and capitalist reaction.'[63] If Marxism was the light that failed, for Cripps it had been flickering since the time of Munich and guttering since his first visit to India. In 1945, admittedly, he had been prominently identified with a policy of friendship towards the Soviet Union and accused the Tories of imperilling this through ideological hostility.[64] Yet Cripps's time in Russia, faced with 'government by secret police and spies which is the only method for a dictatorship', had simply left him 'more than ever convinced of the undesirability of dictatorship and totalitarian regimes'.[65] It was an Orwellian insight *avant la lettre*. It is piquant that when *Nineteen-Eighty-Four* was published in 1949, Orwell had to explain that it was not an attack upon (Crippsian) social democracy, to which the author reaffirmed his own support.[66]

In a negative sense, Cripps's experience of 'actually existing socialism' in the Soviet Union paved the way for his subsequent commitment to 'democratic planning' – a concept more persuasively defined by what it instinctively excluded than what it specifically included. It would not be possible to implement a comprehensive plan, so Cripps assured the Commons in 1946, 'without compulsions of the most extreme kind, compulsions which democracy rightly refuses to accept. That is why democratic planning is so very much more difficult than totalitarian planning.'[67] There is a similar apologia for the notion of democratic planning in the introductory section of the Government's *Economic Survey for 1947*, which we know Cripps to have drafted himself (though, across the floor of the Commons, Churchill sarcastically commended 'the civil servant who wrote this for his Socialist masters').[68] In his 1950 Budget speech Cripps reiterated that it was neither possible nor desirable 'to use the violent compulsions that are appropriate

63. Estorick, p. 362.

64. This provoked a rare clash between Cripps and Eden. See McCallum and Readman, *General Election of 1945*, pp. 138, 183, 195.

65. RSC to Diana, 8 September 1940; quoted above, pp. 195–6.

66. 'Members of the present British government, from Mr Attlee and Sir Stafford Cripps down to Mr Aneurin Bevan, will never willingly sell the pass to the enemy,' he said in a press release dictated to his publisher; see Crick, *Orwell*, pp. 563–70, at p. 566.

67. 5 HC Debs., vol. 430, col. 1086 (21 November 1946); and see Toye, *The Labour Party and the Planned Economy*, ch. 8.

68. Cairncross, *Years of Recovery*, pp. 304ff.

to totalitarian planning'.[69] Instead, he equated democratic planning with the new Budget doctrine.

In a positive sense, then, it was Keynesianism that came to fill the ideological vacuum. Cripps's 1950 Budget speech referred to 'a revolution in economic thinking and in Government responsibility, a revolution so complete that it is often entirely overlooked'.[70] This intellectual reorientation has usually been attributed to Keynes's ideas. Although Cripps and Keynes had been on cordial terms since Popular Front days, a direct ascription of influence will simply not do as the explanation of Cripps's conversion – for two complementary reasons.

The first is general, applying to the ideas themselves. There is now a vast literature devoted to the historical Keynes, focusing on his own intentions in his own historical context; though rather less attention has been devoted to the reception of his theories, which is a separate issue. The result is dissonance. Readers of the *General Theory*, as is widely recognized, are introduced to a kind of economic analysis premised on the inescapability of acting under conditions of imperfect information: an analysis therefore that grapples with the elusive problems of uncertainty, expectations and confidence. The practical impact of Keynesianism, by contrast, came chiefly through the manipulation of policy from above by an administrative elite, in a mode that was more obviously hydraulic than psychological. Keynesianism was thus imperfectly faithful to the ideas of the historical Keynes.

Such a process of ideological distortion can be regarded as an inevitable price for the social purchase that any successful 'ism' comes to exert. It can also be seen as a necessary response to the problem of operationalizing theory as policy. Keynes himself had led the way with his tract of 1940, *How to Pay for the War*, which turned his theoretical analysis to the new problem of excess demand by using the fiscal system to restrain inflationary pressure; and this, of course, became the key post-war problem. Here was the practical conception of demand management – 'actually existing Keynesianism' – that came to be argued in Whitehall by busy administrators who would not necessarily have found the *General Theory* a useful handbook, even if they had had time to peruse it.

These generalizations apply *a fortiori* in the particular case of Cripps. If he had become the most famous Marxist convert of his generation without ever reading Marx, why should it be supposed that he needed to read Keynes in order to become the leading exponent of Keynesian policies? There is

69. 5 HC Debs., vol. 474, cols. 39–40 (18 April 1950).
70. 5 HC Debs., vol. 474, col. 38 (18 April 1950).

some suggestive evidence on this point in the public records. In 1949 an autodidact called Isidore Ostrer sent the Chancellor a summary of a projected book ('which I feel basically solves the mystery of money for all time') – perhaps supposing that a fellow crank might readily be ensnared. Cripps looked at it and evidently suspected fallacies. In due course, a polite reply was dispatched: 'I read it with interest, and feel that your main idea is very like one of those set out at length in the late Lord Keynes's books.' But the overburdened Chancellor, reasonably enough, was here simply approving a letter drafted for him by a trusted economic adviser who was safe in his inference that Ostrer was wholly unfamiliar with Keynes's work.[71]

The implication, that Cripps was equally unfamiliar with Keynes in the original, is surely plain – and unsurprising. If his inveterate literary habits had not changed, nor had his facility for picking up a new brief, from cold, through papers prepared for him with a professional expertise that he could trust. If the fine analytical mind that he had turned to law and the natural sciences had happily seized upon a schematic, determinist version of Marxism in the early 1930s, it is hardly surprising that it readily mastered a finite, determinate model of Keynesianism in the late 1940s.

What Cripps was uniquely placed to achieve was the implementation of these ideas as policy. Here his role cannot simply be discounted, despite his own lack of first-hand intellectual engagement or technical economic expertise. Budget-making under Cripps shows him taking command of the process, step by step. He mastered all the arguments and laid down the lines of approach at an early stage, for example in conceiving that of 1948 as a 'capital budget', so that the impact upon investment could be made more transparent. The institution of a weekend house-party for the Chancellor and his officials some ten weeks before Budget Day was a Cripps innovation, henceforth established as part of the British Budget ritual. He would take Isobel Cripps and a dozen of his advisers, including both Hall and Plowden, to the rehabilitation centre at Roffey Park in Sussex, and, as Jay put it, 'plenty of innocent mirth was excited among the participants at the thought of public reactions to the news that the annual Budget was being constructed in a rest-home for nervous wrecks'.[72] It was at Roffey, as Hall well recognized, that officials had their best chance to canvass and explore their

71. The correspondence with Ostrer, 24 and 29 August 1949, and a comment and draft reply from Robert Hall, 4 October 1949, are all in PRO, CAB 127/142. Ostrer claimed to have anticipated in 1932 what Keynes later wrote in the *General Theory*, but apparently published no book on economics between 1932 and 1964; see Ostrer, *Modern Money and Unemployment* (with a foreword by Lord Beaverbrook).

72. Jay, *Change and Fortune*, p. 175.

favourite proposals – 'though whether any of them are adopted will depend on whether S. C. can persuade his colleagues'.[73]

Cripps's red ink is copiously splashed over the Treasury papers produced at each successive stage in his first two Budgets; for instance, an early draft of the 1949 Budget speech is annotated, 'as written by the Chancellor himself on the basis of the material which he has had over the weekend'.[74] There is thus plenty of evidence of his eager participation in thrashing out the details. Yet Cripps also had clear principles about delegating, based simultaneously on knowing his own limitations and trusting his own experts. Before his first Budget, faced with a last-minute plea from Bevan over the financing of the National Health Service, Cripps minuted: 'This is too complex a matter for me to go into personally in detail, and I must rely on my advisers.'[75]

It was already the case, under Dalton, that fiscal policy was being used to restrain inflation. It is true that the old hands in the Treasury, long conditioned to resisting Keynesian proposals for more spending in a deflationary era, did not have the same antipathy to Keynesian arguments for restraining spending and tightening taxation in the post-war era of incipient inflation. Even so, it was the new rationale, not the inveterate Treasury stance, that was used to justify an autumn Budget in 1947. 'Its sole purpose, if it were decided to have one, would be to lessen the inflationary pressure by "mopping up" some purchasing power,' Dalton had told Bridges, who duly turned the message into a Treasury note: 'The purpose is, not the old-fashioned one of extra taxation to balance the Budget, but a reduction of the inflationary pressure which threatens to prevent the emergency measures from achieving their objective.'[76] The way that the Budget was presented to the Cabinet expressed the full, symmetrical doctrine: 'If there is heavier inflationary pressure, we need a larger Budget surplus, just as, if there were heavy deflationary pressure, we should require a large Budget deficit.'[77]

There is, in fact, abundant evidence that Cripps inherited Dalton's Budget framework, and specifically his Budget surplus. This remains true, as

73. Hall diary, 7 February 1949, in Cairncross (ed.), *Hall: Diaries*, p. 52.
74. PRO, T 171/399, note on second draft.
75. RSC note, 24 March 1948, PRO, T 171/395, f. 17.
76. Dalton to Bridges, 11 August 1947; note by Bridges, n.d., PRO, T 171/392, ff. 1, 13–15. For a general appraisal, somewhat sceptical of the Keynesian convictions here, see Tomlinson, *Democratic Socialism*, ch. 10; and for a recent summary of the debate on Keynesian influence, Booth, 'New revisionists and the Keynesian era'.
77. Note for Cabinet, PRO, T 171/392, f. 123. Dell is thus plainly wrong in saying that there was, even by 1950, 'as yet no suggestion that demand management might, at times, require a Budget *deficit* [his emphasis].' *Chancellors*, p. 111.

Dalton's biographer has rightly argued, despite the fact that Dalton had personal reservations in accepting Keynes's ideas and consistently sought to give the agenda his own redistributive twist.[78] If this was what was distinctive of Dalton's approach, what was distinctive of Cripps's was the overarching way that Keynesianism was meshed with planning. The annual Economic Survey thus became part of the Budget (even though one was for the calendar year and the other for the financial year beginning in April). Here was a decisive triumph for the macroeconomic strategy of thermostatic control over the microeconomic emphasis of 'Gosplan'.

In this, of course, Cripps had picked up his cue from Hall and Plowden, his *eminences grises* and his loyal lieutenants. Hall wrote in March 1948:

In the past 3 months there has been a revolution in Government policy since Stafford Cripps has been the undisputed master in the field and on the whole Plowden has been his prophet. All the old barriers are coming down between the Treasury and other policy and there is very little of a rearguard action. In many ways it has been rather frightening since E. P. and I get almost anything we want and we don't really know enough to justify this faith in us, or more truly lack of faith they have in themselves.[79]

Following the presentation of the 1948 Budget, Cripps gave his advisers a dinner where, Hall recorded, 'Plowden made a little speech of congratulation telling him this was the first "planning" Budget.'[80]

This sort of evidence of how Cripps worked with his advisers has an obvious bearing on a question posed earlier: what exactly was Cripps's own contribution to the formulation of policy? The content and exposition of his canonical 1950 Budget speech has already been examined; but further insight can be gained by exploring its origins.

In March 1950 Cripps received a letter from the veteran Leader of the House of Lords, Lord Addison (who had first been a Cabinet minister under Lloyd George). Addison, normally a warm supporter of Cripps, was conscious that his thoughts might prove, as he put it, 'offensive to the orthodox economists' – now meaning Keynesian economists – but he was unabashed in querying the use of the Budget to restrain demand rather than simply to finance Government expenditure.[81] Moreover, the Prime Minister

78. See Pimlott, *Dalton*, esp. pp. 472–3, 521–2.
79. Hall diary, March 1948, in Cairncross (ed.), *Hall: Diaries*, p. 19.
80. Hall diary, 8 April 1948, ibid., p. 22.
81. Addison to RSC, 10 March 1950, PRO, T 171/400.

weighed in. 'I am not highly skilled in these matters and some of my colleagues are in like case,' Attlee wrote. 'I think that we should welcome an exploration of this subject in Cabinet before the main lines of the Budget are settled.'[82] Since it was fully a month after the Roffey Park meeting, and little more than a month before Budget Day, this was a potentially destabilizing challenge to the whole Budget strategy. It therefore made a statement of its rationale an urgent task.

Cripps turned at once to his advisers. Plowden provided him with a draft reply to Addison – 'All in words of one syllable' – explaining the nature of his misconception: essentially that remission of taxation would boost consumption rather than saving, thus fuelling inflation.[83] Hall took the same line. He was rueful when the memorandum that he drafted for circulation to the Cabinet was amended by Gaitskell ('leaving out all the argument') and himself supplied a covering note as a brief for the Prime Minister.[84] In none of this did Cripps take the initiative, contenting himself with commending the Treasury memorandum to the Cabinet.

Hall's covering note puts the matter best. 'The subject is intensely difficult to understand,' he admitted, 'and though the paper is put in simple language, it is rather doubtful whether in the end there will not have to be an act of faith.' He argued that the Government had 'adopted in 1947 and 1948 a revolution in British practice, when they took responsibility for maintaining full employment, but avoiding inflation. It is the best argument in favour of this policy that the revolution passed almost unnoticed.' The restraint of inflation through the Budget, then, was the alternative to using unemployment to regulate the economy. Hence Hall's argument that departure from this approach would constitute 'an abandonment of the principles of planning', which was obviously a claim with resonance for a Government elected on the planning ticket. In sending a copy of his handiwork to Cripps's private office – 'The Chancellor of the Exchequer may care to see a copy of the attached brief' – Hall displayed his autonomy as Director of the Economic Section, doing his own job, just as Cripps did his.[85]

Here, then, is the origin of the famous Keynesian declaration in the 1950 Budget. Having gained Cabinet approval for his policy, Cripps turned immediately to Hall for 'a section dealing with the general philosophy of

82. Attlee to RSC, 11 March 1950, PRO, T 171/400.
83. Plowden for RSC, 11 March 1950, PRO, T 171/400.
84. See Hall diary, 16 March 1950, in Cairncross (ed.), *Hall: Diaries*, pp. 107–8; the Cabinet Paper is CP (50) 35, with the brief over Hall's name, 16 March 1950, all in PRO, T 171/400.
85. Hall note for the Prime Minister, 16 March 1950, with covering note for William Armstrong, PRO, T 171/400.

the Budget'; and it was this draft that became, with only verbal amendments, the substance of a speech that Cripps happily made his own.[86]

In it, he justified the need to run a large Budget surplus:

for the nation as a whole, spending on capital account must be balanced by savings on income account. If the voluntary savings of individuals and firms are insufficient, then the Government must itself make up the deficiency in the nation's savings by accumulating a Budget surplus, which in effect helps to pay for capital development, such, for instance, as that provided by loans to local authorities.

Clearly, since saving is the opposite of spending, to say that a Budget surplus is necessary to remedy a deficiency in saving is simply to re-state the earlier propostion that a surplus is necessary to curb excessive spending.[87]

This is faithful to the analysis of the *General Theory* in demonstrating the necessary equality between saving and investment – but not by saying that prior saving necessarily ensues in investment, or that these are simply different names for the same activity, which pre-Keynesian economists generally assumed. Instead Cripps asserts that investment, or what he terms 'spending on capital account', must be balanced by saving, given that inflation is not to fill the gap. Moreover, by supplying the definition that 'saving is the opposite of spending', he can show that 'saving' is the residual amount of aggregate income that is not consumed. Hence by using the Budget to restrain aggregate consumption, it is indeed possible to finance aggregate investment, even though individuals never chose to make these notional 'savings'.

Few other Chancellors would have been so enraptured by this process, with its necessary identities disclosed through careful analysis. Certainly no other Chancellor has approached such problems with Cripps's scientific bent and training. Perhaps no other Chancellor would have chanced his arm in insisting upon expounding these complexities at length to the House of Commons. The fact that Cripps was ready to do so helps us to appreciate the judgement on him that Hall later offered in his diary:

He was a wonderful man to work for especially if he respected you: once he was convinced he made much more of one's arguments than one could oneself, and he was almost over-loyal to his subordinates: not only would he take their faults on

86. Hall to Armstrong, 29 March 1950, and Hall's draft with Cripps's pencil amendments, 3 April 1950, PRO, T 171/400;
87. 5 HC Debs., vol. 474, col. 63 (18 April 1950).

himself but he tended to think more of them because he was defending them. This, like his advocacy of his brief, was partly due to his experience as a barrister. He did not really understand the basis of economic planning as we developed it under his regime, but he was entirely responsible for its development.[88]

The end of the beginning

How good a Chancellor was Cripps? And what did people think of him? The answer to each question changes distinctly over time. When Cripps resigned in October 1950, he had been Chancellor for just short of three years. His performance in the first eighteen months had not only been impressive in itself but had been received with extravagant praise. His last eighteen months in office were increasingly painful – literally so since his health collapsed, with an impact on his effectiveness that is difficult to specify exactly but was undoubtedly deleterious. At this stage, moreover, once Cripps's reputation began to ebb, it did so in a savage rip-tide torn by a pent-up gale of prejudice that was both partisan and personal. His virtues were literally caricatured as he became the butt of the frustrations of the long-suffering British electorate, with the achievements of the Labour Government opportunistically denigrated by an Opposition led by an old man in a hurry to return to office himself.

In 1947 as in 1942, Cripps was initially the beneficiary of the situation in which he found himself. His pre-eminence was remarkable, acknowledged in Whitehall, at Westminster and in Fleet Street. The contrast with Dalton worked in his favour and was played up by the Tories. Leo Amery, for example, contrasted Cripps's predilection for 'the harsh truth' with Dalton's for 'half-lies' in the course of a conversation with Harold Nicolson, who himself observed: 'It is extraordinary how much respect Cripps arouses. He is really the leading figure in the country today.'[89] The palpable sense of destiny around Cripps was widely disseminated. 'At the moment he overshadows everyone else in the Government,' as even Beaverbrook's *Daily Express* conceded. 'It may be partly because he has aroused expectations rather than satisfied them so far. But in him alone we occasionally

88. Hall diary, 29 April 1952, in Cairncross (ed.), *Hall: Diaries*, p. 222; cf. ibid., 19–20 October 1950, p. 132.
89. Nicolson diary, 8 October 1947, in Nicolson (ed.), *Harold Nicolson: Diaries and Letters*, iii, p. 111.

hear the authentic note of leadership which Mr Attlee makes no claim to strike.'[90]

Though Cripps's stock went up and down over the years, there was considerable consistency in how he was perceived; what changed was how that perception was evaluated in different contexts. After 1942 he was always liable to be labelled austere. In complimenting him on his parliamentary performance at the end of 1945, the *Daily Mail* said: 'Nor did his speech confirm the legend that Austerity and Misery are his middle names; he was witty and worldly.'[91] A couple of months later the same paper pointedly juxtaposed two comments on Cripps. The Prime Minister tried straightforward rebuttal: 'You don't know how happy a nature he really has.' But John Belcher, Parliamentary Secretary at the Board of Trade, tried outflanking tactics. 'Sir Stafford Cripps is a rather austere man,' he conceded, 'but he does not desire to impose his austerity on other people.'[92]

The trouble was that this was exactly the task assigned to the Board of Trade while Cripps was there. One headline in the Liberal *News Chronicle*, generally sympathetic to Cripps, ran: 'We Must Do Without Half the Clothes We Want, says Cripps'.[93] When Cripps parried a question as to when clothes rationing would end by saying, with a smile, 'I hope it will be in our lifetime', the *Daily Express* printed a straight-faced headline: 'Clothes off ration "in our lifetime"'.[94]

Perhaps Cripps was unwise to make a joke of clothes rationing. He himself, like Anthony Eden, was always well dressed, as was often noted, especially on trips abroad. Interviewed on this point in Ottawa, after mentioning that his suit was 'an old brown Shetland Tweed', he pointed out that he was 'wearing a pre-war shirt – of good British quality – which could take it'.[95] This was double-edged, since one popular grievance against clothes rationing was that only wealthy people had been able to stock up on good clothes with this sort of durability. Moreover, there were clear gender differences here. In taking the offensive against the Housewives' League as 'a political instrument encouraged and misdirected by our opponents', Cripps hit a fair target; but he risked missing the underlying significance of women's felt needs. When he made a well-publicized denunciation of the

90. William Barkley, 'The enigma of Cripps', *Daily Express*, 15 November 1947.
91. *Daily Mail*, 14 December 1945.   92. ibid. 28 February 1946.
93. RSC speech at Nottingham, *News Chronicle*, 9 February 1946.
94. *Daily Express*, 19 February 1946.
95. Interview with RSC, *Men's Wear of Canada*, October 1948; cf. *Toronto Globe and Mail*, 23 September 1948.

New Look, with its unnecessarily full skirts, or joked that 'women – as usual – seem to have got away with it at the expense of the mere man' over textile allocations, not all women voters may have found it funny.[96]

The new chairman of the Conservative Party, Lord Woolton, who had himself been responsible for food rationing during the war, set the tone early.

Sir Stafford Cripps believes in austerity. He practises it himself almost as though it was a religious cult. That might be very good for him, but it is of no use to us. He knows nothing about the ordinary fun of life which you and I want, and I shudder for the condition of England when Sir Stafford comes back after spending three months with Gandhi. He is a bit of saint, but we are not apostles of austerity. If Britain is going to prosper the people must have more food, more clothes, more to spend their money on.[97]

It is a tribute to Woolton's electioneering instinct that this speech, barely six months into the new Parliament, was rarely bettered – or indeed varied – in subsequent propaganda over the next five years. 'Cartoonists lampoon him as an English fakir, reclining with virtuous self-mortification on a bed of utility nails,' one profile noted in May 1947. 'The saloon bars know him as "Misery" Cripps.'[98] Yet, within a matter of months, Cripps's career blossomed as never before. The reason is surely that, especially in the crisis atmosphere of that year, there were more damning charges than that of austerity – complacency or incompetence, for example, self-indulgence or refusal to face awkward facts. Indeed Cripps had himself gone on the attack in a widely reported parliamentary speech at the beginning of the 1946–7 session, countering the charge that Labour 'had put forward a case of ease and simplicity, that little effort was necessary and that Utiopia would be likely to appear round the corner'.[99] He had little difficulty in citing his own utterances; and it was precisely his readiness to confront a stark situation with a stark response that distinguished him.

Cripps temporarily squared the political circle. In August 1947 he received an ovation from Labour MPs when he resisted Tory demands for the Government to abandon the 1945 programme in face of the dollar drain. But within days the Cross-Bencher column in the *Sunday Express*, often the

96. *Reynolds News*, 14 June 1947; *Manchester Guardian*, 10 July 1947. See Zweiniger-Bargielowska, *Austerity in Britain*, esp. pp. 48–52, 92–5.
97. Woolton at Manchester, *Daily Mail*, 23 February 1946.
98. Frederick Mullaly, 'A real saint', *Sunday Pictorial*, 23 March 1947.
99. *The Times*, 22 November 1946.

voice of Beaverbrook, tried an alternative teasing tactic: 'Sir Stafford Cripps has become so reasonable, so restrained and so well-intentioned, that he is now regarded as being above politics, which raises him to a splendid but rather lonely pinnacle.'[100] He was seen as the man for a crisis that Britons needed to face united. 'Now we are all in it and we are all going without and dividing between us what there is,' Cripps explained in a radio broadcast.[101] In a review of the year entitled 'Sir Stafford's Session', the Conservative *Sunday Times* wrote: 'His public exposure of our economic needs has been frank and salutary. He has now to show that with his commanding position in the Cabinet he can bring the whole Government behind the necessary decisions.'[102]

Cripps's major problem was simple: too few dollars. His solution, as we have seen, was also essentially simple: to use the Budget to squeeze resources out of domestic consumption into exports. This was austerity with a fiscal face. It meant running a Budget surplus year by year until the balance of payments was in the black. In this objective, Cripps was eventually successful; but not entirely in the way that he envisaged at the outset – in particular because the exchange rate of sterling meanwhile required a fundamental adjustment. Indeed it was the devaluation crisis of 1949 that marked the watershed in his chancellorship.

In the first phase, Cripps largely continued Dalton's work. At a personal level this was obviously the reason for the good relations that they maintained, despite gossip to the contrary (some of which provoked Isobel Cripps to approach Attlee, who in turn tackled Dalton).[103] 'Good luck in your Budget-making!' Dalton wrote in 1948. 'And in your much more difficult task of stopping the frightful drain.'[104] Even when faced with this chronic problem on the foreign exchanges, neither of them resorted to high interest rates to do the trick. Instead, consistent with Keynes's priority for facilitating investment at low and stable rates, thereby encouraging the 'euthanasia of the rentier', a policy of 'cheap money' was pursued. Admittedly, Dalton's quest for even cheaper money became unsustainable when the markets refused to take up the government stock he issued ('Daltons') and Cripps's

100. Cross-Bencher, *Sunday Express*, 17 August 1947; cf. *Daily Herald* 8 August 1947.
101. BBC speech, *News Chronicle*, 2 November 1947.
102. *Sunday Times*, 18 January 1948.
103. See IC to Attlee, 20 May 1948 (copy) and Attlee to IC, 24 May 1948; Dalton diary, 26 May 1948, in Pimlott (ed.), *Dalton: Political Diary*, p. 434; cf. ibid., 11 September 1948, p. 438. Dalton had no motive to disparage Cripps since, as he well knew, this would simply delay his own return to the Government.
104. Dalton to RSC, 2 March 1948

monetary policy was accordingly less ambitious. None the less, bank rate remained set at 2 per cent until Labour lost office.[105]

Cripps also followed Dalton in making his fiscal measures explicitly redistributive. This was particularly true of the 'special contribution' of 1948, payable largely out of capital. Here Cripps moderated his zeal to the extent of exempting those who were dead – 'Let us tax only the living.'[106] The Beaverbrook press acknowledged that, with the possible exception of George Strauss, 'no member of the Government has been hit harder by Cripps's "once for all" capital levy than the Chancellor himself'.[107] To this extent, Cripps was a tax-and-spend Chancellor, taxing members of his own class in order to finance the post-war welfare state. His characteristic emphasis, in tune with his longstanding antipathy to 'state philanthropy', was that social services were not free and had to be paid for by the taxpayer. Conversely, there is no reason (except political sour grapes) to suppose that Cripps's protection of the social services vitiated his declared strategy of putting economic recovery first, still less his claims to fiscal probity.[108]

One reason for raising revenue was to cover government expenditure (swollen more by the aftermath of wartime defence spending than by the incipient welfare state). But the reason for maintaining an unprecedentedly large surplus from 1948 onwards was the Keynesian logic of restraining inflation. The overall impact can be seen from the figures for revenue and expenditure as a proportion of Gross Domestic Product (per cent of GDP).[109]

	revenue	expenditure	balance
1946–7	41.3	47.8	−6.5
1947–8	43.1	36.0	7.1
1948–9	40.5	32.2	8.3
1949–50	37.6	32.3	5.3
1950–51	36.6	30.1	6.5

105. There is evidence that Gaitskell latterly contemplated a rise in long-term interest rates to counter inflation. See Howson's authoritative study *British Monetary Policy*, esp. pp. 134–5, 149, 152, 191–5, 291–2, 305–7.
106. RSC note on Gregg to Burke Trend, 24 March 1948, PRO, T 171/395. On this measure see Whiting, *Labour Party and Taxation*, pp. 77–80.
107. Bernard Harris, 'Cripps: his wealth and his taxes', *Sunday Express*, May 1949.
108. This is the central (but unsupported) contention of Dell, *Chancellors*, ch. 3, 'The uncertain austerity of Sir Stafford Cripps', esp. pp 105–6; reiterated in his *Strange Eventful History*, pp. 136–8. Marquand, 'Sir Stafford Cripps', remains much more perceptive.
109. Clarke, *Keynesian Revolution and its Economic Consequences*, table on p. 210.

It is readily apparent that the tax burden came to a peak in the fiscal year ending April 1949 and declined thereafter. The fact is that Cripps's Budgets maintained, rather than increased, the level of taxation imposed by Dalton's final, fatal Budget of November 1947. The verdict of the economist J. C. R. Dow, who had worked under Hall in the Economic Section in these years, can still stand: 'Sir Stafford Cripps, despite his name for austerity, and despite the tenacity with which he strove to disinflate by fiscal means, in fact reduced taxes affecting consumption at each of his three budgets; and in three years, more or less undid Dr Dalton's last act of disinflation.'[110]

The Budget papers, as well as the Budget arithmetic, bear this out. The preliminary notes for Dalton's Budget speech for 1947 show him uncompromising:

(ix) *Alcohol.* No one need drink . . .
(x) *Smokes.* No one need smoke.

It was Dalton who denied that heavy taxes on these items could be seen as 'pressing with undue weight on anything which can be accurately described, in these days of austerity, as a prime necessity of life'.[111] Cripps, by contrast, although likewise raising alcohol duties in 1948, took pleasure in implementing a major cut in duties on light wines in 1949 (just as Mr Gladstone had done in the previous century). 'I propose to make a substantial reduction in these duties, and I hope that this will, in due course, bring about an increase in consumption,' Cripps said in his Budget speech.[112] He had negotiated personally with the French Finance Minister, who thanked Cripps for 'l'effort que vous envisagez pour faciliter, du point de vue fiscal, la vente des vins françaises en Angleterre'.[113] This reduction of £32 million in drink duties was the biggest in any post-war Budget until the cut of £33 million in 1959; but it is safe to say that few imbibers then claimed that they had never had it so good since the days of Stafford Cripps.

'Stafford has saved the country from a complete débâcle,' was Robert

110. Dow, *Management of the British Economy*, p. 201, with invaluable tables substantiating this judgement on pp. 198–200, which are my source for all tax changes.
111. Draft notes, November 1947, PRO, T 171/392, 154ff., 160ff. He put £56m. extra on alcohol and £15m. on entertainment and betting; and had already increased tax on tobacco by £77m. in April 1947.
112. 5 HC Debs., vol. 463, col.2092 (6 April 1949).
113. Petsche to RSC, 29 March 1949, PRO, T 171/298, f.25. One reported complaint from Labour loyalists about the Budget was: 'If tax reductions were possible would it not have been better to have kept the full tax on beer, and to have prevented some of the increase in the price of food?' M. Stockwood to RSC, 9 April 1949.

Hall's opinion in 1948, perhaps not unbiased.[114] But this became a common-place view, echoed in many non-Labour newspapers. 'The Chancellor of the Exchequer is a somewhat lonely public figure,' wrote *The Times*. 'No one else in his party sticks so untiringly to the single, austere theme of national salvation from a peril which too few see even yet – the peril of permanent impoverishment.'[115] The *Yorkshire Observer* remarked on the fact that Cripps attracted more attention than any other minister: 'That is not only because his duties touch every one of us more intimately; it is also because he is trusted better.'[116]

Cripps exploited this personal trust in persuading the unions to endorse a wage freeze, which was to last, with relatively minor erosion, from 1948 to 1950 (though voluntary restraint on profits, which he also called for, was less obviously effective). Cripps thus underpinned his fiscal policy, which averted the threat of inflation by suppressing demand, by an incomes policy which directly tackled cost-push inflation. There was a clear intellectual case for such a policy, consistent with Keynesian teaching, once the time-honoured means of checking wage increases – unemployment – was ruled out by a Government now committed to running the economy near to full capacity. In this sense, public acquiescence might be considered as a triumph for enlightened self-interest, reinforced by continuing invocations of toil and sweat, if no longer blood and tears. This suited Cripps's style nicely. 'Quite a lot of wise folk thought it was pretty hopeless to ask people to do these sort of things voluntarily,' he told radio listeners. 'Well they were wrong. The British People are an intelligent and understanding lot and if you tell them frankly what the position is they'll take notice and try and help.'[117]

What was also needed, however, to secure the cooperation of the TUC was the political muscle of the union bosses, which Bevin was uniquely able to mobilize. Just as he actively supported Cripps's domestic policies, so Bevin found his increasingly Atlanticist foreign policy now embraced by a Chancellor who saw an instructive contrast between the Soviet Union's suppression of social democracy in Czechoslovakia and the United States' adoption of Marshall Aid. The *Daily Worker* took to sniping at Cripps, alleging that his objective was to cut working-class living standards.[118]

---

114. Hall diary, 24 March 1948, in Cairncross (ed.), *Hall: Diaries*, p. 21.
115. 'The Warning Voice', *The Times*, 13 August 1948.
116. Leader, *Yorkshire Observer*, 3 November 1948.
117. Text of broadcast, 28 October 1948. On profits, see Francis, *Ideas and Policies*, pp. 173–4.
118. For example William Rust, *Daily Worker*, 3 January 1948; cf. Bullock, *Bevin*, iii, pp. 456–7, 556.

Cripps's popular image was constructed, especially through the press, in a double-edged way. Newspaper cartoons showed him as an invariably severe authority-figure, for example as a schoolmarm wielding her cane, and naturally exaggerated his physical features to fit the stereotypes. Vicky, the most inventive cartoonist of the era, and by no means politically hostile, drew him anthropomorphically as a hatstand, as an elongated lamp-post, as a plank stretched across a ravine and as a stark and leafless tree in winter. Even when not actually depicted in the classic Puritan garb, with a tall black hat, he was always a thin, zealous figure, standing apart from other ministers. He was recognizable in ways that could easily be given a partisan twist, rueful if not hostile. The Conservative front-bencher Walter Elliot was playing up to this in an after-dinner speech delivered, with the sort of Scots humour sometimes called pawky, during Cripps's ascendancy:

God made man, then, thinking that he needed a companion, made woman. Thinking that something ought to be done for man, made tobacco. Then, thinking that he had done too much for man, made Sir Stafford Cripps.[119]

Cripps, with his usual informal relations with journalists, to some extent colluded with them in the way that he was expected to respond. On leaving New York after an official visit, he was asked if he had any 'goodies' to take home and was quoted in all the papers as saying: 'My dear fellow, we have no dollars for luxuries for the Chancellor of the Exchequer.'[120]

'There is only one way to describe it,' wrote the American columnist Joseph Alsop in February 1949. 'In the last year the British people have accomplished a miracle.' He pointed not only to the encouraging economic statistics that showed the 'dollar gap' steadily closing but to the impact of Cripps himself, 'the strange, coolly intelligent, ruthlessly determined leader, who described himself as "sometimes discouraged, but never depressed"'.[121] From his own perspective as a Conservative front-bencher, Rab Butler, who privately described Cripps as 'superb', sought to warn him that things might change. 'You do not realise how adaptable I am,' was Cripps's amused riposte. 'I could become the champion of luxury and private enterprise overnight.'[122]

Cripps's image was indeed austere, even at the height of his acclaim,

119. Walter Elliot, speaking as Rector of Glasgow University, *Newcastle Journal*, 11 September 1948.
120. *Daily Mail*, 6 October 1948.
121. 'The British Miracle', *New York Herald Tribune*, 11 February 1949.
122. Nicolson diary, 15 March 1949, in Nicolson (ed.), *Harold Nicolson, Diaries and Letters*, iii, p. 166.

and his message was uncompromising. He laid out his policy with no concessions, telling the Labour Party:

We know many people feel the pinch of difficulty in making ends meet. But as long as we are in this impoverished state our own consumption requirements have to be the last in the list of priorities. First are exports; second is capital investment in industry. Last are the comforts and amenities of the family.[123]

Listening to his master introducing his 1949 Budget, Hall thought that 'clearly the Government benches disliked the very plain statements that we had to pay for our social services, while the opposition applauded'.[124] Cripps's speech – evoking Eden's tribute to its 'really outstanding brilliance even for him' – struck one experienced political correspondent as masterly in its lucid handling of big themes: 'Not since I first sat in the Gallery at Westminster have I heard a speech so ruthlessly stripped of party camouflage, so indifferent to the traditions of the Parliamentary game.'[125] Moreover, this was more than a parliamentary reputation, as the Gallup Poll confirmed. When asked whether Cripps was doing a good job as Chancellor, 57 per cent of respondents said Yes, only 24 per cent No. This was an even higher approval rating than for Bevin as Foreign Secretary, hitherto Labour's biggest popular asset, let alone for Attlee as Prime Minister.[126]

Until this point, Cripps was riding high, able to master the House, the Labour Party and the pound sterling simultaneously – and all on his own terms. The balance of payments, which had once looked so shaky, had improved dramatically. We now know that the reported deficits in the post-war years were exaggerated, because invisible exports were undercounted. Thus the swing reported at the time from a deficit of £675 million in 1947 to a surplus of £229 million in 1950 rather overstates the transformation. Yet even the corrected figures show a change over this period from a deficit of £381 million to a surplus of £307 million; and they show Britain virtually in balance for 1949.[127]

This marks a considerable achievement by any standards. The unsolved problem was that the United Kingdom continued to run a deficit with the

123. RSC speech at Workington, *Daily Telegraph*, 11 January 1949.
124. Hall diary, 6 April 1949, in Cairncross (ed.), *Hall: Diaries*, p. 55.
125. Douglas Clark, *Bristol Evening Post*, 8 April 1949.
126. Gallup, *Gallup International Public Opinion Polls*, i, p. 196. Bevin and Cripps were now neck-and-neck in the polls as Labour successors to Attlee, who still, however, led Cripps by 31 to 13 per cent as the preferred Prime Minister for a Labour second term.
127. Cairncross, *Years of Recovery*, pp. 153-4.

USA, producing a dollar shortage that was only made good in 1948 when Marshall Aid came through. This American aid was vitally important; it was much appreciated by Cripps and undoubtedly coloured his view of the world; but it was not accepted as a means of subsidizing the welfare state or allowing the country to live 'on tick'. Cripps's objective was to reach the point 'at which we cease to live on American charity, with all that this freedom implies for national self-respect and for our independent position in the world'.[128]

The actual means of reaching this objective was to be devaluation of the pound against the dollar. It was the classic response for economists trained in Keynesian analysis, confronted with a situation where one price (that of the currency) could be adjusted so as to make British goods more competitive and American imports less attractive, thus righting the balance of trade. Little wonder that, successively, Alec Cairncross, Robert Hall, Edwin Plowden, Douglas Jay and Hugh Gaitskell were converted by July 1949. But not the Chancellor. It is difficult to escape the force of Jay's suggestion that 'he never fully understood in the crisis of 1949 the arguments for and against devaluation, though he could of course have recited them with great lucidity'.[129] According to Plowden, it was Cripps's 'conviction that such a policy was morally wrong' that made him unreceptive to this line of thinking.[130] Cripps thus saw in devaluation an intractable moral issue rather than a soluble technical problem; and, by the time he had to confront the dilemma, it was as a sick man who was to be largely excluded from the decision-making process.

Devaluation

There is a letter of early 1949, carefully copied and preserved in the Cripps papers. The writer was Burke Trend, a future Cabinet Secretary, at this time running Cripps's private office.

Bluntly, the way in which you've been living and working, for the last year at least, is lunacy. But there is nobody apart from yourself who can tackle your job, can make

128. RSC to the Cabinet in September 1948, quoted Barnett, *Lost Victory*, p. 371. Barnett is, of course, the foremost critic of 'New Jerusalem' for allegedly building a welfare state 'on foreign tick': Barnett, *Lost Victory*, p. 42n. A more balanced account of Cripps's views can be found in Hogan, *Marshall Plan*, esp. pp. 239–41.
129. Jay, *Change and Fortune*, p. 177; cf. ibid., p. 187, for the moral dimension; there is a magisterial account in Cairncross, *Years of Recovery*, ch. 7.
130. Plowden, *Industrialist in the Treasury*, p. 53.

sense of it as you do, and can get the official machine to toil willingly and happily in spite of the very heavy weight of its burden . . . The concern that you are overloading yourself is very great, and the desire to help lighten the burden is very genuine. But ultimately it all depends on you. We can make a plan to reduce the strain; but we must know that, if we work it, you will be content! It would be very easy – fewer weekend engagements, rather less public speaking, a good deal less sheer reading, a rigorously preserved long weekend away from the office at regular intervals, *and* more devolution . . .

I suppose that a Private Secretary should not write this to the greatest Minister in Europe; but if a Private Secretary can't there are very few other people who can.[131]

Trend was using his special access to articulate worries about two concerns: Cripps's heavy workload and his increasingly precarious health. That the two were linked seemed only common sense.

This was by no means a new problem. In the summer of 1943, Cripps had had to take a fortnight's rest from his duties at MAP, telling Churchill that his doctor was 'quite satisfied with me except that my heart is a bit tired and flabby and my blood pressure very low'.[132] In 1946, of course, Cripps had had a breakdown in India; and on his return had spent a month at the Bircher-Benner Clinic in Switzerland. Raymond Streat, observing him on his return to the Board of Trade, found Cripps 'still a slightly tired man' in September, and a few weeks later observed further evidence not only of strain but of how Cripps dealt with it.

He is far from well, in my opinion. He keeps going because it has become a routine with him to do so. He isn't weary (he says to himself) because his mind, that precision instrument, has charge of the body, and the mind believes itself capable of holding the body on the job. So long as the mind retains that conviction, Stafford will continue to work at full blast.[133]

From November 1947, moreover, Cripps amalgamated his ambitiously demanding task at the Ministry of Economic Affairs with the responsibilities of the Treasury too. A year later, Dalton was reflecting that 'only my resignation made possible the coordination of the Treasury and the Planning Machine' but added: 'this is only possible, effectively, because Cripps is so

131. Trend to RSC, 16 February 1949 (copy).
132. RSC to Churchill, 13 July 1943, Churchill papers, CHAR 20/95B.
133. Streat diary, 26 September, 1 November 1946, in Dupree, *Lancashire and Whitehall*, pp. 367, 272–3.

brilliantly on top of his form. I am sure this set-up can't last. None of the Opposition could carry this double burden.'[134] Nor, in the long run, could Cripps himself. From February 1949 he was dogged by illness in a way that neither his self-imposed regime of abstinence, nor the teachings of F. Mathias Alexander, nor his own formidable will-power could adequately combat; and he began hinting that he might have to retire.

The Budget out of the way, two weeks' holiday in Italy in May 1949 offered respite but no cure. 'Stafford has found it hard to give in,' Isobel Cripps wrote to the Prime Minister after their return, 'but we have both realized this last few weeks that the position had to be faced if he was to continue to give the best service he can.'[135] In public Cripps kept up a brave façade, rushing off to Paris for an all-night meeting over Marshall Aid. 'Lack of a night's sleep had left no trace,' reported the London *Star*. 'Sir Stafford is like that . . . He can go on like that for months.'[136]

He could go on no longer. The reality was that Cripps had spent the previous weekend in bed, preparing for the meeting, and was about to leave his post – for six weeks, it was hoped – to seek further treatment in Switzerland. The Commons received the request for the necessary foreign currency with bipartisan goodwill. 'I hope that the Chancellor will have the most expensive treatment in the most expensive way,' said Rab Butler. Even the *Daily Express* was sympathetic, with an Opinion column entitled 'He Pays the Price'. The *Daily Mail* ran an editorial: 'The Pace that Kills'. The press reflected the general surprise: 'We had begun to take his fantastic stamina for granted.'[137]

Had Cripps pushed his fragile constitution too hard? 'He has no tricks, like some have, of resting for short periods by having a doze or just ceasing to bother,' Streat had observed in 1946.[138] 'He drives himself like a galley-slave,' one friendly journalist had written in 1947.[139] Gaitskell had noted in 1948 that 'you do feel also that he never really relaxes'.[140] In retrospect it is hard to ignore the warning signs, though Cripps himself did so at the time. Even in the summer of 1949 he found it hard to let go, determined to participate in a series of ministerial meetings that still left the

134. Dalton diary, 14 November 1948, in Pimlott (ed.), *Dalton: Political Diary*, p. 444.
135. IC to Attlee, 14 June 1949, copy.   136. *Star*, 1 July 1949.
137. Douglas Clark, *Bristol Evening Post*, 22 July 1949; *Daily Mail*, *Daily Express*, n.d. but late July 1949.
138. Streat diary, 26 September, 1 November 1946, in Dupree, *Lancashire and Whitehall*, pp. 367, 272–3.
139. John Addison, 'Cripps: politician – or saint?', *The People*, 9 November 1947.
140. Gaitskell diary, 16 February 1948, in Williams (ed.), *Gaitskell: Diary*, p. 56.

central issue of devaluation unresolved when he left for Zurich on 18 July.

'If Stafford Cripps had not been a sick man during this period would the outcome have been different?' Plowden wondered. 'I do not think so.'[141] Unless it is interpreted very narrowly, this judgement is hard to reconcile with what Gaitskell recorded at the time. If the July meetings had been so inconclusive in facing up to the impending sterling crisis, Gaitskell wrote, 'the main explanation is undoubtedly to be found in the Chancellor's state of health'. What he called Cripps's 'vacillations', so out of character, showed that 'he was not capable of thinking the problems out for himself'.[142] When Cripps had prepared a draft for the Commons, Hall dismissed it as 'no good', considered it 'wrong in many places', and helped organize a deputation 'to tell him his speech was lousy'. It was only at this point that Hall was informed by Plowden that 'Stafford Cripps was in such bad shape that he was going off on Monday for six weeks' holiday – alas! the horsemen of Israel and the chariots thereof'.[143]

Cripps's disciples thus saw their prophet taken from them; or, to adopt a secular metaphor, the devaluation drama was *Hamlet* without the prince. Attlee nominally took charge of the Treasury but in reality the decision was devolved, in Cripps's absence, upon Gaitskell and Jay, together with Harold Wilson, the President of the Board of Trade, advised by Hall and Plowden. It was the plan which they devised that provided a lifeline for the Government and rescued Cripps's own strategy – despite his intermittent back-pedalling once he was told what was proposed by Wilson, who made a clandestine visit to the sanatorium under cover of his own holiday arrangements in Switzerland.

'One cannot exaggerate the seriousness which S.C.'s illness has been to all our affairs in this period,' Hall ruminated. 'The one man who had them in hand to go off and actually to become the chief obstruction – it ought to be a general lesson that if the leader gets unfit he should step right out until he is better or resigns.'[144] Cripps was suddenly out of his depth, thrust from convalescence into acting as spokesman for a policy not of his own devising. For this deplorable state of affairs, of course, the Prime Minister was at least as much responsible as Cripps.

The dilemma was that he was widely supposed the indispensable

141. Plowden, *Industrialist in the Treasury*, p. 70; cf. ibid., p. 58.

142. Gaitskell diary, 3 August 1949, in Williams (ed.), *Gaitskell: Diary*, p. 126.

143. Hall diary, 11 July 1949, in Cairncross (ed.), *Hall: Diaries*, p. 65. When Elisha saw a chariot of fire appear and Elijah taken up by a whirlwind to heaven, he cried, 'My father, my father, the chariot of Israel, and the horsemen thereof.' 2 Kings 3:12.

144. Hall diary, 26 August 1949, in Cairncross (ed.), *Hall: Diaries*, p. 71.

Chancellor. This was a tribute not only to the Rolls-Royce purr of his past record at the Treasury but to a continuing ability to clock up an impressive performance even when not firing on all cylinders. For he was henceforth at times an invalid, carried by his own team. It was at this point that he gave up smoking, to save his own health (though mythology sometimes had it that it was to save the country dollars). Stafford and Isobel had made the most of their time in Zurich; but this respite lasted only a month in the end, and hardly a restful one. On his premature return, Cripps went to Chequers on 19 August to meet Bevin and Attlee – as though the Big Three could now pick up on a matter that they imperfectly apprehended, entirely without reference to the younger ministers who had a better grasp on what they were doing. Thanks to Bridges, Gaitskell was invited too (along with Wilson) but found the meeting depressing. 'The Chancellor looked very thin,' he noted, 'and it was a thoroughly bad omen when in my presence he handed to Bridges all the papers Bridges had given him and said, "I am not going to do any work for a week. I must go home and sleep." '[145]

The Chequers meeting took the final decision for devaluation of sterling. Obviously, if this were to be done, it were best done quickly. Cripps, however, asserted his authority to ensure that it would have to wait until after he had paid a forthcoming visit to Washington – a decision that baffled Gaitskell at the time but which in hindsight he thought was 'because the Chancellor's health simply did not permit of his doing the necessary work, such as preparing the broadcast, etc.'.[146] On 29 August the Cabinet endorsed the plan. Cripps now seemed rather better but again told Gaitskell, 'I have not slept.'[147] Two days later, Cripps and Bevin sailed the Atlantic – Bevin could not fly because of heart trouble – charged with setting a new exchange rate against the dollar.

Whether Cripps or Bevin or sterling was in worst shape was by this point unclear. Hall, who preceded the ministers by air to the USA, discovered from Plowden that the voyage out had not been used to flesh out the detail on devaluation; instead, 'S.C. had come most unwillingly to the view that we were going to do it at all; wanted as little as possible; and wanted to ask the U.S. and Canada what rate they suggested.'[148] On shipboard, he had risen at 4 or 5 a.m. to begin pacing round the deck and would go back to bed around 4 or 5 p.m. – by which time Bevin, nursing his heart in bed, was

145. Gaitskell diary, 21 September 1949 (reporting 19 August 1949), in Williams (ed.), *Gaitskell: Diary*, pp. 136–7.
146. ibid., p. 137.   147. ibid. (reporting 29 August 1949), p. 138.
148. Hall diary, 8 September 1949, in Cairncross (ed.), *Hall: Diaries*, p. 78.

not yet up; so it was not until three or four days out in the Atlantic that the officials got them both together.[149]

And yet, even under these unpromising circumstances, Cripps showed his extraordinary ability to grasp the main issues, to seize the initiative, and to set the tone for discussions in which the British started on the defensive. In this he was helped by Bevin, their mutual confidence now complete. They worked together to counter the impression that this was simply another British begging mission for more dollars. It was only when the talks moved from increasingly exasperating open sessions, crowded with advisers, into a small meeting confined to ministers and ambassadors that Cripps was able to broach the secret of devaluation as evidence that the balance of payments problem would be solved by British efforts rather than American handouts. The British ambassador reported that 'the Chancellor's utterance at the first ministerial meeting made a profound impression both in content and in manner. It went right home and was responsible for the evident goodwill and helpfulness of both Americans and Canadians throughout the talks.'[150]

How large a devaluation was optimal, once it was finally admitted to be necessary? Cripps's advisers favoured something of the order of 30 per cent, implying a reduction of the rate from $4.03 to under $3.00 against the pound. Much of the necessary drafting had to take place on the spot in Washington, with breakneck improvisation. 'The whole thing was a good example of the folly of leaving it all until the last minute,' Hall noted, 'but I suppose S.C.'s health made it essential.'[151] In the end Cripps and Bevin, closeted in the British embassy, took the decision together for $2.80. It is a mark of their Atlanticism that they were ready to share this secret with the Americans and the Canadians but not the French, whose Foreign Minister and Finance Minister (Schuman and Petsche) were in Washington, and both friends of Cripps – a slight not forgotten in Paris. Impressively, there was no significant leak of plans that had now been under discussion for the best part of two months, and the embargo held until Cripps was back in London to make the announcement on 18 September.

Devaluation was a success for the economy. The UK deficit in its current account with the dollar area had been £510 million in 1947, £252 million in 1948 and – with an American recession producing a worrying setback – £296 million in 1949; this was cut to £88 million in 1950. Since the rest of

---

149. Plowden, *Industrialist in the Treasury*, p. 62.
150. Oliver Franks telegram, 19 September 1949, PRO, CAB 129/36, app. C; and see Bullock, *Bevin*, iii, pp. 716–19.
151. Hall diary, 8 September 1949, in Cairncross (ed.) *Hall: Diaries*, pp. 78–9.

the sterling area now moved into surplus with the dollar area, and capital also began flooding into Britain, the most dramatic switch was seen in the gold and dollar balance. This had been in the red by several hundred millions in every post-war year (except 1947, when the deficit plunged to over a billion); but in 1950 the balance was £308 million in the black. This allowed the gold and dollar reserves to be rebuilt by 70 per cent in the first nine months after devaluation. By 1950 Britain did not need Marshall Aid.[152]

None the less, devaluation was a defeat for Cripps – mainly because he made it so. Plainly he had disliked the whole thing, perhaps did not fully understand the exchange rate complexities, was demonstrably slow to grasp the implication that there had to be cuts in Government spending, and undoubtedly failed to strike the right note in explaining himself to the public. It was a real difficulty for a politician whose reputation was founded on iron rectitude to execute a tactical manoeuvre of this kind. It was not devaluation itself but the pre-existing weakness of sterling that had already made Cripps vulnerable to reproach for much the same characteristics that had previously been praised, or at least tolerated. 'Vegetarian, teetotaller, early riser, unremitting worker, he lacks, it often seems, the human sympathy to sense the real impact of his measures on ordinary people,' was one comment. 'His intellectual self-confidence seems to scorn not only the arguments of others, but their feelings too.'[153] In the spring of 1949, Gallup had recorded a net approval rating for Cripps (positive minus negative) of 33 per cent; after devaluation this margin, though still favourable, was cut to 11 per cent.[154]

There could hardly have been a worse moment for the publication of Eric Estorick's fulsome biography. For two years the author had been fed with documents from the Cripps archive, many of them specially photographed for him, and given introductions to colleagues, in a process closely superintended by Isobel Cripps. The delicacy of the enterprise was well appreciated by Clem Leslie, with his responsibility for the Treasury's relations with the press, especially in the book's manifestly privileged and overtly partisan treatment of the pre-war in-fighting in the Labour Party. 'Told, as the story is,' Leslie advised Isobel Cripps, 'without psychological

---

152. All figures from Cairncross, *Years of Recovery*, Table 7.3, and see his discussion, pp. 199–211.
153. Portrait of Cripps, *Sunday Times*, 5 September 1949 (very likely by H. V. Hodson).
154. In April 1949, as has been noted above, 57 per cent had said Cripps was doing a good job, as against 24 per cent bad. In October, 45 per cent said good, 34 per cent bad; and whereas 24 per cent said the effects of devaluation were likely to be good, 40 per cent said bad. Gallup, *Gallup International Public Opinion Polls*, i, p. 209.

depth, or any attempt (so far as I have read) to show a development in Sir S.'s political outlook and experience – told merely as a succession of sayings and doings by a static Hero, if you see what I mean – these episodes, recalled to memory just now, will not at all fit in with the impression of mature, dispassionate judgment which his record as Chancellor is building up in the public mind.'[155]

This was not a particular, isolated or remediable problem with the book. Its brief was all too apparent in the pre-publication publicity: 'Mr Estorick shatters the myth which has embalmed the Chancellor as an ascetic, joyless personality who consumes statistics and carrots for lunch and spends his evenings planning to increase taxes.'[156] Woodrow Wyatt might loyally assure readers of the *Daily Herald* that Estorick had succeeded; but Malcolm Muggeridge (who had himself married into the Potter clan) made the tellingly restrained comment in the *Daily Telegraph*: 'For some tastes, his biography will seem oppressively adulatory.'[157] Estorick's epilogue was dated 18 August 1949. 'With superb energy and serenity of mind, with patience, persistence and politeness he forges ahead, self-confident, self-controlled,' ran this encomium.[158] The serialization of the book, however, a month later, began in the same week that sterling was devalued.

Devaluation came as the nemesis notoriously courted by perceptions of hubris. W. J. Brown, MP, always a bitter critic, went for the jugular in Beaverbrook's *Evening Standard*:

What was devalued last Sunday was more than the pound sterling. It was the reputation of the most respected figure in the Cabinet; it was public faith in the integrity of Government . . . No wonder Sir Stafford has been sick. Such a divorce between public profession and private intention could upset a stronger stomach than Sir Stafford's.[159]

The controversy that ensued was thus, in many ways, wholly predictable. Virtually everyone expected the Opposition to say that ministers had lied, in defending the currency until the last minute, just as virtually everyone expected the Government to say that they had had to lie, in the public interest. It was when the Leader of the Opposition weighed in to question the Chancellor's integrity that the stakes were raised. Cripps took the attack

155. S. C. Leslie to IC, 2 July 1949.   156. *Leader Magazine*, 17 September 1949.
157. *Daily Herald*, 31 October 1949; *Daily Telegraph*, 4 November 1949.
158. Estorick, p. 369.
159. 'Sir Stafford devalues his own Reputation', *Evening Standard*, 21 September 1949.

personally and immediately declared that he withdrew his consent to receive an honorary degree at Bristol University, where Churchill was Chancellor.

Cripps's name continues to be remembered because of his strong image – usually the image of austerity – reinforced by the attendant personal characteristics and anecdotes that lend it verisimilitude. He is, however, remembered relatively seldom for specific public acts. It is piquant that two of the incidents concerning Stafford Cripps that have entered the folklore both concern intrinsically trivial episodes in which he clashed with Churchill. One was the supposedly crucial warning to Stalin in 1941, a legend originating in Volume 3 of Churchill's *Second World War*. When this was published in July 1950, the review in the *Daily Express* carried the headline: 'I did my best to warn Stalin ... but Cripps did not deliver my note.'[160] The other specific story which Cripps's name continues to trigger concerns devaluation: the fact that a politician who was a byword for impeccable morality got so upset at being accused of lying for his country.

Why did Churchill press this charge? And why did Cripps take it so amiss? That their relationship was peculiarly charged is evident. Throughout the 1940s, Cripps was the one British politician by whom Churchill was continually fascinated, with a peculiar mixture of emotions: respect and even affection, spiced with fear and loathing. Moreover, as a professional politician all his life, Churchill was inured to reconciling public ambition with private affability. In his personal contacts with Cripps, all the evidence is that they got on well. Their meeting on the Sunday of devaluation, when the Chancellor briefed the Leader of the Opposition about the pending announcement, showed Churchill little moved – until he indulged in a flood of nostalgic reminiscences about their comradeship in the Second World War. Then he left, saying: 'But I shall make the utmost political capital out of it.'[161]

Previous partisan encounters indicate an animus on Churchill's part that was to infuse later attacks upon Cripps. 'Mr Churchill astounded the House of Commons last night,' ran a report of the 1946 India debate, 'by suggesting that Sir Stafford Cripps, whom Mr Churchill himself sent to India on a special mission during the war, was biased in favour of the Hindus.'[162] Churchill's truncated recrimination – 'we had to pull him up because of

160. *Daily Express*, July 1950; cf. *Daily Worker*, 24 July 1950, also seizing on 'this astonishing piece of political jugglery and insubordination by Cripps'.
161. Jay, *Change and Fortune*, p. 191; Wyatt, *Turn Again*, pp. 179–80n. 'This story I had from Cripps himself,' added Wyatt, who may have improved it but was surely faithful to the spirit of the exchange.
162. *Daily Mirror*, 13 December 1946.

his . . .' - was delivered, so another report continued, 'his voice shaking passionately, as a roar of Labour protests drowned his words, and Sir Stafford, white lipped, jumped to his feet'.[163] Returning to the Commons for periodic bursts of oratory, the busy author of *The Second World War* read the present into the past and the past into the present. In 1949, after a good summer's progress on Volume 3, now almost ready for publication, he snatched himself away from taunting Cripps for not delivering a cryptic message to Stalin in 1941 and instead set to teasing Cripps for delivering an insufficently cryptic message in the summer of 1949.

For Churchill, on one level the whole thing was an agreeable charade, legitimated by its transparent partisan function. He did his best to defuse the conflict, in private correspondence, recalling his words in Parliament that it was 'a necessary process of deception' in which Cripps had necessarily been involved – just like in the war.[164] Yet at another level the controversy was in deadly earnest. Talk of an election was in the air. Hall was surely right to think that the Conservatives were now 'trying very hard to exploit the loss of confidence in Cripps, as he was the great asset of the Labour party as far as the middle vote was concerned'.[165] Above all, Churchill, at nearly seventy-five, knew that this might be his last chance.

If Churchill's attack did not come out of the blue, then, Cripps's touchiness was also not a complete surprise. He had already displayed sensitivity about his personal honour in earlier parliamentary exchanges. He wanted vindication, conscious of the need to justify his stewardship. His overwrought reaction to criticism, too, can hardly be understood except by reference to his health. As Bevan told Dalton, 'Cripps was in a very strained condition. He now had a persecution mania, and was taking very hard charges of dishonourable conduct over devaluation.'[166] His pressure on Attlee to call an immediate General Election, a course which other economic ministers supported, was perhaps taken less seriously because his own judgement now seemed rather erratic.

In the event the General Election was held in February 1950. When Cripps had become Chancellor, in the Government's bleakest hour, the Conservatives had jumped to a 12-point lead over Labour in the Gallup Poll. The gap was narrowed in 1948 and in the spring of 1949 Labour was actually ahead. In the three months around devaluation, the Conservatives'

163. *Daily Graphic*, 13 December 1946.
164. For a full account of this incident see Burgess, *Cripps*, pp. 294–302.
165. Hall diary, 5 October 1949, in Cairncross (ed.), *Hall: Diaries*, p. 89.
166. Dalton diary, 11 October 1949, in Pimlott (ed.), *Dalton: Political Diary*, p. 459.

lead was a steady 6 per cent and there is no reason to conclude that they would have failed to win an election. As it was, Labour entered the campaign trailing the Conservatives but were neck-and-neck by polling day.[167] The Chancellor faced the election, as Hall observed, 'determined to give up office in any event'.[168] Like Attlee, Cripps was considered an asset to the Labour Party in reinforcing a simple, sensible, moral appeal. His party political broadcast at the beginning of the campaign was very much the Treasury view of what the people ought to know, reaching an audience only half as big as Churchill had commanded a fortnight earlier. 'If you still want full employment, fair shares and decent standards,' he told listeners, 'stick to the policies and the Party which have so far given them to you.'[169]

The Gallup Poll slightly underestimated a swing back to the Government that was enough to give an overall Labour majority of a mere six. Cripps and austerity both played their part in producing this result. What Edward Hulton of *Picture Post*, previously a potent Government supporter, described as 'an inescapable drabness and sadness, to say nothing of austerity', undoubtedly worked against the Labour Party.[170] Cripps himself, with his belated decision to put a good face on devaluation and talk up the economy, had to some extent repositioned himself. He had started speaking in public with more optimism – well justified as it turned out – about economic prospects: 'My austerity approach and my present view of the situation are, I believe, both of them accurate and realistic.'[171] Naturally the Opposition press did not acknowledge the change; the *Daily Express* ran a write-in feature on 'Miserabilism' in the summer of 1950, featuring Cripps alongside such contemporary radio personalities as Doris Arnold ('whose programme "These You Have Loved" is described by one reader as "The Mood of Moonlight on the Morgue" ').[172]

During the General Election, Cripps and Churchill had another fine row: their last. Churchill's platform barb that Cripps's 'clear mind sees so plainly the harm he has wrought his country' again found its mark, as was shown by the stinging retort: 'I regret that a person whom I have admired for his

---

167. Butler and Butler, *Political Facts*, pp. 247–8, 259.
168. Hall diary, 31 January 1950, in Cairncross (ed.), *Hall: Diaries*, p. 102.
169. Text of broadcast, 2 February 1950. BBC figures show that Cripps was heard by 21 per cent of the adult population, Churchill on 21 January by 40 per cent. Listening figures for later election broadcasts were inflated by the fact that they were repeated later in the evening; 51 per cent heard Churchill's final appeal, 44 per cent Attlee's. Nicholas, *General Election of 1950*, p. 127.
170. See Zweiniger-Bargielowska, *Austerity in Britain*, pp. 226–34, Hulton quoted at p. 226.
171. RSC speech at Bristol, *Bristol Evening Post*, 29 November 1949.
172. *Daily Express*, July 1950.

wartime leadership, and, indeed, friendship, should sink to quite this level of guttersnipe politics.'[173] This remark was widely quoted, generally against Cripps. In the judgement of the subsequent Nuffield College study of the General Election, this marked the highest point in the 'fever chart' of a campaign notable for its low temperature.[174]

The result of the election pleased neither man, keeping Labour in power but with only a knife-edge majority in the Commons. Plowden recalls Cripps as saying: 'Edwin, I'm trapped. I intended to go after the election, but with a majority of six I can't possibly do so now.'[175] Dalton was not alone in assuring Attlee that 'Cripps was absolutely irreplaceable as Chancellor'.[176] Cripps was persuaded to carry on with the support of Gaitskell, who took over the post of Minister of Economic Affairs, but subordinate to the Chancellor (in a way that Cripps had never been to Dalton) with the status of Minister of State. But the fact was that the devaluation crisis had been the making of Gaitskell as a substitute Chancellor, should Cripps's health not sustain him in the resumption of his duties, which was an eventuality always in the background thereafter.

The beginning of the end

In April 1950 Cripps received a memorandum from three junior ministers who knew him well: Woodrow Wyatt, John Freeman and Fred Lee. It was virtually a carbon copy of Burke Trend's letter a year previously. It was written on the assumption that 'the Chancellor of the Exchequer is mentally tired and in danger of permanently impairing his health unless he can be persuaded to rest'. Arguing that it was 'almost certain that, in spite of jokes about austerity, etc., the personal prestige of the Chancellor is the decisive factor in swinging moderate opinion behind the Labour Government', the memorandum wanted 'the outstanding statesman of the Western World' restored to its counsels. It proposed an arrangement whereby Cripps would, in effect, take six months off, perhaps assuming nominal duties as Lord Privy Seal while he sought to recuperate.[177] Whether more sinecure or rest cure, this was actually very much what Attlee was to do with Bevin in the last weeks of his life a year later.

173. RSC at Edinburgh, *Evening Standard*, 15 February 1950.
174. Nicholas, *General Election of 1950*, p. 109.
175. Plowden, *Industrialist in the Treasury*, p. 105.
176. Dalton diary, 27 January 1950, in Pimlott (ed.), *Dalton: Political Diary*, p. 466.
177. Wyatt, Lee and Freeman to RSC, 4 April 1950.

The 1950 Budget saw Cripps markedly less active than previously, as the Treasury papers amply demonstrate.[178] He did not attend the Roffey Park house-party in February, held during the General Election campaign. Admittedly, nor did Gaitskell, who now increasingly deputized for Cripps, taking early meetings with the officials either in his own room or, significantly, in the Chancellor's office. Initially, the trouble was that Gaitskell, although consulted often, was always consulted *ad hoc*, and had never been given clearly delegated responsibilities. 'So he does not know where he is,' Hall observed, 'does not always deal with the same issues, and it wastes officials' time routing things through S.C.'[179] The fact that this fundamentally unsatisfactory administrative arrangement worked so harmoniously is a tribute to a flourishing personal relationship, in which Gaitskell's increasingly ungrudging respect was reciprocated by Cripps's increasingly confident trust.

The implications of the Gaitskell–Cripps partnership were to be far-reaching for the Attlee Government. During its first term of nearly five years, if Cripps was thought to have a protégé or favourite son among the rising generation of ministers, it was Bevan who was naturally cast in this role. His role as creator and champion of the experimental National Health Service inevitably depended upon a hard-pressed Chancellor meeting new claims for expenditure. Although manifestly reluctant (as several of their colleagues noted) to reject the pleas for supplementary estimates that Bevan, as Minister of Health, had successively made, Cripps finally drew the line here. In October 1949, as part of the post-devaluation measures to cut Government spending, he had proposed making charges to patients for prescriptions; but though Bevan reluctantly acceded to the principle, he made clear that the real battle would be over implementation.[180]

It was to be on this issue that Cripps's successor as Chancellor, Gaitskell, subsequently clashed with Bevan, whose resignation from the Cabinet in April 1951 precipitated an internal conflict between Bevanites (as they were soon called) and Gaitskellites (as they were later identified) that tore the Labour Party apart during a decade of debilitating acrimony. Where did Cripps himself stand? The crisis over the twin issues of Health Service costs and charges was unresolved when he left office. But his own position seems quite clear; and the course of events during the twenty months of the second term of the Attlee Government was strongly influenced by the emergence of Gaitskell rather than Bevan as Cripps's closest ally.

178. PRO, T 171/400–2.
179. Hall diary, 22 March 1950, in Cairncross (ed.), *Hall: Diaries*, p. 108.
180. Morgan, *Labour in Power*, pp. 400–401.

In the spring of 1950, now with Gaitskell's assistance at the Treasury, Cripps returned to the problem of financing the Health Service, again raising the option of making charges and again encountering opposition led by Bevan. 'I begged Stafford to insist on two things,' Gaitskell wrote. 'First, Treasury control should be established as effectively as it is over other Government expenditure and secondly there should be a definite limit placed on the total National Health Service expenditure.' There is no reason to doubt the evidence of his diary that Gaitskell was himself instrumental in forcing the issue: 'We had a very energetic 48 hours trying to get the Chancellor, and then one or two other Ministers, to back this.'[181] The final compromise, that a ceiling was imposed in the Budget for the coming year while the National Health Service was monitored, arguably fell short both of Gaitskell's agenda, in seeking to establish the necessity for charging, and of Bevan's, in making opposition to charges a point of principle.[182] But it achieved Cripps's own objective in restraining overall expenditure for another year: an issue which, as he wryly warned Attlee, 'may in certain events lead to the (real) resignation of the Minister of Health'.[183]

There is clear evidence that this conflict led to a personal breach with Bevan: an exchange of letters in June 1950, in which he was reproached by Cripps for refusing to attend any more of their weekly dinners, in turn provoking an explicit affirmation from Bevan that the imposition of Health Service charges was the breaking point: 'I am not such a hypocrite that I can pretend to have amiable discourses with people who are entirely indifferent to my most strongly held opinions.'[184] That Cripps was included with Gaitskell in this stricture seems inescapable; and if the Prime Minister continued to rely upon his hunch that 'Nye was much attached to Stafford, who could talk to him like an uncle', it showed him latterly somewhat out of touch.[185]

How long Cripps could carry on as Chancellor remained unclear. 'As to his health, it is extremely difficult to judge,' Gaitskell noted. 'He certainly regards himself as almost an invalid, and Edwin Plowden mentioned to me

---

181. Gaitskell diary, 21 March 1950, in Williams (ed.), *Gaitskell: Diary*, p. 174.
182. See the trenchant analysis in Campbell, *Bevan*, pp. 216-20, 247-8.
183. RSC to Attlee, 2 April 1950, Attlee papers.
184. The exchange, dated to the end of June 1950, is printed in Foot, *Bevan*, ii, pp. 296-7. It has not been found in the Cripps archive.
185. Attlee's comment in Williams, *A Prime Minister Remembers*, p. 249. 'He cut loose after Stafford went,' Attlee added; but the signs are that he would have cut loose anyway, faced with Cripps's determination to hold the line.

the other day that he thought he was rather a hypochondriac.'[186] This apparently uncharitable opinion, shared also by Jay, reflects longstanding prejudices that Stafford, abetted by Isobel, was a tiresome health crank whose troubles were at least partly self-inflicted. 'And he has such queer doctors,' Gaitskell muttered to Dalton.[187] Once the Budget was out of the way at the end of April, Cripps decided to resign at the end of the parliamentary session in three months' time. 'My doctors have been pressing this on me for some time now,' he told Attlee, 'but I have continued on in my job owing to the difficult position of the Party.'[188] Gaitskell gamely tried to secure Isobel Cripps's help in shielding the Chancellor. 'I certainly seem to have plenty to do – and I hope this does mean something like a corresponding reduction in the burden on Stafford,' he told her. 'But you should refuse to allow him to work outside the office and you must stop him worrying.'[189]

Matters came to a head in the summer of 1950. Cripps told Gaitskell and Plowden that he had decided to leave office because he needed a complete rest for at least a year, and had gone as far as writing a letter of resignation, with effect from the beginning of August. The two of them were equally appalled and enlisted Isobel Cripps's help in persuading Stafford, yet again, to carry on. 'It was essential for him to remain Chancellor,' Gaitskell records telling Cripps, 'but that he could quite well go away for a long holiday in the summer.'[190] On this basis, Attlee implemented a variant of the rest cure; it was publicly announced that Cripps would take three months' leave, on the assumption that he would then resume. Privately, Cripps put it more conditionally. 'If I was not ready to take up my work I would then resign, otherwise I would return to my work,' he wrote to Attlee. 'You asked me to proceed upon this basis which I will therefore do.'[191] At Cripps's suggestion, Gaitskell made the symbolic move into the Chancellor's imposing office; and in effect never moved out until the fall of the Attlee Government.

With the Government now racked by arguments over rearmament, once the Korean War had begun, Cripps's absence could not help but undermine his authority. 'True, he has a trustworthy lieutenant in Mr Gaitskell,' the *Manchester Guardian* commented, 'but no Chancellor of the Exchequer who was able to avoid it would have left such a battle to any subordinate,

186. Gaitskell diary, 26 May 1950, in Williams (ed.), *Gaitskell: Diary*, p. 187; cf. Jay, *Change and Fortune*, p. 187.
187. Dalton diary, 11 September 1950, in Pimlott (ed.), *Dalton: Political Diary*, p. 485.
188. RSC to Attlee, 26 April 1950, Attlee papers.   189. Gaitskell to IC, 26 April 1950.
190. Gaitskell diary, 11 August 1950, in Williams (ed.), *Gaitskell: Diary*, p. 192.
191. RSC to Attlee, 11 July 1950, Attlee papers.

however good.'[192] Rumours of his resignation had to be denied. Stafford and Isobel withdrew to Frith, before going to the Bircher-Benner Clinic in September. Then there was a walking holiday in Italy, publicized as the final step in recuperation; but already Cripps had written to Attlee with the medical verdict, telling him that 'unless I now go off for a prolonged rest I shall probably do irreparable harm to my health'.[193]

Cripps returned to England on 16 October and formally resigned from the Government. Within days he stepped down too as a Member of Parliament. The valedictory notices covered the front pages. 'Sir Stafford Cripps will be forever identified with austerity,' the pro-Labour *Daily Mirror* conceded. 'But it was austerity with a purpose.'[194] In its sister paper, the *Sunday Pictorial*, the Labour MP Richard Crossman seized on recent good news about the economy to claim that Cripps had 'won through by austerity and the wage freeze'.[195] The predictable riposte came from the *Daily Express*:

Why did Sir Stafford go wrong? Perhaps because, while he knew so much about economics, he knew little about human beings.

He believed in harsh, dry austerity not only for himself. He enforced the same harsh, dry austerity on the whole country . . .

He pegged the wages of the working man in a time of rising prices. In doing so, he created misery.[196]

Other judgements were more nuanced, perhaps because Cripps's absence had already distanced him from immediate controversy. Thus an article in the Conservative *Daily Mail* began: 'It was as "Austerity" Cripps that he was known, and because he was also a teetotaller on moral grounds, and a vegetarian by compulsion of health, the term seemed apposite also to his personal character.' But it immediately countered: 'In that he has been misjudged.'[197] Political censure did not preclude personal respect; and a number of genuinely sympathetic voices were heard. The *Observer*, now under the editorship of David Astor, was naturally pro-Cripps, acknowledging that 'the word "austerity" has been his shadow, and the better-known aspects of his life have sustained the legend', yet suggesting that 'the word, as a label for the whole period of his Chancellorship, is not

192. *Manchester Guardian*, 23 August 1950.
193. RSC to Attlee, 4 October 1950, in Williams, *A Prime Minister Remembers*, p. 244.
194. Harold Hutchinson, 'The Iron Chancellor', *Daily Mirror*, 20 October 1950.
195. 'Triumph in his final hour', *Sunday Pictorial*, 22 October 1950.
196. Leader, *Daily Express*, 20 October 1950.
197. Montague Smith, *Daily Mail*, 20 October 1950.

very apt'.[198] The *Manchester Guardian*, calling him 'a great Chancellor of the Exchequer', took a more ambivalent view: 'Loyalty to set ideas has been Sir Stafford's strength as a man and his weakness as a Minister. He has always in his public life ignored worldly forces such as human feelings or the trends of the market.'[199]

Cripps's unworldliness had often been remarked before; but it was in his final years that it began to verge on other-worldliness. As Chancellor, Cripps took pride in taking no heed of conventional political considerations. He pushed aside a dossier analysing by-election results since 1945 with the brisk comment, 'no time to read this!'.[200] He touchily refused to introduce anything that could be considered an 'election Budget', thus constraining Attlee's timing of the 1950 General Election.[201] After his Budget in April 1949, which had disappointed many Labour supporters, those letters from members of the public that Cripps not only kept, but had copied, and answered personally, evidently struck a chord with him. One was from four 'poor prospective Tax Payers', currently serving in the forces, saying that 'we would like to compliment and thank you for the courage which you have shewn in presenting your Budget'.[202] Another was from a Labour canvasser in Bristol, reporting: 'The universal reaction to the Budget was "we had hoped for easement, but if it cannot come just now without peril to the Country's economy, then we must carry on as we are going".'[203] A clergyman's widow in Tamworth confessed that she had first felt 'not a little incensed' on hearing Cripps's Budget broadcast; but 'after giving serious thought to this I altered my ideas and I should like to express my admiration for a Chancellor of the Exchequer *and the Party he represents* (mark this) that he should put forward such an austere Budget the year before a General Election'.[204] She was not the only listener to be impressed. 'You combined both the gentle sternness of a father and the wisdom of an Archbishop!' wrote a Canon of Leicester Cathedral, adding: 'It was to me a real co-incidence that all this has happened in Passion Week.'[205]

The explicitly religious register in Cripps's public utterances sometimes served to eclipse the political content. 'Our standards must be spiritual, and

198. 'The Cripps Era', *Observer*, 22 October 1950.
199. 'A New Chancellor', *Manchester Guardian*, 20 October 1950.
200. RSC note, 28 March 1948.   201. Morgan, *Labour in Power*, p. 402.
202. John Heathfield *et al.* to RSC, 7 April 1949.
203. R. Lyne to RSC, 7 April 1949 (emphasis in original).
204. Muriel Cameron to RSC, 7 April 1949.
205. A. Linwood Wright to RSC, 7 April 1949.

not material,' he told the Band of Hope Union in 1947.[206] In hailing the Marshall Plan in 1948, he made a characteristic plea: 'We need as well – side by side with the others – a Christ plan for world peace and happiness if we are to succeed.'[207] It was the same commitment that led Cripps into joining forces with Lord Halifax, now a Conservative elder statesman, in the Christian Action movement that Canon John Collins had founded in post-war Oxford and relaunched in London in 1948. 'We must not only employ democratic methods, but we must use them for Christian ends,' Cripps proclaimed to its vast inaugural meeting in the Albert Hall, with his plea: 'The romance of life lies in self-sacrifice for others.'[208] He again cooperated with Halifax at a service in St Paul's Cathedral, where Collins was now installed as Canon, at the outset of the General Election campaign in February 1950, replete with a sermon from the Archbishop of Canterbury. In the previous month, at Collins's invitation, Cripps had himself preached there, the first layman to do so, packing in a congregation estimated at 3,500. The *Daily Worker* headline read: 'Cripps: New Pulpit But Old Sermon'.[209] His message was indeed familiar. 'There is nothing that matters so much in the world today,' he implored, 'as that we should get back to the standards which Christ set for us by his example and by his teachings in our *public as well as in our private* life.'[210]

The political implications of Cripps's commitment raise ambiguous issues. Since he had published a collection of addresses under the title *Towards Christian Democracy* in 1945, he was later understandably sensitive about the appropriation of religion by the right-wing Christian Democrats of Catholic Europe, which he regarded as 'a complete misuse of the term Christian'.[211] Hence the care with which Collins stage-managed a meeting between Cripps and the Pope in Rome in April 1949, under the auspices of Christian Action. It would be wrong to suggest that Catholic Europe became Cripps's spiritual home. American attempts to make closer ties between Britain and the continent a condition of Marshall Aid found repeated resistance from Cripps, who apparently admitted privately to an.

206. RSC speech at the centenary of the Band of Hope Union, *Sunday Times*, 11 May 1947.
207. RSC address at St Mary Redcliffe, Bristol, *British Weekly*, 1 April 1948.
208. *Daily Telegraph*, 26 April 1948. Full text in *A Call to Action by Christians*, pp. 33–7, at p. 36; and Cripps's speech reprinted in *God in Our Work*, at p. 48. On Christian Action, see Collins, *Faith under Fire*, ch. 6.
209. *News Chronicle*, *The Times*, *Daily Worker*, 9 January 1950.
210. Text of sermon at St Paul's Cathedral, 8 January 1950 (emphasis in original).
211. Cripps interview, *News Chronicle*, 25 January 1949. Correspondence on the Italian visit in the Cripps papers.

American friend 'that he would much rather go it alone, and not be obligated to make agreements with the other European nations'.[212]

None the less, there was an implicit conception of Christendom behind much of Cripps's later religious rhetoric. The origin of the big Christian Action meeting in 1948 was an effort to rally Christians behind moves towards Western European unity in face of the threat of Soviet expansion, notably in Czechoslovakia. The meeting was held in the same week that the adjourned London Conference on Germany (in which several of the continental European speakers were involved) recommenced its work; and this is the more significant since there are good grounds for arguing that the Schuman Plan for a Coal and Steel Community, that key step in European integration, 'was in essence already there at the end of the London confer-ence'.[213] The Schuman Plan was to be rejected by the British Government in June 1950. In hindsight it is easy to exaggerate the significance of Cripps's absence from this Cabinet meeting; but it is still worth noting the fact that he was the only senior minister with a good word for the Plan and that there was a pro-European dimension in his thinking that was unusual at the time.[214]

When Cripps again published his lay sermons between hard covers in 1949, it was in a book entitled *God in Our Work*. In his last audience with the King before going off to convalesce, the Chancellor had presented a copy to His Majesty; a polite hand-written letter of acknowledgement from Princess Elizabeth also survives; and, following the Washington talks on devaluation, President Truman assured Cripps that he was reading the new work 'with a great deal of interest and a lot of satisfaction'.[215]

Those who worked with Cripps sometimes wryly observed that he imported a providential sense into his decision-making. The implication that a decision 'had been imparted to him by some higher wisdom' struck

212. Walter Lippmann to J. William Fulbright, 11 March 1949, in Blum, *Public Philosopher*, p. 534. 'They don't regard themselves as Europeans,' Lippmann wrote, 'they do not wish to stand in the same queue with the others, and they have as a matter of policy manoeuvred themselves out of a collective effort for European recovery.' This perception is echoed by comments on Cripps by Harriman and others in *FRUS*, 1950, iii, *passim*.
213. Milward, *The Reconstruction of Western Europe*, pp. 145–64; and see Collins, *Faith under Fire*, esp. pp. 103–5, 135, 139–40.
214. I think Richard Lamb suggests too much in writing that 'without Cripps the Labour Government spurned the ambitious and wide-ranging French plans'. Lamb, *Failure of the Eden Government*, p. 61. For a shrewd account see Hennessy, *Never Again*, pp. 390–404, endorsing the economic appraisal in Milward, *Reconstruction of Western Europe*, pp. 405–7; also Burgess's likeminded analysis, *Cripps*, pp. 308–11, taking issue with the exhaustive treatment in Dell, *Schuman Plan*, esp. pp. 127–32, 158–9, 229, 298–9.
215. Truman to RSC, 13 September 1949.

Douglas Jay as disconcerting; and it was only when he read Philip Magnus's life of Gladstone, published after Cripps's death, that he came to appreciate the full force of the affinity here.[216] The charge classically levelled against politicians who have paraded the moralistic language of judgmental religiosity – against Thatcher as much as against Gladstone – is that of humbug. It is true that the early Cripps, the red squire of Goodfellows, encountered taunts of political hypocrisy. But what is remarkable is that the later Cripps, leading his exemplary life of Christian reformism, so completely escaped innuendo about his personal integrity. 'Why was it that Sir Stafford Cripps gained such a reputation for humourless and self-righteous bearing in public life?' asked one Conservative paper. 'The answer is simple: his sincerity.[217]

It is not the purity of his intentions that is finally in question but the robustness of his political strategy. What Gladstone and Thatcher had, that Cripps lacked, was an ability to inspire a moral populism that potently subserved their political interests. Other politicians have reconciled strong Christian beliefs with the practice of political guile in coping with the problems of an imperfect world. Lord Salisbury countered Gladstone with an equable cynicism premised on the pervasiveness of original sin; Lord Halifax did not acquire the sobriquet 'Holy Fox' purely out of assonance; Harold Macmillan displayed a ruthless Machiavellian instinct licensed by his sense that the things of this world were finally insubstantial. Cripps, by contrast, as his sermon at St Paul's in 1950 reiterated, took another view of Christ's lesson: 'His teaching largely concerned itself with the actions of men and women here and now, on this earth.'[218] Faithful to this lifelong conviction, Cripps's political career thus remained focused, as it always had been, upon 'bringing about the Kingdom of God *on earth*'.[219] 'The rule of God is destined to come here on earth,' he affirmed, looking to the Church 'as the means of perfecting the rule of God on earth'.[220]

Whether it is a more damaging charge for a politician to be thought ingenuous than to be called disingenuous is a moot point. Mervyn Stockwood, as an Anglican priest, claimed to have defended his friend Stafford against bar-room slights (literally, with a glass in his hand) by saying: 'Yes, he isn't quite ordinary, I agree. You see he believes that Jesus Christ really meant what he said.'[221] Although Cripps did not claim Christ for the British

216. Jay, *Change and Fortune*, pp. 177–8.   217. *Daily Graphic*, 20 October 1950.
218. Text of sermon at St Paul's Cathedral, 8 January 1950.
219. Emphasis supplied. Address by RSC, Westminster Chapel, 5 January 1948, in *Evangelical Christendom*, January–March 1948, pp. 9–13, at p. 11; quoted more fully above, p. 8.
220. RSC, *Towards Christian Democracy*, pp. 8–9.
221. Stockwood to RSC, 4 August 1948.

Labour Party, his political proposition that 'Socialist Democracy is the true barrier against Communism' had a clear religious core.[222] 'The only real force that we have to oppose the enthusiasm of Communism,' Cripps testified, 'is the greater and truer enthusiasm of Christian living.'[223]

Cripps was reinforced in bearing witness by encouragement from his immediate circle. 'It was magnificent and inspiring,' Geoffrey Wilson wrote of Christian Action's inaugural meeting, 'and I was more thankful than I can say to hear a public figure speaking in the way you spoke.' In affirming that 'there is no solution to any of our major problems on the purely material plane and that it is only spiritual forces that are strong and pure enough to see us through', Wilson showed constancy in following his master.[224]

Above all, Isobel Cripps shared Stafford's faith, as she shared his life, in sickness and in health. While Stafford was in India in 1946, she reported visits to the Attlees in Downing Street and at Chequers, and heady consultations about 'Bishop Making', involving both the Prime Minister and the Archbishop of Canterbury. 'I feel so grateful that Clem and he have "believed",' she wrote, with the sense that she had 'lived thro' a deep spiritual experience'.[225] Their valetudinarian regime at 11 Downing Street meant that Isobel was living above the shop, sharing more of Stafford's busy days, and monitoring both his private and his public life. In a rare press interview, she admitted: 'I'm afraid people don't understand him. He is trying to introduce moral and spiritual ideas into politics, and this is not easy in these sceptical times.' It was Gandhi, 'one of the world's truly great men', whose example she cited: 'He is gone, but his message will ring down the centuries.'[226]

The notion of Cripps as the English Gandhi had often been aired, sometimes inspired more by satire than reverence. 'He is an unaccountable person and when he gets these ideas in his head is as stubborn as an ox because he is convinced that he is right and no arguments will move him,' Cripps had once written of Gandhi, in words that might have applied to himself.[227] In his public encomium on Gandhi in Westminster Abbey, he put it slightly differently, but again with a provoking self-referential implication. 'He was a formidable opponent in argument, and would often take up the attitude that his views and the policy he was advocating had come to him in his mediations from God, and then no reasoning upon earth could make him

222. Estorick, p. 360.   223. RSC interview, *News Chronicle*, 25 January 1949.
224. Wilson to RSC, 2 May 1948.   225. IC to RSC, 2, 10 May 1946.
226. Ranjee Shahani, 'The Lady behind Sir Stafford', *Bristol Evening Post*, 20 January 1949.
227. RSC diary, 18 June 1946; for the context see above, p. 447.

depart from them,' Cripps said. 'He knew he was right.'[228] The irony here is that, when he was actually in India, Cripps discerned that Gandhi's uncompromising prophetic stance had become deeply unhelpful in addressing problems for which pragmatic political solutions were now more appropriate. Yet in Britain Cripps ended his career with aspirations more obviously those of a prophet rather than a politician. Cripps brought distinctive *values* to politics; and he showed impressive grasp of *policy*; but he rarely matched this with comparable attention to political *process*.

Dark vale

'My trouble is a tired heart,' Cripps said upon leaving Parliament. 'There is nothing else wrong.'[229] Newspaper pictures already suggested another story, showing a thin and prematurely aged figure. Diagnosis in Switzerland in November confirmed the presence of further afflictions, notably a tubercular abscess in the spine, bringing an abrupt end to plans for further travel. 'Perhaps the Almighty thought our proposed trip was going to be too restless and that we needed the still disciplined beauty of the mountains for re-creating,' Isobel told the family.[230] Treatment required Stafford to be isolated in a plaster cast, so as to give the bones a chance to knit together. By February 1951, there were signs of progress and he started to take an interest in the outside world again. The family learnt that there was no further tubercular infection; the outlook was a further six months in the cast, followed by a year in a special jacket, after which Stafford might take four months to learn to walk again. 'I need hardly tell you how anxious we have been about Stafford's health,' wrote Nehru. 'We had all been looking forward to him coming to India during this winter and it was a great disappointment to learn that he was not well enough to come.'[231]

The initial idea of simply taking a year's rest was mocked by critical developments in Cripps's health during 1951. At first there was a false sense of complacency, with some old colleagues in the Labour Cabinet refusing to acknowledge that his absence was more than temporary. As the Health Service issue became rolled up with Cabinet divisions over the financing of rearmament for the Korean War, Gaitskell made considerable efforts to

---

228. Service of intercession for the people of India, Westminster Abbey, 17 February 1948, reprinted in RSC, *God in Our Work*, p. 35.
229. Guy Eden, *Daily Express*, 20 October 1950.   230. IC diary letter, 20 November 1950.
231. Nehru to IC, 28 February 1951; and see Peggy Cripps to family, 1 February 1951.

keep Cripps posted about developments; and in turn heard what he no doubt wanted to hear. 'Stick to what you believe to be right and don't allow anyone to divert you by arguments of political expediency,' Cripps enjoined from his sickbed, as the arguments over the April 1951 Budget came to a head.[232] The account that Gaitskell gave, running to ten pages in his own hand, written before Bevan finally resigned, conveys the collusive tone.

I hope you will think I was right to stand out. I really have no doubt myself. The risk of Nye resigning and wrecking the government was a very grave one – but if I had given way we should have had the position of Nye overthrowing a clear cabinet decision on a matter of financial policy simply by the threat of breaking up the government.[233]

Cripps was not alone in seeing Gaitskell as his faithful successor. Indeed Attlee passed on his wife Violet's comment to Cripps, that 'if she shuts her eyes she sometimes thinks that it is you speaking because he has proved such an apt pupil'.[234]

The crisis in the Cabinet was overshadowed by a continuing crisis in Stafford's own health. There are conflicting accounts in print of exactly what was wrong, partly because Isobel became acutely conscious of a need for secrecy in face of press intrusion. 'NOT ONE SINGLE PERSON MUST KNOW THESE DETAILS,' she enjoined her family in April when confirming pre-existing fears of the onset of cancer – 'It *is* the lympho-sarcoma' – which now required intense radiation treatment in Lausanne.[235] Stafford's trusted doctor at the Bircher-Benner Clinic, Dr Dagmar Liechti, kept in touch through frequent and affectionate letters from Zurich. Stafford had not only stomach problems but also further swellings in his legs, identified as phlebitis. The aggressive treatment that he was undergoing, Isobel reported, 'had exhausted him so much that he felt at times as if he were just fading out and this made the pains and discomfort more intense'.[236] News of his grave condition, if not accurate diagnosis, could no longer be suppressed. 'Sir S. Cripps: Great and Continuing Anxiety' was a typical headline in the British press.[237] Isobel remained at his side throughout, sitting with Stafford during his waking hours; and she was often joined by

232. RSC to Gaitskell, 31 March 1951, in Williams, *Gaitskell*, p. 258.
233. Gaitskell to RSC, 17 April 1951.   234. Attlee to RSC, 23 May 1951.
235. IC to family, 6 April 1951. I am grateful to Dr David Rubenstein for advice on interpreting the evidence on Cripps's condition.
236. Ibid, 29 April 1951.   237. *Daily Telegraph*, 17 May 1951.

Peggy, who typed press releases which contrived to give as optimistic a view as possible of her father's progress.

Indeed, by May, Stafford was back in the Bircher-Benner Clinic under Liechti's care. A visit from Theresa, accompanied by her husband Robert Ricketts, found her father in good spirits and able to enjoy the mountain views from his new room: ready even for political gossip with Geoffrey Wilson, who also made the journey to the clinic in June. When Isobel was released for a short rest, the indispensable Liechti kept her informed of Stafford's progress by letter; and he himself added, in shaky handwriting: 'All well here, very spoiled! God bless you, Daddy.'[238]

Others now came to pay their respects. At the end of July a visit by the pianist Myra Hess gave the patient both the chance and the incentive to test his mobility in his new steel corset, battling on sticks to the car, and successfully negotiating the two or three steps necessary to enter the room where the recital was held. A visit to Cripps from 'Monty' (Viscount Montgomery of Alamein), then at the height of his celebrity, sent a thrill through the clinic. Later in August a series of reports in British newspapers told of a remarkable recovery, attested by the fact that Stafford could now go out for afternoon drives in the countryside, walking to the car on a single stick now, flanked by Isobel and Peggy. 'Sir Stafford is a man with two qualities: He never knows when he is wrong and he never knows when he is licked,' read a leader in the *Daily Express*, adding the double-edged comment: 'May his restoration be so complete and so rapid that he can take his place on the Front Opposition Bench in the next Parliament.'[239]

Cripps recovered sufficiently to fulfil his ambition to come home to Frith. He was back by the time of the General Election in October 1951, which returned Churchill as Prime Minister (though more narrowly than had seemed likely). 'Smiling Sir Stafford Is on the Mend' had been one headline, above a photograph of an emaciated Cripps, with the evasive comment that 'he is still weak from his spine infection'.[240] Isobel Cripps had kept 'cancer' out of the press, even if she found it a nuisance that 'cure' sometimes crept in – 'this is a word we never use and it rouses scepticism in the medical world unnecessarily'.[241] None the less, within the family the recovery was invested with precariously expansive faith: 'It really is miraculous but one has got so used to miracles these days that perhaps one is not as excited as one should be.'[242]

238. See Liechti to IC, 2 July 1951.   239. *Daily Express*, 16 August 1951.
240. *Daily Mail*, 11 September 1951.   241. IC to family [September 1951].
242. Peggy to family, 17 September 1951.

'You have indeed fought the good fight and kept the faith through these hard months,' Gaitskell told Cripps in welcoming him home, 'and I have never forgotten your hope, in a letter you wrote me when you went away, that you and I would be working together again in 1952. So may it be!'[243] The fact was that Cripps was a desperately sick man, fighting for his own life rather than pining for a chimerical return to Westminster. Isobel Cripps continued to protect him from the press, insisting that Stafford had ceased all political activity on leaving office and ensuring that his name was not used for campaigning purposes.

Once the election was over, and Gaitskell too was out of office, he visited the convalescent at Frith in November 1951. As usual, there was no mention of cancer.

Certainly he looked to me much better than the photographs taken when he arrived here from Switzerland six weeks ago. He was fatter, or not so devastatingly thin, and had put on weight . . . The Doctors at Lausanne, Isobel told me, gave him up for lost. But at Zurich they never gave up and somehow pulled him through. One gets no clear idea of how this happened, and I rather imagine that they both look on it as a kind of miracle . . . We were talking about Winston, and Stafford said, 'He often sends me flowers and books and has also written quite a lot.'[244]

This was quite true. Early in the year Churchill had sent Cripps a copy of the American edition of the fourth volume of *The Second World War*, with its carefully edited account of the Cripps Mission to India in 1942. 'I do hope however that you will not burden yourself with reading it if you find it tiring or boring,' Churchill wrote. 'Still, we have a great story in common of those days we went through together.'[245] A few months later, inspired by 'the gallant fight you are making', he seized on 'the opportunity to send a few flowers from me and Clemmie'.[246] In November, he evidently thought it time for a different kind of olive branch. As Chancellor of the University of Bristol, he renewed the entreaty for Cripps to accept an honorary degree, given, as he tactfully put it, that 'electioneering upset the arrangement' when it had been proffered two years previously.[247] This time there was to be no upset; Cripps gratefully accepted by return of post, though deciding, rather significantly, to take the degree *in absentia*. Thus,

243. Gaitskell to RSC, 6 October 1951.
244. Gaitskell diary, 23 November 1951, in Williams (ed.), *Gaitskell: Diary*, pp. 309–10.
245. Churchill to RSC, 26 February 1951.   246. ibid., 4 June 1951.
247. ibid., 22 November 1951.

in December 1951, their great public feud was publicly healed, and with little time to spare, as it turned out, despite the Prime Minister's optimistic effusions. 'Clemmie and I send you both our love,' he wrote. 'We are so glad to know the reassuring news of your wonderful progress.'[248]

The remission proved only temporary. Though fit enough to receive the Attlees during the Christmas holidays, Cripps was already in constant pain and on 3 January 1952 was flown back from Gloucestershire to Zurich on a stretcher. The radiation therapy was resumed. Isobel Cripps's reports to the family were bleak, if brave, noting that it had been 'one of the "hard" times since we came back, for various reasons and so full of pain'. The immediate aim, she explained, was to reduce the level of drugs and to alleviate the debilitating effects of the X-rays, adding: 'One has to school oneself all the time to concentrate on the "overall" picture and not these moments of pain and discomfort.' Looking always for positive signs, she did not flinch in admitting to bad moments: 'I was out for some time and got back to find D. *wretched*.'[249]

As winter stretched out into spring, there were ups and downs from day to day. Bad on 5 March: 'The pain has been terrible . . .' Better on 6 March: 'There *are* progressive signs of improvement bringing at least slight relief.' Worse again on 7 March: 'Last night was a curious one. It was a non-stop-no-sleep one and I don't think I slept for half an hour. It shows how one judges things as good or bad.' The gamut of emotions on 8 March:

Such a wonderful day. We woke to a white world but in this sun the snow will soon go. There was a good deal of pain in the night. This is *such* a hard time for D. There is something which has to resolve within himself and all we can do is to 'stand by' with the greatest love we can give. I feel soon some new strength and peace will come.[250]

No longer did she disguise from the world the gravity of Stafford's condition: 'He has a radio set in his room, but listens only to music – never news or talks.'[251] Peggy went out to Zurich whenever she could, and also John, to support Isobel in the long vigil at Stafford's bedside. 'I know that Stafford was upheld by an intense spiritual life and by unshakeable faith,' Clementine Churchill later wrote to Isobel. 'And I feel that you share all this with him in this world and the next.'[252]

248. ibid., 4 December 1951.   249. IC to family, 16, 17, 20 January 1952.
250. ibid., 5–8 March 1952.
251. Associated Press release, agreed by IC with Richard Anderegg, 10 April 1952.
252. C. Churchill to IC, 30 April 1952.

Stafford Cripps died on 21 April 1952. Three days later, on what would have been his sixty-third birthday, a short funeral service was held in Zurich, attended by his brother Fred as well as Isobel and her children, Peggy and John. Peggy, who had arrived just too late to see her father for the last time, kept a record of the crowded events in which she was swept up.

Everything had to be done in a rush and the next two days were filled with telephoning, arranging, the continual arrival of wreaths and flowers and a stream of telegrams, later to be followed by packet after packet of letters, some of them very wonderful and remarkable for the fact that they came from all the ends of the earth. Somehow those from India brought one especially near to Daddy.[253]

A month later a memorial service took place in Westminster Abbey, in the presence of a large congregation including the Prime Minister. It was observed by the Cripps family party (whom Isobel had specially asked Joe Appiah to join in the Abbey) that Churchill wept, as he was prone to do on such occasions.[254] At the funeral the hymn 'To be a Pilgrim', adapted from Bunyan, had concluded the service, following the reading from Psalm 23. This is perhaps best known in the version given in the Church of England's *Hymns Ancient and Modern*, in words familiar to Stafford Cripps throughout his life.

> Perverse and foolish oft I stray'd,
> But yet in love He sought me,
> And on His Shoulder gently laid,
> And home, rejoicing, brought me.
>
> In death's dark vale I fear no ill
> With Thee, dear Lord, beside me;
> Thy rod and staff my comfort still,
> Thy Cross before to guide me.

253. Peggy note, Zurich, 27 April 1952.
254. Appiah, *Autobiography*, p. 196. See also F. H. Cripps, *Life's a Gamble*, p. 52; but there is a slip in saying that his brother was buried in the Abbey; the ashes had been flown from Switzerland and were kept privately in Sapperton Church for some time before a subsequent interment, conducted by Mervyn Stockwood, in the new burial ground.

Abbreviations

RSC	Richard Stafford Cripps
IC	Isobel Cripps
DNB	*Dictionary of National Biography*
FRUS	*Foreign Relations of the United States*, ed. E. R. Perkins, vol. 1: Diplomatic papers 1942, and vol. 3: Diplomatic papers 1950 (Washington, DC, 1960)
5 HC Debs.	Parliamentary Debates (Hansard), House of Commons, 5th series
LPACR	Labour Party Annual Conference Reports
Mansergh, *TOP*	*Transfer of Power* (see below, under 'Works cited')

Sources

Archives

CRIPPS PAPERS

The Cripps Papers comprise the collection formerly in the possession of Nuffield College, Oxford, together with the family papers passed to me from Sir Maurice Shock, of which the most significant sections are:

Correspondence of Stafford Cripps
Correspondence of Isobel Cripps
Stafford Cripps diaries
Isobel Cripps Moscow diary, 1940–41
Peggy Cripps (Appiah) Moscow diary (extracts), 1941
Theresa Cripps (Ricketts) Moscow diary, 1940–41
Lord Parmoor diary, 1889–1928
Volumes of newspaper cuttings, 1931–52

PUBLIC RECORD OFFICE

CAB 127/57–154, papers of Cripps's private office, including:
  CAB 127/70–73, 80–81 (Cripps Mission; also CAB 120/577–8) and CAB 127/88, 96–109 (Cabinet Delegation); CAB 127/117–54 (personal correspondence, 1942–50, filed alphabetically)
  BT 91/1 and 7, Board of Trade papers on India and Marshall Aid
  FO 371/24843–9, 29463–72, 32941, Foreign Office papers on Cripps's ambassadorship, 1940–42
  T171/392–402, Chancellor of the Exchequer's Budget papers, 1947–50

OTHER COLLECTIONS CITED

A. V. Alexander diary, Churchill College, Cambridge
Clement Attlee papers, Bodleian Library, Oxford, and Churchill College, Cambridge
Robin Barrington-Ward diary, in the possession of Mr Mark Barrington-Ward
Ernest Bevin papers, Churchill College, Cambridge

R. A. Butler papers, Trinity College, Cambridge

Winston Churchill papers, Churchill College, Cambridge

Reginald Coupland diary, Rhodes House Library, University of Oxford

Lionel Elvin diary, in the possession of Professor Lionel Elvin

Wilfrid Freeman papers, in the possession of Mr Anthony Furse

Harold Laski papers, Brynmor Jones Library, University of Hull

Frederick Pethick-Lawrence papers, Trinity College, Cambridge

Graham Spry papers, National Archives of Canada

Frank Turnbull diary, Churchill College, Cambridge

Beatrice Webb diary, British Library of Political and Economic Science

Edgar Young papers, Brynmor Jones Library, University of Hull

Works cited

(by author or editor as given in the footnotes;
place of publication is London unless otherwise stated)

Addison, Paul, *The Road to 1945* (1975)

Ahmed, Akbar S., *Jinnah, Pakistan and Islamic Identity* (1997)

Akbar, M. J., *Nehru: the making of modern India* (1988)

Alford, B. W. E., Lowe, Rodney, and Rollings, Neil, *Economic Planning, 1943–1951: a guide to the documents in the Public Record Office* (1992)

Appiah, Joseph, *Joe Appiah: the autobiography of an African patriot* (1990)

Appiah, Peggy, *The Attic of My Mind*, in 'Something about the Author' Autobiography Series, vol. 19 (1995)

Azad, Abul Kalam, *India Wins Freedom: the complete version* (Delhi, 1988)

Barnes, John, and Nicholson, David (eds.), *The Empire at Bay: Leo Amery diaries, 1929–45* (1988)

Barnett, Correlli, *The Audit of War: the illusion and reality of Britain as a great nation* (1986)

—— *The Lost Victory: British dreams, British realities, 1945–1950* (1995)

Blaazer, David, *The Popular Front and the Progressive Tradition: socialists, liberals and the quest for unity, 1884–1939* (Cambridge, 1992)

Blum, John Morton (ed.), *Public Philosopher: selected letters of Walter Lippmann* (New York, 1985)

Bohlen, Charles E., *Witness to History, 1929–1969* (New York, 1973)

Booth, Alan, 'New revisionists and the Keynesian era in British economic policy', *Economic History Review*, liv (2001), pp. 346–66

Bottome, Phyllis (ed.), *Our New Order – or Hitler's? a selection of speeches by Winston Churchill, the Archbishop of Canterbury, Anthony Eden, Franklin D. Roosevelt and others* (Harmondsworth, 1943)

Bridges, Edward, *The Treasury* (1964; 2nd edn., 1966)

Brittain, Vera, *Pethick-Lawrence: a portrait* (1963)

Brittan, Samuel, *The Treasury under the Tories, 1951–64* (Harmondsworth, 1964)

SOURCES

—— *Steering the Economy: the role of the Treasury* (Harmondsworth, 1971)

Brogan, Colin, *Our New Masters* (1947)

Brooke, Stephen, *Labour's War: the Labour Party during the Second World War* (Oxford, 1992)

Brown, Judith M., *Gandhi: prisoner of hope* (1989)

Bryant, Chris, *Stafford Cripps: the first modern Chancellor* (1997)

Bullock, Alan, *Life and Times of Ernest Bevin*, 3 vols. (1960–83)

Burgess, Simon, *Stafford Cripps: a political life* (1999)

Burridge, Trevor, *Clement Attlee: a political biography* (1985)

Butler, David E., *The Electoral System in Britain, 1918–51* (Oxford, 1951)

Butler, David E., and Butler, Gareth, *Twentieth Century British Political Facts, 1900–2000* (Basingstoke, 2000)

Caine, Barbara, *Destined to be Wives: the sisters of Beatrice Webb* (Oxford, 1986)

Cairncross, Alec, *Years of Recovery: British economic policy, 1945–51* (1985)

—— (ed.) *The Robert Hall Diaries 1947–53* (1989)

—— 'How British aircraft production was planned in the Second World War', *Twentieth Century British History*, ii (1991), pp. 352–3

Cairncross, Alec, and Watts, Nita, *The Economic Section 1939–1961: a study in economic advising* (1989)

Calder, Angus, *The People's War: Britain 1939–45* (1969)

Campbell, John, *Nye Bevan and the Mirage of British Socialism* (1987)

Cantril, Hadley (ed.), *Public Opinion, 1935–46* (Princeton, 1951)

Cassidy, Henry Clarence, *Moscow Dateline, 1941–3* (1943)

Castle, Barbara, *Fighting All The Way* (1993)

Chadha, Yogesh, *Rediscovering Gandhi* (1997)

Chatterji, Joya, *Bengal Divided: Hindu communalism and partition, 1932–47* (Cambridge, 1995)

Chisholm, Anne, and Davie, Michael, *Beaverbrook: a life* (1992)

Churchill, Winston S., *Great Contemporaries* (1937; Fontana, 1959)

—— *The Second World War*, vol. 1: *The Gathering Storm* (1948)

—— *The Second World War*, vol. 2: *Their Finest Hour* (1949)

—— *The Second World War*, vol. 3: *The Grand Alliance* (1950)

—— *The Second World War*, vol. 4: *The Hinge of Fate* (1951)

Citrine, Walter (Lord), *In Russia Now* (1942)

Clarke, Peter, *Liberals and Social Democrats* (Cambridge, 1978)

—— *The Keynesian Revolution and its Economic Consequences: selected essays* (Cheltenham, 1998)

Collins, L. John, *Faith under Fire* (1966)

Colville, John, *The Fringes of Power: Downing Street diaries, 1939–1955* (1985)

Cooke, Colin Arthur, *The Life of Richard Stafford Cripps* (1957)

Coupland, Reginald, *The Cripps Mission* (1942)

—— *Indian Politics, 1936–42* (1943)

Craig, F. W. S. (ed.), *British Parliamentary Results, 1918–49* (Glasgow, 1969)

Crick, Bernard, *George Orwell: a life* (1980; 1982 edn.)

Cripps, F. H., *Life's a Gamble* (1957)

Cripps, Richard Stafford, 'Can Socialism Come by Constitutional Methods?' in Addison, Christopher, *et al.*, *Problems of a Socialist Government* (1933)

—— *Why This Socialism?* (1934)

—— 'Alternatives before British Labour', *Foreign Affairs*, xiii (1934–5), pp. 122–32

—— 'The political reactions of rearmament', in Fabian Lectures for 1937, *Dare We Look Ahead?* (1938)

—— *Democracy Up-to-Date* (1939)

—— *Shall the Spell be Broken?* Rectorial address to the University of Aberdeen delivered on 6 February 1943 (1943)

—— *Towards Christian Democracy* (1945)

—— *In This Faith We Live*, statement by the Parliamentary Socialist Christian Group, foreword by RSC, April 1948

—— *God in Our Work: Religious Addresses* (1949)

Curtis, Sarah (ed.), *The Journals of Woodrow Wyatt*, vol. 1 (1998)

Dalton, Hugh, *The Fateful Years: memoirs 1931–45* (1957)

—— *High Tide and After: memoirs 1945–60* (1962)

Danchev, Alex, and Todman, Daniel (eds.), *Field Marshal Lord Alanbrooke: war diaries, 1939–1945* (2001)

Das, Durga (ed.), *Sardar Patel's Correspondence 1945–50*, vol. 3 (Ahmedabad, 1972)

Davenport, Nicholas, *Memoirs of a City Radical* (1974)

Davison, P. H. (ed.), *The Complete Works of George Orwell*, vols. 12 and 13 (1998)

Day, David, *Menzies and Churchill at War* (1986)

Dell, Edmund, *The Schuman Plan: the British abdication of leadership in Europe* (Oxford, 1995)

—— *The Chancellors: a history of the Chancellors of the Exchequer, 1945–90* (1996)

—— *A Strange Eventful History: democratic socialism in Britain* (2000)

Dilks, David (ed.), *The Diaries of Sir Alexander Cadogan, O.M., 1938–1945* (1971)

Donoughue, Bernard, and Jones, G. W., *Herbert Morrison: portrait of a politician* (1973)

Dow, J. C. R., *The Management of the British Economy, 1945–60* (Cambridge, 1964)

Dupree, Marguerite (ed.), *Lancashire and Whitehall: the diary of Sir Raymond Streat* (Manchester, 1987)

Eatwell, Roger, 'The Labour Party and the Popular Front Movement in Britain in the 1930s', Oxford D. Phil. dissertation, 1975

Eden, Anthony (Lord Avon), *The Eden Memoirs*, vol. 2: *The Reckoning* (1965)

Edgerton, David, *England and the Aeroplane* (1991)

—— 'The prophet militant and industrial: the peculiarities of Correlli Barnett', *Twentieth Century British History*, ii (1999), pp. 360–79

Estorick, Eric, *Stafford Cripps: prophetic rebel* (New York, 1941)

—— *Stafford Cripps: a biography* (1949)

Fielding, Steven, 'The Second World War and popular radicalism: the significance of the "movement away from party"', *History*, ixxx (1995), pp. 38–58

Fischer, Louis, *A Week with Gandhi* (New York, 1942)

—— 'Why Cripps failed', 2 parts, *Nation*, 19 September 1942, pp. 230–32, and 26 September 1942, pp. 255–9

—— 'Gandhi, Cripps and Churchill', *Nation*, 5 December 1942, pp. 619–21

—— *The Life of Mahatma Gandhi* (New York, 1950; 1983 edn.)

Foot, Michael, *Aneurin Bevan*, 2 vols. (1962–73)

Francis, Martin, *Ideas and Policies under Labour, 1945–1951: building a new Britain* (Manchester, 1997)

French, Patrick, *Liberty or Death: India's journey to independence and division* (1997)

Fröhlich, Elke (ed.), *Die Tagebücher von Joseph Goebbels, Teil 2, Diktate 1941–1945, Band 3, Januar-März 1942* (1994)

Furner, Mary O., and Supple, Barry, *The State and Economic Knowledge: the American and British experiences* (Cambridge, 1990).

Furse, Anthony, *Wilfrid Freeman* (Staplehurst, 2000)

Gallup, George H., *The Gallup Poll: public opinion 1935–1971*, vol. 1: *1935–1948* (New York, 1972)

—— *Gallup International Public Opinion Polls: Great Britain*, vol. 1: *1938–1964* (New York, 1976)

Gandhi, M. K., *The Collected Works of Mahatma Gandhi*, vols. 75 and 84 (New Delhi, 1979, 1981)

Gandhi, Rajmohan, *India Wins Errors: a scrutiny of Maulana Azad's 'India Wins Freedom'* (Delhi, 1989)

Gardner, Lloyd C., *Spheres of Influence: the partition of Europe, from Munich to Yalta* (1993)

Ghosh, Sudhir, *Gandhi's Emissary* (1967)

Gilbert, Martin, *Winston S. Churchill*, vol 6: *Finest Hour, 1939–41* (1983), and vol. 7: *Road to Victory, 1941–45* (1986)

Glendevon, J., *The Viceroy at Bay: Lord Linlithgow in India* (1971)

Gopal, Sarvepalli, *Jawaharlal Nehru: a biography*, 3 vols. (1975–84)

—— (ed.), *Selected Works of Jawaharlal Nehru*, first series, vols. 8–15 (New Delhi, 1976–80), and second series, vols. 6–11 and 20 (New Delhi, 1991–7)

Gorodetsky, Gabriel, *Stafford Cripps' Mission to Moscow, 1940–42* (Cambridge, 1984)

—— *Grand Delusion: Stalin and the German invasion of Russia* (1999)

Gunther, John, *Inside Europe* (1936)

Gupta, D. C., *The Indian National Movement* (Delhi, 1970)

Gupta, Partha Sarathi, *Imperialism and the British Labour Movement, 1914–64* (1975)

Hanak, H., 'Sir Stafford Cripps as British ambassador in Moscow', two parts, May 1940 to June 1941 and June 1941 to January 1942, *English Historical Review*, xciv (1979), pp. 48–70 and xcvii (1982), pp. 332–44

Harriman, W. Averell, and Abel, Elie, *Special Envoy to Churchill and Stalin, 1941–1946* (New York, 1975)

Harris, Kenneth, *Attlee* (1982; 1984 edn.)

Harvey, John, *The War Diaries of Oliver Harvey* (1978)

Hennessy, Peter, *Never Again: Britain 1945–51* (1992)

Hinsley, F. H., *British Intelligence in the Second World War*, 5 vols. (1979–90)

Hodson, H. V., *The Great Divide* (1969; 1985 edn.)

Hogan, Michael J., *The Marshall Plan: America, Britain, and the reconstruction of Western Europe, 1947–52* (Cambridge, 1987)

Hollis, Patricia, *Jennie Lee: a life* (Oxford, 1997)

Howard, Anthony, *RAB: the life of R. A. Butler* (1987)

Howard, Michael, *Grand Strategy*, vol. 4: *August 1942 – September 1943* (1972)

Howson, Susan, *British Monetary Policy, 1945–51* (Oxford, 1993)

Howson, Susan, and Moggridge, Donald (eds.), *The Collected Papers of James Meade*, vol. 4: *Cabinet Office diary, 1944–46* (1990)

Hyde, H. Montgomery, *Walter Monckton* (1991)

Ismay, Hastings Lionel (Baron Ismay), *The Memoirs of General the Lord Ismay* (1960)

Jalal, Ayesha, *The Sole Spokesman: Jinnah, the Muslim League and the demand for Pakistan* (Cambridge, 1985)

Jay, Douglas, *Change and Fortune: a political record* (1980)

Jefferys, Kevin (ed.), *Labour and the Wartime Coalition: from the diary of James Chuter Ede, 1941–1945* (1987)

—— *The Churchill Coalition and Wartime Politics, 1940–1945* (Manchester, 1991)

Jenkins, Roy, 'Stafford Cripps', in *Nine Men of Power* (1974), pp. 81–105

Jones, Mervyn, *Michael Foot* (1994)

Keynes, J. M., *The General Theory of Employment, Interest and Money* (1936)

Kimball, Warren F. (ed.), *Churchill and Roosevelt: the complete correspondence* (1984)

King, Anthony (ed.), *British Political Opinion, 1937–2000: the Gallup Polls*, compiled by Robert I. Wybrow (2001)

Kipling, Rudyard, 'The Brushwood Boy', in *The Day's Work* (1904)

Kitchen, Martin, *British Policy towards the Soviet Union during the Second World War* (1986)

Lamb, Richard, *The Failure of the Eden Government* (1987)

Lawlor, Sheila, 'Britain and Russia's entry into the War', in Richard Langhorne (ed.), *Diplomacy and Intelligence during the Second World War* (Cambridge, 1985), pp. 168–83

Levine, Alan J., *The Strategic Bombing of Germany, 1940–1945* (New York, 1992)

Listowel, William Francis Hare, Earl of, 'The Whitehall dimension of the transfer of power', *Indo-British Review*, vii (1979), pp. 22–31

Louis, William Roger, *Imperialism at Bay, 1941–1945: the United States and the decolonization of the British Empire* (Oxford, 1977)

—— *In the Name of God, Go!: Leo Amery and the British Empire in the age of Churchill* (1992)

Low, Anthony (ed.), *Congress and the Raj* (1977)

McBean, Alison, 'A. V. Alexander and the 1946 Cabinet Mission to India', Cambridge Historical Tripos dissertation, 1986

McCallum, R. B., and Readman, Alison, *The British General Election of 1945* (1947)

MacDonogh, Giles, *A Good German: Adam von Trott zu Solz* (1989)

MacKenzie, Norman (ed.) *The Letters of Sidney and Beatrice Webb*, vol. 3: *Pilgrimage, 1912–1947* (1978)

MacKenzie, Norman and Jeanne (eds.), *The Diary of Beatrice Webb*, 4 vols. (1982–5)

McLachlan, Donald, *In the Chair: Barrington-Ward of The Times, 1927–1948* (1971)

Mansergh, Nicholas, and Lumby, E. W. R. (vols. 1–4); Mansergh, Nicholas, and Moon, Penderel (vols. 5–12), *The Transfer of Power 1942–7: constitutional relations between Britain and India*, 12 vols. (1970–83)

March, Michael, *A New Way of Life* (1942)

Marquand, David, 'Sir Stafford Cripps', in Sissons, Michael, and French, Philip (eds.), *Age of Austerity 1945–1951* (1963; 1964 edn.), pp. 173–95

Menon, V. P., *The Transfer of Power in India* (New Delhi, 1957; 1968 edn.)

Messenger, Charles, *'Bomber' Harris and the Strategic Bombing Offensive, 1939–45* (1984)

Milward, Alan, *The Reconstruction of Western Europe, 1945–51* (1984)

Miner, Steven Merritt, *Between Churchill and Stalin: the Soviet Union, Great Britain and the origins of the Grand Alliance* (1988)

Mishra, B. K., *The Cripps Mission: a reappraisal* (Delhi, 1982)

Moggridge, Donald (ed.), *The Collected Writings of John Maynard Keynes*, vol. 21: *Activities 1931–1939* (1982)

Molesworth, G. N., *Curfew on Olympus* (1965)

Montague Browne, Anthony, *Long Sunset: memoirs of Churchill's last private secretary* (1995)

Moon, Penderel, *Divide and Quit* (1961; 1998 edn.)

—— (ed.), *Wavell: the Viceroy's journal* (1973)

Moore, R. J., *Churchill, Cripps and India, 1939–45* (Oxford, 1979)

—— *Escape from Empire: the Attlee government and the Indian problem* (Oxford, 1983)

—— *Endgames of Empire: studies of Britain's Indian problem* (Delhi, 1988)

Moran, Lord (Charles Wilson), *Churchill: the struggle for survival, 1940–65* (1966; 1968 edn.)

Morgan, Kenneth O., *Labour in Power 1945–1951* (Oxford, 1984)

—— *Callaghan: a life* (Oxford, 1997)

Mountbatten, Louis (Earl), 'Reflections on the transfer of power and Jawaharlal Nehru', the Second Jawaharlal Nehru Memorial Lecture (Cambridge, 1968)

Nehru, Jawaharlal, *The Discovery of India* (1946)

—— *A Bunch of Old Letters: written mostly to Jawaharlal Nehru and some written by him* (1960)

—— *Correspondence, 1903–47: a catalogue*, Nehru Memorial Museum and Library (Delhi, 1988)

Nicholas, H. G., *The British General Election of 1950* (1951)

Nicolson, Harold, *Diaries and Letters, 1930–64* (1980 condensed edn.)

Nicolson, Nigel (ed.), *Harold Nicolson: diaries and letters*, 3 vols. (1966–8)

Ostrer, Isidore, *Modern Money and Unemployment and the Law of Barter* (1964)

Overy, Richard, *The Air War, 1939–45* (1980)

—— *Russia's War* (1997)

Owen, Nicholas, ' "Responsibility without power": the Attlee Government and the end of British rule in India', in Nick Tiratsoo (ed.), *The Attlee Years* (1991), pp. 167–89

Parker, R. A. C., *Churchill and Appeasement* (2000)

Parmoor, Lord, *A Retrospect* (1936)

Patel, Harbans, *The Cripps Mission: the whole truth* (Delhi, 1990)

Patil, V. T., *Jawaharlal Nehru and the Cripps Mission* (Delhi, 1984)

Pearce, Robert (ed.), *Patrick Gordon Walker: political diaries, 1932–1971* (1991)

Peden, George, *The Treasury and British Public Policy, 1906–1959* (Oxford, 2000)

Pelling, Henry, *The Labour Governments, 1945–51* (1984)

—— *Britain and the Marshall Plan* (1988)

Philips, C. H., and Wainwright, M. D. (eds.), *The Partition of India: policies and perspectives, 1935–47* (1970)

Pimlott, Ben, *Labour and the Left in the 1930s* (Cambridge, 1977)

—— *Hugh Dalton* (1985)

—— (ed.), *The Political Diary of Hugh Dalton, 1918–40, 1945–60* (1986)

—— (ed.), *The Second World War Diary of Hugh Dalton 1940–45* (1986)

Plowden, Edwin, *An Industrialist in the Treasury* (1989)

Postan, M. M., *British War Production: civil history of the Second World War* (1952; 1975 revised edn.)

Pritt, D. N., *The Autobiography of D. N. Pritt*, vol. 1: *From Right to Left* (1965)

Rhodes James, Robert, *Anthony Eden* (1986)

Ritschel, Daniel, *The Politics of Planning: the debate on economic planning in Britain in the 1930s* (Oxford, 1997)

Rizvi, Gowher, *Linlithgow and India: a study of British policy and the political impasse in India, 1936–43* (1978)

Roberts, Andrew, *'The Holy Fox': a biography of Lord Halifax* (1991)

—— 'Lord Mountbatten and the perils of adrenalin', in *Eminent Churchillians* (1994), pp. 55–136

Ross, Graham (ed.), *The Foreign Office and the Kremlin: British documents on Anglo-Soviet relations 1941–5* (Cambridge, 1984)

Rzheshevsky, Oleg A. (ed.), *War and Diplomacy: the making of the Grand Alliance, Documents from Stalin's archives* (Amsterdam, 1996)

Said, Edward W., *Orientalism* (New York, 1978; Harmondsworth, 1985)

Sarkar, Sumit, *Modern India, 1885–1947* (1983)

Schuster, George, 'Richard Stafford Cripps', in *Biographical Memoirs of Fellows of the Royal Society*, vol. 1 (1955), pp. 11–32

Singh, Anita, *The Origins of Partition, 1936–47* (Delhi, 1987)

Soames, Mary (ed.), *Speaking for Themselves: the personal letters of Winston and Clementine Churchill* (1998)

Spry, Graham, 'A British reply to Louis Fischer', *Nation*, 14 November 1942, pp. 501–4

—— (ed.), 'The Cripps Mission to India', *International Conciliation* (New York, 1942)

Stokes, Eric, 'Cripps in India', *Historical Journal*, xiv (1971), pp. 427–34

Strauss, Patricia, *Cripps: Advocate and Rebel* (New York, 1942; 1943)

Taylor, A. J. P., *Beaverbrook* (1972)

—— (ed.), *W. P. Crozier. Off the Record: political interviews, 1933–1943* (1973)

Tomlinson, B. R., *The Indian National Congress and the Raj, 1929–42: the penultimate phase* (1976)

Tomlinson, Jim, *Employment Policy: the crucial years 1939–1955* (Oxford, 1987)

—— *Democratic Socialism and Economic Policy: the Attlee years, 1945–1951* (Cambridge, 1997)

Toye, Richard John, *The Labour Party and the Planned Economy, 1931–1951* (forthcoming, 2002)

Tyler, Froom, *Cripps: a portrait and a prospect* (1942)

Verrier, Anthony, *The Bomber Offensive* (1968)

Webb, Beatrice, *My Apprenticeship* (1926; Cambridge, 1979)

—— *Our Partnership* (1948; Cambridge, 1978)

Webster, Charles, and Frankland, Noble, *The Strategic Air Offensive against Germany, 1939–45*, vol. 1 (1961)

Whiting, Richard, *The Labour Party and Taxation: party identity and political purpose in twentieth-century Britain* (Cambridge, 2000)

Williams, Francis, *A Prime Minister Remembers: the war and post-war memoirs of the Rt. Hon. Earl Attlee* (1961)

Williams, Philip M., *Hugh Gaitskell: a political biography* (1979)

—— (ed.), *The Diary of Hugh Gaitskell, 1945–56* (1983)

Williamson, Stanley, *Gresford: the anatomy of a disaster* (Liverpool, 1997)

Wilson, Geoffrey, 'My Working Life', manuscript in the possession of the author (1996)

Woodward, Sir Llewellyn, *British Foreign Policy in the Second World War*, vols. 1 and 2 (1970–71)

Wyatt, Woodrow, *Turn Again Westminster* (1973)

—— *Confessions of an Optimist* (1985)

—— 'Richard Stafford Cripps', *DNB* 1951–60 (1971), pp. 270–74

Ziegler, Philip, *Mountbatten: the official biography* (1985)

Zweiniger-Bargielowska, Ina, *Austerity in Britain: rationing, controls and consumption, 1939–1955* (Oxford, 2000)

Acknowledgements

I am most grateful to the following for talking to me about their memories of Stafford Cripps: Her Majesty the Queen, Professor Lionel Elvin, the Right Hon. Michael Foot, Mrs Margaret Meade, Sir Robert and Lady Ricketts (Theresa Cripps), Mr Peter Stursberg, Mrs Alice Sutton and Sir Geoffrey Wilson. I have enjoyed full cooperation – but also total freedom from interference – in all my cordial dealings with the family of Stafford and Isobel Cripps, notably the late Lady Ricketts (daughter) and Mrs Sara Mason, Dr Judith Heyer and Professor Anthony Appiah (grandchildren). I am happy to acknowledge their permission for use of the Cripps papers, and that of Nuffield College, Oxford. Likewise the help of Mr Mark Barrington-Ward, as holder of the copyright in the diary of his father, is gratefully acknowledged, as is the action of Mr Anthony Furse in freely making available his copies of the papers of Sir Wilfrid Freeman. I am also grateful to Professor Kenneth O. Morgan (Lord Morgan) for a transcript from the Callaghan papers.

In due course the Cripps papers will, at last, be fully integrated and properly catalogued by the Bodleian Library, Oxford. As a result, I fully expect future discoveries to revise some of my own findings, which have been based on exploring a rich but disorganized archive by methods that have had to rely upon intuition and improvisation. This book was begun in 1997, when Sir Maurice Shock handed over not only the part of the Cripps papers in his custody but also his working notes – a generous action which eased my own task. Chris Bryant, MP, as a previous biographer of Cripps, showed himself helpful at a later stage.

The Cambridge History Faculty facilitated the project throughout, notably by temporarily housing the Cripps archive. St John's College, as always during my twenty years as a Fellow, ensured that I had conditions under which to combine research with my teaching responsibilities; and when I moved to Trinity Hall in October 2000, I was able to rely upon a similarly humane understanding within my new College in reconciling the duties of the Mastership with the claims of scholarship. I gratefully acknowledge, too, a personal research grant from the Leverhulme Trust which latterly gave me the two years' relief from undergraduate teaching that enabled this biography to be completed on time.

The scholarly apparatus of the book was overhauled for me by Paul Corthorn and Mark Roodhouse; and drafts were also read for me by Christopher Bayly, Stefan Collini, Ewen Green, David Reynolds, Duncan Tanner and John Thompson. I owe many improvements to their shrewd suggestions. My debt to Richard Toye is heavier still; not only did he work closely with me in jointly writing the entry on Cripps for the *New Dictionary of National Biography* but his collaboration extended to supplying me with many references for the present volume. Finally, my editor, Stuart Proffitt, has adroitly guided this project through the shoals; and my initiation as biographer would, like much else, have been impossible without the unrelenting scrutiny and unstinting support of Maria Tippett.

The Master's Lodge,
Trinity Hall,
Cambridge
November 2001

Index

fascism 73, 190; and capitalism 60, 61, 62, 80, 90; and the National Government 65; and class 81; Nehru's opposition to 347

Fernacres Cottage, Fulmer, Buckinghamshire 27

Filkins, Oxfordshire 28, 197, 246, 262; parish church 30, 43–4; Women's Institute 31; village club 31, 33

Finland 113–14, 156–7, 159, 162, 184

Finno-Soviet agreement 166, 183

First World War 106, 381, 382; undermines C's health 21, 24–5, 26; C volunteers 21; C's ambulance service 22–3; in the Ministry of Munitions 23–5, 373; and the Labour Party 40–41; British political crises 365

Fischer, Louis 352, 354–5, 369, 440; 'Why Cripps Failed' 352–3

Florence, C visits (1906) 15

Fonteyn, Margot 485–6

food rationing 273, 505

Foot, Isaac 68

Foot, Michael 186; on C 36, 54; at Oxford with John Cripps 68–9; refuses editorship of *Tribune* 75; on C's demotion 368

Foreign Office 101, 111, 112, 119, 120, 122, 159, 162, 166, 170, 179, 183–6, 189–94, 197, 198, 203–10, 213, 215–18, 221, 225, 230, 235, 240, 480

Forest of Dean Miners' Gala 100

Formosa, C visits 145, 167

Fourth Hussars 22

Le Franc-Tireur xi

France: Blum's electoral victory (1936) 73; C on holiday (1939) 102, 103–5; declares war on Germany 105; German invasion of 185; fall of 189

Frank, Waldo 53, 168, 169

Frankfurter, Felix 112

free trade 13

Freeman, John 523

Freeman, Sir Wilfrid 375–6, 378–80, 488

French Revolution 108

French Riviera 103

Frith Farm, Far Oakridge 177, 246, 247, 262, 527, 535

fuel crisis (1947) 480

fuel rationing 356

Gaiety music hall, London 15

Gaitskell, Hugh xiii, xvii, 10, 480, 482, 487, 489, 490, 491, 495, 501, 512, 514, 515, 516, 523, 524, 525–6, 533–4, 536

Gaitskellites xiii, 524

Gallup polls 384, 511, 518, 521

Gandhi, Indira (née Nehru) 69, 117, 298

Gandhi, Mahatma Mohandas Karamchand 116, 126, 130, 131, 137, 143, 207, 251, 262, 310, 351, 388, 438–9, 443–4, 461, 505; perceived social conservatism 90; C visits at Wardha (1939) 123, 135–6, 301–2; followers in Congress 115; and joint electorates for the 'depressed classes' 132; and Congress's non-cooperation campaign 142; non-violence 277, 305, 347; and the Bardoli resolutions 277; asks C to 'perform a miracle' 289; visits C in Delhi 295–6, 301–2; anti-war 300; unimpressed by the Cripps Mission 301, 304–5, 306, 323; 'fast unto death' threat 313, 314; and Japan 324, 349; 'Quit India' campaign 336, 342; blamed for the Cripps Mission failure 344, 346, 347, 409; and the Working Committee 347–8, 349; C his declared enemy 348; C tries to use propaganda against 350; and Fischer 352, 354; C on 390, 447, 532–3; compared with C 390; improved relations with C 399, 409, 419; meets the Cabinet Delegation 410–12; and Nehru 416, 422; at Simla 423, 424–6, 427; and the first Delegation Statement 432–6, 437, 439; Isobel and 440, 442, 532; on the

State for India 397; personality 397; view of Gandhi 397, 439; and the Cripps Declaration 397; relationship with C 399; Chequers weekend 404, 405; and Wavell 408, 455, 462; meets Gandhi 411–12; official interviews programme 412; and Jinnah 415, 454; threatens to resign 431; Turnbull on 432; and C's breakdown 437, 439–40; meeting with Patel 450; at the London conference (1946) 464
Le Petit Parisien 269–70
Petsche, Maurice 517
'phoney war' 159, 170
Picture Post 119, 522
Pimlott, Ben xiii, 52
Pisa cathedral 44
Placentia Bay conference 225, 228
Playne, Arthur (C's uncle) 4, 12
Playne, Mary (née Potter; C's aunt) 4, 9, 12
Plowden, Edwin 489, 490, 492–5, 498, 500, 501, 512, 515, 516, 523, 525–6
Poland 103, 113, 214; German invasion and occupation 105, 159, 204; Russian invasion of 158; Chamberlain's failure to offer proper guarantees 158
Pollitt, Harry 65–6
Poole, Dorset 186
Poona 410
Popular Front 73, 74, 75, 78–81, 82, 97, 98, 99, 155, 156, 178, 332
Portugal, C visits 9
'post-war consensus' xv, 484
Postan, Munia 185, 186, 188
'Postscript' series (radio broadcasts) 263–4
Potter, Richard (C's maternal grandfather) 4, 167
Potter family 12, 31, 519
Prague, occupation of 99
Prasad, Rajendra 337
Priestley, J. B. 263, 368
Pritt, D. N. 10, 66, 81, 82

Privy Council, Judicial Committee of the 33
Punjab 403, 409, 473, 474

Quakers 116
Queen Victoria Road, Delhi (No. 3) 295, 301, 304, 305, 314, 317, 318
Queensferry, near Chester 24–5, 28
'Quit India' campaign 336, 342, 348, 349–50, 370, 394–5

R101 airship disaster 47
Racial Unity 92
Raigarh, Rajah of 136
Railway Rates Tribunal 46
Rajagopalachari, Chakravarti 115, 135, 277, 295, 300, 306, 307, 314, 315, 317, 336, 342, 347, 351, 409, 421, 433, 446, 448, 451, 469
Ramsay, Professor Sir William 11, 24
Rangoon 151, 283, 291
Rao, Shiva 130, 300, 307, 311–12, 314, 399, 402, 403, 409, 444
Realpolitik 190, 194
rearmament 64, 158, 526
Red Army xii, 107, 114, 220, 226, 262, 359, 361
Red Army Parade, Sheffield (1943) 378
Reigate, Surrey 10
rentier class 57, 58, 108
Resistance xi
Reuters 276
Ribbentrop, Joachim von 104, 206
Ricketts, Robert (C's son-in-law) 246, 535
Ricketts, Theresa (née Cripps; C's daughter): birth (1919) 30; on her mother's lack of domestic skills 27n; education 30, 72; in Moscow xviii, 45, 179, 188, 194, 200–203, 206, 208, 218; and vegetarianism 68; at Goodfellows 69; and Geoffrey Wilson 72; Jamaican holiday 75–6; and Peggy's marriage 92; and C's visits to India, China and Russia (1939) 120;